THE LIFE

OF

JOHN MILTON:

NARRATED IN CONNEXION WITH

THE POLITICAL, ECCLESIASTICAL, AND LITERARY

HISTORY OF HIS TIME.

BY

DAVID MASSON, M.A., LL.D., Litt.D.,

PROFESSOR OF RHETORIC AND ENGLISH LITERATURE
IN THE UNIVERSITY OF EDINBURGH
AND HISTORIOGRAPHER ROYAL FOR SCOTLAND

INDEX VOLUME

NEW YORK
PETER SMITH
1946

First published 1894

Reprinted 1946 by special arrangement with
THE MACMILLAN COMPANY

PRINTED IN THE UNITED STATES OF AMERICA

PREFATORY NOTE.

THIS Index has been the kindly undertaking, at intervals through several years, of three members of my own household, conjointly or in succession. It has necessarily been a work of exceptional difficulty and patience. The references in the Index to Volume I. are to the revised and enlarged edition of that volume, published in 1881.

D. M.

EDINBURGH : *August* 1894.

INDEX

ABBOT, George, Archbishop of Canterbury, i. 107, 347; his Calvinistic tendencies and unpopularity at Court, i. 348; his retirement from Court and loss of power, i. 349, 354, 356; his opinion of Laud, i. 360-1, 364; suspended from his archbishopric and banished from Court, i. 371, 377, 387, 388, 522, 545; ii. 518, 544; his death, i. 664, and iii. 195; his portrait by Marshall, iii. 456.

ABBOT, Dr. Robert, King's Divinity Professor at Oxford, i. 360.

ABELL, Richard, witness, vi. 92.

ABERDEEN: Marischal College at, founded, i. 511; reputation of, as a seat of letters in 1632, i. 512; opposition of, to the Covenant of 1638, i. 732, ii. 27-8; demonstration for the King's Covenant at, ii. 34; its part in the First "Bishops' War," ii. 56, 57, 59, 60, 63; third Scottish General Assembly since 1638 meets at, ii. 136; "The Aberdeen Doctors," i. 715, 732; ii. 27-8, 29, 34, 38, 56.

ABERDEENSHIRE: state of, during First "Bishops' War," ii. 56-7.

ABERGAVENNY, John Nevill, 8th Baron of, ii. 429.

ABERGAVENNY, George Nevill, 10th Baron of, subscriber to the fourth edition of Paradise Lost, vi. 785.

ABERNETHY, John, Scottish bishop, i. 697, 701; ii. 42.

ABOYNE, Viscount, second son of Marquis of Huntley, ii. 34; in First "Bishops' War," ii. 57; with the King at Newcastle, ii. 60, 63, and at Oxford, iii. 344; with Montrose in Scotland, 345, 347, 357, 360, 361, 367.

"ACADEMIARUM EXAMEN" by Webster, i. 265-6.

ACADEMIES, Italian, i. 763-5: the Apatisti, of Florence, i. 772, 776-8, 779, 780, 782; the Delfici, of Rome, i. 795; the Della Crusca, of Florence, i. 765, 772, 774, 777, 779; the Fantastici, of Rome, i. 795, 796, 797, 806; the Florentine, i. 765, 766 note, 772, 773, 775, 777, 779; the Gelati, of Bologna, i. 765; the Incogniti, of Venice, i. 831; the Intricati, of Rome, i. 795; the Lincei, of Rome, i. 765, 766, 795; the Malinconici, of Rome, i. 795; the Negletti, of Rome, i. 795; the Ordinati, of Rome, i. 765, 795; the Oziosi, of Naples, i. 812, 815; the Partenii, of Rome, i. 795; the Svogliati, of Florence, i. 773, 775, 777, 779; the Umoristi, of Rome, i. 765, 795, 801; Milton among them, i. 782, 821-2.

ACADIE: see Nova Scotia.

"ACCEDENCE COMMENC'T GRAMMAR," see Milton, writings of.

"ACCOMMODATION ORDER" of the Long Parliament, iii. 274-5, 391-3.

ACHESON, Sir Archibald, of Glencairn, Secretary of State for Scotland, i. 706.

ACHESON, James, Parliamentarian officer, ii. 444.

ACHILLINI, Italian poet, i. 797, 806.

B

ACTON, Samuel, Baptist pastor, vi. 746-7.

ACTORS and ACTRESSES of the Restoration, vi. 349-52.

ADAIR, Archibald, Irish bishop, i. 420.

ADAMS, Alderman of London, ii. 447.

ADAMSON, Scottish Presbyterian minister, ii. 38.

ADDISON, Hon. Galston, Governor of Madras, vi. 758.

ADDISON, Joseph, visits Milton's daughter, vi. 752; his papers on *Paradise Lost* in the *Spectator*, vi. 787.

ADIMARO, Alessandro, Florentine poet, i. 787.

AGAR, Ann, daughter of Thomas Agar and his first wife, ii. 100, vi. 771.

AGAR, Ann, daughter of Thomas Agar and his second wife, and wife of David Moore, ii. 100, vi. 772.

AGAR, Anne, second wife of Thomas Agar: see *Milton*.

AGAR, John, witness with Thomas Agar, i. 637.

AGAR, Mary, daughter of Thomas Agar and his second wife, ii. 100.

AGAR, Mary, first wife of Thomas Agar: see *Rugeley*.

AGAR, Thomas, Deputy-Clerk of the Crown, second husband of Anne Milton, i. 637-8, ii. 100-1, 150; his later life and will, vi. 770-4; his death, vi. 763.

AGAR, Thomas, jun., nephew of Thomas Agar, vi. 772-4.

AGNEW, Alexander, called *Jock of Broad Scotland*, v. 92-4.

AGNEW, of Lochnaw, ii. 38.

"AGREEMENT OF THE PEOPLE," Republican document of 1648-9, iv. 7-10, iv. 10 note, 11, 19.

AGRICOLA, John, ii. 574.

AINSWORTH, Henry, Brownist preacher, ii. 539, 542, 556.

AINSWORTH, Robert, his Latin dictionary, vi. 813.

AIRLIE, James, Lord Ogilvie, 1st Earl of, iii. 352, 357, 361, 367, 421; v. 706.

"AIRLY, House o'," ii. 137.

AITZEMA, Leo de, Ambassador from the Hanse Towns, iv. 378-9, 482; his correspondence with Milton on the subject of Divorce, v. 169-71; Milton's letter to, v. 170, vi. 723.

ALABLASTER, Dr., prebendary of St. Paul's, Cambridge scholar and dramatist, i. 215, 448, 509.

ALBEMARLE, Duke of: see *Monk*.

ALBEMARLE (Nan Clarges), Duchess of, vi. 17.

ALDAM, Thomas, Early Quaker, v. 26.

ALDERSGATE Street, London, Milton's house in, ii. 203-12.

ALDERS' GATE, the, London, ii. 205.

ALDRICH, Edward, Parliamentarian officer, ii. 444.

ALDRIDGE, Colonel, under New Model, iii. 326.

ALDRIDGE, Thomas, of Christ's College, Cambridge, i. 149.

ALEXANDER III., Pope; Bellings's secret mission to, vi. 240-1 and note.

ALEXANDER, Sir William, of Menstrie: see *Stirling*, Earl of.

ALEXANDER, William, Lord (son of Earl of Stirling), i. 707.

ALEXIS, Emperor of Russia; State letter to, v. 292-4 and note.

"ALEXIS, The Secrets of," an Italian publication of the 16th century, ii. 256 and note.

ALFONSO V. of Portugal, State letters to, v. 576, 589-90.

ALFORD, Battle of, iii. 359.

ALFORD, Major, under New Model, iii. 327.

ALFRAY, Thomas, of Catsfield, Sussex, ii. 209.

ALGARDI, sculptor, i. 763.

ALINGTON, Sir Giles, fined for marrying his niece, i. 407.

ALLATIUS, Leo, bibliographer, i. 796-7.

ALLECOCK, John, of Nantwich, vi. 747.

ALLEINE, Joseph, ejected Nonconformist, vi. 232 note.

ALLEN, Adjutant-General: his account of the prayer-meeting in the Parliamentary army, iii. 612-13; involved in Republican plottings, v. 33.

ALLEN, Alderman Francis, one of the King's judges, iii. 720 note; in Councils of State of the Commonwealth, iv. 273, 355; at Cromwell's Dissolution of the Rump, iv. 413; one of the Regicides dead before the

Restoration, vi. 28; excepted in the Indemnity Bill of 1660, vi. 54; mentions of, in the Council Order Books, iv. 314, 315, 449, 450.

ALLEN, John, i. 557.

ALLEN, Sir Thomas, vi. 255.

ALLEN, William, army agitator, iii. 534-5.

ALLEN, William, assumed name by author of "Killing no Murder," v. 141-2.

ALLESTREE, James, London bookseller and publisher, vi. 203, 339, 398 note, 403, 404, 514, 642, 646-7 and note, 648.

ALLHALLOWS, Bread Street, London, baptisms and burials of the Milton family at, i. 30, 39, 40, 44, 104, 105.

ALLINGTON, London actor, vi. 349.

ALL SOULS COLLEGE, Oxford, i. 625.

ALMONT, Viscount (Lord Livingstone and Almond): see Callander, 1st Earl of.

ALPHONSO V. of Portugal, v. 576, 589.

ALPHONSO VI. of Portugal, vi. 161.

ALSOP, John, fellow of Christ's College, Cambridge, i. 112, 123, 200; ii. 76.

ALTHORP, Lord Spencer's seat at, iii. 515.

ALURED, Christopher, supposed executioner of Charles I., vi. 94 note.

ALURED, John, case of, ii. 43-5 and note.

ALURED, John, Parliamentarian officer, ii. 445; signs death-warrant of Charles I., iii. 720; one of the Regicides dead before the Restoration, vi. 28; excepted in the Indemnity Act of 1660, vi. 54.

ALURED, Lawrence, Parliamentarian officer, ii. 444.

ALURED, Matthew, Colonel in the Republican army, iv. 402; in Scotland, iv. 551-2; in Republican plottings against Cromwell, v. 33; precautions against, v. 107; in service under Fleetwood, v. 470, 495, 517, 522, 537.

AMBROSE, Daniel, tutor of St. John's College, Cambridge, i. 121.

AMERICA, first British settlements in, i. 428-31: see New England.

AMES, Dr. William (Amesius), ii. 579.

AMSTERDAM, English Brownists in, ii. 538, 542; reputation of, as a nursery of heresies, iii. 163.

ANABAPTISTS or BAPTISTS: their first activity in England, i. 58, 342; ii. 539-40, 543-4; in New England, ii. 574; growth of, in the Parliamentary army and in England generally, iii. 89-91; origin and development of the principle of Religious Toleration among, iii. 99, 101-7; account of, as a recognised English sect in 1644-5, iii. 138-41, 146-9; outbreak against Cromwell, iv. 547-8; in 1654, v. 15; among the clergy of Cromwell's Established Church, v. 56-7; in Scotland, v. 92; after 1662, vi. 235.

"ANARCHIA ANGLICANA," Clement Walker's, iv. 121.

ANCHORAN, John, translator of Comenius, iii. 201.

ANCRAM (or Ancrum), Lord (Charles, 2nd Earl of), in the Restored Long Parliament of Monk's Dictatorship, v. 545, 552; in the Convention Parliament, vi. 51.

ANDERSON, Sir Edmund, i. 603 note.

ANDREW, Robert, Scottish "Protester," vi. 134.

ANDREWES, Lancelot, Bishop of Winchester: i. 368-9, 522; his death celebrated by Milton in Latin verse, i. 168; his pulpit oratory, i. 515, 518; author of a portion of the volume of Oxford Tracts replied to by Milton in his Reason of Church Government, ii. 364, 369-70; Charles I. and, iii. 515.

ANDREWS, Edward, Parliamentarian officer, ii. 444.

ANDREWS, Robert, in the Restored Rump, v. 453.

ANDREWS, Dr. Roger, Master of Jesus College, Cambridge, i. 116, 120.

ANDREWS, Alderman Thomas, one of the Regicides, iii. 720 note; knighted by Cromwell in 1657, v. 354 note; dead before the Restoration, vi. 28; excepted in the Indemnity Bill of 1660, vi. 54.

ANGEL, London actor, vi. 350.

ANGELONI, numismatist in Rome, i. 796.

ANGLESEY, Charles Villiers, 2nd Earl
of (deceased in 1660), ii. 429.
ANGLESEY, Arthur Annesley, Earl of:
see *Annesley, Arthur*.
ANGUS, Archibald Douglas, Earl of
(son of Marquis of Douglas), Scottish Privy Councillor in 1638, i.
707; 722; ii. 15; iv. 208, 561.
"ANIMADVERSIONS on the Remonstrant's Defence against Smectymnuus," Milton's, ii. 257-68.
ANLABY, John, in Second Council of
the Barebones Parliament, iv. 525;
in the Restored Rump, v. 453, 544
note.
ANNAN, Mr., Scotsman in Paris in
1638, i. 758.
ANNAN, William, Scottish prelatic
minister, i. 721.
ANNANDALE, Earl of, ii. 15, iii.
344.
ANNE, of Denmark, Queen of James
I., i. 61, 595; iii. 513.
ANNE, Princess, daughter of James I.:
Cambridge verses on her birth, i.
649.
ANNE, daughter of James II., Queen of
England, vi. 272, 605.
ANNE, Queen of Louis XIII. of France,
i. 744, 755, 756.
ANNESLEY, Arthur: his concern with
projected Royalist insurrection against
the Restored Rump, v. 472; in the
Council of State of Monk's Dictatorship, v. 544; in the Restored Long
Parliament, v. 545, 546, 549; co-
adjutor with Monk before the Restoration, v. 554; at the reception
of the Breda Letters from Charles II.,
v. 695-6; in the Privy Council of
Charles II. at the Restoration, vi.
19; in the Convention Parliament,
vi. 23, 24; in a Committee on the
Indemnity Bill, vi. 30, 32; in the
debates on the Indemnity Bill, 41,
43, 49, 51, 173; on the Commission
for Trial of the Regicides, vi. 77, 78,
89; in Conference respecting Charles
II.'s Ecclesiastical Declaration, vi.
99, 100; and Irish affairs, vi. 127;
created Earl of Anglesey (1661), vi.
152; his possible co-operation in
Milton's escape from punishment
after the Restoration, vi. 187, 189;

in the Clarendon Administration, vi.
222; made Lord Privy Seal, vi.
598; his acquaintance with Milton
in Milton's later years, vi. 637-
38.
ANNESLEY, Dr. Samuel, London Nonconformist minister, and grandfather
of the Wesleys, v. 541 note; vi. 232
note, 408, 416.
"ANNUS MIRABILIS," Dryden's, vi.
376-8.
ANSELME, William, Parliamentarian
officer, ii. 446.
ANSTIE, Stephen: author of Latin
verses on the death of Edward King,
i. 651.
ANSTRUTHER, Philip, fined by Cromwell, iv. 561.
ANSTRUTHER, Sir Robert, father of
Philip Anstruther, iv. 561.
"ANTAPOLOGIA" of Thomas Edwards,
iii. 130-5, 230.
ANTHOLIN, Church of St., London,
iii. 18.
ANTIGUA, colonisation of, v. 103.
ANTINOMIANS and ANTINOMIANISM,
ii. 559, 574; iii. 89-91; account of,
as a recognised English sect in 1644,
iii. 150-1; v. 15, 18.
ANTINORI, Florentine, i. 822.
ANTI-SABBATARIANS, English sect of,
iii. 155, v. 15.
ANTI-SCRIPTURISTS, English sect of,
iii. 158, v. 15.
ANTI-TRINITARIANS, English sect of,
iii. 157; Cromwell's toleration of,
v. 64-6: see also *Socinians*.
ANTRIM, Randal Macdonnell, Earl of;
his invasion of Argyleshire, ii. 23,
26-7; in the First Bishops' War,
ii. 51, 56; in the episode of Montrose in Scotland, iii. 344, 345, 347,
348.
APOLLO TAVERN, see *Taverns*.
"APOLOGETICAL NARRATION," the, of
the Five Independents of the Westminster Assembly, iii. 23-6, 128,
129, 130, 131.
"APOLOGIA *contra Johannis Polyprag-
matici, alias Miltoni Angli, Defen-
sionem*," by an anonymous author,
and Reply to the same for Milton by
his nephew John Phillips, entitled
Johannis Philippi Responsio ad Apolo-

giam Anonymi cujusdam tenebrionis,
iv. 470-4.

"APOLOGY" for Smectymnuus, Milton's, see *Milton,* Writings of.

APPLEBOOM, Harold, Swedish Ambassador in London, iv. 378.

APPLETON, Captain, iv. 485.

APPLETREE, Matthew, the Powell property and, iii. 477-8, 482, 639; iv. 237-8.

APPLETREE, Richard, iii. 479.

APPLETREE, Thomas, iii. 479.

"ARCADES," Milton's Masque, entitled, i. 578 — 602; occasion of the Masque and account of the heroine, i. 587-97; probable date of, i. 599 note, and 604 note: argument of, i. 599-602.

"ARCADIA", Sir Philip Sidney's, plagiarism from, in the *Eikon Basilike,* iv. 248-9 and note.

ARCHDALE, the family of, ii. 493 and note.

ARCHER, Giles, son-in-law of Cæsar Calandrini, v. 174 note.

ARCHER, John, in Southwark, story of, and of the warrant for his torture, ii. 133-4.

ARCHER, Puritan divine, suspended by Laud, i. 402; reputed a Millenary, iii. 153.

ARDERNE, James, one of the Rota Club, v. 485.

ARDGLASS, Earl of, Royalist peer, ii. 429.

"AREOPAGITICA," Milton's: immediate occasion of his writing it, iii. 266-75; the pamphlet itself, iii. 275-91; its literary character and style, iii. 278-9; abstract and extracts, iii. 279-90; its indications of Milton's personal relations to the Presbyterians and the Independents, iii. 285-7; nature and limits of its doctrine of Toleration, iii. 287-90; effects of, upon the English public mind, iii. 431-4; see also under *Milton,* Writings of.

ARGYLE, Archibald Campbell, 7th Earl of, i. 707; sketch of the life and character of, in his later years, by the Roman Catholic poet Habington, ii. 10-12; his death in 1638, ii. 13, 41 and note.

ARGYLE, Archibald Campbell, 8th Earl of; Scottish Privy Councillor, as Lord Lorne, i. 707, 710, 724; estates transferred to him while still Lord Lorne, i. 707, ii. 11; becomes 8th Earl by his father's death, ii. 13; his position towards the King and Covenanters previous to the First Bishops' War, ii. 10, 12-4, 15, 16; his character, as painted by Clarendon and by Scott, ii. 11, 13-4; during the Marquis of Hamilton's Mission, ii. 21, 28, 33; his hereditary feud with the Clandonald, ii. 23, 26-7; his correspondence with Wentworth, ii. 26-7; takes part in the Glasgow Assembly of 1638, and becomes an open Covenanter, ii. 41, 42; his influence with the Privy Councillors, ii. 55; correspondence with Earls Pembroke and Holland, ii. 61; joins the Scottish camp at Dunse, ii. 65; at the pacification of Birks, ii. 71; in Second Bishops' War, ii. 137; his importance in Scottish affairs in 1641, ii. 292-3; early distrust of Montrose, ii. 295; plots against, in 1640-1, ii. 296-301; during the King's visit to Scotland in 1641, ii. 303-6; in Scottish Government of 1641, ii. 307, 416-7; created Marquis by Charles I., ii. 308; his policy of sympathy with the English Parliament, ii. 417, 418; opposes neutrality, iii. 7; is an occasional lay-commissioner in the Westminster Assembly, iii. 17; accompanies the Scottish auxiliary army into England, iii. 37; in the episode of Montrose in Scotland, iii. 340-3, 347, 348-9, 351, 352, 353, 354, 355, 356, 357, 361, 367; re-establishment of his supremacy after Philiphaugh, iii. 368-9; in negotiations with Charles I. at Newcastle, iii. 412; a glimpse of, as a British politician, in his speech to a committee of the English Parliament, iii. 418-20; presents the Nineteen Propositions to the King, iii. 421, 422; in continued negotiations with Charles I. at Newcastle, iii. 498, 499; in English and Scottish disputes concerning the King, iii. 509; opposes

the Scottish *Engagement*, and refrains from any part with Hamilton in the Second Civil War, iii. 589, *et seq.* ; leader of the *Anti-Engagers* and Whigamores in Scotland (1648), iii. 620-1 ; in a deputation of Scottish Committee of Estates to Cromwell, iii. 621-2 ; his understanding with Cromwell, iv. 20-22 ; his relations to the Kirk and Government in 1649, iv. 62 ; his part at the trial and execution of Montrose, iv. 185-7 ; at the head of the Committee of Estates when Cromwell invades Scotland, iv. 196, 199 ; the " Argyle, or Government, Party " after Dunbar, iv. 201-6 ; his dealings with Charles II. in Scotland, iv. 207-10, 299 ; places the Crown on Charles II.'s head at Scone, iv. 212 ; in the seventh session of the second Triennial Scottish Parliament, iv. 281 ; opposes march of Charles II. into England, and refuses to accompany him, iv. 290 ; his ruined condition in Scotland after the Battle of Worcester, iv. 299 ; reflections on his character and career, iv. 299-302 ; at the incorporation of Scotland with the English Commonwealth, iv. 365 ; his extreme poverty under the Protectorate, v. 87 ; grant to, by the Council of the Protectorate, of half the excise of wines and strong waters in Scotland, v. 94-5 note ; in London, on a suit to the Protector, and visits Evelyn, v. 94-5, 97 ; favours Cromwell's Kirk policy for Scotland, v. 345 ; in Richard's Parliament, v. 430, 435 ; back in Scotland, under the Restored Rump (1659), v. 459 ; appears at Whitehall after the Restoration, and is committed to the Tower, vi. 131-2 ; state of feeling in Scotland respecting him after the Restoration, vi. 135 ; removed from the Tower to Edinburgh Castle, vi. 140 ; in Edinburgh Castle, vi. 142 ; his trial, vi. 150 ; his execution, vi. 160.

ARGYLE, Lady Anne Douglas, Countess of (wife of Archibald, 7th Earl), ii. 11.

ARGYLE-WARRISTON GOVERNMENT, their " Act of Classes," and proclamation of Charles II., iv. 19-22 ;

their negotiations with Charles II. at the Hague, iv. 26-7 ; and Treaty of Breda (May 1650), iv. 180, 182 ; character of the, iv. 187.

ARIANISM, Milton's, vi. 823.

ARIANS, English : two burnt, i. 60 ; account of, in 1644-5, iii. 157 ; in 1654-5, v. 15.

ARISTOTLE, in the Universities, i. 263-6 ; references to, by Milton in his Academic exercises, i. 280, 282, 283, 288, 295 and note, 305-6.

ARLINGTON, Henry Bennet, Earl of : ambassador in Spain for Charles II. in his exile, v. 503-4 ; succeeds Sir Edward Nicholas as English Secretary of State, vi. 237 ; among the crypto-catholics at the court of Charles II., vi. 239-40 ; his part in the Toleration Edict of 1662, vi. 242, 244 ; a favourite with Charles II., vi. 245 ; raised to the peerage as Lord Arlington, vi. 253 ; at Clarendon's fall, vi. 263-4, 271 ; licenser of the *London Gazette*, vi. 331 ; in the Cabal Administration, vi. 562-3, 565 ; in the Secret Negotiation with France for undoing the Triple Alliance, vi. 569, 570-1 ; in the Cabal from 1670, vi. 574-5, 591 ; his concern in the Secret Treaty of Dover between Charles II. and Louis XIV., vi. 576, 579-80 ; made Earl of Arlington, vi. 582 ; during the Dutch War, vi. 585 ; at the break-up of the Cabal, vi. 597 ; principal Secretary of State, vi. 598, 600 ; his unpopularity with the " No Popery " party, vi. 600, 602 ; is appointed Lord Chamberlain in the Danby Cabinet, vi. 603, 729 ; occasionally licenses a book, vi. 616 ; Milton's nephew, Edward Phillips, some time in his household, vi. 765-7 ; his mansion of Euston described by Evelyn, vi. 765-6 ; his only daughter, and her marriage with Henry Fitzroy, one of the natural sons of Charles II., vi. 766-7.

ARMANI, Giuseppe, suit against, by John Hosier, for swindling, v. 386-7.

ARMINIANISM, condemned by the Synod of Dort, i. 61 ; at Cambridge

University, i. 129 ; declared against by Charles I.'s Third Parliament, i. 215-6 ; Milton's college tutor, William Chappell, accused of, ii. 76-7 : among the Brownists at Amsterdam, ii. 539.

ARMINIANS, i. 518.

ARMINIUS, theologian of Leyden, i. 59, 529.

ARMSTRONG, Archie, court-fool to Charles I., ii. 5-6 and note.

ARMSTRONG, John, corrector to Dugard's printing-press, iv. 152.

ARMY, the King's English : in the First Bishops' War, ii. 50-1, 58, 62-5, 70 ; in the Second Bishops' War, ii. 135-42 ; "Army Plot" for the release of Strafford, ii. 183.

ARMY, the English Royalist : in the First Civil War, ii. 421-4 : composition and officering of, at the commencement of the War, ii. 440-3, 448-53 ; through the War, ii. 453-71 ; iii. 96, 176-7, 329-38, 370-2, 374 ; in the Second Civil War, iii. 590-605.

ARMY, English Parliamentarian : in the Civil War, ii. 421-2 ; composition and officering of, at the commencement of the War, ii. 443-8, 448-53 ; through the War, ii. 453-71, iii. 96-8, 176-80 ; Parliamentary Ordinance for new modelling of the, iii. 181-3, 325 ; composition and officering of the New Model, and view of the work lying before it, iii. 325-30, 328 note ; first actions of the New Model, iii. 330-2 ; successes of, iii. 332-8, 369-72 ; at the close of the First Civil War, 377-81 ; Independency and Sectarianism in, iii. 384-6 ; proposal of the Presbyterians in Parliament for disbandment of, iii. 516, 521-2 ; general account of, in 1647, iii. 522-6 ; objections of the, to being disbanded, iii. 526-9 ; votes in Parliament for disbanding the, iii. 529-32 ; resistance of the, to the same, iii. 532-4 ; "Agitatorships" in the, iii. 535 ; futile attempts at mediation by the, iii. 535-7 ; cause of, against Parliament adopted by Fairfax and other leaders of the, iii. 537-8 ; Cromwell's "Flight to the Army,"

iii. 538, 538 note ; general Rendezvous of the, under Fairfax, iii. 538-9 ; at the abduction of the King by Joyce, iii. 538-43 ; movements of the, iii. 547-9 ; denunciation of eleven chiefs of the Commons by the, iii. 548 ; march of the, under Fairfax, on London, iii. 553-4, 560 ; *Heads of Proposals* by the, to the King and Parliament, iii. 557-9, 559 note, 565-6 ; headquarters of the, shifted to Putney, iii. 561-2 ; interference from Scotland with the, iii. 562-4 ; suspicions in the, of Cromwell's integrity, iii. 569 ; "Levellers" in the, and their Army-tracts, iii. 570, 610 ; mutiny of the, iii. 571-4 ; the King escapes from the, iii. 574-5 ; the mutiny suppressed, iii. 583 ; Concordat of, with the Parliament, iii. 584, 610 ; in the Second Civil War, iii. 590-605 ; the mastery of affairs assumed by the, iii. 611-6 ; Grand Army Remonstrance, iii. 616-20 ; headquarters of the, near London, iii. 625-6, 629-30 ; the King in the custody of, iii. 625-30 ; the two Houses in the grasp of the, iii. 692-5 ; "Pride's Purge" of Parliament by the, iii. 696-9 ; resolution of the, for the capital punishment of the King, iii. 699 ; the King's removal to Windsor by the, iii. 699-702 ; estimation of the available military forces in England and Wales in March 1648-9, iv. 41 ; in Cromwell's expedition into Scotland (1650-1) : see *Scotland ;* in the pursuit of Charles II. : see *Charles II. ;* supreme power of the, and of its officers, in the affairs of the Commonwealth, iv. 401-3 ; dissatisfaction of the, with the government of the Rump, iv. 402-3, 403-4 ; at the dissolution of the Rump, iv. 408-14 ; payment of arrears to the, under the Protectorate, v. 32, 35, 139 ; at the accession of Richard Cromwell, v. 418 ; Monk's advice to Richard concerning the, v. 419-20 ; the *Army,* or *Wallingford House, Party,* v. 421 ; the, through the Protectorate of Richard, v. 421-51 ; action of the, under Fleetwood, at Richard's

downfall, v. 459-60 ; remodelling of the, by the restored Rump, v. 468 71, 497 ; struggle for supremacy between the Rump and the, v. 486-95 ; arrangements for the officering and discipline of the, by the Council of Safety, v. 495-7 ; condition and mood of the, immediately before the Restoration, v. 561-2 ; Monk's manipulation of the, v. 562-4 ; devices of Parliament for disbanding the, vi. 57, 69 ; final disbanding and dispersion of, and the survival of three of the regiments as the "King's Guards," vi. 76.

ARMY, Cromwell's English Auxiliary, to co-operate with the French in Flanders : see *Flanders*.

ARMY, Monk's English, in Scotland : see *Scotland* and *Monk*.

ARMY, the English, for the subjection of Ireland, iv. 41, 56 : see under *Ireland*.

ARMY, Scottish Covenanting ; under General Leslie, in the First Bishops' War, ii. 52-8, 63-8, 70, 293, 295-6 ; in the Second Bishops' War, ii. 135-42 ; offer of the Scottish Parliament to Charles I. of a portion of the, for service in Ireland, ii. 317 : see *Scotland*.

ARMY, Scottish Auxiliary ; in the First Civil War under General Leslie (Lord Leven), iii. 35-8, 40, 84-7, 96-8, 177, 339-40 ; iv. 205 ; at Newcastle with the King, iii. 372-4, 411-22, 491-510 : see *Scotland*.

ARMY, Scottish Royalist ; in the Second Civil War, commanded by the Duke of Hamilton, iii. 589-92, 597 ; at the Battle of Preston, iii. 604.

ARMY, Scottish Royalist, of Charles II. ; under command of David Leslie, at the English Invasion of Scotland, iv. 196-201 ; at the Battle of Dunbar, iv. 200-1 ; after Dunbar, iv. 203, 284, 287-94 ; at Worcester, iv. 294 : see *Charles II.*

ARMY, the Irish Insurgent, or Army of the Confederate Catholics of Ireland, in the Insurrection of 1641 : see *Ireland*.

"ARMY'S MODEST INTELLIGENCER," the, iv. 39.

ARMYN, Sir William, ii. 273, 464 ; iii. 8, 41, 510, 599 note ; iv. 12, 83, 87, 147, 223, 224, 229, 230, 231, 313-4, 273.

ARNALD, army-mutineer, shot by order of Cromwell, iii. 583, iv. 43.

ARNOLD, Christopher, Professor of History at Nuremberg : his stay in London, and account of Milton, iv. 350-3, 417.

ARNOTT, of Fernie, fined by Cromwell, iv. 561.

ARRAN, Earl of : see *Hamilton*, Marquis of.

ARRAN, Isle of, ii. 56.

ARROWSMITH, John, Puritan divine : at Cambridge, i. 121 ; account of, ii. 516 ; member of Westminster Assembly, ii. 605 ; appointed master of St. John's College, Cambridge, iii. 93, 95 note ; iv. 514, 571 ; v. 74.

ARTHINGTON, Henry, fined by the Restored Rump, v. 478.

ARTHUR, Prince of Wales, son of Henry VII., i. 607.

ARTILLERY WALK, Milton's house in, vi. 481-86, 498-500, 636, 728, 731 : see *Bunhill Fields*.

"ARTIS LOGICÆ PLENIOR INSTITUTIO" : see *Milton*, Writings of.

ARUNDEL and SURREY, *Thomas Howard*, 2nd Earl of : i. 378, 383, 384, 385, 666 ; ii. 9 note, 24, 46, 50, 57, 62, 63, 64, 68, 128, 144, **152,** 179, 184, 278, 280, 283, 429, **430.**

ARUNDEL, Countess, i. 523.

ARUNDEL, Mr. John, Cornish gentleman, ii. 466.

ARUNDEL, of Wardour, 2nd Lord, ii. 429 ; vi. 570-1, 576.

ASCHAM, Anthony, English resident in Madrid, iv. 126, 160-1 ; his assassination, iv. 193, 234, 235-6 ; vi. 179 note.

ASH, James, Restored Rumper, v. 453.

ASHBURNHAM, Colonel William : in Long Parliament, ii. 173, 284 ; treasurer of Royalist Army, ii. 441 ; his regiment, ii. 442.

ASHBURNHAM, Mr. John, ii. 415 ; groom of the bedchamber to Charles I., iii. 373, 561, 568, 574, 587 ; committed to the Tower in 1656, v. 107.

ASHE, Simeon, army-chaplain, ii. 444; member of Westminster Assembly; account of, ii. 516, 593; chaplain to Earl of Manchester, iii. 92, 677; iv. 71; correspondence with Baillie, v. 98, 115; after the Restoration, vi. 62; one of the ejected Nonconformists, vi. 232 note, 416.

ASHFIELD, Colonel Richard: in New Model, iii. 326, iv. 402, v. 470, 487, 490, 521, 547.

ASHLEY, Baron: see *Cooper*, Sir Anthony Ashley.

ASHMOLE, Elias, vi. 459.

ASHTON, Peter, of Trinity College, Cambridge, i. 237.

ASHURST, William, v. 5.

ASHWORTH, Edward, ii. 496; iii. 474-5, 634-5; iv. 240-1.

ASHWORTH, Mrs., wife of Edward Ashworth, iv. 241-2.

ASHWORTH, Walter, Parliamentarian officer, ii. 444.

ASSEMBLY, Scottish General: of 1638, ii. 36-42, 70; of 1639, ii. 71, 122, 130; of 1640, ii. 136-7; of 1641, ii. 271, 287-91, 368 note, 418-20, 509-10; of 1642, ii. 418-20; of 1643-4, iii. 7, 8, 10; of 1644-5, iii. 175-6, 357; of 1646, iii. 417; of 1647, iii. 509, 563; of 1649, iv. 122; of 1650, iv. 190, 197; of 1651, iv. 288-9; of 1653, dispersed by Colonel Cotterel, iv. 509-10.

ASSEMBLY, Supreme, of Notables: called by Cromwell, iv. 500-2.

ASSEMBLY, Westminster: convention of, by the Long Parliament, ii. 509-14; meeting of, ii. 514-5; list of the members, with biographical sketches, ii. 515-24; composition of, ii. 524-7, 602-8; Presbyterians and Independents in, ii. 604-5; Erastians in, ii. 605-8; opening of, and forms of procedure, iii. 3-4; first business of, iii. 4-6; the Solemn League and Covenant adopted by, iii. 11-2; Scottish Commissioners to, list of, with biographic sketches, iii. 16-8; first debates in, between the Presbyterians and the Independents, iii. 18-26; the five leading Independents in, iii. 22-3; proceedings in, iii. 31; debates on Independency continued in, with growing horror of sects and sectaries, and question of Toleration, iii. 87-91; denunciation of picked sectaries and heretics, iii. 160-6; attention to cases of heresy and blasphemy, iii. 170; progress of its main work, and results as far as to end of 1644, iii. 171-6; and Milton's second Divorce tract, iii. 258-60; attack on Milton, by Mr. Herbert Palmer, iii. 262; continued controversy in, over Independency, the Sects, and Toleration, iii. 382-3; and the case of Paul Best, iii. 384-5; Toleration Controversy continued in, iii. 394-6; proceedings of, through 1645, and progress of Presbyterian Settlement, iii. 396-400; difference between, and Parliament on "The Power of the Keys," and the Assembly rebuked, iii. 405-9 and note, 410-1; Presbyterian remonstrance to Parliament, iii. 416; Marquis of Argyle in, iii. 420; reconciliation of, with the Parliament, iii. 422-6; continued work of, iii. 425-6, 511-3; the *Confession of Faith* completed by, and presented to Parliament, iii. 512, 545, 567; also their *Larger Catechism*, iii. 568; members of, still zealous against sects and heretics, iii. 677; cessation of the, iv. 58-60; its bequests to England and to Scotland, iv. 60-3.

ASTLEY, Sir Jacob (created Lord Astley of Reading in 1664), ii. 62, 440; iii. 335, 372.

ASTON, Sir Arthur, Royalist officer, ii. 441, 442, 464-5.

"ASTRÆA REDUX," Dryden's, vi. 16, 317.

"AT A SOLEMN MUSIC," see *Milton*, Writings of.

"AT A VACATION EXERCISE IN THE COLLEGE," see *Milton*, Writings of.

ATHEISTS, English, iii. 159, v. 15.

ATHERSTON MOOR, Battle of, iii. 6.

ATHOLL, 2nd Earl of, iv. 205, 206, 212, 508, 560.

ATKINS, Alderman Thomas, ii. 166, 466; iv. 88; knighted by Cromwell, v. 354 note; in the Restored Rump, v. 453; mentioned in *Treason Arraigned*, v. 666.

ATKINS, Judge, v. 67-8.

ATTAINDER, Bills of: against Strafford, ii. 182; against the Regicides, vi. 112, 114.

ATTAWAY, Mrs., Baptist preacher, iii. 149, 153; story of, and her sympathy with Milton's Divorce Doctrine, iii. 189-92.

ATTERBURY, Francis, afterwards Bishop: a subscriber to the fourth edition of *Paradise Lost*, vi. 785.

AUBIGNY, Lord (Abbé), vi. 229; and Bellings's Mission, vi. 240-1, 247; and the Toleration Edict, vi. 242; and Morus, vi. 422.

AUBIGNY, Lord, brother of Duke of Richmond: killed at Edgehill, ii. 455.

AUBREY, John: his accounts of Milton's father, i. 50, of Suckling, i. 504, of Waller, i. 506, of Henry Marten, ii. 166; under the Protectorate, v. 76; in the Rota Club, v. 485; among Men of Letters of the Restoration, vi. 314; a Fellow of the Royal Society, vi. 396; visits Milton, vi. 638.

AUDLAND, John, Quaker, v. 26.

AUDLEY, Lady, i. 597 note.

AUDLEY, Lord: see *Castlehaven*, Earl of.

AUGIER, René, iv. 227, 381, 482; v. 178.

AULDEARN, Battle of, iii. 359.

AUSTEN, licenser of books, i. 550 note.

AUSTIN, George, Parliamentarian officer, ii. 445.

AVERY, Mr., iii. 218.

AXTELL, Daniel, captain in New Model, iii. 326; Major, iii. 524, 534, 537; Colonel, iii. 619; at "Pride's Purge," iii. 696; at the King's trial, iii. 707; arrests Levellers, iv. 45; in army of Ireland, iv. 401; in Oliver's First Parliament, v. 5; and Republican remodelling of the army, v. 471; with Lambert at Daventry, v. 566; excepted from Indemnity Bill, vi. 39, 44-5, 46-8, 50-1, 54; his trial, vi. 80, 87-8, 94; his execution, vi. 97; attainted, vi. 115.

AYLMER, Brabazon, publisher of Milton's *Epistolæ Familiares* and *Prolusiones Oratoriæ*, i. 273-4; vi. 719-22; publisher of Milton's *Translation of Letters Patent of Election of King of Poland*, vi. 725; and Jacob Tonson, vi. 781-2; subscriber to the fourth edition of *Paradise Lost*, vi. 785; publisher of Milton's *History of Moscovia*, vi. 812.

AYSCOUGH MSS. in the British Museum, i. 101; v. 603 note.

AYSCOUGH, Sir Edward, ii. 232, 445.

AYSCOUGH, Admiral, Sir George: in the war with the Dutch, iv. 374-5; vi. 254-5; Swedish expedition of, v. 428, 571-2.

AYTOUN, Sir Robert (Scottish poet), i. 462.

B

BAAS, M. de, French diplomatic agent, and Cromwell, iv. 554-6.

BABINGTON, John, iv. 578.

BABTHORPE, Major, Royalist officer, ii. 442.

BACHILER, John, licenser for the press, iii. 270, 432 and note.

BACHILTON, Laird of, iv. 561.

BACON, Lord Chancellor, i. 29; his trial and sentence, i. 106; his intention to endow a Natural Philosophy Lectureship at Cambridge, i. 155, 267; his *Instauratio Magna* presented by himself to the Cambridge University Library, i. 265; first signs of the Baconian spirit at Cambridge, i. 265-6; his Latin prose compared with Milton's, i. 298, 348, 351, 352; Ben Jonson's reverence for, i. 438-9; i. 514, 527, 528, 529, 530, 540, 541; referred to by Milton, ii. 284; his views on Brownism, ii. 538.

BACON, Mr. Justice, in the prosecution of Milton by Stationers' Company, iii. 295-6.

BADDELEY, Admiral, iv. 485.

BADDELEY, Richard, publisher, iv. 520.

BAGSHAW, Edward (lawyer), in Long Parliament, ii. 173; and the *Root and Branch* Bill, ii. 217; opposes "Grand Remonstrance," ii. 321.

BAGSHAW, Edward, member of the Rota Club, v. 485.

BAHAMAS, the, v. 103.

BAILDON, Cuthbert, Lieutenant to Cromwell in 1642, ii. 446.

BAILLIE, of Lamington, ii. 38.

BAILLIE, Mr. Robert, minister of Kil-

winning near Glasgow, i. 712 ; his " Letters " referred to, i. 712 note, 718, 719, 727 ; in the Negotiations with the Marquis of Hamilton, ii. 13, 16 ; in the Glasgow Assembly of 1638, ii. 37, 38, 39 ; his account of the " First Bishops' War," ii. 63, 65-9 ; pamphlets by, ii. 126, 218, 382, 382 note ; with the Scottish preachers at Newcastle, ii. 142 ; in the Scottish Commission to London, from Nov. 1640 to June 1641, ii. 191, 288 ; present at the Trial of Strafford, ii. 180, 191-3 ; in the English Church Reform Movement, ii. 202, 215, 224, 591 ; letter of Henderson to, in 1642, ii. 419 ; his account of the *Solemn League and Covenant*, iii. 9-10 ; is Professor of Divinity in the University of Glasgow, iii. 16 ; in the Westminster Assembly from Nov. 1643 to Dec. 1646, iii. 16, 87, 91 and note, 121, 130, 142-59, 160, 162, 184, 264 note, 393, 406-9, 412-3, 501 ; his *Dissuasive from the Errors of the Time*, iii. 142-59 ; in the General Assembly at Edinburgh in 1645, iii. 175-6, 357 ; his opinion of Milton's Doctrine of Divorce, iii. 264 note, 467-8 ; the epithet " Scotch What d'ye call " applied to, by Milton, iii. 468-70 ; vi. 214 ; return of, to Glasgow, iii. 511-3 ; at the death of Henderson, iii. 428, 429 note, 430 ; his admiration of Morus, iv. 460 note ; with Charles II. at the Hague in 1649, iv. 20, 26, 180 ; a "Resolutioner," iv. 203, 209, 213 ; v. 97 ; at the dispersion of the General Assembly in Edinburgh in 1653, iv. 510 ; his account of Cromwell's policy in 1654, iv. 569 ; his description of Glasgow city and University in 1656, v. 88 ; his interest in Sharp's mission to London, v. 97-8 ; Sharp's letter to, from Breda, vi. 5 ; his state of feeling after the Restoration, vi. 135-7, 141 ; appointed Principal of Glasgow University in 1660, vi. 141-2 ; his reference to the fates of the Regicides and to "blind Milton," vi. 214 ; special reference to the *Letters and Journals* of, iii. 16.

BAILLIE, William, Lieutenant-General to the Scottish Covenanting Army in First Bishops' War, ii. 55 ; with Scottish auxiliary army in England, iii. 37 ; during the episode of Montrose in Scotland, iii. 353, 355, 357-9, 360-1 ; in the Scottish invasion of England during the Second Civil War, iii. 596.

BAINBRIGGE, Christopher, i. 171, 651, 654.

BAINBRIGGE, Dr. Thomas, Master of Christ's College, Cambridge, and in 1627-8 Vice-Chancellor of the University, i. 116, 123, 160, 167, 170, 181, 182, 183 note, 186, 187, 193 ; his letter to the Duke of Buckingham, i. 205, 239-40 note, 267, 269, ii. 76, 401 note ; at the visitation of Cambridge University in 1644, iii. 93.

BAKER, Cambridge antiquary, i. 116, 234, 238, 255.

BAKER, George, Bishop of Waterford and Lismore, vi. 128.

BAKER, James, in the Restored Rump, v. 453.

BAKER, Mr., book-licenser, iii. 198 ; iv. 152, 156.

BAKER, Richard, merchant, v. 271.

BAKER, Sir Richard : his Chronicle of the Kings of England, iii. 446 ; vi. 463, 481, 765, 767.

BAKER, Thomas, v. 625.

BAKERS of Bayfordbury, Herts, the family of, and Milton's portraits, vi. 754-8 note.

BALCANQUHAL, Dr. Walter, ii. 10, 17, 35, 40, 51, 301.

BALCARRES, Lord Lindsay of : in the "First Bishops' War," ii. 65.

BALCARRES, Alexander, 1st Earl of (1651), in the Scottish General Assembly of 1642, ii. 418 ; against Montrose, iii. 360, 361 ; with Charles I. at Newcastle, iii. 412 ; with Charles II. in Scotland, iv. 290, 302 ; 365 ; agitating in the Highlands for the King, iv. 508-9.

BALDWIN, James, of Suffolk, i. 112.

BALDWIN, Thomas, fellow-student of Milton at Christ's College, Cambridge, i. 112, 218, 258.

BALFOUR, Sir James, Lyon King of Arms, iii. 357.

BALFOUR, Sir William, Lieutenant of the Tower of London in 1640, ii. 133-4, 330; Lieutenant-General in the Parliamentarian Army, ii. 445; iii. 168.

BALFOUR, William, Parliamentarian officer, ii. 445.

BALIANI of Genoa, i. 767.

BALL, John, treatises by, ii. 593, 595.

BALL, William, and the Royal Society, vi. 394, 396.

BALLARD, Colonel Thomas, Parliamentarian officer, ii. 444.

BALMERINO, John, 2nd Lord: Covenanter, i. 710, 722, 723, ii. 16; in the Glasgow Assembly of 1638, ii. 38; in the Committee of Estates in 1640, ii. 292; in the Westminster Assembly, iii. 17; in a deputation to Charles I. at Newcastle, iii. 499.

BALVAIRD, Lord, iv. 561.

BAMPFIELD, Colonel (Royalist), iii. 593.

BAMPFIELD, John, sergeant-major in the Parliamentarian army, ii. 444.

BAMPFIELD, Thomas, in Richard's Parliament, v. 432.

BAMPFIELD, William, Colonel in the Parliamentarian army, ii. 444.

BANBURY, burning of the town of, iii. 482.

BANCROFT, Archbishop of Canterbury (1604 to 1610), i, 347; ii. 543, 545.

BANCROFT, Bishop of Oxford (1632 to 1641), i. 399; ii. 150, 151, 498 and note, ii. 324.

"BANDERS," the Scottish, of 1642, ii. 417, 418.

BANDS (Covenants): use of, in Scottish History, i. 726; the Earl of Montrose's, called "the, of Cumbernauld," ii. 296.

BANER, General, i. 743.

BANFF (Sir George Ogilvy), 1st Lord, iv. 561.

BANISTER, Mr., i. 627.

BANKS, Sir John, Attorney-General, ii. 159; Lord Chief Justice, ii. 279-81, 283, 337.

BAPTISTS: see Anabaptists.

BARBADOES, v. 103.

BARBER, Edward, Baptist preacher, iii. 148.

BARBER, English Presbyterian, ii. 532.

BARBERINI, Cardinal Antonio, the elder, i. 795, 797.

BARBERINI, Cardinal Antonio, the younger, i. 795.

BARBERINI, Carlo, i. 795.

BARBERINI, Cardinal Francesco, i. 795, 798-800; his reception of Milton at Rome, i. 802-3; Milton's salutations to, i. 823; vi. 240.

BARBERINI, Maffeo: see Urban VIII.

BARBERINI, Taddeo, i. 795.

BARBICAN: the town-house of the Bridgewater family in London in the, ii. 80, 208; Milton's house in the, iii. 437-8, 442-4, 486-7.

BARBONE: see Barebones.

BARCLAY, Colonel, in the New Model Army, iii. 326.

BARCLAY, David, Scottish Cromwellian, iv. 562; v. 108; vi. 134.

BARCLAY of Towie, ii. 38.

BARCLAY, Robert, apologist for the Quakers: account of his book, v. 22-5.

BARCLAY, Robert, Provost of Irvine, agent in London for the Scottish Covenanters, ii. 132; iii. 40, 175, 510, 578.

BAREBONES (or BARBONE), Praise God, London leather-dealer and Baptist preacher, iii. 147; iv. 505; v. 533, 561, 666, 671; vi. 179 note.

BAREBONES PARLIAMENT, the, iv. 505; its proceedings and collapse, iv. 510-7: see Parliaments.

BARGENY (Sir John Hamilton), 1st Lord, iv. 560.

BARKER, Colonel John, in the Restored Rump, v. 453.

BARKER, Independent divine, v. 497.

BARKSTEAD, Colonel John, Regicide, iii. 720; officer under the Commonwealth, iv. 323, 402, 403; in Cromwell's First Parliament, v. 5; one of Cromwell's major-generals, v. 49; in Cromwell's Second Parliament, v. 107; Lieutenant of the Tower, v. 259, 320; knighted by Cromwell, v. 303 note; one of Cromwell's lords, v. 324, 338; supports Richard's Government, v. 418, 469; at the quest of the Regicides, vi. 28; excepted from the Indemnity Bill, vi. 31, 54; fugitive, vi. 115 and

note ; captured in Holland, brought home, and executed, vi. 228-9.

BARLAEUS, Caspar, iv. 165.

BARLOW, Lucy : see *Waters*.

BARLOW, Mary, and the Irish Massacre of 1641, ii. 312-3.

BARLOWE, Randolph, Irish archbishop, i. 420.

BARNARD, Nathaniel, Puritan lecturer at St. Sepulchre's, London, i. 407.

BARNET, Henry, London sectary, i. 402.

BARNEVELDT, reference to, in account of Grotius, i. 746.

BARNSTAPLE, surrender of, to the Parliament, iii. 371-2.

BARON, Richard : his edition of Milton's *Eikonoklastes*, v. 603 note.

BARONI, Adriana, Italian singer, i. 803.

BARONI, Catherine, Italian singer, i. 803.

BARONI, Leonora, Italian singer, i. 803-4 and note; Milton's three Latin poems of compliment to, i. 804, 821 note ; iii. 650.

BARRET, Edward : see *Newburgh*, Baron.

BARRIÈRE, M. de, envoy in London from the Prince of Condé, iv. 381.

BARRIMORE, David Barry, 1st Earl of : in First " Bishops' War," ii. 62 ; his wife, Lady Alice Boyle, iii. 660.

BARRIMORE, Richard Barry, 2nd Earl of : his relations to Milton, iii. 658-60 ; v. 233-4, 235 and note.

BARRINGTON, Sir Thomas, in Long Parliament, ii. 173 ; lay member of Westminster Assembly, ii. 524.

BARRON, Dr. Robert, one of the " Aberdeen Doctors," i. 715, 716 note ; ii. 28, 29, 69.

BARROW, Henry, leader of the Brownists or *Barrowists*, ii. 537, 539, 569 ; iii. 101.

BARROW, Isaac : his matriculation at Cambridge, i. 243 ; under the Protectorate, v. 76 ; after the Restoration, vi. 315, 388, 617 ; and Daniel Skinner, vi. 791, 803.

BARROW, Robert (or William), Colonel in the Irish Army, iv. 401 ; at the Republican officering of the army, v. 470, 490, 496 ; in disgrace, v. 521.

BARROW, Dr. Samuel, physician to Monk's army in Scotland, v. 476, 499, 500, 528, 534 ; and Milton's *Paradise Lost*, vi. 714-5 and note.

BARTAS : see *Du Bartas*.

BARTELSON, Lambert, v. 250.

BARTHOLOMEW CLOSE, place of Milton's hiding at the Restoration, vi. 162-3.

BARTHOLOMEW'S DAY, St., 1662, ejection of English Nonconformist clergy on, vi. 225-6.

BARTHOLOMEW'S, Little St., residence of the Diodati family, i. 100.

BARTOLOMMEI, G., Florentine, i. 822.

BARTON, Colonel, iv. 525.

BARTON, Mr. William, minister of St. John Zachary, Aldersgate : author of metrical version of the Psalms, iii. 425, 485, 512, 634, 635 note, 674 note.

BARTON, W., mathematician, i. 569.

BARWELL, Edmund, Milton's fellow-student at Christ's College, Cambridge, i. 149, 218, 258.

BARWICK, Dr., Episcopalian divine, vi. 99.

BASCON, a Frenchman, v. 576.

BASING HOUSE, storming of, iii. 369.

BASSECOUR, Nicolas de la, pastor of Amsterdam in 1654, v. 196.

BASTWICK, Dr. John, Puritan pamphleteer, i. 543, 681-2 ; ii. 175, 176 note ; his antipathy to Independency and Toleration, ii. 588-9 ; iii. 130, 386, 390.

BASTWICK, Susanna, wife of the above, ii. 176 note.

BATCHCROFT, Dr., of Caius College, Cambridge, i. 171, 172 ; iii. 93.

BATEMAN, London actor, vi. 349.

BATES, Dr., London physician, attends Cromwell in Scotland, iv. 278 ; sent by Cromwell to visit the Quaker Nayler, v. 317.

BATES, Dr. William, Nonconformist divine, vi. 62, 232 note, 417.

BATH, Henry Bouchier, Earl of (died in 1654), ii. 159, 428, 443, 465.

BATH, John Granville (spelt also Greenville), Earl of.

BATH, surrender of, to the Parliament, iii. 338.

BATHURST, Dr., at Oxford, v. 231, vi. 392, 394.

BATHURST, Thomas (or Theophilus) : in the Westminster Assembly, i. 516.

BATTEN, Lady, friend of Pepys, vi. 123.

BATTERSBY, Mr., friend of Pepys, vi. 339.

BAXTER, Richard, leading Nonconformist : his residence at Ludlow in his youth, i. 608-9 ; minister at Kidderminster, ii. 590, 595; iii. 29; his account of Sectarianism in the New Model army, iii. 385-6 ; becomes chaplain in that army, iii. 386, 525 ; his friendship with the Republican James Berry, iii. 535; preaches against the Republican *Engagement*, iv. 178; on the *Commission of Ejectors* under the Protectorate, iv. 571 ; one of the ecclesiastical advisers of Cromwell's First Parliament, v. 12; his interviews with Cromwell and their opinions of each other, v. 13 note ; favours toleration of Episcopacy under the Protectorate, v. 63; among Men of Letters of the Protectorate, v. 76, 79, 98; appointed one of the King's chaplains in 1660, vi. 62 ; preaches before the Commons, vi. 425 ; his censure of the King's Ecclesiastical Declaration of 1660, vi. 99-101 ; declines a bishopric, vi. 105 ; his part in the Savoy Conference of 1661, vi. 159 ; his testimony to Dr. Gauden, vi. 433 ; among the ejected Nonconformists of 1662, vi. 232 note, 417, 567 ; an anti - Hobbist, vi. 290 ; among Men of Letters of the Restoration, vi. 299, 302, 322, 388, 514, 616 ; his contest with Dr. Samuel Parker, vi. 700-1.

BAYLY, Dr. Lewis, Bishop of Bangor, i. 388.

BAYLY, Thomas, appointed of the Westminster Assembly, ii. 516.

BAYLY, William, Irish bishop, vi. 127, 129.

BAYNTON, Mr., on the "Committee for Printing" in 1644, iii. 266.

BAYNTON, Sir Edward, ii. 166, 445.

BEACONSFIELD, Bucks, vi. 492-3.

BEALE, Edward, English merchant, v. 243.

BEALE, Dr. Jerome, Master of Pembroke College, Cambridge, i. 116, 120, 157.

BEALE, Dr. William, Master of St. John's College, Cambridge, i. 121 ; iii. 93, 95 note.

BEARD, Dr., Cromwell's schoolmaster at Huntingdon, i. 215.

BEARE, Richard, merchant, v. 250.

BEARGARDEN, the, in London, i. 49.

BEAUCHAMP, Sieur, Parisian advocate, v. 369.

BEAUCLERK, Charles : see *St. Albans*, Duke of.

BEAUMONT, Francis, the dramatist (Beaumont and Fletcher) : lines by, on the Mermaid Tavern, i. 45 and note, 433, 434, 570 ; iii. 449 ; vi. 352, 353, 355, 358 ; in Dryden's *Essay on Dramatic Poesy*, vi. 379-81 : see also *Fletcher*, John.

BEAUMONT, Sir John : poem by, to a Marchioness of Winchester, i. 245 note.

BEAUMONT, Joseph, of Peterhouse, Cambridge, i. 649 ; verses by, on the death of Edward King (Lycidas), i. 652.

BEAUMONT, Thomas, one of Cromwell's baronets, v. 354 note.

BECKE, Mr., neighbour of Milton in Artillery Walk, Bunhill, vi. 717.

BEDELL, William, Irish bishop, i. 420, 422 ; ii. 124.

BEDFORD, Francis Russell, 4th earl of, Parliamentarian peer, ii. 48, 142-3 ; in the Long Parliament, ii. 153, 156, 161 ; in the matter of Strafford's trial, ii. 185 ; his part in the English Church Reform movement, ii. 201 ; his death, ii. 272, 281.

BEDFORD, William Russell, 5th Earl and 1st Duke of, ii. 273 ; second in command to the Earl of Essex in the Parliamentarian army, ii. 422, 430 and note, 443, 465, 466 ; and the Westminster Assembly, ii. 523 ; at the close of the Civil War, iii. 377 ; at Count Bundt's supper, v. 249, 336.

BEDFORD, Lucy, Countess of (wife of the 3rd Earl), i. 130.

BEDFORD, Mr., schoolmaster of Aderston, i. 111.

BEDFORD HOUSE, London, ii. 153.

BEESTON, actor, vi, 349.

BEHN, Mrs. Aphra, vi. 611.

BEKE, Captain, knighted by Richard Cromwell, v. 416 note.

BELHAVEN, John, 1st Lord, Scottish Privy Councillor in 1638-9, ii. 15.

BELL, Robert, student of Christ's College, Cambridge, i. 149.

BELL, Scottish minister, ii. 38.

BELLAMY, John, London publisher, iii. 164 note.

BELLASIS, H., ii. 326.

BELLASIS (Belasyse), Lord John, in the King's army in 1642, ii. 442, 449.

BELLASIS, Sir Rowland, brother of Viscount Falconbridge, vi. 151.

BELLEAU, in Lincolnshire, country-seat of Sir Henry Vane, iv. 532, v. 107.

BELLENDEN, Adam, Scottish bishop and Privy-councillor, i. 697, 704, 706, 707, 715 ; ii. 42.

BELLIÈVRE, French ambassador, iii. 503, iv. 380.

BELLINGS, Sir Richard, Roman Catholic diplomatic agent, vi. 240-1 and note, 247, 571, 576.

BELL INN, the, in London, ii. 208.

BELTON, Dr., of Queen's College, Cambridge, i. 199-200.

BEMERTON, in Wiltshire, George Herbert's rectory, i. 414-5.

BENBOW, Mr. John, of the Crown Office, died in 1625, i. 104 and note.

BENBOW, Captain John : his execution in 1651, iv. 297.

BENCE, Alexander, merchant, v. 576.

BENDISH, Mr. Thomas, iv. 150.

BENET COLLEGE, Cambridge : see Corpus Christi.

BEN JONSON : see Jonson.

BENNET, Henry, nephew of the Earl of Arlington, vi. 766.

BENNET, Sir Henry : see Arlington, Earl of.

BENNET, John, musical composer, i. 51.

BENNETT, Sir Humphrey, Royalist conspirator, v. 337.

BENNETT, Jervas, iv. 525.

BENNETT, Justice of the Peace in Buckinghamshire, vi. 495.

BENNETT, Philip, fellow-graduate of Milton's at Cambridge, i. 218.

BENNETT, Colonel Robert, iv. 94 note, 498 ; in the Barebones Parliament, iv. 501, 506, 514, 523 ; in the Restored Rump, v. 453 ; on the Committee of Safety, v. 494.

BENNETT, Thomas, v. 178.

BENSON, Early Puritan, ii. 531.

BENTIVOGLIO, Cardinal, i. 795, 796, 799.

BENTIVOGLIO, Italian historian, i. 762.

BENTLY, Richard, publisher, vi. 786.

BERE, Sidney, under-Secretary of State, ii. 336.

BERGE, Ernst Gottlieb vom, translation of Paradise Lost into German by, at Zerbst in 1682, vi. 783.

BERKELEY, Lady (mother of the 8th Lord), i. 596.

BERKELEY, George, 8th Lord, Parliamentarian peer in 1642, ii. 431 ; iii. 297 note, 554, 693 ; v. 700 ; his new mansion in London in 1664, vi. 250.

BERKELEY, Sir Charles : see Falmouth, Earl of.

BERKELEY, Sir John (1st Lord of Stratton), with Charles I. in 1647, iii. 561, 574-5.

BERKELEY CASTLE, iii. 338.

BERKSHIRE, Thomas Howard, 1st Earl of, i. 158 ; ii. 48, 68, 128, 152, 180, 278, 337, 428, 429 ; vi. 18.

BERKSHIRE, Thomas Howard, 3rd Earl of (son of the preceding), in the Privy Council of Charles II., vi. 18, 77, 152, 314, 367.

BERMUDAS, the, v. 103.

BERNARD, Dr. Nicholas, editor of Usher's Reduction of Episcopacy, v. 64.

BERNARD, lawyer, i. 630.

BERNARD, physician, iv. 249 note.

BERNARDI, Francesco, Genoese agent in London, iv. 379.

BERNERS, Josiah, v. 456, 519.

BERNHARD, of Weimar, i. 743.

BERNINI, sculptor, i. 763, 797.

BERRIFF, William, Parliamentarian officer, ii. 444.

BERRY, Edward, Parliamentarian officer, ii. 445.

BERRY, James, captain in the New Model, iii. 327 ; president of the

Army-Agitators, iii. 535 ; colonel, iv. 402 ; one of Cromwell's major-generals, v. 49 ; in Cromwell's Second Parliament, v. 107, 127, 129 ; one of Cromwell's lords, v. 324 ; supports Richard's Government, v. 418 ; during Richard's Protectorate, v. 422-3 ; under the Restored Rump, v. 449, 456, 470, 479, 490 ; in the Wallingford House Government, v. 494, 495, 624 ; at the second Restoration of the Rump, v. 516-7, 521 ; under Monk's dictatorship, v. 563.

BERTIE, Lord Robert, 1st Earl of Lindsey : see *Lindsey*.

BERWICK, during First "Bishop's War," ii. 62, 64, 67, 68, 69, 70-1.

BEST, Paul, anti-Trinitarian, iii. 157, 384-5, 389, 677-8.

BETHEL, Colonel Hugh, knighted by Richard Cromwell, v. 416 note.

BETHELL, Major in the New Model Army, iii. 327 ; killed, iii. 338 note.

BETHELL, Slingsby, in Council of State of the Second Restored Rump, v. 520.

BETTERTON, Thomas, actor, vi. 186, 350, 353, 354, 609, 611, 785.

BETTERTON, William, actor, vi. 350.

BEVERNING, Dutch ambassador, iv. 502 ; his reception by Cromwell, iv. 572 ; in connection with the Morus controversy, iv. 632.

BEZA, i. 529 ; ii. 250 ; iv. 459.

BIBLE, authorised English version of, i. 60 ; Diodati's Italian, i. 99 ; Walton's Polyglott, i. 105, 119.

BIDDLE, Mr. John, anti-Trinitarian, iii. 157, 677, 687 ; author of *A Two-fold Catechism*, v. 13-4, 59 note ; tried for blasphemy, v. 64-6, 350.

BIGOT, Emeric, account of, and of his correspondence with Milton, v. 283-5 ; vi. 723.

BILLINGSLEY, Henry, Parliamentarian officer, ii. 444.

BINGHAM, Colonel John, iv. 525 ; v. 453, 544 note.

BIRCH, John, and his wife, resident in Aldersgate Street, ii. 207.

BIRCH, Colonel John, in Cromwell's first Parliament, v. 7 ; in the Restored Rump, v. 453, 455 ; in the Restored Long Parliament, v. 544 ; in the Convention Parliament, v. 695 ; vi. 51.

BIRCH, Dr. Thomas, his contributions to the biography of Milton, i. ix ; iii. 483 note ; iv. 335 note ; vi. 497-8 and note, 759-61, 763 note.

BIRD, John, Parliamentarian officer, ii. 445.

BIRD, Theophilus, actor, vi. 349, 350.

BIRKENHEAD, John, editor of the *Mercurius Aulicus*, iii. 546 ; iv. 38 ; under the Protectorate, v. 76 ; after the Restoration, vi. 202, 299, 308 ; as censor of the Press and book-licenser for the Restoration Government, vi. 325-6, 339.

BIRKS, near Berwick, ii. 62 ; Pacification of, ii. 70.

BISCOE, John, v. 470.

BISHOPS, English : list of, in 1628-1632, i. 388-90 ; changes in the body between 1632 and 1638, i. 673-4 ; alarms among, in 1638-40, ii. 122-6 ; in the House of Lords at the opening of the Long Parliament, ii. 150-1 ; Bishops Exclusion Bill in the Long Parliament, ii. 222 ; rejected by the Lords, ii. 227 ; Bishop Williams's proposed substitute, ii. 235 ; impeachment of thirteen, by the Commons, ii. 269-70, 272-3 ; reintroduction of the Exclusion Bill, ii. 316 ; appointment of new, by Charles in 1641 to fill vacancies, ii. 324-5 ; arrest of twelve, by the Long Parliament, ii. 333-5 ; disappearance of, from Parliament, ii. 336 ; Women's Petition against, ii. 348-9 ; Bishops Exclusion Bill passed by the Lords, ii. 349 ; King's assent to the Bill, and virtual cessation of Episcopacy in England (Feb. 1641-42), ii. 351-3 ; survivors at the Restoration, vi. 61 ; in the English Church of the Restoration, vi. 104-5, 118 ; attendance of, at the Coronation of Charles II., vi. 153-7 ; readmission of, into Parliament, vi. 223, 224 : see also under *Church*.

BISHOPS, Scottish : i. 424-5 ; list of, in 1632, i. 697 ; in the Scottish Privy Council, i. 706 ; their *Declinator* in the General Assembly of Glasgow,

ii. 39-40 ; deposition of them collectively by that Assembly, and abolition of Episcopacy in Scotland, ii. 42 ; unpopularity of the ex-Bishops, ii. 61, 69 ; single survivor of the body at the Restoration, vi. 151 : see also under *Church.*

BISHOPS, Irish Protestant : list of, in 1632, i. 420 ; during Wentworth's viceroyalty, i. 691-2 ; survivors of the body at the Restoration, and revival of the Irish Protestant Episcopate, vi. 127-9 : see also under *Church.*

"BISHOPS' WARS": history of the First, ii. 3, 43-71 ; history of the Second, ii. 3, 135-142.

BITTLESTONE, tanner, of Newcastle, ii. 43.

BLACKBOROUGH, a relation of Milton : his concern in the reconciliation of Milton and his wife, iii. 437, 440.

BLACKFRIARS (London), fatal vespers in, i. 107 ; the Diodatis in, ii. 80-3.

"BLACK SATURDAY," i. 425.

BLACK SPREAD EAGLE COURT (London), the site of Milton's birthplace, i. 41, 42.

BLACKWELL, John, of Mortlake, vi. 39, 47, 55.

BLACKWOOD, Christopher, Baptist preacher, iii. 148.

BLAEU, John, of Amsterdam : his Atlas, Milton's inquiries about, v. 281.

BLAGDEN, London actor, vi. 349.

BLAGDEN, Thomas, servant of Cromwell's Council, v. 625.

BLAGRAVE, Daniel : Regicide, iii. 720 ; v. 453, 666 ; vi. 28 ; excepted in the Indemnity Bill, vi. 44, 54 ; escape of, 115, 115 note.

BLAIR, Robert, Scottish Presbyterian divine, ii. 38, 191, 202, 218 ; iii. 87, 427, 717 ; and the incorporation of Scotland into the Commonwealth, iv. 363 ; his position between the Resolutioners and Protesters, v. 90.

BLAKE, Robert, Parliamentary colonel in the First Civil War, iii. 379 ; elected as a recruiter to the Long Parliament, iii. 401 ; one of the Generals of the Fleet of the Commonwealth, iv. 41, 42, 56, 124, 217-8, 233 ; member of the fourth

Council of State of the Commonwealth, iv. 310, 354 ; his encounters, as Admiral in the naval war of the Commonwealth against the Dutch, with the Dutch Admiral, Van Tromp, iv. 372-4, 375-7 ; supposed rivalry with Cromwell, iv. 408 ; mention of, in the Council Order books, iv. 451 ; his adhesion to Cromwell's Dictatorship, iv. 499 ; nominated one of Cromwell's " Supreme Assembly" (Barebones Parliament), iv. 501 ; fresh naval victories over the Dutch, iv. 502, 507 ; in the first Parliament of Oliver's Protectorate, v. 5 ; his services in the Mediterranean, v. 37-8 ; in the second Parliament of the Protectorate, v. 107, 108 ; more naval exploits in the war with Spain, v. 113-4, 141 ; his death and burial in Westminster Abbey, v. 309-10 ; disinterment of his body after the Restoration, vi. 227.

BLAKISTON, John, Regicide, iii. 720 ; vi. 28 ; dead in 1660, vi. 54.

BLANCHE-TETE, Henry, of Amsterdam, v. 196.

BLANOT, M. de, envoy in London to the Commonwealth from the city of Bordeaux, iv. 381.

BLAUGDEN, Barbara, early Quaker, v. 27.

BLOMFIELD, Dr., of Trinity Hall, Cambridge : commits suicide, i. 153.

BLONDELL, David, French Protestant theologian, i. 759 ; iv. 343, 461, 463.

"BLOODY TENENT, the" (i.e. *Bloody Tenet*), Roger Williams's Toleration Treatise, iii. 112, 124, 131, 162, 264, 299.

BLOUNT, Colonel, iv. 514.

BLOUNT, Thomas, author of the *Glossographia*, v. 383.

BLUNDELL, Colonel, iv. 402.

BLUNDEN, Elizabeth, wife of Sir Thomas Moore, vi. 775.

BLUNDEN, Humphrey, publisher, v. 20.

BLUNDEN of Basingstoke, William, vi. 775.

BOCHART, Samuel, French savant, iv. 269.

C

BODIN, French writer, cited by Milton, ii. 381.

"BODY OF LIBERTIES, the," of Massachusetts, ii. 559.

BOECLERUS, departure from Sweden of, iv. 344.

BŒHME, Jacob, and the sect of Bœhmenists, i. 746 ; iii. 448 ; v. 20-2.

BOGGIS, John, Baptist preacher, iii. 159.

BOHEMIA and the BOHEMIANS, i. 61.

BOLD, Mr., i. 627.

BOLDE, William, apprentice to Milton's father, i. 4.

BOLINGBROKE, Oliver St. John, 1st Earl of, i. 589 ; ii. 48, 142, 154, 354, 430, 439, 523 ; iii. 40, 297 note, 377, 405, 406.

BOLSOVER CASTLE, Charles I. and his Queen entertained at, in 1634, ii. 152.

BONAR, James, Scottish Presbyterian divine, ii. 38.

BOND, Dennis, in successive Councils of the Commonwealth, iv. 13, 14, 150, 151, 223, 224, 225, 226, 227, 228, 229, 231, 273, 309, 313, 314, 315, 321, 354-5, 394, president of Council, iv. 447, 449, 450, 483 ; in Oliver's First Parliament, v. 5 ; in Oliver's Second Parliament, v. 107.

BOND, John, of Exeter, member of Westminster Assembly, ii. 522.

BONHAM, English Presbyterian, ii. 532.

BONMATTEI : see Buommattei.

BONNEL, Benjamin, Swedish Resident in London, iv. 378.

"BONTIA," waiting-maid of Madame de Saumaise ; scandal concerning her and Morus, and Latin epigram thereon, iv. 462 - 5 ; use of the scandal, and mention of Bontia by Milton in his Defensio Secunda, iv. 587-8 ; sequel of the Bontia and Morus story, iv. 628 ; Morus's own account of the affair, v. 194-5 ; sarcastic recurrence by Milton to the subject in a passage in his Pro Se Defensio, v. 205-6.

"BOOK OF SPORTS," the, iii. 26.

BOOKSELLERS, London : see Book Trade.

BOOK TRADE, British, account of, with statistics, in and about 1632 : i. 544-51 ; from 1640 to 1645, iii. 446-8 ; in 1656, v. 257-60 ; of the Restoration, with statistics of, from 1660 to 1667, and comparison with the book trade of the Commonwealth and Protectorate, vi. 322-5, 398-405 ; in 1667, vi. 514-6 ; from 1667 to 1674, vi. 615-7.

BOOKER, Mr., a book-licenser, iii. 271.

BOONE, Thomas, Restored Rumper, v. 453, 467, 478.

BOOTE, maiden name of the mother of Milton's third wife, vi. 474.

BOOTH, student of Corpus Christi, Cambridge, i. 220.

BOOTH, Sir George (Presbyterian Royalist), leader in Cheshire of a Royalist Insurrection in 1658, v. 472, 474, 475, 476, 477, 478 : see Delamere, Baron.

BORDEAUX, M. de, French envoy to London, iv. 382, 500 ; full ambassador from Mazarin in negotiations between France and the Protectorate, iv. 554-5 ; v. 37, 244 ; Milton's State letters to, for Cromwell, v. 372, 376-7 ; during the Protectorate of Richard, v. 426 ; during the anarchy after Richard's abdication, v. 460, 463, 502 ; correspondence of, with Mazarin, v. 507 note ; and General Monk, v. 556.

BORELLI, of Naples, pupil of Galileo, i. 767.

BORLACE, Sir John, ii. 309.

BOROMINI, architect at Naples, i. 763, 797.

BORTHWICK, Mr., Scottish preacher, ii. 191.

BOSC, M. du, at Paris, i. 758.

BOSTOCK, Robert, bookseller, iii. 335 note ; iv. 123.

BOSWELL, Francis, rector of Horton, i. 559, and note.

BOSWELL, Sir William, of Jesus College, Cambridge, i. 115, 120, 147.

BOULD, Thomas, i. 115, 147.

BOULTER, Robert, bookseller, vi. 403, 516, 622-3, 625-6.

BOULTON, Samuel, at Cambridge, i. 218, 258 ; account of, as member of Westminster Assembly, ii. 516.

BOURBON, Charlotte de, wife of William of Orange, ii. 158.

BOURCHIER, Sir John, King's judge and Regicide, iii. 720; Councillor of State of the Commonwealth, iv. 273; 314, 315, 321, 355, 449; in the Restored Rump, v. 453; in the Restored Long Parliament, v. 545; after the Restoration, vi. 28, 43; death of, vi. 49, 54.

BOURNE, Samuel, of the Stationers' Company, iii. 271.

BOUTEL, Mrs., actress, vi. 350, 351, 607.

BOUTFLOWER, John, fellow-graduate of Milton at Cambridge, i. 218, 258.

BOW CHURCH, London, i. 43.

BOW LANE, Old Cheapside, i. 48.

BOWDEN, Thomas, churchwarden of Horton, i. 640.

BOWER, Jeffrey, scrivener, i. 339 note.

BOWER, Thomas, apprentice to Milton's father, i. 62; made his partner in the business, i. 338 and note; story of lawsuit against, in the case of Cotton v. Milton and Bower, i. 627-38, 659-61.

BOWER, William, scrivener, apprentice of Milton's father, i. 338 note.

BOWERMAN, Captain, commandant at Carisbrooke Castle, iii. 626-8.

BOWERS, widow, neighbour of Milton in Bunhill, vi. 717.

BOWLES, Edward, chaplain to Fairfax, iii. 326; vi. 232 note.

BOWLES, Dr. John, Bishop of Rochester, i. 390, 674.

BOWLES, Oliver, member of the Westminster Assembly, ii. 516.

BOWMAN, Cambridge printer, i. 738 note.

BOWYER, punished for libelling Laud, i. 673.

BOYD, Andrew, Bishop of Argyle, i. 697; ii. 42.

BOYD, Lord, i. 722; ii. 16, 65; iv. 561.

BOYD, Zachary, Scottish Presbyterian divine, ii. 38.

BOYES, Philibert Emanuel de, Lieutenant-General of Ordnance in Essex's Army, ii. 443.

BOYLE, Francis: see Shannon, Lord, v. 230.

BOYLE, Michael, Bishop of Waterford and Lismore, i. 420, vi. 129.

BOYLE, Richard, Bishop of Cork, Cloyne, and Ross, i. 420.

BOYLE, Sir Richard: see Cork, 1st Earl of.

BOYLE, Richard, son of the Earl of Cork, pupil of Peter du Moulin, v. 225, 235, in Oxford, v. 267, killed, vi. 254.

BOYLE, Roger, Lord Broghill: see Orrery, Earl of.

BOYLE, the Hon. Robert, son of the 1st Earl of Cork, and remembered as the founder of English Chemistry: iii. 659-60; his connection with Hartlib and "The Invisible College," iii. 663; among Men of Letters under the Protectorate, v. 76; further account of, v. 230-1; his friendship with Rev. Peter du Moulin, v. 235 note; in Oxford, v. 266, 267; in correspondence with Hartlib, iii. 215 note, with Henry Oldenburg, v. 365, 6, 631-2, vi. 458-9, with his sister Lady Ranelagh, vi. 456, 458, with Hooke, vi. 289, and with his nephew, Richard Jones, vi. 459-60; an anti-Hobbist, vi. 290-1; among Men of Letters of the Restoration, vi. 314-5, 387, 616; and the Royal Society, vi. 392, 394, 396; satirised by Butler, vi. 618.

BRABOURNE, Theophilus, Puritan minister in Norfolk, and a founder of the sect of Anti-Sabbatarians or Traskites, iii. 155.

BRACCIOLINI, Italian poet, i. 762, 797.

BRACKLEY, John Egerton, Viscount, son of the 1st Earl of Bridgewater, i. 587-9, 598, 609; one of the performers in Milton's Comus at Ludlow Castle, i. 611-21; edition of Comus dedicated to him by Lawes, i. 641; in 1639-40, ii. 80; his marriage, ii. 430; succeeds to the Earldom in 1649, iv. 531; his inscription in a copy of Milton's Defensio Pro Populo Anglicano, iv. 531; vi. 151.

BRACKLEY, John Egerton, Viscount (son of the preceding), at the Coronation of Charles II., vi. 151.

BRADFORD, William, of New Plymouth, ii. 548.

BRADLEY, officer of the City Trained Bands, ii. 447.

BRADLEY, Quaker, schoolmaster in London, vi. 472.

BRADLEY, John, of the Protector's household, v. 625.

BRADSHAW : supposed connection of Milton's mother with the family of, i. 30-3, 38 note.

BRADSHAW, Henry, nephew and heir of the Regicide, v. 630.

BRADSHAW, Sir John, of Bradshaw in Lancashire, common progenitor of the Bradshaws, i. 32.

BRADSHAW, John, the Regicide : tradition of Milton's cousinship with, i. 32 ; v. 630 note ; his presidency at the King's trial, iii. 706-7, 708-11, 712 note ; heads the signatures to the death warrant, iii. 720 ; vi. 28 ; President of the first Council of State of the Commonwealth, iv. 12, 13 note, 17 ; concern with the appointment of Milton to the Latin secretaryship, iv. 79, 82, 83 ; empowered to sign warrants, iv. 43, 120 ; his intercourse with Milton, iv. 105 ; in the trial of Lilburne, iv. 46, 120 ; at a City Banquet, iv. 54 ; his official salary, iv. 55 ; present in Council, iv. 87, 88, 89 ; his Press Act, iv. 116-8, 324-5, 386 ; present in Council, iv. 145, 146, 147, 150 ; and Marchamount Needham, iv. 156 ; his warrant for the custody of State-papers by Milton, iv. 157 ; mentioned in a letter of Milton to Mylius, v. 705 ; President of the second Council of State, iv. 177 ; present in Council, iv. 223-31 ; signs some of Milton's State Letters, iv. 232, 235 ; story of, in connection with Milton, Dugard, and the Eikon Basilike, iv. 249 note ; present in Council, iv. 313-21 ; in correspondence with Cromwell, iv. 280 ; cessation of his permanent Presidency of the Council, iv. 310 ; in the third Council of State, iv. 273, 421 ; in the fourth Council of State, iv. 355, 446 ; in the fifth Council of State, iv. 449 ; Milton's letter to, in favour of Marvell, iv. 478-9, 479 note ; his behaviour at the dissolution of the Rump, iv. 413 ; Milton's eulogy on, in the Defensio Secunda, iv. 600-1, 606 ; mentioned in a letter of Marvell to Milton, iv. 620-2 ; in the First Parliament of the Protectorate, v. 5, 7 ; quits the Parliament, v. 9 ; in anti-Oliverian plottings, v. 33 ; precautions taken against, v. 107 ; reference to his library in a letter of Milton to Bigot, v. 284, 285 note ; member for Cheshire in Richard's Parliament, v. 430 ; in the Parliament and Council of the Restored Rump, v. 456 ; Commissioner for the new Great Seal, v. 465 ; present in Council, v. 479 ; his death, v. 495 ; his legacy to Milton, v. 630-1 ; one of the four dead Regicides attainted for High Treason, vi. 30, 54, 114 ; disinterment of, vi. 113-4, 122-3 ; his head, with those of Cromwell and Ireton, set on Westminster Hall, in 1661, vi. 123-4.

BRADSHAW, Mrs., wife of the preceding ; disinterment of her body, vi. 228.

BRADSHAW, Richard, agent of the English Commonwealth at Hamburg, iv. 125, 217, 224-5, 233, 234 ; envoy, to Denmark, iv. 484, to Russia, v. 293, 294, 314, 386, 395.

BRADSTREET, Mrs. Anne, writer of the first original work printed in America, ii. 564.

BRAINE, denounced as a heretic in the Second Beacon Fired in 1654, v. 59 note.

BRAMHALL, John, Bishop of Derry, ii. 78 ; his criticism of Milton's Irish Pamphlet, ii. 361 note ; goes into exile, iii. 96 ; denounced as a "Delinquent," iii. 421 ; anti-Presbyterian tract by, iv. 27 ; reputed author of the Apologia against Milton, and of the Eikon Aklastos, iv. 348 and note, 349 and note, 536 and note ; attack on, in Phillips's Apologia, iv. 471-2, vi. 213-4 ; and John Lilburne, iv. 502 ; during the Protectorate, v. 76, 81 ; Archbishop of Armagh after the Restoration, vi. 127-8 ; in the Cavalier Parliament, vi. 158 ; an anti-Hobbist, vi. 290, 292, 322 ; a posthumous treatise of, vi. 701.

BRANDENBURG, Frederick William, Marquis of ("the Great Elector") iv. 31 ; v. 246, 313, 314 ; Milton's State letters to, v. 371, 373 ; vi. 115.

BRANDON, Richard, executioner of Charles I., vi. 91, 92, 94 note.

BRANDON, Mary, wife or daughter of the above, vi. 91, 94 note.

BRANDRETH, Henry, in the Committee of Safety, v. 494.

BRANTHWAIT, Michael, King's Agent in Venice, i. 738 note, 752 note, 831.

BRASENOSE COLLEGE, Oxford, i. 526.

BRASS, Mr. Henry de, letters of Milton to, v. 363-5, 379-80 ; vi. 645, 723 : see also under *Milton*.

BRATHWAYTE, Richard, poet, iii. 456.

BRAY, Lieutenant, Parliamentarian officer, iii. 583.

BRAYFIELD, Colonel Alexander, in Ireland, v. 471.

BREAD STREET, London : Milton's birthplace in, and its notabilities and associations, i. 3-5, 30, 41-6, 50, 564, 629 ; Milton's property in, vi. 444, 504.

BREAKSPEAR, Nicolas (Pope Adrian IV.) : his family, i. 603 note.

BRECKNOCK, Earl of : see *Ormond*, Duke of, vi. 17.

BREDA, Charles II. at, and his Treaty there with the Scottish Covenanting Government, iv. 180-2, 187 ; Charles again at Breda, v. 560 ; his " Breda Letters " preparing for the Restoration, v. 560, 695-7 ; peace between Charles II. and the Dutch concluded at, vi. 269.

BREMEN, Consuls and Senate of the City of, v. 166, 371.

BRENT, Sir Nathaniel, judge of the Prerogative Court and book-licenser, iii. 270, 450, 546, 640 ; iv. 118.

BRENTFORD, Middlesex, Dr. Diodati at, i. 100, 101 ; King's march to, ii. 456.

BRENTFORD, Patrick Ruthven, Earl of (and Earl of Forth in the Scottish Peerage), ii. 440, 460, 465 ; iii. 421.

BRERETON, Mr. Peter, Auditor to the Commission for Sequestration in 1650-1, iv. 244.

BRERETON, Sir William, Parliamentarian officer, ii. 460 ; iii. 334 and note ; at close of Civil War, iii. 379, 381 ; one of the King's judges, but avoids the trial, iii. 708 note ; in third Council of State of the Commonwealth, iv.. 273 ; and in the fifth, iv. 355 ; mentions of, in the Council order books, iv. 315, 321, 449 ; in the Restored Rump, v. 453, also 604.

BRERETON, William, fellow of the Royal Society, vi. 396.

BREREWOOD, Edward, first Professor of Astronomy in Gresham College, London, ii. 365-9.

BRESSIEUX, French optician, v. 632.

BRETON, of Emanuel College, Cambridge, i. 257.

BREWER, Separatist, i. 678-9.

BREWSTER, Robert, one of the Restored Rump, v. 453, 479.

BREWSTER, Thomas, bookseller, iv. 246, 433 ; trial of, for sedition, vi. 478-80.

BREWSTER, William, of New Plymouth, ii. 546, 551, 554.

BRIDGE, William, Independent minister, member of the Westminster Assembly, ii. 516, 580, 585, 591, 605 ; iii. 22, 23, 87, 111, 127-8, 131, 392 ; and the Toleration question under the Commonwealth, iv. 392 ; and the Racovian Catechism, iv. 438 ; one of the ejected Nonconformists of 1662, vi. 232 note, 416.

BRIDGEMAN : see *Bridgman*.

BRIDGES, Edward, sèrvant of Councils of State, v. 625.

BRIDGES, Tobias, one of Cromwell's major-generals, v. 49, 418.

BRIDGES, William, younger son of the fifth Lord Chandos, i. 591, 598.

BRIDGES : see *Chandos*.

BRIDGEWATER, John Egerton, 1st Earl of, son of Lord Chancellor Ellesmere: i. 587-9 ; in the Privy Council of Charles I., i. 380, 567 ; accounts of him and his family, i. 587-9 ; ii. 79 ; iii. 462-4 ; Lord President of the Council in Wales, i. 604 ; at Ludlow, i. 608-10 ; Milton's *Comus* acted before, i. 610 ; his subscription towards the First

Bishops' War, ii. 48; correspondence with Windebank previous to the Second Bishops' War, ii. 129-30; and the Long Parliament, ii. 152; a non-effective Royalist peer, ii. 430; signs the Covenant reluctantly, iii. 39-40; his town house in Barbican, iii. 443; death of, iv. 531.

BRIDGEWATER, John Egerton, 2nd Earl of: see *Brackley*.

BRIDGEWATER, 3rd Earl of: see *Brackley*.

BRIDGEWATER, Countess of, wife of 1st Earl, i. 588, 589, and 610 note.

BRIDGEWATER, storming of, iii. 338.

BRIDGMAN, Dr. John, Bishop of Chester, i. 390; ii. 151, 335.

BRIDGMAN, Sir John, Chief-Justice of Chester, i. 609.

BRIDGMAN, Sir Orlando, in the Long Parliament, ii. 321; and the Treaty of Newport, iii. 606; in the Convention Parliament, vi. 22; Chief Baron of the Exchequer after the Restoration, vi. 74; presides at the trials of the Regicides, vi. 77-9; Lord Keeper, and in the Cabal Administration, vi. 562, 564, 567, 575; his resignation of the Lord Keepership, vi. 590.

BRIDGMAN, Mr., secretary to Sir Joseph Williamson of the Foreign Office, vi. 804.

"BRIEF NOTES on Dr. Griffith's Sermon": see *Milton*, writings of.

BRIERLY, W., Latin verses by, on the death of Edward King ("Lycidas"), i. 651.

BRIGGES, Samson, Latin verses by, on the same, i. 653.

BRIGGS, Henry, mathematician, v. 153-4.

BRIGGS, Thomas, early Quaker, v. 26.

BRIGHT, John, Parliamentarian in Suffolk, ii. 421.

BRISBANE, Mr., a Scotsman in Paris, i. 758-9.

BRISTOL, storming and surrender of, iii. 338.

BRISTOL, John Digby, 1st Earl of: during the "Bishops' Wars," ii. 48, 143; account of, in the Long Parliament, ii. 157, 167, 279, 283, 337; in the Royalist army, ii. 428,

442; one of the "Delinquents" denounced by Parliament, iii. 421; in exile, iii. 494; and the Second Civil War, iii. 591.

BRISTOL, George Digby, 2nd Earl of: in 1659, v. 473; with Charles II. in Spain, v. 503; at the Coronation of Charles II., vi. 151; is an avowed Roman Catholic, vi. 238; is sent by Charles II. on a private mission to Parma, vi. 239; and the crypto Catholicism of the Court, vi. 239; and the Toleration Edict, vi. 239-44; attack on Clarendon by, vi. 245-9; takes part in promoting the war with the Dutch, vi. 254; letters of Bishop Gauden to, vi. 435-8; excepted, with his countess, from the conditions in the Test Act of 1673, vi. 595.

BRISTOL, Countess of, and the Test Act, vi. 595.

BRITTEN, Richard, sizar, and fellow-student of Milton, at Christ's College, Cambridge, i. 111, 149.

BRITTEN, William, of Essex, i. 111.

BROAD WINDSOR, in Dorsetshire, Thomas Fuller, rector of, ii. 359.

BRODICK CASTLE, in Arran, taken by Argyle in First Bishops' War, ii. 56.

BRODIE, Alexander, one of the five members for Scotland in Cromwell's Supreme Assembly of Notables, iv. 502.

BROGHILL, Roger Boyle, Lord: see *Orrery*, Earl of.

BROME, Alexander, relative of Brome the dramatist, vi. 312; Cavalier songs by, vi. 333.

BROME, Edmund, of Foresthill, ii. 493 and note.

BROME, Henry, publisher, v. 689; vi. 806.

BROME, Richard, dramatist, i. 447, 451; iii. 446; vi. 312.

BRONCKARD, Sir William, muster-master in the Royalist army in 1642, ii. 441.

BROOK, John van den, mentioned in a State letter of Milton, v. 275.

BROOKE, Fulke Greville, 1st Lord: in Charles I.'s Cabinet Council in 1625, i. 383 note 2: i. 448; his literary works, i. 484; death of, ii. 156.

BROOKE, Robert Greville, 2nd Lord,

ii. 156, 445 ; home of, at Warwick Castle, ii. 463, 519 ; his sister married to Sir Arthur Haselrig, ii. 164 ; his supposed plan of emigrating to New England baulked, i. 680 ; associated with Lord Saye and Sele as a Puritan leader, ii. 49 ; refuses to assist the King in the First "Bishops' War," ii. 49 ; is summoned to join the Royal army, refuses the oath, and is committed to custody in consequence, ii. 58, 67 ; petitions for the assembling of a Parliament in 1640, ii. 142, 143 ; in the Long Parliament, ii. 156, 201, 236 ; publishes a tract on the *Nature of Episcopacy* in November 1641, ii. 362, 362 note, 596 ; Milton's high admiration of, and of the said pamphlet, ii. 362, 596 ; iii. 284 ; appointed Lord Lieutenant for Warwickshire, ii. 439 ; in the Parliamentarian army of the Earl of Essex, ii. 444, 445 ; defends Brentford, and retires before the Royal forces, ii. 456 ; is killed at the siege of the Cathedral Close of Lichfield, ii. 431 ; iii. 377.

BROOKE, Robert Greville, 4th Lord : in a deputation of the Lords to Charles II. in May 1660, v. 700.

BROOKE, Mr. Peter, accomplice of Sir George Booth, v. 478.

BROOKES, Nathaniel, stationer, publisher, and bookbinder, v. 229 note, 259, 262-3 ; v. 383 ; vi. 400, 403 ; trial and sentence of, vi. 478-80.

BROOKS, Mr. Thomas, divine, iv. 370 ; Nonconformist, vi. 232 note.

BROUGHTON, in Oxfordshire, house of Viscount Saye and Sele at, ii. 155.

BROUGHTON, Andrew, member of the Council of State in the Barebones Parliament, iv. 506 ; included in the Quest of the Regicides as having been one of the clerks of the court at the trial of Charles I., vi. 27, 31, 33, 34 ; one of the thirty living Regicides absolutely excepted in the Act of Free and General Pardon, vi. 54 ; is a fugitive, and included in a Bill of Attainder against the unpardoned Regicides, vi. 115 ; subsequent fate of, vi. 115 note.

BROUNCKER, Henry, 3rd Viscount, groom of the chamber to the Duke of York, vi. 256 note ; in the Royal Society, vi. 392, 394, 396, 458-9.

BROUNCKER, Viscountess, a subscriber to the fourth edition of *Paradise Lost*, vi. 785.

BROWN, George, of Ashford, Kent, i. 558.

BROWN, Sir John, of Fordel in Fifeshire, a major-general in Charles II.'s Scottish army, iv. 283 ; taken prisoner at the Battle of Inverkeithing, and dies of his wounds, iv. 288.

BROWN, John, merchant and shipowner in London, v. 254.

BROWN, Mildred : see *Bulstrode*.

BROWN, R., author of Latin verses on the death of Edward King, i. 651, 654.

BROWN, Robert, founder of *Brownism* : ii. 536-7, 568-9 ; iii. 100-1, 149.

BROWN, Robert, a London merchant, v. 275.

BROWNE, John, clerk of the Parliament in 1640, ii. 173-4.

BROWNE, John, a fellow-graduate of Milton at Cambridge in 1628-9, i 218, 258.

BROWNE, John, M.P. for Dorsetshire, and colonel of dragoons in the Parliamentarian army in 1642, ii. 445 ; major-general at the close of the Civil War, iii. 379 ; one of the Commissioners to the King from the Scots, iii. 510, 541 ; and Presbyterian tumults in London, iii. 552 ; in Richard's Parliament, v. 430 ; and the projected Royalist Insurrection, v. 473 ; in the plot to bring in the King, v. 516 ; in the Restored Long Parliament, v. 545 ; at the Restoration, vi. 10 ; in the Convention Parliament of 1660, vi. 23 ; Lord Mayor-elect of London, vi. 85 ; at the trial of the Regicides, vi. 85.

BROWNE, Sir John, officer in the Parliamentarian Army, ii. 446.

BROWNE, Richard, Major-general : member for Wycombe in the recruited House of Commons in 1645, iii. 401.

BROWNE, Samuel, member of Parliament, and in the " Committee of

the Two Kingdoms," iii. 41 ; at the Treaty of Newport, iii. 605.

BROWNE, Samuel, printer, at the Hague, v. 218.

BROWNE, Thomas, of Norwich: among Men of Letters under the Protectorate, v. 76, 79; after the Restoration, vi. 294, 296, 304, 322.

BROWNE, William, poet, author of *Britannia's Pastorals*, i. 453, 455-6, 456-8, 467-8, 474, 575.

BROWNE, Mrs., her daughter married to Howlett of Sidney Sussex College, Cambridge, ii. 78.

BROWNISTS, the, and BROWNISM, i. 58; rioting against Laud by, ii. 144; 289; account of, ii. 534-8; in Amsterdam, ii. 578; iii. 149; v. 15.

BROWNRIGG, Dr. Ralph, Master of Catherine Hall, Cambridge, i. 120; mentioned in a letter of Hartlib, iii. 218; and the Bishops' Exclusion Bill controversy, ii. 225; is appointed Bishop of Exeter, ii. 411; a member of Westminster Assembly, ii. 516, 522, 525; is ejected from Cambridge University, iii. 94; 218; and the Treaty of Newport, iii. 609; in correspondence with Baxter, v. 63.

BRUCE, of Whorlton, Lord : see *Elgin*, Earl of.

BRUCE, Lord, a Cromwellian peer, iii. 297 note, 405, 406; v. 249, 473, 700; in the Convention Parliament, vi. 23.

BRUCE, Mr., at the foundation of the Royal Society, vi. 394.

BRUDENEL, Lord, in Royalist army, ii. 429.

BRUDENELL, Thomas, Baron : see *Cardigan*, Earl of.

BRUERTON, Lieutenant-Colonel, Royalist officer, ii. 442.

BRUSLON, Count de, courtier of Louis XIII., i. 755, 756.

BUCCLEUCH, Francis Scott, Earl of, with Scottish auxiliary army in England, iii. 37, 509; iv. 208; his heirs fined by Cromwell, iv. 560.

BUCCLEUCH, 1st Duke of: see *Monmouth*, Duke of.

BUCCLEUCH, Ann Scott, Countess of, her marriage to the DUKE of Monmouth, vi. 248-9.

BUCER, Martin, ii. 365; iii. 218; and Milton's Second Divorce Tract, iii. 255-61.

BUCHAN, James, Earl of, iv. 561.

BUCHAN, William, Parliamentarian officer, ii. 446.

BUCHANAN, George, Milton's early readings in, i. 96, 511-2; mentioned in Milton's *Defensio Secunda*, iv. 596.

BUCHANAN, Mr., a London correspondent of Sir Kenelm Digby, i. 758.

BUCHLERUS, Joannes, author, vi. 635.

BUCK, John, Esquire Bedel of Cambridge University, i. 199 note.

BUCKENHAM, Richard, fellow-graduate of Milton at Cambridge, i. 218, 258.

BUCKHURST, Lord : see *Dorset*, Earl of.

BUCKINGHAM, George Villiers, 1st Duke of, i. 60; rise of, to 1621, i. 348; unpopularity of, with the English, on account of the foreign policy of himself and King James, i. 61; Dr. John Preston and, i. 117; at the Spanish Court with Prince Charles in 1623, i. 105, 366; supremacy of, in affairs, i. 348-9; Lord Keeper Williams and, to 1625, i. 351-3; Laud and, to 1625, i. 364-6, 367-8; relations of Laud and, after the accession of Charles I., i. 148, 368-72; in Charles's Cabinet Council, i. 383-4 note; impeachment of, by Charles's Second Parliament, i. 157-9; appointed by Charles I. to succeed the Earl of Suffolk in the Chancellorship of Cambridge University in May 1626, i. 157-9; his Installation in March 1627, i. 181-2; in the war with France and the expedition to Rochelle in June 1627, i. 204-5; at the calling of Charles's Third Parliament, i. 187; Meade's account of the determined attitude of the Parliament towards, in June 1628, i. 191-2; in correspondence with Bainbrigge on University matters in July 1628, i. 205-6; assassination of, in August 1628, i. 206-7, 211,

213-4, 373; his successor in the Chancellorship of Cambridge University, i. 213; his place in affairs filled by Laud, now Bishop of London, i. 214, 373-4.

BUCKINGHAM, George Villiers, 2nd Duke of: ii. 150, 156; non-effective Royalist peer during his minority, ii. 429; a sister of, married to Lord Butler of Bramfield, iii. 59; active Royalist in the Second Civil War, iii. 591, 596; in Scotland with Charles II., and with Charles in the march of the Scottish Royalist Army from Stirling into England, and at the Battle of Worcester, iv. 188, 189-90, 206, 284; his escape to France, iv. 299; and John Lilburne, iv. 502; mention of, among Men of Letters under the Protectorate, v. 76; his marriage to Mary Fairfax, v. 320-2; arrested by Cromwell, v. 357; removed from the Tower to Windsor Castle, v. 359; his release on Fairfax's bail, v. 436; concern of, in the projected Royalist Insurrection of 1659, v. 473; is again arrested, v. 478; at the Restoration of Charles II., vi. 8, 10; in the Convention Parliament, vi. 22; in the Privy Council, vi. 237; and the Toleration Edict of 1662, vi. 244; his popularity with the King, vi. 245; his share in the attack on Clarendon, vi. 249; and in the war with the Dutch, vi. 254; mention of, among Men of Letters of the Restoration, vi. 314, 320, and among the Restoration Dramatists, vi. 355; as a member of the Cabal Administration, vi. 562-4, 565-6, 569, 572, 574-5, 579-80, 585, 591, 593; at the break-up of the Cabal in 1673, vi. 597, 600; his unpopularity then, vi. 600; in the Danby Administration, vi. 602-3; his "Rehearsal," vi. 611, 613-5; vi. 617-8.

BUCKINGHAMSHIRE, Duke of (Earl of Mulgrave): vi. 782-3.

BUCKLEY, Richard: see Bulkeley.

BUCKNER, licenser of books, i. 550 note.

BUCKRIDGE, Dr. John, Bishop of Rochester and afterwards of Ely, i. 389.

BUCKWORTH, Theophilus, Irish bishop, i. 420.

BUFFIELD, John, merchant, v. 396.

BULKELEY, John, in a Parliamentary Commission for carrying the Four Bills to the King in the Isle of Wight, iii. 579; in a Commission of Lords and Commons for the Treaty of Newport, iii. 605.

BULKELEY, Lancelot, Irish archbishop, i. 420.

BULKLEY, Peter, New England minister, ii. 555.

BULKLEY (or BUCKLEY), Richard, member of Westminster Assembly, ii. 516.

BULL, musical composer, i. 51.

BULL INN, Bishopsgate Street, London: see Taverns.

BULMER, Thomas, messenger to the Council, iv. 578.

BULSTRODE, Bridget, widow of John Allen, and second wife of Henry Bulstrode (elder), i. 557-8.

BULSTRODE, Cicely, daughter of Henry Bulstrode (elder), married to Philip Smith, i. 558.

BULSTRODE, Cecil or Cicely, daughter of Sir John Croke, and wife of Edward Bulstrode (elder), i. 557.

BULSTRODE, Coluberry, daughter of Simon Mayne, and wife of Thomas Bulstrode, i. 558.

BULSTRODE, Dorothy, daughter of Henry Bulstrode (younger), i. 557.

BULSTRODE, Edward (elder), of Hedgerly-Bulstrode and Upton, i. 557.

BULSTRODE, Edward, son of John Bulstrode, i. 557 note.

BULSTRODE, Edward, younger son of Edward Bulstrode (elder), and a lawyer of the Inner Temple, i. 557, 558, 562.

BULSTRODE, Edward, son of Henry Bulstrode (elder), i. 557, 558.

BULSTRODE, Elizabeth, daughter of Edward Bulstrode (elder), wife of James Whitlocke, and mother of Bulstrode Whitlocke, i. 557.

BULSTRODE, Elizabeth, daughter of Henry Bulstrode (elder), i. 557.

BULSTRODE, Henry, of Hedgerly-Bul-

strode and of Horton, eldest son of Edward Bulstrode (elder), i. 557-8, 752 note.

BULSTRODE, Henry (younger), son of Henry Bulstrode (elder), i. 557.

BULSTRODE. John, i. 557 note.

BULSTRODE, Margaret, daughter of John Bulstrode, i. 557 note.

BULSTRODE, Mary, daughter of Thomas Read, and first wife of Henry Bulstrode (elder), i. 557.

BULSTRODE, Mary, daughter of Henry Bulstrode (elder), married to Thomas Knight of Reading, i. 558.

BULSTRODE, Mildred, daughter of George Brown, wife of Edward Bulstrode, i. 558.

BULSTRODE, Samuel and Simon, sons of Thomas Bulstrode, i. 558.

BULSTRODE, Thomas, eldest son of Henry Bulstrode (elder), i. 558.

BULSTRODE, lieutenant-colonel under New Model, iii. 326.

BUNDT, Count Christian, ambassador from Sweden, v. 247-50 ; his relations with Milton, v. 254-6 ; end of his embassy, v. 270.

BUNHILL FIELDS, Milton's residence in Artillery Walk, near : Dissenters' Burial Ground at, vi. 499-500, 731.

BUNYAN, John : in Bedford jail, vi. 122 ; his release from prison, vi. 590 ; his grave in Bunhill Fields, vi. 499 ; his Pilgrim's Progress, vi. 616-7 ; mention of, among Men of Letters under the Protectorate, v. 76, and of the Restoration, vi. 315.

BUOMMATTEI, Benedetto, Florentine scholar, i. 773 ; account of, and of Milton's acquaintance with him in Florence, i. 778-9, 821, 822 ; Latin letter from Milton to, i. 789-92 ; mentioned in Milton's Defensio Secunda, iv. 637 ; vi. 723.

BUONNAROTI, Michel Angelo, i. 787.

BUONVISI, Anna, wife of Michel Diodati, i. 99.

BURFORD, Earl of : see St. Albans, Duke of.

BURGES, Dr. Cornelius, rector of St. Magnus, London, and vicar of Watford, ii. 201, 225, 228 ; a member of the Westminster Assembly, ii. 516, 605 ; iii. 5, 22 ; his sister

marries " Patriarch White," ii. 523 ; and the Solemn League and Covenant, iii. 11 and note ; 84, 160, 161 ; iv. 71 ; vi. 232 note.

BURGESS, Anthony, a member of the Westminster Assembly, ii. 516.

BURLAMAQUI, Madeleine, wife of Giovanni Diodati, i. 100.

BURLEIGH, Lord (Queen Elizabeth's), i. 380 ; ii. 536, 537, 569.

BURLEY (Burleigh), Lord, Scottish Covenanter, i. 722 ; ii. 16, 38 ; President of the Scottish Parliament of 1641, ii. 291, 292 ; 418 ; defeated by Montrose in 1644, iii. 352, 361.

BURLINGTON, Earl of : see Cork, 2nd Earl of.

BURNELL, Edmund Dunch, Baron : see under Dunch.

BURNELL, Robert, Parliamentarian officer, ii. 445.

BURNET, Bishop Gilbert, in London, vi. 619.

BURNETT, Alexander, Council licence to, iv. 228.

BURNTISLAND, surrender of, to Cromwell, iv. 288.

BURREL, Abraham, in fourth Council of State of the Commonwealth, iv. 354, 446.

BURROUGH, Edward, early Quaker, v. 26, 317 ; his letter to the Lady Protectress, v. 360.

BURROUGH, John, cabinet-maker, vi. 742.

BURROUGHS, Jeremiah, member of Westminster Assembly, ii. 516, 580, 585, 591, 605 ; iii. 22, 23, 111, 127-8, 131, 153, 393.

BURT, Nicholas, actor, vi. 349, 350.

BURTON, Henry, rector of Little St. Matthew's, Friday Street, London, and Puritan pamphleteer, i. 542-3 ; prosecuted in the Star-chamber, i. 681-2, ii. 175, 588-9, 591-3, 595 ; in the Toleration Controversy, iii. 109-11, 125, 127, 149, 386-7, 389, 396 note.

BURTON, Sara, wife of Henry Burton, petition from, ii. 176 note.

BURTON, Robert, author of Anatomy of Melancholy, i. 526-7, 547-8, 570.

BURTON, William, author of History of Leicestershire, i. 526.

BURTON, William, excepted from the general pardon in the Indemnity Bill of 1660, vi. 38, 47, 55.

BUSBY, Dr., master of Westminster School, vi. 317.

BUSHER, Leonard : his tract on Religious Liberty, iii. 102-3, 432 note.

BUSSEL, Thomas, English merchant, v. 250.

BUTLER, Joseph, messenger to the Council, iv. 578 ; his salary, v. 625.

BUTLER, Samuel, author of *Hudibras* : his early employment by the Countess of Kent and by Selden, i. 523 ; supposed original of the character of his *Hudibras*, ii. 167 ; v. 549 ; mentions of, among Men of Letters under the Protectorate, v. 76, 79, and account of, among Men of Letters of the Restoration, vi. 299-300 ; his *Hudibras*, vi. 339-42, 387, 388 ; his part in the authorship of *The Rehearsal*, vi. 613 ; in his later days, vi. 617-8 ; *Hudibras* remains unfinished, vi. 618-9 ; reference to Milton by, vi. 636 note ; new edition of *Hudibras* in 1674, vi. 730.

BUTLER, William, colonel of horse under the New Model, iii. 327 ; at the Battle of Naseby, iii. 336 ; and the question of the disbandment of the Army, iii. 537 ; his Paper presented to the Committee of Parliament for the Propagation of the Gospel, and Cromwell's approval of it, iv. 393 and note ; one of Cromwell's major-generals, v. 49 ; member of Cromwell's Second Parliament, v. 107, 125 ; a supporter of Richard's Government, v. 418 ; in the Trials of the Regicides, vi. 39.

BUTLER, of Bramfield, Lord, non-effective Royalist peer, ii. 430.

BUTLER, Jane, third wife of James Ley, Earl of Marlborough, iii. 59.

BUTTER, Nathaniel, bookseller in London ; publisher of a weekly news-sheet in 1622 called "Butter's *Coranto*," i. 542 ; publisher of Bishop Hall's *Humble Remonstrance to the High Court of Parliament* in 1640, ii. 214 ; 391 note.

BUTTON, an early Puritan or Non-conformist, ii. 531.

BUTTS, Dr. Henry, Master of Corpus Christi College, Cambridge, i. 120 ; and Vice-Chancellor of the University, i. 226 ; his exertions and bravery during the Plague visitation at Cambridge in 1630, and his letter to Lord Coventry about the Plague, i. 235 ; his reappointments to the Vice-Chancellorship, i. 237, 247 ; his connexion with the royal visit to Cambridge in 1631, i. 252 ; his death by suicide, i. 254-7 ; anonymous letter describing its manner, i. 255-6 ; only literary relic of, *Dyet's Dry Dinner*, i. 257 note.

BUXTORF, an edition of a Hebrew grammar by, in 1645, iii. 448.

BYFIELD, Adoniram, M.A. (Cantab.), chaplain to a Parliamentarian regiment, ii. 444 ; one of the scribes or clerks of the Westminster Assembly, ii. 515, iv. 392 ; in the Enquiry by the Council and the Parliament concerning the Racovian Catechism, iv. 438 ; notice of, in the Council Order Books, iv. 228.

BYFIELD, Richard, member of Westminster Assembly, brother of Adoniram Byfield, ii. 518.

BYRD, a contributor with Milton's father in 1614 to *Teares and Lamentations of a Sorrowfull Soul*, i. 1.

BYRD, Barnaby, legatee of Jeffrey of Holton, i. 21.

BYRON, Sir John, 1st Lord (ancestor of the poet), appointed Lord-Lieutenant of the Tower in 1641, ii. 331 ; his supposed part in Charles's *Coup d'Etat*, ii. 346 ; removed from his lieutenancy, ii. 351 ; in the King's army in 1642, ii. 442 ; in the Second Civil War, iii. 591 ; with Charles II.'s Court at the Hague, iv. 27.

BYRON, Sir Nicholas, commander of the city of Chester for Charles I., ii. 460.

BYRON, Sir Thomas, brother of Lord Byron, and commander of a royal troop of horse in 1642, ii. 442.

BYRON, Lord, the poet : his maternal ancestors, ii. 57.

BYZANTINE HISTORIANS, the : Milton's inquiries concerning certain works of the, v. 284-6.

C

CABAL : administration of affairs, after the fall of Clarendon, by the, vi. 561-2 ; constitution of the, for English affairs, vi. 562-3 ; the *Protestant Liberal* section of the, with the Duke of Buckingham as pseudo-premier, vi. 564-5, 575 ; the *crypto-Catholic* section of the, represented by the Duke of York, vi. 565, 575 ; the Church policy of the, from 1667 to 1670, vi. 563-8 ; the foreign policy of the, in connection with the Triple Alliance, and the Secret Negotiation with France, vi. 568-72 ; temporary disintegration into two halves, and re-coalescence of the, in 1670, vi. 574-5 ; the name "Cabal" explained, vi. 575 ; action of the, from April 1670 to June 1673, vi. 574-96 ; methods of Charles and the, for deferring the reassembling of Parliament, vi. 590 ; changes of office within the, 590-1 ; the final breaking-up of the original, of five, in 1673, vi. 596-8 ; formation of a new Cabal of seven members, vi. 597-8, 602-3 : see also under *Councils*.
CABINET : see *Councils*.
"CABINET COUNCIL," an edition of Raleigh's, by Milton : see *Milton, Writings of.*
CADE, Jack, in 1450, i. 48.
CAERLAVEROCK, Castle of, ii. 56.
CÆSAR, Sir Julius, Master of the Rolls since 1614, died in 1636, i. 381.
CAIUS COLLEGE, Cambridge, i. 171, 172.
CAIUS, Dr., Founder of Caius College, vi. 162.
CALAMY, Edmund (1600-66), Minister at St. Edmundsbury, Suffolk, in 1630, i. 419 ; minister of St. Mary, Aldermanbury, London, in 1640-41, ii. 201 ; is one of the authors of the *Smectymnuus* pamphlet, ii. 219, 605 ; in the Bishops Exclusion Bill controversy, ii. 225-6 ; as a member of the Westminster Assembly, ii. 517, 605, iii. 20, 160 ; preaches an anti-Toleration sermon before Parliament, iii. 170, 184 ; a book-licenser, iii. 270 ; signs the Presbyterian "Testimony" against Toleration, in 1647, iii. 677 ; visits Charles I. in his last hours, iii. 721 ; is Moderator of the fourth half-yearly Provincial Presbyterian Synod of London in May 1649, iv. 60 ; signs *A Vindication* in favour of the recently executed King, iv. 71 ; in correspondence with Baillie, iv. 510 ; v. 98 ; mentioned among the Men of Letters under the Protectorate, v. 75, 77 ; interviews Charles II. at the Hague, vi. 4 ; preaches a sermon before the Convention Parliament, 1660, vi. 425 ; is one of ten Presbyterian divines who are sworn in among the King's chaplains after the Restoration, vi. 62-3 ; Charles II.'s Ecclesiastical Declaration submitted to, for criticism, vi. 99, 100 ; declines the Bishopric of Coventry and Lichfield, vi. 105 ; is ejected for nonconformity, in 1662, from his perpetual curacy of Aldermanbury, London, vi. 232 note, 416.
CALAMY, Edmund (junior), ejected for nonconformity in 1662, vi. 232 note.
CALAMY, Edmund (1671-1732), author of the *Nonconformist's Manual*, vi. 232 note.
CALANDRIN, Jean Louis, a Genevese merchant, called by Milton "Calandrini," v. 172, 173 note.
CALANDRINI, the family of, at Geneva in 1575, v. 174 note.
CALANDRINUS, Cæsar (a student at Exeter College, Oxford, and afterwards minister of the parish of Peter le Poor in London), account of, and of his descendants, v. 173 note 2.
CALDERON, the Spanish dramatist, i. 745 ; vi. 357.
CALDERWOOD, David, Scottish historian, i. 711, 712 ; present in the Glasgow Assembly of 1638, ii. 38.
CALENDAR, explanation of the method of double dating used in this work, and account of the system of dating

in use in England before 1752, i. 111 note ; the same old system extinct in Scotland from the beginning of the seventeenth century, i. 705 note.

CALLANDER (or Calendar), Lord Almont, 1st Earl of, in the Marquis of Hamilton's Mission, ii. 15 ; joins the Covenant in 1638, ii. 55 ; lieutenant-general to Leslie in the Second Bishops' War, ii. 136 ; joins the "Band of Cumbernauld" in 1640, ii. 296; in "The Incident," ii. 306 ; mentioned as second in command under Leslie, ii. 307 ; raised to the Scottish peerage as Earl of Callander in 1641, ii. 307 ; appointed lieutenant-general to the Duke of Hamilton in the Scottish army of 1648, iii. 589, 596-7 ; is with Charles II.'s Court at the Hague, iv. 25, 27 ; admitted with other Malignants to the Scottish Parliament of 1650, iv. 212 ; is one of the Exceptions from Cromwell's Ordinance of Pardon and Grace in 1654, iv. 506.

CALPRENÈDE, French romance writer, vi. 359.

CALTON, Thomas, of Dulwich, i. 4.

CALVINISTS, at the Synod of Dort, i. 61.

CAMBRIDGE, Charles, Duke of, son of James II., vi. 107-8, 119.

CAMBRIDGE, Earl of: see *Hamilton*, 3rd Marquis of.

CAMBRIDGE UNIVERSITY :—List of the sixteen colleges of, in the order of their numerical importance in 1621, i. 113 ; number of students at, in 1622, i. 115 note ; government of the University distinct from that of the town, i. 115 ; list of the chief authorities and office-bearers of, in the year 1624-5, i. 115-8 ; statutes of Elizabeth regulating the Terms of the University, i. 133-4, 138 ; puritanical opinions and practices at, especially in certain colleges of, i. 138-40 ; order of the curriculum, and system of graduation, i. 140-5, 195 note ; matriculation, i. 141 footnote; Milton's matriculation in, i. 149 ; doings at, upon the occasion of the death of James I. and acces-sion of Charles I., i. 150; and at the marriage of Charles I. with Princess Henrietta Maria, i. 151-2 ; intended bequest of Lord Bacon to the University, i. 155 ; movement for internal reform in, and decree by the Vice-Chancellor and heads of colleges, i. 156-7 ; death of the Chancellor, the Earl of Suffolk, i. 157-8 ; corporal punishment at, i. 160, 161 footnote ; annual election of Vice-Chancellor and Proctors, i. 172 ; appointment of the Duke of Buckingham to the Chancellorship in 1626, i. 205 ; death of the Vice-Chancellor, Dr. Gostlin, in 1626, i. 172-3; celebration of the 5th of November at, i. 173 footnote ; courtesies of the King to the University, and their motive, i. 187 ; the leading doctors of, invited to preach at the Court of Charles I., i. 187; visit of Charles I. in Milton's fourth year at, i. 187 ; ceremonies of *Commencement*, i. 193-9, and 193 note ; the Commencement of the year 1628, i. 193-4, 199-203 ; dispute with the London stationers as to the right of the University Press to the exclusive printing of certain books, i. 205 ; Earl of Holland appointed Chancellor at the death of the Duke of Buckingham, i. 213, 379 ; formula of subscription to the Articles of Religion required of graduates, i. 217 ; Milton graduates as B.A. at, in March 1629, i. 217-8 ; Commencement of 1629, i. 219; custom of dramatic performances at, i. 221-6 ; royal injunction concerning laxity of discipline at, i. 231 ; closed on account of the Plague in 1630, i. 232-4 ; royal interferences with the exercise of College and University patronage in the matter of granting fellowships, i. 239 and note ; a theatrical performance at, i. 244 ; a volume of academic verses published at, on the births of Prince Charles and Princess Mary, i. 247-8 ; another visit of Charles I. and Queen Henrietta Maria to, i. 251-4; more theatricals at, i. 251-4; suicide of Dr. Butts, the Vice-Chancellor, i. 254-7 ; he is succeeded in

the Vice - Chancellorship by Dr. Comber of Trinity, i. 257; ceremony of the *Commencement* of 1632, i. 257; Milton's graduation as M.A. at, i. 257-8; *Quadriennium* of undergraduateship, and *Triennium* of Bachelorship, i. 260; lectures and text-books, i. 261; transition at, from the old scholastic discipline to the modern system of studies, i. 263-6; Laud's influence in the University, i. 408-9; disputes of, in 1629, with the London printers, and with the Cambridge chandlers, i. 408-9; reference to theatricals at, in Elizabeth's reign, i. 448-9; the privilege of licensing books conferred upon the Chancellor of, in 1559, i. 544; the custom in the University of annual incorporation in the degree of Master of Arts of men from other Universities, i. 624-5; account of Edward King ("Lycidas"), and of a volume of verses by men of, on the occasion of his death in 1637, i. 647-65; Ordinance for regulating the University by the Long Parliament in January 1643-4, and the Earl of Manchester commissioned to make a visitation to it, iii. 32-3, 92-6; ejection of fellows of colleges and heads of houses, and new appointments, iii. 92-4; a new era in the history of, dating from 1644, and extending to the Restoration, iii. 95-6; condition of the, under the Protectorate, v. 73-5; Henry Cromwell a member for the, in 1654, v. 5.

CAMBRIDGE, town of: Hobson, the carrier, i. 134-5, 240-3; taverns in, i. 138, 140; bathing in the river Cam, i. 139; the Plague in, in 1624, i. 153-4; and again in 1630, i. 232-6; members for, in Long Parliament, ii. 164-5.

CAMDEN, William: his death in 1623, i. 107-8.

CAMERONS of Lochiel, iii. 354.

CAMFIELD, Colonel, and the army remodelling, v. 522.

CAMM, John, early Quaker, v. 26.

CAMPBELL, Archibald: see *Argyle*, Earl of.

CAMPBELL, Sir Duncan, of Auchin-

breck, in the Episode of Montrose in Scotland, iii. 355, 356.

CAMPBELL, Neil, Scottish bishop, i. 705; ii. 42.

CAMPBELLS of Breadalbane, the, iii. 354.

CAMPBELLS of Glenorchy, iii. 354.

CAMPDEN, Viscount, in Royalist army: his death, ii. 429.

CAMPSIE, John, merchant, v. 372.

CAMPVERE, in Holland, ii. 65; iii. 91, 121 and note.

CANNE, John, Independent divine and printer in Amsterdam, ii. 578, 580, 585, 593; iii. 156; in the Council Order Books, iv. 229; regicide pamphlet by, iv. 94 note; succeeds Needham in editorship of *Mercurius Politicus*, v. 671.

CANT, Mr. Andrew, minister of the parish of Pitsligo in Aberdeenshire, i. 712-3, 716; takes part in the Marquis of Hamilton's Mission, ii. 16; in a deputation of Covenanting leaders to Aberdeen, and preaches there, i. 732; ii. 27-8; a member of the Glasgow General Assembly of 1638, ii. 37; in the General Assembly at Edinburgh in 1641, ii. 289-90; reference to his having been in a commission of Presbyterians from the General Assembly to the King at Newcastle, iii. 427; Moderator of the General Assembly at Edinburgh in 1650, iv. 190; a leader of the *Anti-Resolutioners*, or *Protesters*, in the General Assembly of 1651 at St. Andrews, iv. 288-9; v. 90; in danger of State prosecution with other leading Protesters in 1660, vi. 135.

CANTERBURY, Charles I. at, in 1642, ii. 351.

CAPEL, Arthur, Lord (Baron of Headham in 1641), account of, in the Long Parliament, ii. 169; in the Royal army, ii. 429, 442; sent to Shrewsbury as lieutenant-general of the King in the west shires, ii. 460; accompanies the Prince of Wales to Jersey, iii. 375, 494; in attendance on the King at Hampton Court, iii. 561; in a plot for the escape of the King to Berwick, iii. 573; joins in the Second Civil War, iii. 591;

at the siege and surrender of Colchester, iii. 594, 605; sentenced to banishment, iii. 615; trial and execution of, in March 1648-9, iv. 40.

CAPEL, Richard, member of the Westminster Assembly, account of, ii. 517.

CAPPONE, Vincenzo, Florentine, i. 787.

CARANT, Morice, of Looner in Somersetshire, iii. 58.

CARBERY, Richard Vaughan, 2nd Earl of, husband of Lady Alice Egerton, iv. 246 note; v. 78; appointed by Charles II. to the revived Presidency of Wales, vi. 300.

CARDAN, Jerome, i. 265.

CARDENAS, Alphonso de, Spanish Ambassador in London in 1649, iv. 30-1, 221, 234-5, 274, 275, 314, 379-80, 555; State letters of the Council addressed to, in 1650-3, iv. 235-6, 481, 483, 485, 486, 528; negotiates with Cromwell in 1654, v. 37; is recalled to Madrid upon the occasion of the rupture with Spain in 1655, v. 46.

CARDI, Captain, of Leghorn, iv. 485.

CARDIGAN, Thomas Brudenell, Earl of: at the coronation of Charles II., vi. 152.

CARDOUIN : see Cerdogni.

CARELESS, Captain, escapes with Charles II. after Battle of Worcester, iv. 295.

CAREW, Sir Alexander, execution of, by the Long Parliament, iii. 185.

CAREW, John: signs the death warrant of Charles I., iii. 720; a member of the third Council of State of the Commonwealth, iv. 273, 314; and of the fourth Council of State, iv. 309; mention of, in the fourth Council of State, iv. 354, 523, 525; a member of Cromwell's Interim Council of Thirteen, iv. 499, and v. 707; summoned by Cromwell to be of his Supreme Assembly, or "Barebones Parliament," iv. 501, 506; in Oliver's First Parliament, v. 5; concerned with Republican plottings, v. 33; arrested for disaffection to Cromwell's system of government, v. 335; a member of the "Restored

Rump," v. 454, 544 note; fined by the Rump, v. 478; in the quest of the Regicides, vi. 28, 44; excepted from the Indemnity Bill, vi. 49, 53, 54; trial of, vi. 81, 85; execution of, vi. 96-7; in the Bill of Attainder, vi. 115.

CAREW, Thomas, poet : Gentleman of the Privy Chamber to Charles I., i. 502-3, 506, 532, 567, 586, 621; iii. 446, 449; vi. 515.

CAREY, George : see Hunsdon.

CAREY, Henry: see Falkland, 1st Viscount.

CAREY, Sir Henry, Royalist, ii. 442.

CAREY, Horatio, Parliamentarian officer, ii. 445.

CAREY, Sir Lucius : see Falkland, 2nd Viscount.

CAREY, Mr. N., brother of Lord Falkland, i. 800.

CARISBROOKE Castle, Charles I. at, iii. 575, 576-7; the Princess Elizabeth at, iv. 214; Vane at, v. 107.

CARLELL, Ludovick, dramatist, i. 449; iii. 449; vi. 311.

CARLETON, Sir Dudley, ambassador to Holland in 1618, i. 536 : see Dorchester, Viscount.

CARLINGFORD, Earl of : see Taffe.

CARLISLE, James Hay, 1st Earl of, Gentleman of the Bedchamber to James I., i. 379 : see Hay.

CARLISLE, James Hay, 2nd Earl of (1642), ii. 428.

CARLISLE, Charles Howard, Earl of (1661): see Howard, Colonel Charles.

CARLO EMANUELE II., Duke of Savoy and Prince of Piedmont : the Piedmontese Massacre, v. 38, 40, 42, 43; State letters of Milton, for Cromwell, to, v. 184-8, 372-3.

CARLO II., Duke of Mantua, i. 745.

CARLOS II. of Spain, son of Philip IV., and his successor in 1665, vi. 568.

CARLTON, an officer of the City Trained Bands, ii. 447.

CARLYLE's Cromwell: among the many references to, see i. 215, ii. 159 note, iii. 166, 384, 391, 538 note, 568 note, 571, 625; iv. 201 note, 409 note; v. 136-7 note, 307-8 note, 311 note, 361 note, 455 note, and vi. 345-6.

CARLYLE, William, bailie of Dumfries at the execution of Agnew for blasphemy in 1656, v. 93.

CARMICHAEL, Sir James, Justice-Clerk and Treasurer-Depute of Scotland, i. 706; ii. 15; in Cromwell's Ordinance of Pardon and Grace, iv. 561.

CARNARVON, Robert Dormer, 1st Earl of: at Oxford in 1624, i. 456, 535; a peer of the Long Parliament, ii. 158; killed in the Battle of Newbury in 1643, ii. 428, iii. 35.

CARNEGIE, David: see Southesk, Earl of.

CARNEGIE (of Ethie), Sir John: see Northesk, Earl of.

CARNEGIE, Lord, in the Scottish Parliament of 1650, iv. 212.

CARNEGIE, Magdalene, daughter of the Earl of Southesk, and wife of the Marquis of Montrose, ii. 293.

CARNWATH, the 3rd Earl of: at the Battle of Marston Moor, iii. 96; in the Episode of Montrose in Scotland, iii. 344; a "Delinquent," iii. 421; is taken prisoner in the Battle of Worcester, iv. 294, 298.

CAROLINE, Princess of Wales, her contribution to a fund for the relief of Milton's daughter, vi. 754.

CARR, Thomas, fellow-graduate of Milton at Cambridge, i. 218, 258.

CARTER, Colonel, and Monk's manipulation of the army, v. 563.

CARTER, Thomas, a member of Westminster Assembly, ii. 517.

CARTER, William, Independent preacher in London, member of Westminster Assembly, ii. 517; iii. 392 and note; v. 392.

CARTER, Mr., of Yorkshire, licenser of books in 1643, iii. 270.

CARTERET, Philip, of the Isle of Guernsey, member of the Rota Club, v. 485.

CARTERET, Sir George, member of the Privy Council of the Restoration, vi. 18.

CARTWRIGHT, Thomas, English Presbyterian leader, ii. 532.

CARTWRIGHT, William, of Christ Church, Oxford, poet, i. 508, 647;

publication of his works by Humphrey Moseley in 1646, iii. 449.

CARTWRIGHT, William, actor in the King's Company in 1660-8, vi. 349, 350.

CARVER, John, first Governor of New Plymouth, ii. 548.

CARY, Dr. Valentine, master of Christ's College, Cambridge, i. 123.

CARY, Mr. N.: see Carey, Mr. N.

CARYL, Joseph, member of Westminster Assembly, ii. 517, 605; iii. 392 note; book-licenser, iii. 231 note, 270; attacked by Milton in his Colasterion in 1645, iii. 300, 313-5, 315 note; preaches before Parliament, iii. 483 note; iv. 118; accompanies the Commissioners at the surrender of Charles I. by the Scots, iii. 510; with the King at Holmby House, iii. 514; accompanies the Commissioners to the Isle of Wight, and is present at the wreck of the Treaty of Newport, iii. 606; offers his services to the King on the night before his execution, and is dismissed with thanks, iii. 721; licenses the Eikon Basilike, iv. 148; mentions of, iv. 229, 322, 370, 421; in connexion with the Barebones Parliament, iv. 514; in the Commission of Triers, iv. 571; summoned by Cromwell to attend the Council, v. 31; Cromwell's liking for, v. 77; is at the Savoy Synod of the Congregationalists, v. 424; takes part in the negotiations with Monk, v. 497; and is at a Conference at Holyrood House, v. 499; signs a manifesto against the Venner Rebellion, vi. 122; is ejected in 1662 from St. Magnus, London Bridge, for nonconformity, vi. 232 note, 417; his Commentary on Job, vi. 509.

CASAUBON, Meric, Scholar, i. 529; resident in London in 1651, iv. 351.

CASE, Thomas, minister of St. Mary Magdalen, London, member of Westminster Assembly, ii. 571; a member of the Sion College Conclave, iii. 677; iv. 71; implicated in a Presbyterian conspiracy in aid of Charles II., and committed to the

Tower, iv. 285 ; pardoned after the victory of Worcester, iv. 304 ; interviews Charles II. at the Hague, vi. 4 ; is sworn in as one of his Majesty's Chaplains, vi. 62 ; is ejected for nonconformity in 1662, vi. 232 note, 416.

CASSILIS, John Kennedy, 6th Earl of, called "the grave and solemn Earl," a leading Presbyterian in 1634, i. 710, 712, 722 ; is one of the Covenanting Chiefs in 1638, ii. 16 ; attends the Glasgow General Assembly of 1638, ii. 38 ; in the First Bishops' War, ii. 65 ; in the Committee of Estates, ii. 292 ; iv. 202 ; at the General Assembly at St. Andrews in 1642, ii. 418 ; signs the Solemn League and Covenant of 1643, iii. 10, 15 ; with the Scottish auxiliary army in England, iii. 37 ; is in a deputation from the Committee of the Scottish Estates to the King at Newcastle in 1646, iii. 499 ; in the Commission of the General Assembly of the Kirk of Scotland, iii. 509 ; iv. 202 ; joins the "Anti-Engagers" in opposition to the "Engagement" of the Hamiltonians, iii. 589, 621 ; is in a special embassy to Charles II. at the Hague in 1648-9, iv. 20, 26 ; is a Commissioner from the Scottish Parliament at the Treaty of Breda in 1649-50, iv. 180 ; returns to Scotland with Charles II., iv. 188 ; is present at a meeting of the Committee of Estates at Perth, iv. 208, 281 ; in the Scottish Parliament held at Perth and Stirling in 1650-1, iv. 282 ; is nominated one of Cromwell's peers in 1657-8, v. 323 ; refuses to take the Oath of Allegiance to Charles II. in the Scottish Parliament of 1661, vi. 145, 148-9.

CASIMIR, John : see *John II.* of Poland.

CASSINI, Italian scientist, i. 768.

CASTELL, Edmund, Cambridge Oriental scholar, i. 122.

CASTELLI, of Brescia, mathematician, i. 767, 796.

CASTLEHAVEN, Mervin Tuchet, Lord Audley, 2nd Earl of, marries Lady Chandos in 1624, and is executed in 1631 for scandalous criminality, i. 591, 597 note.

CASTLEHAVEN, Lord Audley, Earl of, non-effective Royalist peer : in Ireland, ii. 430 ; at the capture of Limerick in 1650, iv. 303.

CASTLEMAINE, Lady : see *Cleveland,* Duchess of.

CASTLETON, Baldwin, scrivener, i. 26.

CASTLETON, Lord, in a deputation from the Commons to King Charles II. in May 1660, v. 700.

CASTON, Mr. James, i. 64 note.

CASTON, family of, supposed connection of Milton's mother with the, i. 30-1, 38 note, 64 note.

CASTRO, A., Senator of Hertogenwald, iv. 538.

"CATECHISM, a Twofold," by John Biddle, v. 14.

CATHERINE of Braganza, daughter of King Alphonso VI. of Portugal, and wife of Charles II., vi. 161, 238-9, 604 ; her arrival in England and marriage in May 1662, vi. 229 ; the royal honeymoon at Hampton Court, vi. 229-30 ; the increase of the crypto-Catholic mood of the Court after the royal marriage, vi. 239-41 ; negotiations with the Pope to secure for the Queen's Almoner a Cardinal's hat, vi. 240-1 ; the Queen's Court, as described in the *Memoirs of the Count Grammont,* vi. 461 ; plots at Court for enabling Charles to obtain a divorce, vi. 572, 639 ; portrait of the Queen by Faithorne, vi. 648.

CATHERINE HALL, Cambridge, i. 114, 116, 120, 180, 516 ; ii. 225.

CATHOLICS, English, their contribution to the expenses of the First Bishops' War, ii. 50 ; their condition and action under the Protectorate, v. 98-100 ; see also under *Ireland.*

CATON, William, early Quaker, v. 27.

CATZ, Jacobus, Dutch Ambassador in London, iv. 371, 422 ; vi. 782.

CAULFIELD, Lord G., Baron Charlemont, i. 651 ; his wife, Anne King, i. 172, 651.

CAVALCANTI, a Florentine, i. 822.

D

CAVALIERI, scientist at Milan, i. 767.
"CAVALIERS,"introduction of the term,
ii. 331.
CAVALIER SONGS, vi. 333-5
CAVENDISH, Mr. Charles, i. 758.
CAVENDISH, Sir Charles, brother of
the Marquis of Newcastle, at the
Battle of Marston Moor, iii. 96.
CAVENDISH, Colonel, brother of Earl
of Devonshire, ii. 469.
CAVENDISH, Lady Elizabeth, daughter
of the 1st Duke of Newcastle, iii. 462.
CAVENDISH, Lord, 9th Earl and 1st
Duke of Devonshire, vi. 785.
CAWDREY, Daniel, a member of West-
minster Assembly and Nonconformist,
ii. 519 ; iv. 71 ; vi. 232 note.
CAWLEY, William, signs the death-
warrant of Charles I, iii. 720 ; in
third Council of State, iv. 273 ; in
fifth Council of State, iv. 355 ;
mentioned in Council Order Books,
iv. 313, 321, 449 ; member of the
Restored Rump, v. 454, 544 note ;
prosecuted as one of the Regicides,
vi.· 28, 44 ; is excepted from the
Indemnity Act, vi. 54 ; fugitive in
Switzerland, vi. 115, and 115 note.
CAWTON, Mr. Thomas, Presbyterian
minister in the City of London, iv.
47; arrested for treasonable speeches
in the pulpit, iv. 47, 122-3.
CECIL, Edward : see Wimbledon, Viscount.
CECIL, Lucy, Marchioness of Winches-
ter, i. 245 footnote.
CECIL, Mr. Robert, second son of the
Earl of Salisbury, member of the
Restored Rump in 1659-60, v. 519.
CECIL, Sir Thomas, a neighbour of
Milton in Aldersgate Street, ii. 207,
357.
CECIL, William, 2nd Earl of Salis-
bury : see Salisbury, Earl of.
"CENTURY OF INVENTIONS," the, by
the Marquis of Worcester, ii. 462.
CERDA, John Lewis de la, Duke of
Medina Celi, letter of State to, vi.
235.
CERDOGNI (or Cardouin), Camillo,
resident in Geneva, i. 833.
CERVANTES (1547-1616), i. 744.
CESARINI, Cardinal, in Rome, i.· 795.
CHALFONT ST. GILES, in Buckinghamshire, the rector of, at the Westminster Assembly in 1643, ii. 522 ;
the Quaker Ellwood takes a house
for Milton to retire to during the
visitation of the Plague in 1665-6,
vi. 490-8 and 498 note ; Ellwood's
visit to Milton there, and his report
of Paradise Lost as then finished,
and of his suggestion of Paradise
Regained to Milton as a sequel, vi.
652, 654.
CHALFONT ST. PETERS, in Buckinghamshire, vi. 467, 469, 472-3.
CHALGROVE FIELD, the skirmish of,
ii. 471.
CHALLONER, James, Regicide, vi. 35,
37, 55 ; his ultimate penalty, 98
note, 224.
CHALLONER, Mr. Thomas, a Recruiter
for Richmond in Surrey, iii. 507 ;
signs the death-warrant of Charles
I., iii. 720 ; is a member of the
Restored Rump, v. 454, 544 note ;
in successive Councils of State, iv.
273, 354-5 ; v. 456, 519 ; is mentioned in the Council Order Books,
iv. 152, 156, 177, 224, 225, 230,
313, 315, 449 ; is included in the
quest of the Regicides, vi. 28-9 ;
excepted from the Indemnity Bill, vi.
35, 37, 45, 54 ; Bill of Attaint
against, vi. 115 ; subsequent fate of,
vi. 115 note.
CHAMBERLAINE, Thomas, a merchant
living near London Wall, and a
captain of the Trained Bands in
1642-3, ii. 483 ; created a baronet
by Cromwell, v. 354 note.
CHAMBERLAYNE, William, among Men
of Letters of the Restoration, vi.
299, 309.
CHAMBERS, Abbé, Scottish chaplain
to Cardinal Richelieu,·i. 758.·
CHAMBERS, David, diplomatist, resident in Rome, i. 798.
CHAMBERS, Humphrey, member of
Westminster Assembly, ii. 517.
CHAMBERS, Richard, merchant of London, tried by the Star-Chamber,
and kept in prison for several years,
i. 385 ; refuses ship-money, i. 670 ;
is compensated by the Long Parliament, ii. 176 ; mentioned in the
Council Order Books, iv. 225.

"CHAMPIONS of England, the Great," iii. 376-81.

CHANCERY, office of Clerk of the Crown in, i. 104 and note; see *Phillips* and *Agar*.

CHANCERY, office of Clerk of the Commonwealth in, v. 110-1.

CHANDOS, Grey Bridges, 5th Lord, i. 591, 596.

CHANDOS, Anne, Lady, widow of the 5th Lord : see *Stanley*, Lady Anne.

CHANDOS, George Bridges, 6th Lord, i. 591, 597 note, 598, 603 note; his part in the Civil War, ii. 429; his wife, i. 603 note.

CHAPMAN, Livewell, publisher, and probable author of *Plain English*, v. 670, 678 note; vi. 399, 480, 403; v. 605, 645.

CHAPMAN, George, poet and dramatist, i. 445, 451, 453, 579; plays by, vi. 352.

CHAPPELL, William, Milton's first tutor at Christ's College, Cambridge, i. 112, 123, 128, 129; his supposed quarrel with Milton, i. 160, 167, 170; tutor to Roger and Edward King, i. 171; mentions of, at Cambridge, 237, 243, 266, 267, 268, 270, 651, 656; his relations with Laud and Wentworth, and his career in Ireland as Dean of Cashel, Provost of Trinity College, Dublin, and Bishop of Cork, Cloyne, and Ross, i. 129, 692; further account of, ii. 76-9; ii. 401 note.

"CHARACTER of the Long Parliament and Assembly of Divines": see *Milton*, writings of.

CHARENTON, near Paris; the Protestant Church of, v. 368-9.

CHARING CROSS, demolished in 1647, iv. 107.

CHARLES I., King of England—
UNTIL HIS ACCESSION TO THE THRONE (*1600-1625*) :—His birthplace described, iii. 413 note; death of his elder brother Henry, i. 60; his chaplains when Prince, i. 115, 117; the proposed Spanish Marriage, i. 61, 105-6, 107, 353, 366; betrothed to Henrietta Maria, i. 106; in Laud's Diary, i. 367; dissuades Sir Henry Wotton from writing a Life of Luther,

i. 530; theological scholarship before the reign of, i. 518-9; his accession to the throne, i. 149-50, 368.

FIRST FOUR YEARS OF HIS REIGN (*March 1625-March 1629*):—His affection for Buckingham, i. 368; Church government under, and Laud, to 1632, i. 340-4, 368-73, 373-419; adopts Laud's theory of Anglican orthodoxy as the Royal rule in Church matters, i. 368; his marriage to Queen Henrietta Maria, i. 151-2; his kindnesses to Ben Jonson, i. 432, 435, 438; the brothers William and Henry Lawes in the service of, i. 566-7; Thomas Carew is a Gentleman of his Privy Chamber, i. 502; Sir John Suckling's father is his Comptroller of the Royal Household, i. 504; his First Parliament, i. 156, 368-9; dissolution of Parliament on the Tonnage and Poundage Question, i. 368, 369; Bishop Williams deprived of the Great Seal, i. 370; in University business, i. 156-9; his Second Parliament, i. 157, 369-70; his Coronation at Westminster, i. 370; Bishop Williams forbidden to be present at the Coronation, and his place occupied by Laud, i. 370; dissolution of his Second Parliament, i. 159, 369, 370; royal proclamation to all persons, lay or clerical, against controversy on subtle points, i. 370; Sir Henry Wotton's panegyric on, i. 531; "twenty-one months of experimental government without Parliament," i. 370-2; Archbishop Abbot's letter to, i. 371; and Dr. Mainwaring's two Court sermons on the King's rights and powers, i. 371-2; Laud's always increasing influence with, i. 411; his Third Parliament and the Petition of Right, i. 187-8, 204, 213-16, 370, 372, 375-6; courtesies of, to the University of Cambridge, i. 187; cedes the Petition of Right, i. 188, 192-3, 688; tries a similar arrangement with the Irish, i. 688-9; prorogation of his Third Parliament, i. 213, 372, 373; Arthur Johnston of Aberdeen, poet and scholar, is appointed King's Physician in 1628: see *Johnston*; raises Lord Scudamore

to the peerage in 1628, i. 749 ; and
the assassination of the Duke of
Buckingham, i. 206, 213, 373 ;
Waller's poem on "His Majesty's
receiving the news of the Duke
of Buckingham's death," i. 506 ;
"wild words," upon that event, of
Alexander Gill the younger, i. 207-
13, 214-15, 510 ; Laud's influence
with the King increases after the
death of the Duke, i. 373-5 ; his
Declaration prefixed to the Thirty-
nine Articles in the Book of Common
Prayer, i. 374-6 ; his Third Parliament reassembles, i. 215-6, 375-6 ;
his leaning to the Roman Catholics,
i. 341 ; birth and death of his first
child, i. 216, 247 ; his chaplains,
Dr. Mainwaring, and Dr. Peter
Heylin, i. 213-4, 400-1 ; grants a
Charter to "The Governor and Company of Massachusetts Bay in New
England," i. 430-1 ; his Third Parliament is dissolved with ignominy, i.
216.
*FIRST TEN YEARS OF PERSONAL
RULE BY CHARLES WITHOUT AN
ENGLISH PARLIAMENT (March
1629-Dec. 1638)* :—Laud now the
King's chief adviser, i. 376, 664 ;
the Privy Council of, from 1628 to
1632, i. 377-83, 383 note, 383-4
note, 403 ; always increasing influence of Laud with the King in
Council, i. 384-7 ; assists Laud in
the Council by the issuing of measures
in the guise of Royal Proclamations
and Instructions, i. 392-5, 402, 408 ;
birth of his second child, afterwards
Charles II., i. 247, 648 ; birth of the
Princess Mary, i. 247, 648 ; grants
a fellowship of Christ's College, Cambridge, to Edward King, i. 239 ; is
with his Court at Wilton when George
Herbert takes holy orders, i. 414-5,
414 note ; the Fairfaxes of Yorkshire
and, ii. 171 ; knights Sir Simonds
D'Ewes, ii. 172 ; Gill's dedication to,
of his Latin verses, i. 510 ; present at
a trial of three Oxford men for breaking the King's Instructions, i. 408 ;
visits Cambridge with Queen Henrietta Maria, i. 251-4 ; list of bishops
appointed by, since his accession to
1632, i. 391 ; Dr. Juxon is sworn
Clerk of the King's Closet, i. 400 ;
in Laud's projects for the Irish
Church, i. 423, and for a farther extension of Prelacy among the Scots,
i. 425 ; his interference with the
Dutch Synod, i. 427.—The "Reign
of Thorough" (1632-40), i. 664-9 ;
in the Government of England,
with Laud for his chief Minister,
from 1632 to 1638, i. 669-87 ; in
the Government of Ireland, with
Wentworth as Lord Deputy, from
1632 to 1638, i. 687-96.—Cambridge
verses on his recovery from smallpox
in the winter of 1632, i. 648 ; the
passion of the Court of, for dramatic
amusement, i. 578, 579 ; Royal
Letter of Instructions to the Earl
of Bridgewater, 12th May 1633, i.
609 ; account of the King's Coronation Visit to Scotland in June 1633,
i. 699 ; ii. 8, 11, 152 ; is crowned in
Holyrood Abbey, i. 699-700 ; opposition to the Royal Acts in the
Scottish Parliament of 1633, i. 701-
4 ; the King's return to London in
July, 1633, i. 648, 664, 666 ; pro-
motes Laud to the Archbishopric of
Canterbury, i. 664-5, 673 ; his private
letters to Wentworth in Ireland, i.
666, 689 ; character and habits of, in
Council business, and his fixed resolution to govern England without
parliaments, i. 667-8 ; after his
return to London, i. 704-6 ; at the
Masque of the Inns of Court in the
Banqueting House at Whitehall, i.
583 ; himself acts in a masque by
Carew, i. 586-7 ; abets Laud in his
Church innovations, i. 676, 677 ;
consents to Wentworth's advice and
calls a Parliament in Dublin, in
1634, i. 690 ; decree of, establishing
the Book of Canons, dated Greenwich, May 23, 1635, i. 716-7 ; in
correspondence with Wentworth, i.
691 ; proclamation to forbid emigration by Puritans, i. 680 ; constitution of his Scottish Privy Council, i. 706-8 ; in correspondence by
post with the Scottish Privy Council,
i. 708 ; grants a royal warrant for a
Scottish Court of High Commission,

i. 708-9 ; in further correspondence with Wentworth, i. 690-1 ; refuses Wentworth an earldom, i. 691 ; in his relations to European Governments, specially of France and Spain, i. 748-9 ; appoints Lord Scudamore his Ambassador to the French Court, i. 749-50 ; appoints Juxon Lord Treasurer in succession to the Earl of Portland, i. 671 ; royal grant to Laud of right of Visitation of the two Universities, i. 678 ; again refuses an earldom to Wentworth, i. 695-6 ; missive letters of, to the Scottish Privy Council in May 1637 concerning the New Service Book, i. 718 ; displeasure of, at the news of the Jenny Geddes Riot and failure of his scheme of Scottish Episcopacy, i. 721, 723, 724, 725 ; royal proclamation at Stirling, i. 725-6 ; his and Laud's system of absolutism defied in the Scottish Covenant of March 1638, i. 728-32 ; his and Laud's dealings with the Scottish Covenanters, ii. 4-8 ; the surprise of, and of his Court at Whitehall, at the news of the Covenant, and the King's fool expelled, ii. 5-6 ; Wentworth's advice to, on the Scottish difficulty, ii. 6 ; is resolved on sending English forces into Scotland if necessary, ii. 7 ; his Councillors are in favour of more moderate measures, ii. 8 ; sends the Marquis of Hamilton on a mission to Scotland as his Commissioner to treat with the Covenanters, ii. 8-36 ; summons the Marquis of Lorne to the English Court to advise on Scottish affairs, ii. 13 ; Royal Declaration of, ii. 17-20, 25 ; private correspondence with Hamilton, ii. 18-9, 21 ; his secret commission to the Earl of Antrim, ii. 23-4, 27 ; calls a Council at Theobalds to decide on the question of peace or war with the Scots, ii. 24 ; new *Instructions* to Hamilton, dated London, July 27, ii. 25-6 ; his proposed changes in the Scottish Covenant, ii. 28, 31-2 ; his letters of thanks carried by Lord Gordon to the Aberdeen magistrates and doctors, ii. 29 ; revokes the Service Book, and calls a General As-

sembly, ii. 30-4 ; proposes a new or revised Covenant, ii. 31-2 ; his difficulties with the Covenanting party increase, ii. 34-5 ; during the Glasgow Assembly of 1638, ii. 36-42 ; is represented there by the Marquis of Hamilton, ii. 37 ; the *Instructions* insisted upon and rejected, ii. 40-1 ; the Earl of Argyle and, ii. 41 ; the Assembly annulled by proclamation direct from the King at Whitehall, but continues to sit, ii. 42.

LAST YEARS OF " THOROUGH," WITH THE TWO "BISHOPS' WARS" AGAINST THE SCOTS (*Dec. 1638-Nov. 1640*) :—The King resolves on war with Scotland (" First Bishops' War "), ii. 46, 47 ; Laud's dream of "K. C.", ii. 49-50; arranges the command of his army, ii. 50-1, 154 ; issues proclamation of war, ii. 51 ; account of his march to the Borders, ii. 56, 58-65 ; his treaty with the Scots, ii. 67-71 ; is dissatisfied with the treaty, refuses to open the Assembly and Parliament, and returns to Whitehall, ii. 71 ; in correspondence with Wentworth, ii. 127 ; changes in his Council, ii. 127-8; the "Short Parliament" of 1640, ii. 128-30; his Council of War, ii. 128 ; creates Wentworth Earl of Strafford, ii. 129 ; loan of money to, among the members of the Cabinet, ii. 129 ; commits Lord Loudoun to the Tower for the letter, "Au Roy," ii. 130-1 ; his eldest daughter affianced to William of Nassau, Prince of Orange, May 2, 1640, ii. 350, 353; dissolves the " Short Parliament," ii. 131; requires Convocation to continue its sitting for three weeks after the dissolution of Parliament, ii. 131-3 ; causes the arrest of the Puritan leaders of the late Parliament, ii. 132 ; grants a warrant for torturing John Archer, ii. 133-4 ; knights the younger Vane in June 1640, ii. 165 ; at the commencement of the " Second Bishops' War," ii. 3, 135-42 ; his desperate methods for obtaining money for the war, 135-6 ; hurries north with Strafford, ii. 140-1 ; is petitioned

for another Parliament, ii. 142 ; summons a " Great Council of Peers" to York, and calls a Parliament at Westminster, ii. 143-4 ; treaty of peace with the Scots, ii. 143-4 ; Laud's prayer for, to be delivered at the opening of the new Parliament, ii. 145.
FROM THE MEETING OF THE LONG PARLIAMENT TO THE OUT-BREAK OF THE CIVIL WAR (Nov. 1640-Aug. 1642) :— Opens the Long Parliament at Westminster, ii. 149-50 ; nominates Lenthall for the Speakership, ii. 149-50 ; assents to the Bill for Triennial Parliaments, ii. 186 ; his liking for Hall's Humble Remonstrance, ii. 215 ; assents to the Bill for the Indissolubility of Parliament except by its own Act, ii. 187 ; his behaviour in the matter of Strafford's impeachment, trial, and execution, ii. 176-84 ; his approval of Dr. Hackett's speech to the Commons, ii. 229 ; at the conclusion of the Scottish Treaty, ii. 189-90 ; negotiations with the Scottish Commissioners in London, ii. 191-3 ; Bishop Hall and, ii. 253-4 ; his first interview with Edward Hyde, ii. 286-7 ; his second Visit to Scotland, in 1641, ii. 271-3, 287-308 ; is in secret correspondence with Montrose and Napier, ii. 298-9, 300, 302 ; choice of new Councillors and Ministers, ii. 278-85 ; distrust of him by his English and Scottish subjects, ii. 277-8 ; in the Scottish Parliament of August-October 1641, ii. 303-4 ; his concern in the plot in Edinburgh, known as "The Incident," ii. 304-6, 315-6, 318 ; procures the release of Montrose and his associates from their imprisonment in Edinburgh Castle, ii. 307, iii. 340 ; Scottish honours conferred by, ii. 307-8 ; and the Insurrection in Ireland, ii. 308-12 ; declines the offer of the Scottish Parliament to send 10,000 men into Ireland, ii. 317 ; references to, in letters of the English Parliament to the Scottish Parliament, on Irish affairs, ii. 318-9 ; instructions from, to the English Parliament concerning

the Grand Remonstrance, ii. 320 ; changes the lieutenancy of the Tower, ii. 330-1 ; entry of the King and royal Family into London upon his return from Scotland, ii. 323-4 ; fills up vacant bishoprics, and dismisses the guard from the Houses of Parliament, ii. 325 ; receives at Hampton Court a deputation from the Commons to present the Grand Remonstrance and Petition, ii. 325-7 ; present in Parliament at Westminster, ii. 327 ; his breach of Parliamentary privilege, ii. 328-9 and note, 330 ; remodels his Privy Council, ii. 336-7 ; his part in the blunder of Archbishop Williams, ii. 334 ; his Coup d'Etat, or attempted arrest of the Five Members, ii. 336-45 ; quits London, ii. 345-55 ; assents, by commission, to the Bishops' Exclusion Bill and a Bill for pressing soldiers in Ireland, ii. 351 ; is at Dover at the Queen's departure with the Crown jewels to the Continent, and thence proceeds north, ii. 353-5, 410 ; is firm in his resistance to the Militia Bill, ii. 355, 410 ; establishes himself at York, ii. 410 ; appoints several new bishops, ii. 411 ; threatens to go into Ireland and assume the command against the rebels there, ii. 411 ; location of his family, ii. 413 ; acts of, in the three months preceding the Civil War, ii. 411-2, 511-2 ; is refused admittance into Hull, ii. 412 ; flocking of the chief Royalists towards the King at York, ii. 412-6 ; is bidding for the help of the Scots in the war, ii. 416 ; his letter to the General Assembly of 1642, and the answer of the Assembly, ii. 420 ; arrival of a ship for, on the north English coast, with arms and ammunition from Holland, ii. 421 ; grants Commissions of Array, ii. 421, 440 ; gives the Earl of Lindsey the command of his army, ii. 422 ; his nephew, Prince Rupert, is summoned from the Continent, ii. 422 ; issues proclamation " for suppressing the present Rebellion, etc.," ii. 422 ; raises his standard at Nottingham, ii. 422-4, 427 ; iii. 341.

THROUGH THE FIRST CIVIL WAR (*Aug. 1642-Aug. 1646*) :— His Army at the beginning of the Civil War, ii. 440-3 ; in first weeks of the war, ii. 453-8 ; his first success, called the fight of Powick Bridge, ii. 454 ; the Battle of Edgehill, and the march towards London, ii. 454-6 ; takes and occupies Reading, ii. 455 ; takes Brentford, ii. 456 ; retires from Brentford, ii. 458 ; his headquarters at Oxford, ii. 458, 464 ; advances to the relief of the town of Reading, ii. 465 ; Royal Proclamation from Oxford forbidding the Westminster Assembly, ii. 514 ; rejoined by the Queen, iii. 6 ; tries to induce the Scots to adopt a policy of neutrality and mediation, iii. 7 ; his success in the war and that of the Parliamentary army evenly balanced previous to the joining of the Scottish auxiliary army, iii. 35-7 ; issues a Royal Proclamation from Oxford forbidding the Solemn League and Covenant, iii. 12 ; summons an Anti-Parliament to meet him at Oxford, iii. 83 ; prorogues the same, iii. 84 ; disastrous results to, of the Battle of Marston Moor, iii. 96-8 ; defeats Essex in Cornwall, iii. 167-8, 176-7 ; Dr. Daniel Featley is discovered to be acting as a spy in the interest of, iii. 15, 138 ; negotiations of Parliament with the King, issuing in the Treaty of Uxbridge, and finally broken off, iii. 183 ; the strength of, in the various war districts in the early months of 1645, iii. 329-30 ; Oxford still his headquarters, and first actions of New Model against, iii. 331-2 ; leaves Oxford with his artillery train, etc., takes the field with Prince Rupert, and is pursued by Cromwell, iii. 333 ; relieves Chester, and takes Leicester by storm, iii. 334 ; commands in person at the Battle of Naseby, iii. 335, 335 note ; Montrose's attempt to recover Scotland for, iii. 340-69 : see *Montrose* ; is steadily losing ground in the Midlands and elsewhere in England, iii. 370 ; is again in headquarters at Oxford, iii. 368-70 ; is negotiating with Parliament for a personal treaty, iii. 371 ; intrigues with Ireland and France, iii. 372, 519-21 ; escapes in disguise from Oxford, iii. 373 ; takes refuge with the Scottish army, iii. 374, 114, 423, 491 ; issues from Newcastle Orders of Surrender to English cities, towns, and fortresses, and concludes the war (June 10, 1646), iii. 374 ; disposal of the royal family at the close of the Civil War, iii. 375.

THE FOUR STAGES OF THE KING'S CAPTIVITY :—I. In the custody of the Scots at Newcastle (*May 1646-Jan. 1647*), iii. 411-22, 491 ; efforts of the Scots to induce him to take the Covenant, iii. 413-4, 417 ; real motive of, in coming to the Scots, iii. 414-5 ; corresponds in cipher with the Queen, iii. 415, 417, 418, 422 ; in close intercourse with Henderson, iii. 426-8, 429-30 note ; his Letters to the Parliament and to the City of London, iii. 415-7, 422, 424 ; referred to by the Marquis of Argyle in his speech to the Commons of England, iii. 419-20 ; declines to accept the *Nineteen Propositions* of the Parliament, iii. 421-2, 496-7 ; Henrietta-Maria and, iii. 491-6, 502-6 ; balancing of, between the two parties of Presbyterians and Independents, iii. 496-8 ; his scheme of concessions refused by the Scottish deputation, iii. 499-501 ; in a private treaty with the Independents, iii. 501-2 ; his draft Answer to the "Nineteen Propositions" suppressed, iii. 504-6 ; his dealings with the Irish to Jan. 1647, iii. 517-21 ; surrender of, by the Scots to the English, iii. 506-10. II. At Holmby House in the custody of the English Parliamentary Commissioners (*Feb.-June 1647*) :—iii. 513-16, and notes ; sends his answer to the *Nineteen Propositions* to the English Parliament, iii. 539 ; its reception by the two opposed parties there, iii. 539-40 ; abduction of, by the Army, iii. 540-3. III. The King in keeping of the Army (*June-Nov. 1647*) :—iii. 547, 556-7 ; in confer-

ences with the Army chiefs, iii. 557; the Army's *Heads of Proposals* and the Parliament's *Nineteen Propositions* compared, iii. 557-60; at Hampton Court, iii. 561-8; new propositions from Army and Parliament to, iii. 566; in conferences with Cromwell and Ireton, iii. 568-73; new set of Parliamentary Propositions intended for, iii. 573-4. IV. *In the Isle of Wight (Nov. 1647-Nov 1648)*: — Escapes to Carisbrooke Castle, iii. 574-7; the Four Bills and the Propositions of the Parliament delivered to, by a Commission of the two Houses, iii. 584; a Protest against the same delivered to, by the Scottish Commissioners, iii. 584; the "Engagement" or Secret Treaty, between, and the Scottish Commissioners, iii. 586, 590; Answer of, to the English Commissioners, resulting in his final rupture with the Parliament, iii. 584-5; is kept in stricter seclusion, iii. 587-8; in the period of the Second Civil War, iii. 590-605; the Parliament and, in the Treaty of Newport, iii. 603, 605-9; demand of the Army to bring him to justice, iii. 609-10, 616-20; removed to Hurst Castle, iii. 625-30, 694; last efforts of the Presbyterian party in Parliament against the Army and in behalf of the King, iii. 694-5; Prynne's speech in behalf of reconciliation with, iii. 695.
END OF THE REIGN OF CHARLES: — Brought from Hurst Castle to Windsor, iii. 699-702, 705; Resolution and Ordinance for his trial passed by the Commons, but rejected with vehemence by the Lords, iii. 702-5; the Court appointed to try, iii. 705-7; is brought from Windsor to St. James's Palace, iii. 707; his trial and sentence, iii. 707-12; last three days of his life, iii. 712-19; the death warrant, iii. 719-20 and note; his last night, iii. 721-3; procession to Whitehall, iii. 723-4; on the scaffold, iii. 724-6 and note; his burial, iii. 726-9 and note.
POSTHUMOUS AND MISCEL-

LANEOUS MENTIONS OF CHARLES: — His literary tastes, and special liking of Shakespeare, iii. 515; iv. 137; the *Eikon Basilike*, iv. 33-7, 129-32; *Memories of Charles I.*, *etc.*, by Mercier, iv. 155 note; Royalist Pamphlets after his death, iv. 37-71, 155 note; references to, in Milton's *Tenure of Kings and Magistrates*, iv. 65-70, in the *Eikonoklastes*, iv. 133-144, in the *Defensio Prima*, iv. 260-261, and in the *Defensio Secunda*, iv. 591-2; Marvell's verses on his death, iv. 477; celebrations of the Anniversary of King Charles the Martyr after 1660, vi. 122-4, 422.
CHARLES JAMES, Prince, eldest son of Charles I., died in infancy, i. 216.
CHARLES II. — *DURING THE LIFE-TIME OF HIS FATHER (1630-49)*: —Birth of (29th May 1630), i. 247, 648; Lord Scudamore suggests a future alliance between, and a princess of France, i. 755; his tutor, Brian Duppa, i. 625-6; his Governor, the Earl of Newcastle, ii. 152-3; "the Prince of Wales's own troop" furnished by the Earl of Newcastle, ii. 153; the King sends him to the Lords with a last message on behalf of Strafford, ii. 184; mentioned in the Scottish Treaty, ii. 271; accompanies the King on his departure from Whitehall in January 1641-2, ii. 345; joins the King at Greenwich in his journey to York, ii. 353; is with Charles I. at York, ii. 413; present at Nottingham at the raising of the King's standard, ii. 423; mentioned in the list of peers, ii. 428; is in the extreme south-west of England at the fag-end of the Civil War, iii. 369-70; takes refuge in the Scilly Isles, iii. 371; goes to Jersey, and thence to join the Queen at Paris, iii. 375; with the Queen at the French Court, iii. 494-5, 495 note; the King offers to the peers to send for, from France, iii. 422; his proposed part in the programme of the second Civil War, iii. 592, 593; he joins the revolted fleet at Helvoetsluys in Holland, iii.

595 ; brings the fleet from Holland to the south-east coast of England, and blocks the Thames, iii. 597-8 ; at the end of the Second Civil War, he withdraws the fleet to Holland, iii. 604 ; mentioned in the Grand Army Remonstrance, iii. 618 ; the King is willing to abdicate in favour of, iii. 705, 711 ; the King, in his farewell interview with his younger children, tells them of their duty to, iii. 714 ; the King leaves his Bible as a dying gift to, iii. 723.

AS KING OF THE SCOTS (1649-51): — Proclaimed at Edinburgh (5th Feb. 1649) by the Argyle-Warriston Government, and Envoys despatched to him at the Hague, iv. 19-22 ; is proclaimed also in Ireland, and invited thither by the Marquis of Ormond, iv. 23-5 ; his Court at the Hague, iv. 25-9 ; his chaplain in exile, John Earle, i. 527 ; arrival of the Scottish Commissioners at the Hague, iv. 26-9, 63 ; attitudes of the various Foreign Powers to Charles, and his chances at this juncture, iv. 29-31, iv. 63 ; orders Latin and French translations of the *Eikon Basilike* to appear at the Hague, iv. 36, 131 ; Dr. Richard Watson preaches a sermon before, at the Hague, eulogising the *Eikon Basilike*, iv. 131 ; is asked to leave the Hague, after the murder of Dr. Isaac Dorislaus, iv. 55-6 ; joins his mother in France, and proceeds thence to Jersey, iv. 125 ; removes to Breda in North Brabant, and renews negotiations with Scotland, iv. 125, 180 ; mentioned by Milton in his *Eikonoklastes*, and in the first of his State Letters, iv. 143, 160 ; appoints Montrose his Lieutenant-Governor and Captain-General of Scotland, and also Ambassador-Extraordinary to the northern foreign Powers, iv. 181-2 ; the *Defensio Regia* of Salmasius is dedicated to, iv. 150-1, 166 ; resumes negotiations with Argyle, iv. 180-2; Presbyterianism in Scotland and England is favourable to, iv. 122 ; the Irish, in their despair, talk of throwing him aside,

in favour of the Roman Catholic Duke of Lorraine, iv. 125 ; signs the Treaty of Breda, iv. 180-1 ; public and private letters to Montrose from, iv. 182, 182 note ; eulogy of, by Montrose in his address on the scaffold, iv. 185-6 ; letters of, from Breda, concerning Montrose, read in the Scottish Parliament, iv. 187 ; for further references to, in connexion with Montrose's expedition into Scotland, see *Montrose ;* Fairfax retires from the Commandership-in-Chief, rather than head an offensive war against, iv. 192, 194 ; arrival of, in Scotland, iv. 188-90, 192 ; signs both the Covenants, June 23, 1650, iv. 189 ; goes from Falkland to Perth, to Dunfermline, to Stirling, to Leith, and thence back to Dunfermline, iv. 196-7 ; mentions of, in Cromwell's Declarations and Proclamations to the Scots, iv. 197, 198 ; signs the Declaration of the Committee of Estates and the Kirk, iv. 199-200 ; his relations with the Marquis of Argyle after the Battle of Dunbar, iv. 202-6 ; his Court at Perth purged by the Committee of Estates at Stirling of twenty-two of his English attendants, iv. 206-7 ; the incident of "The Start" and its consequences, iv. 207-10 ; the Scotland of Charles II. is reduced to the portion of the kingdom north of the Firths, iv. 210-11 ; present at a meeting of a Scottish Parliament at Perth (26th Nov. 1650), iv. 211-12 ; 279, 281, 282 ; his Coronation at Scone, on 1st Jan. 1650-1, iv. 212-3 ; split of the Scottish Presbyterian clergy round, in 1650, into the *Resolutioners* and the *Remonstrants* or *Protesters*, iv. 213-4, 281-3 ; the officering of his Scottish army, iv. 283-4 ; his march into England, iv. 289-92 ; defeated at the Battle of Worcester, 3rd Sept. 1651, iv. 294-9 ; his escape to France, iv. 299, 299 note.

EIGHT YEARS AND A HALF OF RENEWED EXILE ON THE CONTINENT (*Oct. 1651 - May 1660*): — Resident at, or near, Paris, a pen-

sioner of the French Crown, iv. 380-2, 369 note; his cause at its lowest ebb in England in Dec. 1651, iv. 359; his cause in Scotland, iv. 361-3; his attendance when in Paris at the Protestant church at Charenton, v. 369 note; dedications to, of royalist publications, iv. 436, 453; v. 214, 218, 222; royalist insurrection in Scotland, iv. 508; v. 32, 34, 165 note; excepted (April 1654) from Cromwell's Ordinance of Pardon and Grace, iv. 559; issues a "Secret Proclamation," dated at Paris, May 3, 1654, authorising the assassination of Cromwell, iv. 550; two Royalist risings in England, v. 34-5; Spain adopts the cause of, v. 46; early associations of, with Hobbes and Cowley, v. 80-3; prayers discontinued by the clergy in Scotland for, v. 89; compact between Spain and, for a landing in England, v. 109, 119-20, 141-2; feelings towards of certain Presbyterian Royalists, v. 125; a letter of, to Colonel Overton in 1654, v. 165 note; casual glimpses of, through Oliver's Second Protectorate, v. .306, 321, 332; account of the renewed project, in 1658, of landing a Spanish army in England with Charles and his refugees among them, v. 335-6; discovery by Thurloe and Cromwell of the Royalist Secret Association called "the Sealed Knot," v. 336-8; disappointment of Charles and his friends at the undisputed accession of Richard Cromwell, v. 416-17; revival of their hopes after Richard's abdication, v. 463-5; new projected Royalist Insurrection, v. 472-3; the scheme bungled, v. 474; Sir George Booth's rising in Cheshire crushed by Lambert, v. 475-7; movements of Charles in exile during these events, v. 503-4; growth meanwhile of feeling in his favour in England, v. 504-5; Monk's design to bring in the King is discussed by Whitlocke and Fleetwood, v. 515-17; inquiry into Monk's real intentions with regard to the restoration of Charles, v. 526-8; letter of Mordaunt to Charles concerning this matter (Feb. 17, 1659-60), v. 541 note; the question of Restoration of Charles is not openly discussed in the Parliament of Secluded Members, v. 550-1, 553-4; popular feeling declares itself with enthusiasm for Charles, v. 556-8; agreement between Charles and Monk, v. 559-60; quits Spain and returns to Breda, v. 560; the Restoration certain, v. 567-8, 666, 667; in Milton's latest pamphlets, v. 676-7, 680-1, 684-5, 686-7; vi. 166; dedication to, of a pamphlet by G. S., v. 691-4; account of his sojourn at Breda until his departure to England, v. 560-8; vi. 3-6; recognition by the English Council of State and by the two Houses of Parliament of the King's Breda Letters, v. 694-8; references to, in a summary of incidents immediately preceding and leading up to the Restoration, v. 698-700; the Restoration settled, and arrangements made for the King's voyage from the Hague to Dover, v. 700-2; vi. 6-9.

FOURTEEN YEARS AND A HALF OF THE RESTORED REIGN OF CHARLES II. (May 1660 - Nov. 1674): — I. First year of the Restoration and of the Hyde (Clarendon) Administration (May 1660 - May 1661): — Royal progress to, and entry into, London (May 29), vi. 9-11; rejoicings throughout the British Islands, vi. 11-17; his Privy Council and Ministry in June 1660, vi. 17-19; the Junto or Cabinet, vi. 19-21; relation of the King and his Councillors to the Parliament, vi. 21; arrangement by, for the Lords, vi. 21-2; his first appearance in the Convention Parliament, vi. 22-5; the Royal Declaration of Indemnity, vi. 25-6; in the business of the Indemnity Bill and the Quest of the Regicides, vi. 26-53; gives his Assent to the Bill (29th August 1660), vi. 53; five other Bills assented to by, vi. 56-8; the King makes fruitless efforts to promote conciliation between the two contending Church Parties in Parlia-

ment, vi. 58-67 ; in business of the Parliament immediately preceding the Recess, vi. 67-8 ; addresses the two Houses and adjourns the Parliament for a Recess of eight weeks (Sept. 13 to Nov. 6), vi. 68 ; extolled by Hyde in his speech to the Lords, vi. 69-70 ; in full practice and enjoyment of his royalty during the Recess, vi. 70 ; the Royal Family of the Restoration, vi. 71-2 ; the Court of the Restoration, vi. 72-4 ; touches for the King's Evil, vi. 74-5 ; origin of the regiments known as the "Guards," vi. 76, 121 ; the King's *Declaration* concerning Ecclesiastical Affairs (Oct. 25, 1660), vi. 99-104 ; arrangements of, with Hyde for filling up the Episcopate, vi. 104-6 ; recognises the marriage of Anne Hyde and the Duke of York, vi. 106-8 ; proposes to dissolve the Convention Parliament and confers a peerage on Hyde, vi. 108 ; at the reassembling of the Convention Parliament (Nov. 6), vi. 108-10 ; collapse of the King's *Declaration*, vi. 110-2 ; mentions of, in the process of the Bill of Attainder and the "Disinterring" Order through Parliament, vi. 112-5 ; in measures for raising revenue, vi. 115-7 ; appoints several new bishops, and dissolves the Convention Parliament (29th Dec. 1660), vi. 117-8 ; events in the royal family, vi. 118-9 ; royal proclamation (10th Jan. 1661), on the occasion of the Venner Riot, against meetings for worship except in parish churches and authorised chapels, vi. 121-2 ; Davenant's revived laureateship in 1660, vi. 273; the King's connexions with Hobbes, v. 80-1, vi. 290; anti-Puritan reaction in the Court and Literature of the Restoration, vi. 345; the King's Theatre, vi. 353-6 ; the King's taste for comedy and farce, vi. 357 ; his taste for mechanics and for chemistry, vi. 395 note ; his connexion with the Royal Society of London, vi. 395 and note ; referred to in Bishop Gauden's letters to Clarendon, vi. 425-39, 433 note ;

references to, in account of the State of Ireland at the Restoration, vi. 124-9; the Re-severance of Scotland from England at the Restoration, and the views of Charles and of Hyde upon that matter, vi. 129 ; management of Scottish affairs by the King with a Scottish Council sitting at Whitehall, vi. 130-2 ; arrest of the Earl of Argyle at Whitehall, vi. 132 ; further acts of the King and his Scottish Council, vi. 132-3; references to, in the further account of Scotland at the Restoration, vi. 133-51 ; account of the Coronation of, at Westminster (April 23, 1661), vi. 151-8 ; first meeting of the new (Cavalier) Parliament (8th May 1661), vi. 158 ; Act of Parliament for the first anniversary of Thanksgiving for the Restoration (May 29, 1661), vi. 160 ; dealings of the King and Hyde with Scottish delinquents, vi. 161 ; the King announces to the new Parliament his intended marriage, vi. 161. —II. *Through the First Six Sessions of the Cavalier Parliament to the Fall of Clarendon* (*May 1661-Aug. 1667*), vi. 221-72 :—The royal marriage on 21st May 1662, vi. 229-30 ; and the execution of Sir Harry Vane, vi. 230-1 ; and the Act of Uniformity, vi. 235-6, 237 ; changes in the Privy Council, vi. 236-7; the King secretly a Roman Catholic, vi. 237-42; the King's Toleration Edict in opposition to the anti-Toleration policy of Clarendon, vi. 243-5; resentment of Charles at the opposition of Clarendon, vi. 245 ; at the impeachment of Clarendon and restoration of Clarendon to power, vi. 245-8; marriage at Whitehall of Mr. James Crofts, the King's natural son, to Anne Scott, vi. 248-9 ; continued antagonism of the "crypto-Catholics" to Clarendon's supremacy, vi. 249; mentioned in account of two Acts of the third session of the Cavalier Parliament, vi. 249-50 ; royal gift to Clarendon of a town-mansion, vi. 250-1 ; during the war with the Dutch, vi. 251-6 ; is driven, with his Court, from

Whitehall by the Great Plague in June 1665, vi. 256-8 ; the fifth session of the Parliament (Oct. 9-31) is held at Oxford for the convenience of the King and the Court, vi. 258 ; his behaviour during the Great Fire of London, vi. 261-2 ; in Dryden's *Annus Mirabilis*, v. 377 ; Dryden and, vi. 371, Nell Gwynn and, vi. 355 ; Court scandals concerning, vi. 261-4 ; interference of Parliament with the King's expenditure of public money, vi. 262 ; Clarendon's influence with the King on the wane, vi. 263-5 ; still at war with the Dutch, vi. 265 ; the Dutch in the Thames, and the country indignant against the King and Clarendon, vi. 266-8 ; summary assembling of the Parliament, vi. 269 ; in the Treaty of Breda, vi. 269 ; dismisses Clarendon from the Chancellorship, and sends him into exile, vi. 269-72. —III. *Through the Cabal Administrations to 1674* :—Composition of the Cabal, or Cabinet, after the Fall of Clarendon, vi. 562-3 ; Church policy of, from 1667 to 1670, vi. 565-8 ; in the seventh session of the Cavalier Parliament, vi. 566; in the eighth session, vi. 567 ; in the *Triple Alliance* and the *Secret Negotiation with France*, vi. 568-72 ; and the *Lord Roos Divorce Bill*, vi. 572-4 ; disintegration of the Cabal, vi. 574-5 ; *Secret Treaty of Dover*, and proposed Declaration of Catholicity by the King, vi. 575-82 ; alliance with Louis XIV. against the Dutch, vi. 582-6 ; the Prince of Orange at the English Court, vi. 585 ; the Declaration of Religious Indulgence, vi. 586-90 ; in the tenth session of the Cavalier Parliament, vi. 590-8; the Test Act, vi. 594-5 ; break-up of the Cabal, vi. 596-8; in the eleventh session of the Cavalier Parliament, vi. 598-600; in the twelfth session, vi. 600-2 ; makes peace with the Dutch, vi. 601; at the beginning of the Danby Administration in 1674, vi. 602-3 ; the Court and Royal Family in 1674, vi. 604-5.

CHARLES V., Emperor of Germany, i. 99.

CHARLES X., or Charles Gustavus (Karl Gustav), King of Sweden in succession to Queen Christina, i. 832; iv. 554 ; State Letters to, iv. 636 ; v. 40, 166, 189, 246-50, 252, 269, 270-1, 274, 289, 370, 385-6, 395-6 ; Cromwell's admiration of, v. 313-4, 427 ; more State Letters to, v. 570-2, 575, 590 ; his relations with the Restored Rump, v. 467, 502, 595.

CHARLES XI. of Sweden : his birth, v. 249.

CHARLTON, in Wiltshire, Dryden in retirement at, vi. 368, 376.

CHARLTON, actor in Killigrew's Company, vi. 349.

CHARLTON, Dr., author, and friend of Dryden, vi. 366; satirised by Butler, vi. 618.

CHARLTON, Mr., member of the Convention Parliament, vi. 173.

CHARNOCK, Stephen, Nonconformist, vi. 232 note.

CHARTER HOUSE, The, ii. 208.

CHARTERIS, Thomas, Scottish divine, v. 346 note.

CHASE, of Sidney Sussex College, Cambridge, i. 199-200.

CHATEAUNEUF, French Ambassador Extraordinary : his visit to Cambridge with Lord Holland, i. 220, 223, 225.

CHAUCER, Milton's early readings in, i. 97, 180, 514.

CHAUNCY, Charles, Puritan preacher at Cambridge, i. 121 ; at Ware, i. 407 ; New England minister, ii. 555, 574.

CHEAPSIDE (or West Cheap), in Milton's boyhood, i. 46-9.

CHEEVERS, Sarah, early Quaker, v. 27.

CHELSEA COLLEGE, ii. 225 ; iii. 222 ; v. 341.

CHERUBINI, Alexander, Roman friend of Milton, account of, i. 801-2 ; Milton's mention of, i. 802.

CHERUBINI, Laertius, Roman lawyer, i. 801.

CHESS, Charles I. and the game of, iii. 510.

CHESTER, Colonel J. L., his researches into the Milton genealogy, i. 11 note, 23 note, 33-7, 830 note ; his re-

searches concerning the Diodati family, i. 102 note.

CHESTERFIELD, Earl of, in Royalist army, ii. 428 ; capture of, v. 477.

CHEYNEL, Francis, member of Westminster Assembly, ii. 517, 605.

CHIABRERA, Italian poet, i. 762.

CHICHESTER, Charles, Parliamentarian officer, ii. 445.

CHICHESTER, Thomas Leigh (first Lord Dunsmore), Earl of, in 1644 : ii. 143, 158, 337, 429.

CHIDLEY, Katherine, Brownist, pamphlet by, ii. 595 ; iii. 110-1, 130, 149.

CHIDLEY, Samuel, pamphlet by, v. 132 note.

CHIESLEY, Sir John, clerk to Scottish Commissioners, iii. 580, 717 ; iv. 22 ; vi. 132-3.

CHIGI, Cardinal, Charles II.'s letter to, vi. 240.

CHILIASTS : see *Millenaries.*

CHILLENDON, Edmund, Independent, ii. 587.

CHILLINGDON, Captain, his "church meeting-place," v. 64.

CHILLINGWORTH, William, Fellow of Trinity College, Oxford, i. 208, 210, 212, 533, 537-8, 685 ; ii. 169, 413-4 ; iii. 107-8, 126 and note.

CHIMENTELLI, Valerio, Florentine friend of Milton, i. 773, 779, 780, 821; iii. 654, 690 ; mentioned in Milton's *Defensio Secunda,* iv. 637.

CHIVERTON, Alderman Sir Richard, knighted by Cromwell, v. 354 note ; supporter of Richard's Protectorate, v. 418.

"CHOICE DROLLERY, Songs and Sonnets," v. 260.

CHOLMLEY, Sir Henry, colonel in the Parliamentarian Army, ii. 444 ; v. 700.

CHOMLEY, Sir Hugh, his desertion to the King, ii. 470.

CHOTE, Thomas, fellow-student of Milton at Christ's College, Cambridge, i. 111, 218.

CHRIST CHURCH, Oxford, i. 501, 508, 526, 535, 626.

"CHRISTIAN PARADOXES, The," ii. 520-1.

CHRISTIAN IV. of Denmark, i. 741, 747.

CHRISTIAN, Mr. Charles, i. 309 note.

CHRISTINA, Queen of Sweden, iv. 31, 183, 268-71, 317, 344-6, 377-8, 424, 481, 553-4 ; Milton's panegyric addressed to, iv. 597-9, 597 note, 624.

CHRISTINE, daughter of Henry IV. of France, and Duchess - Regent of Savoy, v. 38, 42.

CHRIST'S COLLEGE, Cambridge: i. 111 ; account of, in 1621, i. 113, 114, 116, 118, 122-32 ; in Milton's time, i. 111, 132-3, 133, 136-7, 140, 149, 150-1, 171, 182, 183 note, 186, 218, 225, 238-9, 248, 258 ; further mentions of, i. 275, 285, 354, 377, 490, 562, 647 note.

CHUDLEIGH, Mr., secretary to the Embassy at Nimeguen, vi. 797-9, 801.

CHURCH and RELIGION—

To the Glasgow Assembly of 1638 :—Religious education in old St. Paul's School i. 75 ; a Protestant Italian congregation in Geneva in 1572, i. 99 ; the Scottish Presbyterian Kirk system in 1576, i. 69 ; retrospect of English Church Government to 1603, i. 340-4 ; account of the same continued from 1603 to 1625, i. 344-68 ; Hampton Court Conferences of 1603 and Canons of 1604, i. 344-7 ; High Church Primacy of Bancroft from 1604 to 1610, i. 347 ; anti-Episcopal *Protestation at Perth* in 1606, i. 69-70 ; Scottish students in Protestant Universities of Northern Germany in 1606, i. 70 ; Diodati's Bible in 1607, i. 99 ; Low Church Primacy of Abbot from 1611 onwards, i. 347-9 ; Archbishop Usher and the Irish Church, in 1615, i. 519-20 ; Bishop Williams's Broad Church policy, i. 349-54 ; growth of English anti-Calvinism, i. 354-8 ; promotions of Laud, i. 358-67 ; English Protestant feeling roused in prospect of the proposed Spanish Match, i. 105-6, 366 ; *the Fatal Vespers in Blackfriars,* i. 107, 366 ; prelates and theologians at Christ's College, Cambridge, i. 114, 123-31 ; *English Church Government* from 1625 to 1632, i.

368-419; Church incidents to 1632, 139-40, 143, 155, 168-9, 173-4, 174-9, 195-201; Laud's work during Buckingham's Premiership (1625 to 1628), i. 368-73; relations of Charles and Laud after the assassination of Buckingham, i. 373-5; the Committee of Religion in the third Parliament of Charles I. in 1628-9, i. 215-6, 375-6; University Tests, i. 217 and note; composition of the English Privy Council from 1628-32, i. 377-83; Laud in the Council and Star-Chamber, i. 384-6; Secretary Windebank, i. 386-7; Dr. Henry More and the doctrine of Calvinistic Predestination, i. 249; Laud's supremacy in the Church in 1632, i. 387-8; the English Episcopate, i. 388-90; Laud's Ecclesiastical Legislation and Administration, i. 391-407, 409-18; religious statistics in England in 1632, i. 340-4; Milton and Laud, i. 257-8, 323-7, 413, 418-9; poets of the popular Calvinism, i. 490-1; poets of the anti-Puritan or Laudian school, i. 485, 491-501, 525-6; religious prose literature on both sides, i. 515-25; the Irish Protestant Church in 1632, i. 419-23, 520; the Scottish Kirk in 1632, i. 423-6; Foreign Chaplaincies, i. 426-8; the Colonial Church or Church of the Puritan settlements in America, i. 428-31; the principle of *Thorough* applied to Church government, i. 669, 697; Church government in England (1632-8), i. 673-87; in Ireland (1632-8), i. 690-6; in Scotland (1632-8), i. 697-726; the National Scottish Covenant of 1638, see *Covenants;* the Scottish Covenanters, ii. 3-36; the General Assembly at Glasgow in 1638, ii. 36-42, 122.

To the cessation of the Westminster Assembly in 1649 :— Calvinistic Protestantism in Geneva in June 1639, i. 831-2; the First Bishops' War or *Bellum Episcopale* with the Scots, ii. 3, 43-71, 122; the General Assembly of 1639 in Edinburgh, ii. 42, 71, 122, 124, 130; Episcopal alarms in England, ii.

122-3; Bishop Hall's *Episcopacy by Divine Right,* ii. 123-6, 214; Convocation of the Clergy at Westminister, ii. 131-2; arrest of Puritan leaders of the Parliament, ii. 132-3; riots in London, ii. 133-4; the Second Bishops' War, ii. 3, 126-31, 135-42; iv. 20; Baillie, Henderson, and other Scottish preachers, at Newcastle, ii. 142; during the Scottish occupation of the North of England, ii. 142; Laud's prayer for the opening of the Long Parliament, ii. 145; list of the Episcopal Bench in 1640, ii. 150-1; the English Church Reform Movement in 1640, ii. 193-202; extraordinarily religious character of the Long Parliament, ii. 194-5; Pym's speech on "Prejudice of Religion," ii. 194; the three parties in England on the Church Question, ii. 195; the High Church Party, ii. 195-6; the Moderate Party, ii. 196-9; the Root-and-Branch Party, ii. 199-202; the Church question in and out of Parliament, ii. 212-36; pamphlets by Henderson and Baillie and other Scottish divines, ii. 218; Bishop Hall and "Smectymnuus," ii. 214-5, 218-22; the Bishops Exclusion Bill : ii. 222-31, 269, 349; Bishop Williams's Scheme, ii. 224-6, 235; Archbishop Usher's Scheme, ii. 229-30, 235; the Root-and-Branch Bill, ii. 231-6, 269; redistribution of parties in England, ii. 236; Milton's Anti-Episcopal pamphlets, ii. 237-68, 356-409; impeachment of thirteen Bishops, ii. 269-70; regulation of public worship in parishes and cathedrals, ii. 273-4; state of parties on the Church Question, ii. 274-87; the General Assembly of 1641, and Scottish Parliament during the King's visit in that year, ii. 287-308; the Irish Rising of 1641, and "the Oath of the Confederate Catholics of Ireland," ii. 311; new appointments of bishops, ii. 324-5; the Grand Remonstrance of Dec. 1641, ii. 316-30, 509; Archbishop Williams's blunder and its consequences, ii. 330-6; the Women's Petition against

bishops, ii. 348-9; the Bishops' Exclusion Bill passed, ii. 349-54; appointment of several new bishops by the King, ii. 411; account of the calling of the Westminster Assembly in July 1643, ii. 509-27, 603-8; English Presbyterianism, (1564-1643), ii. 531-4 : see *Presbyterianism;* English Independency to 1643, ii. 534; Brownism and the first Brownists (1580-92), ii. 534-8; the English Separatists in Holland (1592-1620), ii. 538-42; Separatist congregations in London, etc. (1610-32), ii. 543-4; the New England emigration, and Church of New England (1620-40), ii. 545-77; continuation of English Independency in Holland (1620-40), ii. 578-80; its persistence in England (1632-40), ii. 580-4; its reinvigoration (1640-3), ii. 584-602; Presbyterianism and Independency in July 1643 : their prospects in the Westminster Assembly, ii. 602-8; first meeting of the Westminster Assembly, iii. 3-4; revision of the Thirty-nine Articles of, iii. 4-6; Scottish Commissioners in the Assembly, iii. 6-10, 16-8; the Solemn League and Covenant, iii. 10-15, 38-40; questions debated in the Assembly, iii. 18-26; visitation of the University of Cambridge, iii. 32-3, 92-6; Milton's first Divorce Treatise, iii. 43-56, 61-78; struggle between Presbyterianism and Independency in England, iii. 84-90; correspondence of Baillie and William Spang at Campvere, iii. 91; the Toleration Controversy in 1644, iii. 98-136; synopsis of English Sects and Sectaries in 1644, iii. 136-60; denunciation by the Westminster Assembly of picked sectaries and heretics, iii. 160-6; Cromwell's interference for Toleration, iii. 166, 169-71, 177-8; progress of the Assembly's work, iii. 171; *Confession of Faith,* or *Articles of Religion,* iii. 171, 172; the *Catechisms* of the Westminster Assembly, iii. 171, 425; the Westminster Assembly's *Frame of Discipline or Church Government,* in lieu of Episcopacy, iii.

171, 172, 173, 396-400, 425; the *Directory of Worship* of the Westminster Assembly to supplant a Liturgy, iii. 172, 173, 425; Presbyterian Settlement voted by both Houses on Jan. 28, 1644-5, iii. 175; Scottish General Assembly of 1645 at Edinburgh, iii. 176; ratification of the Westminster *Directory of Worship* and *Frame of Church Government* by the Scottish General Assembly, iii. 176; Presbyterians desire execution of Laud, iii. 184-5; Milton among the Sectaries, iii. 186-9; Mrs. Attaway, iii. 189-92; Milton's projected *Body of Divinity,* iii. 254-5, 671-2; Milton's Divorce Treatises, iii. 255-61, 262-5, 297-301, 301-13, 313-21; continued Church controversies, iii. 382-3; Independency and Sectarianism in the New Model, iii. 384; Cromwell and Toleration, iii. 385-6; religious democratic opinion in English society, and in London, iii. 386; pamphlets and pamphleteers, iii. 386-90; Presbyterian methods for suppression of Toleration, iii. 389-96; Sion College and the Londoners, iii. 394-5, 676-80, Parliament rebukes the Westminster Assembly, iii. 403-11; Milton's anti-Presbyterian outburst, iii. 466-71, 673-80; resumption of the Church Question in the Commons, iii. 544; successive Provincial Presbyterian Synods of London, iii. 423-4, 544-5, 568; visitation of the University of Oxford, iii. 546; Parliament and the Westminster Assembly reconciled, iii. 422; new work for the Assembly, iii. 425-6; Rous's Metrical Version of the Psalms, iii. 425; death of Alexander Henderson, iii. 426-9 and note; balancing of Charles between the Presbyterians and the Independents, iii. 496-506; progress of the Presbyterian Settlement, iii. 511-3; the "Army of Fanatics," iii. 522-6; Church incidents in Parliament, iii. 567-8; the King's proposals for settlement of the Church question, iii. 577; the Scottish Envoys, iii. 580-2;

Charles's Secret Treaty with the Scottish Commissioners on the Religious Question, iii. 586, 588-90; Royalist tendencies among the Presbyterians in England, iii. 590; revision by the two Houses of the Westminster *Confession of Faith* and *Larger Catechism*, iii. 599 and note; Presbyterian feeling against the Second Civil War, iii. 599-602; the Treaty of Newport wrecked on the Episcopacy question, iii. 605-9; Presbyterians and Independents in Parliament (1648), iii. 619-20; religious controversies on the Continent to 1649, i. 100; horror of the Scottish Presbyterians at the execution of Charles I., iv. 21-2; Ormond's Treaty with the Roman Catholics of Ireland, iv. 23; union of all varieties of Catholics and Protestants in Ireland for the purposes of a Royalist alliance, iv. 23-4; the Presbyterians of Ulster denounce the English Sectaries, iv. 23-4; theological antipathies to the Commonwealth within England, iv. 32-3; the *Eikon Basilike* and Milton's *Eikonoklastes*, iv. 33-7, 129-44; cessation of the Westminster Assembly, and its Bequests to England and Scotland, iv. 58-60.

To the Dissolution of the Rump in 1653 :—The Scottish Kirk in 1649, iv. 60-3; the Presbytery of Belfast, iv. 102-4; Clement Walker's *History of Independency*, iv. 121; the General Assembly of 1649 at Edinburgh, iv. 122; Presbyterian royalism, iv. 122-4; the "Engagement" of the Commonwealth to supersede the *Solemn League and Covenant* of 1643, iv. 124; Salmasius and his *Defensio Regia*, iv. 162-75; Acts for the Propagation of the Gospel in Wales, England, and Ireland, iv. 178-9; other Acts and Resolutions of the House, iv. 179-80; Charles II. signs both the Covenants in Scotland, iv. 189, 212-3; penance and excommunication in Scotland, iv. 213; Cromwell's reduction of Kilkenny, iv. 190; emigration of Roman Catholic officers to France and Spain, iv. 191; Cromwell in Scotland, iv. 196-8; the *Commission of the Kirk*, iv. 197, 202, 211; the Super-Ultra Presbyterian party of the west of Scotland, iv. 203-5; Order, in 1650, to view and inventory the records of the Westminster Assembly, iv. 228-9; changes in the chaplaincy of Council of State, iv. 229; second edition of *Eikonoklastes*, iv. 246-9; the *Pro Populo Anglicano Defensio*, iv. 250-67; Scottish Presbyterianism in south Scotland shaken by the influence of the English army there, v. 279-81; Presbyterianism north of the Firths also broken down, iv. 281-4; split of the Scottish Presbyterian clergy in 1650 into *Resolutioners* and *Anti-Resolutioners*, iv. 213-4, 281-4, 288-9, 361-3; conspiracy of Presbyterians and Royalists in London, iv. 284-7, 304; Scottish General Assembly of 1651, iv. 288-9; Christopher Arnold's account of church matters in London, iv. 350-3; Scottish Church parties at the incorporation of Scotland with the Commonwealth, iv. 360-3; prospects of Scottish Presbyterianism, iv. 369-70; measures for the Government of Ireland, iv. 366-71; the "Racovian Catechism," iv. 423; 438-39, 439 note; Acts for "the Propagation of the Gospel," iv. 387-95, 397-8, 438; the Church of the Colonies and Roger Williams, iv. 395-6; Milton's sonnet to Cromwell, and its relation to Church affairs, iv. 440-2; question of a new State Church, iv. 398; a new Translation of the Bible projected by the Rump Parliament, iv. 524; Scottish General Assembly of 1653 dispersed, iv. 509-10; death of Salmasius, iv. 538-9; collapse of the Parliament in 1653 on the Ecclesiastical Question, iv. 513-5; Cromwell's idea of an Established or State-paid Church, iv. 515-7.

To the Restoration of Charles II. (*1653-60*) :—Ordinances of Cromwell affecting religion and morals, iv. 559, 562, 563, 564, 565 and note;

Cromwell's scheme for the Propagation of the Gospel in England and Wales, iv. 566; Cromwell's two fixed ideas : an Established Church, and toleration of dissent round that Church, iv. 566-71, 613-6; Church measures in Cromwell's first Parliament, v. 11-14; new sects since 1644, v. 15-28; the Piedmontese Massacre, v. 38-44, 175, 183-90, 191, 244-6, 269-75; Cromwell's Church policy from 1654 to 1656, v. 52-72; Church matters in Cromwell's Second Parliament, v. 106-18, 132-6, 290-2; through the Second Protectorate, v. 315-20, 341-43, 343-5, 345-50, 370, 387-90, 395-6; condition of religion in Scotland through the Protectorate, v. 89-98; Milton's Treatise of Civil Power addressed to Richard's Parliament, v. 580-7; letter of Moses Wall to Milton, v. 601-3; Milton's private letters to Jean Labadie, v. 590-5; Church policy of the Restored Rump, v. 466, 616; Milton's "Means to remove hirelings out of the Church," v. 605-16; Monk and the "Fanatics," v. 639-40, 641; re-establishment of Presbytery by the Restored Long Parliament (1659-60), v. 548; alarm of the Independents and Sectaries, v. 549; the Solemn League and Covenant revived by the Commons, v. 549; other Presbyterian measures, v. 550; Church measures of the same Parliament, v. 657-8; Dr. Matthew Griffith and his Sermon, v. 667, 675.

After the Restoration: — The Church Question in 1660, vi. 58-67; touching for the King's evil, vi. 75; *Declaration of the King concerning Ecclesiastical Affairs*, vi. 99-104, 110-2; the English Episcopate in Nov. 1660, vi. 104-6; additional bishoprics, vi. 118; the Venner Riot and John Bunyan, vi. 120-2; religious celebration of the Anniversary of King Charles the Martyr, vi. 122-3; a Protestant Parliament restored to Ireland, vi. 124; the Irish Episcopal Church restored, vi. 127-9, 160;

Church affairs in Scotland at the Restoration, vi. 133-158; meeting of the new English Parliament, and prospects of Episcopacy in England, vi. 158-60; burning of the Solemn League and Covenant in London and Westminster, vi. 159; Act of 1661, repealing an Act of the Long Parliament, and restoring bishops to their places in the House of Lords, vi. 223; Act against Quakers, vi. 225; Act of Uniformity, vi. 225-7; St. Bartholomew Sunday, 1662, and the ejection of 2000 of the clergy of the Church of England from their livings for Nonconformity, v. 231-5, 237; vi. 414, 416; Anti-Puritanism in the literature of the Restoration, vi. 335-6; Cowley's *Vision of Cromwell*, vi. 336-9; Butler's *Hudibras*, vi. 339-42; the "atheism" of Thomas Hobbes, or "Hobbism," defined, vi. 279-91; Crypto-Catholicism of the Court, vi. 237-41; the King's Toleration Edict, vi. 241-45; Milton's prophecy of the Acts of the Restoration Government, and his "warnings," contained in the *Ready and Easy Way*, fulfilled, vi. 408-16; Clarendon's opposition to the King's Popish tendencies, vi. 245-8; trials of John Twyn and others, printers, for high treason, vi. 477-81; the Conventicles Act (May 17, 1664), vi. 249-50; the Five Miles Act (Oct. 31-1665), vi. 258-9; Church policy of the Cabal Government from 1667-70; vi. 563-7; the Triple Alliance, and the Secret Negotiation with France, vi. 568-72; the Secret Treaty of Dover, and the proposed Declaration of Catholicity by the King, vi. 575-82; Charles's Declaration of Home Policy, with suspension of all coercive laws in religion, and granting indulgence of separate worship to Nonconformists, vi. 586-90; Church measures in the Tenth Session of the Cavalier Parliament, vi. 591-6; the Test Act, vi. 594-5; Milton's Tract on True Religion and Toleration in 1673, vi. 690-9; controversy between Samuel Parker and Andrew Marvell, vi.

E

699-708; the No-Popery enthusiasm continued through the Twelfth Session of the Parliament, vi. 600-2 ; Milton's Treatise of Christian Doctrine, vi. 817-40.

CHUTE, Chaloner, in Richard's Parliament, v. 431-2.

CIAMPOLI, Italian poet in 1638, i. 797.

CIPRIANI, engraver of Milton's portrait, i. 310 note ; vi. 754 note.

CITY of LONDON, the : see *London ;* for list of Milton's residences in and near, see *Milton.*

CIVIL WAR : the "First" (1642-6) :— First actual bloodshed in, ii. 57 ; first field-action of the, ii. 57 ; preparations for, ii. 410-24 ; statistics of the two sides, ii. 428-38, 438-53 ; first few weeks of, and fight of Powick Bridge, ii. 453-4 ; Battle of Edgehill, ii. 454-6 ; the March to Turnham Green, ii. 457-8 ; events till midsummer 1643, ii. 458-70 ; progress of the, iii. 6 ; 33-41 ; Scottish Auxiliary army, iii. 35-7 ; 83-91 ; Battle of Marston Moor, iii. 96-8 ; Royalist victory in Cornwall, iii. 167-8 ; new modelling of the Parliamentarian army, iii. 176-83 ; Treaty of Uxbridge, iii. 183 ; survey of the state of the, after formation of *New Model,* iii. 329-30; 330-8 ; 339-40 ; fag-end of the, iii. 369-74 ; state of things at the end of, iii. 374-81.—the " Second," (May-Aug. 1648) :—iii. 590-605 ; chance of a Third, v. 459-60.

CLANRANALD, the Chief of, with the Earl of Montrose, iii. 353.

CLANRICARDE, Ulick de Burgh, 2nd Earl of St. Albans, and Marquis of : his subscription towards First Bishops'·War, ii. 47 ; non-effective Royalist peer, ii. 430 ; Ormond's substitute in Ireland, iv. 303, 368.

CLARE, Earl of, ii. 162 ; his subscription towards First Bishops' War, ii. 48; in the Long Parliament, ii. 159 ; in the Civil War, ii. 430 ; iii. 377.

CLARE HALL, Cambridge, i. 114, 116, 120, 129, 182, 213, 221, 416.

CLARENDON, Edward Hyde, Earl of : account of, to 1632, i. 531-2 ; his acquaintance with the poet Davenant, i. 348, 363, 524, 533, 580, 581 ; vi. 273-4 ; his story of Argyle, ii. 11, 13 ; his picture of the national prosperity during the reign of Thorough, ii. 22, 24 ; his account of English ignorance about Scotland previous to First Bishops' War, ii. 43 ; account of, in composition of Long Parliament, ii. 168 ; his descriptions of members of the Long Parliament, ii. 152-8, 161-5, 166-70; 174 ; at Strafford's trial, ii. 185 ; 187 ; his account of Scottish Commissioners in London, ii. 191 ; in the Church Reform movement, ii. 197 ; his part in the Bishops' Exclusion Bill, ii. 226 ; 233, 274 ; on Charles I.'s character, ii. 277 ; first interview with Charles I., ii. 286-7 ; 308 ; opposes the "Grand Remonstrance," ii. 319, 320, 321, 322 ; 328, 337, 350, 351 ; joins Charles I. before Civil War, ii. 413-5 ; with the Prince of Wales in Jersey at the close of Civil War, iii. 375, 376 ; one of the nineteen "Delinquents," iii. 421 ; in Jersey writing his History, iii. 493-4, 504 ; at commencement of Second Civil War, iii. 591 ; his anonymous answer to the *Declaration* of the Commons against Charles I., iii. 598 ; with Charles II.'s Court at the Hague, iv. 25, 27, 28 ; with Cottington at the Spanish Court, iv. 31, 125 ; correspondence with Lord Hatton, iv. 131 ; his servant murders Ascham at Madrid in 1650, iv. 193 ; is dismissed from Madrid, iv. 220 ; references, in letters of ·(1652-3), to Milton's *Defensio Prima,* vi. 187-8 ; said to have drawn up for Charles II. a "Secret Proclamation" at Paris, May 3, 1654, iv. 550 ; on the accession of Richard to the Protectorate, v. 416-7 ; revived hopes of his party, v. 464 ; in list of Men of Letters under the Protectorate, v. 76 ; in correspondence with the Secret Association called the "Sealed Knot," v. 336 ; advises a Royalist Insurrection, v. 472 ; watches the growing Royalist enthusiasm,

v. 557 ; goes to Breda from Brussels with Charles II., v. 560-1 ; at the Restoration of Charles II., vi. 9 ; member of Privy Council of the Restoration, vi. 17 ; his premiership, vi. 19 - 21 ; and the Convention Parliament, vi. 22 ; his part in the King's *Declaration of Indemnity*, vi. 25, 40, 50-1, 52 ; his share in Milton's escape, vi. 187-9, 240 ; and the Restoration Church Question, vi. 59, 60 note, 61, 62, 64 ; his speech before the Recess, vi. 69-70 ; his correspondence with Bishop Gauden, vi. 425-8, 432-3 and note, 434-5, 437-8 ; his History, vi. 617 ; at the trials of the Regicides, vi. 77 ; drafts the King's Ecclesiastical Declaration, and appoints new bishops, vi. 99-101, 104-5 ; his daughter's clandestine marriage with the Duke of York, 106-8 and note ; accession to the peerage, vi. 108 ; at reassembling of the Convention Parliament, vi. 109-11 ; his speech at dissolution of the Convention Parliament, vi. 118 ; his daughter's marriage recognised, vi. 118-9 ; his discontent at the severance of Scotland from England, vi. 129 ; associated with the Scottish Council in London, vi. 131, 138-9, 141 ; his son, Henry Hyde, knighted at the Coronation of Charles II., vi. 151 ; created Earl of Clarendon, vi. 152 ; at the Coronation, vi. 156 ; in the Cavalier Parliament, vi. 158 ; his administration continued in the period of Charles II.'s Second Parliament, vi. 221-2 ; and Lady Castlemaine, vi. 230 note ; his part in the sentence and execution of Vane, vi. 231 ; sends, with the King, for Butler on the first appearance of *Hudibras*, vi. 340-1 ; his part in the Church and State policy of the Government to the end of 1662, vi. 235 - 7 ; in connection with the crypto-Catholicism of the Court and Charles's secret Catholicism, vi. 238-45 ; Bristol's attack on, vi. 245-8 ; his new house in Piccadilly, vi. 250 ; opposes the war with the Dutch, vi. 253 ; one of chief promoters of the Five Miles Act, vi.

258 ; his influence with the King waning, vi. 263-5 ; his fall, vi. 267-72 ; in the list of Men of Letters of the Restoration, vi. 294 - 5, 319 ; Milton and, vi. 411-4.

CLARGES, Nan : see *Albemarle*, Duchess of.

CLARGES, Sir Thomas, in Cromwell's Second Parliament, v. 108 ; in Richard's Parliament, v. 430 ; with Monk, v. 476, 497-9, 500, 525, 534, 535, 538, 556, 563, 698, 702, 490 ; in the Convention Parliament, vi. 23, 24, 38, 41, 43, 173 ; knighted at the Restoration, vi. 73 ; his possible part in Milton's escape, vi. 185, 187, 189, 481-2.

CLARK, a connexion of Hartlib, iii. 193.

CLARKE, Abraham, of Spitalfields, husband of Milton's daughter Deborah, i. 6 note ; vi. 741, 751.

CLARKE, Abraham, jun., son of Caleb Clarke, vi. 758.

CLARKE, Agnes, i. 15.

CLARKE, Caleb, son of Deborah Clarke, vi. 752 ; vi. 755-9.

CLARKE, Mrs. Deborah : see *Milton*, Deborah.

CLARKE, Elizabeth, daughter of Deborah Clarke, iii. 483 note ; married to Thomas Foster, vi. 751-2; account of, vi. 759-61.

CLARKE, Francis, Parliamentarian officer, ii. 444.

CLARKE, Mr. Hyde : his examination of the books of the Scriveners' Company, i. 25, 27 note ; researches in the biography of Milton's father, i. 338 note.

CLARKE, Isaac, son of Caleb Clarke, vi. 758.

CLARKE, Mary, at Forest Hill, ii. 505 note.

CLARKE, Mary, daughter of Caleb Clarke, vi. 758.

CLARKE, Mary, daughter of Abraham Clarke jun., vi. 758.

CLARKE, Peter, member of Westminster Assembly, ii. 517.

CLARKE, Samuel, of Benetfink, member of Westminster Assembly, and afterwards Nonconformist, iii. 677, vi. 232 note.

CLARKE, Sir Simon, of Warwickshire, baronet, married to a daughter of Hobson the Cambridge carrier, i. 240.

CLARKE, Dr. Timothy, of the Royal Society, vi. 396.

CLARKE, Urban, son of Deborah Clarke, vi. 751-2; his death, vi. 759.

CLARKE, an anti-Trinitarian, iii. 157.

CLARKE, author of *General Martyrologie* (1677), ii. 518, 519, 521, 522.

CLARKE, Mr., envoy with Roger Williams to England, iv. 395, 533.

CLARKSON, Laurence, Anabaptist and Seeker, iii. 153, 677.

Clavis Apocalyptica, by Joseph Meade, i. 126.

CLAYPOLE, Lady : see *Cromwell*, Elizabeth.

CLAYPOLE, John, knighted by Cromwell in 1657, v. 354 note.

CLAYPOLE, John : account of, in the family of the Protector, v. 305 ; in Cromwell's Second Parliament, v. 108 ; one of Cromwell's Lords, v. 323 ; 354 note.

CLAYPOLE, Oliver, youngest son of Lady Claypole : his death, v. 355.

CLAYTON, Richard, member of Westminster Assembly, ii. 517.

CLAYTON, Sir Thomas, of "the Vache," at Chalfont St. Giles, vi. 494, 495.

CLAYTON, Sir William : and the "Sealed Knot," v. 336.

CLEMENTS, Gregory : signs the death warrant of Charles I., iii. 720 ; vi. 28 ; in the Indemnity Bill, vi. 34 note, 54 ; his trial, vi. 80, 81, 85 ; his execution, vi. 96-7 ; in the Bill of Attainder, vi. 115.

CLENDON, Thomas, member of Westminster Assembly, ii. 520.

CLERKE, John, one of Cromwell's Lords, v. 324 ; supports Richard's Government, v. 418; in Republican remodelling of the army, v. 470 ; on the Committee of Safety, v. 494.

CLETHERO, Samuel, fellow-graduate of Milton at Cambridge, i. 218.

CLEVELAND, Lady Castlemaine and Duchess of (Barbara Villiers, and wife of Mr. Palmer), at the Restoration and Coronation of Charles II., vi. 11, 158 ; present at Charles II.'s marriage, vi. 229-30 and note, 239; 261, 262-4; and Lord Clarendon, vi. 271, 353, 354, 355 ; and Nell Gwynn, vi. 356, 367 ; Dryden's verses to, vi. 369 ; in *Memoirs of Count Grammont*, vi. 461 ; her portrait by Faithorne, vi. 648 ; and her rivals, vi. 578 ; in the Royal Court and Family in 1674, vi. 604.

CLEVELAND, Thomas Wentworth, 1st Earl of, in Royalist army, ii. 428; his son, ii. 429; in Scotland with Charles II., iv. 188; dismissed from the Scottish Court, iv. 206; his return to Court, iv. 212; in Charles II.'s Scottish army, iv. 284 ; taken prisoner at Battle of Worcester, iv. 294; his trial, iv. 297.

CLEVELAND, John, satirist : admission to Christ's College, Cambridge, i. 186 ; his Latin oration on occasion of Lord Holland's visit to Cambridge, i. 225-6; at Christ's College, i. 250; 297, 508, 647 ; verses on the death of Edward King, i. 652 ; ii. 43 ; epitaph on Strafford, ii. 185 ; verses on *Smectymnuus*, ii. 219-20 ; 522 ; in list of Men of Letters under the Protectorate, v. 76, 80-2.

CLEVELAND, Thomas, father of the satirist, i. 186.

CLIFFORD, Lord, commander of a horse regiment in the First Bishops' War, ii. 62 : see *Cork*, 2nd Earl of.

CLIFFORD, Matthew, takes part in a controversy with Dryden, vi. 612-3.

CLIFFORD, Sir Thomas : a crypto-Catholic, and M.P. for Totness, vi. 264; in the Cabal Administration, vi. 562-3, 565 ; in the Secret Negotiation with France, vi. 570-1, 574-5 ; one of the signatories of the Secret Treaty of Dover, vi. 576, 579-80; is created Baron Clifford of Chudleigh, vi. 582 ; appointed to the office of Lord Treasurer, vi. 591 ; in the Tenth Session of the Cavalier Parliament, vi. 593 ; resists the Test Act, becomes an avowed Catholic, resigns his office, and dies, vi. 597, 610.

CLIFTON, Captain, captain of the Castle of Edinburgh, iv. 509.

CLIFTON, Sir Gervase, i. 590; his

wife, the Lady Alice, daughter of the Earl of Huntingdon, i. 590.

CLIFTON, Richard, Brownist minister, ii. 539.

CLOBERY, John, a colonel in Monk's army, stationed at Stirling, v. 470; sent by Monk on a deputation to London, v. 498, 501; is with Monk in London, v. 535, 540, 541 note, 562; in the Convention Parliament, vi. 23.

CLODIUS, German chemist, married to the daughter of Hartlib, v. 236; vi. 200.

CLOTWORTHY, Sir John, member for Malden in the Long Parliament, ii. 173; takes part in the debates on the "Grand Remonstrance," ii. 320; is a lay-member of the Westminster Assembly, ii. 524; is of the pro-Scottish party in Parliament during the negotiations at Newcastle, iii. 416; is one of the eleven Presbyterian leaders denounced by the Army, iii. 548-9; escapes abroad, iii. 554.

CLUNN, Walter, actor in Killigrew's company, vi. 349, 350.

CLUTTERBUCK, Thomas, case of, in letters of Council, v. 387.

COBBET, Ralph (an officer in Robert Lilburne's foot regiment), is rebuked by Cromwell for attempt to mutiny, iii. 583; conducts the removal of the King to Hurst Castle, iii. 626-9; and also his later removal to Windsor, iii. 701; receives an honorary degree at "The Fairfaxian Creation" at Oxford University, iv. 52, 402; v. 470, 487, 490, 496-7, 498; is in disgrace with the chiefs of the "Wallingford House Interregnum," v. 521, 547; and the escape and recapture of Lambert, v. 566; in the Tower, v. 567; excepted from pardon in the Indemnity Bill, vi. 40, 41, 47; under perpetual Incapacitation, vi. 55.

COCHET, correspondent in Paris of Philaras, iv. 639.

COCHRANE, Lord, fined £5000 by Cromwell, iv. 560.

COCHRANE, Scottish refugee in Hamburg, iv. 160.

COCHRANE, Colonel Sir John, brother of Sir William Cochrane of Cowdon, joins Charles I. before the Civil War, ii. 418; his part in "The Incident," ii. 305, 306.

COCHRANE of Cowdon, Sir William, ancestor of the Dundonald family, ii. 418.

COCKAYNE, Sir Aston, in list of writers under the Protectorate, v. 76; at the Restoration, vi. 294, 297.

COCKBURN, Sir Patrick, fined £2000 by Cromwell, iv. 561.

COCKIN, William, English merchant, v. 244.

CODDINGTON, an Antinomian, ii. 577.

COKE, one of the Cambridge writers of Latin verses upon the death of Edward King, i. 651.

COKE, Bridget, daughter of Sir Edward Coke, iii. 657.

COKE, Sir Edward, High Steward of Cambridge University, i. 115; opposes Buckingham in Charles I.'s third Parliament, i. 192; his share in drawing up the Petition of Right, i. 522; ii. 560.

COKE, Francis, member of Westminster Assembly, ii. 517.

COKE, Dr. George, Bishop of Hereford, i. 389, 399 and note, 674; ii. 150; impeachment of, ii. 270; 334, 335 and note, 336.

COKE, Sir John, Secretary of State, i. 382, 386, 389, 668; ii. 24, 61, 68, 69, 128; iii. 510, 541; iv. 82 note.

COKE, Roger, a member of the Rota Club, v. 485.

"COLASTERION," Milton's pamphlet entitled: see Milton, Writings of.

COLBERT, the French economist, iv. 381.

COLBRON, James, scrivener in London in 1600, i. 25-7, 338 note.

COLCHESTER, member for, in the Long Parliament, ii. 173; siege of, in the Second Civil War, iii. 594, 596, 604-5.

COLE, Peter, printer, iii. 726 note; iv. 96, 313.

COLEMAN, Thomas, member of Westminster Assembly, ii. 517, 531, 606; iii. 20.

COLEPEPPER, Sir John, member for

Kent in the Long Parliament: character of, by Clarendon, ii. 167 ; in Strafford's trial, ii. 185 ; is associated with Falkland and Hyde in Parliamentary business, ii. 187, 197, 319, 321, 328, 340 ; in the Privy Council of Charles I., ii. 337, 350 ; joins Charles I. before the Civil War, ii. 413 ; in the mock negotiation at the beginning of the war, ii. 453 ; with the Royal Family in France, iii. 375, 376, 421, 494, 495 note ; in correspondence with Charles I., iii. 502-3 ; King Charles's opinion of, iii. 504 ; at the beginning of the Second Civil War, iii. 591, 595 ; with Charles II.'s Court at the Hague, iv. 25 ; in intercourse with John Lilburne, iv. 502 ; at Richard's accession, v. 416 ; as Lord Colepepper and Privy Councillor to Charles II., vi. 19 ; his death immediately after the Restoration, vi. 19 ; his views on the Church Restoration question, vi. 59.

COLET, Sir Henry, mercer, twice Lord Mayor, i. 74.

COLET, John, Dean of St. Paul's, and founder of St. Paul's School, i. 74, 77.

COLLAIRNEY, the younger, fined by Cromwell, iv. 561.

COLLETT, married sister of Nicholas Ferrar, i. 416.

COLLIER, William, ii. 599.

COLLINS, Dr. Samuel, Provost of King's College, and Regius Professor of Divinity, Cambridge, i. 116, 118, 120, 150, 152, 267, 648 ; ejected from the University, iii. 94.

COLLKITTOCH, Alexander Macdonald, called the, iii. 347-8.

COLLKITTOCH, Alexander Macdonald, called the younger : iii. 348, 351, 352, 353, 357, 361, 362, 367, 368 ; in disgrace, iii. 421 ; mentioned by Milton, iii. 461 and note.

COLONIES, the, during the Protectorate, v. 101-4 : see also under Church.

COLOURS, the Scottish, at Duns Law, ii. 65.

COLQUHOUN of Luss, iv. 561.

COLTELLINI, Agostino, Florentine friend of Milton, i. 773, 776-8, 780, 821, 828 ; iii. 654, 690, 691 note ; iv. 637.

COLVILL, mentioned by Pepys, vi. 261.

COLWELL, Thomas, involved in the lawsuit against Milton's father, i. 628, 629, 635, 636.

COMBER, Dr. Thomas, Master of Trinity College, Cambridge, i. 121, 247, 253 ; appointed Vice-Chancellor of the University, i. 257 ; also i. 648.

COMBERBACH, Roger, of Chester, i. 9.

COMENIUS, Joannes Amosus (John Amos Komensky), iii. 198-215 ; Hartlib and, iii. 202-4 ; his views on Education, iii. 204-10, 205 note ; his method for languages, iii. 210-12, his Pansophic Speculations, iii. 213-5 ; reproduction of his *Didactica Magna* by Hartlib, iii. 220 ; in London, iii. 221-5 ; in Sweden, iii. 225-6 ; in Elbing, iii. 227-8 ; Milton's opinion of, iii. 232-4 and note, 235 and note, 237-9 ; his Latin Didactics recast, iii. 661-2 ; concerned in project for a London College of Science, iii. 221-4 ; vi. 394.

COMMISSION of the Kirk of Scotland, iv. 190, 202, 211.

"COMMISSIONS of Array," ii. 421, 440.

COMMITTEE of the Two Kingdoms, the, iii. 331 and note, 579 ; dissolution of, iii. 585.

COMMITTEE of Religion in Charles I.'s Third Parliament, i. 215.

COMMITTEE of Safety, in the Wallingford House Government, v. 494-5 ; in negotiation with Monk, v. 497, 501 ; growth of Stuartism in the, v. 505 ; New Republican Constitution debated in the, v. 506-10 ; 520.

COMMONPLACE Book, Milton's, i. 303 ; vi. 790 note.

COMMONWEALTH, THE ENGLISH : I. *Foundation and Beginnings of the Commonwealth :*—Votes in the Rump Parliament for the Abolition of Kingship and the House of Lords, iv. 3-5 ; Draft Constitution for the new Republic in Ireton's *Agreement of the People*, iv. 6-12 ; the First Council of State of the Commonwealth, iv. 12-19 ; dangers to **the**

Infant Commonwealth from Scotland and from Ireland, iv. 19-25; sentiments of the various Foreign Powers towards the English Commonwealth, iv. 29-31; opposition to the Commonwealth within England itself, iv. 32-3; pamphlets denouncing the, iv. 37; scurrilities against Cromwell and the Commonwealth in Royalist journals, iv. 37-9; trials of Royalist delinquents in the Second Civil War and executions of the Duke of Hamilton, the Earl of Holland, and Lord Capel, iv. 40; other early acts of the Commonwealth, iv. 40-1; military forces of the Commonwealth estimated, iv. 41-2; resolution of Parliament to send an army to Ireland, with Cromwell as Commander-in-Chief, Fairfax retaining the supreme generalship for the Commonwealth, iv. 42; action of the Council of State against the Royalist press, iv. 42-3; outburst of Lilburne and the Levellers, iv. 43-5; Lilburne arrested and brought before the Council, iv. 45-8; assassination of Dr. Dorislaus, envoy of the Commonwealth to the Hague, iv. 48-9; complete suppression of the Levellers and confirmation of the Commonwealth, iv. 50-1; University honours at Oxford for Fairfax, Cromwell, and other army officers, and grand City Banquet in the City of London to the Commonwealth magnates, iv. 51-4; removal of the Council of State from Derby House to Whitehall, iv. 54-5; Cromwell in Ireland, iv. 111-3; Bradshaw's Press Act, iv. 116-8; pamphlets of Lilburne and the Levellers, iv. 115-6; trial of Lilburne, iv. 118-20; Clement Walker's attacks on the Commonwealth in his *History of Independency*, and his arrest in consequence, iv. 121; disaffection of the Presbyterians in London to the Commonwealth, iv. 121-4; imposition of the "Engagement" or promise of loyalty to the Commonwealth on officials, civil and military, iv. 124; relations of the Commonwealth to Foreign Powers, iv. 124-6; question of a New Parliament mooted and postponed, iv. 126-7; appearance of the *Defensio Regia* of Salmasius, iv. 150-1; see also under *Milton*. II. *Second Year of the Commonwealth (Feb. 1650-Feb. 1651)* :—The Council of State, iv. 177; the "Engagement" enforced, iv. 177-80; the Irish Rebellion suppressed by Cromwell, and Cromwell recalled for service in Scotland, iv. 190-1; appointment of Cromwell to be Chief of the Forces of the Commonwealth in place of Fairfax, resigning, iv. 192; Ludlow and Ireton in Ireland, iv. 192-3; assassination of Anthony Ascham, envoy of the Commonwealth to Spain, iv. 193; Cromwell's campaign in Scotland ending in the battle of Dunbar (Sept. 3, 1650), and complete shattering of the Scottish Royalist army, iv. 200-1; relations of the Commonwealth with the United Dutch Provinces, iv. 215-6; relations of the Commonwealth with Hamburg, iv. 217; relations with Portugal and Spain, iv. 217-21; question of a New Parliament again postponed, iv. 221-2. III. *Third Year of the Commonwealth (Feb.-Dec. 1651)* :—Council of the year, iv. 273-4; in foreign business, iv. 275-8; Cromwell still in Scotland, iv. 278-89; Charles's march into England, and Cromwell's pursuit of him to Worcester, iv. 289-94; the Battle of Worcester, and subsequent events, iv. 294-303; condition of Ireland under Ireton and Ludlow, iv. 304; "the First Navigation Act," iv. 305; relations with Foreign Powers, iv. 305-6; the question of a New Parliament discussed, iv. 306-9. IV. *Fourth Year of the Commonwealth, with Fragment of a Fifth Year (1st Dec. 1651-20th April 1653)* :—Councils of State for those years, iv. 354-5; death of Ireton, iv. 356-7; Lilburne banished, iv. 357-8; Waller pardoned, iv. 359; Cromwell at the centre of affairs, iv. 359-60; question of the Incor-

poration of Scotland, iv. 360-6; in Irish affairs, iv. 366-71; difficulties with the Dutch, iv. 371-4; war with the Dutch, iv. 374-7; synopsis of the relations of the Commonwealth with other foreign powers through 1652 and 1653, iv. 377-83; discussions in the Rump and Council of State on various matters of home government, iv. 383-7; discussion of the subject of "The Propagation of the Gospel," iv. 387-98; the Quarrel of the Army and the Parliament, ending in the forcible Dissolution of the Rump and of the Council of State by Cromwell, iv. 398-414.

COMMONWEALTH, THE RESTORED (of the Rump and Time of Anarchy). I. *Five Months of the Restored Rump* (*May 25-Oct. 13, 1659*):—the Restored Rump and the Council of State, v. 453-9; expectations of a Civil War between the Cromwellians and the Republicans, v. 459-63; veering of the Cromwellians to a junction with the Royalists, v. 463-4; energetic procedure of the Restored Rump in both home and foreign business, v. 465-8; Republican remodelling of the Army and Navy, v. 469-72; intended general insurrection of Royalists, v. 472-5; negotiations of Charles II. with Monk, v. 476; Sir George Booth's insurrection crushed by Lambert, v. 477-9; question in the Rump of a new system of Government to succeed itself, v. 479-81; account of Harrington and of the "Rota Club," v. 481-6; renewal in Sept. 1659 of the Quarrel of the Army and the Parliament, ending in the dissolution of the Rump by the Council of State under coercion of Lambert and the Army chiefs, v. 486-92. II. *The Wallingford House Interregnum, or Ten Weeks of Military Oligarchy* (*Oct. 13-Dec. 26, 1659*):—a fortnight of continued government by the Council of State of the Dissolved Rump in association with the Wallingford House Council of Officers, v. 493-4; coalescence of

the Council of the Rump with the Council of Officers in a new supreme Executive called *The Committee of Safety*, v. 494-5; new Army arrangements, v. 495; difficulties and negotiations between Monk and the Wallingford House Government, v. 496-501; foreign relations, v. 501-3; renewed attempts of Charles and the Royalists, v. 502-5; the question of a future Constitution again under discussion, and proclamation made for a new Parliament, v. 505-12; Monk's march into England to suppress the Government, and counter-movements of the Wallingford House leaders, v. 512-4; the proposed New Parliament superseded by the reassembling of the Restored Rump, v. 514-7. III. *Two Months of the Rump after its Second Restoration* (*Dec. 26, 1659-Feb. 21, 1660*):—the House and the new Council of State, v. 518-20; immediate action of the Rump and its Council, v. 520-4; during the advance of Monk from Coldstream to St. Albans, v. 524-8; Monk's entry into London (3rd Feb. 1660), v. 528-9; events in London from that date leading up to the resuscitation of the Long Parliament, v. 529-41; (see also under *Monk*). IV. *Through Monk's Dictatorship to the Restoration* (*Feb.-May 1660*):—Government by the resuscitated Long Parliament to 16th March 1660, v. 543-54; interval between the Long Parliament and the meeting of the Convention Parliament on 25th April 1660, v. 554-68; first fortnight of the Convention Parliament to 8th May 1660, v. 694-8; the Commonwealth defunct on 1st May, and government by King, Lords, and Commons decreed, v. 698; incidents and formalities of the next seven days to the 8th May, v. 698-700.

COMMONWEALTH, THE GOVERNMENT OF THE: a Constitutional Instrument of forty-two Articles, defining the powers and duties of the Protectorate, signed by Cromwell at his Installation, iv. 542-7, v. 5, 7-11.

"COMMONWEALTH of Oceana," v. 482.

COMPACT, the Merchiston House, ii. 296-301.

"COMPLETE ANGLER, THE," v. 79 : see *Walton, Izaac.*

COMPREHENSION, theory of, in Church matters, vi. 60.

COMPTON, Anne, Lady : see *Spencer,* Anne.

COMPTON, Anthony, servant of the Council, salary of, v. 625.

COMPTON, Henry, 1st Lord, i. 591.

COMPTON, Sir William, a member of the "Sealed Knot," v. 336.

"COMUS," Milton's Masque of : see under *Milton;* also *Milton,* Writings of.

CON, George, Papal agent at the Court of Charles I., i. 684, 798 ; ii. 50.

CONANT, John, B.D., Rector of Limington in Somersetshire, a member of the Westminster Assembly, ii. 517, 605.

CONANT, Dr. John, Archdeacon of Norwich, nephew of the above, ii. 517 ; a leading divine in Oxford University under the Protectorate, v. 73 ; Nonconformist in 1662, vi. 232 note.

CONCORDAT between the Army and Parliament, iii. 582-4, 610.

CONDE, Prince of, i. 834 note ; v. 340.

CONDELL, editor of the First Folio Shakespeare, i. 330, 378.

CONFESSION OF FAITH of the Westminster Assembly, iii. 171-2, 599 and note.

CONGREGATIONALISM : see *Independency.*

CONNECTICUT - River Settlement, ii. 549 ; v. 101.

CONSERVATORS OF LIBERTY, office of, proposed by Ludlow, v. 511.

CONSTABLE, Sir William, Bart., his regiment, ii. 444 ; signs the death warrant of Charles I., iii. 720 ; a member of the first Council of State of the Commonwealth, iv. 12, 13, 354 ; a member of the Second Council, iv. 354 ; present at the appointment of Milton to the Latin Secretaryship, iv. 83 ; in Council business, iv. 87, 150, 224, 225, 226, 231, 446, 448 ; appointed a member of the fourth Council of State, iv. 354-5 ; deceased in 1660, vi. 28 ; excepted from the Indemnity Act, vi. 54.

CONSTITUTIONAL INSTRUMENT of the Commonwealth, iv. 542-4.

CONTINENT, the, general condition of, in 1638, i. 739-51.

CONTRARIANTS, v. 122 : see also *Oliverians, Quakers.*

CONVENTICLES ACT, the, vi. 249-50.

CONVOCATION of the Church, i. 391 note ; Charles I. and, in 1640, ii. 131-2.

CONWAY, Edward, 1st Viscount, i. 380, 383 note 2, 385.

CONWAY, Edward, 2nd Viscount : in the Second Bishops' War, ii. 129 ; at Newcastle, ii. 135-6, 140, 168 ; a witness in Strafford's Trial, ii. 180 ; in the Civil War, ii. 429 ; lay member of the Westminster Assembly, ii. 523 ; iv. 82 note.

CONY, a merchant : his suit-at-law against the Protectorate, v. 35-6.

CONYERS, Sir John, appointed Lord Lieutenant of the Tower, ii. 351.

COOK, a head-master of St. Paul's School, i. 78.

COOK, Colonel (royalist), with the King at Newport, iii. 627-8.

COOK, John, one of the counsel for the prosecution in the King's trial, iii. 706, 708, 709 ; among the Regicides, vi. 27 ; in the Indemnity Bill, vi. 31, 33, 34, 54 ; his trial, vi. 80, 85-7 ; his execution, vi. 96-7 ; in the Bill of Attainder, vi. 115.

COOK, Thomas, press licenser, vi. 514-5.

COOKE, Major, afterwards Lieutenant-Colonel, iii. 326, 619 ; his regiment in Ireland, iv. 56.

COOKE, Edward, servant of the Council of State, v. 625.

COOKE, Francis, fellow and tutor of Christ's College, Cambridge, i. 111, 123.

COOKE, Robert, servant of the Council of State, v. 625.

COOPER, Sir Anthony Ashley, afterwards Lord Ashley and 1st Earl of Shaftesbury : account of, iv. 385-6 ;

in Cromwell's Supreme Convention or Assembly of Notables, iv. 501 ; in the Councils of State of the Barebones Parliament, iv. 506, 525 ; in the Barebones Parliament, iv. 514 ; member of Council under the Protectorate, iv. 545, 575 ; becomes an anti-Oliverian and withdraws from the Council, v. 32 note, 308 ; in Cromwell's Second Parliament, v. 108, 111, 329 ; in Richard's Parliament, v. 430 ; in the Council of State of the Restored Rump, v. 456-7 ; charged with complicity in a Royalist Insurrection, v. 478 ; not included in the Committee of Safety, v. 495 ; co-operates with Monk, v. 514 ; member of the new Council of State, v. 519 ; member of the Rump Parliament after its second restoration, v. 519, 537 ; in the Council of State of the restored Long Parliament, v. 543, 545, 549 ; his part at the Restoration, v. 700 ; member of Charles II.'s Privy Council, vi. 9, 19 ; in the Convention Parliament, vi. 23, 24 ; his part in the debates on the Indemnity Bill, vi. 43, 51 ; and on a Bill for the settlement of the Church question, vi. 64 ; is one of the thirty-four Commissioners for the trials of the Regicides, vi. 77 ; created Baron Ashley at the Coronation of Charles II., vi. 152 ; appointed Chancellor of the Exchequer and Under Treasurer in Charles II.'s Government, vi. 222 ; supports the crypto-Catholic policy of the King, vi. 244 ; his popularity with Charles II., vi. 245 ; in the intrigues against Clarendon, vi. 249, 264 ; appointed Treasurer of the prizes in the war with the Dutch, vi. 253-4 ; opposes the Five Miles Act, vi. 258 ; a member of the Cabal Administration, vi. 562, 563, 564, 565, 574, 575, 579, 580 ; created Earl of Shaftesbury, vi. 582 ; office of Lord Chancellor conferred upon, in succession to Clarendon, vi. 591 ; in the Tenth Session of the Cavalier Parliament, vi. 593, 598 ; one of the reformed Cabal, vi. 597 ; in the Eleventh Session of the Cavalier Parliament, vi. 598 ; is dismissed from the Chancellorship, ceases to be a member of the Cabal, and becomes the leader of the infant party of English Whigs, vi. 599, 600 ; is assisted in his theory of politics by Locke, vi. 619, 729.

COOPER, Charles Henry : his *Annals of Cambridge* and *Athenæ Cantabrigienses*, i. 146 note.

COOPER, Marmaduke, Parliamentarian officer, ii. 445.

COOPER, Robert, fellow-graduate of Milton at Cambridge, i. 218, 258.

COOPER, Colonel Thomas, in Cromwell's army, iv. 402 ; v. 86, 87 ; one of Cromwell's lords, v. 324, 354 ; supporter of Richard's Government, v. 418, 422, 471.

COOPER, Samuel, his supposed miniature of Milton, vi. 754 note ; his miniature of Pym, ii. 161.

COOPER, William, minister, v. 274-5.

COOTE, Sir Charles (afterwards Earl of Mountrath), colonel in the English Parliamentary army in Ireland, and President of Connaught, iii. 518, 519 ; iv. 24, 42 ; assists Cromwell in Ireland, iv. 111, 112, 303, 366; in Oliver's First Parliament, v. 5 ; in Oliver's Second Parliament, v. 108 ; in Richard's Parliament, v. 431 ; is back in Ireland, v. 459, 471 ; co-operates with Monk, v. 514, 520 ; joins in impeachment of Ludlow, v. 521 ; in Ireland, v. 564 ; President of Connaught, vi. 124 ; created, at the Restoration, Earl of Mountrath in the Irish peerage, and made one of the Lord Justices of Ireland, vi. 127.

COPERNICUS : i. 746.

COPINGER, Edward, of Nottinghamshire, i. 63.

CORBET, Clement, LL.D., master of Trinity Hall, Cambridge, i. 116, 120.

CORBET, Edward, member of Westminster Assembly, ii. 517 ; iv. 71.

CORBET, John, author of " The Epistle Congratulatorie of *Lysimachus Nicanor*," ii. 126.

CORBET, Sir John : his part in the " Grand Remonstrance," ii. 326 ; in Councils of State of the Common-

wealth, iv. 354 ; v. 519 ; in the Restored Rump, v. 454.

CORBET, Miles, signs the death warrant of Charles I., iii. 720 ; one of the Council of Assessors to Lord Deputy Fleetwood in Ireland, v. 98 ; one of the Commissioners for the civil government of Ireland under Lieutenant-General Ludlow, v. 471 ; in disgrace with Ludlow, v. 521 ; 666 ; is included in the trials of the Regicides, vi. 28, 44, 54 ; escapes to Germany, vi. 115, 115 note ; taken in Holland, and executed at Tyburn, vi. 228-9.

CORBET, Dr. Richard, Bishop of Oxford and of Norwich, i. 389, 419, 501-2, 674.

COREY, Mrs., actress, vi. 350, 351.

CORITON, William, i. 216 ; ii. 163.

CORK, headquarters of Cromwell at, iv. 113.

CORK, Richard, Lord Boyle, 1st Earl of : Lord High Treasurer of Ireland in 1632, i. 689 ; account of his career and family connexions, iii. 659 ; his son, Richard : see Cork, 2nd Earl of ; his son, Roger : see Orrery, Earl of ; his son, Francis : see Shannon, Viscount ; his son, Robert : see Boyle, the Hon. Robert ; his daughter, Alice : see Barrimore, 1st Earl of ; his daughter, Catherine : see Ranelagh, Lady.

CORK, Richard Boyle (Viscount Dungarvan), 2nd Earl of, and afterwards created Lord Clifford of Lanesborough and Earl of Burlington in the English peerage, iii. 659 ; in Ireland, v. 230 ; his two sons at Oxford, v. 267 ; his new mansion in Piccadilly, vi. 250.

CORNEILLE, the French tragedian, i. 744 ; vi. 360-1.

CORNWALL, Francis, Baptist preacher, iii. 148.

CORNWALLIS, Sir Frederick, Bart., Treasurer of the Household to Charles II., created Baron Cornwallis at the Restoration, vi. 18, 152, 222 ; his death, vi. 237.

CORONATIONS : of Charles I. at Westminster, i. 369-70, at Edinburgh in 1633, i. 699 ; of Charles II. at

Scone in 1651, iv. 212-3, and at Westminster in 1661, vi. 151-8.

CORPUS CHRISTI (or Benet) College, Cambridge, i. 114, 116, 120, 221, 226, 237, 238, 247, 254, 255.

CORPUS CHRISTI College, Oxford, i. 535 ; ii. 249.

CORTONA, Pietro da, Florentine artist, i. 763.

COSINS, Dr. John, partisan of Buckingham at Cambridge, i. 158 ; ejected from the University, iii. 94, 95 note.

COTES, Richard, printer, iii. 164 note.

COTTEREL, Lieut.-Colonel : disperses General Assembly at Edinburgh, iv. 509-10.

COTTERILL, James, printer, v. 259.

COTTESWORTH, Lieut.-Colonel, in the New Model Army, iii. 326.

COTTINGTON, Lord, of Hanworth, member of Charles I.'s Privy Council, Chancellor of the Exchequer, and Master of the Court of Wards, i. 381, 383, 384, 410, 666, 668, 671, 684, 691, 695 ; his handwriting, ii. 9 note, 24 ; in the First "Bishops' War," ii. 46, 47 ; in the King's Cabinet, previous to the Short Parliament, ii. 127, 144 ; one of the lay ministerial peers in the Long Parliament, ii. 152 ; included with Strafford among delinquents to be proceeded against by the Long Parliament, ii. 176, 178 ; takes part in Strafford's trial, ii. 181, 278 ; resigns the Mastership of the Wards, ii. 281 ; resigns the Chancellorship of the Exchequer, ii. 337 ; with Charles I. at York, ii. 429 ; one of the "delinquents" proposed by the Parliament to be outlawed, iii. 421 ; an exile in France, iii. 494, 591 ; with Charles II.'s Court at the Hague, iv. 25 ; with Hyde at the Spanish Court, iv. 31, 125 ; their servant assassinates Mr. Anthony Ascham, iv. 193 ; is dismissed from Madrid, iv. 220.

COTTON, Charles, one of Hyde's literary associates in 1628-32, i. 532.

COTTON, Charles, Restoration writer, vi. 316, 388.

COTTON, John, i. 627, 628.

COTTON, John, B.D., of Cambridge University, Nonconformist minister

of Boston in Lincolnshire, and afterwards a leading New England divine, ii. 555-6, 556-7, 557, 559, 562; his part in Mrs. Hutchinson's heresy, ii. 574-6 ; a treatise by, ii. 598 ; declines to attend the Westminster Assembly at the request of Cromwell and others, ii. 605; further account of his Anti-Toleration writings and of his controversy with Roger Williams, iii. 114, 128 ; iv. 396.

COTTON, Sir Robert, antiquary and collector of MSS., deceased in 1631, i. 525.

COTTON, Sir Thomas, of Sawtrey in Huntingdonshire, Bart., nephew and executor of John Cotton ; story of the lawsuit *Cotton* ver. *Milton and Bower*, i. 627-37, 659-61, 661 note.

COUNCILS : *The English Privy*, of Charles I., from 1628 to 1632, i. 377-83 ; ii. 68, 142, 144 ; certain members of, released from their Oath of ·Secrecy at Strafford's trial, ii. 180 ; changes and additions in, attempted by Charles I. in 1641-2, ii. 278-85, 336-7 ; a Committee of, elected for Scottish affairs, ii. 24, 46, 68, 181.—*The Privy, of Scotland*, i. 704, 705 ; constitution of, in 1634-8, i. 706-7, 708, 709, 718, 719, 721, 722, 723, 724, 725, 726, 727 ; policy of, previous to the Civil War, ii. 416-8.—*For the Principality and Marches of Wales*, i. 604-5.—*Of Covenanting Chiefs* at Edinburgh, for the temporary government of Scotland, instituted previous to the First Bishops' War, ii. 54 ; constitution of, ii. 54-5, 59.—*Great, of English Peers*, summoned by Charles I. at York, ii. 143-4.—*Of State, the First, of the English Commonwealth*, iv. 11-2 ; constitution of, iv. 12-3; minute of the first meeting of, in Derby House, and account of subsequent meetings of, iv. 12-6 ; forms and routine of the, iv. 16-8, 16 note ; first Acts of the, in connection with the Rump Parliament, iv. 39 - 49 ; removal of the, from Derby House to the Palace of Whitehall, iv. 51, 54-5 ; during Cromwell's absence in Ireland, iv. 57 ; Bradshaw first present as President of

the, iv. 79 ; appointment of Milton to the Latin Secretaryship of, iv. 79-80, 82-4 ; activity of the, in all matters of the government, iv. 114-27 ; dissolved, iv. 127-8 ; *Second, of the Commonwealth*, iv. 127-8 ; constitution of, iv. 177 ; Acts of the, in connexion with the Parliament, to please the Presbyterians, iv. 177-80; during the war with the Scots, iv. 180 ; *Third, of the Commonwealth*, iv. 221-2, 273; constitution and first meeting of, 273-4 ; v. 705; a committee of the, manages negotiations with Portugal, iv. 275 ; sends, by desire of the Parliament, two London physicians and an apothecary to attend Cromwell at Edinburgh, iii. 278; certain of the chief prisoners of the war with the Scots recommended by the, for trial and capital punishment, iv. 297 ; respectful treatment by, of Lord Leven, iv. 297-8 ; allowances by the, to prisoners in the Tower and elsewhere after the war with the Scots, iv. 298 ; disposition by, of the whole residue of prisoners, iv. 298-9 ; revision of the work, iv. 306-7 ; dissolution of, and election of a new, iv. 309-10; regulation by the expiring council for future Presidencies, iv. 310 ; *Fourth, of the Commonwealth*, iv. 354 ; constitution of, iv. 354 ; Presidents after Bradshaw, iv. 355 ; incidents in the history of the, iv. 356-9, 364, 369, 370, 372, 373, 374, 377 ; *the Fifth, of the Commonwealth*, its constitution, iv. 355; incidents in its history, 377, 378, 379, 380, 381, 382, 383, 386, 399, 402 ; recommendation by the, to the Parliament, to remove the Duke of Gloucester from the Isle of Wight, and to send him abroad to his relatives, iv. 406 ; dismissed by Cromwell immediately after the dissolution of the Rump, iv. 413-4.—*Council of Officers* during Cromwell's Interim Dictatorship, iv. 402-6, 410, 498-9.—Council called *of the Thirteen*, iv. 499 ; Acts of, 499-505, 517.—*The First, of the Barebones Parliament*, iv. 505 ; its constitution, iv. 506 ; incidents in its history, iv. 506-7,

511; *the Second, of the Barebones Parliament*, iv. 511-3, 575-80; its collapse, 513.—Incidents in Milton's secretaryship in the successive councils of the Commonwealth, iv. 77-107, 129-61, 221-36, 250-2, 311-35, 341-53, 414-94, 519-40, 574-642; v. 150-68, 168-225, 240-57, 269-76, 289-98, 362-79, 384-99, 402, 569-96, 597-631, 636-74: see also *Milton*.—Council *of the First Protectorate*, iv. 542-3, 575.—Council *of the Eighteen*, iv. 545; arrangements and habits of, iv. 545-7; action of, during the first nine months of the Protectorate, 547-57; Ordinances of, 558-73; revision of the, under Thurloe, iv. 574; Milton's services retained in the, 575-7; new arrangements, 575 80; a revision of its Acts, v. 11; position of Cromwell and his Council during period of "Arbitrariness," v. 31; first meeting of, after the dissolution of Parliament, v. 31-2; management of Commonwealth affairs by Cromwell and the, v. 32, 35, 240, 241, 243, 276, 294.—*Of the Second Protectorate*, v. 308; constitution of, 308-9; administration of affairs by, v. 309-23, 333, 342; restrictions of the press by, v. 351-2; meetings of, at Hampton Court during Cromwell's last days, v. 355-6, 357, 358, 359, 360, 361 note.—*A Council for the Protestant Religion*, contemplated by Cromwell as a desirable European institution, v. 341-2.—*Of Richard's Protectorate*, v. 415-17; composition of, v. 417; 421, 422, 423.—*Of the Restored Rump Parliament during the period of the Anarchy*, v. 519-20.—*Monk's General, of Officers*, v. 539-40.—*The, of the Restored Long Parliament*, v. 543-4, 554-5.—*The Wallingford House, of Officers*: see *Wallingford House*. —*Of the Army and Navy*, appointed by the Wallingford Committee, v. 510.—*The English Privy*, of Charles II. at the Restoration, vi. 17-21: see also *Cabal, Junto, Cabinet.—The Scottish Privy*, in London, at the Restoration, vi. 130-42.

"COUNTRY PARTY," the, in the Cabal, vi. 589, 598.
COURLAND, Duke of, iv. 383; v. 292.
COURT: of Chancery, Bill for its reform, v. 11; ordinance for regulating the, v. 36; of the County Palatine of Chester, abolished, ii. 189; of High Commission, its constitution and powers, i. 406-7; prosecutions by the, i. 678-80; abolished, ii. 188; Scottish, of High Commission, in 1634, i. 708; of the Duchy of Lancaster, abolished, ii. 189; of the President and Council of the North, abolished, ii. 189; of the President and Council of Wales, abolished, ii. 188.
"COURT PARTY," the, in Richard's Government, v. 421.
COURTNEY, Hugh, in the Council of the Barebones Parliament, iv. 506; arrested, v. 335.
COVELL, Captain, officer of City Trained Bands, ii. 447.
COVENTRY, Sir Henry, younger brother of Sir William, member of the Cabal Administration, vi. 265, 590, 598, 600; of the Danby Administration, vi. 602.
COVENTRY, Thomas, 1st Lord: High Steward of Cambridge, i. 235; Lord Keeper of the Great Seal, i. 317, 383, 384, 535, 668; death of, ii. 128; iii. 158.
COVENTRY, 2nd Lord: in Royalist army, ii. 429; his arrest, v. 50.
COVENTRY, Mr. or Sir William (Royalist), opposes the "Grand Remonstrance," ii. 321; during the Dutch war, vi. 254-5, 263-64, 265; in the Cabal Administration, vi. 563, 590.
COVENANTS: *The National Scottish*, of 1638:—its origin in previous Covenants of 1581 and 1590, and the story of its introduction in 1638, i. 726-7; the first signing in the Greyfriars Churchyard, i. 727-8; the wording of the Document, i. 728-32; its reception over Scotland, i. 732; ii. 4-8; the Marquis of Hamilton's Mission to treat with the Covenanters, ii. 8-36; Charles I. and the "damnable Covenant," ii. 31; discussed and further established

in the debates of the Glasgow Assembly of 1638, ii. 36-42 ; its part in the "First Bishops' War," ii. 43-71; the, in connexion with the "Solemn League and Covenant," iii. 9, 10, 13 ; the Earl of Montrose and the, iii. 363-5 ; iv. 186 ; Charles II. and the, iv. 27, 63, 212 ; vi. 101, 142 note ; continues in force in Scotland after the Restoration, vi. 133, 135, 136 ; Act against the, in the Scottish Parliament of 1661, vi. 145.—*The Solemn League and*, of 1643, constructed for Scotland and England, iii. 6-18 ; Henderson, the author of, iii. 9-10, 18, 36, 342 ; inaugurated in the English House of Commons, iii. 34, 38 ; made stringent throughout England and Scotland, iii. 38-40 ; in the business of the Westminster Assembly, iii. 172, 406, 408 ; the Earl of Montrose and, iii. 342, 343, 364 ; iv. 186 ; in the negotiations of the Scots and Charles I. at Newcastle, iii. 413-8, 496, 499-500 ; the Earl of Argyle and, iii. 419 ; in the Nineteen Propositions of the Parliament to the King, iii. 421, 496, 499-500, 502, 50ς Oxford squibs against, iii. 546 ; Presbyterian petition to the Houses for the strict observance of, iii. 549 ; in the army's *Heads of Proposals* to the King, iii. 558, 563 ; the Scottish envoys in the Isle of Wight and the, iii. 581-2 ; in the Engagement or Secret Treaty of Charles with the Scots, iii. 586 ; the King and, in the Treaty of Newport, iii. 607 ; in the movement of the Kirk and the Argyle government for Charles II., iv. 22, 27, 63 ; is superseded, as a test of allegiance to the Commonwealth, by the "Engagement" test of the Parliament of England, iv. 124; the Earl of Montrose and, in 1649, iv. 186, 199-200 ; in the Treaty of Breda (1650), iv. 181, 189, 190 ; Fairfax and the, iv. 192 ; Cromwell and the, iv. 197-8 ; Charles II. and the, iv. 27, 63, 212 ; vi. 101, 281, 142 note, 362, 363 ; its revival by the restored Long Parliament in 1659-60, v. 549, 551, 552 ; after the Restoration, vi. 63, 101, 135, 136, 138, 139, 145 ; declared null and void by the Scottish Parliament of 1661, vi. 146, 149. See *Bands*.

COWARD, William, M.D., vi. 763.

COWELL, Major, under *New Model*, iii. 326, 534.

COWLEY, Abraham : his boyhood, i. 489, 649, 683 ; iii. 449 ; under the Protectorate, v. 76, 80, 83, 83-4 note ; the Duke of Buckingham's marriage and, v. 320-1 ; Restoration verses by, vi. 13-4 ; connexion with Davenant, vi. 276 ; after the Restoration, vi. 299, 309-11, 387, 388 ; and the "matchless Orinda," vi. 317, 322 ; his Vision of Cromwell, vi. 336-8 ; the Restoration drama and, vi. 358 ; in Dryden's *Essay on Poetry*, vi. 380 ; the Royal Society and, vi. 394, 396 ; *Ode* by, in honour of the Royal Society, vi. 398 ; his death, vi. 405 ; registration of works by, vi. 515 ; Milton and, vi. 682.

COWPER, William, Clerk of the Parliament, i. 9.

COWPER, William, the poet : his translations of Milton's Latin poems, i. 174.

COX, Dr., physician : his visit to Nayler, v. 317.

COX, Benjamin, Baptist preacher, iii. 148, 395-6.

Cox, Robert, player, vi. 347.

Cox, William, vi. 91.

COYET, Peter, Swedish resident in London, v. 246, 249, 253.

CRADOCK, a Baptist minister, ii. 581.

CRADOCK, Francis, and the Rota Club, v. 485 ; his poetical tribute to Milton, vi. 782.

CRADOCK, Samuel, vi. 232 note.

CRAGGE, John, fellow-graduate of Milton at Cambridge, i. 258.

CRAIG, John, Scottish Presbyterian divine, i. 726.

CRANE, of Roehampton, English Presbyterian, ii. 532.

CRANSTOUN, John, 2nd Lord, i. 710, 722 ; ii. 16, 38 ; iv. 212.

CRANSTOUN, William, 3rd Lord, iv. 560.

CRANTZIUS, Dr. George : his preface to the Hague edition of the *Defensio Secunda*, v. 151-2 ; in the Morus Controversy, v. 203, 206 ; and Salmasius's reply to Milton, vi. 203.

CRASHAW, Richard, poet, i. 248, 499-500, 648, 649 ; iii. 449.

CRAVEN, Mr., at Cambridge, i. 182 ; of Trinity College, Oxford, i. 208.

CRAVEN, of Hamstead-Marshall, Lord, in Royalist army, ii. 429.

CRAWFORD, James, licenser for the press, iii. 233 note, 270, 272 ; iv. 123.

CRAWFORD, Countess of, provision for, iv. 560.

CRAWFORD, Ludovic Lindsay, Earl of, ii. 305-6, 442 ; iii. 361, 367, 421, 499, 509 ; iv. 212, 290, 296, 298, 560 ; v. 547 ; vi. 130-1 ; in the Scottish Parliament of 1661, vi. 148-9.

CRAWFORD, Major-General : in the Battle of Marston Moor, iii. 97, 166-7.

CRAWFORD, Colonel, under *New Model*, iii. 326.

CREED, Major Richard, v. 470, 490, 521 ; in the Restored Long Parliament, v. 547, 566-7 ; in the Indemnity Bill, vi. 40, 47, 55.

CREIGHTON, Robert, public orator and professor of Greek at Cambridge, i. 121, 152, 220, 267, 409.

CREQUI, Duke de, in an embassy to Cromwell, v. 340, 392-3.

CREWE, John, iii. 41, 510, 541, 605 ; one of Cromwell's Lords, v. 324 ; on Council of State, v. 543 ; in the Restored Long Parliament, v. 545, 554 ; in the Convention Parliament, vi. 23, 24 ; made a Baron at the Coronation of Charles II., vi. 153.

CRICHTON, William : see *Dumfries*, Earl of.

CRIPPS, Henry, publisher, iv. 107 note.

CRISP, one of the "heretics" of Sion College, iii. 678.

CROFTS, James : see *Monmouth*, Duke of.

CROISSY, M. Colbert de, French ambassador in London, vi. 571, 576, 580, 582, 593.

CROKE, Sir John, of Chilton, Bucks, i. 557.

CROMPTON, Thomas, v. 454, 544 note.

CROMWELL, Lord : see *Ardglass*, Earl of.

CROMWELL, Mrs., "living near Shere Lane," ii. 44.

CROMWELL, Bridget, Cromwell's eldest daughter, in correspondence with Cromwell, iii. 155 ; marries Ireton, iii. 478 ; provision for, on her husband's death, iv. 357 ; marries Fleetwood, iv. 366-7 ; v. 304.

CROMWELL, Catherine, Cromwell's sister, married to (1) Roger Whetstone, (2) Colonel John Jones, v. 307.

CROMWELL, Elizabeth, wife of Oliver Cromwell : iv. 55 note ; through the Protectorate, iv. 573 ; v. 304 ; in Cromwell's last days, v. 358, 360 ; settlement of money on, v. 450 ; her petition in 1660, vi. 113 ; scurrilities against, vi. 462.

CROMWELL, Mrs. Elizabeth, Cromwell's mother : her death, v. 304 and note ; disinterred, vi. 227.

CROMWELL, Elizabeth (Lady Claypole), Cromwell's daughter, iii. 155 ; in Cromwell's Protectorate, v. 305 ; her death, v. 355-6.

CROMWELL, Elizabeth, Cromwell's sister, v. 306.

CROMWELL, Lady Frances, Cromwell's daughter, proposed marriage of, with William Dutton, iv. 617 ; marries Mr. Robert Rich, v. 306 ; in Cromwell's last days, v. 355.

CROMWELL, Henry, Cromwell's son, iii. 626 ; iv. 401 ; called to Cromwell's Supreme Assembly, iv. 502 ; in the Barebones Parliament, iv. 512 ; in Council Order Books, iv. 525 ; in Ireland in 1654, iv. 551 ; in Oliver's First Parliament, v. 5 ; in Ireland in 1655, v. 98-100, 304-5 ; Lord Deputy of Ireland, and one of Cromwell's lords, v. 323 ; in Cromwell's last days, v. 358-9 ; correspondence with Thurloe, v. 402 ; supports Richard's Government, v. 418 ; in correspondence with Lord Falconbridge, v. 420-1 ; his letter to Fleetwood, v. 423-5 ; 436, 438, 459, 461-3, 464 ; his retirement, v. 515.

CROMWELL, Jane, Cromwell's sister, married to Major John Desborough, iii. 327; v. 307; disinterred, vi. 227.

CROMWELL, Margaret, Cromwell's sister, married to Valentine Walton, v. 307.

CROMWELL, Mary, Cromwell's daughter, married to Lord Falconbridge, v. 305-6; *Epithalamium* by Davenant on her marriage, vi. 274 note; in Cromwell's last days, v. 355; at the theatre after the Restoration, vi. 353-4.

CROMWELL, Robina, Cromwell's sister, married to (1) Peter French, D.D., (2) Dr. John Wilkins, v. 307.

CROMWELL, OLIVER : at Sidney Sussex College, Cambridge, in 1617, i. 121, 142; ii. 78; in Charles I.'s Third Parliament, in 1628, i. 187, 215, 375; related to the poet Waller, i. 505, to John Hampden, ii. 161, 164, to Oliver St. John, ii. 163, 164, and to Sir Thomas Barrington and Sir William Masham, ii. 173; his meditated emigration to New England in 1635, i. 680.

From the calling of the Long Parliament in Nov. 1640 to August 1642 :—As member for Cambridge, ii. 164; sketch of, at this date, and of his appearances in the House, ii. 164-5; his usual place in the House, ii. 174; presents Lilburne's petition to the Commons, ii. 175; supports the Bill for Triennial Parliaments, ii. 186; joins the Root-and-Branch party in the English Church-reform movement, ii. 201, 231-2, 236; in the Party of Movement, ii. 277, 318, 319; his motion in the Commons to give the Earl of Essex power to assemble the Trained Bands, ii. 318-9; in the debates on the "Grand Remonstrance," ii. 319-22; carries a motion for stopping investiture of new bishops, ii. 324-5; in the House at the attempted arrest by the King of the Five Members, ii. 343; attendance in Parliament, ii. 416; raises a troop of horse in Cambridgeshire, ii. 421.

Through the Civil War to Aug.

1646 :—Captain of horse in Essex's Parliamentarian army, ii. 446, 449, 450-3; signs a letter to invite certain New England Independents to join the proposed Westminster Assembly, ii. 605; his "Ironsides," and his first notable action in the Civil War, ii. 469; signs the Solemn League and Covenant, iii. 12; is a colonel in the Parliamentarian army, iii. 35; in a commission for the management of the Colonies, iii. 119; on the "Committee of Peers and Commoners of the two Kingdoms," iii. 41, 331; promoted to be lieutenant-general and second in command in the Associated Eastern Counties under the Earl of Manchester, iii. 85, 166, 177; recognised as the head of Army-Independency, iii. 85-7; at the Battle of Marston Moor, iii. 96-8, 160; his interference for Independency and Toleration, and his increased influence after Marston Moor, iii. 166-71; his Accommodation, or Toleration, Order in Parliament, iii. 168-70, 177-80, 274-5, 391-3; in the second Battle of Newbury, iii. 177; in the impeachment of the Earl of Manchester, iii. 179-80, 388; in the *Self-denying Ordinance* and *Ordinance for New-Modelling of the Army*, iii. 180-3 and notes; composition of the *New Model Army*, iii. 325-8 and notes, 402; in the first actions of the New Model, iii. 331; retained in command, iii. 333; in the Battle of Naseby and other successes of the New Model, iii. 335-7, 369, 390-1; in the Toleration Controversy, and at the head of the party of Independents in the Army and in the Commons, iii. 384-95, 416; his adherents among the Recruiters of the Commons in Aug. 1645, iii. 402; is back in London, and thanked in the House for his services in the War, iii. 411; marriage of his eldest daughter, Bridget, to General Ireton, iii. 420; in a Parliamentary Commission of Lords and Commons for establishing Presbytery in England, iii. 423; at the siege and surrender

of Oxford, iii. 420, 471-2; at the close of the First Civil War in Aug. 1646, iii. 369, 372, 378, 381, 411, 416.

From the close of the First Civil War to the Execution of the King (Aug. 1646 to Jan. 29, 1649):—In the quarrel between the Parliament and the Army, iii. 521-38; his so-called "Flight to the Army," iii. 538, and note; his part in Joyce's abduction of the King, iii. 542-3, 543-4 note; in a Commission of Officers to treat with the Parliament, iii. 549; mediates with Parliament for civilities to Charles I., iii. 556-7; his alleged part in the Army's *Heads of Proposals*, iii. 559-60 note; his *Middle Course* with the King, iii. 565-9, 569 note; in the Council of War at Putney, during the mutiny of the Army, iii. 569-73; in the "Concordat," iii. 573, 583-4, 610-1; suppresses the Army mutiny, iii. 583-4; story of the prayer-meeting of officers held in Windsor Castle previous to the outbreak of the Second Civil War (May-Aug. 1648), iii. 611-3; suppresses the Royalist rising in Wales, iii. 592-3, 595, 597, 600, 601; proceedings of the Parliament in absence of, ending in charges of high treason against, iii. 601-3; in the three days' Battle of Preston against the Scots and English, iii. 604, iv. 20-1; further actions in the north after Preston, iii. 620; proceeds to Scotland, iii. 621; in Edinburgh, iii. 622; on the return journey southwards, iii. 622-3; in correspondence with Colonel Robert Hammond, Governor of the Isle of Wight, iii. 624-6; is back in London, and receives the thanks of the House for his recent services in Wales, Scotland, and the north of England, iii. 698-9; in the Commission for the King's Trial, iii. 703, 704, 707, 712 note; at the signing of the death-warrant, iii. 718, 720-1 note, vi. 28; story of his concern with the actual execution, vi. 87-8.

To the Dissolution of the Rump in April 1653:—In the *Agreement*

of the People, iv. 10; in the First Council of State of the English Commonwealth, iv. 12-16, 25, 25 note, 38-9, 46-54, 69, 77, 79-80, 82-3, 87, 89, 102, 105-6: for appointment of, to subsequent Councils of State, see *Councils*; appointed (March 30, 1649) to be Commander-in-Chief of an army for the reconquest of Ireland, iv. 41-2; his speech in Council against Lilburne and the Levellers, iv. 46-7; assists Fairfax in suppressing an army mutiny and a rising of Levellers, iv. 49-51, 51 note; at the *Fairfaxian Creation* at Oxford, and at the London City Banquet, iv. 51-4; at the removal of the Council of State from Derby House to Whitehall, iv. 54-5; squibs against, in current literature, iv. 55 note, 56, 57 note; leaves London for Ireland, iv. 56; the Council in his absence, iv. 57-8; in the Irish Campaign (1649), iv. 111-3; disaffection to, among Royalists and Levellers, iv. 115-6, 119-21, 158; effect of his Irish victories on the attitude of Foreign Powers towards the Commonwealth, iv. 125; in the Second, or continued, Campaign in Ireland (1650), iv. 190-1; honours to, on his return to London, iv. 191-2; Andrew Marvell's Horatian ode to, iv. 477-8; invades Scotland in 1650, iv. 192-3, 194, 196, 196-200; victory of Dunbar, iv. 200-1; in Edinburgh, iv. 201; his policy after Dunbar, iv. 210-1; is master of all Scotland south of the Firths, iv. 211, 279-81; effect of the Scottish victories upon the relations of the Commonwealth with Foreign powers, iv. 216; appointed to the Chancellorship of the University of Oxford, iv. 278; detained by illness at Edinburgh, iv. 278-84; in the case of Love and Gibbons, iv. 285-7; crosses the Firth of Forth into Fifeshire, iv. 287-8; is at Perth, iv. 289-90; pursues Charles II. into England, iv. 290-4; Battle of Worcester, iv. 294-6; back in London, iv. 296-8; in debates of the House on the Question of a new Parliament, iv. 308-9; at the death

of Ireton, iv. 356-7 ; his relations to the Government, iv. 359-60; and the Incorporation of Scotland with the Commonwealth, iv. 361, 362 ; in the government of Ireland, iv. 366-71 ; marriage of his daughter (Ireton's widow) to Fleetwood, iv. 367 ; in foreign affairs, iv. 377, 423 ; in internal questions, iv. 383-7, 449 ; in the question of the Propagation of the Gospel, iv. 387-98 ; and the Rump, iv. 399-401 ; his Army and his Council of Officers, iv. 401-2 ; the Petition of the Officers to the Rump in Aug. 1652, iv. 402-5 ; references to, in the *Regii Sanguinis Clamor*, in Aug. 1652, iv. 457-8 ; his part in the Bill for Dissolution of the existing Parliament and Election of a new Representative, iv. 405-9, 409 note ; his conferences with the chiefs of the Rump, iv. 409-11 ; forcibly dissolves the Rump Parliament and the Council of State, in April 1653, iv. 411-4, 411-2 note, 519-23, 616.

Through his Interim Dictatorship (April-Dec. 1653) :—General adhesion to, after the dissolution of the Rump, iv. 498 ; his Declarations, iv. 498-9 ; his Interim Council of Thirteen, iv. 498-500, 502-4, 523-4, 616 ; his separate military Council of Officers, iv. 499, 500 ; Lilburne and, see *Lilburne*, John ; Supreme Assembly of Notables summoned by, iv. 500-2, 504-5 ; his "First Speech" to the Assembly, iv. 505 ; constitution of the "Parliament of the Commonwealth of England" known as the Barebones Parliament, iv. 505-6 ; Councils of State of this Parliament, iv. 506, 512, 524-5, 616 ; conservative policy of, at this date, in the Church question, iv. 515-7 ; collapse of the Parliament, iv. 516-7 ; Installation of, as Lord Protector of the Commonwealth, Dec. 16, 1653, iv. 517-8.

First nine months of the First Protectorate (to Sept. 3, 1654) :—Change of titles and signature of, at the Protectorate, iv. 542 ; powers of the Protector, and his relations to Council and Parliaments, iv. 542-4 ; his Council of State, iv. 544-7, 577-8, 580, 636; discontent of Republicans, and Stuartist plots against, iv. 547-52 ; dealings with Ireland and Scotland, iv. 551-2 ; in Treaties with Foreign Powers, iv. 552-7, 572-3, 580 ; legislative activity of, and his first eighty-two Ordinances, including the Ordinance of Pardon and Grace for the People of Scotland, with names of persons excepted, and amounts of Fines to be imposed on Delinquents, iv. 557-66 ; of the Conservative policy of the Protectorate, and of its relations to the Church, iv. 566-7 ; in Court incidents of the Protectorate, iv. 572-3 ; in passages of Milton's *Defensio Secunda*, with subsequent discussion on Milton's advices to, iv. 560-93, 602-5, 605-16.

Through the First Parliament of the Protectorate (to Jan. 22, 1655) :— iv. 572, 642 ; meeting of the First Parliament of the Protectorate, Sept. 3rd, 1654, v. 3-6 ; his "Fortunate Day," v. 6 ; his "Second Speech," v. 6 ; unmanageable constitution of the Parliament, v. 6-7 ; the Parliament attempts a revision of the Constitution, and challenges the authority of, and his right to "negatives," v. 7-13 ; his "Third Speech," v. 8-9 ; in Council letters, v. 166-7 ; his "Fourth Speech," and dissolution of his First Parliament, v. 29, 32, 165.

Between the Parliaments or "Period of Arbitrariness" (to Sept. 17, 1656) :—His Council, v. 31-2 ; Republican plottings and Royalist risings against, v. 32-5 ; his arbitrariness in the matter of supplies and revenue, v. 35-6 ; foreign policy of, v. 36-7 ; sends two fleets under Blake and Penn to the Mediterranean, v. 37-8 ; his indignation on the occasion of the Piedmontese Massacre in 1655, v. 38-44, 183-4, 295 ; at the failure of Penn's West India Expedition, v. 44-6 ; in Irish affairs, v. 99-100 ; alliance with France and rupture with Spain, v. 46-7, 240-1, 243 ; his policy

and management in colonial matters, v. 101-4 ; his government by major-generals, v. 48-53; his Established Church of England and Wales, v. 53-8 ; his toleration of dissent from the Established Church, v. 58-72 ; his encouragement of literature and the arts, v. 72-86; in the government of Scotland, v. 86-98; Letters of State of, to Foreign States and Princes, v. 243-54, 269-75 ; in Council business, v. 259-60.

In the First Session of his Second Parliament (to June 26, 1657):— He resolves to call another Parliament, v. 106 ; its constitution and first meeting, Sept. 17, 1656, v. 107-8 ; Cromwell's "Fifth Speech," v. 108-10 ; his arbitrary exclusion of anti-Oliverians, 110-11 ; Act of Parliament for the personal safety of, v. 112 ; confines himself and Council to matters of administration, war, and diplomacy, v. 114-6 ; his part in the case of the Quaker James Nayler, v. 116-18 ; in Council letters, v. 289-94; abandons the major-generalships, v. 118-9 ; the Sexby-Sindercombe Plot against, v. 119-20; his "Sixth Speech," v. 120; Sir Christopher Pack's motion for a *Humble Address and Remonstrance* to, v. 121-3 ; kingship offered to, and refused by, v. 123-32, 296-7 ; his "Seventh" and "Eighth Speeches," v. 128 ; his "Ninth Speech," v. 128 ; his "Tenth," "Eleventh," and "Twelfth Speeches," v. 129 ; his "Thirteenth Speech," v. 129-30, 135 ; gives his assent to the *Petition and Advice*, v. 136, 136-7 note ; his "Fourteenth Speech," v. 137 note; his past ordinances confirmed, v. 137-9 ; his "Fifteenth Speech," v. 139 ; his Treaty "Offensive and Defensive" with Louis XIV. against Spain, v. 140, 295 : see *France ;* his idea of a League or Union of the Protestant States of Europe, 295-6; in *Killing no Murder*, v. 141-2 ; account of the new Protectorate Constitution, v. 142-9, 296-7 ; Cromwell's Upper House, v. 147 ; his second Installation (June 26, 1657), v. 147-9 ; adjourns the House for seven months, v. 149.

Through the Second Protectorate (to Sept. 3, 1658):—Increased ceremonial of the Court in the second Protectorate, v. 302-4 ; list of knighthoods conferred by, in the first Protectorate, v. 303 note, 354 note ; his family and relatives v. 304-7 ; his new Privy Council for his second Protectorate, v. 308; in foreign business, v. 311-5, 370-4, 376-9, 386-98, 399-401 ; his Established Church brought to a satisfactory condition, v. 315-7 ; in relation with the Quakers, v. 317-8; orders the arrest of the Duke of Buckingham, v. 322; marriages of his daughters to Viscount Falconbridge and Mr. Rich, v. 323 ; his Peers or Lords, v. 323-5 ; in the second session of his Second Parliament, and his experiment of Two Houses (Jan. 20 to Feb. 4, 1657-8), v. 325-33 ; his "Sixteenth Speech," v. 327 ; his "Seventeenth Speech," v. 330 ; his "Eighteenth Speech," v. 331 ; dissolves the Parliament, v. 331-3 ; in a meeting of army officers at Whitehall, v. 334 ; is only occasionally present in Council after the dissolution, 333-4 ; his activity against Royalist conspiracy and the proposed insurrection of old Commonwealth's men, v. 334-8 ; correspondence with the Earl of Warwick, v. 338-9 ; his continued charge of the French Alliance, v. 339-41 ; his interest in the scheme of a great Protestant League, v. 341-3 ; his chief home concern still "the Propagation of the Gospel," and conservation of the Church Establishment, v. 343-5 ; his schemes for Scotland, v. 345-50 ; his scheme for Religious Toleration, v. 350-1 ; and proposed restrictions of the Press, v. 351 ; his thoughts of another Parliament, v. 353-4 ; his last days, and death at Whitehall on Sept. 3, 1658, v. 354-61 ; embalming and interment of, v. 415 ; in the Indemnity Bill, vi. 28, 30, 54 ; disinterment of, vi. 113-4 ; his head, with those of Bradshaw

and Ireton, set upon the top of Westminster Hall, vi. 123-4; recollections of, in 1667, vi. 267; Cowley's Vision of, vi. 336-8; Faithorne's emblematical print of, vi. 648; Milton's sonnet to, vi. 688; Milton and the Cromwell papers, vi. 813-6. For his intercourse and private connexions with Milton, Marvell, Overton, Lilburne, the Count of Oldenburg, Sir Harry Vane, George Fox, the poet Cleveland, William Allen, etc., see these names.

"CROMWELL LETTERS, THE," consisting of Letters and Addresses to Cromwell from 1649 to 1658, found among the Political Collections of Milton, and edited by John Nickolls in 1743, vi. 740 note, 814-6.

CROMWELL, Sir Oliver, Cromwell's uncle, iii. 542.

CROMWELL, Oliver, Cromwell's son, killed, ii. 445.

CROMWELL, Sir Philip, uncle of Cromwell, iii. 326.

CROMWELL, Philip, son of Sir Philip Cromwell, and major in New Model, iii. 326.

CROMWELL, RICHARD: in his father's First Parliament, v. 5; in his father's Second Parliament, v. 107; at his father's second installation, v. 149; under the Protectorate, v. 304-5, 308, 323; in the Privy Council after dissolution of the Second Parliament, v. 333, 346; present at his father's last illness, v. 355; succeeds his father as Lord Protector, v. 414-19; contending parties round, v. 420-3; his Foreign Policy, v. 426-8; State letters of Milton for, v. 570-2, 575-6, 589-90; his Parliament, v. 428-38; dissolution of Parliament forced upon him, v. 441-2; state of his finances, v. 443-4; his abdication, v. 450-1; continues at Whitehall after abdication, v. 459, 463; in the Indemnity Bill, vi. 40.

CROMWELL, Robert, eldest son of Oliver Cromwell, his death, ii. 165.

CROOK, Samuel, English Presbyterian, ii. 513 note, 532.

CROOK, Major Upton, v. 34, 470.

CROOKE, Andrew, publisher, iii. 219; vi. 403.

CROOKSHANK, William, of Loncardy, Perthshire, i. 70.

CROONE, Henry, physician and member of the Rota Club, v. 485.

CROSS, the, Old Cheapside, i. 48.

CROSSE, Robert, member of Westminster Assembly, ii. 517.

CROULLÉ, M. de, French agent and spy in London, iv. 381.

CROWN OFFICE in Chancery, i. 104 and footnote.

CROWNE, John, plays by, vi. 611-2; vi. 730.

CROXTON, Colonel, sentenced to death by the Convention Parliament in 1660, vi. 47.

CRUSOE, Timothy, ii. 483.

CRYPTO-CATHOLICISM of the Court of Charles II., vi. 238-40: see Charles II.

CUDWORTH, Nicholas, fellow-graduate of Milton at Cambridge, i. 218.

CUDWORTH, Ralph, at Cambridge, i. 248; at the Visitation of Cambridge University, iii. 94, 95; v. 71, 73; among Men of Letters under the Protectorate, v. 75, 77; among Men of Letters of the Restoration, vi. 299; and the Platonists, vi. 306-7; 388, 616, 617.

CULVERWELL, Nathaniel, Cambridge Platonist, vi. 306.

CUMBER, Dr. Thomas, ejected from Cambridge University, iii. 93.

CUMBERLAND, Henry Clifford, 5th Earl of, ii. 428, 442-3, 468.

"CUMBERNAULD, the Band of," ii. 296.

CUNNINGHAM, Presbyterian divine, ii. 38.

CUNNINGHAM, Adam, Parliamentarian officer, ii. 444.

CUNNINGHAM, Henry, in the Council Order Books, iv. 228.

CUPAR, Lord, i. 710; ii. 38, 292; in Cromwell's Ordinance of Pardon and Grace, iv. 561.

CURLE, Dr. Walter, Bishop of Winchester, i. 388, 390, 399, 674, 677; in the Long Parliament, ii. 150; impeachment of, ii. 270, 335, 349.

CURRENT INTELLIGENCER, the, vi. 331.

CURZON, Sir John, mentioned in Mr. Powell's will, iii. 637, 639.
CUTTS, Sir John, iii. 542.
CYRIL, Paul, petition of, v. 312.

D

DACRES, an actor, vi. 350.
DACRES, Lord, Parliamentarian Peer, ii. 431 ; iii. 405 ; last efforts for the King, iii. 692 ; in Oliver's First Parliament, v. 5.
DAILLÉ, French Divine, v. 368 ; co-pastor with Morus, vi. 420.
DALBIER, John, a Dutchman, Parliamentarian officer, ii. 443, 445; teaches drill to Cromwell, ii. 450 ; killed in Second Civil War, iii. 596.
DALGARNO, George, author of *Ars Signorum*, vi. 314.
DALGLEISH, Presbyterian divine, ii. 38.
DALHOUSIE, Earl of, i. 722 ; ii. 65 ; with Scottish auxiliary army in England, iii. 37 ; fined by Cromwell, iv. 561.
DALKEITH, Lord, i. 722.
DALKEITH, Earl of, son ot Duke of Monmouth, vi. 604.
DALKEITH HOUSE, in First Bishops' War, ii. 56 ; General Monk resident at : see *Monk*.
DALYELL, Thomas, of Binns, in Charles II.'s Scottish army, iv. 283 ; prisoner in England, iv. 298 ; fined by Cromwell, iv. ᶜ60.
DALZELL, Lord (afterwards 2nd Earl of Carnwath), i. 722 ; ii. 15.
DALZIEL, Sir John, iii. 367.
DANBY, Henry Danvers, 1st Earl of, ii. 48 ; his death in Jan. 1643-4, ii. 430 ; his brother, Sir John Danvers, iii. 401.
DANBY, Sir Thomas Osborne, Earl of, account of, as Viscount Latimer of Danby, in 1673, vi. 597 ; member of the Cabal, and Lord High Treasurer, vi. 597-8, 600 ; Earl of Danby in 1674, vi. 602, at the head of the " Danby Administration " after the Cabal, vi. 602-3 ; advises Charles II. in favour of the marriage of Princess Mary to the Prince of Orange, vi. 729.

DANIEL, Samuel, Elizabethan poet, i. 432, 451.
DANIEL, Colonel, in Cromwell's army, iv. 402 ; his regiment, v. 498.
DANTE, i. 98 ; vi. 518-22, 532-6.
DANTZIG, Letters of State to the Senate of the City of, v. 292.
DANVERS, Sir John, brother of the Earl of Danby, and M.P. for Malmesbury in the recruited Parliament of 1645-6, iii. 401 ; at the King's Trial, iii. 712 note ; signs the death-warrant of Charles I., iii. 720 ; in Councils of State of the Commonwealth, iv. 12, 13, 79, 83, 87 ; not re-elected for 1650-1, iv. 177 ; a Voluntary and Tolerationist, iv. 393 ; member of the Barebones Parliament, iv. 515 ; arrested with Harrison in the Venner Riot, v. 134 ; included among the dead Regicides, vi. 28 ; in the Indemnity Bill, vi. 54.
D'ARCY and CONYERS, Sir Conyers D'Arcy, Lord : in Royalist army, ii. 429.
D'ARCY, Elizabeth (daughter of Earl Rivers, and wife of Viscount Savage), i. 244.
DARLEY, Henry, member of the Long Parliament, iii. 8 ; in Councils of State, iv. 273, 313, 314, 321 ; a recruiter in the Restored Rump, v. 454, 544 note.
DARLEY, Richard, recruiter in the Restored Rump, v. 454.
DARLINGTON, John, yeoman, vi. 747.
DARREL, Mr., barrister of Lincoln's Inn, i. 581.
DARTMOUTH, storming of, iii. 371.
DATI, Carlo, i. 772 note, 773, 774-6, 780 ; his Latin letter to Milton, i. 783, 785, 785 note, 821, 822 note, 828 ; ii. 90 and note ; iii. 455 ; in correspondence with Milton, iii. 650-3 and note, 654 and note, 655, 680-3, 689-91, 691 note ; mentioned in Milton's *Defensio Secunda*, iv. 637 ; intimate with Morus, v. 212 and note ; Milton's letter to, vi. 723.
DAVENANT, Charles, son of the poet, vi. 609.
DAVENANT, Dr. John, Bishop of Salisbury, President of Queen's College,

Cambridge, i. 117; Margaret Professor of Divinity at Cambridge, i. 267, 364, 390, 400, 403, 414, 677, 684; ii. 124, 150-1, 324; iii. 218.

DAVENANT, John, Mayor of Oxford, account of, vi. 278.

DAVENANT, Lady, wife of the poet, vi. 351, 609-10.

DAVENANT, Sir William, the poet, tradition of his birth, vi. 278-9; i. 245, 448, 451, 504, 567; appointed Poet Laureate in 1637, i. 646; his part in the "Army Plot," ii. 183; knighted in 1643, iii. 503; his mission to Charles I., in 1646, iii. 503-4 and note; and the publisher, Moseley, iii. 449; under the Protectorate, iv. 193; v. 76, his Italian Opera, v. 80-1, 81 note: in *Wit and Drollery*, v. 261-2 and note; concerned with the Royalist insurrection in 1659, v. 478; in connexion with Milton's escape, vi. 186, 189; his revived Laureateship, vi. 14-5, 273-9; his literary relations to Hobbes and Hobbism, vi. 279, 290; his contemporaries in literature in 1660, vi. 294, 299-302; in the Drama of the Restoration, vi. 347-9, 350-6, 361-2, 365-6; in Dryden's *Essay on Poetry*, vi. 383; his death in 1668, vi. 273, 405, 606; mentioned, vi. 515, 610.

DAVENPORT, John, New England minister, ii. 556, 558, 582, 605.

DAVENPORT, the Misses, actresses, i. 350-1.

DAVIES of Hereford, writer, i. 596.

DAVIES, Sir John, poet, i. 485.

DAVIES, Thomas, publisher, vi. 647 note.

DAVIES, W., Parliamentarian officer, ii. 444.

DAVIS, shoemaker in St. Martin's, iv. 395.

DAVIS, Dr., and his daughters, iii. 436-8, 438 note.

DAVIS, Miss Mary (Moll), actress, vi. 350, 351; and Charles II., vi. 578, 604; her daughter: see *Tudor*, Mary.

DAVIS, Robert, officer of Trained Bands, ii. 446, 483.

DAVIS, Walter, vi. 89.

DAWKINS, one of Cromwell's major-generals, v. 49.

DAWSON, warden of the Stationers' Company, iv. 148.

DAWSON, Richard, ii. 207.

DAWSON, Robert, Irish bishop, i. 420.

DAWSON, Samuel, merchant, v. 372.

DAY, John, printer, ii. 205.

DEAN, Colonel, taken in a Royalist plot, v. 338.

DEAN, Cornet, mutineer, iv. 50.

DEAN, Mr., v. 497.

DEAN, Richard, Admiral: signs the death-warrant of Charles I., iii. 720; vi. 28; General of the Fleet of the Republic, iv. 41, 42, 124; in Ireland, iv. 56; at the incorporation of Scotland with the Commonwealth, iv. 303, 360, 365; 375-6, 401; at the dissolution of the Rump, iv. 499, v. 706; killed in a sea-battle with the Dutch in 1653, iv. 502; his body disinterred, vi. 54, 227.

DEAN, Richard, an Anabaptist, in the Indemnity Bill, vi. 40-1, 47, 55.

DEAN, Richard, v. 624, 625 note.

DECKER, dramatist, i. 434, 445, 569; vi. 352.

"DE CORPORE POLITICO," of Hobbes, vi. 280.

DEE, Francis, Bishop of Peterborough, i. 674.

DEERING, Sir Edward, in Long Parliament, ii. 167, 178; his part in the Root-and-Branch Bill, ii. 231-5, 286; his part in the "Grand Remonstrance," ii. 320-1, 326; expelled the House," ii. 346; his pro-Episcopacy Agitation, ii. 412; a licenser of books, iii. 268; in the Convention Parliament, vi. 23.

"DEFENSIO PRIMA": see *Milton*, Writings of.

"DEFENSIO REGIA," see *Salmasius*.

"DEFENSIO SECUNDA": see *Milton*, Writings of.

DEFOE, Daniel, his grave in Bunhill Fields, vi. 499.

"DE IDEA PLATONICA, *quemadmodum Aristoteles intellexit*": see *Milton*, Writings of.

DEINCOURT, Francis Leake, 1st Lord: see *Scarsdale*, Earl of.

DELAHAY, Henry, witness, iii. 637.

DELAMERE, Baron (Sir George Booth until 1661), excluded from the Rump, v. 448; his Cheshire Insurrection, v. 472, 474-7; his imprisonment, v. 477; his release, v. 505, 547; at the Restoration, v. 700; in the Convention Parliament, vi. 23; in the debates on the Indemnity Bill, vi. 41, 49, 51, 173; Baron Delamere in 1661, vi. 152: see *Booth*.

DELAWARR, Charles West, Lord, 14th Baron, ii. 430; iii. 555 note.

DELL, William, M.A., Baptist preacher and army chaplain, iii. 148, 524-5, 721; iv. 568; v. 59 note; vi. 232 note.

DELMÉ, Philip, member of Westminster Assembly, ii. 520.

DENBIGH, William Fielding, 1st Earl of (Royalist Peer), made M.A. at Cambridge, i. 181; failure of his expedition to relieve Rochelle, i. 204, 380; his subscription towards First Bishops' War, ii. 48; a private in the King's Life Guards, ii. 441; killed, while serving under Prince Rupert, at the taking of Birmingham, ii. 428, 463.

DENBIGH, Basil Fielding, 2nd Earl of, a Parliamentarian, ii. 431, 445; lay-member of Westminster Assembly, ii. 523; in the prosecution of Milton by Stationers' Company, iii. 297 note, 406, 510, 555 note, 579, 584, 703; iv. 4; in Councils of State, iv. 12, 14, 79, 83, 150, 223, 224, 227; in the reconstituted House of Peers, 1660, v. 695.

DENDY, Edward, Sergeant-at-arms in the Council of the Commonwealth, iv. 17, 89, 147, 177, 224, 226; v. 178, 179; his salary, iv. 575, 578; v. 624, 625 note; and the quest of the Regicides, vi. 27; in the Indemnity Bill, vi. 31, 34, 54; in the Bill of Attainder, vi. 15.

DENHAM, Baron, English judge, i. 675.

DENHAM, Sir John, his "Cooper's Hill" and "Tragedy called the Sophy," iii. 447; poems by, iii. 449; under the Protectorate, v. 76; Surveyor of Works, vi. 151; and court scandals, vi. 262; at the Restoration, vi. 299, 309, 322; in Dryden's *Essay on Poetry*, vi. 380, 383-4; and the Royal Society, vi. 394, 396, 459; registration of works by, vi. 515; and *Paradise Lost*, vi. 628-9, 632.

DENMARK and Norway: in 1638, i. 747; Scottish officers in, ii. 52; King of, in 1649, iv. 183, 378; Treaty between the Commonwealth and, iv. 484, 554; v. 40.

DENN, Mr., Chaplain of the Council of State, v. 31.

DENNE, Henry, Baptist preacher, iii. 148.

DE QUINCEY, his criticism of the poet Donne, i. 487.

DERBY, Alice, Countess-Dowager of, daughter of Sir John Spencer of Althorpe, and wife of (1) Lord Strange, afterwards 5th Earl of Derby, and (2) Lord Chancellor Ellesmere, i. 588; account of, and of her literary associations, i. 590-602 and notes, 602-3 note; ii. 158.

DERBY, Charlotte de la Tremouille, Countess of, daughter of the Duke of Thouars, and wife of the 7th Earl of Derby, ii. 158; her two years' defence of Latham House, iii. 339.

DERBY, Henry Stanley, 4th Earl of, his death in 1593, i. 592.

DERBY, Ferdinand Stanley, 5th Earl of, i. 588, 590; known as Lord Strange until 1593, i. 592; his death in 1594, i. 593; account of, i. 593-4 notes.

DERBY, William Stanley, 6th Earl of, i. 595; ii. 158; his death in 1642, ii. 429, 430.

DERBY, James Stanley, 7th Earl of, as Lord Strange in 1636, i. 627; account of, in composition of Long Parliament, ii. 158; succeeds his father, the 6th Earl, ii. 429, 430; Lord-Lieutenant for Cheshire, ii. 439; in the King's army, ii. 443, 468; his wife's defence of Latham Castle, iii. 339; a "Delinquent" in 1646, iii. 421; resident in the Isle of Man, iv. 285; joins Charles II. in his march into England, iv. 292; defeated at Wigan, iv. 293-4; taken prisoner at Worcester, iv. 294; executed, iv. 297.

DERBY, Charles Stanley, 8th Earl of,
in the Royalist Insurrection of 1659,
v. 473, 474; capture of, v. 477.

DERWENTWATER, Francis Radcliffe,
2nd Earl of, married to Mary Tudor,
daughter of Moll Davis and Charles
II., vi. 605.

DESBOROUGH, John, quartermaster, in
1642, to Cromwell, ii. 446; major
under the *New Model*, iii. 326-7; in
the quarrel of the Parliament and
the Army, iii. 534, 535, 537, 549;
not at the King's trial, iii. 708 note;
iv. 402; in the Interim Council of
Thirteen, iv. 498; in the Barebones
Parliament, iv. 505-6, 512; in
the Council, iv. 512, 525, 545
and note; Milton's mention of him
in the *Defensio Secunda*, iv. 602,
606, 612; one of Cromwell's major-
generals, v. 49, 57; in Cromwell's
Second Parliament, v. 107, 124-6,
128, 130-1; in Councils of State, v.
31, 183-4, 305; married to Cromwell's sister, v. 307; in the Privy
Council of the Second Protectorate,
v. 308; one of Cromwell's lords, v.
323; in the Privy Council after the
dissolution of Cromwell's Second
Parliament, v. 333, 352, 354; his
intercourse with Milton, v. 381;
supports Richard's Government, v.
417-8, 421, 422, 423, 425; in
Richard's Parliament, v. 430; in
the Wallingford House Convention,
v. 438-40, 439, 441-2; at the restoration of the Rump, v. 445, 449,
469; in the Council of State, v. 456,
459; Colonel of Horse at the re-
officering of the army, v. 470, 479;
in the General Petition of Officers, v.
488-9, 490; on the Committee of
Safety, v. 494, 495; in the Representative Council of the army and
navy, v. 510; at the second restoration of the Rump, v. 516-7; in disgrace, v. 521, 522, 563; in the Indemnity Bill, vi. 38, 47, 55; among
Milton's old friends and associates,
vi. 197.

DESBOROUGH, Samuel, brother of John,
one of the Commissioners of Forfeited
Estates in Scotland, iv. 56; in Cromwell's Scottish Council in Edinburgh,

v. 86-7, 88; in Cromwell's Second
Parliament, v. 108, 349; supports
Richard's government, v. 418; in
Richard's Parliament, v. 430.

DESCARTES, i. 265, 744; iv. 269.

DESKFORD, James Ogilvy, Lord, Scottish Privy Councillor, i. 707.

D'ESPAGNE, Jean, French preacher in
London, iv. 351.

D'ESPERNON, the Duke, vi. 152.

D'ESTRÉE, Marshal, i. 757.

DE RUYTER: see *Ruyter, De*.

DETHICKE, Sir John, Lord Mayor of
London, iv. 315; v. 71, 253, 281,
290, 589.

DE TRANCOUS, envoy in London from
the city of Bordeaux, iv. 381.

DEVIZES CASTLE, surrender of, iii. 338.

DEVON, Earl of, at Count Bundt's
supper, v. 249.

DEVONSHIRE, Countess-Dowager of,
widow of the 2nd Earl, and mother
of the 3rd Earl, ii. 158, 192, 302.

DEVONSHIRE, William Cavendish, 1st
Earl of, ii. 152.

DEVONSHIRE, William Cavendish, 2nd
Earl of, i. 359, 541.

DEVONSHIRE, William Cavendish, 3rd
Earl of, ii. 152; account of, in composition of Long Parliament, ii.
158; in Royalist army, ii. 428; his
brother, Colonel Cavendish, ii. 469;
v. 81; vi. 288-9, 295.

D'EWES, Sir Simonds, i. 113 note;
his account of his work and readings
at St. John's, Cambridge, i. 261-3,
266, 410; account of, in composition
of Long Parliament, ii. 172, 174;
his part in the "Grand Remonstrance," ii. 326; his interest in the
Irish Distress Fund, ii. 358 note;
in last efforts for the King, iii. 694;
in "Pride's Purge," iii. 696.

DE WITT, Cornelius, assassination of,
vi. 584-5.

DE WITT, John, Dutch Admiral, in
the war between the Dutch and
English, iv. 375, 507; vi. 260, 265-
6, 569; assassinated, vi. 584-5.

DEWSBURY, William, Early Quaker, v.
26-7, 67-8.

DICAS, Thomas, bookseller and publisher, vi. 203, 646-7, 648.

DICKENS, John, merchant, iv. 486.

DE WOLZOGNE, v. 594.

DEY of Tunis, the, in an engagement with Blake's fleet, v. 37.

DICK, William, Mr., of Edinburgh, money borrowed from, by the Scottish Covenanters, ii. 54.

DICKSON, Alexander, son of Mr. David Dickson, and Professor of Hebrew in Edinburgh University, v. 349.

DICKSON, Mr. David, minister of Irvine in Ayrshire, i. 712, 714, 715, 722, 723, 727, 732; ii. 16, 27, 37, 122, 289; iv. 213, 509-10; Professor of Divinity, Edinburgh, v. 90, 95, 349.

DICKSON, John, vi. 134.

"DIDACTICA MAGNA," of Comenius, iii. 203, 204, 210, 212, 220.

"DIES DOMINICA," by Thomas Young, ii. 75.

DIGBY, George, Lord, account of, in the Long Parliament, ii. 167; in Strafford's trial, ii. 185, 185-7; in English Church-reform movement, ii. 197; is for Limited Episcopacy, ii. 215-6, 284, 286; his part in the "Grand Remonstrance," ii. 319, 337; his part in the attempted arrest of the Five Members, ii. 339-40, 344, 346; his flight, ii. 350; in the Royalist army, ii. 429, 442; in the episode of Montrose in Scotland, iii. 345-6, 362-3; at the fag end of Civil War, iii. 370, 375, 376; a "Delinquent," iii. 421; with Henrietta Maria at the French Court, iii. 494. For further references to, see Bristol, 2nd Earl of.

DIGBY, Sir John (afterwards 3rd Earl of Bristol), ii. 442.

DIGBY, Sir Kenelm : i. 532, 627; his conversion to Rome, 686; at Paris, i. 757-9; on a Catholic committee to raise contributions towards the First "Bishops' War," ii. 50; treatises and works by, iii. 448, 449; under the Protectorate, v. 76; connexion with the Royal Society, vi. 394, 396; mentioned among Men of Letters of the Restoration, vi. 294, 296-7.

"DIGGERS, the," a sect, iv. 48.

DIGGES, Leonard : his verses on Shakespeare, i. 236, 330, 331.

DILLINGHAM, Thomas, of Dean, ii. 573 note.

DILLON, Wentworth, Lord, iv. 23 : see Roscommon, 4th Earl of.

DILLON, a pirate, v. 244.

DIODATI, the family of, i. 98-102; v. 173 note.

DIODATI, Anne, i. 99.

DIODATI, Carolo, of Geneva, i. 99, 101; Marie Mei, his wife, i. 99; his children, i. 99.

DIODATI, Charles (Milton's friend), his connexions and early life, i. 98, 101, 102, 103, 103 note; at Trinity College, Oxford, i. 161-2, 210, 626; Latin verses by, in 1623, i. 107; meetings and correspondence with Milton, i. 161-6 and notes, 226-8, 623, 642-6 : see also Milton; incorporated M.A. at Cambridge, i. 219; his death, i. 829-30, 830 note, 832-3; ii. 80-5; Milton's Epitaphium Damonis in memory of, ii. 85-94 and notes; Milton's letters to, published in 1674, vi. 723.

DIODATI, Dr. Jean or Giovanni, Genevese theologian and translator of Bible, uncle of Charles Diodati, i. 99, 100, 102; his wife, Madeleine Burlamaqui, i. 100; his reception of Milton at Geneva, i. 832-3; v. 173; mentioned in Milton's Defensio Secunda, iv. 637; in the Morus Controversy, v. 160-1, 173, 193-4, 206, 208.

DIODATI, John, brother of Charles, i. 101, 103, 645 note.

DIODATI, Joseph, i. 99.

DIODATI, Madeleine, i. 99.

DIODATI, Marie, i. 99.

DIODATI, Michele, Gonfaloniere of Lucca, i. 99; Anna Buonvisi, his wife, i. 99.

DIODATI, Philadelphia, sister of Charles Diodati, i. 101, 103, 645 note; her death, i. 829.

DIODATI, Pompeio : his wife, Laura Calandrini, i. 99.

DIODATI, Samuel, i. 99.

DIODATI, Dr. Theodore, London physician and father of Charles Diodati, i. 100-2; his second marriage, i. 645 note, 827; account of, ii. 81-3, 83 note; 207, 357.

DIODATI, William, emigrant to America, i. 102 note.

" DIRECTORY OF WORSHIP," iii. 172-3 : see *Assembly, Westminster.*

" DISCOURSE ON EPISCOPACY " : see *Brooke*, 2nd Lord.

" DISINTERRING " ORDER, the, of 1660, vi. 113-5.

DISNEY, Mr., and the boy-portrait of Milton, i. 309 note.

DIVES, Sir Lewis: colonel in the King's army, ii. 442.

DIVORCE : Milton's *Tracts on the Doctrine and Discipline of*, see *Milton*, Writings of.

DIVORCERS, sect of, iii. 155; v. 15.

DIXON, actor, vi. 350.

DIXWELL, John (Regicide), signs the death-warrant of Charles I., iii. 720; in the Fourth Council of State of the Commonwealth, iv. 354 ; v. 456, 519; in the Restored Rump, v. 454 ; in the Quest of the Regicides, vi. 28, 44 ; in the Indemnity Bill of 1660, vi. 54 ; in Bill of Attainder, vi. 115 ; subsequent fate of, vi. 115 note.

DOCEMIUS, of Hamburg, iii. 202.

" DOCTRINAL PURITANS," a term of reproach invented and circulated by Laud, i. 358, 364.

DOD, Rev. Mr., Puritan minister, suspended by Laud, i. 402.

DODD, William, master of the Scriveners' Company, i. 62.

DOGE of Venice, State letter to the, v. 243.

DOGGE, Edward, fellow-graduate of Milton at Cambridge, i. 218.

DOLBEN, Dr. David, Bishop of Bangor, i. 388, 674.

DOLBEN, Dr. John, nephew of Archbishop Williams, vi. 419.

DOLLAM, Mr., of Blackfriars, i. 829.

DOLLE, W., engraver, vi. 684, 687, 713.

DOMENICHINO, Italian painter, i. 763, 815.

" DON QUIXOTE," John Phillips's English translation of, vi. 768.

DONI, Giovanni Battista, Florentine, i. 797, 799, 822, 823 note.

DONNE, Edward, fellow-student of Milton at Christ's College, Cambridge, i. 111.

DONNE, Dr. John, poet, i. 451, 470 ; account of, i. 485-9, 491, 492, 493, 496, 498, 500, 503, 516, 521, 528, 590 note ; his portrait by Marshall, iii. 455, 459 note ; v. 261-2 note ; vi. 515.

DONNE, Marmaduke, Presbyter of London, i. 111.

DOOLITTLE, Thomas, Nonconformist, vi. 232 note.

DORCHESTER, Dudley Carleton, Viscount; in the Privy Council of Charles I., i. 240 note, 381, 597 note ; his death in 1632, i. 386.

DORCHESTER, Henry Pierrepoint, Marquis of (son of 1st Earl of Kingston), in the Privy Council of the Restoration, vi. 18 ; in the Convention Parliament, vi. 22 ; his daughter Anne married to Lord Roos, vi. 639.

DORCHESTER, Marchioness of (Lady Catherine Stanley, daughter of 7th Earl of Derby, and wife of the preceding Earl), v. 263.

DORISLAUS, Dr. Isaac, Advocate of the Parliamentarian army, ii. 443 ; in the King's trial, iii. 706 ; assassination of, iv. 49 ; vi. 179 note ; his body dug up, vi. 227.

DORMER, John, in the Restored Rump, v. 454.

DORSET, Anne, Countess of : see *Spencer, Anne.*

DORSET, Thomas Sackville, Lord Buckhurst, 1st Earl of, i. 378.

DORSET, Robert Sackville, 2nd Earl of, son of the above, i. 378.

DORSET, Richard Sackville, 3rd Earl of, i. 378, 591.

DORSET, Edward Sackville, 4th Earl of, in Charles I.'s Privy Council, i. 378-9, 383, 384, 385, 438, 448 ; account of, in the Long Parliament, ii. 152; 168, 278, 280, 283, 336 ; in Royalist army, ii. 428 ; in exile, iii. 561 ; rejoins Charles I. at Hampton Court, iii. 561 ; his death in 1652, i. 379.

DORSET, Richard Sackville, 5th Earl of, v. 660 note ; in the trials of the Regicides, vi. 77 ; his son, Lord Buckhurst, vi. 321.

DORSET, Charles Sackville (Lord Buckhurst), 6th Earl of : in Restoration literature, vi. 321 ; and Nell

Gwynne, vi. 356; and Dryden, vi. 378, 389; his lyrics, vi. 390-1; and *Paradise Lost*, vi. 628-32, 785; and Milton's portrait, i. 309 note.

DORT, Synod of, i. 61, 100, 355-6, 369, 536, 832.

DOUGLAS, Alexander, Parliamentarian officer, ii. 445.

DOUGLAS, Angus, son of the Marquis of Douglas, v. 87.

DOUGLAS, Archibald, Earl of (son of the Marquis of), Scottish Privy Councillor in 1638, i. 707, 722; ii. 15; iv. 208, 561.

DOUGLAS, Lady Anne, Countess of Argyle, ii. 11.

DOUGLAS, the Marquis of, in the Scottish Parliament of 1633, i. 701; in the Scottish Privy Council of Charles I., i. 707; ii. 8; in the episode of Montrose, iii. 367; fined by Cromwell, iv. 561; under the Protectorate, v. 87; his son the Earl of Selkirk : see *Selkirk*.

DOUGLAS, Robert, Presbyterian minister, and Moderator of General Assembly of 1642, ii. 418; iii. 10, 15; in the negotiations at Newcastle, iii. 427; iv. 209; preaches the sermon at the Scottish Coronation of Charles II., iv. 212-3; Moderator of the Scottish General Assembly of 1651, iv. 288; taken prisoner and sent to England, iv. 296; at the dispersion of the General Assembly, iv. 509; v. 90, 95; at the Restoration, vi. 5, 137-8, 149.

DOUGLAS, William : see *Morton*, 9th Earl of.

DOUGLAS of Cavers, Sir William, in the First Bishops' War, ii. 16, 38, 68; in the Second Bishops' War, ii. 130, 132, 143, 190.

DOUNE, James Stewart, Lord of (son of Earl of Moray), Scottish Privy Councillor, i. 707.

DOVE, Major, in the *New Model*, iii. 326.

DOVE, John, in the Restored Rump, v. 454; in the Indemnity Bill, vi. 35, 37, 56 note.

DOVE, Dr. Thomas, Bishop of Peterborough, i. 390.

DOVER, Charles I. at, ii. 353.

DOVER, Henry Carey, 1st Earl of, ii. 48, 332, 428, 441; his son, Viscount Rochfort, ii. 431.

DOVER, Simon, his trial, vi. 478-80.

DOWETT, Francis, Parliamentarian officer, ii. 445.

DOWLAND, musical composer, i. 51.

DOWNAM (or Downham), George, Prælector of Logic in Cambridge University, afterwards Bishop of Derry, i. 265 note, 420; ii. 390, 390 note; vi. 685-6.

DOWNER, Anna, Early Quaker, v. 27.

DOWNES, Andrew, of St. John's College, Regius Professor of 'Greek at Cambridge, i. 118, 152, 262, 267.

DOWNES, Colonel John, signs the death-warrant of Charles I., iii. 720, vi. 28; in Councils of State of the Commonwealth, iv. 354, v. 456, 465, 480; in the Restored Rump, v. 454; at Quest of the Regicides, vi. 44, 49, 54; his trial, vi. 80, 93; his death, vi. 98 note; in Bill of Attainder, vi. 115.

DOWNHAM, John, book-licenser, iii. 255 note, 270, 272, 300, 432, 677; iv. 92, 118, 149 and note.

DOWNING, Calibute, member of Westminster Assembly, ii. 517; and book-licenser, iii. 270.

DOWNING, Emanuel, in Cromwell's Government of Scotland, v. 86.

DOWNING, George, Commissioner to Louis XIV. from the Protector, v. 43-4, 191; Resident for the Protector in the United Provinces, v. 312, 314, 342, 378; account of, v. 378 note, 386, 395; supports Richard's Government, v. 419, 467, 502; dishonourable conduct of, v. 557 and note; knighted, vi. 74; after the Restoration, vi. 199, 228-9; Minister at the Hague, vi. 252, 253.

DRAKE, Dr., physician, iv. 304.

DRAKE, John, Parliamentarian officer, ii. 444.

DRAKE, William, pamphleteer, vi. 109.

DRAMA, the : Ben Jonson and his School, i. 442-4; Dramatists alive in 1632, i. 444-9; first appearance of women on the English stage, i. 449; influence of Puritanism upon,

i. 449-50 ; Prynne's *Histriomastix*, i. 450-1, 579 ; Milton's *Arcades*, and Masques generally, in 1633, i. 578-9, 597-602 ; the great Masque of the Inns of Court entitled *The Triumph of Peace*, i. 580-6; Carew's Masque, *Cœlum Britannicum*, i. 586-7 ; Milton's *Comus*, i. 604, 610-23; the English dramatists of the reign of Charles I., and Davenant's place among them, vi. 276-9; Ordinance for closing theatres, Sept. 1642, v. 81 ; reopened in 1660, vi. 72-3; the Drama of the Restoration, vi. 346-75 ; Dryden and the London theatres in 1667-74, vi. 605-12 ; reaction against Heroic Plays, and the Duke of Buckingham's *Rehearsal* in 1671-2, vi. 612-15 ; Milton's *Samson Agonistes*, vi. 662-78 ; Milton's connexion with dramatic literature and the Acted Drama, i. 578 ; vi. 662-4.

DRAPER, Matthew, Parliamentarian officer, ii. 445.

DRAX, James, Barbadoes merchant, knighted by Cromwell, v. 354 note.

DRAYTON, Michael, poet, i. 451, 453, 464, 474 ; iii. 447.

DRELINCOURT, French Protestant divine, v. 368.

DRING, Thomas, publisher of the 2nd Edition of Milton's Minor Poems (1673), vi. 400, 402, 403, 514, 687, 784.

DROGHEDA, in Ireland, ii. 311 ; storming of, iv. 112.

DRUMLANRIG, the Earl of, vi. 785.

DRUMMOND of Balloch, with the Earl of Montrose, iii. 360, 367.

DRUMMOND of Mackensy, iv. 561.

DRUMMOND of Maderty, David, with the Earl of Montrose, iii. 351.

DRUMMOND of Riccarton, ii. 143, 190.

DRUMMOND, . John : see *Perth*, 2nd Earl of.

DRUMMOND, Lord, iii. 351.

DRUMMOND, Sir John, son of Earl of Perth, with the Earl of Montrose, iii. 351 ; fined by Cromwell, iv. 560.

DRUMMOND of˙ Hawthornden, Sir John, father of the poet, i. 465.

DRUMMOND of Hawthornden, William,

Scottish poet : visit of Ben Jonson to, i. 434, 439, 486 ; account of his life and writings, i. 465-8, 511, 512, Milton's readings in, i. 575; Edward Phillips's edition of his Poems, v. 263.

DRYDEN, Sir John, uncle of the poet, member for the County of Northampton in the Long Parliament, ii. 173.

DRYDEN, John, Poet : his opinion of Sylvester's *Du Bartas*, i. 91 ; 437, 439, 470, 484, 514; his opinion of Milton, i. 575 ; ii. 173 ; iii. 326 ; in official employment under Thurloe for Oliver Cromwell, v. 375-6 ; vi. 15 ; among Men of Letters under the Protectorate, v. 76, 77 ; his Stanzas to the memory of Cromwell, vi. 15-6; Restoration Verses by, vi. 15-6; in the Literature of the Restoration, vi. 316-7; early dramas by, vi. 353-6, 366-75; as chief of the Restoration dramatists, vi. 375-6; his *Annus Mirabilis*, vi. 376-8, 388; his *Essay of Dramatic Poesy*, vi. 378-87, 388, 633-5; Fellow of the Royal Society, vi. 396; registration of works by, vi. 514-5; from 1667 to 1670, vi. 605-7; as Poet-Laureate, vi. 608-10 ; in the Blank Verse Controversy, vi. 633-4; visits Milton, vi. 709-10; from 1670 to 1674, vi. 611-2; reaction against his Heroic Plays, vi. 613-5 ; satirised by Butler, vi. 618 ; in connexion with Milton and *Paradise Lost*, vi. 629, 631-2, 633-5, 637, 682, 776-8, 785 ; his Opera from *Paradise Lost*, vi. 711-2, 717 note.

DU BARTAS, Guillaume de Salluste, French poet, i. 89, 91-4, 457 ; vi. 530, 544.

DUCKINFIELD, John, Lieutenant-Colonel, v. 470, 487 ; v. 491.

DUDHOPE, John Scrimgeour, 3rd Viscount, fined by Cromwell, iv. 561.

DUDLEY, Edward Sutton, 9th Lord, deceased in 1643, ii. 430.

DUDLEY, Thomas, Governor of Massachusetts in 1634, ii. 549, 599.

DUFFUS, Alexander Sutherland, 1st Lord, iv. 561.

DUGARD, William, printer, prints the *Eikon Basilike*, iv. 148 ; is com-

mited to Newgate by Order of Council, Feb. 1649-50, for printing Salmasius's *Defensio Regia*, iv. 152, 225; his friendship with Milton, and the story of " Pamela's Prayer " in *Eikon Basilike*, iv. 249-50 note; prints for the Council Milton's *Pro Populo Anglicano Defensio*, iv. 251, 312, 313; also the Racovian Catechism, iv. 423, 438; in other Council printing business, iv. 447, 448; prints Phillips's *Apologia*, iv. 470-4; account of his career, vi. 399, 403; his wife, Mrs. Dugard, iv. 252; his daughter, Lydia, vi. 403.

DUGDALE, William, the Antiquary, v. 76; vi. 294, 296.

DUKE, actor, vi. 349.

DUKE HUMPHREY'S WALK, in Old St. Paul's Church, i. 48.

DUMBARTON CASTLE held by Scottish army in First Bishops' War, ii. 56.

DUMFRIES, William Crichton, Earl of, Scottish Privy Councillor, i. 707; ii. 15.

DU MOULIN, the family of, v. 215-6, 218 note.

DU MOULIN, Dr. Peter (elder), French Protestant theologian, v. 215, 218 note; referred to by Milton in his letter to Jean Labadie as Du Moulin of Nismes, v. 592.

DU MOULIN, Peter, D.D. at Leyden, eldest son of the preceding (Royalist and Episcopalian), account of, and of his authorship of the *Regii Sanguinis Clamor*, v. 216-25, 218 note; his intimacy with the Boyle family, v. 234-5, 235 note, 267; vicar of Bradwell in Bucks, v. 276, 276 note; his preferments at the Restoration, vi. 212-3.

DU MOULIN, Lewis, Doctor of Physic at Leyden, younger son of Dr. Peter (elder), a Parliamentarian and Independent, v. 73, 113, 215-6, 218 note; his degradation at the Restoration, vi. 213.

DU MOULIN, Mary, daughter of Dr. Peter (elder), her interview with Charles II. at Breda, v. 218, 218 note.

DUN, the Laird of, i. 732.

DUN, Mr., of Berwick, iv. 491.

DUN, William, fellow-graduate of Milton at Cambridge, i. 218, 258.

DUNBAR, Battle of, iv. 200-1.

DUNCH, Edmund, of Little Wittenham, Berks, relative of Cromwell, and created by him Baron Burnell, v. 354 note.

DUNCH, Mr. Edmund, in projected Royalist Insurrection, v. 473; in the Restored Rump, v. 454; v. 478.

DUNCHES of Berkshire, the: relations of the Protector, v. 307.

DUNCOMBE, scholar of St. Paul's, and afterwards a colonel of dragoons at Edgehill, i. 82.

DUNCOMBE, Sir John, Chancellor of the Exchequer, vi. 264, 591.

DUNDAS, Walter, Governor of Edinburgh Castle in the war with Cromwell, iv. 201.

DUNDAS, the young Laird of (Cromwellian), iv. 283.

DUNDAS, William (Cromwellian), vi. 135.

DUNDEE, siege of, by Monk, iv. 295-6.

DUNDONALD, the family of, ii. 418.

DUNFERMLINE, the Earl of, Commissioner for the Scots in First " Bishops' War," ii. 68; in the deputation to Charles I. from Scottish Committee of the Estates, ii. 130, 143, 190, 292; Commissioner to the General Assembly of 1642, ii. 418; with Scottish Auxiliary Army in England, iii. 37; in the Negotiations at Newcastle, iii. 412; in English and Scottish disputes, iii. 509; with Charles I: at Holmby, iii. 540-2; in the Scottish Parliament of 1650, iv. 212.

DUNGANNON, Lord (Colonel Marcus Trevor), a subscriber to the fourth edition of *Paradise Lost*, vi. 785.

DUNGARVAN, Charles Boyle, Viscount, son of the 2nd Earl of Cork, and pupil of Dr. Peter Du Moulin, v. 224, 235, 267.

DUNKELD, Bishop of, deposed in 1638, ii. 42.

DUNKIRK, siege of, v. 340; captured, v. 392; 426-7; sale of, vi. 251.

DUNMORE, John, stationer, vi. 647 note.

DUNNING, William, member of Westminster Assembly, ii. 518.

DUNSMORE, Lord : see *Chichester*, Earl of.

DUNSTER, Charles, his investigation of Milton's early readings, i. 89 note, 96.

DUNSTER, Henry, ii. 563.

DUNTON, John, bookseller, vi. 769.

DUPORT, James, Professor of Greek at Cambridge and Master of Magdalen, i. 121, 152, 247, 253, 509-10, 624, 648, 649.

DUPPA, Dr. Brian, Dean of Christ Church, and Tutor to Prince Charles, i. 625-6, 647; Bishop of Chichester, i. 674; in the Long Parliament, ii. 150; Bishop of Salisbury, ii. 325, 335; his interest in Shotover Forest, ii. 498; at the Treaty of Newport, iii. 606; in the Church Question after the Restoration, vi. 61; Bishop of Winchester in Nov. 1660, vi. 105, 245; his connexion with the *Eikon Basilike*, vi. 429, 432; death of, vi. 434-6.

DUREL, John, native of St. Helier's in Jersey, and author of one of the Oxford Tracts for Episcopacy, ii. 367-9, 367-8 note.

DURHAM : Charles I. at, ii. 58; English forces at, during Second Bishops' War, ii. 141; foundation of a College in, v. 75.

DURHAM, James, Presbyterian minister, iv. 209; v. 90.

DURIE, John (called sometimes DURÆUS or DUREE): account of, in footnote, ii. 367-8; ii. 367; as member of Westminster Assembly, ii. 517-8; iii. 229, 392 note; his Church-conciliation Scheme, ii. 517; iii. 663; v. 291, 295; vi. 199; minister of the English Merchants' Kirk at Rotterdam in 1645, ii. 518; Hartlib and, iii. 194-7, 217-8, 221, 228, 230; Prynne and, iii. 298; in the Council Order Books, iv. 228; Keeper of the Library of St. James's in succession to Mr. Patrick Young, iv. 229-30, 315, 351; translates into French Milton's *Eikonoklastes*, v. 315, 448; vi. 188; Christopher Arnold in London and, iv. 351;

in Church Questions, iv. 392, 438; secretary to Whitlocke in the embassy to Sweden in 1653, iv. 513; ordinance for donation of land or income to, iv. 565 note; Morus at Amsterdam in 1654 and, iv. 630-1; in correspondence with Milton, iv. 631; v. 158, 200; agent for the Protectorate in Switzerland, v. 41-2, 244; letter of, to Hartlib, in 1656, v. 72 note; Milton in Petty France and, v. 230, 236; as a member of the *Invisible College*, v. 235; his daughter marries Henry Oldenburg, v. 236; vi. 459; reference to, in Milton's letter to Labadie, v. 592, 594; after the Restoration, vi. 199; abroad, vi. 452.

DURY, Giles, appointed by the Council to write the *Weekly Intelligence*, v. 672; becomes a Restoration journalist, vi. 202, 324-5.

DUTCH, the: see *United Provinces*.

DUTTON, John, of Sherborne in Gloucestershire, Esq., brother of Sir Ralph Dutton, iv. 617; v. 306.

DUTTON, Sir Ralph, of Gloucestershire, iv. 616.

DUTTON, William, son and heir of Sir Ralph, a ward of Cromwell, iv. 616-20, 619-20 note; his marriage, v. 306 and note.

DUVAL, Sir Gustavus, knighted by Cromwell in 1656, v. 270.

DYER, Mrs., a New England Antinomian, iii. 150, 151-2 note.

DYMOCK, Captain, Parliamentarian officer, ii. 445.

DYMOCK, Sir Edward, the King's Champion at Coronation of Charles II., vi. 157.

DYSART, Earl of : see *Murray, Will.*

E

EACHARD, Dr., a subscriber to the fourth edition of *Paradise Lost*, vi. 785.

EARLE, Augustin, of Lincoln, i. 112.

EARLE, Sergeant Erasmus, in the Restored Rump, v. 454.

EARLE, Dr. John, of Bishopstone, Wilts: author of *Microsmography*

in 1628, i. 527 ; ii. 513 note ; one of the Falkland-Hyde coterie, i. 533, 534 ; his Latin translation of the *Eikon Basilike*, iv. 131 ; under the Protectorate, v. 76 ; at the Restoration, vi. 7 ; in the Church Question, vi. 61 ; Dean of Westminster, vi. 227, 294-5 ; Bishop of Worcester, vi. 439.

EARLE, Richard, fellow-commoner of Christ's College, Cambridge, and Milton's fellow-student, i. 112, 149.

EARLE, Sir Walter, in the Long Parliament, ii. 172 ; Parliamentarian officer, ii. 445 ; at the surrender of Charles I. by the Scots, iii. 510 ; in Oliver's First Parliament, v. 5.

EAST INDIA COMPANY, in London ; factories, of at *Surat* and on the *Gambia*, v. 101.

EASTLAND, an actress in the King's Company, vi. 350.

EATON, John, Antinomian preacher, iii. 151, 678.

EATON, Nathaniel, first Principal of Harvard College, ii. 563.

EATON, Theophilus, first Governor of Newhaven in New England, ii. 550, 599.

ECHLIN, Robert, Irish Bishop, i. 420, 421.

ECLECTICS, or quasi - Presbyterians, v. 55.

EDEN, Dr., of Trinity Hall, Cambridge, iii. 93.

EDINBURGH : Charles I.'s Coronation at, in 1633, i. 699 ; the Parliament of 1633 at, i. 701 ; royal command sent to official persons in, to attend Holy Communion, i. 704 ; creation of a new bishopric for, with St. Giles's Church for a Cathedral, i. 705 ; the first two bishops of, i. 705-6 ; Johnstone of Warriston a lawyer in, i. 711 ; Andrew Ramsay and Henry Rollock ministers in, i. 711-2 ; the historian, Calderwood, in, after return from exile, i. 712 ; printing of the new Service Book by the King's printer in, i. 717, 718 note ; the Jenny Geddes riot at, in July 1637, i. 719-21 ; the Scottish Supplicants in, i. 722 ; Royal Proclamations at the Cross of, i.

723 ; Montrose joins the Supplicants at, i. 724 ; one supreme or central *Table* permanent in, i. 724 ; royal proclamations and counter-proclamations of the supplicating nobles, at, i. 725-6 ; appeal of Archibald Johnstone to the people of Scotland delivered in the High Street of, i. 726 ; the Tables summoned again to, i. 726 ; the *Scottish Covenant* of 1638 signed at Greyfriars Church in, i. 727-32 ; the Marquis of Hamilton as King's Commissioner stays at, ii. 15 ; the Covenanters at, ii. 15 ; the Covenanting chiefs meet at, ii. 19 ; the Marquis of Hamilton back in, after his return to Court, ii. 20-1, 26 ; Lord Lorne and the Aberdeen Deputation in, ii. 28 ; the Marquis of Hamilton back in, after his second return to the English Court, ii. 30 ; Royal Proclamations ii. 32-5 ; the Judges of the Court of Session and the "King's Covenant," ii. 35 ; preparations of the Covenanters at, for the coming General Assembly to be held at Glasgow, ii. 35-6 ; references to, in the account of the Glasgow Assembly of 1638, ii. 38, 42 ; the General Assembly of 1639 appointed to be held in, ii. 42 ; Royal Proclamation read at the Cross of, ii. 42 ; an incident of the First "Bishops' War," in the High Street of, ii. 43 ; General Leslie among the Covenanting chiefs in, ii. 53 ; preparations for the First "Bishops' War" in, ii. 54, 55 ; the seizing of the Castle of, by the Scottish army, ii. 56 ; Marquis of Huntley and Lord Gordon imprisoned in the Castle of, ii. 57 ; Council of Covenanting chiefs at, ii. 59 ; strengthening of the approaches to, ii. 59 ; Dr. Moysley, English Vicar of Newark, on a visit at, is entrusted by Henderson with letters to Charles I. at Newcastle, ii. 60-1 ; Baillie's letter to Spang, describing the position of the Scottish army on Dunse Law, commanding the direct road from Berwick to, ii. 65 ; the army's money-supplies from, i. 66 ; lawyers of, serve as covenanters

in the First Bishops' War, ii. 66; the
King appoints Traquair as his Commissioner at the proposed Assembly
and Parliament at, ii. 71 ; General
Assembly of 1639 meets at, ii. 122;
meeting of the Parliament of 1639
at, ii. 122; the King places General
Ruthven as Commander of the
Castle of, ii. 137 ; the General Assembly of 1641 at, ii. 287, 290 ;
incident of the Earl of Montrose in
his youth in the High Street of, ii.
293-4 ; Montrose's lodgings in the
Canongate of, ii. 296 ; Napier's
mansion of Merchiston near, ii. 296 ;
trial and execution of the Laird of
Ladywell at, ii. 301 ; the King's
visit to, in 1641, ii. 291, 301-2 ; iii.
17, 304, 427 ; the Earl of Montrose
imprisoned in the Castle of, iii. 340-
1; the Sub-Committee of Estates, and
the Earl of Argyle at, ii. 292-3 ; the
Incident, ii. 304-6; final business of
the Parliament of 1641, and Charles's
departure from, ii. 307-8 ; the *Solemn
League and Covenant* drafted by
Henderson, iii. 12 ; v. 549 ; and
signed by the Scottish nobles in, iii.
13 ; joint embassy of the Westminster
Assembly and the English Parliament to the Scottish Convention of
Estates and to the Scottish General
Assembly sitting at, iii. 7, 10, 36 ;
negotiations concerning the Solemn
League and Covenant between London and, iii. 38 ; Henderson and
other Commissioners sent to the
Westminster Assembly, iii. 15 : see
Assembly, Westminster ; a stationary
Committee of Estates appointed at,
iii. 40; sentence of excommunication
pronounced against Montrose in the
High Church of, iii. 346; the Marquis
of Argyle leaves, with a commission
from the Parliament, in pursuit of
Montrose, iii. 349 ; Argyle returns
alone to, and resigns his commission,
iii. 353 ; the Parliament at, pro-
nounces sentence of high treason on
Montrose, iii. 357 ; submission of,
to Montrose, after the Battle of
Kilsyth, iii. 361 ; the death of
Alexander Henderson at, iii. 428-9,
429 note ; v. 549 ; a snatch vote of

the Scottish Parliament or Convention of Estates at, in favour of the
King's interests, iii. 508-9 ; Baillie's
comments written from, upon the
Presbyterian Rising in London, iii.
562-3 ; Lord Loudoun and Lauderdale and the other Scottish Commissioners return to, at the dissolution of the Committee of the Two
Kingdoms and the ending of the
Scottish Alliance, iii. 585, 588,
589 ; Charles II. proclaimed at
the Cross of, iv. 19 ; movements
of the two Scottish armies, of the
Committee of Estates and of Anti-
Engagers, round about, iii. 621 ;
Cromwell's first visit to, iii. 622; iv.
21 ; reference to the annual General
Assemblies in, iv. 62 ; General Assembly of 1649 at, iv. 122 ; death of
the poet Drummond at, in 1649, v.
263; Montrose's last days and execution at, iv. 184, 185, 186 ; meeting
of General Assembly of 1650 at,
iv. 190 ; Cromwell with his army
approaches, iv. 197, 198 ; Leslie's
army on the hills round about, iv.
198 ; Cromwell in possession of,
after Dunbar, iv. 201, 210, 211,
279 ; Cromwell's illness at, iv.
278-9 ; behaviour of the " Army of
Sectaries " at, iv. 279 ; prosperous
condition of, described by Cromwell
in a letter to Bradshaw, iv. 280 ;
contentment of the inhabitants while
under Cromwell's management of, iv.
362; traces of English Puritanism
left in, since 1650-1, iv. 281 ; Cromwell breaks up his camp near, and
marches north, iv. 287 ; English
judges administer justice in, after the
union with Scotland, iv. 364 ; the
English army has one of its four
chief stations at, iv. 365 ; the
General Assembly of 1652 at, iv.
509 ; the General Assembly of
1653 at, dispersed by an order
of the English Parliament, iv. 509-
10 ; Mr. Robert Leighton, Principal
of the University of, v. 88, 90, 349 ;
General Monk's Council sitting in,
v. 86; his army in, v. 87 ; leaders
of the *Resolutioner* clergy and
of the *Protesters* living in, v. 90 ;

members of the Scottish Privy Council sent back from London to their posts at, by order of the Protector, v. 115; the Provost of, in 1656-7, v. 129, 349 note; order of the English Council for a grant of money to the University of, v. 348-9; officering of the regiments at, v. 470; negotiations with Monk at, v. 496-501; Monk's departure from, v. 512; after the Restoration, vi. 129, 132-3; arrests of Chiesly, Stewart, and Govan in, vi. 133; escape of Johnstone of Warriston, and arrest of the twelve Protesters, vi. 133-4, 135, 137; letters of the King to the Presbytery of, vi. 137, 140, 141; the Parliament of 1661 at, vi. 140, 142-9, 143, 145, 149, 158; State trials at, vi. 140, 150; loss of the Scottish Records on their way to, vi. 141; execution of Argyle at, vi. 160; and of Guthrie and Govan at, vi. 160-1.

EDGEHILL, battle of, Oct. 23, 1642, ii. 454-6.

EDMUNDS, Sir Thomas, i. 381.

EDWARD III. (England), a statute of, referred to, i. 180.

EDWARD IV. (England), at the Battle of Mortimer's Cross, i. 607.

EDWARD V. (England), as Prince of Wales, i. 607.

EDWARD, Prince, younger son of the Queen of Bohemia, and brother of Prince Rupert, iv. 276-7; vi. 71; at Coronation of Charles II., vi. 152.

EDWARDS, Humphrey, signs death-warrant of Charles I., iii. 720, vi. 28; deceased in 1660, vi. 54.

EDWARDS, Mr., a lecturer, suspended by Laud, i. 402.

EDWARDS, Thomas, account of, ii. 594-5; iii. 110; his anti-toleration writings, iii. 130-5, 142-3, 146, 149, 190, 298; his Gangraena, iii. 141-2, 191-2 and notes, 393, 536; his notice of Milton's Divorce Doctrine, iii 467-8; mentioned by Milton, iii. 469-70; denounced by the Army Agitators, iii. 536.

EGERTON, Lady Alice, daughter of the 1st Earl of Bridgewater: her part in Milton's Comus, i. 588, 589, 598, 609, 611, 614; ii. 80; married to Earl of Carbery, iv. 246 note; vi. 300.

EGERTON, Lady Arabella, sister of the above, married to Lord St. John of Bletso, i. 588, 589.

EGERTON, Lady Catherine, sister of the above, i. 588.

EGERTON, Colonel, in projected Royalist rising in 1649, v. 473, 474, 477.

EGERTON, Lady Elizabeth, daughter of the 1st Earl of Bridgewater, i. 588.

EGERTON, Lady Frances, sister of the above: married to Lord Hobart, i. 588, 589, 596.

EGERTON, John, 1st Earl of Bridgewater: see Bridgewater, 1st Earl of.

EGERTON, John, Viscount Brackley, son of the above: see Bridgewater, 2nd Earl of.

EGERTON, John, Viscount Brackley, son of the above: see Bridgewater, 3rd Earl of.

EGERTON, Lady Magdalen, daughter of the 1st Earl of Bridgewater, i. 588.

EGERTON, Lady Mary, sister of the above, i. 588, 589, 598.

EGERTON, Mr., a leader in the English Presbyterian Movement, ii. 532.

EGERTON, Lady Penelope, daughter of the 1st Earl of Bridgewater, i. 588.

EGERTON, Sir Thomas, father of the 1st Earl of Bridgewater: see Ellesmere, Lord Chancellor.

EGERTON, Mr. Thomas, younger son of the 1st Earl of Bridgewater, and one of the actors in Comus, i. 587, 588, 589, 598, 609, 611; ii. 80: see Bridgewater, 2nd Earl of.

EGERTON, Sir William, younger son of the 2nd Earl of Bridgewater: at the Coronation of Charles II. in 1661, vi. 151.

EGLINTOUN, Alexander Montgomery, 6th Earl of, i. 710, 722; ii. 16, 38, 65; at the General Assembly of 1642, ii. 418; with the Scottish Auxiliary Army in England, iii. 37; one of the anti-Engagers in Scotland, iii. 589, 621; after Dunbar, iv. 202, 208; 212, 560, 561; in London, v. 94.

"EIKON AKLASTOS," iv. 349-50; vi. 188.

"EIKON BASILIKE," the, iv. 33-7, 129-45; account of trade history of, iv. 147-9, 149 note; story of Bishop Gauden's authorship of the, vi. 423-40.

"EIKONOKLASTES": see *Milton*, Writings of.

EIZEN, Albert van, v. 290.

EJECTORS and TRIERS, Cromwell's, v. 52-4, 139, 315, 343-4.

ELCHO, David, Lord, son of the 1st Earl of Wemyss, in the General Assembly of 1642, ii. 418; in the Episode of Montrose in Scotland, iii. 351, 361; in a deputation to Cromwell in the North, iii. 621-2.

ELDRIDGE, Mr., sequestration of his effects, iii. 478.

ELECTOR PALATINE, the, ii. 52, 342, 343, 345; iii. 712; iv. 79.

"ELEGIARUM LIBER": see *Milton*, Writings of.

"ELEMENTA PHILOSOPHICA DE CIVE," by Hobbes, vi. 280.

ELGIN, Bruce of Whorlton, 1st Earl of, Parliamentarian peer, ii. 431.

ELIOT, Sir John, indicted in Star Chamber and committed to the Tower, i. 216; in Charles I.'s Third Parliament, i. 375, 522; his death in 1640, ii. 160, 161, 163.

ELIOT, John, New England minister, ii. 556.

ELIZABETH, Queen, i. 4, 87, 595.

ELIZABETH, Princess, daughter of James I. of England, married to the Elector Palatine Frederick, and known as the "Ex-Queen of Bohemia" and "Queen of Hearts," i. 60, 100; Cambridge verses on her birth, i. 649; in correspondence with Charles I., i. 748; with Charles II.'s Court at the Hague, iv. 25, 28, 29 note; at the Restoration of Charles II., vi. 6-7; her friendship with Salmasius, iv. 166; in correspondence with Montrose, iv. 181.

ELIZABETH, Princess, daughter of Charles I., iii. 375, 556, 714, 723; her death, iv. 214.

ELLESMERE, Lord Chancellor (Sir Thomas Egerton), i. 348, 350, 380, 438, 485, 587, 588, 594 and note.

ELLIOT of Stobbs, fined by Cromwell, iv. 561.

ELLIS, Howard, member of Westminster Assembly, ii. 518.

ELLIS, John, a book-licenser, iii. 270.

ELLIS, Joseph, ii. 587.

ELLIS, Robert, son of Robert Ellis in Essex, a sizar and fellow-student of Milton at Christ's College, i. 112.

ELLIS, Sir William, v. 354 note; created a baronet, v. 356; supports Richard's Protectorate, v. 418; in Richard's Parliament, v. 430; in the Restored Rump, v. 454; Solicitor-General in the Restored Long Parliament, v. 545.

ELLIS, William, master of a ship called *The Little Lewis*, charged with a robbery, v. 372, 378-9.

ELLSTON, John, in Mr. Powell's will, iii. 636-7, 639 and note.

ELLWOOD, Thomas, account of, vi. 467-8, 469-73; his part in Milton's stay at Chalfont St. Giles, vi. 490-3, 495; his imprisonment at Aylesbury, vi. 495-6; his visits to Milton at Chalfont St. Giles, and the story of the completion of *Paradise Lost* and of his suggestion of *Paradise Regained*, vi. 496, 654; his connexion with the family of the Penningtons, vi. 497; his *History of his own Life* and his connexion with the Cromwell Papers, vi. 815-6.

ELPHINSTONE, Alexander, Lord, member of the Scottish Privy Council, i. 707; ii. 15; in Cromwell's Ordinance of Pardon and Grace, iv. 561.

ELPHINSTONE, Sir William, Justice-General of Scotland, and member of the Scottish Privy Council, i. 706; ii. 16.

ELSYNG, Henry, sen., clerk of the House of Lords, v. 285 note.

ELSYNG, Henry, jun., clerk of the Commons in the Long Parliament, ii. 174; iii. 703; v. 285 note.

ELY, Cromwell's place of residence from 1636 to 1640-1, ii. 164.

ELY, Lord, Lord Chancellor of Ireland, i. 689.

ELZEVIR, Dutch printer and publisher,

iv. 158, 164, 166, 318; vi. 792, 795, 796, 797, 798, 799; letter from, to Sir Joseph Williamson, in 1676, concerning the publication of the Milton Manuscripts, vi. 800; 802, 803, 805, 805 note.

EMANUEL, Duke of Savoy, Prince of Piedmont, Letters of State to, v. 40, 184-8, 372-3.

EMANUEL COLLEGE, Cambridge: its constitution in 1621, i. 114; 117, 118, 121, 122, 220, 248, 394; ii. 225.

EMBREY: his salary for service to the Council of State, v. 625.

EMDEN, in Holland, Brownists in, ii. 539.

EMERSON, Elizabeth, of Lambeth, wife of the poet Wither, i. 475.

ENGAGEMENT, the Scottish, or Secret Treaty between Charles I. and the Scottish Commissioners, iii. 586, 588-9, 597; iv. 124, 178 and note.

ENGLAND and the ENGLISH PEOPLE: Religious Statistics of, in 1632: see *Church*; Church Government of, through the reigns of James and Charles: see *Church*; Episcopate of, i. 388-90; vi. 104; Privy Councils of: see *Councils*; Universities of: see *Universities*; in the "period of Thorough": see *Charles I.* and *Laud*; the effects upon, of the Presbyterian Revolt in Scotland in 1638-40, ii. 3-71; in the First and Second "Bishops' Wars" with the Scots: see *Wars*; Charles I.'s government of, without Parliaments: see *Charles I.*; the Parliament of 1640-1 ("Long Parliament"), ii. 150-73; Church-reform Movement in, ii. 193-202; Parties in, in 1641, ii. 274-85; the First and Second Civil Wars in: see *Wars*; the Solemn League and Covenant between the Scots and: see *Covenants*; the "Committee of the Two Kingdoms," iii. 40-1, 584-5, Sects and Sectaries in 1644, iii. 136-59; imagined map of, as it appeared to the Parliamentarians in 1645, iii. 328-30; the Peerage of: see *Peerage*; Republic of: see *Commonwealth*; Councils of State: see *Councils*; foreign relations of: see *Holland*,

France, Spain, Portugal, Netherlands, Savoy; "bequests" of the Westminster Assembly to, iv. 58-61; the Great Seal of, iv. 100; v. 465; war with Scotland in 1650: see *Wars*; the south of Scotland becomes a province of, iv. 211; changes in the relations of, with Foreign Powers in 1650, iv. 215; occupation of Scotland by, iv. 279-81, 284; incorporation of Scotland with, iv. 302-3, 360-6, 561; retrospect of three years of the history of (1649-51), iv. 306; foreign relations of, in 1653, iv. 377-83; internal affairs of, after the Battle of Worcester, iv. 383-7; Cromwell's supremacy in the government of, iv. 399-407; represented in Cromwell's Supreme Assembly, iv. 501; government of, by Cromwell as Protector (1653-8): see *Cromwell*; through the Protectorate of Richard, the period of Anarchy, and to the Restoration, v. 413-542; in the year of the Restoration, vi. 3-162; through the Clarendon Administration, 1661-7, ii. 221-72; government of, by the Cabal (1667-74), vi. 561-98; division of parties in, into "Whig and Tory," vi. 619: see also under *Church*, *Colonies*, *Wars*, etc.

ENGLAND, New: see *New England*.

"ENGLAND'S REMEMBRANCER," Republican pamphlet in 1656, v. 106.

ENT, Dr. George, and the Royal Society, vi. 396.

EPISCOPACY, ii. 122-3, 124-6; iii. 492, 497-8, 502; a *Treatise on*, by *Divine Right*, by Bishop Hall: see *Hall*; *Discourse on*, by Lord Brooke: see *Brooke*; see also under *Church*, *England*, *Scotland*, *Ireland*.

EPISCOPALIANS, Cromwell's toleration of the, v. 61-4.

"EPISTOLÆ FAMILIARES": see *Milton*, Writings of.

"EPITAPH on the Marchioness of Winchester": see *Milton*, Writings of.

"EPITAPHIUM DAMONIS": see *Milton*, Writings of.

"EPITHALAMIUM upon the marriage

of the Lady Mary Cromwell," by Davenant, vi. 274 note.

ERASMUS, his connexion with Dr. John Colet of St. Paul's, i. 74, 75, 76.

ERASTIANISM in the Westminster Assembly, ii. 606; in the Parliament, iii. 397; alliance of Independency and, iii. 403-4.

ERBURY, William, Anabaptist preacher, iii. 153, 678; iv. 568.

ERISY, Richard, iii. 58, 59.

ERROLL, Gilbert Hay, 10th Earl of, in Cromwell's Ordinance of Pardon and Grace, iv. 561.

ERSKINE, Sir Charles, Scottish Covenanting Commissioner, iii. 510, 578, 579-82.

ERSKINE, Lord, with the Earl of Montrose in 1645, ii. 64-5; iii. 367.

ERSKINE, William, and the Royal Society, vi. 396.

ERYTHRŒUS, James Nicius (G. Rossi), i. 801, 804 note.

ESPAGNE : see D'Espagne.

ESPERNON : see D'Espernon.

"ESSAY OF DRAMATIC POESIE": see Dryden.

ESSEX, Earl of (in Queen Elizabeth's reign), i. 528.

ESSEX, Robert Devereux, 3rd Earl of, Lieutenant-General of the English Army in the First Bishops' War, ii. 50-1, 60, 62, 68; signs a petition to Charles I. to call a Parliament in 1640, ii. 142, 143; in the Long Parliament, ii. 153-4, 157, 168; at Strafford's trial, ii. 185; in Charles's Privy Council, ii. 279, 281; has power to assemble the Trained Bands, ii. 316, 319; sets an armed guard round the two Houses, ii. 325; is Lord Chamberlain in succession to the Earl of Pembroke, ii. 336; 338; refuses to join Charles I. in the Civil War, ii. 413; Commander-in-Chief to the Parliamentarian army, ii. 422, 430, 443; Lord Lieutenant for Staffordshire, ii. 439; character of his regiment, ii. 444; Parliamentarian leader, ii. 448-9; during the first weeks of the Civil War, ii. 453; at the Battle of Edgehill, ii. 454-6; in the March to Turnham Green, ii. 457-8; in winter quarters at Windsor, ii. 458; in the Civil War, ii. 458, 459, 460, 463; at the siege of Reading, ii. 464-5; 466, 467; blamed by the Parliamentarians, ii. 471; is a lay-member of Westminster Assembly, ii. 523; in the Civil War, iii. 35; 39; in the "Committee of the Two Kingdoms," iii. 41; 84, 85; defeated in Cornwall, iii. 167-8, 176-7, 178; is acting against Cromwell, iii. 180; in the prosecution of Milton by Stationers' Company, iii. 297 note; in the debate on "The Power of the Keys" question, iii. 405, 406; retires into private life, iii. 183; 333; proposals of rewards to, iii. 378, 380; his death (Sept. 14, 1646), iii. 381.

ESSEX, Arthur, Baron Capel, created Earl of, at the Coronation of Charles II., vi. 152.

ESSEX, Colonel Charles, his regiment, ii. 444; killed, ii. 455.

ESSEX, Thomas, Parliamentarian officer, ii. 444.

ESSEX, Sir William, Parliamentarian officer under his son, Colonel Essex, ii. 444.

ESSEX HOUSE, ii. 154.

ESTATES : Committee of, in Scotland, ii. 130, 136, 137, 138, 139, 143, 291-2; iii. 588-9, 620-1; iv. 196, 202; the Scottish Convention of, iii. 7, 8, 175, 499, 508-9.

ETCETERA Oath, the, ii. 132.

ETHEREGE, Sir George, among Men of Letters of the Restoration, vi. 320; Plays by, vi. 611.

ETHIE, Earl of : see Northesk, Earl of.

ETON COLLEGE, i. 529-31; ii. 73.

"EUPHUES'S GOLDEN LEGACY," iii. 447.

EUNSON, Mr. James, minister at Airth, v. 115.

EURE, Lord (Royalist), i. 605; killed in the Royalist Army, ii. 429.

EURE, Lord, one of Cromwell's lords, v. 5, 323, 326.

EUSTACE, Sir Maurice, vi. 127.

EUSTON, Earl of : see Grafton, Duke of.

EVANS, Catherine, Early Quaker, v. 27.

EVANS, Thomas, English shipmaster, v. 289.

EVELYN, Colonel Arthur, Parliamentarian officer, ii. 445 ; v. 540.

EVELYN, Sir John, Member for Bletchingley in Surrey, in the Long Parliament, and uncle of Mr. John Evelyn, ii. 173 ; in the Convention Parliament, vi. 23.

EVELYN, Sir John (of Wilts), Member for Ludgershall in Wilts, in the Long Parliament, ii. 173, 416 ; lay member of Westminster Assembly, ii. 524 ; teller for votes of the anti-Presbyterians in Parliament, iii. 408 ; an "Independent," iii. 510 note, 530, 531 ; 565, 566 ; in General Monk's Council of State, v. 544 ; in the Restored Long Parliament, v. 545, 546 ; in the Convention Parliament, vi. 23.

EVELYN, John, author (nephew of Sir John of Surrey), among Men of Letters under the Protectorate, v. 76, 78, 80 note ; his Reply to the "News from Brussels," v. 672 note ; his acquaintance with Clarendon, vi. 250 ; among Men of Letters of the Restoration, vi. 299, 308 ; member of the Royal Society, vi. 392, 394, 396, 459 ; account of his connexion with Edward Phillips, vi. 481, 765-6.

EVENIUS, of Weimar, iii. 202.

EWER, Isaac (Regicide), Lieutenant-Colonel under New Model, iii. 326-328 note ; at the King's Trial, iii. 707 ; in the quarrel between Parliament and Army, iii. 534, 537, 569, 583, 584, 619 ; succeeds Hammond in the Isle of Wight, iii. 626 ; signs death-warrant of Charles I., iii. 720, vi. 28 ; departure of his regiment for Ireland, iv. 56 ; mentions of, in the Council Order Books, iv. 576, 578 ; in Indemnity Bill, vi. 54.

EWINS, Lieutenant-Colonel under New Model, iii. 326.

EXETER, surrender of, iii. 371-2.

EXETER COLLEGE, Oxford, i. 625 ; ii. 225.

EXETER, Thomas Cecil, 1st Earl of, i. 245 note.

EXETER, William Cecil, 2nd Earl of, i. 380 ; ii. 142, 430.

EXETER, John Cecil, 3rd Earl of, ii. 430.

EXPARCH, William, one of the assassins of Anthony Ascham, iv. 234.

EYRE, Colonel William, in the Restored Rump, v. 454, 522 ; at the restoration of the Long Parliament, v. 540.

EYTON, publisher, vi. 514.

F

FAGG, Colonel John, in the Restored Rump, v. 454 ; in the new Council of State, v. 519, 523 ; in the Convention Parliament, vi. 23.

FAGIUS, Paul, professor of Hebrew in Cambridge University in 1549, iii. 256-7.

FAIRBANK, Matthew, under-clerk of Council, iv. 576, v. 624, 625 note.

FAITHORNE, portrait painter, i. 309 note, 567 ; his portraits of Milton, vi. 647-8, 754 note.

FAIRFAX, Colonel Charles, in Cromwell's English army, iv. 402 ; v. 470, 563 ; in Monk's army, vi. 563.

FAIRFAX, Edward, translator of Tasso (brother of the 1st Lord Fairfax), i. 97, 451, 462 ; ii. 171 ; iii. 515.

FAIRFAX, Francis, Parliamentarian officer, ii. 444.

FAIRFAX (of Denton in Yorkshire), Sir Thomas, created 1st Lord (Baron of Cameron in the Scottish Peerage) : in the First Bishops' War, ii. 62 ; account of, ii. 171.

FAIRFAX, Ferdinando, 2nd Lord, son of the 1st Lord, in the First "Bishops' War," ii. 62 ; in the Long Parliament, ii. 171-2 ; his part in the "Grand Remonstrance," ii. 326 ; appointed General-in-Chief for Yorkshire and the Northern Counties in the Parliamentary army, ii. 447-8, 467-9 ; defeated at Atherston Moor, iii. 6, 35, 379-80 ; his death, iii. 593.

FAIRFAX, Lady Mary, daughter of Lord Sheffield, and wife of the preceding, ii. 171.

FAIRFAX, Sir Thomas (afterwards 3rd

Lord), son of the 2nd Lord ; account of, in composition of Long Parliament, ii. 171-2 ; at Cambridge, i. 116 ; with his father in the army of the North, ii. 448, 467-9 ; in the Civil War, ii. 467-9 ; iii. 35, 86 ; at the siege of York, iii. 96 ; at Marston Moor, iii. 97 ; appointed Commander-in-Chief of the New Model Army, iii. 182-3, 182 note ; 326, 331, 331 note, 332, 333 ; at the siege of Oxford, iii. 334 ; at the Battle of Naseby, iii. 335-7 ; at the resumed siege and surrender of Oxford, iii. 471-2 ; at the close of the Civil War, iii. 369, 371, 374, 378, 380 ; in the recruited House of Commons, 402 note ; meets Charles I. on his journey to Holmby House, iii. 514 ; his relations to Presbyterianism, iii. 384 ; in the quarrel between the Parliament and the Army, iii. 522, 531-5 ; his *Rendezvous*, iii. 536-41 ; his displeasure at Joyce's abduction of the King, iii. 543, 543-4 note ; in negotiations between the Army and the Presbyterians, iii. 548 ; his march on London, iii. 553-4 ; reinstates the Houses, iii. 555 ; in conferences with Charles I., iii. 556-7 ; and the Army's *Heads of Proposals*, iii. 557 ; in correspondence with Cromwell, iii. 568 note ; with the Council of War at Putney, iii. 573 ; his remonstrance with the mutinous army, iii. 582-3 ; succeeds his father and becomes Lord Fairfax, iii. 593 ; in the Second Civil War, iii. 593-605 ; besieges Colchester, iii. 594, 596, 601 ; surrender of Colchester to, iii. 605 ; Milton's sonnet to, iii. 688, vi. 688 ; army petitions to, iii. 614-6 ; presides over a General Council of the officers of the army at St. Alban's, iii. 616 ; the Grand Army Remonstrance, with a letter by, presented to the Commons, iii. 619-20 ; letters of Cromwell to, on Scottish affairs, iii. 622 ; his part in the removal of the King to Hurst Castle, iii. 625-6, 627, 630-1 ; removes his headquarters from St. Alban's to Whitehall, iii. 629-30 ; his part in

"Pride's Purge," iii. 695-7 ; on the Commission for the trial of the King, iii. 703 ; attends only the first meeting of the Commission, iii. 706 ; is not present at the King's trial, iii. 707, 708 note ; petitions to, on behalf of the King during the King's last days, iii. 716, 718 ; and the *Agreement of the People*, iv. 7, 10, 11 ; elected among the "Recruiters" to the Rump, v. 456 ; in the First Council of State of the English Republic, iv. 12, 14, 15 ; appointed Supreme General of the Parliamentary Forces, iv. 42 ; in the suppression of the Levellers, iv. 48, 49-51 ; at the *Fairfaxian Creation* at Oxford, iv. 51-2 ; receives the thanks of the House, and is entertained at a great city banquet in London, iv. 53-4 ; allusion to, in Milton's "Tenure of Kings and Magistrates," iv. 70-1 ; present at the appointment of Milton to the Latin Secretaryship, iv. 79, 82 ; present in Council, iv. 87, 145, 147 ; probable intercourse with Milton in 1648-9, iv. 105 ; is attacked in a pamphlet by Lilburne, iv. 119 ; declines to conduct an expedition into Scotland, and resigns his Commission of General-in-Chief of the Army, iv. 192 ; his retirement into private life, iv. 194-6 ; Milton's eulogy of him in the *Defensio Secunda*, iv. 601-2, 606 ; sits in Oliver's First Parliament, v. 5 ; his daughter's marriage to the Duke of Buckingham, v. 320-22 ; his inclination towards a Restoration, v. 337 ; arrest of his son-in-law, and his last interview with Cromwell, v. 357 ; represents Yorkshire in Richard's Parliament, v. 430, 435 ; stands bail for his son-in-law, the Duke of Buckingham, v. 436 ; is at the forced dissolution of Richard's Parliament, v. 442 ; is one of ten non-Parliamentary members of the Council of State of the Restored Rump, v. 456 ; he withdraws into Yorkshire, v. 457 ; reported to be implicated in a projected Royalist Insurrection, v. 473 ; his regiment and General Monk, v. 498 ; in negotiation with Monk, v.

499; is organising a movement in Yorkshire in combination with Monk, v. 514; reappointed to the Council of State at the second restoration of the Rump, v. 520; retires from the Council, v. 523; is in conference with Monk at York, v. 524, 528; is in the new Council of State, v. 543; at the settling of Restoration, v. 700; member of the Convention Parliament, vi. 23; his portrait by Faithorne, vi. 648.

FAIRFAX, Lady Anne, daughter of Lord Vere, and wife of the preceding, ii. 171, 448; her remonstrance at the trial of the King, iii. 707; in her husband's retirement, iv. 192, 194, 195.

FAIRFAX, Mary, daughter of the preceding Lord General Fairfax and his wife Lady Anne: her education by Andrew Marvell, iv. 194-6, 477; her marriage to the Duke of Buckingham, v. 320-2.

FAIRFAX, Sir William, colonel of foot in the Parliamentarian Army in 1642, and killed in 1644, ii. 444.

FALCONBRIDGE (Fauconberg), Thomas Bellasis, 1st Lord: his subscription to the King for the First "Bishops' War," ii. 48; in the Long Parliament (1640), ii. 159; in Royalist Army (made Viscount), ii. 429; escapes with Prince Rupert from the Battle of Marston Moor, and does not return till the Restoration, iii. 96.

FALCONBRIDGE, Thomas Bellasis, Viscount, married to the Lady Mary Cromwell, v. 305-6; Epithalamium, by Davenant, on his marriage, vi. 274 note; is one of Cromwell's lords, v. 323, 326; in embassies to Louis XIV., v. 340, 390-1, 392; in Cromwell's last days, v. 355; supports Richard's Government, v. 417; in correspondence with Henry Cromwell, v. 420-1; during the Protectorate of Richard, v. 421, 426, 438, 439; during the Anarchy, v. 459, 464, 469, 473; his imprisonment in the Tower, v. 477; accepts a colonelcy under Monk, v. 563; in the Convention Parliament, vi. 22;

absent from the Commons at the "Disinterring Order," vi. 113; his brother, Sir Rowland Bellasis, knighted, vi. 151; at the theatre with his wife, vi. 353-4; at the break-up of the Cabal, vi. 598.

FALKLAND, Henry Carey, 1st Viscount, i. 380; Lord-Deputy of Ireland, i. 532-3, 688-9.

FALKLAND, Sir Lucius Carey, 2nd Viscount (eldest son of the Lord-Deputy): at Cambridge, i. 116; succeeds to the title in 1633, ætat. 23, and becomes the centre of the group of Latitudinarians, i. 532-5; Clarendon's account of him, i. 538-40; sonnet by, i. 590 note; one of the writers in Jonsonus Verbius, i. 647; i. 685-6; account of, in the composition of the Long Parliament, ii. 168-9, 174; at Strafford's trial, ii. 185, 187, 188; in the English Church reform movement, ii. 197; in favour of a limited Episcopacy, ii. 215; opposes the "Grand Remonstrance," ii. 319, 320, 321, 322, 328; in the Privy Council, ii. 337; at Charles's Coup d'État, ii. 340, 352; in Charles's Council, ii. 350; joins Charles I. at York, ii. 413; goes to London on business for the King, ii. 453; in a Committee of the House on Westminster Assembly business, ii. 511; killed at the Battle of Newbury, iii. 35.

FALKLAND, 3rd Viscount: his arrest by the Major-Generals, v. 50; reported to be implicated in Projected Royalist Insurrection, v. 473; his release from imprisonment on this account, v. 505; at the Restoration, v. 700; in the Convention Parliament, vi. 23; in the debates on the Indemnity Bill, vi. 40, 173.

FALKLAND, Dowager-Viscountess, widow of 1st Viscount, i. 686.

FALMOUTH, the Earl of (Sir Charles Berkeley), in Privy Council of the Restoration as Comptroller of the Household, vi. 18; his conduct on the occasion of Anne Hyde's marriage, vi. 108, 118; Treasurer of the King's Household, vi. 237; 239; Lord Fitzharding and Earl of Falmouth

in 1664, vi. 253; killed in the war with the Dutch, vi. 254.

FAMILISTS, the Sect of, i. 58; in 1632, i. 342; iii. 152; v. 18.

FANSHAWE, Sir Richard : among Men of Letters under the Protectorate, v. 76, and after the Restoration, vi. 294, 297; registration of his poems in 1667, vi. 515.

FARLEY, Colonel William, in General Monk's army, v. 540.

FARLOWE, landlord of the *Mitre* at Cambridge, i. 138.

FARNABIE, a book-licenser, iii. 270.

FARNABIE, Thomas, schoolmaster in Cripplegate, i. 73, 83, 108, 171; poem of, on death of Edward King, i. 651.

FARNSWORTH, Richard, Early Quaker, v. 26-7; denounced as a heretic, v. 59 note.

FARQUHAR, Sir Robert, fined by Cromwell's Ordinance in 1654, iv. 561.

FARQUHARSONS of Braemar, the, in the episode of Montrose in Scotland, iii. 354.

FARRE, Laurence, servant or agent to Sir Robert Pye, iii. 475; iv. 242.

FARRINGTON, Colonel, under *New Model*, iii. 326.

FAST-DAYS in London, iii. 162.

FAUCHEUR, French Protestant, v. 368.

FAULKE, Colonel, in Cromwell's Irish army, iv. 401, 401 note.

FAWKARD, Rowland, servant of the Council of State, iv. 578.

FAWKES, Guy, i. 174, 179.

FAWNE, Luke, London bookseller, v. 59 note.

FAWNE, Mr. Warden, in the Stationers' Register, vi. 339.

FEAK, Christopher, Anabaptist preacher, iv. 547-8; v. 59 note; in Fifth Monarchy Riot, v. 136.

FEATHERSTONEHAUGH, Sir Timothy, beheaded at Chester after the Battle of Worcester, iv. 297.

FEATLEY, Dr. Daniel, Provost of Chelsea College and Rector of Lambeth, ii. 225; account of, in the list of the Westminster Assembly, ii. 518; 523, 525; his expulsion from the Westminster Assembly, iii. 15; anti-

Toleration tract by, iii. 138, 139, 146, 148; attack on Milton by, iii. 300-1; answered in Milton's *Tetrachordon*, iii. 311-2 and note; his portrait by Marshall, iii. 456, 459 note.

FEILD, William, servant to the Council of State, v. 625.

FELL, Dr., Vice-Chancellor of Oxford University : his resistance to the Parliamentary Visitation and imposition of the Covenant, iii. 546; iv. 51-2.

FELL, Mrs., wife of the Vice-Chancellor, iv. 51.

FELTHAM, Owen, author of *Resolves* (1628, 1631), i. 527-8; one of the writers of *Jonsonus Verbius*, i. 647; among Men of Letters of the Restoration, vi. 294, 297-8.

FELTON, the assassin of the Duke of Buckingham, i. 206-7; ii. 134; hanged at Tyburn, i. 214, 373.

FELTON, Nicholas, Bishop of Ely : his death celebrated by Milton in Latin verse, i. 168.

FELTON, N., verses by, on Edward King's death, i. 651.

FENNER, of the sect of Separatists, i. 679.

FENWICKE, fellow of Christ's College, Cambridge, i. 187, 200.

FENWICKE, merchant of Newcastle, ii. 43.

FENWICK, George, one of the eight Commissioners at the first establishment of the federation of the New England Colonies in 1643, ii. 599.

FENWICK, Colonel George, at the Incorporation of Scotland with the Commonwealth, iv. 303, 360, 363; with Lilburne and the army in Scotland, iv. 402.

FERDINAND II., German Emperor, revolt from allegiance to, by the Bohemians, i. 61.

FERDINAND III. of Germany, v. 315.

FERDINANDO II., Grand Duke of Tuscany, i. 745; Letters of State to, iv. 422, 480, 483, 484, 485, 485-6; Blake's demands on, v. 37; more State Letters to, v. 372, 378-9, 386-7, 391-2, 589.

FERGUS, the chair of, ii. 68.

FERGUSSON, of Craigdarroch, ii. 38.

FERMAT, mathematician, i. 744.

FERNANDEZ, Antonio, v. 377.

FERNE, Dr. Henry, master of Trinity College, Cambridge, and Bishop of Chester, i. 122, 247 ; iii. 609.

FERRAR, John, i. 416.

FERRAR, Nicholas, account of, i. 416-7, 492, 493, 498, 500.

FERRER, Constantine, Parliamentarian officer, ii. 444.

FIDES PUBLICA, or *Public Testimony*, by More, in reply to Milton's *Defensio Secunda*, v. 151, 156-62.

FIELD, Mr., Presbyterian lecturer at Wandsworth, ii. 532.

FIELD, John, printer to Cromwell, v. 351 ; vi. 399.

FIELD, Nathaniel, dramatist, i. 446.

FIELD, Dr. Theophilus, bishop, i. 389, 674.

FIELDEN, Colonel John, in Third Council of State, iv. 273, 314, 315, 322 ; in Fifth Council of State, iv. 355, 449, 450 ; in the Restored Rump, v. 454, 522 ; in the Restored Long Parliament, v. 545.

FIELDING, William : see *Denbigh*, 1st Earl of.

FIELDING, Basil, Lord : see *Denbigh*, 2nd Earl of.

FIELDING, Colonel Richard, Royalist officer, ii. 441 ; at siege of Reading, ii. 465.

FIENNES, Francis, Parliamentarian officer, ii. 445.

FIENNES, Hon. John (third son of Viscount Saye and Sale), Parliamentarian officer, ii. 445 ; Colonel under *New Model*, iii. 327 ; at Battle of Naseby, iii. 335 ; member for Morpeth in the Recruited Commons, iii. 401 ; in the Council Order Books, v. 183-4 ; one of Cromwell's lords, v. 324.

FIENNES, the Hon. Nathaniel (2nd son of Viscount Saye and Sele), called "Young Subtlety" : account of, in Long Parliament, ii. 163-4, 217 ; in a Commission of the Commons to follow Charles I. into Scotland, ii. 273, 315 ; officer in the Parliamentarian army, ii. 445 ; signs a letter of the two Houses to New England Independents, ii. 605 ; his inefficient defence of Bristol, iii. 6 ; his sentence, his pardon, and his restoration to Parliament, iii. 402-3 ; his Parliamentary declaration against Charles I., iii. 598 ; at "Pride's Purge," iii. 696-7 ; during last days of Charles I., iii. 718 ; in Cromwell's Council, iv. 545 ; v. 31, 64 ; in Cromwell's Second Parliament, v. 107, 111, 118, 128, 327 ; in the negotiations of Cromwell with Count Bundt, v. 248, 252-3, 270 ; called "Lord Commissioner," v. 304 ; one of the Privy Council of Second Protectorate, v. 308, 333, 354 ; one of Cromwell's lords, v. 324 ; supports Richard's government, v. 417-8, 421 ; Speaker of the Upper House in Richard's Parliament, v. 429, 442.

FIENNES, William, 1st Viscount Saye and Sele, ii. 49 ; account of, ii. 155 ; vi. 17.

FIFE, regiments from, in First "Bishops' War," ii. 65.

FIFTH Monarchy Riot, v. 132-4 ; Cromwell on the, v. 135-6 : see *Millenarians*.

FILMER, Sir Robert, anti-Milton Tract by, iv. 434-6 and note.

FINCH, Sir Heneage, in the Convention Parliament, vi. 24 ; and the Indemnity Bill, vi. 26, 30-1, 43, 173, 181 ; in the Church Question, vi. 63 ; at the Court of the Restoration, vi. 74 ; at trials of the Regicides, vi. 77, 82 ; in Parliament, vi. 109, 110 ; his opinion of Milton, vi. 195 ; Attorney-General in 1670, Lord Keeper in 1673, vi. 600, 602.

FINCH, John, barrister of Gray's Inn, and actor in the Masque of the Inns of Court, i. 580 ; Speaker in Charles I.'s Third Parliament, and forcibly held in his chair during the passing of the "Three Resolutions," i. 216 ; ii. 162 ; Chief Justice of the Common Pleas, i. 671 ; at the trial of Bishop Williams, i. 683 ; succeeds Lord Keeper Coventry, ii. 128 ; in Charles's Privy Council, ii. 144, 190 ; in the Long Parliament, ii. 149, 152, 173 ; proceedings against, and his escape to Holland, ii. 178

278, 279 ; non-effective Royalist Peer, ii. 430.

FINCH, William, fellow-graduate of Milton at Cambridge, i. 218, 258.

FINDLATER, James Ogilvie, 1st Earl of, in the episode of Montrose in Scotland, iii. 359 ; iv. 561.

FIORETTI, Benedetto, Florentine writer, i. 777, 787.

FIRE of London (1666), vi. 260-2.

FISHER, Jesuit, i. 365-6.

FISHER, John, witness to Milton's signature, vi. 511.

FISHER, Samuel, student at Oxford, i. 210-11.

FISHER, Elizabeth, maid-servant in Milton's house, vi. 717 ; her memories of Milton, vi. 728-31 ; and Milton's nuncupative will, vi. 735-9.

FISHER, Mary, sister of Elizabeth Fisher, her memories of Milton, vi. 731 ; and of Milton's nuncupative will, vi. 737.

FITCH, Colonel Thomas, iv. 402 ; v. 470.

FITHY, David, merchant, v. 590.

FITZHARDING, Lord : see Falmouth, Earl of.

FITZ-HERBERT, Sir Anthony, lawyer of Henry VIII.'s time, i. 327 note.

FITZJAMES, Colonel, v. 121.

FLANDERS, an Auxiliary army sent to, by Cromwell in 1657 to co-operate with the French against Spain, v. 140-1, 295, 339-41.

FLATMAN, Thomas, among Men of Letters of the Restoration, vi. 319, 387 ; 462 ; his lines on Faithorne, vi. 648 ; and the fourth edition of Paradise Lost, vi. 785.

FLAVEL, John, Nonconformist, vi. 232 note.

FLECKNOE, Richard, vi. 311.

FLEETWOOD, Anne, infant grand-daughter of Cromwell : her body dug up, vi. 228.

FLEETWOOD, Charles, of Northampton, vi. 763.

FLEETWOOD, Lieutenant-General Charles (younger brother of the Regicide, and son-in-law of Cromwell) : his family connexions, v. 493, 546 note ; Colonel under New Model, account of, iii. 327 ; at

Battle of Naseby, iii. 336 ; in the recruited House of Commons, iii. 401 ; in the quarrel of Parliament and Army, iii. 534, 536, 537-8 ; with Cromwell's army in Scotland, iv. 192 ; marries Ireton's widow, iv. 366-7 ; Lord Deputy of Ireland, iv. 369-70 ; Commander-in-Chief in Ireland, iv. 401-2 ; in the government of Ireland, iv. 551, v. 98-100 ; appointed one of the major-generals, v. 49 ; in Cromwell's Second Parliament, v. 107 ; opposes the Petition and Advice, v. 124-6, 130-1 ; grant of lands in Ireland to, v. 139 ; at Count Bundt's supper, v. 249; in Cromwell's Court, v. 303-4; at the arrest of Buckingham, v. 322; one of Cromwell's lords, v. 323; sent to Dover to meet the French Embassy, v. 341 ; in successive Councils of State :—in the Third, iv. 273, 314, 315, 321, in the Fourth, 354, in the Council of the Barebones Parliament until 3rd Nov. 1653, iv. 506, 512, 525, in the Councils of the First and Second Protectorates, iv. 545, v. 32 note, 259-60, 308, 333, 345, 346, 352, 354, 374 ; one of Cromwell's Lords, v. 324; intimacy with Milton, v. 381 ; in correspondence with Henry Cromwell during Cromwell's last days, v. 359 ; supposed nomination of, by Cromwell to the Protectorate, v. 414 ; in Richard's Council, v. 417-8 ; a leader of the Wallingford House Party, v. 421, 422, 438-40 ; in Richard's speech to the officers, v. 423 ; in a letter of Henry Cromwell, v. 423-5 ; in Richard's Parliament, v. 430, 441-2 ; at the Restoration of the Rump, v. 445-6, 449, 454, 456, 459, 468, 479, 624 ; at the Republican re-modelling of the army, v. 468-70 ; 480, 487-8, 490, 529; on Committee of Safety, v. 494, 495, 505, 506, 510 ; in correspondence with Monk, v. 496, 497, 499 ; at the Second Restoration of the Rump, v. 514-7, 521 ; removal of his regiments from London, v. 525-6, 528, 562 ; is incapacitated for army service, v. 563 ; is absent from the Restored Long

Parliament, v. 544 note; after the Restoration, vi. 40, 47, 55; among Milton's old friends and associates, vi. 197; in Milton's *Defensio Secunda*, iv. 606, 612.

FLEETWOOD, Edward, messenger to the Council, iv. 578.

FLEETWOOD, Sir George, knight (son of Thomas and grandfather of the Regicide), vi. 493.

FLEETWOOD, George (Regicide), iii. 401; at the trial of Charles I., iii. 712 note; signs the death-warrant, iii. 720, vi. 28; in Cromwell's Second Council of the Barebones Parliament, iv. 525; one of Cromwell's Lords, v. 324; in the Quest and Trials of the Regicides, vi. 43, 49, 54, 80, 81, 94; his subsequent fate, 98 note; in Bill of Attainder, vi. 115; mention of, vi. 493.

FLEETWOOD, Martha, daughter of Charles Fleetwood of Northampton, married to (1) Thomas Milton, (2) Dr. William Coward, vi. 763.

FLEETWOOD, Thomas, first proprietor, in 1564, of the manor-house of the Vache in the parish of Chalfont St. Giles, vi. 493.

FLEMING, Lord (Scottish), one of the Scottish Supplicants in 1637, i. 722; in the First "Bishops' War," ii. 64-5.

FLEMING, John, Lord (3rd Earl of Wigton), iii. 367.

FLEMING, Sir William (Scottish), sent, as bearer of Charles II.'s Breda despatch, to Edinburgh, iv. 187: see *Wigton*, Earls of.

FLEMING, Basil, Lord, (English) Colonel of Horse in Essex's army, ii. 445.

FLEMING, Sir Oliver, (English) Master of Ceremonies at the court of the Commonwealth, iv. 219, 221, 422, 447, 483, 525; v. 247, 399; supports Richard's Protectorate, v. 418.

FLESHER: see *Fletcher*.

FLETCHER, Sir Andrew, fined by Cromwell's Ordinance, iv. 560.

FLETCHER, Bishop, father of the dramatist, i. 458.

FLETCHER, Elisabeth, early Quaker, v. 27.

FLETCHER, Giles, father of the poets Giles and Phineas, i. 458.

FLETCHER, Giles, poet (brother of Phineas), i. 73, 453; account of, i. 458-60, 489, 575.

FLETCHER, John, dramatist (Beaumont and Fletcher), son of Bishop Fletcher, i. 45, 433, 434, 444, 453, 570, 575, 579, 622; iii. 449; vi. 352, 353, 355, 358, 379; in Dryden's *Essay of Dramatic Poesy*, vi. 379-81.

FLETCHER, Major, vi. 141-2 note.

FLETCHER (Flesher), Mr., licenser of books, iv. 149 note.

FLETCHER (Flesher), Miles, publisher and printer, vi. 403, 784, 812.

FLETCHER, Phineas, poet (brother of Giles), i. 453; account of, i. 458-9, 460-2, 489, 575.

FLOYD, actor, vi. 350.

FLUDD, Robert, Rosicrucian philosopher, i. 540.

FOGG, John, presbyterian minister, iii. 424.

FOOT, Alderman, Thomas, iii. 415; knighted by Cromwell, v. 354 note; in Council of State, v. 520.

FORBES, family of, ii. 56; iii. 352.

FORBES, the Master of, ii. 57.

FORBES, Dr. John, one of the Aberdeen Doctors, i. 715; ii. 28.

FORBES, Mr. John, minister at Kincardine, v. 346 note.

FORBES, Patrick, Scottish Bishop, i. 715, 697, 701, 706.

FORBES, William, Scottish Bishop, i. 706.

FORD, musical composer, i. 51.

FORD, Henry, member of the Rota Club, v. 485.

FORD, John, dramatist, i. 446, 451, 569, 647; iii. 449; vi. 352.

FORD, Thomas, expelled from Oxford for Puritanism, i. 408.

FORESTER, Lord, fined by Cromwell, iv. 561.

FORSTER, a shoemaker, first victim of the plague in Cambridge in 1630, i. 233.

FORTESCUE, Colonel, iii. 326, 332, 537; major-general in Penn's West India Expedition, and left by Penn in charge of Jamaica, v. 45, 103.

FORTESCUE, Sir Faithful, ii. 442, 444, 446.

FORTESCUE, Mr. N., guest with Milton at the English College at Rome in 1638, i. 800.

FORTH, Earl of: see *Brentford*, Earl of.

FOSTER, Edmund, officer of City Trained Bands, ii. 447.

FOSTER, Matthew, officer of City Trained Bands, ii. 447.

FOSTER, Thomas, at Holloway, married to a grand-daughter of Milton, i. 6 note, vi. 751.

FOSTER, Dr. William, Bishop of Man, i. 674.

FOULIS, Sir David, punished by the Star-Chamber, i. 673.

FOUNTAIN, one of the Commissioners for a new Great Seal of the Restored Rump, v. 465.

"FOUR BILLS," the, sent by Parliament to Charles I. at the Isle of Wight, iii. 578-9, 579, 580, 584, 586.

FOWLER, a London merchant, father of "the Matchless Orinda," vi. 317: see *Philips, Katherine*.

FOX, Mr., mention of, in a letter of Christopher Arnold, iv. 351.

FOX, George, founder of the Quaker sect ; his early career and first interview with Cromwell, v. 26-7, 60, 66-70, 317, 318 ; his last interview with Cromwell, v. 356-7 ; presents an address to Charles II. on behalf of the Quakers imprisoned for the Venner Riot, vi. 122 ; his activity in writing and publishing, vi. 313.

FOXCROFT, John, member of Westminster Assembly, ii. 518.

FRANCE, marriage of Prince Charles to Henrietta Maria, sister of Louis XIII., i. 106, 151 ; war with, in 1626-9, i. 159, 204 ; concluded by proclamation of peace, i. 216 ; French ambassador to the Court of Charles I., see *Chateauneuf ;* in Sir Henry Wotton's letter to Milton, i. 738 ; account of, in 1638, i. 742-4 ; Milton in, i. 751-9, 834 ; British ambassadors at Court of, in 1641, ii. 308 ; the English Queen and royal family in, iii. 375-6, 422, 491 ; relations of, with the English Commonwealth in 1651-3, iv. 380-3 ;

the Queen's interference in English affairs from, iii. 502-3 ; ambassadors from, to England, iii. 503, 715 ; the Queen, resident in, continues acting in the affairs of the King, iii. 491-5, 502 ; iv. 30, 380 ; Davenant's mission from, to King Charles, iii. 503-4 ; vi. 273 ; in the titles of Charles II. proclaimed at Edinburgh, iv. 19 ; Claude de Saumaise (called Salmasius), a native of, iv. 162 ; escape of Charles II. to, after Worcester, iv. 299 ; relations of, to the Commonwealth, iv. 380-2 ; Alexander Morus, a native of, iv. 459, 586 ; Royalist plots in, iv. 550-1 ; alliance of Cromwell with, in 1655, iv. 554-5 ; v. 36-7, 46 ; Cromwell's intercessions with the King of, on the occasion of the Piedmontese Massacre, v. 40, 43, 189, 341-3, 387-9 ; the family of Du Moulin, v. 215 ; Council letters on various business to Louis XIV. and Mazarin, v. 244, 253-4, 271-2, 275, 290, 390-1 ; Treaty of Cromwell with Louis XIV. against Spain, in 1657, v. 140, 251, 295, 339-41, 392-5 ; M. de Bordeaux, ambassador for Louis XIV. to the Commonwealth, see *Bordeaux, M. de ;* William Lockhart, ambassador for the Commonwealth to Louis XIV., see *Lockhart ;* letters of Richard Cromwell to Louis XIV. and Mazarin, v. 570, 575, 576 ; the alliance with, continued through Richard's Protectorate, v. 426-7, but brought to an end by the government of the Restored Rump, v. 467 ; in the Treaty of the Pyrenees, v. 502-4 ; return of Henrietta Maria from, to the Court of Charles II., vi. 71, 107, 119 ; the English ambassador of Charles II. at the Court of, see *St. Albans, Earl of ;* the French ambassador to Charles II., see *Ruvigny ;* in the Triple Alliance, vi. 568-9 ; Secret Negotiation of Charles II. with, v. 569-72, 574 ; in the Secret Treaty of Dover, vi. 575-81 ; English alliance with Louis XIV. against the Dutch, vi. 582-6, 591 ; the alliance concluded, vi. 601.

FRANCESCO I., Duke of Modena, i. 745.

FRANCINI, Antonio, Florentine friend of Milton, i. 773, 780; his ode to Milton, i. 783-5; references to, i. 821, 822 note, 828, ii. 90 and note, iii. 455, 650, 652, 690, 691 note; mentioned in Milton's *Defensio Secunda*, iv. 637.

FRANCIS, Lieutenant-Colonel, under the *New Model*, iii. 326.

FRANCIS, Benjamin, a witness, vi. 90.

FRANKLIN, Benjamin, the philosopher, vi. 162.

FRASER, the clan of, iii. 352.

FRASER, of Philorth, ii. 38.

FRASER, Andrew, 2nd Lord, ii. 56-7.

FRASER, Dr., physician to Charles II., iv. 189, 207.

"FRAUS HONESTA," a Cambridge comedy, by Philip Stubbe, i. 220, 221-5.

FREDERICK, Elector Palatine, husband of Princess Elizabeth, daughter of James I., i. 60, 61, 105, 740.

FREDERICK HENRY of Orange, i. 746.

FREDERICK III., King of Denmark, iv. 31, 378, 481-2, 484; v. 40, 189, 250, 290-1, 313, 596: see *Denmark and Sweden*.

FREDERICK WILLIAM, Marquis of Brandenburg (the "Great Elector"), v. 371, 373-4.

FREEMAN, master at St. Paul's School, i. 78.

FREEMAN, John, London merchant, v. 250.

FREEMAN, Richard, messenger to the Council of State, iv. 578; v. 625.

FREINSHEIM (Freinshemius), librarian to Queen Christina of Sweden, iv. 269, 344.

FRENCH, Peter, D.D., husband of Cromwell's sister, v. 307.

FRENDRAUGHT, Viscount, in Montrose's Expedition to Scotland (1649-50), iv. 184.

FRESCOBALDI, Pietro, Florentine friend of Milton, i. 773, 779-80, 821; iii. 654, 690, 691 note; iv. 637.

FRESHWATER, Edward, fellow-student of Milton at Christ's College, Cambridge, i. 112.

FRESHWATER, Richard, of Essex, i. 112.

FREWEN, Dr. Accepted, President of Magdalen College, and Vice-Chancellor of Oxford University, i. 210, 625; Bishop of Lichfield and Coventry, vi. 61; Archbishop of York, vi. 105.

FRIENDS, Society of: see *Quakers*.

FRIESLAND, Letters of State to the States of West, v. 575.

FRITH, John, author of *A Mirror or Glass to know thyself*, i. 155.

FRODSHAM, Henry, Parliamentarian officer, ii. 444.

FROST, Gualter, elder, Secretary to the Council of State, iv. 12, 13, 18, 79, 83, 84-5, 87, 146, 147, 154-5, 177, 224, 226, 228, 229, 230, 231, 273-4, 313, 315, 323, 325-6, 417; his death, iv. 425, 433; v. 705.

FROST, Gualter, younger, Assistant-Secretary to Council of State, iv. 17, 18, 83, 84-5, 177, 224, 273-4, 313, 421, 425, 426, 450, 523, 525, 526; in the Interim Council of Thirteen, iv. 499; Treasurer to Cromwell's Council, iv. 546, 575-9, v. 177, 182, 624, 625 note; in the Council of the Rump, v. 624, 625 note.

FROST, John and Joseph, under-clerks to Council of State, iv. 576.

FRY, John, present at the King's trial in 1639, vi. 35, 37; in the Indemnity Bill, vi. 54.

FULLER, Arthur, of Bradfield, Herts., Esq., iii. 58.

FULLER, Dr. Thomas; as student at Cambridge, i. 122, 248, 410, 525-6, 648; as Church Historian and Rector of Broad Windsor in Dorsetshire, ii. 224, 359-61; iii. 126; through Oliver's Protectorate, v. 53, 76, 78-9, 98; at the Hague, vi. 6; among the Writers of the Protectorate surviving into the Restoration Period, 294-5, 322; death of, in Aug. 1661, vi. 418.

FULWAR, Thomas, Archbishop of Cashel, vi. 127-8.

FURSEMAN, George, ii. 496.

FUSSEL, Nicholas, bookseller, iii. 449.

G

GACHES, French Protestant preacher, v. 368.

GADDI, Jacopo, Florentine scholar, account of, i. 773-4; 821, 822, 828; iv. 637.

GADDIAN Academy at Florence, the, iii. 651, 654.

GAINSFORDE, Thomas : his *Historie of Trebizonde*, i. 596.

GALILEI, Vincenzo (Florentine scholar), iii. 690, 691 note.

GALILEI, Thomas (ship captain in the Venetian service), case of, v. 377.

GALILEO, the Astronomer, i. 265; account of, in 1638, i. 766-8; 780-1; Milton's visit to, i. 788, 821; Milton's allusions to, in *Paradise Lost*, i. 789; 795; Milton's reminiscence of, iii. 283; 651; his Copernicanism and Milton's, vi. 534.

GALLOWAY, James, 2nd Earl of, iv. 560.

GALLOWAY, Sir James, Master of Requests in Scotland, i. 706.

GAMMON, Hannibal, member of Westminster Assembly, ii. 518.

"GANGRAENA" : see *Edwards*, Thomas.

"GARDEN OF CYPRUS," Sir Thomas Browne's, iv. 296.

GARDINER, engraver, i. 310 note.

GARDINER, Mr., English Presbyterian leader, ii. 532.

GARDINER, James, English Puritan preacher, i. 402.

GARDINER, Sir Thomas, in attendance on Charles I. in the Isle of Wight, iii. 606.

GARDINER, Sir Thomas, of Essex, pupil of Milton, iii. 658.

GARLAND, Augustine (Regicide), iii. 720, vi. 28; iv. 316; in the Restored Rump, v. 454, 523; after the Restoration, 43, 49, 54; his trial, vi. 80, 93; subsequent fate of, vi. 98 note, 114, 115.

GARRARD, letter-writer, i. 638.

GARTHE, Richard, Milton's contemporary at Cambridge, i. 218, 258.

GARTHWAIT, London publisher, vi. 403.

GASSENDI, i. 744; iii. 494.

GATAKER, Rev. Thomas (Puritan divine), as Rector of Rotherhithe, i. 54 and note, 71, 559; as member of the Westminster Assembly, with further account of him, ii. 518, 605; iii. 19; a book-licenser under the Long Parliament, iii. 270; one of the Presbyterians of the Sion College Conclave, iii. 677; joins in the Presbyterian demonstration in behalf of Charles I., iv. 71; and Bradshaw's Press Act, iv. 118; his attack on Lilly, the astrologer, v. 21; his death, v. 75.

GATFIELD, Lionel, of Jesus College, Cambridge, i. 247.

GAUDEN, Charles, son of Bishop Gauden, vi. 433 note.

GAUDEN, Dr. John, Rector of Bocking, his efforts on behalf of Charles I. in his last days, iii. 716, 719; allusions to, in Milton's *Tenure of Kings and Magistrates*, iv. 71; made Bishop of Exeter after the Restoration, vi. 105; sketch of, vi. 423-5; in letters to Lord Chancellor Hyde, vi. 426-8; and the story of the *Eikon Basilike*, vi. 429-31; more correspondence with Chancellor Hyde, vi. 432-3 note; his part in the Savoy Conferences of 1661, vi. 433-4; his relations with the Earl of Bristol, vi. 435-6; Bishop of Worcester, vi. 437; his death and burial, vi. 438-9; note on his claims to the authorship of the *Eikon Basilike*, vi. 439.

GAUDEN, Mrs., wife of the Bishop, vi. 427, 429-30, 438.

GAULMIN, Gilbert, French writer, iv. 343.

GAWDY, Framlingham, member for Thetford in the Long Parliament; his notes in the House, ii. 172.

GAWEN, Thomas, of New College, Oxford, i. 800 and note.

GAYE, Percivall, i. 15.

GAYWOOD, R., engraver, vi. 213 note.

"GEDDES, Jenny," story of, and of the Riot in Edinburgh of 23rd July 1637, i. 719-21.

GEERE, major in the London Trained Bands, ii. 447.

GEERING, William, v. 625.

GELL, Sir John, Parliamentarian, ii. 463.

GELL, Dr. Robert, Fellow of Christ's College, Cambridge, during Milton's residence there, i. 111, 123-4, 237, 248, 267, 649; ii. 76; as Rector of St. Mary Aldermary, London, after the Restoration, vi. 476.

GELLIBRAND, Henry, Professor of Astronomy in Gresham College, i. 566; v. 154.

GELLIBRAND (or Gellebrand), Samuel, London publisher, iii. 143 note, 198; v. 59 note.

GENEVA, a branch of the Diodati family resident at, i. 99; Milton's visit to, in 1639, i. 833; his reminiscences of, and subsequent communications with, v. 171-5; State Letter to the City of, v. 190.

GENOA, the Republic of, in 1638, i. 745; agent for, in London, in 1651, iv. 379.

GENTILLOT, French envoy in London, iv. 381, 382.

GEORGE, David, founder of the Familists, iii. 152.

GERARD, Lord, a former Lord President of Wales, i. 605

GERARD of Bromley, Lord (a minor), non-effective Royalist Peer, ii. 430.

GERARD, John, Royalist conspirator, iv. 550, 556-7.

GEREE, John, M.A., Presbyterian pamphleteer, ii. 593.

GERLING, Mr., barrister of Lincoln's Inn, i. 580.

GERMANY in 1638, i. 746; cadets of Scottish families serving in, ii. 52-3; iv. 378-9; Emperor of (1667-70), and the Triple Alliance, vi. 569.

GERRARD, Sir Gilbert, Parliamentarian Treasurer at War, ii. 443; on the "Committee of the Two Kingdoms," iii. 41; one of Cromwell's lords, v. 324; on the Council of State of Monk's Dictatorship, v. 543; in the Restored Long Parliament, v. 545.

GERRARD'S Hall, Old Bread Street, London, i. 44, 45.

GESLING, Richard, engineer, his pamphlet on Artificial Fuel, iii. 36-7.

GHERARDI, Raffaelle, Florentine scholar, i. 780.

GIBBON, John, member of Westminster Assembly, ii. 518; iii. 5.

GIBBON, Robert, Republican Colonel, v. 470.

GIBBONS, Ellis, musical composer, i. 51.

GIBBONS, John, English Presbyterian conspirator, case of, iv. 285-7; execution of, iv. 293.

GIBBONS, Orlando, musical composer, i. 51.

GIBBS, actress, vi. 350.

GIBBS, alderman, iii. 395.

GIBBS, Nathaniel, feltmaker, executed for treason, vi. 471.

GIBSON of Durie, Scottish Covenanter, ii. 16.

GIBSON, Samuel, of Burleigh, Rutlandshire, member of Westminster Assembly, ii. 518.

GIFFARD, Henry, keeper of the Treasury-Room of Oliver's Council, iv. 578; v. 177.

GILBERT, Dr., of Cambridge University, i. 257.

GILL, Alexander, sen., head-master of St. Paul's School, i. 76; account of, i. 78-82; his various writings, i. 79-82; Aubrey's mention of him, i. 82; 108, 112; 214, 215, 215 note, 243, 272, 305; his feud with Ben Jonson, i. 481, 565; his death, i. 626; ii. 79; iii. 242.

GILL, Alexander, jun., under-master of St. Paul's school, i. 79; account of, i. 82-3; Milton's intimacy with him, i. 97-8; his Latin poems, i. 107, 108; Milton's letters to, i. 188, 190-1, 193-4, 305, 623-4; vi. 723; story of his scrape at Oxford in connexion with Felton's assassination of Buckingham, i. 207-12, 214; publication of his Latin poems in 1632, i. 510; his English lampoon on Ben Jonson's Magnetic Lady, and Jonson's lampoon in reply, i. 565-6; v. 261; admitted D.D. at Oxford, i. 626; succeeds his father as head-master of St. Paul's School, i. 626, ii. 79; 207, 357.

GILL, George, another son of Alexander Gill, the elder, i. 211.

GILLESPIE, George, Scottish Presbyterian divine, i. 712; his treatise

Against the English-Popish Cere-
monies, i. 723 ; minister of Wemyss
and a Covenanter, ii. 16, 38 ; one
of the Scottish clerical deputation to
London in 1640-1, ii. 191, 202 ;
his pamphlet *On the Grounds of*
Presbyterial Government, ii. 218 ;
sent as one of the Scottish assessors
to the Westminster Assembly, iii.
10, 11 ; further account of him, iii. 16 ;
in the Westminster Assembly, and his
notes of what was done there, iii.
22, 23 note, 84 ; his anti-Toleration
activity, iii. 130, 160 ; in the Scottish General Assembly of 1644-5,
iii. 175 - 6 ; and the episode of
Montrose in Scotland, iii. 357 ;
again in London, iii. 413 ; supposed
mention of, by Milton, iii. 461 and
note ; and the case of Will Murray,
iii. 501, 513 ; his return to Scotland
in August 1647, iii. 568.
GILLESPIE, Patrick, of Glasgow, one
of the Scottish ultra-Presbyterians
after Dunbar, iv. 203-4, 209 ; a
leader among the Remonstrants or
Protesters, iv. 213 ; deposed by the
Scottish General Assembly of 1651,
iv. 289 ; and the incorporation of
Scotland with the English Commonwealth, iv. 363 ; as Cromwellian
Principal of Glasgow University, v.
88, 90 ; in London, v. 115 ; sermon
by, before the Protector, v. 120 ;
and Cromwell's Government of
Scotland, v. 345, 348 ; after the
Restoration, vi. 134-5 ; deprived of
his Principalship, vi. 142 ; his trial,
vi. 150.
GIPPES, George, member of West-
minster Assembly, ii. 518.
GIROLAMI, Florentine scholar, i. 822.
GITTENS, Richard, vi. 89.
GLADMAN, Major John, v. 335, 470.
GLAMORGAN, Earl of, ii. 47 ; his
Treaty with the Irish Roman Catho-
lics, iii. 519.
GLANVILL, Joseph, Platonist, vi. 307.
GLANVILLE, John, in the Long Parlia-
ment, ii. 173.
GLAPTHORNE, dramatist, iii. 446 ; vi.
352.
GLASGOW, General Assembly of 1638
at, ii. 36-42, 70-1.

GLENCAIRN, William Cunningham, 9th
Earl of, ii. 418 ; iii. 509 ; as leader
of Royalist movement in Scotland,
iv. 508-9, 552, 560 ; v. 512 ; as
Chancellor of Scotland after the
Restoration, vi. 131, 133, 138, 143,
145, 161.
GLENDINNING, William, Scottish Commissioner in London, iii. 717 ; iv.
22.
GLENGARRY, chief of, with Montrose
in Scotland, iii. 360.
GLENHAM, Sir Thomas, ii. 442, 467 ;
iii. 374, 593.
GLISSON, the physician, i. 120.
GLOBE THEATRE, the, i. 49.
GLOUCESTER, petition from, for Church-
reform, ii. 214.
GLOUCESTER, Henry, Duke of (third
son of Charles I.), ii. 428 ; iii. 375,
556, 705, 714, 723 ; iv. 214, 406 ;
v. 340 ; at the Restoration, v. 701 ;
vi. 6, 10 ; after the Restoration, vi.
17, 22, 67 ; his illness and death,
vi. 70.
GLOVER, Cornelius, servant of Hugh
Peters, vi. 86.
GLYNN (or Glynne), John, lawyer, in
the Long Parliament, ii. 173, 181,
321, 334 ; lay-member of the Westminster Assembly, ii. 524 ; on the
" Committee of the Two Kingdoms,"
iii. 41 ; among the eleven Presbyterian leaders denounced by the
Army, iii. 548-9, 554 ; at the Treaty
of Newport, iii. 605, 606 ; counsel
for Lilburne, iv. 508 ; in Oliver's
First Parliament, v. 5 ; one of
Oliver's judges, v. 36 ; story of
Glynne and George Fox, v. 70 ; in
the Conference as to Toleration of
the Jews, v. 71 ; in Cromwell's
Second Parliament, v. 107 ; supports
Sir Christopher Pack's motion for
Cromwell's Kingship, v. 122, 124,
125-6, 128 ; one of Cromwell's
lords, v. 324 ; supports Richard's
Protectorate, v. 418 ; in the Con-
vention Parliament of the Restora-
tion, vi. 23, 30, 53.
GOAD (or Good), William, member of
Westminster Assembly, ii. 518.
GOADE, Dr. Thomas, of Cambridge, i.
120, 226.

GOARE, Thomas, Baptist preacher, iii. 148.

GODDARD, Dr. Jonathan, physician, one of the members of the "Invisible College," iii. 662; attends Cromwell in Scotland, iv. 278; in the Second Council of the Barebones Parliament, iv. 525; as head of an Oxford College, v. 73, 231; and the beginning of the Royal Society, vi. 391-4, 396.

GODEMAN, Dr. (Swede), ii. 368 note; iii. 194.

GODOLPHIN, Sidney, i. 532, 534, 538; in the Long Parliament, ii. 172, 185.

GODWIN, Dr. Francis, Bishop of Hereford, i. 389, 400, 674.

GOFFE, William (Regicide), iii. 720; iv. 402, 403, 514, 571; one of Cromwell's major-generals, v. 49; in Cromwell's Second Parliament, v. 107, 127, 129; one of Cromwell's lords, v. 324, 354; supports Richard's Protectorate, v. 418, 422, 423; in the Wallingford House Convention, v. 439, 440, 442; under the Restored Rump, v. 469; negotiations with Monk, v. 497; fugitive after the Restoration, vi. 28, 44, 54, 115 and note.

GOLD, Mr., one of the Rota Club, v. 660 note.

GOLD, James, London merchant, v. 589.

GOLD, Nicholas, in the Restored Rump, v. 454, 544 note.

"GOLDEN GROVE, the," Earl of Carbery's seat in Caernarvonshire, v. 78.

GOMBERVILLE, French romance writer, vi. 359.

GOMERSALL, dramatist, i. 449.

"GONDIBERT," Davenant's, vi. 274-6.

GONVILLE and Caius College, Cambridge, i. 114, 116, 120.

GOOCH, Dr. Barnaby, master of Magdalen College, Cambridge, i. 116, 171.

GOOD, William : see Goad.

GOOD, chaplain to the Earl of Manchester, iii. 92.

GOODAL, Rev. Edward, rector of Horton during Milton's residence there, i. 559-60, 560, 640; ii. 73.

GOODAY, Faith, captain in London Trained Bands, ii. 483.

GOODMAN, actor, vi. 349.

GOODMAN, Dr. Godfrey, Bishop of Gloucester, i. 389, 519, 677; ii. 150, 270, 334-6.

"GOOD OLD CAUSE," the, v. 444-6.

GOODSON, Vice-Admiral, v. 45, 103.

GOODWIN, Arthur, Parliamentarian officer, ii. 445.

GOODWIN, John, Arminian theologian, and vicar of St. Stephen's, Coleman Street, London, account of, to 1640, ii. 582-4; his anti-Presbyterianism and advocacy of Toleration, iii. 112-3, 120 and note, 121 and note, 122, 125, 126, 127, 128, 129, 131; attacked in Edwards's Gangræna, iii. 157-8; attacked by the Westminster Assembly, iii. 163, 165, 170; denounced by the Westminster Assembly to Parliament, iii. 262, 288; defended by Hezekiah Woodward, iii. 294; mentioned by Prynne, iii. 298; continued advocacy of Toleration and free thought, iii. 386-7; ejected from his vicarage of St. Stephen's, Coleman Street, iii. 389; iii. 392 note; denounced by Sion College, iii. 677-8, 679; seeks an interview with Charles I. on the night before his execution, iii. 721; iv. 6; his Regicide pamphlet, called The Obstructors of Justice, iv. 95 note, 106; 130; vi. 39, 174, 181, 191; and the constitution of the Church of the Commonwealth, iv. 392; under the Protectorate, v. 58, 59 and note, 75, 77; his relations to Cromwell's Established Church, and attack upon him by Needham, v. 316-7; conjoined with Milton for prosecution after the Restoration, vi. 39; vi. 40, 41; excepted from the Indemnity Bill, and incapacitated for life, vi. 47, 55, 173, 177, 183-5; copy of the Proclamation against Milton and him, vi. 181-2; burning of his and Milton's pamphlets, vi. 193, 197, 417; after the Act of Uniformity, vi. 232 note, 292-3.

GOODWIN, Robert, in Parliament, iii. 579; in Third Council of State of the Commonwealth, iv. 273, 314,

H

321 ; and in the Fifth, iv. 355, 449 ; in office in Ireland, v. 98 ; in the Restored Rump, v. 454, 471, 537.

GOODWIN, Thomas (English Independent divine), notices of, before 1643, ii. 368 note, 578, 580, 585, 591 ; as member of the Westminster Assembly, with account of his antecedents, ii. 518 ; one of the Five original Independents of the Westminster Assembly, ii. 605 ; iii. 22, 23, 87, 111 ; his Millenarianism, iii. 153 ; in the course of the Toleration Controversy, iii. 286, 391, 392 ; thanksgiving sermon by, after the establishment of the Commonwealth, iv. 53 ; his popularity with the First Council of State of the Commonwealth, iv. 61 ; chaplain to the Council of State, with lodgings in Whitehall, iv. 106, 149, 153 ; President of Magdalen College, Oxford, iv. 177 ; on a committee with Milton, iv. 228 ; thanksgiving sermon by, after Worcester, iv. 296 ; and the question of the constitution of the Church of the Commonwealth, iv. 392 ; and the Barebones Parliament, iv. 514 ; and the Established Church of the Protectorate, iv. 566 ; on the *Commission of Triers*, iv. 571 ; his sermon at the opening of Cromwell's First Parliament, v. 6 ; through Oliver's Protectorate, v. 12, 71, 73, 75 ; Oliver's liking for him, v. 77 ; supports Richard's Protectorate, v. 418 ; in the Savoy Synod of Congregationalists, v. 424 ; in Milton's *Treatise of Civil Power*, v. 585 ; after the Restoration, vi. 121, 232 note, 292-3, 416 ; his grave in Bunhill Fields, vi. 499.

GOODWYN, John, in the Restored Rump, v. 454, 455, 544 note.

GOODYERE, Henry, English judge in Scotland, v. 86.

GORDONS, the, as adherents of Montrose in Scotland, iii. 351, 352, 368 ; mentioned by Milton, iii. 461.

GORDON, Lord, eldest son of the Marquis of Huntley, ii. 29, 34, 57 ; with Montrose, iii. 358 ; killed, iii. 360.

GORDON, Lord Lewis, third son of Marquis of Huntley, ii. 60 ; iii. 352, 358, 359.

GORDON, Colonel Nathaniel, iii. 360, 361, 367, 368.

GORDONS of Gicht, anti-Covenanters, ii. 57.

GORDON, younger, of Straloch, iv. 491.

GORING, Colonel George (son of Lord Goring), member for Portsmouth in the Long Parliament, ii. 173, 284 ; in Civil War, ii. 461, 468 ; iii. 330, 332, 337, 338.

GORING, George, Lord (afterwards 1st Earl of Norwich) ; subscription towards the First Bishops' War, ii. 47 ; in the First Bishops' War, ii. 62, 63 ; as peer in the Long Parliament, ii. 152, 173, 279, 283 ; created Earl of Norwich, ii. 429 ; iii. 591, 594, 605, 615 ; trial of, iv. 40.

GORTON, Samuel, New England Antinomian and Anarchist, ii. 601 ; iii. 467, 678.

GOSTLIN, John, M.D., master of Gonville and Caius College, Cambridge, i. 116, 120, 153 ; Vice-Chancellor of the University, i. 154, 156, 157 ; his death in the Vice-Chancellorship, and Milton's commemoration of that event, i. 172-3.

GOTHERICHE, Sir George, Royalist colonel, ii. 442.

GOTHOFRIDIUS, Genevese lawyer, v. 194.

GOTSO, or Joce, de Dinan, i. 606.

GOUGE, Thomas, Nonconformist of 1662, vi. 232 note.

GOUGE, Dr. William, Puritan divine at Cambridge, i. 120 ; member of the Westminster Assembly, ii. 518, 558, 605 ; Moderator of the First Provincial Presbyterian Synod of London, iii. 544 ; one of the Presbyterians of the Sion College Conclave, iii. 674, 677 ; iv. 71.

GOUGH, Francis, Irish bishop, i. 420.

GOULDMAN, Francis, in the affair of the Racovian Catechism, iv. 438.

GOULDSMITH, Nicholas, mercer of Nantwich, great-grandfather of Milton's third wife, Elizabeth Minshull, vi. 473 ; his wife, Dorothy, his

daughters, Margery Gouldsmith and Ellen Gouldsmith, and their descendants, the Pagets and the Minshulls, vi. 473-5.

GOVAN, Captain William, Scottish Protester, vi. 132-3; hanged, vi. 160-1.

GOWER, Stanley, member of the Westminster Assembly, ii. 518; iv. 71.

GRAEF, C. de (of Amsterdam), v. 196.

GRAFTON, Isabella, Duchess of, vi. 766-7.

GRAFTON, Henry Fitzroy, Earl of Euston and Duke of, natural son of Charles II., vi. 604; his marriage, vi. 766-7.

GRAHAM, of Fintray, ii. 38.

GRAHAM, Sir Frederick, of Netherby, Cumberland, possessor [of Milton's Commonplace Book, i. 303.

GRAHAM, James: see *Montrose*.

GRAHAM, Lord, eldest son of Montrose, iii. 351; his death, iii. 358.

GRAHAM, John, Bishop of Orkney, i. 697; ii. 42.

GRAHAM, Patrick, elder, of Inchbrakie, iii. 349.

GRAHAM, Patrick, younger, of Inchbrakie, iii. 349-50, 357.

GRAHAM, Sir Robert, of Morphie, iv. 561.

GRAIN, Robert, Parliamentarian officer, ii. 444.

GRAINGER, Mrs. Christian, preserver of the Scottish Regalia, iv. 366.

GRAMMONT, Memoirs of Count, vi. 460-1.

GRANDISON, Oliver St. John, Viscount, i. 380; ii. 62, 442; iv. 188.

GRANDISON, William Villiers, Viscount, vi. 71.

GRANTHAM, Colonel Thomas, in the Long Parliament, ii. 444.

GRANVILLE (Greenville), Sir Bevis, ii. 466.

GRANVILLE, Sir John (son of the preceding), his plotting for the Restoration, v. 472, 473; his negotiations with Monk and with Charles II., v. 476, 559-61, 568; his delivery of the Breda Letters, and final action in the Restoration, v. 695-7, 698-9, 701; vi. 25; made Earl of Bath at the Coronation of Charles II., vi. 152.

GRASWINKEL, Dutch Publicist, iv. 319, 342.

GRAVELINES, taking of, v. 341.

GRAVES, Richard, *New Model* Colonel, iii. 327, 332, 514, 537, 540, 541, 543 note.

GRAY, Lord (Scottish), iv. 561.

GREAT Seal, a new, iii. 705.

GREAVES, John, Professor of geometry in Gresham College, i. 566; and Christopher Arnold, iv. 351.

GRECIAN Coffee-House, the, vi. 629-30.

GREEN, of Magdalen College, Cambridge, i. 221.

GREEN, Baptist preacher, iii. 147.

GREENE, dramatist, i. 592.

GREENE, Benjamin, Milton's servant, vi. 511.

GREENE, John, member of the Westminster Assembly, ii. 518.

GREENHILL, William, member of the Westminster Assembly, iii. 518; one of the Independents, iii. 392; iv. 392, 438; one of the Nonconformists of 1662, vi. 232 note.

GREENVILLE, see *Granville*.

GREENWAY, Mr., iv. 556.

GREENWOOD, John, English Brownist, ii. 537, 539, 569; iii. 101.

GREGSON, Thomas (of New England), ii. 599.

GRENVILLE, Richard, captain of a troop of horse in the Parliamentarian army, ii. 445.

GRENVILLE, Sir Richard, v. 176.

GRESHAM COLLEGE, London, ii. 366; iii. 222, 662; vi. 392-3, 394-5, 433, 436, 438, 458.

GREVILLE, Fulke: see *Brooke*, *1st Lord*.

GREVILLE, Robert: see *Brooke*, *2nd Lord*.

GREY, Henry : see *Stamford*, *1st Earl of*.

GREY, John, Lord, ii. 155.

GREY of Groby, Lord (in 1603), son of the above, ii. 155.

GREY of Groby, Thomas, Lord (son of the Earl of Stamford), ii. 155; in the Long Parliament, ii. 326; in the Parliamentarian army, ii. 445, 463; on the Committee of the Rump for the King's trial, iii. 699; one of the Regicide judges, iii. 707, 712 note;

signs the death-warrant, iii. 720; votes for the abolition of the House of Peers, iv. 5; in the First Council of State of the Commonwealth, iv. 12, 13, 89, 120, 145; in the Second Council of State, iv. 223; in the Council Order Books, iv. 231; in the Third Council of State, iv. 273, 313, 314, 315, 321; in the Fifth Council of State, iv. 355; in Oliver's First Parliament, v. 5; imprisoned for Republican plottings against Oliver, v. 33; dead before the Restoration, vi. 28; posthumous indemnity for his concern in the Regicide, vi. 36, 38, 52.

GREY of Ruthen, 13th Lord, ii. 429.

GREY of Ruthen, 16th Lord, among the subscribers for the 4th edition of *Paradise Lost*, vi. 785.

GREY, William, 1st Lord Grey of Wark, in the Long Parliament, ii. 159; in the Parliamentarian army, ii. 431, 445; his "Eastern Counties Association," ii. 459; lay member of the Westminster Assembly, ii. 523; chairman in the Lords' House during the prosecution of Milton there by the Stationers' Company, iii. 291, 297 note; continues among the Peers through 1647, iii. 555 note; among the Erastian Presbyterians of that House, iii. 406; in the last sittings of the House of Peers, iv. 4; on the First Council of State of the Commonwealth, iv. 12, 14, 15; not re-elected, iv. 177; reappears in the Convention Parliament, v. 695.

GRIFFIN, actor, vi. 349.

GRIFFITH, George, Bishop of St. Asaph, vi. 104.

GRIFFITH, Dr. Matthew, account of, and of his Royalist sermon in March 1660, v. 667-9 note; Milton's *Brief Notes on Dr. Griffith's Sermon*, v. 675-7.

GRIFFITHS, Edmund, Bishop of Bangor, i. 673.

GRIFFITHS, Robert, warden of the Scriveners' Company, i. 62.

GRIFIANDER, Christopher, envoy of the Count of Oldenburg, iv. 635.

GRIMES, Ellis, Lieutenant-Colonel in the *New Model*, iii. 326, 534; v. 470.

GRIMSTONE, Sir Harbottle, in the Long Parliament, ii. 173, 197, 216; in the Treaty of Newport, iii. 605; last efforts for the King, iii. 694; in Oliver's Second Parliament, v. 107, 110; in the Council of State of the Restored Long Parliament, v. 544, 545; speaker of the Commons' House in the Convention Parliament, v. 694; concern in the Restoration, v. 696-7; vi. 11; continues Speaker in the Convention Parliament, vi. 24; on the Commission for the Trials of the Regicides, vi. 77.

GRINDER, Mary, complaint of, v. 575.

GRINKIN, William, of Jesus College, Oxford; his trial by the Star-Chamber, i. 211-2, 214, 510.

GRISMOND, John, London printer, v. 259.

GRONOVIUS, John Frederick, iv. 317, 319, 342, 343, 434, 465, 474, 539, 540.

GROSART, Dr. A. B., his "Lord Bacon not the author of the Christian Paradoxes," ii. 520-1.

GROSVENOR, Colonel, iv. 402.

GROTIUS, Hugo, i. 523; account of, i. 746; ambassador for Sweden at the Court of Louis XIII. of France, i. 747; his scheme for a union of all the non-Calvinistic Protestant Churches, i. 752-4; Milton's introduction to him in Paris, i. 752, 754, 759, 834; ii. 367, 368 note; his *De Jure Belli*, iv. 434; his *Mare Liberum*, iv. 450; Milton's mention of him in the *Defensio Secunda*, iv. 637.

GROTIUS, Madame, i. 746, 747, 755.

GROVE, Francis, London publisher, vi. 400.

GROVE, Captain Hugh, his execution, v. 35.

GRUB Street, vi. 484-5.

GRUELERS, the (club of Oxonians), vi. 454.

GUARINI, i. 529.

GUÉBRIANT, i. 743.

GUERCINO, i. 763.

GUIDO, i. 763.

GUILD, William, one of the Aberdeen Doctors, i. 715 ; ii. 38.

GUIMARAES, Don Joseph de, Portuguese ambassador to the Commonwealth, iv. 218-9 ; Milton's State correspondence and interviews with, iv. 235, 275, 315.

GUMBLE, Dr. Thomas, Presbyterian Chaplain to Monk in Scotland, v. 476 ; his negotiations with and for Monk, v. 499, 525, 528, 538.

GUNN, Thomas, Baptist preacher, ii. 587 ; iii. 148.

GUNNING, Dr., Anglican Divine, vi. 61, 99.

GUNPOWDER Plot, the, Milton's long Latin Poem on (with translation of it), and his Latin epigrams on the same subject, i. 173-80, 493-4.

GUNTER, John, Parliamentarian officer, ii. 445, 450 ; killed, ii. 471.

GÜNTZER, Christopher, of Strasburg, his academic dissertation against Milton, v. 402-4.

GURDON, Brampton, Restored Rumper, v. 454.

GURDON, John, in the Second Council of State of the Commonwealth, iv. 177, 224, 225, 227, 230 ; in the Third Council of State, iv. 273, 314, 321 ; in the Fourth Council of State, iv. 354 ; and in the Fifth, iv. 355, 449, 450 ; in the Restored Rump, v. 454, 544 note, 666.

GURNEY, Lord Mayor, ii. 323, 328, 412.

GUSTAVUS ADOLPHUS, i. 382, 741-3, 747 ; ii. 9 ; Scottish officers in the army of, ii. 52-3.

GUTHRIE, James, of Stirling (Scottish Protester or ultra-Peresbyterian), iv. 203-4, 209, 213, 283 ; deposed by the Scottish General Assembly of 1651, iv. 289 ; during the Protectorate of Oliver, v. 90, 115, 345 ; after the Restoration, vi. 133, 134, 135 ; his trial, vi. 150 ; hanged in Edinburgh, vi. 160-1.

GUTHRIE, John, Bishop of Moray, i. 697, 701, 706 ; ii. 42.

GUZMAN, Don Pedro de Carillo de, iv. 324.

GWILLIAMS, Major, iii. 327.

GWYNN, Nell, actress in the King's Theatre, vi. 350, 351-2, 354, 355, 356 ; in Dryden's *Maiden Queen*, vi. 355, 368-9 ; as mistress of Charles II., vi. 578 ; her son, vi. 604, 605 ; story of her acting in Dryden's *Tyrannic Love*, vi. 607-8 ; and Fleet Shepherd, vi. 630.

GWYNNE, Dr. Owen, master of St. John's College, Cambridge, i. 116, 121, 349.

H

HAAK, Theodore, his connexion with the origin of the Royal Society, iii. 662 ; v. 235 ; and vi. 391, 783 ; proposed provision by Parliament for, iv. 107 ; mentions of, in the Council Order Books of the Commonwealth, iv. 228, 229, 448, 482 ; naturalised as an English subject, v. 113 ; his translation of part of *Paradise Lost* into German, vi. 783-4.

HABINGTON, William, Roman Catholic poet, account of, and of his poetry, i. 493-8 ; his wife, Lucy Herbert, i. 494 ; mentions of, i. 569, 647 ; ii. 12 ; iii. 446.

HACKER, Colonel Francis, at the King's Trial, iii. 707 ; has custody of the King in his last days, iii. 712, 713 ; death-warrant of Charles delivered to, iii. 720 and note ; at the execution of Charles, iii. 723-6 ; as an army officer through the Commonwealth, the Protectorate, and the Anarchy, iv. 402, 403 ; v. 27, 470, 522 ; one of the Regicides examined during the debates on the Indemnity Bill, and excepted from that Bill, vi. 45-8, and 54, 87-9 ; his trial, vi. 80, 87-9 ; his sentence, vi. 94 ; his execution, vi. 97 ; included in the Act of Attainder on the Regicides, vi. 115.

HACKER, Mrs., and the death-warrant of Charles I., vi. 45-6.

HACKET, Dr. John, Bishop of Lichfield and Coventry, his Biography of Archbishop Williams, i. 352 note, 353, 401 ; his Cambridge comedy, *Loyola*, i. 410, 449, 683 ; ii. 151 and note, 516, 525 ; iii. 218 ; Rector of St. Andrews, Holborn, ii. 225,

228 ; nominated a member of Westminster Assembly, ii. 518 ; iii. 674 note; under the Protectorate, v. 76 ; after the Restoration, vi. 61, 99, 292 ; mentions of Milton by, vi. 636 note.

HADDINGTON, Thomas Hamilton, 1st Earl of, i. 706.

HADDINGTON, Thomas Hamilton, 2nd Earl of, ii. 15.

HAEX, David, a Dutchman resident in Rome, i. 797.

HAGUE, The : see under *Charles II.*

HAINES, actor, vi. 349.

HAKEWILL, Dr. George, Archdeacon of Surrey, and author of *Apologie of the Power and Providence of God*, i. 200-1, 519.

HALE, John, Parliamentarian officer, ii. 445.

HALE, Matthew (lawyer and judge), on the Law Reform Commission of the Commonwealth, iv. 385-6, 508 ; appointed by Cromwell Judge of Assize for Lancaster, iv. 558 ; in Oliver's First Parliament, v. 5, 7 ; as judge in Trials of Quakers, v. 68 ; in the Convention Parliament, vi. 24, 30, 43, 58 ; in the Trials of the Regicides, vi. 77 ; as Chief-Justice under Charles II., vi. 567.

HALES, Mr., Royalist insurgent in Kent, iii. 594.

HALES, John, of Eton, account of, i. 533, 535-7, 538, 539, 540, 564 ; his probable acquaintance with Milton, i. 738 ; ii. 74, 169 ; iii. 107-8, 126 and note ; during the Protectorate, v. 76, 78.

HALHEAD, Miles, Early Quaker, v. 26.

HALIFAX, Viscount, English Plenipotentiary in Holland, vi. 585 ; 598.

HALINGHAM, Early English Presbyterian, ii. 531.

HALL, Mr., his Utopian speculations, iii. 663.

HALL of Trinity College, Cambridge, i. 220.

HALL, George, son of Bishop Hall, iii. 674 note.

HALL, Henry, member of Westminster Assembly, ii. 519.

HALL, Henry, Bishop of Killala and Achonry, vi. 129.

HALL, John, a pamphleteer in pay of the Commonwealth, iv. 88, 146, 147 ; v. 177 ; edits Drummond's *History of Scotland*, v. 264 ; licenser for the press, vi. 515.

HALL, Dr. Joseph, Bishop of Exeter, i. 389, 399 note, 400 ; his Satires, i. 470-1, 508 ; his prose writings before 1632, i. 516-7, 527, 569 ; in correspondence with Laud, i. 678 note, 684 ; ii. 123-5 ; his *Episcopacy by Divine Right asserted*, ii. 125-6 ; in the Long Parliament, ii. 150-1 ; leader of the High Church Party in the Parliament, ii. 196 ; his *Humble Remonstrance*, ii. 214-5, 391 ; answer to it by Robert Blair, 218 ; answer to it by the Smectymnuans, ii. 219-222, 391 ; in the conferences and discussions on the Bishops Exclusion Bill, ii. 225-229 ; his *Defence of the Humble Remonstrance against the Smectymnuans*, ii. 253-4, 391 ; reply of the Smectymnuans to the same, ii. 255-6, 369-70, 391 ; Milton's *Animadversions upon, etc.* (Third Pamphlet), see *Milton*, Writings of, ii. 256-62 ; impeachment of, ii. 270 ; Bishop of Norwich, ii. 325 ; shares in Archbishop Williams's blundering Protest, and is imprisoned in consequence, ii. 334, 335 and note, 336 ; his correspondence with John Durie, ii. 367 ; his *Modest Confutation* of Milton's *Animadversions*, ii. 394 ; Milton's reply to the same in his *Fifth Pamphlet*, ii. 398-409 ; 543 ; 593, 595 ; iii. 110 ; his reference in his *Cases of Conscience* to Milton's Divorce Doctrine, iii. 62 ; correspondence with Durie and Hartlib, iii. 217, 218 ; his life as Ex-Bishop under the Protectorate, v. 76, 78.

HALL, Rev. Robert, Canon residentiary of Exeter, and son of Bishop Hall ; his share in his father's controversy with Milton, ii. 390-9, 399-405.

HALL, W. (of Cambridge), verses on the death of Edward King, i. 653.

HALLAM, the historian, his criticism of the *Ode on the Nativity*, i. 228.

HALLOWS, Nathaniel, in the Restored Rump, v. 454, 544 note.

HALSALL, Edward, one of the assassins of Anthony Ascham, iv. 234.

HAMBURG, Letters of State to the Senate of, iv. 159-60, 160, 233, 234, 482; v. 290, 371, 371-2: see *Hanse Towns*.

HAMILTON of Preston, fined by Cromwell's Ordinance, iv. 561.

HAMILTON, Colonel Alexander, Scottish Covenanting officer, ii. 55, 59.

HAMILTON, Count Anthony, his *Memoirs of Count Grammont*, vi. 460-1.

HAMILTON, Archibald, Archbishop of Cashel, i. 420.

HAMILTON, Archibald, brother of Robert Hamilton of Milburn, iv. 283.

HAMILTON of Orbiston, Sir John, Justice-Clerk of Scotland, i. 706; ii. 16.

HAMILTON of Milburn, Robert, iv. 283.

HAMILTON, Thomas: see *Haddington*, Earl of.

HAMILTON, James, 3rd Marquis and 1st Duke of (also Earl of Cambridge, and Earl of Arran): account of, and of his relations to King Charles before 1638, i. 382-3, 667, 701, 708; account of his mission to Scotland, in 1638, to negotiate with the Covenanters, ii. 8-36; as Lord High Commissioner for Charles in the Glasgow General Assembly, ii. 36-42; acquiesces in war with the Scots, ii. 46; in command of the fleet sent against the Scots in the First Bishops' War, ii. 51-63; his castle of Brodick taken by Argyle, ii. 56; letters to, ii. 60; one of the Commissioners for a Treaty with the Scots, ii. 69; declines farther service against the Covenanters, ii. 71; at the calling of the Short Parliament, ii. 127; in the Long Parliament, ii. 152, 178; in the Trial of Strafford, ii. 180; accompanies Charles I. in his second visit to Scotland in August 1641, ii. 272, 278, 283; plot against, in Scotland, by Montrose and his friends, ii. 300-6; in Scottish Privy Council of 1641, ii. 307; in Scotland before the outbreak of the Civil War, ii. 417-8; at the commencement of the Civil War, ii. 428; in Scottish affairs in the first year of the Civil War, iii. 341-2; committed to prison at the instance of Montrose as unfaithful to the King, iii. 343; liberated, iii. 371; with Argyle in London, iii. 420; regained to the cause of the King, iii. 498-9; in negotiations with and for the King at Newcastle, iii. 499-501; action of, and of his party, for the King in Scotland, iii. 509; as the head of the *Scottish Engagement* or Secret Treaty with the King, iii. 586-90; his preparations for a second Civil War in the King's behalf, iii. 593; his march into England, iii. 596-7; defeat of, by Cromwell in the Battle of Preston, iii. 604; a prisoner in England, and fined £100,000 by the Parliament, iii. 615; his trial and execution after the establishment of the Commonwealth, iv. 40.

HAMILTON, William Hamilton, 2nd Duke of (brother of the preceding, and known as Earl of Lanark until 1649), Secretary of State for Scotland, in 1640-1, ii. 128; admitted of the English Privy Council, ii. 279; with the King in his visit to Scotland in 1641, ii. 303-7; arrested, with his brother, on suspicion of disloyalty to the King, but escapes to the Continent, iii. 342-3; with the King at Newcastle, iii. 412, 498-500 and note, 501; in Scotland and in correspondence with the King at Newcastle, iii. 505-9; in continued efforts for the King, iii. 572, 578, 579-82, 584-5; one of the agents in *The Engagement* or Secret Treaty of the Scots with Charles, iii. 586 and note; with the relics of the *Engagers* in Scotland after his brother's defeat at Preston, iii. 620-1; at the Hague with Charles II., iv. 25, 27, 28, 182; succeeds his brother as 2nd Duke of Hamilton, iv. 40; in Scotland with Charles II., iv. 188, 189; his activity in Scottish politics after the Battle of Dunbar, iv. 205, 212, 282; taken prisoner at the Battle of Worcester, iv. 294; his death, iv. 267, 560.

HAMILTON, Lord William Douglas,

styled Duke of, vi. 130, 148 : see *Selkirk, Earl of.*

HAMILTON, Dowager-Marchioness of, (mother of the 3rd Marquis), ii. 9, 59.

HAMILTON, Duchess of (widow of the 2nd Duke), iv. 560.

HAMILTON, Anne, Duchess of, heiress of James, 1st Duke of, vi. 130.

HAMILTONIANS, or *Engagers*, the, iii. 588-9 ; v. 143-4.

HAMMOND, Independent minister, v. 497.

HAMMOND, Dr. Henry, nominated to the Westminster Assembly, ii. 519, 525, 526 note ; Chaplain to Charles I., iii. 556, 587, 575, 678-9, 716-9 ; allusion to, in " Tenure of Kings and Magistrates," iv. 71, 131, 434 ; among Men of Letters under the Protectorate, v. 76, 78-9 ; his death, vi. 61, 424.

HAMMOND, John, Parliamentarian officer, ii. 445.

HAMMOND, John, printer, iii. 229.

HAMMOND, Colonel Robert (nephew of Dr. Henry Hamond), iii. 326 ; at the Battle of Naseby, iii. 336 ; in the quarrel between Parliament and the Army, iii. 533, 534, 537 ; in an interview with the King, iii. 543 ; in a Council of War, iii, 549 ; governor of Isle of Wight, iii. 575, 577, 587 ; at the Treaty of Newport, iii. 609 ; in correspondence with Cromwell, iii. 524-5 ; relieved of his command in the Isle of Wight, iii. 625-6 ; in the case of Love and Gibbons, iv. 286 ; mention of, in Milton's *Defensio Secunda*, iv. 592 ; in Ireland, v. 98.

HAMMOND, General Thomas (Regicide), brother of Dr. Henry Hammond, ii. 445 ; iii. 326, 378, 537 ; at the King's Trial, iii. 707, 712 note, 720 note; iv. 7 ; vi. 28 ; in the Indemnity Bill, vi. 54.

HAMON, landlord of the *Dolphin* at Cambridge, i. 138.

HAMPDEN, John, i. 505; his resistance to Charles I.'s methods of raising money without Parliaments, i. 670, 680, 696; loses his ship-money lawsuit, i. 735 ; ii. 155; account of, in composition of Long Parliament, ii. 161-2, 164; in Strafford's Trial, ii. 179, 188; in English church-reform movement, ii. 201 ; appointed to attend Charles I. in Scotland, ii. 273, 281, 315 ; his part in the " Grand Remonstrance," ii. 319, 322 ; attempted arrest of, by the King in Parliament, ii. 339-45 ; his regiment, ii. 444, 449 ; Cromwell's mention of, ii. 451-2 ; on the Committee of the House for calling the Westminster Assembly (April 1642), ii. 511 ; defends Brentford, ii. 456 ; is mortally wounded at Chalgrove Field in Bucks, ii. 471 ; his daughter married to Colonel Robert Hammond, iii. 575.

HAMPDEN, Mrs., widow of Hampden, iv. 146.

HAMPDEN, Mrs. Elizabeth, mother of Hampden, ii. 583 ; v. 307.

HAMPDEN, Richard, eldest son of Hampden, v. 307 ; one of Cromwell's lords, v. 324.

HAMPTON COURT, reference to Conferences at, in 1603-4, i. 58 ; Charles I. at, previous to the Civil War, ii. 345, 550, and again, in 1647, as prisoner with the Army of the Parliament, iii. 556, 561-2 ; residence of Cromwell at, iv. 296 ; Lady Claypole's death at, in 1658, v. 355-6.

HANCOCK, actor, vi. 349.

HANMER, Dr. John, Bishop, i. 388.

HANNAY, Dr. James, Dean of Edinburgh, i. 720.

HANSE TOWNS, relations with England, iv. 378-9 ; Letters of State to the, iv. 482.

HARBORD, Sir Charles, v. 176.

HARBY, Edward, v. 454.

HARDING, English Divine, ii. 422 note.

HARDINGE, Richard, neighbour of Milton, vi. 717.

HARDWICKE, Humphrey, member of Westminster Assembly, ii. 519.

HAREFIELD, Middlesex, seat of Countess-Dowager of Derby, and scene of the *Arcades*, i. 588, 591, 595, 597 note, 598, 600 note, 603 note, 752 note ; vi. 491.

HARLEY, Edward, Colonel of Foot in

the *New Model* Army, iii. 327 : see *Harvey*.

HARLEY, Lord (in 1721), i. 309 note.

HARLEY, Sir Robert, in Long Parliament, ii. 173 ; lay member of Westminster Assembly, ii. 524 ; in Presbyterian tumults in London, iii. 552, 694, 696.

HARMAN, Captain, vi. 256 note.

HARNETT, William, one of the assassins of Anthony Ascham, iv. 234.

HARO, Don Luis Mendez de, Prime Minister to Philip IV. of Spain, iv. 220, 379 ; State-Letter to (Sept. 4, 1654), v. 165-6 ; in the Treaty of the Pyrenees, v. 468, 502-4.

HARPER, John, trustee for forfeited lands in Scotland, iv. 562.

HARRINGTON, translator of Ariosto, i. 115 ; iii. 515.

HARRINGTON, Lord, of Exton, i. 130.

HARRINGTON, Mr. James, author of *Oceana*, accompanies the King in his removal to Hurst Castle, iii. 629 ; dismissed from the King's service, iii. 700 ; among Men of Letters under the Protectorate, v. 75 ; his club, called "Harringtonians," or the "Rota," v. 481-6, 507, 508-9 ; Pamphlets by, v. 531 ; end of his club, v. 555 ; censure of the *Rota* on Milton, v. 659-60 note, 663; mentioned in Milton's *Ready and Easy Way*, v. 682-4 ; among Men of Letters of the Restoration, vi. 299, 307-8.

HARRINGTON, Sir James, a Recruiter in 1645, iii. 401; at the surrender of Charles I. by the Scots, iii. 510; in Councils of State of the Commonwealth, iv. 12, 14, 83, 145, 273, 308, 354-5, 225, 229, 230, 315, 321, 390, 449; in Oliver's First Parliament, v. 5 ; in the Restored Rump, v. 454, and its Council, v. 456 ; on the Committee of Safety, v. 494 ; on the New Council of State, v. 519, 544 note, 624; after the Restoration, vi. 35, 37, 55, 224 ; his death, vi. 98 note.

HARRIS, Dr., named as possible author of the *Eikon Basilike*, iv. 131.

HARRIS, Dr. John, member of Westminster Assembly, ii. 519.

HARRIS, Joseph, actor, vi. 350-1, 354, 609.

HARRIS, Dr. Robert, member of Westminster Assembly, ii. 519, 605; in the reformed Oxford University under the Protectorate, v. 73.

HARRISON, master at St. Paul's School, i. 78.

HARRISON, schoolmaster of Eton, i. 248.

HARRISON, Colonel Thomas (Regicide), Major under *New Model*, iii. 327, 328 note ; in the recruited House of Commons, iii. 402 note ; accompanies Lord Lisle to Ireland, iii. 521 ; his religious views, iii. 523; back from Ireland and joins Fairfax's Army, iii. 537, 549 ; his regiment mutinous, iii. 582-3; at the King's removal to Windsor, iii. 700-2 ; at the King's Trial, iii. 707, 712 note ; signs death-warrant of Charles I., iii. 720, vi. 28 ; iv. 12, 52; Commander-in-Chief in England during Cromwell's war in Scotland, iv. 192 ; in Councils of State, iv. 273, 355 ; in command of the English Militia during the march of Charles II. into England, iv. 291, 292, 294; his intercourse with Roger Williams, iv. 396, 548-9 ; one of Cromwell's officers, iv. 402 ; in the Officers' Petition to the Rump, iv. 403, 408 ; at the dissolution of the Rump, iv. 411-3 ; in Interim Council of Thirteen, iv. 498, 499, 500, 523; in the Barebones Parliament and its Council, iv. 505-6, 512 ; disapproves of Cromwell's assumption of the title of Protector, iv. 518, 606; in Oliver's First Parliament, v. 5 ; leader of the sect of Fifth Monarchy men, v. 16 ; alleged to be in anti-Oliverian plottings, v. 33; in Cromwell's Second Parliament, v. 107 ; in Fifth Monarchy riot, v. 132-4, 134-5; concerned in Royalist agitation, v. 335 ; ejected by the Restored Rump, v. 479, 508 ; after the Restoration, vi. 23, 30-1, 34 note, 54 ; his trial, vi. 79-80, 81-5 ; his execution, vi. 95-6 ; in Bill of Attainder, vi. 115

"HARRY, Dean," ii. 523.

"Harry, Long," ii. 523.

Harsnet, Dr. Samuel, Archbishop, i. 377, 387, 390, 392, 392-4, 399.

Hart, Charles, actor, vi. 349, 350, 356, 368, 607, 609.

Hart, John, case of, iii. 170.

Hartfell, James Johnstone, 1st Earl of, iii. 367 ; iv. 561.

Hart Hall, at Oxford, i. 521.

Hartlib, Samuel, merchant in London ; warrant for examining him and searching his house, on suspicion of his complicity with the Scots in the First Bishops' War, ii. 45 and note ; account of, and of his friendship with John Durie, iii. 193-9 ; first publications by, iii. 198-9 ; his part in introducing the system of Comenius in England, iii. 198, 199, 201-3, 215 ; his passion for New Lights, iii. 215-21, 662 ; letter of, dated Aug. 10, 1640, iii. 217 ; further publications of, in 1641-2, iii. 219-21 ; in correspondence with Comenius, concerning a scheme for a Pansophic College in London, iii. 222-5, 662 ; account of, in 1643-4, iii. 228-31 ; his friendship with Mr. Hezekiah Woodward, iii. 231, 294-5 ; his friendship with Milton, iii. 231-3 ; Milton's Tract "Of Education" addressed to, iii. 233, and 233 note, 235, 239, 661, vi. 687, 690 ; his connexion with the "Invisible College," iii. 661-5 ; v. 235 ; proposed provision for, by the Parliament of the Commonwealth, iv. 107 ; order in Council for payment of £50 to, iv. 229 ; in correspondence with the printer Ulac, iv. 466-7, 627 ; v. 153 ; order in Council for payment of arrears to, iv. 525 ; letter of Durie to, on the subject of Toleration of the Jews in a Christian Commonwealth, v. 72 note, 365, 374, 601 ; after the Restoration, vi. 199, 200 ; his connexion with the beginnings of the Royal Society, vi. 392 ; is reduced to extreme poverty at the Restoration, vi. 452 ; petitions the Convention Parliament, vi. 452, 453 note ; his death in 1662 ; vi. 452, 453 note

Hartlib, Mrs., wife of Samuel Hartlib ; a Cure for the Stone suggested by, iii. 663-4.

Hartlib, Samuel, jun., probable nephew of Hartlib, vi. 453 note.

Hartmann, Adam Samuel, petition of, to Cromwell's Council, v. 312.

Harvard, John, founder of Harvard University, ii. 563.

Harvard College, ii. 587.

Harvey, the Anatomist, i. 120 ; vi. 648.

Harvey, Cromwell's groom of the bedchamber, v. 356, 359, 360.

Harvey, Edmund, Captain of Trained Bands, and one of the Regicides, ii. 483 ; present at the King's Trial, but does not sign the warrant, iii. 720 note ; vi. 28 ; surrenders to the House in 1660, vi. 43, 49 ; excepted with a saving clause from the Indemnity Bill, vi. 54 ; his trial, vi. 80, 93 ; his death, vi. 98 note ; in the Bill of Attainder, vi. 115.

Harvey (or Harley), Edward, Colonel of Foot under Fairfax in the New Model, iii. 327, 537 ; is one of the eleven Presbyterians denounced by the Army, iii. 548-9 ; in Oliver's Parliament, v. 5 ; in the Restored Rump, v. 454, 455 ; in Monk's Council of State, v. 544, 544 note.

Harvey, John, fellow-graduate of Milton at Cambridge, i. 218.

Haselrig, Sir Arthur, Bart., i. 680 ; member for County Leicester in the Long Parliament, ii. 164, 174, 231-2, 236, 326, 328 ; and Charles's Coup d'État, ii. 339-45 ; officer in the Parliamentarian Army, ii. 445 ; lay member of Westminster Assembly, ii. 524, 605 ; in "Committee of the Two Kingdoms," iii. 41 ; in Commission of Lords and Commoners for management of the Colonies, iii. 119 ; vote of Parliament to, at the close of Civil War, iii. 381 ; a Recruiter in the Commons, iii. 404 ; a leader of the Party of Independents in the House, iii. 408, 410, 416, 418, 510 note, 530, 531, 565-6 ; Governor of Newcastle in the Second Civil War, iii. 593 ; is with Cromwell in Scotland, iii. 622 ; is one of the judges absent from the King's Trial, iii. 708 note ; in Councils

of State of the Republic, to April 1653, iv. 12, 14, 15, 87, 200, 223, 224, 273, 313, 315, 354-5, 449; President of Council in 1652, iv. 423; his dealings with John Lilburne, iv. 357-8, 503; one of Cromwell's officers, iv. 402, 406, 407; at the Dissolution of the Rump, iv. 413, 512; in Oliver's First Parliament, v. 5, 7, 9, 33; in Cromwell's Second Parliament, v. 107, 110, 112, 326, 329, 331; one of Cromwell's Lords, v. 324; in Richard's Parliament, v. 430, 432-3, 441; at the Restoration of the Rump, v. 445, 448, 449, 454, 455; in the Council of the Restored Rump, v. 456, 465, 470, 478, 479, 480, 488, 490, 495, 497, 505, 512, 514; in the Council of the Rump at its second Restoration, v. 519-20, 522, 523-4, 529, 533, 534, 537, 538; in the Restored Long Parliament, v. 544, 545, 556, 561, 604, 666; in the Indemnity Bill, vi. 38, 46-8, 50-2, 55, 224; in prison, vi. 98; his death, vi. 98 note.

HASTINGS, Colonel Henry (Royalist), a younger son of the Earl of Huntingdon, ii. 442, 463.

HASTINGS, Lady Alice: see under Clifton, Sir Gervase.

HASTINGS, Lady Elizabeth, married to Sir Hugh Calverley, i. 599 note.

HASTINGS, Ferdinando, Lord, Earl of Huntingdon: see Huntingdon, Earl of.

HASTINGS, Henry, Lord, Earl of Huntingdon: see Huntingdon, Earl of.

HATCHER, Thomas, Parliamentarian officer, ii. 446; iii. 8.

HATFIELD, Charles I. at the Earl of Salisbury's mansion of, iii. 556.

HATTON, Lord Chancellor: Holmby House built by, in reign of Queen Elizabeth, iii. 513.

HATTON, Lord: with the Queen-mother in France, iv. 131; and the Royal Society, vi. 394.

HATTON, John, apprentice to Milton's father, i. 63, 338 note.

HAUGHTON, alleged name of Milton's paternal grandmother, i. 9, 20-3.

HAUGHTON, Edmund, of Goddington, Oxfordshire, i. 21-2; his children, Jane, Isabel, Henry, Edward, Nicholas, i. 22.

HAUGHTON, Thomas, of Nethermorton; Thomas and Ellen, his children, i. 21.

HAUSTED, Peter, of Queen's College, Cambridge, author of Senile Odium, i. 244, 247, 448, 649; his Rival Friends, i. 251-3.

HAWES, Captain, subordinate to Colonel Hammond in the Isle of Wight, iii. 626-7.

HAWKE, Michael, pamphlet by, v. 142 note.

HAWKINS, Sir John, historian of music, his account of York tune, i. 52.

HAWKINS, John, churchwarden of Horton, i. 640.

HAY, legend of the origin of the name of, and of the family of Earls of Errol, i. 69.

HAY, of Bowsey, fined by Oliver in 1654, iv. 561.

HAY, of Lands, Sir John, Clerk of Register in the Scottish Council, i. 706; ii. 16, 301, 307.

HAY, of Naughton, fined by Oliver in 1654, iv. 561.

HAY, George: see Kinnoull, Earl of.

HAY, James, 1st Earl of Carlisle (in 1622): A Panegyricke to, by Weckerlin (in 1619), as Viscount Doncaster, and English Ambassador in Germany, iv. 32 note.

HAY, John: see Yester, Lord.

HAY, William, in fourth Council of State of the Commonwealth, iv. 354; in the Restored Rump, v. 454.

HAYMAN, Sir Peter, indicted in Star Chamber, and committed to the Tower, i, 216.

HAYNES, Colonel Hezekiah, in Cromwell's Army, iv. 402, 514; appointed Deputy-Major-General, v. 49, 82; in Cromwell's Second Parliament, v. 107.

HAYNES, John, Governor of Massachusetts, ii. 549, 561.

HAYS, James, Patrick, and Alexander, case of, v. 290.

HAYWARD, J., Canon-residentiary of Lichfield, i. 651, 654.

HAYWARD, Sir John, his Life and Raigne of King Edward VI., ii. 266.

HAYWOOD, licenser of books, i. 551 note.

HAZARD, Independent minister, and his wife, ii. 581.

HEANE, Major-General, killed off St. Domingo in 1655, v. 45.

HEARNE, William, goldsmith of London, ii. 495.

HEATH, Attorney-General, i. 209, 212.

HEATH, or HETH, Richard, pupil of Milton, iii. 657 ; Milton's Latin Familiar Epistle to, iv. 469 ; Nonconformist, vi. 232 note, 417 and note.

HEATH, Sir Robert, i. 627 ; ii. 134.

HEATH, Thomas, iii. 292.

HEATH's Chronicle, vi. 636 note.

HEAVENS, Elizabeth, early Quaker, v. 27.

HEIGHEHAM, Thomas, of Bethnal Green, i. 4.

HEIMBACH, Peter, his correspondence with Milton, v. 279-81, 380-1 ; vi. 500-2 and note, 723.

HEINSBERG, Peter, a Dutch merchant in Amsterdam, v. 575.

HEINSIUS, Daniel, iv. 319.

HEINSIUS, Nicholas, son of the above, i. 771-2, 775, 779, 780 ; iii. 681 and note ; iv. 269 ; his correspondences with Vossius and others, iv. 317-20, 341-4, 434, 474, 475, 539-40, 463-5, 633 ; his friendship with Bigot, v. 285.

HELDER, T., bookseller, vi. 627, 630-2.

HELWISSE, Thomas, Baptist pastor in London, ii. 540, 544, 581 ; his Toleration principles, iii. 102-3, 147.

HEMINGE, editor of First Folio Shakespeare, i. 330, 378.

HENCHMAN, Humphrey, Bishop of Salisbury and of London, i. 120 ; vi. 99, 100, 105.

HENDERSON, Alexander, parish minister of Leuchars in Fife, i. 712, 714, 722, 727 ; a leader of the Covenanters, i. 732 ; ii. 16, 17 ; his Paper of Reasons, ii. 19; the Marquis of Hamilton confers with, ii. 20 ; in a deputation from the "Tables" to Aberdeen, ii. 27; his Protest against the King's Rival Covenant, ii. 33 ; Moderator of the Glasgow Assembly of 1638, ii. 38-42 ; incites Scotland to undertake the First Bishops' War, ii. 54;

a "supplication" to the King drawn up by, ii. 61; one of the Scottish Commissioners for the Treaty of the Pacification of Birks, ii., 68-9, 126-7 ; liking of Charles I. for, ii. 69 ; in Newcastle, at the close of the Second Bishops' War, ii. 142 ; in the negotiations at Ripon, ii. 143 ; with the Scottish Commissioners in London, ii. 190-3, 202 ; anti-Episcopal pamphlets by, ii. 218, 226 ; Moderator of the General Assembly of 1641, held at Edinburgh, ii. 287-91 ; in communication with the English Puritan ministers, ii. 290, 509 ; acts as chaplain to Charles I. during his visit to Scotland in 1641, ii. 302, 304, 308 ; present at General Assembly of 1642, held at St. Andrews, ii. 418-20 ; is Moderator of General Assembly of 1643, held at Edinburgh, iii. 7 ; is the probable author of the Solemn League and Covenant, iii. 9-10 ; sent with it to the Westminster Assembly in London, iii. 10-8 ; takes part in the business of the Assembly, iii. 22, 84, 176 ; his standpoint in the Toleration controversy in 1640 and onwards, iii. 108, 136, 160 ; in correspondence with Hartlib, iii. 219-20 ; leaves London to attend the Negotiations at Newcastle, iii. 412-3 ; his discussions with the King there, iii. 417, 426 ; his death at Edinburgh in Aug. 1646, iii. 426-9 and note, 430.

HENDRINCX, Jacob, vi. 803.

HENRIETTA-MARIA, Queen; marriage to Charles I., i. 106, 151-2, 232 ; visits Cambridge with the King, i. 251-4, 341, 379, 447, 506, 580, 583, 587 ; her private palace, Denmark House in the Strand, i. 685 ; intrigues with Rome, i. 685, 748, 756, 799; during the First Bishops' War, ii. 50, 51, 152 ; during Strafford's Trial, ii. 179, 183, 187 ; political intrigues, ii. 282-4, 352 ; during the Irish Insurrection, ii. 311-2, 317, iii. 517 ; her entry into London with Charles I. on his return from Scotland, ii. 323, 345, 346 ; leaves the kingdom with the Crown Jewels, ii. 350, 353, 421 ; re-

turns to England, after a year's absence, ii. 468 ; the "Queen's Army," *alias* the "Popish Army," ii. 468 ; her interview with Montrose, iii. 341, 343, 344 ; with Charles I. at Oxford, iii. 6 ; during the first Civil War, iii. 335 ; at the close of the Civil War, iii. 376 ; birth of her youngest child at Exeter, iii. 375 ; escapes to France and is resident there for two years, acting as the King's agent, iii. 375 ; in correspondence with Charles I. during the Newcastle Negotiations, iii. 415, 417, 418, 422 ; her influence over Charles during his captivity, iii. 491-6 ; in continued correspondence with Charles I., iii. 498-9, 501, 502, 506, 507, 558 ; during the Second Civil War, iii. 590, 591-2 ; encourages Montrose, iv. 181 ; her letter to Parliament in the last days of Charles I., iii. 715 ; continues to take part in English affairs after the death of the King, iv. 27, 56, 131, 180, 380-2 ; excepted from Cromwell's Ordinance of Pardon and Grace, iv. 560 ; Cowley, the poet, is her Secretary in France, v. 83 ; after the death of Cromwell, v. 416 ; votes of money to, by Parliament in 1660, vi. 67, 109 ; return of, to England, and the Court of her son, vi. 71-2, 239 ; her action in the matter of Anne Hyde's marriage, vi. 107-8, 118-9 ; her Almoner the Abbé Lord Aubigny, vi. 240 ; her portrait by Faithorne, done in Paris, vi. 648.

HENRIETTA, Princess, youngest child of Charles I., birth of, iii. 375 ; in exile with the Queen, her mother, iii. 494 ; after the Restoration, vi. 71, 72 ; as wife of Philip, Duke of Orleans, vi. 571, 575-6 ; death of, vi. 578.

HENRY, Prince, eldest son of James I., i. 60, 100 ; iii. 724, 727.

HENRY IV., of France, i. 106.

HENRY VII., of England, i. 607.

HENRY, Matthew, son of Philip Henry, vi. 232 note.

HENRY, Philip, Nonconformist, vi. 232 note.

HENSCH, Gerard, v. 190.

HENSHAW, Thomas, in the first Council of the Royal Society, vi. 396.

HENSLOWE, theatrical manager, i. 432.

HEPBURN, Sir Patrick, ii. 143, 190.

HERBERT, Edward, of Cherbury, 1st Lord, author of *De Veritate*, i. 540-1, 546 ; ii. 48, 429, 430 note ; iii. 377, 448, 555 note.

HERBERT, Edward, 3rd Lord of Cherbury, in the First Parliament of the Protectorate, v. 5 ; in the projected Royalist Insurrection of 1659, v. 473, 474 ; his imprisonment, v. 477 ; his release, v. 505 ; after the Restoration, v. 700.

HERBERT of Raglan, Edward Somerset, styled Lord, i. 182 ; account of, as eldest son of the 1st Marquis of Worcester, ii. 462.

HERBERT, Sir Edward, member of the Inner Temple in 1633, i. 580 ; in the Long Parliament, ii. 159 ; Solicitor-General, and, in 1640, Attorney-General, ii. 279, 283 ; his part in Charles I.'s *Coup d'Etat*, ii. 338, 346.

HERBERT, George, religious poet, i. 73 ; public orator of Cambridge, i. 119 ; as Professor of Rhetoric at Cambridge, i. 262 ; 267, 413-5, 430, 486, 492, 496, 498, 500 ; iii. 515 ; Izaak Walton's Life of, vi. 700.

HERBERT, Sir Henry, Master of the Revels, and licenser of plays in London, i. 450, 546, 550 note, 587.

HERBERT, Henry, in the Fourth Council of State of the Commonwealth, iv. 354.

HERBERT, Hon. James, second son of the Earl of Pembroke, and member for Wilts in 1645-6, iii. 401.

HERBERT, Lucy : see *Habington.*

HERBERT, Mr., member of the Restored Long Parliament in 1659-60, and teller in a division with Lord Ancram, v. 552.

HERBERT, Philip : see *Pembroke*, Earls of, and *Montgomery*, 1st Earl of.

HERBERT, Sir Thomas, favourite attendant of Charles I., iii. 514 note ; his *Memoirs of the last Two Years of Charles I.*, iii. 588, 588 note, 629,

700-1 ; in the last days of Charles I., iii. 712, 713, 721-7, 726 note.

HERBERT, William, Parliamentarian officer, ii. 444 ; Colonel, iii. 537.

HERBERT, William : see *Pembroke*, Earls of.

HERBERT, William : see *Powis*.

HEREFORD, Viscount, v. 700.

HERLE, Charles, member of Westminster Assembly, ii. 519, 605 ; iii. 20, 22, 160 ; a book-licenser, iii. 270, 298, 391 ; Prolocutor of the Westminster Assembly, iii. 426.

HEROIC Plays, or Rhyming Tragedies, vi. 358-63.

HERRICK, Richard, member of Westminster Assembly, ii. 519 ; iii. 425 note ; iv. 285, 304.

HERRICK, Robert, the poet, i. 506-8, 513, 567 ; ii. 79 ; iii. 446 ; under the Protectorate, v. 76 ; after the Restoration, vi. 292,'322.

HERRINGMAN, Henry, printer and publisher, v. 258, 262 note ; vi. 13, 14 note, 16 and note, 365 note, 369 note, 376, 378, 400, 402, 403-5, 460, 508-9, 514-5, 710, 730.

HERTFORD, William Seymour, 1st Marquis of : see *Somerset*, Duke of.

HETH : see *Heath*, Richard.

HETHERINGTON, John, of the sect of Familists, iii. 152.

HEVENINGHAM, William (Regicide), at the King's Trial, iii. 720 note, vi. 28 ; in Councils of State, iv. 13, 79, 82, 83, 147, 150, 151, 223, 224, 231 ; v. 544 note ; in the Restored Rump, v. 454 ; after the Restoration, vi. 43, 49, 54 ; trial of, vi. 79-80, 94 ; death of, vi. 98 note ; in the Bill of Attainder, vi. 115.

HEWIT, Dr. John, trial and execution of, v. 337-8.

HEWLET, Captain William, supposed to be the executioner of the King, vi. 41-2, 54 ; trial of, vi. 81, 87-92, 94 ; in the Bill of Attainder, vi. 115.

HEWSON, Colonel Sir John, under the *New Model*, iii. 326, 328 note, 524, 534, 536, 537,'696 ; at the King's trial, iii. 707, 712 note ; signs death-warrant of Charles I., iii.

720 ; at the *Fairfaxian Creation* at Oxford, iv. 52 ; in Ireland, iv. 56, 370, 401 ; in the Barebones Parliament, iv. 501, 506, 512, 514 ; in Oliver's First Parliament, v. 5, 128 ; one of Cromwell's lords, v. 324 ; knighted by Cromwell, v. 354 note ; supports Richard's Government, v. 418 ; in Republican remodelling of the Army, v. 470 ; on the Committee of Safety, v. 494, 514 ; at Second Restoration of the Rump, v. 522 ; after the Restoration, vi. 44, 54 ; in Bill of Attainder, v. 115 ; subsequent fate of, vi. 115 note.

HEYDON, Sir John, Royalist officer, ii. 441.

HEYGATE, James, Irish Bishop, i. 420.

HEYLIN, Peter, biographer of Laud, i. 361, 400-1, 525 ; ii. 167 ; among Men of Letters under the Protectorate, v. 76, 78-9 ; at the Restoration, vi. 292, 325, 387.

HEYRICKE : see *Herrick*, Richard.

HEYWOOD, the dramatist, i. 445, 569 ; iii. 446.

HEYWOOD, Oliver, Nonconformist, vi. 232 note.

HIBBENS, William, ii. 586.

HICKES, Jasper, member of Westminster Assembly, ii. 519.

HICKMAN, Spencer, publisher, vi. 647 note, 684-5.

HICKSON, Samuel, of Trinity College, Cambridge : University Proctor, i. 171.

HIERON, John, fellow-graduate of Milton at Cambridge, i. 218, 258.

HIGGINSON, Puritan emigrant to America, i. 430 ; ii. 551-4.

HIGHAM, John, pupil of Joseph Meade at Christ's College, Cambridge, i. 150, 180, 181, 231-2.

HIGH HOLBORN, Milton's house in, iii. 667.

HILDERSHAM, Rev. Samuel, suspended by Laud, i. 402 ; member of Westminster Assembly, ii. 519.

HILL, Abraham, v. 221 ; and the Royal Society, vi. 394, 396.

HILL, Nicholas, servant of the Council of State, v. 625.

HILL, Roger, in the Restored Rump Parliament, v. 454.

HILL, Thomas, scrivener, i. 339 note.
HILL, Rev. Thomas, rector of Titchmarsh, ii. 225 ; member of Westminster Assembly, ii. 519, 605 ; at the Visitation of Cambridge University, iii. 93 ; 162-3, 263-4 ; iv. 352.
HILLS, Henry, printer and publisher, iv. 249 note ; v. 264, 351 ; vi. 399, 403.
HILLS, Dr. John, Master of Catherine Hall, Cambridge, i. 116, 120, 180.
HIPPESLEY, Sir John, iv. 150, 153, 315.
HISPANIOLA : see *St. Domingo*.
" HISTORY OF BRITAIN," etc., by Milton : see *Milton*, Writings of.
" HISTORY OF MOSCOVIA," see *Milton*, Writings of.
" HISTRIOMASTIX," by Prynne, i. 450, 579, 673.
HOBART, Sir John, of Blickling, Norfolk, i. 588-9 ; v. 128, 324.
HOBART, Sir Miles, prosecuted by the Star Chamber, i. 216.
HOBBES, Thomas, i. 538 ; account of, to 1632, i. 541-2 ; is tutor to the 2nd and 3rd Earls of Devonshire, ii. 158 ; is tutor to the Prince of Wales in Paris in 1646, iii. 430, 494, 503, 664 ; his connexions with Davenant in Paris, vi. 275-6 ; references to the works of, iv. 434-5 ; included among Men of Letters of the Period of the Protectorate, v. 76 ; story of his exile from 1641, of his return to England in 1651-2, and of his residence with the Earl of Devonshire, v. 80-1, 295 ; his position and work among Men of Letters at the Restoration, and his place and influence in English Philosophy, vi. 279-91, 290 note, 388, 617 ; reference to Milton and the Salmasian controversy by, vi. 636 note ; his portrait by Faithorne, done in 1664, vi. 648 ; Milton's opinion of, reported by Aubrey, vi. 682.
HOBBISM, vi. 304, 305, 318, 322.
HOBSON, Captain, iii. 58-60, 159, 188, 188 note.
HOBSON, Paul, Baptist preacher, iii. 147, 148, 678.
HOBSON, Thomas, the Cambridge carrier, i. 134-5, 152, 240-1 ; Milton's two epitaphs on, i. 241-3.
HOBSON, Thomas, son of the Cambridge carrier, i. 240.
HOCKCHESTER, Roger, of Pembroke College, Cambridge, University Proctor, i. 237.
HODDER, James, schoolmaster, vi. 516.
HODGES, Giles, expelled from Oxford for Puritanism, i. 408.
HODGES, Thomas, member of Westminster Assembly, ii. 519, 605.
HODGKINS, Roger, in the Venner Riot, vi. 120.
HODGKINSON, James, apprentice of Milton's father, i. 338 note.
HOG, William, his Latin translations from Milton, vi. 790.
HOGHTON, Sir Richard, i. 21.
HOGHTON, Sir Thomas, i. 21.
HOLAC, Count of, a German, v. 249.
HOLBORN, Robert, lawyer, member for Michell, Cornwall, in Long Parliament, ii. 173-4 ; in the Trial of Strafford, ii. 185.
HOLBORN, Colonel, under the *New Model*, iii. 326-7, 361.
HOLCHAR, Thomas, i. 628, 629, 637.
HOLDEN, actress, vi. 350.
HOLDEN, John, bookseller, vi. 186.
HOLDENBY HOUSE : see *Holmby House*.
HOLDING, Dr., of Lancaster, a guest, with Milton, in the English College at Rome, i. 800.
HOLDSWORTH, Mr. Richard, tutor in St. John's, Cambridge, in 1616-8, i. 121, 262 ; afterwards Master of Emanuel and Dean of Worcester, i. 121 ; ii. 225, 519 ; his part in Usher's project for Church management, ii. 230 ; non-acting member of Westminster Assembly, ii. 519, 525 ; ejected from Cambridge University in 1644, iii. 93 ; his death in 1649, ii. 519.
HOLLAND : States of West, iv. 383 ; Letters of State to the States of, in Sept. 1656, v. 274-5, 378.
HOLLAND, Mr. Cornelius, one of the Regicides, iii. 720 note ; in Councils of State of the Commonwealth, iv. 11, 13, 82, 83, 87, 145, 146, 150, 223, 224, 226, 230, 354, 446 ; in

the Restored Rump, v. 454; on the Committee of Safety, v. 494; mentioned in *Treason arraigned*, v. 666; at the quest of the Regicides, vi. 28, 31, 54; subsequent fate of, vi. 115, 115 note.

HOLLAND, Henry Rich, 1st Earl of: Constable of Windsor Castle, i. 22 note; Chancellor of Cambridge University in succession to Buckingham, i. 213, 220, 223, 225; account of his early career, i. 379; in Charles I.'s Council, i. 383, 384, 408; ii. 278, 279, 337; his part in the First Bishops' War, ii. 51, 61, 62, 63-4, 68, 129, 143; in the Long Parliament, ii. 152, 153, 168; in Strafford's Trial, ii. 180; appointed by the Commons Lord - Lieutenant of Berkshire, ii. 354, 439; refuses to join Charles I. in the First Civil War, and is deposed by the King from his various offices, ii. 413; his fickleness in the Civil War, ii. 430; iii. 377, 591; a lay member of Westminster Assembly, ii. 523; commissioned Generalissimo of the King's forces in England in the projected Second Civil War, iii. 591, 596; addresses a Declaration of Motives to Parliament, acts in co-operation with the King's forces, is defeated and taken prisoner, iii. 596; sentenced to banishment by the Commons, iii. 615; executed together with the Duke of Hamilton and Lord Capel in 1649, iv. 40.

HOLLAND HOUSE, at Kensington, i. 379.

HOLLAND, Hugh, his lines on Shakespeare, i. 330, 331.

HOLLAND, Sir John, Parliamentary Commissioner to the King at Oxford, ii. 464; and at Newcastle, iii. 510; in the Council of State of the Restored Long Parliament, v. 544; at the Restoration, v. 700.

HOLLAR, engraver, iii. 457.

HOLLES, Denzil (brother of the Earl of Clare, and brother-in-law of the Earl of Strafford), committed to the Tower for his action in the House of Commons at the dissolution of Charles I.'s Parliament in 1629, i.

216, 522; ii. 162; member for Dorchester in the Long Parliament, ii. 162, 174, 178, 281, 321, 338; his action on the occasion of Charles's *Coup d'Etat*, ii. 339-45; in Commons business, ii. 416; Colonel of a foot-regiment in Essex's army, ii. 444, 449, 456, 465, 466; acts in opposition to Cromwell in debates on the Self-denying Ordinance, iii. 180, 182 note; his hatred to Cromwell, iii. 180, 603; proposals of rewards to, by Parliament at the close of Civil War, iii. 380; is one of the Presbyterian party-chiefs in the Commons in 1645-6, iii. 404, 408, 416, 530, 531, 532, 533, 534, 538, 559 note; one of the eleven Presbyterian leaders denounced by the Army, iii. 548-9; escapes abroad, iii. 554; returns to his seat in the House, and reassumes the Presbyterian leadership, iii. 603; in the negotiations for the Treaty of Newport, iii. 605, 606; among the members excluded from the House by "Pride's Purge," iii. 696-7; 699; concerned in Sir George Booth's insurrection, v. 478; in the Council of State of the Restored Long Parliament, v. 544; at the Restoration, v. 700, vi. 3-4, 7; in the Privy Council of Charles II., vi. 19; in the Convention Parliament, vi. 23, 24, 51, 53, 64; one of the Commissioners for the Trials of the Regicides, vi. 77, 78; in the Conference with Charles II. concerning the Royal Ecclesiastical Declaration, vi. 99, 100; created a Baron at the Coronation of Charles II. vi. 153; in Charles's Council during the Clarendon Administration, vi. 222; one of the English Plenipotentiaries at Breda in the Dutch War, 265; as Lord Hollis, and first Ambassador for Charles II. at Paris, vi. 421; 598.

HOLLIS, Thomas, i. 310 note; vi. 754 note.

HOLLISTER, Mr. Dennis, member of Cromwell's Council in the Barebones Parliament, iv. 506.

HOLMAN, John, Parliamentarian officer, ii. 444.

HOLLOWAY, Christmas, gent., and his wife Elizabeth, mentioned in Mrs. Powell's will, vi. 750.

HOLMBY HOUSE, Charles I. a prisoner at, iii. 510, 513-6, 539-46.

HOLMES, a victim of the plague in Cambridge, i. 233.

HOLMES, Admiral, in the War with the Dutch, vi. 252, 260, 377.

HOLMES, Thomas, Baptist preacher, iii. 148.

HOLMES, Thomas, early Quaker, v. 26-7.

HOLSTEIN, Duke of, iv. 183.

HOLSTENIUS, Lucas, Secretary to Cardinal Francesco Barberini, and one of the Librarians of the Vatican, i. 798; in correspondence with Milton, i. 802-3, 822-3, 823 note; vi. 723.

"HOLY AND PROFANE STATE," by Fuller, ii. 359-61.

HOLYMAN, the first Baptist in New England, ii. 562.

HOLYWOOD, John, his work on Astronomy, iii. 254, and note; vi. 534.

HOME, Sir James Home, 2nd Earl of, ii. 16, 38: see Hume.

HONEYWOOD, Michael, Fellow of Christ's College, Cambridge, i. 123, 213, 267, 649, 651; ii. 76.

HONEYWOOD, Sir Robert, in the Council of State of the Restored Rump, v. 456, 467; a fellow-plenipotentiary with Admiral Montague in the Baltic, v. 478.

HONEYWOOD, Sir Thomas, v. 324.

HOOKE, Robert, in correspondence with Boyle, vi. 289, 392, 397.

HOOKER, Richard, theologian, i. 514, 517, 518; quotations from, in a volume of Oxford Tracts in favour of Episcopacy, ii. 363-4; his Ecclesiastical Polity among Charles I.'s favourite books at Holmby House, iii. 515; a new edition of the Works of, with a Life of, by Dr. Gauden, in 1661, vi. 434.

HOOKER, Thomas, at Chelmsford, suspended by Laud, i. 402; account of, ii. 556-7; as minister at Hartford in New England, ii. 558, 559; declines the invitation of some of the English Parliament to join the Westminster Assembly, ii. 605.

HOORNE, Simon van, v. 196.

HOOTON, Elizabeth, Early Quaker, v. 72.

HOPE of Craighall, Sir Thomas, King's Advocate, and member of the Scottish Privy Council in 1634-8, i. 706, 709, 711; ii. 15, 16.

HOPE of Craighall, Sir John, one of the Trustees for forfeited lands in Scotland in 1653, iv. 561-2.

HOPE of Hopeton, Sir James, iv. 502; in the Council of the Barebones Parliament, 506.

HOPER, J., writer of verses on Edward King's death, i. 651.

HOPKINS, Edward, ii. 549, 599.

HOPTON, Sir Ralph, K.B. (afterwards Lord Hopton), member for Wells in the Long Parliament, ii. 170; account of, ii. 170-1, 326; joins Charles I. in the Civil War, ii. 415, 443, 465; made Baron Hopton of Stratton, ii. 466; his military successes in Cornwall, ii. 466-7; at the close of the Civil War, iii. 371, 375; included among the Delinquents, iii. 421; in exile, iii. 493-4; in the Second Civil War, iii. 591, 595; in correspondence with John Lilburne, iv. 502.

HORNE, Thomas, Master of Eton, iii. 201.

HORSEY, Sir George, mentioned in a lawsuit against Milton's father, i. 267.

HORSMANDEN, Daniel, of St. John's College, Cambridge, i. 111, 121.

HORTON, place of residence of Milton's father and the Milton family, from 1632 to 1640, i. 338-9, 553-6, 556-61, 560 note, 632, 638-40, 640 note; ii. 72-3, 456, 488-9.

HORTON, Mr., Divinity Lecturer at Gresham College, iii. 392 note.

HORTON, Jeremiah, Parliamentarian officer, ii. 444.

HORTON, Thomas, tutor of Emanuel College, Cambridge, i. 121.

HORTON, Major Thomas, one of the Regicides: signs the Petition of Officers, iii. 534; signs the death-warrant of Charles I., iii. 720; departure of his regiment for Ireland, iv. 56; dead at the date of the Re-

storation, vi. 28 ; excepted from the Indemnity Bill, vi. 54.

HORWOOD, Alfred J., his discovery of Milton's Commonplace Book, etc., i. 303.

HOSIER, John, master of a ship called *The Lady*, v. 386.

HOSKYNS, Job, a member of the Rota Club, v. 485.

HOTHAM, Charles, student of Christ's College, Cambridge, i. 248.

HOTHAM, Sir John, in the King's army in the First Bishops' War, ii. 62 ; member for Beverley in Long Parliament, ii. 172 ; at Charles's *Coup d'État*, ii. 340 ; governor of Hull, ii. 412 ; in Fairfax's army, ii. 448 ; at Hull, ii. 467-8 ; is wavering towards the King, ii. 470 ; executed with his son for treachery at Hull, iii. 185.

HOTHAM, John (son of Sir John Hotham), member for Scarborough in Long Parliament, ii. 172 ; captain of a troop of horse in Essex's army, ii. 445 ; in Fairfax's army, ii. 448 ; with his father at Hull, ii. 467-8, 470 ; executed with his father for treachery at Hull, iii. 185.

HOTTON, Gothofrid, minister of the French Church in Amsterdam, iv. 631 ; in the Morus Controversy, v. 196, 200, 205.

HOUBRAKEN, engraver of Milton's portrait, i. 310 note.

HOWARD of Charlton, Lord, eldest son of Earl of Berkshire, ii. 429.

HOWARD of Escrick, Lord, at the calling of the Long Parliament, ii. 143 ; account of, in the composition of Long Parliament, ii. 156-7 ; in Scotland with Charles I., ii. 273 ; Parliamentarian peer, ii. 297 note, 431 ; iii. 555 note, 692 ; lay member of Westminster Assembly, ii. 523 ; iii. 406 ; at the abolition of House of Peers, iv. 4 ; member for Carlisle in the Rump Parliament, iv. 58 ; in Cromwell's Council of State, iv. 177, 224, 227, 230 ; ceases to be in the Council, iv. 273 ; expelled from the House, and punished for receiving bribes, iv. 284.

HOWARD, Charles, 1st Earl of Carlisle :

Colonel in the Royalist Army in 1645, iii. 335 ; in the Barebones Parliament, iv. 501, 506, 512 ; member of Cromwell's Council, iv. 525 ; one of Cromwell's major-generals, v. 49 ; in Cromwell's Scottish Council, sitting in Edinburgh, v. 86, 87, 115 ; in Cromwell's Second Parliament, v. 107, 125, 128, 129 ; one of Cromwell's lords, v. 323 ; created Viscount by Cromwell, v. 354 note ; during Richard's Protectorate, v. 417-8, 421, 439 ; during the period of Anarchy, v. 464, 469, 505, 517 ; Monk gives a regiment to, v. 563 ; in Charles II.'s Privy Council, vi. 19, 222, 598 ; on the Committee for the Indemnity Bill, vi. 30 ; made Earl of Carlisle at the Coronation of Charles II., vi. 152 ; his sister married to Sir George Downing, vi. 229 ; sent, in 1663, as Ambassador-Extraordinary to Muscovy, Sweden, and Denmark, vi. 252 ; his secretary in the Embassy, Andrew Marvell, vi. 252, 482.

HOWARD, Hon. Edward (son of Earl of Berkshire), among Men of Letters of the Restoration, vi. 314, 364-5, 365 note, 367, 515, 610, 618.

HOWARD, Lady Elizabeth, married to Dryden, vi. 367.

HOWARD, Lady Frances, married to the Earl of Somerset, ii. 153-4.

HOWARD, Hon. James, son of Earl of Berkshire, among Men of Letters of the Restoration, vi. 314, 367, 611.

HOWARD, Mr., a neighbour of Milton in Artillery Walk, vi. 717.

HOWARD, Sir Robert, son of Earl of Berkshire, among Men of Letters of the Restoration, vi. 314, 353-4, 358, 363, 365 note, 366-7, 376, 378, 610-1, 612, 633-4, 637-8, 785.

HOWARD, Theophilus : see *Suffolk*, 2nd Earl of.

HOWARD, Thomas : see *Suffolk*, 1st Earl of.

HOWARD, Thomas : see *Arundel*, 2nd Earl of.

HOWE, Mr. John, at Stowmarket in Suffolk, i. 185.

HOWE, John, among Men of Letters under the Protectorate, v. 76 ; chap-

lain to Cromwell, v. 77; at the Restoration, vi. 315-6, 617; ejected for Nonconformity, vi. 232 note, 417.

HOWE, Samuel, Baptist preacher, iii. 147.

HOWELL, James, author : i. 438, 736, note ; ii. 206; iii. 62-3; 446, 448-9; v. 76; vi. 292; reference to his clerkship to the Council and subsequent post of Historiographer to the King, vi. 293; 322; death of, vi. 608.

HOWELL, Thomas, gent., mentioned in Mrs. Powell's will, vi. 750.

HOWGILL, Francis, early Quaker, v. 26-7.

HOWLETT, Richard, Cromwell's tutor at Cambridge, i. 121, 155; ii. 78.

HOWSE, William, of Beckley, Oxfordshire, i. 15, 16.

HOWSON, Dr. John, Bishop of Durham, i. 390.

HOYLE, Alderman, vi. 179 note.

HOYLE, Dr. Joshua, member of Westminster Assembly, ii. 519; iii. 677.

HUBBERTHORN, Richard, early Quaker, v. 26.

HUBBERTHORN, Colonel John, one of Monk's officers, v. 540, 562.

"HUDIBRAS," by Samuel Butler, vi. 339-42, 339 note, 387-8, 730.

HUDSON, Dr., in the King's escape from Oxford to the Scots, iii. 373.

HUET, French courtier of Queen Christina of Sweden, iv. 269.

HUGHES, Mrs., actress, vi. 350, 351.

HUGUENOTS, the, of Rochelle, i. 204-5.

"HUMAN NATURE," by Hobbes, vi. 280.

"HUMBLE REMONSTRANCE to the High Court of Parliament," by Bishop Hall, ii. 214-5.

HUME (Home), 2nd Earl of, i. 722, 725; in the Episode of Montrose, iii. 362.

HUME, John, Scottish "Protester," vi. 134.

HUME, Patrick, Scottish schoolmaster in London, author of a Commentary on Paradise Lost, vi. 787.

HUNCKS, Colonel Hercules, the death-warrant of Charles I. addressed to, iii. 720; turns informer at the trials of the Regicides, vi. 87-8, 97.

HUNGERFORD, Sir George : his anecdotes of Paradise Lost, related to the painter Richardson, vi. 628-9.

HUNSCOT, Joseph, beadle of the Stationers' Company, iv. 152.

HUNSDON, Lord, Parliamentarian peer : see Rochfort, Viscount.

HUNSDON, Lady Elizabeth : see Spencer.

HUNSDON, George Carey, 2nd Lord, i. 591.

HUNTER, Joseph, author of Milton Gleanings, i. 11, 17, 18, 19, 20.

HUNTER, William, Parliamentarian officer, ii. 444.

HUNTINGDON, Cromwell member for the town of, in Charles I.'s Third Parliament, i. 215; Charles I. at, ii. 354.

HUNTINGDON, Elizabeth, Countess of, i. 590, 595-6.

HUNTINGDON, Ferdinando Hastings, 6th Earl of, i. 590; ii. 429, 445.

HUNTINGDON, Henry Hastings, 5th Earl of, i. 590, 595-6; ii. 428, 463.

HUNTINGDON, Colonel Robert, a major under the New Model, iii. 327, 336, 531, 603; mention of, in Milton's Defensio Secunda, iv. 592-3.

HUNTLY (or Huntley), George Gordon, 2nd Marquis of, ii. 4, 7, 8, 13, 15; and the King's Covenant in Aberdeen, ii. 34; in First "Bishops' War," ii. 51, 56-7, 59, 60; in Second "Bishops' War," ii. 137; during the Episode of Montrose in Scotland, iii. 342, 352, 368; a "Delinquent," iii. 421.

HUNTLY, Lewis Gordon, 3rd Marquis of, iv. 205, 206, 282.

HUNTLY, the Marchioness of (daughter of the 7th Earl of Argyll), ii. 11.

HURDIDGE, Francis, merchant, v. 589-90.

HURLOCK, George, publisher, vi. 403.

HURRY, Alexander, Parliamentarian officer, ii. 444.

HURRY, John: see Urry.

HURST Castle, Charles I. confined in, iii. 625-30, 699-702.

HUSBAND, Edwin, printer to the House of Commons, v. 544 note ; vi. 167 note.

HUSSEY, George, messenger to the Council, iv. 578; v. 625.

HUTCHINSON, Mrs. Ann, New England heretic, ii. 165, 574-7, 601; popular myth concerning, and tragic end of, iii. 150, 151 note, 467.

HUTCHINSON, George, Parliamentarian officer, ii. 444.

HUTCHINSON, Colonel John, in the Civil War, iii. 379; member of the recruited Commons, iii. 401; one of the Commissioners for the King's Trial, iii. 707, 712 note; signs the death-warrant of Charles I., iii. 720; in Councils of State of the Commonwealth, iv. 12, 14, 82, 147, 150, 223, 225, 230; in the Restored Rump, v. 454, 479, 522-3; in the Restored Long Parliament, v. 545, 546; in the Convention Parliament, vi. 23; 28; excepted from the Indemnity Bill, vi. 36, 37, 38, 45, 50, 55; dies a prisoner in Deal Castle, vi. 98, 98 note.

HUTTON, Henry, member of Westminster Assembly, ii. 519.

HYDE, Anne, Duchess of York, vi. 71, 106-8, 118-19, 262, 270, 461; her death, vi. 580.

HYDE, Mr. Sergeant, member for Salisbury, ii. 286.

HYDE, Captain David, ii. 332, 342.

HYDE, Edward: see Clarendon.

HYDE, Henry, father of the Earl of Clarendon, i. 532.

HYDE, Sir Henry, eldest son of Clarendon, vi. 74, 151.

HYDE, Sir Nicholas, Lord Chief-Justice, i. 532; ii. 495; vi. 478.

I

IBBETSON, Robert, printer and bookseller, v. 361 note; vi. 399.

"IGNORAMUS," a Cambridge Comedy, by George Ruggle, i. 221.

ILES, Thomas, Professor of Divinity at Oxford, ii. 498 note.

"ILLUSTRIOUS SHEPHERDESS, the," translated from the Spanish by Edward Phillips, v. 263.

"IL PENSEROSO": see Milton, Writings of.

IMBRECOURT, Lord, graduate of Cambridge, i. 181-2.

"IMPERIOUS BROTHER, the," translated from the Spanish by Edward Phillips, v. 263.

"IN ADVENTUM VERIS": see Milton, Writings of.

"INCENDIARIES," a term applied to one class of the national "Delinquents" tried by the Scottish Parliament of 1641, ii. 300-1, 307.

"INCIDENT, The," story of, at Edinburgh, in 1641, ii. 304-6, 315.

INCHCOLM, island of, in the Firth of Forth, ii. 59.

INCHGARVIE, a fortified island in the Firth of Forth, surrender of, to Cromwell in 1651, iv. 288.

INCHIQUIN, Lord, in the war of the Parliament with Ireland in 1643-4, iii. 518, 519; joins the Irish rebels against the Parliament in 1648, iii. 593; in the Treaty of the Marquis of Ormond for Charles II. with the General Assembly of the Roman Catholics of Ireland, iv. 23.

INCHKEITH, island of, in the Firth of Forth, ii. 59.

INDEMNITY, Charles II.'s Declaration of, dated from Breda, April 4, 1660, vi. 25-6; the Bill of, in the Commons, vi. 26-44; in the Lords, vi. 44-48; differences and conferences on, vi. 48-53; the Bill passed, vi. 53; Abstract of the Bill, vi. 54-56; Milton and the Bill of, vi. 167-180; the Act confirmed, vi. 222-3.

INDEPENDENCY: founders of: see Brown, Barrowe, Jacob, Smyth, Helwisse, Robinson, Lathorp; i. 402; congregations of Independents settle in Amsterdam, i. 426-7; the colony of New Plymouth in America founded in 1620 chiefly by English Independents of Holland, i. 428-9; ii. 46; history of English, at home and abroad, to 1643, ii. 534-602; Presbyterianism and, in July 1643, their prospects in the Westminster Assembly, ii. 602-8; iii. 20; the Apologetical Narration of the Independents in the Assembly, iii. 23-6; spread of, in England, iii. 84; Cromwell, the great Independent, iii. 85, 166; Army Independency,

iii. 85-91, 167; the Independents generally and the Baptist section of them part company on the Toleration question, iii. 106; pamphlets of Thomas Edwards against, iii. 110, 130-5; the Congregationalists, or Orthodox Independents, and the chaos of Sects and Sectaries, professing, with them, the principle of Church Independency, iii. 136-7; Edwards's *Gangræna*, iii. 142; Baillie's *Dissuasive* against, iii. 142-3; the Battle of Marston Moor won mainly by Cromwell and the Army Independents, iii. 160; Milton's more extreme Independency, exemplified by passages from the *Areopagitica*, iii. 286-90; and the Toleration Controversy, iii. 382-3; in the *New Model* Army, iii. 384-6, and through English society generally, iii. 386; in the Westminster Assembly, iii. 391-4; Erastianism and, iii. 396-7; alliance of Erastianism and, against the policy of the ultra-Presbyterians, iii. 403-11; 416; differences among the leaders of, on the question of a State Church as conceived by Cromwell, iv. 566; Milton's adherence to the principle of, and his opposition to Cromwell's policy of a State Church, iv. 614-15; extreme sects of, in 1654-5, v. 15; existence of, among the Scottish parish clergy, especially in Aberdeenshire, v. 91; the *Independents proper* form a section of the great Nonconformist party in 1662, vi. 235. See also under *Church* and *Presbyterianism*.

INGELO, Mr. or Dr. Nathaniel, chaplain to Whitlocke in the Swedish Embassy of 1653, iv. 513; and Marvell, iv. 623-4.

INGOLDSBY, Colonel Henry, v. 354 note.

INGOLDSBY, Sir Richard, iii. 326.

INGOLDSBY, Colonel Richard (son of Sir Richard), Parliamentarian officer, ii. 444; under the *New Model*, iii. 326, 332, 402 note, 537, 615; signs the death-warrant of Charles I., but is not present at the sentence, iii. 720 and note, vi. 28-9; at the Fairfaxian

Creation, iv. 52; in the **Fifth** Council of State of the Commonwealth, iv. 355, 449; in the Rump Parliament, iv. 402, 403; member for Buckinghamshire in both the Parliaments of the Protectorate, v. 107, 307; his relationship to the Protector, v. 307; one of Cromwell's Lords, v. 324; supports Richard's Protectorate, v. 417-8, 421; in Richard's Parliament, v. 431, 439, 442; 459, 469, 473, 517, 522; in the Restored Long Parliament, v. 545; his fight with Lambert, v. 564-7; in the Convention Parliament, vi. 23; at the Quest of the Regicides, vi. 29, 45, 48, 50; in the Indemnity Bill, vi. 55; his good fortune, vi. 98; knighted at the Coronation of Charles II., vi. 151.

INGRAM, Sir Arthur, in the Long Parliament, ii. 326.

"IN NOMINE": lost musical composition by Milton's father, i. 51.

"IN OBITUM PROCANCELLARII MEDICI": see *Milton*, Writings of.

"IN OBITUM PRÆCONIS ACADEMICI CANTABRIGIENSIS": see *Milton*, Writings of.

"IN QUINTUM NOVEMBRIS": see *Milton*, Writings of.

INSTRUMENT, the original of the Protectorate, v. 31, 111, 112.

"INTELLIGENCER, the London Public," a newspaper of 1658, v. 94 note.

"INTELLIGENCER, The," a newspaper edited by L'Estrange in 1663, vi. 329-31.

"INTERCURSUS MAGNUS," a document translated by Milton for the Council in 1651, iv. 314.

INVERKEITHING, Battle of, in 1651, iv. 288.

INVERLOCHY, Battle of, in 1645, in which Montrose beat the Marquis of Argyle, iii. 356-7.

"INVISIBLE COLLEGE" (called also the "Philosophical College"), out of which there grew at length the Royal Society of London, iii. 662-5; v. 231, 235; vi. 392.

IRBY, Sir Anthony, Parliamentarian officer, ii. 446; his connexion with

Hartlib, iii. 193 ; in the Long Parment, iii. 599 note ; in Cromwell's Second Parliament, v. 107, 110 ; in the Restored Long Parliament, v. 545 ; in the Convention Parliament, vi. 23; and the Indemnity Bill, vi. 30.
IRELAND : Account of the government of, by Wentworth (1632-8), with a retrospect from 1625 to 1632, i. 666-7, 687-96 ; Laud in the Chancellorship of Trinity College, Dublin, i. 692-4 ; the Irish Insurrection in 1641-2, ii. 308-14, 316-8, 327-8 ; affairs in, from 1642 to 1648, with account of the organisation in, of the Catholic Confederates, iii. 516-22 ; 593 ; dangerous attitude of, towards the Infant Commonwealth, iv. 22-5, 98 : see also under *Ormond, Earl of ;* Milton's Pamphlet on, for the Council of the Commonwealth, iv. 98-102 ; war between the Commonwealth and, iv. 41-2, 56-7 ; Cromwell's first and second campaigns in (1649-50), iv. 111-14, 190-1 : see also under *Cromwell ;* government of, by Lord-Deputy Ireton, iv. 303-4 : see also under *Ireton ;* affairs of, after Ireton's death, iv. 366-7 : see also under *Lambert ;* government of, by Lord-Deputy Fleetwood, iv. 367-71 ; Cromwell's Irish Army, iv. 41-2, 401 : see *Fleetwood ;* attitude of parties in, at the assumption by Cromwell of the Protectorate, iv. 551-2 ; Henry Cromwell in, v. 98-100, 459, 461-2 : see also under *Cromwell, Henry ;* re-officering of the Army of, by the Restored Rump, v. 471, 475 ; account of the civil settlement of, at the Restoration of Charles II., vi. 124-7 ; the Irish Episcopal Church restored, vi. 127-8.
IRETON, Henry, graduate of Oxford, and barrister of the Middle Temple, ii. 445 ; captain of a troop of horse in the Parliamentarian army under the Earl of Essex in 1642, ii. 445 ; account of, as Captain in the *New Model* Army, iii. 327 ; Colonel in command of the left wing of horse at the Battle of Naseby, iii. 336 ; among the favourite military chiefs at the close of the Civil War, iii. 378 ; Commissary-General in Cromwell's army, and Member of Parliament for Appleby, iii. 402 ; marries a daughter of Cromwell, iii. 478 ; in the Army Reform movement, iii. 529 ; in the Quarrel between Parliament and Army, iii. 534, 536 ; with General Fairfax, iii. 537 ; in an interview of the Army leaders with the King at Childersley House, iii. 543 ; his part in the remonstrances of the Army against Parliamentary Presbyterianism, iii. 548, 549 ; with the other Army chiefs in charge of the King's person, and in constant conference with him at Hampton Court, iii. 556-7 ; chief author of the Army's *Heads of Proposals* for the Council of War, iii. 557, 559 note, 610 ; peculiar position of Cromwell and, iii. 568-9; the mutinous pamphlet, *Case of the Army,* signed by agents of his regiment, iii. 571 ; Convener of the Committee of the Council of War for Inquiry into the matter of the Army mutiny, iii. 573, 583, 584, 593, 594 ; in the Second Civil War, iii. 593, 594 ; at the siege of Colchester, iii. 601 ; the *Grand Army Remonstrance,* drafted by, iii. 616 ; a member of the High Court of Justice for the Trial of the King, iii. 703, 704, 705, 707, 712 note ; signs the death-warrant, iii. 720, vi. 28 ; the *Draft Agreement of the People,* written mainly by, iv. 10, 11, 19; excluded from the First Council of State, iv. 12, 16 ; in an incident related by Whitlocke, iv. 15-6 ; is with Cromwell in the first Irish Campaign, iv. 56 ; as Major-General and third in command under Cromwell, iv. 112 ; in Lilburne's *Impeachment against Cromwell and Ireton,* iv. 119 note ; appointed President of Munster, and afterwards Deputy Lord-Lieutenant of Ireland, iv. 191 ; his government of Ireland as Cromwell's Deputy, iv. 303-4 ; lands with £2000 a year voted to, by Parliament, iv. 296, 304 ; his death in 1651 at Limerick, iv. 356-

7 ; buried at Westminster, iv. 357, vi. 113 ; mentioned in *Treason Arraigned*, v. 666 ; excepted, as being one of the four principal Regicides, all deceased, from the Bill of Indemnity, vi. 29-30, 54 ; his disinterment, vi. 113-4.

IRETON, John (brother of Henry Ireton), Alderman of London and member of the Barebones Parliament, iv. 514 ; knighted by Cromwell in 1657, v. 354 note ; one of the City Colonels of Militia, v. 472 ; on the Committee of Safety, v. 494 ; Lord Mayor of London in 1659, v. 472 ; his sentence under the Indemnity Bill, vi. 38, 47, 55.

IRONSIDE, Gilbert, Bishop of Bristol, vi. 118.

IRVINE, laird of Drum, in Aberdeenshire, Sir Alexander : in the first " Bishops' War," ii. 56 ; his appeal to Monk, iv. 362.

ISHAM, Sir John, of Lamport, Northamptonshire, i. 180-4.

ISHAM, Justinian, son of Sir John, and pupil of Meade at Christ's College, Cambridge, i. 181-4.

ISLE OF WIGHT, Charles I.'s escape to the, iii. 574-5.

ISRAEL, Manasseh Ben, his address to Cromwell on behalf of the Jews, v. 71-2.

ISSARD, Charles, of Stanton St. John's, i. 15.

ITALIAN OPERA, beginning of the, v. 81 and note.

ITALIAN SONNETS AND CANZONE of Milton : see, *Milton*, Writings of.

ITALY and the Italians in 1638, i. 745, 759-68 ; iv. 379.

IVES, Mr., in the case of Biddle and the Socinians, v. 65.

IVESON, W., author of verses on Edward King's death, i. 651.

IVY, Simon, musical composer, i. 580, 586.

J

JACKSON, Mr., a leading English Presbyterian in 1572, ii. 532.

JACKSON, Lieutenant - Colonel, under the New Model, iii. 326.

JACKSON, Arthur, Moderator of the Fifth Provincial Presbyterian Synod of London in 1649, iv. 60 ; a Nonconformist, vi. 232 note.

JACKSON, John, member of Westminster Assembly, ii. 519.

JACKSON, William, fellow-student and fellow-graduate of Milton at Cambridge, i. 112, 128.

JACOB, Henry, one of the founders of English Independency, i. 59, 341-2 ; ii. 539, 541, 542, 544, 556, 570, 581, 598 note ; iii. 103-4, 147.

JACOB, Tiddy, v. 575.

JAFFRAY, Alexander, Provost of Aberdeen, iv. 502 ; vi. 134.

JAMAICA, taken by the English, under command of Penn and Venables, in 1655, v. 45-6 ; account of Cromwell's strenuous endeavours to colonise it from New England, v. 103-4.

JAMES I. of Scotland, called the Poet-King, i. 86.

JAMES I. of England (and VI. of Scotland) : signs, in 1581, the National Covenant of Scotland, called "The Second Confession of Faith," i. 726 ; his *Essays of a Prentice in the Divine Art of Poesie*, written in 1585, i. 462 ; his friendship for Sir Henry Wotton before and after his accession to the English throne, i. 528 ; references to his anti - Presbyterian policy for Scotland, i. 69, 423-4 ; proclaimed King of England, and leaves Edinburgh to take possession of his new kingdom, i. 4 ; Millenary Petition to, and the Hampton Court Conferences of, in 1603-4, i. 58 ; declares against the Puritans, and ratifies the 141 Canons passed in the Convocation of 1603-4, i. 344-7 ; account of his policy towards the Puritans and Sectaries in England from the beginning of his English reign to 1610, i. 58-9, 347 ; his difficulties with his English Parliaments, i. 59-60 ; death of Henry, Prince of Wales, in 1612, and marriage of the Princess Elizabeth to the Elector-Palatine, i. 60 ; his treatment of Legate, the Arian, i. 60 ; his first visit to Cambridge in 1614, i. 117, 139 note, 221 ; his second visit to

Cambridge, in 1615, i. 128; his favouritism of George Villiers, afterwards Duke of Buckingham, i. 60; visits Scotland in 1617, i. 60; the Book of Sports, first issued in 1618, i. 675; sends deputies to the Synod of Dort, in 1619, i. 61, 355; death of Queen Anne, i. 61; his subserviency to the Catholic power of Spain, and unpopularity of, and of his favourite, Buckingham, on account of the "Spanish Match" negotiations, i. 61, 105-6; his Councillors in Church and State, i. 348-52, 378; influence of Lord-Keeper Williams in the later policy of the Government of, i. 352; the King's dislike of Laud, and his opposition to Williams in the matter of Laud's appointment, in 1821, to the Bishopric of St. David's, i. 364-5; his "Directions to Preachers" in 1622, i. 356-8; at war with Spain, i. 106; incidents of his later years, i. 106-7; some of his connexions with the English literature of his reign, i. 434, 438-9, 447, 462, 463, 465, 472-3, 483, 505, 509, 512, 517, 518, 522, 528; George Herbert's eulogy of, i. 119; references to, in Milton's writings, i. 173-9, iv. 260; his death and funeral, i. 148, 150, 368; miscellaneous mentions of, i. 70, 101, 119; ii. 152, 153, 154, 155; portraits of, by Jansen, i. 66.

JAMES, DUKE OF YORK (afterwards James II.), Latin elegiacs in a volume of Cambridge verses on the birth of, in 1633, i. 649; with King Charles in his journey to York in 1641-2, ii. 353, 413; mentioned, ii. 428; the Earl of Northumberland has charge of, at the close of the Civil War in 1646, iii. 375; is brought to visit the King at Caversham in 1647, iii. 556; escapes from St. James's Palace to Holland during the Second Civil War, iii. 593; in the Revolt of the Fleet, in 1648, iii. 395; proviso concerning, in the Grand Army Remonstrance, iii. 618; in the last days of King Charles I., iii. 705, 723; with Charles II.'s Court at the Hague, iv. 25; in correspondence with his mother, Queen Henrietta Maria, iv. 382; excepted, with others, from Oliver's Ordinance of Pardon and Grace, iv. 560; with Don John of Austria in an attempt to recapture Mardike from the English, v. 311; at the Battle of Dunkirk, v. 340; in the Projected Royalist Insurrection of 1659, v. 473; at the Restoration, v. 699, 701, vi. 6, 10; in the Convention Parliament, vi. 22; in the Privy Council of the Restoration, vi. 17; vote of money to, vi. 67; at the Court of Charles II., vi. 71; his secret marriage with Anne Hyde, vi. 71, 106-8; birth of his son Charles, Duke of Cambridge, vi. 107-8; mentioned, vi. 110; his marriage with Anne Hyde recognised, vi. 118-9; present at the Coronation of Charles II., vi. 151; mention of, in Dr. Gauden's Letters to Hyde, in 1660, vi. 429, 430, 432; letters of Gauden to, vi. 432, 433 note, 434, 436; his statement to Bishop Burnet concerning the Eikon Basilike, vi. 439 note; hears Morus preach in French in St. James's Chapel, vi. 422; the Manor of the Vache, in the parish of Chalfont St. Giles, given by the King to, vi. 493; Lord High Admiral in the war with the Dutch, in 1665, vi. 252-5, 256 note, 263-5, 376; in Court scandals, vi. 262; returns to town after the Plague, vi. 499; the "Duke's or Davenant's Theatre," vi. 353; with the King at the King's Theatre, vi. 355; at the fall of Clarendon, in 1667, vi. 270; in the Cabal Administration, from 1667 to 1670, vi. 562, 565, 570, 571, 572-3, 639; from 1670 to 1673, 574-5, 576, 583, 594-6; his second marriage to the Duchess of Modena, in 1674, vi. 598-600; in the beginnings of the Danby Administration, vi. 602; his family in 1674, vi. 605.

JAMES, an actress in the "King's Company," vi. 350.

JAMES, Colonel, in the Barebones Parliament, iv. 515.

JAMES, John, of the sect of Seventhday Baptists, vi. 228.

JAMESONE, George, Scottish portrait painter, i. 512, 715.

JAMESONE, John, Scottish shipmaster, v. 292.

JANE, Joseph, author of *Eikon Aklastos*, vi. 188, 213 note.

JANE, Thomas, son of the above, vi. 213.

"JANUA LINGUARUM RESERATA," by Comenius, iii. 200-3, 210, 211, 212.

JANSEN, Cornelius, portrait painter, i. 66, 308 note ; ii. 169.

JANSEN, John, publisher, iv. 318 ; his *Novus Atlas*, v. 280.

"JEALOUS LOVERS, the," Cambridge Comedy, by Thomas Randolph, i. 251-4.

JEFFREY, Jeffery, Jeffraye, Geffrey, or Gefferey, a family of the name of, found in the county of Essex from an early period, i. 33.

JEFFREY, Christopher (son of Jeffrey of Holton), i. 21.

JEFFREY, Christopher (brother of John of Little Bursted), i. 33.

JEFFREY, Ellen, wife of Paul Jeffrey, and maternal grandmother of Milton, i. 30, 31, 35-7, 39.

JEFFREY, Gefferey, of East Hanningfield, yeoman : his will, i. 33.

JEFFREY, George, case of, iii. 292.

JEFFREY, Henry, i. 21.

JEFFREY, Henry, of Little Bursted, i. 36.

JEFFREY, John, of Holton, husbandman, and his wife Elizabeth, i. 21.

JEFFREY, John, of Little Bursted, i. 33.

JEFFREY, John, of East Hanningfield, yeoman, i. 33-4 ; his widow Johan, and their six children, i. 34.

JEFFREY, John (son of the above), i. 34, 35, 36.

JEFFREY, John, of Childerditch in Essex and of Stratford in Suffolk, i. 36 ; his will, i. 37.

JEFFREY, Margaret, i. 21.

JEFFREY, Margaret, of Newton Hall, daughter of Paul Jeffrey, married to Thomas Truelove, i. 35-9, 63.

JEFFREY, Paul (youngest son of John of East Hanningfield), i. 34 ; merchant tailor in London, and grandfather of Milton, i. 35-7.

JEFFREY, Richard (another son of the same), i. 33, 34, 35, 36.

JEFFREY, Richard, of West Hanningfield, yeoman, i. 33.

JEFFREY, Sara, daughter of Paul Jeffrey, and mother of Milton, i. 35-7.

JEFFREY, Thomas, of East Hanningfield, yeoman : his will in 1519, i. 33.

JEFFREY, Thomas (a son of John of East Hanningfield), i. 34, 35.

JEFFREY, Thomas, of Chelmsford (also son of John of East Hanningfield), i. 34-6.

JENKINS, Sir Leoline, judge of the Prerogative Court of Canterbury, in 1674, and afterwards Ambassador at Nimeguen and Secretary of State, vi. 739, 797-9.

JENNEY, Mrs., and her husband William, in the story of Mrs. Attaway, iii. 190-1.

JENNINGS, actress in the "Duke's Company," vi. 350.

JENNISON, Dr., of Durham, in the Westminster Assembly, ii. 513 note.

JENNY GEDDES : see *Geddes*, Jenny.

JEPHSON, Colonel, William, in Oliver's First Parliament, v. 5 ; in Oliver's Second Parliament, v. 108, 128, 129 ; in an embassy to Sweden, v. 312, 314, 342, 370-1, 373, 386, 395 ; supports Richard's Government, v. 419.

JERMYN, Henry, Lord : Master of Horse to Queen Henrietta Maria, and member for Bury St. Edmunds in the Long Parliament, ii. 173 ; a "Delinquent," iii. 421 ; his relations to Henrietta Maria at the French Court, iii. 495 and note ; in correspondence with Charles I., iii. 502 ; in Davenant's Mission, iii. 503-4 ; in the Second Civil War, iii. 591 ; Cowley the poet and, v. 83 ; made Earl of St. Alban's at the Restoration, vi. 18 ; ambassador for Charles II. to Louis XIV., vi. 18 ; in the disputes on the Church question after the Restoration, vi. 62 ; in Charles II.'s Court, vi. 72 ; ambassador at Paris, vi. 252.

JERMYN, Henry, nephew of Earl of St. Alban's, vi. 72.

JERMYN, Sir Thomas, i. 381 ; ii. 159, 278, 283, 337.

JERUSALEM CHAMBER, at Westminster, ii. 225.

JESSEY, Henry, Independent minister, ii. 582, 587 ; iii. 147, 148 ; vi. 232 note, 417.

JESSOP, William, Assistant - Secretary to Cromwell's Council, iv. 524, 525, 526, 526 note, 546, 547, 576, 578, 579 ; v. 111, 182, 178-9, 252, 363, 546, 625 note, 670 ; in Richard's Parliament, v. 630 ; after the Restoration, vi. 198-9.

JESUS COLLEGE, Cambridge, i. 114, 115, 116, 120, 247.

JEWIN STREET, residence of Milton in, vi. 406-8.

JEWS, Cromwell's exertions in behalf of the, v. 71-2.

JOACHIMI, Dutch ambassador in London, iv. 90-1, 215-6.

JOCE, or Gotso, i. 606.

"JOCK OF BROAD SCOTLAND," case of, v. 92-4.

JOHN OF AUSTRIA, Don, at the siege of Mardike, v. 311 ; at the siege of Dunkirk, v. 340.

JOHN II., King of Poland, v. 246, 313 ; vi. 725-7.

JOHN IV., King of Portugal, iv. 30 ; Letters of State to, 161, 217-9, 232, 233, 380, 636 ; v. 269 - 70, 271, 273-4, 289-90, 396 ; 576 note.

JOHNSON, a divine in the Westminster Assembly, ii. 517.

JOHNSON, a baker, and leader of a band of Separatists in Lincoln, i. 678.

JOHNSON, Francis, Brownist pastor in Amsterdam, ii. 539.

JOHNSON, Mrs. Elizabeth, sister of Dr. Paget, vi. 744.

JOHNSON, Dr. Samuel, references to his Life of Milton, i. 159, 270, 437, 484, 485, 489 ; iii. 251-2.

JOHNSON, Thomas, publisher, in St. Paul's Churchyard, London, in 1658-60, v. 405, 667.

JOHNSTON, Arthur, of Aberdeen, Scottish Latinist, i. 511-2, 715.

JOHNSTONE, Lord, in the Glasgow Assembly of 1638, ii. 38.

JOHNSTONE, of Warriston, Archibald, one of the principal leaders in the Scottish struggle for Presbyterianism, i. 710-1, 723, 725-6 ; ii. 16, 17, 21 - 2, 33 ; Clerk of the Glasgow Assembly of 1638, ii. 39 ; Scottish Commissioner in First Bishops' War, ii. 68, 143, 190, 192 ; during the King's visit to Scotland in 1641, ii. 304 ; appointed Lord of Session, ii. 307 ; in the Committee of Estates, ii. 292 ; 323, 416-7 ; in the General Assembly of 1642, ii. 418 ; in the business of the Solemn League and Covenant, iii. 7, 8, 10 ; account of, as deputy to the Westminster Assembly in 1643, and of his career to that date, iii. 17 ; in the "Committee of the Two Kingdoms," iii. 40, 331 note ; in Scottish Convention of Estates, 1644-5, iii. 175 ; in negotiations at Newcastle, iii. 413 ; opposes the Scottish Engagement, iii. 589 ; and the "Act of Classes" of 1648-9, iv. 21 ; with Argyle and Loudoun in the government of Scotland for the absent Charles II. in 1649, iv. 62 ; in the war with Cromwell, iv. 198 ; after Dunbar, iv. 202, 203, 209 ; at the Incorporation of Scotland with the Commonwealth, iv. 363 ; his position in Scottish affairs during Cromwell's government of Scotland, v. 87 ; a leader of the "Protesters" in Scotland, v. 90 ; goes to London on this business, v, 115, 345 ; as "Lord Warriston" in Cromwell's Upper House in 1657-8, v. 324 ; in the Council of State of the Restored Rump, v. 456-7, 465, 479 ; on the Committee of Safety, v. 494, 508, 509, 511, 624 ; in disgrace at the second Restoration of the Rump, v. 521 ; after the Restoration of Charles II., vi. 132, 134-5.

JONAS, Lewis, Irish bishop, i. 420.

JONES, Mr., a lecturer, suspended by Laud, i. 402.

JONES, Colonel Henry, knighted by Cromwell in 1658, v. 354 note.

JONES, Henry, Bishop of Clogher, vi. 127-8.

JONES, Colonel John, member of the Long Parliament for Monmouthshire, and one of the Regicides, iii. 720; v. 307; in Councils of State of the Commonwealth, iv. 13, 14, 83, 87, 145, 146, 147, 150, 223, 224, 225, 226, 229; in Fleetwood's Council in Ireland, iv. 401; in Cromwell's Council, v. 31; in Cromwell's Parliament, v. 107; married to Cromwell's sister, v. 307; one of Cromwell's lords, v. 324; supports Richard's Government, v. 418; ¦ in the Restored Rump, v. 454; in the Council of State of the Restored Rump, v. 456, 465; with Ludlow as his deputy in Ireland, v. 471, 495, 496; in disgrace, v. 521; absent from the Parliament of Secluded Members, v. 544 note; at the quest of the Regicides, vi. 28; in the Indemnity Bill as one of the Seven surviving Regicide Judges, vi. 31, 34 note, 54; his trial, vi. 80, 81, 85; his execution, vi. 96-7; in the Bill of Attainder, vi. 115.

JONES, Colonel Michael, Parliamentary Governor of Dublin in 1647, iii. 379; iv. 24, 42; Ormond threatens, iv. 56; letter from Ormond to, and reply of, to the same, iv. 98; action of Parliament in favour of, iv. 99; repulses Ormond from before Dublin, iv. 111-2; is appointed second in command to Ireton, iv. 112; his death by fever in 1649, iv. 113.

JONES, Peter, servant to Milton's father, i. 4.

JONES, Colonel Philip, in the Interim Council of Thirteen, iv. 498; called to Cromwell's Supreme Assembly, iv. 501; in the Barebones Parliament and its Council, iv. 506, 515, 525; in Cromwell's Council, iv. 545, v. 183-4, 259-60, 273; in the Privy Council of Second Protectorate, v. 308; one of Cromwell's lords, v. 324; in the Privy Council after the dissolution of Cromwell's Second Parliament, v. 333; in Oliver's schemes for Scotland, v. 346-7; in the Council's proposed restrictions of the Press, v. 351, 352; in a Committee of the Council for a New Par-

liament, v. 354; supports Richard's Government, 417, 421; in the Restored Rump, v. 455; fined by the Rump for non-attendance, v. 479; in the Indemnity Bill, vi. 40.

JONES, Mr. Richard: see *Ranelagh*, 1st Earl of.

JONES, Colonel Theophilus, at the Republican remodelling of the army, v. 471; in co-operation with Monk, v. 514; at the Second Restoration of the Rump, v. 520.

JONES, William (or Edward) and Mary, of Sandyford, ii. 493 note.

JONGESTALL, Mynheer, ambassador from Holland to Cromwell, iv. 502, 572-3; his wife, iv. 572-3.

JONSON, Ben (Poet-Laureate): educated at Westminster School, i. 73; and the Mermaid Tavern, i. 45-6, 45 note; folio edition of his works in 1616, i. 88; Milton's early readings in, i. 89, 575; his verses on Shakespeare, i. 236, 330, 331; his elegy on the Marchioness of Winchester, i. 245; 462; his visit to Drummond of Hawthornden (1619-20), i. 465-6, 486; account of, in a Survey of British Literature in 1632, i. 432-44; additional mentions of, in the same Survey, i. 445, 447, 449, 452, 453, 454, 456, 462, 464, 465, 466, 472, 479-82, 483, 485-6, 502, 503, 506, 508, 509, 513, 515, 521, 524, 532, 533; the younger Gill and, i. 565-6, v. 261; references to his Masques, i. 579, 595, 596, 621, 622; death of, in 1637, i. 641; account of his grave, and its famous inscription, in Westminster Abbey, i. 646-7; obituary verses to, i. 647; ii. 163; publication of his Masques and other remains in 1640, iii. 446; his plays acted in 1660, vi. 353; sale of the copyright of his Masques in '1667, vi. 515.

JOPP, William, shipmaster, v. 271.

JORDAENS, Jacob, painter in the Netherlands, i. 746.

JOYCE, George (once a tailor, then a cornet in Fairfax's Life-Guard); appointed for the abduction of Charles I. by the Army, iii. 539-43; nominated at the *Fairfaxian Crea-*

tion, by Cromwell and Fairfax, for an Honorary M.A. degree of Oxford University, iv. 52; in the Council Order Books of 1650-1, iv. 226; at the Quest of the Regicides, vi. 27; his arrest, vi. 32, 33.

JUBBS, Lieutenant-Colonel, under the *New Model*, iii. 326, 534, 537.

"JUDGMENT OF MARTIN BUCER CONCERNING DIVORCE": see *Milton*, Writings of.

JUNIUS, Franciscus, Anglo - Saxon scholar, iv. 351; vi. 557, note.

JUNIUS, Patricius (Patrick Young), keeper of the King's Library in St. James's, London, iii. 645-6; in the Council Order Books, iv. 147, 151; · tirement from Librarianship, iv. 229 - 30; Queen Christina's inquiry concerning, iv. 597 note.

JUNTO of the Restoration, the, vi. 19-21: see *Council*.

JUXON, Dr. William, President of St. John's College, Oxford, and Dean of Worcester, i. 400; Bishop of London in succession to Laud, i. 671, 677, 716; ii. 150; iii. 196; Lord High Treasurer, i. 671, 674; ii. 24, 144; a witness in Strafford's Trial, ii. 180, 184; resigns the Lord High Treasurership, ii. 281; John Durie in correspondence with, iii. 196; at the Isle of Wight during the Treaty of Newport, iii. 606; in the last days of Charles I., iii. 712, 713; in the night previous to the execution, iii. 721; with Charles I. on the scaffold, iii. 723-26; has charge of the burial of the King, iii. 726-8; sermon by, on the death of the King, iv. 37; the Prayer of the King, in the *Eikon Basilike*, alleged to have been delivered to, before the King's death, iv. 139, 248-9; his kindness to the printer Ulac, v. 154, 155 note; after the Restoration, vi. 61; translated to the Archbishopric of Canterbury in September 1660, vi. 104, 425; crowns Charles II. at Westminster, vi. 155; is in the Privy Council of Charles II., vi. 236; death of, in 1663, vi. 237.

K

KEATS, the poet: referred to in connexion with Milton, i. 318, and with William Browne, i. 458.

KEBLE, Sergeant Richard, English lawyer and an Oliverian, iv. 120; vi. 38, 39, 47; among Eighteen Persons Incapacitated in the Indemnity Bill (1660), vi. 55.

KECK, Christianus, his *Phalæcians* against Milton, v. 403-4.

KEECH, William, gold-beater of London, co-surety for Christopher Milton, iii. 633.

KEINTON, fight of: see *Edgehill*, battle of.

KEIR, Sir George Stirling, Laird of, his connexions with Montrose, ii. 296, 298, 300, 301; iii. 341.

KELLIE, Thomas Erskine, 1st Earl of, i. 380; iv. 294, 298, 560.

KELLY, Major, Royalist officer, ii. 442.

KELLY, Mrs.: see *Hazard*.

KELSAY (or Kelsey), Thomas, Major in the *New Model* army, iii. 326, 534, 537, 619; one of Cromwell's Major-Generals, v. 49; in Cromwell's Second Parliament, v. 107; supports Richard's Protectorate, v. 418; in the remodelled army of the Restored Rump, v. 470; in disgrace with the Restored Rump, v. 490, 521; during Monk's dictatorship, v. 536.

KELSO, the Raid of, ii. 64.

KEMP, Francis, warden of the Scriveners' Company, i. 62.

KEMP, John, iii. 579.

KENMURE, John Gordon, Viscount, died in 1634, i. 710, 712; his widow, ii. 11.

KENMURE, Viscount, Scottish Royalist, iv. 508, 560.

KENNEDY, Hugh, burgess of Ayr, ii. 143, 190; iii. 510, 578, 579, 582.

KENNEDY, John: see *Cassilis*, Earl of.

KENSINGTON, Baron, afterwards 1st Earl of Holland : see *Holland*.

KENT, county of, petition from, for Church reform, ii. 213; members for, in the Long Parliament, ii. 167.

KENT, Earl of, Selden's connexion with, i. 523 ; dead in 1643, ii. 430.

KENT, Elizabeth, Countess of, wife of the above, and daughter of the Earl of Shrewsbury, i. 523.

KENT, Henry, Earl of (son of the preceding), Parliamentarian Peer, ii. 430 and note ; iii. 292, 297 note, 377, 406, 555 ; iv. 4 ; vi. 785.

KENTISH KNOCK, sea fight of, iv. 375.

KEPLER, the Astronomer, i. 265, 529, 530, 746.

KER, Scottish Presbyterian divine, ii. 38.

KER, Andrew, Scottish judge during the Protectorate, v. 87.

KER, Colonel Gilbert, iv. 204, 210-11 ; vi. 134.

KER, John, shipmaster, v. 372.

KER, Lord, son of the Earl of Roxburgh, ii. 305.

KER, Robert : see Roxburgh, Earl of.

KER, William : see Lothian, Earl of.

KERWELL, Madame : see Querouaille, and Portsmouth, Duchess of, vi. 604.

KETYNG, English judge, vi. 478.

KIFFIN, William, Baptist preacher, iii. 147, 148 ; iv. 45.

KILBURNIE, Lord, vi. 145.

KILCOP, Thomas, Baptist preacher, iii. 148.

KILLIGREW, Dr. Henry, vi. 308.

KILLIGREW, Thomas, Royalist wit and dramatist, iii. 446, 449 ; in exile, v. 76, 575 ; returns with Charles II., vi. 8 ; at the court of Charles II., vi. 249, 299, 308-9 ; patentee of the King's Theatre, vi. 348 ; his company, vi. 349 ; his connexions with the Drama of the Restoration, vi. 350-6 ; his Parson's Wedding, vi. 358 ; during Dryden's laureateship, vi. 609.

KILLIGREW, Sir William, Royalist officer, and brother of the above, ii. 441 ; vi. 308.

KILLIGREW, Lady, case of, in the Council Order Books of 1649, iv. 150.

" KILLING NO MURDER," pamphlet by Edward Sexby in 1657, v. 141-2, 320 ; vi. 112.

KILMADY, Vincent, Parliamentarian officer, ii. 444.

KILMURRAY, Viscount, ii. 442.

KILPONT, Lord, eldest son of the Earl of Menteith, iii. 351.

KILSYTH, battle of, iii. 360-1.

KIMBER, Rev. Isaac, Baptist minister at Nantwich, vi. 747.

KIMBOLTON, Lord : see Manchester, Earl of.

KINASTON, Anne : see Powell.

KINASTON, Thomas, merchant of London, vi. 750.

KINCARDINE, Earl of, iv. 561.

KINDALL, Samuel, neighbour of Milton in Artillery Walk, vi. 717.

KING, a stray madman of London, intrudes himself into Richard's Parliament, v. 431.

KING, Mr., member of the Barebones Parliament in 1653, iv. 514.

KING (Scotsman) Lieutenant-General in "the Queen's army," ii. 468 ; iii. 96.

KING, Anne (sister of Edward King of Christ's College) : see Caulfield.

KING, Colonel, Lilburne's quarrel with, iii. 388, 390.

KING, Colonel Edward, one of the members for Great Grimsby in the Convention Parliament, befriends Milton, vi. 195.

KING, Edward ("Lycidas"), at Christ's College, Cambridge, i. 171 ; elected fellow of Christ's College by the King's mandate, i. 239 ; incidents of his Cambridge life, i. 244, 248, 250, 253 ; in correspondence with Milton, ii. 401 note ; his death by shipwreck in the Irish Sea, i. 641-2 ; general account of him, with specimens of his Latin academic verses, i. 647-50 ; the collection of Obituary Poems to his memory, i. 650-5 ; Milton's "Lycidas" in that collection, i. 655-9 ; Milton's real relations to, discussed, ii. 82 ; mentioned, vi. 195.

KING, Edward, Bishop of Elphin, uncle of Milton's friend, i. 172, 420, 651.

KING, Henry, brother of Edward King of Christ's College, i. 651, 652.

KING, Dr. Henry, Dean of Christ Church, Oxford, and Bishop of Chichester in 1641, ii. 411 ; vi. 61, 105, 292.

KING, Sir John, father of Edward King of Christ's College ("Lycidas"), i. 171, 651.

KING, John, Parliamentary sequestrator, iii. 476, 478, 479.

KING, Margaret, sister of Edward King of Christ's College : see *Loder*.

KING, Sir Robert, brother of Edward King of Christ's College, i. 651 ; in Oliver's First Parliament, v. 6.

KING, Robert, of Trinity Hall, Cambridge University, Proctor in 1629-30, i. 226.

KING, Roger, brother of Edward King of Christ's College, i. 171.

"KINGDOM'S INTELLIGENCER," a weekly newspaper (1662), vi. 339 note.

KINGDON, Richard, v. 624, 625 note.

KINGHORN, John Lyon, Earl of, i. 707 ; ii. 15 ; joins the Covenant, ii. 55, 56 ; iv. 561.

KING'S COLLEGE, Cambridge, i. 114, 116, 117, 120, 122, 182, 248, 505.

KING'S EVIL, touching for the, after the Restoration, vi. 74-5.

"KINGSHIP, THE DIGNITY OF, ASSERTED : in answer to Mr. Milton's Ready and Easy Way to establish a Free Commonwealth, by G. S." v. 691-4, and 691-2 note.

KINGSTON, Robert Pierrepoint, 1st Earl of, ii. 47-8, 159, 173 ; his house in London, ii. 208 ; and the Bishops Exclusion Bill, ii. 227 ; killed on the King's side in the Civil War in 1643, ii. 428 ; vi. 18.

KINGSTON, Henry, Lord Pierrepoint, and Marquis of Dorchester (son of the above), 2nd Earl of: see *Dorchester*, Marquis of.

KINNAIRD HOUSE, iv. 184.

KINNEILL HOUSE, ii. 304.

KINNERSLEY, Mr., wardrobe-keeper to the Protector, v. 625.

KINNOULL, George Hay, Earl of, High Chancellor of Scotland, i. 702, 706 ; ii. 15, 417 ; iv. 183, 184.

KIRKCUDBRIGHT, Lord, in Scottish Covenanting army, ii. 65.

KIRLE, Robert, Parliamentarian officer, ii. 446.

KIRTON, Joshua, London bookseller, v. 59 note.

KNEPP, Mrs., actress, vi. 350, 351, 355.

KNIGHT, chirurgeon to Charles II., iv. 75.

KNIGHT, Mr., Independent divine, iv. 370.

KNIGHT, Colonel Ralph, officer in Monk's army, v. 498, 501, 540, 541, 562 ; in the Convention Parliament, vi. 23, 173.

KNIGHT, Thomas, of Reading, i. 558 : see *Bulstrode*, Mary.

KNIGHTLEY, Mr. Richard, member of the Long Parliament, iii. 599 note ; in the Restored Long Parliament, v. 543, 545.

KNOLLYS, Hanserd, Baptist preacher, his life in New England from 1638 to 1641, ii. 557, 574, 576 ; returns to England, ii. 586 ; one of the chiefs of the English Baptists, iii. 148 ; denounced as a heretic by the Westminster Assembly, iii. 161, 165 ; champion of Toleration, iii. 387.

KNOWESLY, John, fellow of Christ's College, Cambridge, i. 112, 123.

KNOWSLEY, seat of the Earl of Derby, ii. 158.

KNOX, John, Scottish Reformer, i. 423, 726 ; grave of, ii. 291 ; references to, by Milton, iii. 285 ; iv. 103.

KOMENSKY : see *Comenius*.

KONIGSMARCK, Count, v. 292.

KYGHLEY, Edwin, Parliamentarian officer, ii. 445.

KYNASTON, Edward, actor, vi. 349, 350, 353, 607.

L

LABADIE, Jean, account of, v. 591-2 ; in correspondence with Milton, v. 592-5 ; Milton's letter to, vi. 723.

LA CLOCHE, James (known as Rohan, Henry de), reputed son of Charles II., vi. 605.

LACY, John, actor, vi. 349, 350, 353, 355 ; plays by, vi. 358, 611, 613.

LACY, Lieutenant - Colonel, Royalist officer, ii. 442.

LACY, DE, of Ludlow, i. 607.

LAGERFELDT, Israel, Swedish ambassador in London, iv. 378, 524.

LAING, David, Scottish antiquary, i. 71 note ; iii. 395 note.

"L'ALLEGRO": see *Milton*, Writings of.

LAMB, Andrew, Scottish bishop, i. 697, 705.

LAMBE, Sir John, v. 155 note.

LAMBERT, John, Colonel under Fairfax in the north, iii. 327 ; in the *New Model*, iii. 327 ; with the army chiefs, iii. 534, 536, 537, 543, 548, 549 ; General of the Parliamentary forces in the northern counties of England during the Second Civil War, iii. 593, 595-6, 597, 601 ; Cromwell's junction with, in the Battle of Preston, iii. 604 ; is left by Cromwell in Scotland, iii. 622 ; is absent at the King's Trial, iii. 708 note ; his regiment of horse for the campaign in Ireland, iv. 56 ; Major-General in Cromwell's army in Scotland, iv. 192 ; with Cromwell at the Battle of Dunbar, iv. 200 ; in the victorious action at Hamilton, iv. 210-1 ; Milton's allusion to the same in the *Defensio Secunda*, iv. 602, 606, 612 ; in the passage through Fifeshire and at the Battle of Inverkeithing, iv. 288 ; in the pursuit of Charles II. into England, iv. 291, 292, 294 ; Scottish lands voted to, by Parliament, iv. 296 ; sent to Scotland in the Commission for the Incorporation of Scotland with the English Commonwealth, iv. 303, 360-1, 364 ; appointed by Parliament to succeed Ireton as Lord-Deputy of Ireland under Cromwell's Lord-Lieutenancy, iii. 366 ; declines the office, iii. 367 ; second to Cromwell in the army of England, iv. 402, 408, 413 ; in Cromwell's Interim Council of Thirteen and New Council of State, iv. 498-9, 500, 505-6, 523 ; omitted at re-election of the Council, iv. 512 ; at the installation of the Protectorate, iv. 518 ; in the Council of the Protectorate, iv. 545, 575 ; member of Cromwell's Council after the dissolution of Parliament in 1653, v. 31 ; is styled "Lord Lambert" in the Council Order Books, v. 177,

183-4, 304 ; in the case of Biddle and the Socinians, v. 64 ; moves for a hereditary Protectorship in Cromwell's family, v. 10 ; is one of Cromwell's major-generals, v. 49, 118 ; in the Council of Cromwell, v. 259-60, 273 ; in Cromwell's Second Parliament, v. 107 ; takes part with the Scottish "Protesters," v. 345 ; in the debate on Sir Christopher Pack's motion, v. 121 ; opposes the "Kingship" proposition, v. 124-6 ; his omission from the Council of the Second Protectorate, and his retirement into private life, v. 308-9 ; mentioned, v. 337 ; member for Pontefract in Richard's Parliament, v. 430, 435, 441 ; at the Restoration of the Rump, v. 449 ; in the Council of the Restored Rump, v. 456 ; at the Republican remodelling of the army, v. 470 ; Booth's Insurrection crushed by, v. 475, 477-9, 616 ; petition to Parliament by his Brigade, v. 487-8, 496 ; deprived, with other principal officers of the army, of his commission, v. 489-90 ; his *Coup d'état*, v. 491-2, 493, 496, 515 ; Milton's opinion of the *Coup d'état*, v. 616-20 ; on the Committee of Safety, v. 494 ; appointed, by the Wallingford House Council, Major-General of the forces in England and Scotland, v. 495, 596 ; sent north with a large force against Monk, v. 497, 499, 500-1, 512-3, 514, 524-5 ; in discussions for a New Republican Constitution, v. 506, 515 ; is firm against the design of Whitlocke of recalling Charles II., v. 516 ; in disgrace with the Council of the Rump at its second restoration, v. 521, 522, 538 ; Monk's particular pique against, v. 541 note ; committed to the Tower, v. 547-8, 562, 563 ; his escape, capture by Ingoldsby at Daventry, and recommittal, v. 564-7 ; after the Restoration, vi. 23, 39, 46-8, 50-1 ; sentenced with Sir Harry Vane, and saved by a petition of both Houses, vi. 55 ; remanded to prison, vi. 98, 197 ; capital prosecution of, by Charles's Second Parliament, vi. 224 ; his trial and

sentence, vi. 230-1 ; his death thirty
years later, vi. 98 note.

LAMBERT, Lady, in ceremonies at
Cromwell's Court, iv. 573.

LAMBETH PALACE, residence of the
Bishops of London, squibs and riots
at, ii. 51, 133.

LANCASTER, James, Early Quaker, v.
27.

LANCE, William, member of Westminster Assembly, ii. 519.

LANE, John, versifier, friend of Milton's
father, i. 56-8.

LANEY, Dr. Benjamin, master of Pembroke Hall, Cambridge, i. 120 ;
ejected from the University, iii. 94,
95 note ; Bishop of Peterborough,
of Lincoln, and of Ely, vi. 118.

LANGDALE, Sir Marmaduke, Royalist,
iii. 335, 370, 591, 593, 595-6, 597,
604.

LANGHAM, George, officer of London
Trained Bands, 446, 483.

LANGHERN, Colonel, iii. 592.

LANGLAND, William, early English
poet, i. 470.

LANGLEY, Dr. Henry, Nonconformist,
vi. 232 note.

LANGLEY, John, member of Westminster Assembly, ii. 519 ; book-
licenser, iii. 270.

LANGLEY, Lieutenant-Colonel, Royalist
officer, ii. 442.

LANGRICH, Hercules, Parliamentarian
officer, ii. 445.

LANSDOWNE, battle at, iii. 6.

LASSELL, John, at Second Restoration
of the Rump, v. 519.

LASSELS, Francis, in the Convention
Parliament, vi. 23, 36, 37, 38, 55,
98.

LATHAM, seat of the Earl of Derby,
ii. 158.

LATHORP, John, Independent minister,
i. 341, 402 ; ii. 544, 582 ; iii. 147.

LATIMER, the Reformer, i. 114.

LATIMERS, in Bucks, a mansion of the
Earl of Devonshire, iii. 556.

LATITUDINARIANS, i. 531 - 40 ; iii.
107 ; vi. 235.

LAUD, William, birth of, at Reading
in 1573, i. 359 ; at St. John's
College, Oxford, i. 359 ; successive
appointments at Oxford and in the
Episcopate to 1628, i. 116, 359-65,
371, 388, 389 ; his unpopularity at
Oxford, i. 359-61 ; and pre-deter-
mined anti-Puritanism, i. 361-4 ;
incorporated at Cambridge in 1627,
i. 181 ; his intimacy with Buckingham, i. 365-8 ; his Diary, i. 367-8 ;
the ecclesiastical department of affairs
confided to, by Buckingham, i. 368 ;
his relations with Buckingham from
1625 to 1628, i. 368-73 ; in Charles's
First Parliament, i. 368 - 9 ; in
Charles's Second Parliament, and at
the Coronation, i. 369-70 ; his influence with the King and his successive preferments from June 1626 to
March 1627-8, i. 371-2 ; is opposed
and attacked in Charles's Third
Parliament, i. 372 ; his position in
the Government after the death of
Buckingham in 1628, i. 373 ; as
Privy-Councillor and chief Minister
of Charles I. from 1628 to 1632, i.
376-87 ; his severities in Council and
Star-Chamber, i. 377, 384-6, 404-6 ;
Wentworth and, i. 386 ; Secretary
Windebank and, i. 386-7 ; as Bishop
of London from 1628, i. 205-6, 373,
387, 389 ; in the government of the
Church from 1628 to 1632, i. 387 ;
account of the Ecclesiastical Legislation and Administration of, from
1628 to 1632, i. 391-9, 391 note, 399-
404 ; his notion of the "Beauty of
Holiness," i. 395-8, 401, 415, 417,
492, 748 ; his action in the Court of
High Commission, i. 406-7 ; Chancellor of Oxford University in 1630,
i. 408 ; George Herbert and, i. 413-
5, 492 ; Nicholas Ferrar and, i. 416-
8, 492 ; projects of, concerning the
Irish Church, i. 423, 520 ; interference of, with the Foreign British
Chaplaincies, i. 427, 698 ; becomes,
virtually, Prime Minister of England in 1632, i. 386-7 ; character
of, discussed, i. 409-13 ; his Pa-
tristic learning, i. 513, 515, 518,
519, 538 ; in the Triumvirate of
Laud, Wentworth, and Hamilton
during the Period of Thorough, i.
664-9 ; explanation of the term
"Thorough," i. 668 - 9 ; Crown
patronage of the Church exercised

for Laudian purposes, i. 673; Archbishop Abbot and, i. 360-1, 364, 371, 388; as Archbishop of Canterbury in succession to Abbot, from Aug. 3, 1633, i. 664-5, 673, 704; is offered, and refuses, a cardinalship, i. 665; in correspondence with Wentworth in Ireland, i. 667, 668; appointed a Commissioner of the Treasury, i. 671; procures the full office of Treasurer for Juxon, i. 671; his theory of Anglicanism, i. 674; his legislation (1) in the *Sabbatarian Controversy*, i. 674-5, (2) in the *breaking up of the Dutch and Walloon congregations throughout England*, i. 675-6, and (3) in the *Altar Controversy*, i. 676-7; his measures for enlarging ecclesiastical jurisdiction, i. 677-8; obtains the right of visitation of the Universities, i. 678; in ecclesiastical prosecutions and punishments in England from 1632 to 1638, i. 678-82; in the State prosecution of ex-Keeper Williams, Bishop of Lincoln, i. 682-4; hopeless condition of English Presbyterianism during the supremacy of, ii. 533; persecution of English Independents in England by, ii. 544, 547, 558; activity of, as censor-in-chief of the Press, i. 545; reported at Rome to be in favour of the union of the Churches of England and Rome, i. 684-7; co-operates with Wentworth in the government of the Irish Church from 1632 to 1638, i. 687-96; is elected Chancellor of Trinity College, Dublin, in 1633, i. 691; in correspondence with Wentworth, i. 691-2; sends Chappell to Ireland, i. 692; obtains a new Charter and new body of Statutes for Trinity College, i. 692; restores to the Irish Church all the impropriations held by the Crown, i. 692; abrogates the Irish Articles of 1616 as the separate basis of the Irish Church, and substitutes the Thirty-nine Articles of the English Church, i. 693-4; his policy of *Thorough* for Scotland, i. 698; his ceremonial arrangements for the Coronation of Charles in Edinburgh,

i. 700; with Charles in Scotland, i. 703; attempts to govern Scotland on Laudian principles, i. 704-6, 708, 716-28; Scottish defiance to, in the Covenant of 1638, i. 728; in the struggle with the Scottish Covenanters, ii. 5, 13, 35; resolved on a war with Scotland, ii. 46; requires the English clergy to contribute towards the First Bishops' War, ii. 49; his dream previous to the war, ii. 49-50; in correspondence with Strafford concerning preparations in Scotland for the First Bishops' War, ii. 54; in Irish University matters, ii. 76-8; in correspondence with Wentworth in Irish University affairs, ii. 77-8; in correspondence with Bishop Hall, ii. 123-5; his part in Hall's *Episcopacy by Divine Right*, ii. 195-6; in Charles's Cabinet or Junto, ii. 127, 280; his scheme for revising the Canons of the Church, ii. 131-3; his Diary, ii. 134, 144; and the English emigrants · to America and the West Indies, i. 430, 698; ii. 547, 558; draft of his Archiepiscopal prayer for the opening of the Long Parliament, ii. 144-5; in the Long Parliament, ii. 150, 151, 153; the London booksellers' petition to him against the printer Ulac, v. 154, 155 note; proceedings against, by the Parliament, ii. 176; sent to the Tower in 1640, ii. 178, 278; his former transactions with the King and Strafford, ii. 181; *Laudians*, or the High Church Party, ii. 195-6; his detestation of Williams's scheme of Church management, ii. 224; with Williams and the Bishops in the Tower, ii. 335; his self-vindication at his trial in 1643, i. 361-4; Hartlib a witness against, iii. 229 and note; his trial and execution, iii. 183-5: Mentions of, in connexion with Joseph Meade, i. 125, William Chappell, i. 129, Hyde, ii. 168, Alexander Gill, i. 209, 214, John Durie, ii. 367, iii. 195, Secretary Windebank, i. 387, the poet Shirley, i. 446, Bishop Andrewes, i. 515, Lord Scudamore, i. 749, 750, 753, Grotius, i. 753-4, ii. 368

K

note, Chelsea College, iii. 222 ; other mentions of, i. 510, 535, 537, 673, 758, 759; ii. 167; iii. 107, 218; his handwriting, ii. 9 note ; portrait of, by Marshall, iii. 456.

LAUDER, William : his attempts to prove Milton a plagiarist, i. 89 note.

LAUDERDALE, John Maitland, 1st Earl of, member of the Scottish Privy Council of Charles I., i. 707, 724 ; ii. 15 ; in the General Assembly of 1642, ii. 418.

LAUDERDALE, John Maitland, 1st Duke of (eldest son of the above), in London as one of four Scottish Commissioners to the Westminster Assembly, iii. 10-1, 17, 40 ; succeeds to the Earldom, iii. 143 note ; in the Committee of the Two Kingdoms, iii. 40, 413 ; at the conclusion of the Treaty with the Scots, iii. 510 and note ; alleged insults to, by the officers and soldiers of Fairfax's army, iii. 543, 544 ; in the matter of the Propositions of the Army, iii. 572, and of the Four Bills, iii. 578, 579-82 ; delivers to the King in the Isle of Wight a Scottish Protest against the Bills and Propositions, iii. 584, 586 ; at the dissolution of the " Committee of the Two Kingdoms," iii. 585 ; in the Secret Treaty with Charles, iii. 586, 588 ; his part in the Scottish *Engagement*, iii. 588-90 ; with Charles II.'s Court at the Hague, iv. 25, 27, 28 ; Henrietta Maria and, iv. 181 ; in Scotland with Charles II., iv. 188, 189 ; at the head of the party of Presbyterian Royalists in Scotland, iv. 205 ; in the Scottish Parliament held at Perth in 1650, iv. 212, 282 ; taken prisoner at the Battle of Worcester, iv. 294 ; as prisoner in the Tower of London, in Warwick Castle, and in Windsor Castle, iv. 297, v. 94, 97, 360 ; excepted from Cromwell's Ordinance of Pardon and Grace in 1654, iv. 560 ; discharged from imprisonment by the Restored Long Parliament in 1660, v. 547 ; with the Scottish Council of Charles II. in London, vi. 130-1, 137 ; and Middleton, vi. 138-40 and note ;

continued Presbyterianism of, vi. 139-40, 142 ; in the story of the loss of the Scottish Records, vi. 142 note; his enmity to Clarendon, vi. 249 ; Latin letters of Alexander Morus to, vi. 421-22 ; in the Cabal Government, vi. 574, 579-80, 582, 591, 593, 597, 599, 600, 602 ; raised to the peerage as Duke of Lauderdale, vi. 603.

LAUDERDALE, Countess of, provision for, in Cromwell's Ordinance of Pardon and Grace, iv. 560.

LAURENCE, Colonel, in Fleetwood's army in Ireland, iv. 401.

LAW, James, Scottish Archbishop, i. 697.

LAWES, Henry, musician, account of, i. 566-7 ; his part in the Great Masque of the Inns of Court in 1633, i. 580, 586 ; his connexion with the Bridgewater family, i. 586, 589-90 ; his great reputation, ii. 79-80 ; composes music for Milton's *Arcades*, i. 598, 601 note, and for Milton's *Comus*, i. 610, 611, 640-1 ; ii. 80 ; iii. 445, 454 ; letter of, to Milton, i. 736 ; Waller's songs and, iii. 449 note ; Milton's songs and, iii. 451 ; Milton's sonnet to, iii. 462-5 ; vi. 688 ; music by, at the first London Italian Opera-house, v. 81, 81 note, vi. 347 ; his *Ayres and Dialogues* and *Choice Psalmes*, v. 226 ; death of, vi. 452-3.

LAWES, Thomas, Vicar-choral of Salisbury Cathedral, and father of the two musicians, Henry and William, i. 566.

LAWES, William, musician (elder brother of Henry), i. 566-7 ; his death, iii. 462.

LAWRENCE, Henry, of St. Ives, Hunts, member for Westmorland in the Long Parliament, iii. 402 ; Roger Williams and, iv. 396, 549 ; called to Cromwell's Supreme Assembly, iv. 501 ; in the Barebones Parliament and its Council, iv. 506, 525 ; as President of Council through the First Protectorate, iii. 658, iv. 545, 545-6 note, 547, 549, 572, 575, v. 31, 64, 107, 177, 183-4, 259-60, 273, 304; in the Privy Council of the Second

Protectorate, v. 308 ; one of Cromwell's Lords, iii. 658, v. 324 ; after dissolution of Cromwell's Second Parliament, v. 333, 346-7, 372, 401, 374 ; in Milton's *Defensio Secunda*, iv. 602, 606, 612 ; v. 381; supports Richard's government, v. 417 ; on the Committee of Safety, v. 494 ; after the Restoration, vi. 197.

LAWRENCE, Edward (elder son of President Lawrence), dead in 1657, iii. 658.

LAWRENCE, Henry (younger son and heir of President Lawrence), among Milton's known pupils, iii. 658 ; his friendship with Milton, v. 230 ; 235, 367 ; vi. 453 ; Milton's sonnet to, v. 237-40, vi. 688.

LAWRENCE, Colonel Richard, v. 471.

LAWRENCE, William, one of Cromwell's Commissioners for the forfeited estates in Scotland in 1654, iv. 561 ; one of Cromwell's Supreme Commissioners of Justice in Scotland, v. 86, 92.

LAWSON, Admiral, in the war with the Dutch (1652), iv. 375-6 ; v. 33; in Cromwell's Second Parliament, v. 107 ; in Fifth Monarchy Riot, v. 134; his Swedish expedition, v. 428 ; at the Republican reofficering of the Navy, v. 471 ; in co-operation with Monk, v. 514, 519-20; at the Restoration of the Long Parliament, v. 540, 564, 571-2 ; in the war with the Dutch (1665), vi. 252, 254, 507.

LAYCOCK HOUSE, surrender of, by the Royalists, iii. 338.

LAZON, Martin de, v. 376.

LEA : see *Ley*.

LEACH, Francis, printer and publisher, iii. 376 note ; iv. 520.

LEADBETTER, Joshua, v. 625.

LEARMONT, Sir James, in Cromwell's Government of Scotland, v. 86.

LECHMERE, Nicholas, in the Restored Rump, v. 454, 666.

LECTURERS, a body of men employed for Puritan preaching and teaching, i. 342-3.

LEDSOM, William, v. 625.

LEE, Sir Edward : see *Lichfield*, Earl of.

LEE, Isaac, English agent in Hamburg, iv. 87, 89, 90, 125, 159.

LEE, John, iv. 88, 92.

LEE, Nat, vi. 611 ; Dryden and, vi. 777.

LEE, Samuel, Nonconformist, vi. 232 note.

LEE, William, publisher, iii. 300 ; vi. 402.

LEGATE, Bartholomew, burned for Arianism, i. 60 ; iii. 157.

LEGGE, Mr. William, with Charles I. at Hampton Court and the Isle of Wight, iii. 561, 574-5 ; is dismissed from the King's service, iii. 587 ; v. 472.

LEICESTER, Lady Dorothy Percy, Countess of, i. 751 ; iv. 214.

LEICESTER, Robert Sidney, 2nd Earl of, British Ambassador at Paris, i. 749, 751, 755, 756, 757, 758, 759, 834 ; Lord-Lieutenant of Ireland in succession to Strafford, ii. 281, 308, 310 ; iii. 517, 519 ; has Parliamentarian leanings, ii. 428, iii. 327 ; his two sons : see *Lisle, Viscount ;* and *Sidney, Algernon ;* in the Privy Council of the Restoration, vi. 18.

LEIDA, Marquis of (Spanish Governor of Dunkirk), iv. 528.

LEIGH, Richard, vi. 612, 703.

LEIGHTON, Dr. Alexander, account of the prosecution of, by Laud and the Star Chamber in 1630, i. 404-6, 404 note, 405-6 note, 542 ; released from prison by the Long Parliament, ii. 175, 254, 260, 589.

LEIGHTON, Dr. Robert, Archbishop, son of Dr. Alexander Leighton, i. 404-5 ; minister of Newbattle, and appointed Principal of Edinburgh University in 1653, v. 88, 90, 349 ; as Scottish Bishop, vi. 299, 301.

LEIGHTON, Thomas, Parliamentarian officer, ii. 444.

LEIGHTON, Sir William, gentleman pensioner of James I., i. 51 ; Royalist conspirator, v. 338.

LEITH, town of, in the First Bishops' War, ii. 54, 59.

LELAND, the antiquary, i. 76, 114.

LEMON, Robert, Deputy-Keeper of State Papers, vi. 816.

LEMON, William, in Councils of State, iv. 273, 313, 315, 321 ; in the Restored Rump, v. 454.

LENNARD, John, iv. 579.

LENNOX, Charles : see *Richmond*, Duke of, vi. 605.

LENNOX, James Stuart, Duke of, at Trinity College, Cambridge, i. 122, 152, 701; ii. 8, 25 note; in the Second Bishops' War, ii. 129; in the Long Parliament, ii. 152, 303; in Scottish Privy Council, ii. 307.

LENTHALL, Sir John (son of the Speaker), knighted by Cromwell, v. 354 note; in the Restored Rump, v. 454.

LENTHALL, William, member for Woodstock, and Speaker in the Long Parliament, ii. 149, 173, 174, 342-3; Cromwell's letter to, from Naseby field, iii. 384; 536, 551-2, 554; Cromwell in correspondence with, from Scotland, iii. 622; iv. 54, 89, 156; his signature to some of Milton's State letters, iv. 232, 291, 400; Speaker in Cromwell's First Parliament, v. 5, 6; in Cromwell's Second Parliament, v. 108, 128; is one of Cromwell's lords, v. 324; at the Restoration of the Rump, v. 446-7, 453, 491; in correspondence with Monk, v. 496; at the Second Restoration of the Rump, v. 517, 529; in the Restored Long Parliament, v. 545, 596; his sentence under the Indemnity Bill after the Restoration, vi. 38, 47, 55.

LEONORA (Tasso's), i. 808-9.

LEONORA (Milton's) : see *Baroni*.

LEOPOLD, Archduke of Austria, Letters of State to, iv. 232, 283; v. 176; elected Emperor of Germany, v. 315, 396; in the Dutch War (1665), vi. 596.

LESLIE, General Sir Alexander : see *Leven*, Earl of.

LESLIE, David, Major-General under the Earl of Leven, iii. 37; at the Battle of Marston Moor, iii. 97-8; routs Montrose at the Battle of Philiphaugh, iii. 366-8, 371; with Charles I. at Newcastle, iii. 412; second in command, under the Earl of Leven, of the forces of the anti-Engagers in Scotland, iii. 621; at the capture of Montrose in May 1650, iv. 184; in command of the Scottish

army against Cromwell, iv. 196, 189-200; beaten at the Battle of Dunbar, iv. 200-1; after Dunbar, iv. 203-4, 208, 212; commander of Charles II.'s Scottish army, iv. 283, 290, 293; taken prisoner at the Battle of Worcester, iv. 294-5, 297; in the Tower of London, iv. 298; v. 94; fined by Cromwell, iv. 560-1.

LESLIE, of Balgonie, George (father of the Earl of Leven), ii. 52.

LESLIE (or Lesley), John, Bishop of the Isles in 1628, i. 697; translated to Raphoe in Ireland, i. 420, 705; ii. 124; vi. 128.

LESLIE, Henry, Bishop of Down and Connor, vi. 127, 128.

LESLIE, Robert, Bishop of Dromore, vi. 128.

LESLIE, Robin, Scottish page to Charles I., ii. 67.

LESLIE, Dr. William, of Aberdeen, ii. 28.

LE SŒUR, Hubert, sculptor, vi. 162.

L'ESTRADES, governor of Dunkirk, v. 253, 290.

L'ESTRANGE, Sir Roger, journalist, iii. 185; in the Second Civil War, iii. 594; under the Protectorate, v. 76; author of *No Blind Guides*, v. 689-90; after the Restoration, vi. 299, 308, 326-32, 326 note, 339, 365 note, 478-80; licenser of books, vi. 506-7, 514-6, 613, 710, 764; and the fourth edition of *Paradise Lost*, vi. 785.

"LETTER TO A FRIEND," Milton's, in 1633 : see *Milton*.

LETTERS OF STATE, Milton's Latin ; see under *Milton*.

LEVELLERS, the, iii. 529, 570-1, 610-1; Lilburne and the, iv. 44-7; suppression of the, iv. 49-51 and note; tracts against the, iv. 96-7; their pamphlets against the Commonwealth, iv. 115-6; plottings by the, v. 32-3 : see also under *Lilburne*, John.

LEVEN, Earl of (General Sir Alexander Leslie), Commander-in-Chief of the Scottish Army in the First "Bishops' War," ii. 52-5 and note, 56, 63-7; his signature to a letter from the Scottish Leaders to Louis XIII., ii. 130; in the Second "Bishops' War," ii.

135, 136; invades England, ii. 137-42; during the King's visit to Scotland in 1641, ii. 292, 295, 306, 323; created Earl of Leven, ii. 307; leads Scottish Auxiliary Army into England, iii. 37, 40, 84; Montrose and, iii. 342; at the Battle of Marston Moor, iii. 97; takes Newcastle, iii. 177; through the Civil War, iii. 339, 371; at Newcastle with the King, iii. 374, 412; in command of the forces of the *anti-Engagers* in Scotland, iii. 621; entertains Cromwell in the Castle of Edinburgh, iii. 622; resigns his post of Commander-in-Chief, iv. 196; accompanies the relics of the Army, after Dunbar, to Perth, iv. 203, 212; in the defence of Stirling Castle, iv. 290; taken prisoner by Monk and sent to England, iv. 296, 297-8.

LEVENTHORPE, Sir Thomas, v. 477.

LEVETT, of Ripon, English divine, ii. 513 note.

"LEVIATHAN": see *Hobbes*.

LEWIS, Sir William, among the eleven Presbyterian leaders denounced by the Army, iii. 548-9; escapes abroad, iii. 554; in the Council of State and the Restored Long Parliament, v. 544, 545.

LEXINGTON, Robert Sutton, 2nd Lord, vi, 785.

LEY, Anne, married to Sir Walter Long, iii. 58.

LEY, Dionysia, married to John Harington, iii. 58.

LEY, Elizabeth, married to Morice Carant, iii. 58.

LEY, Henry: see *Marlborough*, 2nd Earl of, iii. 58.

LEY, Hesther, married to Arthur Fuller, iii. 58.

LEY, James: see *Marlborough*, 1st Earl of.

LEY, James, son of the preceding, iii. 58.

LEY, John, member of Westminster Assembly, ii. 519.

LEY (or Lea), Mr., i. 627.

LEY, Lady Margaret, Milton's sonnet to, iii. 57-61, 188, 188 note, 189.

LEY, Martha, iii. 58.

LEY, Mary, married to Richard Erisy, iii. 58.

LEY (or Lea), Matthew, iv. 576, 578; v. 624.

LEY, Phœbe, married to Biggs, of Hurst, in Berkshire, Esq., iii. 58.

LEY (or Lea) Thomas, iv. 576, 578; v. 624.

LEY, William, son of the 1st Earl of Marlborough, iii. 58.

LEYDA, the Marquis of, Governor of Dunkirk; State letters of Milton to, iv. 528; v. 37, 340.

LEYDEN, Brownists in, ii. 539, 541, 542; the University of, i. 100.

"LIBEL FROM WARE" (Herts), a Puritan document so endorsed by Windebank during the First "Bishops' War," ii. 52.

LIBRARY, THE KING'S: see *St. James's Palace*.

LIBRI, Lorenzo, Florentine, i. 787.

LICHFIELD, siege of the Cathedral Close of, ii. 463.

LICHFIELD, Charles Stuart, Earl of, in the Convention Parliament, vi. 45.

LICHFIELD (Sir Henry Edward Lee), Earl of, marries a daughter of the Duchess of Cleveland and Charles II., vi. 604-5.

LICHFIELD, Leonard, printer to the Oxford University, ii. 363.

LIDCOTT, Thomas, Parliamentarian officer, ii. 445.

LIGHTFOOT, Dr. John, theologian and orientalist, i. 519; account of his early career, ii. 519; avowed Erastian in the Westminster Assembly, ii. 606; iii. 20, 160; under the Protectorate, v. 74, 75; at the Restoration, vi. 294, 295.

LILBURNE, Elizabeth, wife of John Lilburne, v. 319-20.

LILBURNE, George, uncle of John, iv. 357.

LILBURNE, Henry, brother of John, iii. 388.

LILBURNE, John, persecution of, in Laud's time, and liberation of, from imprisonment by the Long Parliament in 1640, ii. 175, 589; one of the Root and Branch party in Church matters, ii. 201; in Essex's army, ii. 444, 458, 458 note; at Marston Moor, iii. 387; as a pamphleteer, iii. 387-90; and Crom-

well, iii. 387-8, 570; joins the extreme Independents, iii. 388-9; a reader of the *Areopagitica*, iii. 433; imprisoned for contumacy before the House of Commons, iii. 390; fined and imprisoned by the Lords, in 1646, iii. 528; continues pamphleteering while in prison, iii. 529; a leader of the "Levellers," iii. 529, 570-1; released from the Tower in 1647, iii. 583; iv. 43; his levelling manifesto, *England's New Chains Discovered*, iv. 43, 44, 87; his appearance before the Council of State, and outburst against Cromwell, and his committal to the Tower, iv. 45-7, 49-51, 93, 97; more levelling pamphlets by, iv. 115-6, 118-9, 178 note; tampers with the Army, iv. 119; his prosecution, trial, acquittal, and release, iv. 119-20, 178, 357; banished for life in 1652, iv. 357-8; his continued scurrilities abroad, v. 502-4; returns from exile in 1653, and is recommitted for trial, iv. 504; his second trial and acquittal, iv. 507-8; continued imprisonment of, iv. 508; v. 318-9; release of, and death, v. 319-20.

LILBURNE, Robert (brother of John), cornet in the Parliamentarian army in 1642, ii. 445; colonel under *New Model*, iii. 326, 388, 534, 537, 583; one of the Commissioners at the King's trial, iii. 707, 712 note; signs the death-warrant of Charles I., iii. 720, vi. 28; at the trial of his brother John, iv. 120; in the pursuit of Charles II. into England, and defeats the Earl of Derby at Wigan, iv. 293; in the War with Scotland, iv. 302, 365; left, with Monk and Dean, in Scotland, iv. 401-2, 490, 491, 508-9, 551-2; v. 706-7; in Oliver's First Parliament, v. 5; appointed Deputy to Major-General Lambert, v. 49, 107; in the Second Parliament of the Protectorate, v. 107; supports Richard's government, v. 418; through the period of Anarchy, v. 470, 494, 497, 522; after the Restoration, vi. 43, 49; his sentence under Indemnity Bill (1660), vi. 54; his trial, vi. 80, 93; his

death, vi. 98 note; in the Bill of Attainder, vi. 115.

LILLIESTON, actor, vi. 350.

LILLY, Mr. William (*Merlinus Anglicus*) and his Almanacks since 1644, v. 21; examined by a Committee of the Commons in the Quest of the Regicides, vi. 31-3.

LILY, William, grammarian, first master of St. Paul's School, i. 74, 76.

LIMBERY, John, merchant, v. 589.

LINCOLN, Theophilus Clinton, 4th Earl of, ii. 48, 142, 158, 430; iii. 692; committed to the Tower with other peers in Sept. 1647, iii. 554; in the reconstituted House of Peers in 1660, v. 695.

LINDSAY, John, 1st Earl of (in 1633), Scottish Covenanter, i. 710, 722, 725; ii. 16; in the Glasgow Assembly of 1638, ii. 38; in the First "Bishops' War," ii. 65; on the Committee of Estates, ii. 292; iii. 499; in London, on a Scottish Parliamentary Commission, in 1642, ii. 417; with Scottish Auxiliary army in England, iii. 37; interviews Charles I. at Newcastle in 1646, iii. 499.

LINDSAY, Alexander, Bishop of Dunkeld in 1607, i. 697.

LINDSAY, David, Bishop of Brechin in 1619, i. 697; officiates at the Coronation of Charles I. in Holyrood Abbey, i. 700; Bishop of Edinburgh and Privy Councillor, i. 706; at the "Jenny Geddes" riot, i. 719-20; sentence upon, by the Glasgow Assembly of 1638, ii. 42.

LINDSAY, Patrick, Bishop of Ross in 1613, and Archbishop of Glasgow in 1633, i. 697; at Charles's Coronation in Holyrood Abbey, i. 700; in the Scottish Privy Council, i. 706; sentence upon, by the Glasgow Assembly of 1638, ii. 42.

LINDSELL, Dr. Augustine, Bishop of Peterborough and of Hereford, i. 120, 390, 399, 674.

LINDSEY, Robert Bertie, 1st Earl of (1626), in Charles I.'s English Privy Council, i. 380; in correspondence with Windebank, ii. 58; in the English army in the First Bishops'

War, ii. 62; in the Long Parliament, ii. 152; in command of the King's army in the Civil War, ii. 422, 440; killed in October 1642, ii. 428, 455.

LINDSEY, Montague Bertie, 2nd Earl of (son of the above), ii. 429; at the Treaty of Newport, iii. 606; at the removal of the King to Hurst Castle, iii. 627-9; in the last days of Charles I., iii. 712-3; at the burial of Charles I., iii. 727; his arrest, v. 50; in the Privy Council of the Restoration, vi. 18; at the trials of the Regicides, vi. 77; at the Coronation of Charles II., vi. 152.

LINLITHGOW, George, 3rd Earl of, ii. 15; in the Scottish Parliament of 1650, iv. 212; in Oliver's First Parliament, v. 5.

LIPPI, Lorenzo, Florentine poet and painter, i. 787.

LISKEARD PARK in Cornwall, mines and quarries in, vi. 213.

LISLE, Mr. Daniel (David), special messenger from the Council to Queen Christina, iv. 378.

LISLE, Sir George, at the Battle of Naseby, iii. 335; his death, iii. 605.

LISLE, Mr. John, in a Commission of the Commons to the King in the Isle of Wight, iii. 579; King's Judge and present at the trial, iii. 720 note; in Councils of State of the Commonwealth as "Councillor at Law," iv. 11, 12, 14, 79, 82, 83, 87, 150, 227, 229, 273, 314, 354-5, 425, 449; v. 118; as Commissioner of the Great Seal, iv. 40, 54, 224, 225; v. 128, 324, 346-7; one of Cromwell's lords, v. 324; supports Richard's government, v. 418; in the Restored Rump, v. 454, 479; at the Quest of the Regicides, vi. 28, 31; in the Indemnity Bill (1660), vi. 54; in Bill of Attainder, vi. 115; assassin of, vi. 115 note.

LISLE, Philip Sidney, Viscount, eldest son of the Earl of Leicester; member for Yarmouth in the Isle of Wight, in the Long Parliament, ii. 173; vi. 18; his younger brother, Algernon, iii. 327; Lieutenant-General of Ireland for the Parliament in 1646, iii. 519-21, 531; at the

Resolution of the Commons for the trial of Charles I., iii. 699; not at the trial, iii. 708 note; in the first Council of the Commonwealth, iv. 12, 14, 15, 79, 82; in successive Councils of the Commonwealth, iv. 147, 150, 151, 224, 229, 354-5, 425; appointed Ambassador Extraordinary to Sweden by the Rump, iv. 378; but does not go, iv. 512; called to Cromwell's Supreme Assembly, iv. 501; in the Councils of the Barebones Parliament, iv. 506, 525; in the Council of the First Protectorate, iv. 545, 575; not in the First Parliament of the Protectorate, v. 5; in Cromwell's Council between the Parliaments, v. 31, 64, 183, 184, 259, 288, 374; at Cromwell's Second Installation, v. 149; in Cromwell's Court, v. 303; in the Council of the Second Protectorate, v. 308, 374; one of Cromwell's lords, v. 323; in the Privy Council after the dissolution of Cromwell's Second Parliament, v. 333, 352; in Richard's Council, v. 417; in the Restored Rump, v. 454, 479, 544 note.

LISTER, Esquire, Thomas, member of the Long Parliament, and in Councils of State of the Commonwealth, iv. 313, 314, 315, 355, 449; in the Restored Rump, v. 454, 455, 465, 490; in the Indemnity Bill, vi. 36, 37, 47-8, 55.

LITCHFIELD, Leonard, Cambridge printer, i. 738 note; vi. 331.

LITERATURE, sketch of English, to Milton's time, i. 86-8; survey of British, in 1632, i. 432-51; under the Protectorate, v. 75-86; first seven years of the, of the Restoration, vi. 273-405; from 1667-70, vi. 605-19.

LITTLE CONDUIT, the, Old Cheapside, i. 48.

LITTLE GIDDING, in Northamptonshire, the Protestant nunnery of Nicholas Ferrar, i. 416-7.

"LITTLE NONSUCH," anonymous pamphlet in 1646, iii. 678.

LITTLETON, Dr. Adam: his Latin Dictionary, vi. 813.

LITTLETON, Sir Edward, Keeper of the Great Seal to Charles I., in the Long Parliament, ii. 159, 274, 279, 281, 283, 334, 338 ; conveys the Great Seal to Charles at York, ii. 413-4 ; his death, ii. 429.

LIVESEY, Sir Michael, colonel under *New Model*, iii. 327, 402 ; Parliamentarian officer in the Second Civil War, iii. 596 ; at the King's Trial, iii. 712 note; signs the death-warrant, iii. 720 ; in the Restored Rump, v. 454, 544 note, 666 ; in the Indemnity Bill, vi. 28, 44, 54 ; in Bill of Attainder, vi. 115 ; subsequent fate of, vi. 115 note.

LIVINGSTON OF KILSYTH, Sir James, iv. 561.

LIVINGSTONE, John, Scottish Presbyterian divine, i. 715 ; ii. 38 ; iv. 188-9 ; v. 90.

LIVINGSTONE, William, Covenanting leader, ii. 15 ; member of Assembly of 1638, ii. 38.

LLEWELLEN, Peter, v. 625.

LLOYD, Dr., and Milton's Will, vi. 737.

LLOYD, David, author, vi. 514.

LLOYD, Edward, of St. John's College, Cambridge, University Proctor, i. 186.

LLOYD, Hugh, Bishop of Llandaff, vi. 105.

LLOYD, James, witness, iii. 637.

LLOYD, Lodowick, publisher, iv. 107 note.

LLOYD, Sir Marmaduke, Justice of Chester, i. 609.

LLOYD, Dr. Richard, ii. 513 note.

LLOYD, Walter, Lieutenant-Colonel under *New Model*, iii. 326, 332.

LOCKE, John, the philosopher, under the Protectorate, v. 76 ; at the Restoration, vi. 318-9 ; and Infant Whiggism, vi. 619.

LOCKHART, William, of Lee, afterwards Sir William : one of the five members for Scotland called to Cromwell's Supreme Assembly in 1653, iv. 502 ; one of Cromwell's Trustees of the forfeited lands in Scotland, iv. 562 ; member for Lanarkshire in Cromwell's Parliament of **1654**, v.

5 ; account of, v. 47 ; Ambassador for the Protectorate to Paris, v. 47 ; in Cromwell's Scottish Council in 1654, v. 86, 94 ; in Cromwell's Second Parliament, v. 108, 114 ; in the Treaty with France of 1656-7, v. 140; 141, 251, 310, 468 ; further account of, v. 295 ; in the Treaty of the Pyrenees, v. 342-3, 388, 394, 502-3 ; one of Cromwell's lords, v. 324 ; capture of Dunkirk by, in 1658, v. 340, 392 ; still with the Army in Flanders, but giving his support to Richard's Protectorate, v. 415, 419, 420, 421, 426-7, 438, 459, 570; returns to England in June 1659 to render his accounts, v. 461 ; gives his adherence to the Government of the Restored Rump, v. 463, 464.

LOCKYER, Mr. Nicholas, Independent minister, and one of Cromwell's Commission of Triers and Ejectors, iv. 370, 514, 565 note, 571 ; v. 31, 77, 115, 345 ; Nonconformist, vi. 232 note.

LOCKYER, Robert, a trooper, tried by Court-martial, and shot for mutiny by order of Cromwell (April 1649), iv. 48, vi. 179 note.

LODER (or Lowther), Sir George, Chief Justice of Ireland, married to Edward King's sister Margaret, i. 172, 651, 653.

LONDON : Milton's early connexions with, i. 3-64 ; population of, at Milton's birth, i. 43 note ; public schools in, i. 73-7 ; bishopric and diocese of, i. 205-6, 373, 389, 401 ; Cathedral of St. Paul's, i. 407 ; church of St. Sepulchre, i. 407 ; the post of Chronologer to the City of, i. 432, 436 ; the Court of Aldermen, i. 436 ; population and size of, in 1632, i. 437 ; Taylor "the Water Poet," and the River Thames, i. 482-3 ; Dr. Donne, Dean of St. Paul's, i. 485 ; Nathaniel Butter and the first newspapers of, i. 542 ; the Stationers' Company of, i. 544 ; the sale of books in, in 1632, i. 547, 548-51, 550 note ; Milton on visits to, from Horton, i. 564-5, 566, 567 ; dramatic entertainments in, i. 579-

80 ; the Plague in (1636-7), i. 626-7, 629, 638 ; Lambeth Palace, i. 665 ; Juxon succeeds Laud in the bishopric of, i. 674 ; foreigners resident in, in 1638, ii. 45 note ; contributions of the City of, towards the First " Bishops' War," ii. 50 ; the Diodati family in, ii. 80-2, 81 note ; Milton in, ii. 97, 101-2 ; the Earl of Loudoun imprisoned by Charles I. in the Tower of, ii. 132 ; riots in, following the dissolution of the Short Parliament, ii. 133-4 ; aldermen of, sent to prison, ii. 135 ; loan of, for the Second " Bishops' War," ii. 135 ; petition of the City of, for calling a Parliament, ii. 142 ; Juxon, Bishop of, summoned to the Long Parliament, ii. 150 ; John Glynn, Recorder of, in the Long Parliament, ii. 173 ; other leading citizens of, in the Parliament, ii. 173 ; Strafford committed to prison in the Tower of, ii. 177 ; Laud sent to the Tower of, ii. 178, 335 ; the Scottish Commissioners in London as the guests of the Corporation of the City of, in 1640-1, ii. 191-2, 193, 203, 288 ; Aldersgate Street in, ii. 203-12 ; petition from the City of, to Parliament, in the Church Reform Movement, ii. 213 ; the Plague again in (1641), ii. 272, 274, 315 ; news of the Irish Insurrection reaches, ii. 316-7 ; reception of Charles I. by the citizens of, on his return from Scotland in 1641, ii. 323 ; tumults in, ii. 328, 330-1, 331 note ; Archbishop Williams and the bishops sent to the Tower of, ii. 335 ; application by the Commons to the City of, for a guard of trained bands on the occasion of Charles's *Coup d'Etat*, ii. 338 ; the King's search for the Five Members in the City of, ii. 344 ; the Parliament holds its meetings in the City of, ii. 345 ; the King away from, ii. 345-8, 350 ; petitions to Parliament by the prentices and sailors of, and by the street porters of, ii. 349 ; traces of Milton as a citizen and taxpayer in, ii. 356-8 ; in the first weeks of the Civil War : the King's advance on, ii. 453 ; the Earl of Warwick appointed by Parliament Captain-General for the defence of the City of, ii. 455 ; the march of the Trained Bands and Volunteers to Turnham Green, ii. 455-8 ; Milton and the Trained Bands of the City of, ii. 482-8 ; Henderson and the Solemn League and Covenant in, iii. 11 ; the winter of 1643-4 in, iii. 36-7 ; execution of Laud on Tower Hill, iii. 185 ; project of a University of, iii. 221, 662 ; Comenius in, iii. 223-5 ; the Stationers' Company and Milton in, iii. 265-9, 273-4, 291-7 ; Sion College and the Londoners in Church matters, iii. 394-5 ; Baillie's disappointment at the " Nipshot " of the City, iii. 406-7 ; quarrel and reconciliation of the two Houses and the City of, iii. 407-8 ; the King's letters from Newcastle to the City of, iii. 415 ; the petition of, for peace, iii. 415-7 ; Presbyterianising of, and of Lancashire, iii. 423-5 ; the book trade in, between 1640 and 1645, iii. 447-50 ; the Powell family in, iii. 480-3 ; the army of Fairfax and the City of, iii. 347-54, 593 ; Presbyterian rage in, iii. 549-51 ; a week of mob-dictation in, iii. 551-2 ; Fairfax's march on, iii. 552-4, 593 ; the petitions of the City of, against the Civil War, iii. 602-3, and against the Treaty of Newport, iii. 613-4 ; the " Invisible College " in, iii. 662-4 ; Presbyterian Church government in, iii. 673-80 ; Lilburne and the conspiracy of Levellers in, iv. 45-9, 51, 53 ; the Lord Mayor of, fined, and sent to the Tower, iv. 47 ; a day of Thanksgiving in the City of, and a banquet by the Corporation of, to the House, the Council of State, the Judges, and the Officers of the Army, iv. 53-4 ; the Lord Mayor and Corporation of, in an interview with the House on Church matters, vi. 123-4 ; Presbyterian Royalist plottings in, iv. 285-7 ; the Stationers' Company of, iv. 325 ; Christopher Arnold in, iv. 350-3 ;

foreigners in, in 1651, iv. 353 ; Dutch ambassadors in, iv. 371, 373; the Rota Club in, v. 486 ; Sharp's mission to, v. 96-8, 115-6; the book trade of, and popular literature of, in 1656, v. 257-9 ; new Royalist conspiracy in, and elsewhere, in 1657-8, v. 335 ; loyalty of the City to Cromwell, v. 336 and note ; member for, in Richard's Parliament, v. 430 ; officering of the Militia of, by the Restored Rump, v. 472 ; in the negotiations of the Royalists with General Monk, v. 476, 477, 478, 497, 499, 500, 501 ; in Lambert's *Coup d'Etat*, v. 491 ; the government of, by the Committee of Safety, v. 501, 502 ; the Coffee Club in Bow Street, v. 486, 509 ; Monk's Commissioners in, v. 509 ; anarchy in the City of, and utter discredit of the Wallingford House Government in, v. 514-5 ; General Monk's march from Scotland to, v. 524-30 ; the press of, in criticism on the crisis of affairs, v. 530-2 ; the City of, in open revolt against the Rump Government, v. 532 ; Monk's rupture and reconciliation with the City of, v. 533-9 ; " Roasting of the Rump " in, v. 536 ; " Old George " in, v. 547 - 8 ; Monk appointed Major-General and Commander-in-Chief of the Militia of, v. 555 ; Royalist enthusiasm in, v. 557 ; letters of Charles II. from Breda to the Lord Mayor, Aldermen, and Common Councilmen of, v. 561, 697, 698 ; festive dinners to Monk in, v. 657 ; at the Restoration, v. 700 ; the entry of Charles II. into the City of, vi. 10 ; Gilbert Sheldon, Bishop of, in 1660, v. 105, 425 ; ejections in, on St. Bartholomew Sunday (Aug. 24), 1662, vi. 231, 416-8 ; the Great Plague of 1665-6 in, iv. 256-8, 259-60, 489-90, 498-500 ; the Great Fire of 1666, vi. 260-2, 265, 503-5, 508 ; the Dutch in the Thames, vi. 266-7 ; the newspaper press of, before and after the Restoration, vi. 325 ; the chiefs of the London virtuosi and their meetings in Gresham College and elsewhere

in the City of, before and after the Restoration, vi. 391-2, 458-9 ; booksellers and publishers of, from 1640 to 1660, vi. 398-405 ; Milton's house in Jewin Street in, vi. 407-8 ; the *Mercurius Publicus* of Jan. 3, 1660 - 1, published in, vi. 425 ; Morus in, in 1662, vi. 423 ; Milton's house property in the City of, before and after the Restoration, vi. 444-5 ; his losses in the Great Fire of, in 1666, vi. 718 ; maps of Old, and Cunningham's *Handbook* of, vi. 485 note ; foundation of New St. Paul's Cathedral in, in 1674, vi. 730 ; the London *Gazette*, vi. 331, 332, 730, 790 ; Milton's burial place in St. Giles, Cripplegate, in the City of, vi. 731 - 2 ; eminent persons visiting, go to see Milton's daughter, vi. 752-4 ; famous publishers in, vi. 781 ; Companies of : see *Mercers' Company, Merchant-Tailors' Company, Scriveners' Company.*

LONG, Miss, actress, vi. 350-1.

LONG, Jean, co-pastor of Morus at Middleburg, v. 208-9.

LONG, Sir Lislebone, member for Wells in Richard's Parliament, v. 431.

LONG, Sir Walter, of Draycot-Cerne, Wilts : son-in-law of the first Earl of Marlborough, iii. 58 ; in the Long Parliament, iii. 59.

LONG, Walter, Esq., member for Ludgershall, Wilts, in 1645, and a Colonel in Essex's Army, ii. 445 ; iii. 401 ; among the eleven Presbyterian leaders denounced by army, iii. 548-9 ; escapes abroad, iii. 554.

LONGE, William, indicted in Star Chamber, and committed to the Tower, i. 216.

LONGLAND, Mr. Charles, English agent at Leghorn, in correspondence with the Council of State, iv. 483.

LOPE DE VEGA, Spanish dramatist, i. 745.

LORNE, Archibald Campbell, Lord, afterwards 8th Earl of, and 1st Marquis of Argyle, ii. 10-14 : see *Argyle*.

LORNE, Lord, eldest son of the 8th Marquis of Argyle, a colonel of foot-

guards at the Battle of Dunbar, and with Charles II. after Dunbar, ii. 202, 206, 208 ; in a Royalist insurrection in Scotland, iv. 508-9 ; excepted from Cromwell's Ordinance of Pardon and Grace, iv. 560 ; at the Court of Charles II., vi. 131-2.

LORRAINE, Duke of, vi. 596.

LOTHIAN, Countess of, daughter of the 7th Earl of Argyle, ii. 11.

LOTHIAN, William Ker, 3rd Earl of, Covenanter, i. 710, 722 ; ii. 16 ; in the Glasgow Assembly of 1638, ii. 38 ; in the Committee of Estates, ii. 292 ; one of the Scottish Commissioners in London, ii. 417 ; with the Scottish Auxiliary Army in England, iii. 37 ; in command of the forces sent against Montrose in 1644, iii. 352 ; in the Negotiations at Newcastle, iii. 412 ; in the Commission of the General Assembly of the Kirk, iii. 509 ; a Protester or Anti-Engager, iii. 589 ; still with the Commissioners in London, and pleads for the King's life, iii. 717 ; iv. 22 ; is arrested by the English Parliament, and sent back to Scotland, iv. 22 ; in a Commission from the Argyle Government to Charles II. at Breda, iv. 180 ; his arrival in Scotland with Charles II., iv. 188 ; in the Committee of Estates at Perth, iv. 202, 208, 209 ; in the Parliament of March 1650-51, iv. 282 ; during Cromwell's government of Scotland, v. 87 ; in London, prosecuting lawsuits, v. 94.

LOUDOUN, John Campbell, 1st Earl of, Covenanter, i. 710, 722, 723 ; ii. 16, 22 ; in the Glasgow Assembly of 1638, ii. 38, 40 ; in the First "Bishops' War," ii. 65, 68, 69, 126 ; in a deputation to Charles I. in London from the Scottish Committee of Estates, ii. 130 ; committed for treason to the Tower, ii. 130-1, 132, 292 ; at the calling of the Long Parliament, ii. 143 ; one of the Scottish Commissioners in London, ii. 190-2 ; appointed Chancellor of Scotland in the Scottish Privy Council of Charles I., and created Earl of Loudoun, ii. 307, 323, 416 ;

iii. 7 ; in a Commission from the Argyle Government to the English Parliament, ii. 417 ; in the General Assembly of 1642, ii. 418 ; present in the Westminster Assembly, iii. 17 ; with the Scottish Auxiliary Army in England, iii. 37 ; on the "Committee of the Two Kingdoms," iii. 40, 331 note ; his speech in Essex House against Cromwell, as reported by Whitlocke, iii. 180 ; in the Scottish Parliament of June 1644, iii. 347 ; his exertions for peace between the two nations at the close of the Civil War, iii. 371 ; in the Negotiations at Newcastle, iii. 412, 421, 422, 498, 499 ; with the Scottish Commissioners in London, iii. 507 ; leaves London at the surrender of Charles I. by the Scots, iii. 510, 511 note ; with the Scottish Committees in the Isle of Wight, iii. 578, 579-82, 584-5 ; in the Secret Treaty between Charles I. and the Scottish Commissioners, iii. 586 and note, 588, 589 ; among the Anti-Engagers in Scotland, iii. 620-21 ; in the Argyle Government of Scotland in 1649 for the absent Charles II., iv. 62 ; in correspondence with Salmasius, iv. 166 ; after Dunbar, iv. 202, 208-9 ; President of the Committee of Estates, iv. 211 ; in the Scottish Parliament, at Perth and Stirling, of March 1650-1, iv. 281 ; excepted from Cromwell's Ordinance of Pardon and Grace, iv. 560 ; provision for the Countess of, iv. 560 ; in retirement and poverty under the Protectorate, v. 87.

LOUGHBOROUGH, Lord (Royalist), in the Second Civil War, iii. 594, 615.

LOUIS XIII. of France, i. 106, 744, 755, 756 ; ii. 130.

LOUIS XIV. of France : first mention of, in history, i. 755 ; iii. 375 ; his relations with the English Republic, iv. 30, 381-2, 556 ; and the Piedmontese Massacre, v. 40, 42 ; in Treaty with Cromwell, October 1655, v. 46, 140, 141 ; State letters to, v. 189, 190-1, 244, 251, 253, 271-2, 275, 290, 387, 390-1, 392-5, 570, 575-6 ; and Cromwell's

Government, v. 315, 340, 342, 460, 467 ; in relation to Richard's Government, v. 416, 467 ; and the government of the Restored Rump, v. 463, 467, 503 ; and the Synod of Loudun in Anjou, v. 634 ; sale of Dunkirk to, by Charles II., vi. 251 ; in the War between England and the Dutch, vi. 253, 260, 265, 596 ; and the Triple Alliance, vi. 568-9 ; and the Secret Negotiation between France and England, vi. 569-72 ; and the Secret Treaty of Dover, with the text of the article of *The Declaration of Catholicity*, vi. 576 - 81 ; in alliance with England against the Dutch, vi. 582-3 ; and Charles II.'s Declaration of Religious Indulgence, vi. 593 ; in the peace with the Dutch, vi. 601 ; and the Duchess of Portsmouth, vi. 604.

LOUIS DE BOURBON, Prince of Condé, iv. 381.

LOVE, Alderman, on Council of State, v. 520.

LOVE, Christopher, London Presbyterian minister : account of, ii. 519 ; iii. 677 ; case of, iv. 284-7 ; execution of, iv. 293.

LOVE, Nicholas (Regicide), at the King's Trial, iii. 720 note, vi. 28 ; in Councils of State of the Commonwealth, iv. 273, 309, 313, 314, 315, 321, 354-5, 449 ; v. 519 ; at the dissolution of the Rump, iv. 413 ; in the Restored Rump, v. 454 ; in the Indemnity Bill, vi. 44, 54 ; subsequent fate of, vi. 115, 115 note.

LOVE, Dr. Richard, Dean of Ely and Master of Corpus Christi College, Cambridge, i. 120, 213, 220 ; member of Westminster Assembly, ii. 519 ; iii. 93.

LOVE, Thomas, of Peterhouse, Cambridge, University Proctor, i. 186.

LOVEL, actor, vi. 350.

LOVELACE, Lord, Royalist, ii. 142, 429 ; v. 50.

LOVERING, schoolmaster at Cambridge, i. 171.

LOWE, William, Parliamentarian officer, ii. 444.

LOWER (or LOUR), Lord, ii. 292 : see *Northesk*, Earl of.

LOWER, Thomas and William, case of, v. 254.

LOWNES, Humphrey, publisher, i. 56, 89, 90, 472 : see *Book Trade.*

LOWRY, John, in the Parliament of the Restored Rump, v. 454.

LOWTHER, Sir George : see *Loder.*

LUBECK, Letter of State to the Consuls and State of, v. 371.

LUCAS, Lord, his arrest, v. 50.

LUCAS, Sir Charles, Royalist, ii. 442 ; iii. 594, 605.

LUCAS, Thomas, father of the Marchioness of Newcastle, vi. 313.

LUCCA, Republic of, i. 98, 745, 823.

LUCY, Luke, merchant, v. 376.

LUCY, Sir Richard, in the Restored Rump, v. 454, 455.

LUCY, William, Bishop of St. David's, vi. 105.

LUDLOW, in Shropshire, description and history of the town and castle of, i. 605-8 ; "Comus Hall," i. 610 note ; Samuel Butler at, vi. 300.

LUDLOW, Colonel Edmund, Regicide, ii. 173 ; iii. 379, 402 ; in the King's Trial, iii. 705, 707, 712 note ; signs the death-warrant of Charles I., iii. 720, vi. 28 ; in the First Council of State of the Republic, iv. 11, 12, 13, 47, 82 ; Lieutenant-General under Ireton in Ireland, iv. 192, 303 ; in the Council Order Books, iv. 150, 225, 229 ; not reappointed to Council of State, iv. 273 ; in the management of Irish affairs after Ireton's death, iv. 366, 401-2 ; his account of the dissolution of the Rump by Cromwell, iv. 411-3, and 413 note ; protests, in the Dublin Council, against the assumption by Cromwell of the sovereignty, and withdraws from the government of Irish affairs, iv. 551, v. 98 ; his Republicanism and Milton's, iv. 606 ; not in Oliver's First Parliament, v. 5 ; retains his commission in the Army, v. 100 ; precautions taken against, by Cromwell, v. 107 ; in Cromwell's last days, v. 354, 359 ; member for Hindon in Richard's Parliament, v. 430, 431, 432, 439, 441, 445, 446 ; in the Restored Rump, v. 449, 454, and

its Council of State, v. 456, 465; Commander-in-Chief of the Army of the Restored Rump in Ireland, v. 471 ; in a Commission of seven appointed by the House for the government of the Army, v. 490, 529 ; on the Committee of Safety, v. 494, 495 ; in Irish business for the Rump, v. 496 ; Monk's letters to, v. 496 ; his summary of the various schemes of a new Republican Constitution, v. 480-1 ; in debates of Committee on the New Constitution, v. 505, 505 note, 506, 509, 510; Whitlocke, Vane, and, v. 510-2 ; impeached for high treason by the Officers in Ireland, v. 521, 521 note, 537 ; during Monk's Dictatorship, v. 544, 544 note, 561, 565 ; after the Restoration, vi. 23, 44, 49 ; in the Indemnity Bill (1660), vi. 54 ; one of the nineteen fugitives in the Bill of Attainder, vi. 115 ; further account of, vi. 115 note.

LUDLOW, Sir Henry, father of Edmund Ludlow, ii. 173.

LUKE, Sir Samuel, ii. 167 ; iii. 696 ; supposed original of Butler's "Sir Hudibras," v. 549 ; vi. 311 ; in the Restored Long Parliament, v. 549 ; in the Convention Parliament, vi. 23.

LUMLEY, Lord, i. 350.

LUNCARTY : see Loncardy, ii. 238.

LUNDIE, Laird of, fined by Cromwell's Ordinance in April 1654, iv. 561.

LUNSFORD, Colonel, in the Second "Bishops' War," ii. 141 ; appointed to the Governorship of the Tower of London by Charles I., ii. 330-1, 330 note, 332, 344, 346.

LUSHINGTON, Dr., chaplain to Bishop Corbet, i. 501-2.

LUTHER, Martin, i. 264.

LUTTERWORTH, in Leicestershire (Wycliffe's parish), i. 130, 160, 170; ii. 76.

LYCIDAS, Milton's, occasion of, i. 641-2, 647-55; 656-9, 662-3, 686-7; ii. 211 ; iii. 445.

LYDCOTT, Colonel Leonard, v. 535, 540.

LYFORD, William : account of, ii. 519.

LYON, John : see Kinghorn, Earl of.

LYSACKER, Henry Willemsen Rosenwing de, iv. 481-2.

LYSIMACHUS NICANOR : see Corbet, John.

M

MABBE, dramatist, i. 449.

MABBIT, John, Baptist preacher, iii. 148.

MABBOTT, Gilbert, Deputy-Clerk to the House of Commons, and licenser of pamphlets and newspapers, iii. 431-2, 432 note; iv. 87-8, 93-4, 154 ; v. 227 note.

MACDONALD, Alexander : see Collkittoch.

MACDONNELL, Randal : see Antrim, Earl of.

MACDOWELL of Garthland, iv. 561.

MACGREGOR, The Clan, iii. 354.

MACGUIRE, Lord, in the conspiracy for the Irish Rebellion, ii. 309, 310 ; execution of, iii. 185.

MACKENZIE, Sir George, vi. 320.

MACKENZIES of Seaforth, the, iii. 349.

MACKWORTH, Colonel Humphrey, in Oliver's Council, iv. 545; his death, v. 32 note ; and disinterment, vi. 227.

MACKWORTH, Thomas, v. 478.

MACLEAN of Duart, iii. 361.

MACLEANS, the, iii. 354.

MACLEOD of Assynt, iv. 184.

MACMAHON, Colonel Hugh, Irish conspirator, ii. 309, 310 ; execution of, iii. 185.

MACOCK, John, printer, vi. 167 note, 202, 325, 331.

MACPHERSONS, the, in the Episode of Montrose in Scotland, iii. 354.

MACVAIRD, Robert, Scottish divine, vi. 149-50.

"MADAGASCAR," a poem by Davenant (1648), vi. 274.

MADGE, Mr., of Christ Church, London, i. 407.

MAGDALEN COLLEGE, Cambridge, i. 114, 116, 121, 122, 171, 172, 221.

MAGDALEN HALL, Oxford, i. 24 note, 625.

MAINWARING, Dr. Roger, Chaplain to Charles I., i. 213-4, 215, 371-3 ;

appointed Bishop of St. David's, i. 674; in the Long Parliament, ii. 150, 151; 335.

MAIRE, John, Dutch engraver, iv. 165; v. 274-5.

MAITLAND, John: see *Lauderdale*, Earl of.

MAJOR-GENERALS, Cromwell's, v. 48-50, 51, 118-9.

MALATESTI, Antonio, Florentine poet, i. 773, 780-1, 781 note; dedicates a volume of Sonnets to Milton, i. 786, 786 note, 828; iii. 654.

MALEVRIER, Sir Richard, heads a Royalist rising, v. 34.

MALHERBE, i. 744.

"MALIGNANTS," ii. 346 and note; iii. 28-30, 38; v. 143-4.

MALIM, headmaster of St. Paul's School, i. 78.

MALLET, Michael, a member of the Rota Club, v. 485.

MALLET, Thomas, a Judge of the King's Bench, knighted in 1660, vi. 74.

MALLORY, Henry, in the "Sealed Knot" Conspiracy, v. 337.

MALPIGHI, i. 768.

MALYN, William, Cromwell's Private Secretary, v. 334, 350.

MAN, Isle of, property of the Earls of Derby, ii. 158.

MAN, Samuel, warden of the Stationers' Company, iii. 233 note, 271.

"MAN IN THE MOON," the, a Royalist journal in 1647, iv. 39.

MANCHESTER, Henry Montagu, 1st Earl of (grandson of Sir Edward Montagu), called also Viscount Mandeville and Lord Kimbolton: member of Charles I.'s Privy Council, i. 377-8, 383, 384; ii. 48, his son Walter, ii. 156; 155, 168, 278, 281, 336; a Peer in the Long Parliament, ii. 152, 429; his death in 1642, ii. 430.

MANCHESTER, Edward Montagu, 2nd Earl of (called also by his titles of Viscount Mandeville and Lord Kimbolton), in the First "Bishops' War," ii. 48; in the Petition of the Puritan Nobles to Charles I. for a Parliament in 1640, ii. 142, 143, 161; account of, in the Long Parliament (1640), ii. 155-6; 168; in English Church reform movement, ii. 201; a popular leader in the Lords and member of Charles I.'s Privy Council in 1640-1, ii. 279, 280; and Charles's *Coup d'Etat*, ii. 339-40; succeeds his father, the 1st Earl, in 1642, ii. 430, 431; appointed Lord-Lieutenant for Hunts, ii. 439; his regiment, ii. 444; his military chaplain, ii. 516; in the Westminster Assembly, ii. 523; Commission to, for Cambridge University in 1643, iii. 32, 33; at the Visitation of the University in 1644, iii. 92, 96; v. 73; in the "Committee of the Two Kingdoms," iii. 41; inactivity of the army under, iii. 85, 86; at Marston Moor, iii. 96-7; his relations with Cromwell after Marston Moor, iii. 166-8; impeachment of, by Cromwell in the House of Commons after the second Battle of Newbury, iii. 176-80, 388; retires from service in the Army, iii. 183; in the House of Lords, iii. 297 note; his brother, Sir Sidney Montagu, and his cousin, Colonel Edward Montagu, iii. 326; styled "the late General," iii. 333; parliamentary honours to, at the close of the Civil War, iii. 378, 380; in debates in the Lords, iii. 405, 406; Speaker of the Lords, iii. 551; absent from the House of Lords during the Presbyterian Riots in London, iii. 551, 552; reinstated, iii. 554, 555 note, 585, 692, 695; one of Cromwell's Lords, v. 323, 326; implicated in Sir George Booth's Royalist Insurrection, v. 473; is Speaker of the reassembled House of Lords in April 1660, v. 694, 696; at the Restoration of Charles II., vi. 11; in the Privy Council of the Restoration, vi. 18; in the Convention Parliament, vi. 21-2; in Church questions after the Restoration, vi. 61-2, 65; at the Trials of the Regicides, vi. 77, 78; in the Conference with Charles II. concerning the *Ecclesiastical Declaration*, vi. 99; in the King's Scottish Privy Council in London, vi.

131 ; at the Coronation of Charles II., vi. 151.

MANCINI, nephew of Mazarin, v. 340-1 ; in an embassy from Louis XIV., v. 392.

MANDEVILLE, Lord, in a deputation of the Commons to Charles II. at Breda, v. 700.

" MANE CITUS LECTUM FUGE " (Prolusion on Early Rising) : see *Milton*, Writings of.

MANLEY, of London, Esq., John, the Postage of Letters, inland and foreign, let out to, by Order of Council, iv. 564.

MANLEY, Sir Richard, ii. 161.

MANLEY, Colonel, Royalist conspirator, v. 338.

MANNERING, Thomas, Anabaptist of Norwich, i. 79.

MANNERING, Major, officer of London Trained Bands, ii. 446.

MANSELL, Dr. John, President of Queen's College, Cambridge, i. 115, 116 ; Vice-Chancellor of the University, i. 147.

" MAN'S MORTALITY," by R. O., iii. 678.

MANSO, the Marquis, of Naples, account of, i. 808-20 ; ii. 92, 92 note ; Milton's Latin poem to, ii. 94, iii. 453 ; Latin distich by, iii. 455, 650 ; mentioned in Milton's *Defensio Secunda*, iv. 637 ; deceased in 1647, iii. 651.

MANTON, Dr. Thomas, v. 12, 115 ; at the Second Installation of Cromwell, v. 149 ; in a Presbyterian deputation to Charles II. at the Hague, vi. 4 ; after the Restoration, vi. 62, 99 ; a leading Nonconformist, vi. 232 note, 417, 567.

MAPLETOFT, Robert, Master of Pembroke Hall, Cambridge, i. 122.

MAR, Earl of, ii. 15 ; joins the Covenant, ii. 55.

MARCHE, Jean de la, ii. 517.

MARDIKE, siege of, v. 311, 426-7.

MARENZO, Italian musical composer, ii. 79.

MARGETSON, James, Bishop of Dublin in 1661, vi. 128.

MARIA OF MODENA, Queen of James II., vi. 598-600, 665.

MARIA-THERESA, Spanish Infanta, and Queen of Louis XIV., v. 467, 503 ; vi. 568.

MARINI, Italian poet, i. 762, 763, 810-11.

MARISCHAL, William, 7th Earl, ii. 15 ; joins the Covenant, ii. 55 ; in First " Bishops' War," ii. 56, 60, 296 ; with Scottish Auxiliary Army in England, iii. 37, 358, 509 ; taken prisoner in 1651 and sent to England, iv. 296, 298 ; v. 94 ; excepted from Cromwell's Ordinance of Pardon and Grace, iv. 560.

MARKHAM, Gervase, dramatist, i. 449, 569.

MARKHAM, Colonel Henry, under Ludlow in Ireland, v. 471 ; with Fleetwood in London, v. 517, 519.

MARLBOROUGH, James Ley, 1st Earl of, in the Privy Council of James I. and Lord High Treasurer of England, account of, and of Milton's mention of him, iii. 57-9.

MARLBOROUGH, Henry Ley, 2nd Earl of, deceased in 1638, iii. 58, 59.

MARLBOROUGH, James Ley, 3rd Earl of, a general officer in the army of the King in 1643, iii. 59 ; killed in 1665, iii. 59 ; vi. 254.

MARMION, Shakerley, dramatist, i. 447-8, 569, 647 ; vi. 352.

MARRIETT, Thomas, member of the Rota Club, v. 485.

MARRIOTT, Richard, publisher, vi. 12, 339, 339 note, 400, 403-4.

MARSH, Dr., minister of St. Dunstan's-in-the-East, ii. 513 note.

MARSH, John, lawyer, iv. 364.

MARSHAL, a bricklayer at Hackney, of the sect called *Anti-Scripturists*, iii. 158.

MARSHALL, Ann, actress, vi. 349, 351-2, 354, 368, 607.

MARSHALL, Rebecca, sister of the preceding, actress, vi. 349, 351, 354, 356.

MARSHALL, Stephen, minister of Finchingfield in Essex, ii. 201 ; one of the authors of the *Smectymnuus* pamphlet, ii. 219, 225, 605 ; iii. 169 ; Parliamentarian chaplain, ii. 444 ; member of Westminster Assembly, ii. 519-20 ; iii. 8, 20, 22,

153, 160, 161, 169, 391 ; preaches Pym's funeral sermon in Westminster Abbey, iii. 41 ; with the King at Holmby House, iii. 510, 514; at the Presbyterian Rising in London in 1647, iii. 562; at the Isle of Wight during the negotiations for the Treaty of Newport, iii. 606; at the collapse of the Barebones Parliament, iv. 514; one of Cromwell's *Triers*, iv. 571 ; in Committee business of Cromwell's First Parliament, v. 12; his body dug up in Westminster Abbey in 1661, vi. 227.

MARSHALL, William, engraver, iii. 138 note, 312 note ; account of, and of his portrait of Milton in the First Edition of the Poems, with the story of Milton's Greek epigram affixed to the same, iii. 456-9 and note ; his engraved design for the *Eikon Basilike*, iv. 33, 37 ; Milton's punishment of him in the *Eikonoklastes*, iv. 135.

MARSIN, Count, at the Coronation of Charles II. in 1661, vi. 151.

MARSTON, John, dramatist, i. 327 note, 434, 445, 471, 595-6.

MARSTON MOOR, Battle of, iii. 96-8.

MARTEN, Sir Henry, Dean of the Court of Arches, father of Henry Marten, ii. 166.

MARTEN, Henry (Regicide), member for County Berks in the Long Parliament, ii. 166, 174 ; iii. 388, 402-3, 408, 410, 565, 566, 598 ; at the Treaty of Newport, iii. 613 ; with Cromwell in the North, iii. 623-4 ; in the King's Trial, iii. 699, 705, 707, 712 note ; signs the death-warrant of Charles I., iii. 720, 720 note ; vi. 28 ; at the abolition by the Commons of House of Peers, iv. 5 ; in the First and Second Councils of State of the Commonwealth, iv. 12, 13, 79, 87, 89, 120, 223, 225, 230 ; his witty parable of Moses in the Bulrushes, iv. 40 ; opposes the Act of May 10, 1650, against Moral Offences, iv. 180 and note ; not re-appointed to the Third Council of State in 1651, iv. 273, 308, 310 ; in Fourth Council of State, iv. 354 ; in Parliament measures, iv. 370,

394, 403 ; at the Dissolution of the Rump, iv. 407, 412 ; in the Barebones Parliament, iv. 512 ; *not* mentioned in Milton's *Defensio Secunda*, iv. 606 ; *not* in Oliver's First Parliament, v. 5 ; implicated in Republican plottings, v. 33 ; in the Restored Rump, v. 447, 454, 465, 480 ; v. 519 ; his witty description of Monk, v. 530, 537 ; in the Restored Long Parliament, v. 544, 545, 552 ; at the Quest of the Regicides, vi. 43, 49 ; 54 ; his Trial, vi. 80-1, 93 ; in the Bill of Attainder, vi. 115 ; vi. 136 ; death of, vi. 98 note.

MARTIN, Anthony, Irish Bishop, i. 420.

MARTIN, Christopher, in the Restored Rump, v. 454, 544 note.

MARTIN, Dr. Edward, President of Queen's College, Cambridge, ejected in 1645, iii. 93, 95 note.

MARTIN, Francis, in Essex's Army, ii. 444.

MARTIN, Henry, shipmaster, v. 372.

MARTIN, John, publisher, vi. 203, 339, 403, 404, 514, 646-7, 648, 730.

" MARTIN MARPRELATE TRACTS," a series of Brownist Tracts in 1589, ii. 538.

MARTIN, Rev. William, a Puritan lecturer, suspended by Laud, i. 402.

MARTINI, Martin, Jesuit missionary to China, v. 269 and note.

MARVELL, minister of Hull, father of Andrew Marvell : story of his death, iv. 623.

MARVELL, Andrew, the Poet, i. 649 ; Milton and, iv. 476-80, 616-9, 620-1, 622-5 ; among Men of Letters under the Protectorate, v. 75, 77, 85 ; Milton and, v. 230 ; Assistant Secretary with Milton in the Council of State, v. 374-6, 399-402 ; member for Hull in Richard's Parliament, v. 430 ; still with Milton in the Latin Secretaryship to Richard's Council, v. 570, 603-4, 624-5 and note ; his satirical verses on the Restoration of Charles II., v. 16-7 ; in the Convention Parliament, vi. 23 ; his exertions for the escape of

Milton, vi. 185-6, 189, 195; in continued friendship with Milton, vi. 200, 453-4, 699; accompanies the Earl of Carlisle in a mission to Russia, vi. 252, 482; account of his literary work until the Restoration, vi. 312; from 1668-74, vi. 617; his paper war with Samuel Parker, and his *Rehearsal Transprosed*, vi. 699-708; encomium on Milton by, vi. 714-7.

MARVIN, John, sea captain, v. 589.

MARY, Princess, eldest daughter of Charles I., and mother of William III.: her birth in 1631, i. 247, 648; affianced to Prince William of Orange in 1641, ii. 350, 353; the Duke of Northumberland in charge of, iii. 375; with her husband at the Hague in 1648, iii. 595; a widow, with her son, Prince William, at the Hague in 1660, vi. 6-7; in the Court of Charles II. at London, vi. 71; and the younger Henry Jermyn, vi. 72; and the Duke of York's marriage, vi. 107; her death by smallpox in Dec. 1660, vi. 118.

MARY II., Queen of England, daughter of the Duke of York and his wife Ann Hyde, vi. 272, 605; her marriage to William, Prince of Orange, vi. 729.

MARYLAND, Colony of, in North America, in 1634, v. 102.

MASANIELLO, the Neapolitan, i. 816.

MASHAM, Sir William, member for the County of Essex in the Long Parliament, ii. 173; v. 307; lay member of Westminster Assembly, ii. 524; in the Councils of State of the Commonwealth, iv. 12, 13, 14, 79, 82, 83, 147, 223, 224, 225, 226, 227, 230, 231, 273, 313, 315, 321, 354, 355, 370, 448, 449, 450, 485; in Oliver's First Parliament, v. 307.

MASHAMS of Essex, the, distant kindred of the Protector, v. 307.

MASON, Mr., secretary to the 1st Duke of Buckingham, i. 158.

MASON, C., author of College verses on Edward King's death, i. 651.

MASON, Colonel, in the question of the kingship for Cromwell, v. 132.

MASON, Francis, author of one of the *Oxford Tracts*, ii. 368-9.

MASON, R., author of verses on Edward King's death, i. 651.

MASQUE, the: popularity of this form of dramatic literature in the reigns of Elizabeth and James I., i. 578-80; the Great, of the Inns of Court, in 1633-4, i. 580-7. For further accounts of: see *Carew*, Thomas; *Jonson*, Ben.

MASSACHUSETTS BAY, Settlement of, ii. 165, 549; v. 101.

MASSEY, Colonel (afterwards Major-General), Edward, ii. 444, 462-3; in the Civil War, iii. 337-8, 379; M.P. for Wooton Bassett in 1645, iii. 401; in the quarrel between the Parliament and the Army, iii. 532; among the eleven Presbyterian Leaders denounced by the Army, iii. 548-9; and the Presbyterian tumults in London, iii. 552, 562; in Holland, iii. 554; shut out of the Commons at "Pride's Purge," iii. 696; in Charles II.'s Scottish army, iv. 283-4, 292, 293, 294; taken prisoner at the Battle of Worcester, iv. 294; his trial and escape to France, iv. 297; in the projected Royalist Insurrection of 1659, v. 473, 474, 478; in the Convention Parliament, vi. 23; knighted in 1660, vi. 74.

MASSEY, Captain Hugh, brother of General Massey, iv. 304.

MASSINGER, Philip, dramatist, i. 433, 445, 451, 569; iii. 449; vi. 352-3, 358.

MASSON, Captain, at Speymouth, iv. 491, 492.

MATHER, Cotton, son of Dr. Increase Mather, ii. 557.

MATHER, Dr. Increase, son of Richard Mather, ii. 557; a Nonconformist, vi. 232 note.

MATHER, Richard, New England minister, ii. 557; iii. 114.

MATTHEW, reputed to be one of the King's executioners, vi. 27.

MATTHEWS, Jokay, neighbour of Milton in Aldersgate Street, ii. 207, 358.

MATTHEWS, Sir Toby, son of a former Archbishop of York, i. 685.

L

MATTHIAS, Emperor of Germany, deceased in 1619, i. 61.

MAUCHLINE, Lord, son of the Earl of Loudoun, iv. 560.

MAULE, Henry, son of the Earl of Panmure, iv. 561.

MAULEVERER, Sir Thomas (Regicide), signs the death-warrant of Charles I., iii. 720, vi. 28; deceased in 1660, vi. 54.

MAURICE, Prince (brother of Prince Rupert), in the Civil War, ii. 467; iii. 332, 335, 345, 375; at the surrender of Oxford, iii. 472; in engagements with Blake, iv. 217-8.

MAWE, Dr. Leonard, Bishop of Bath and Wells, i. 115, 117, 119, 157, 252 note, 388.

MAXWELL, Usher of the Lords in the Long Parliament, ii. 178.

MAXWELL, Mrs. Ann, authoress, vi. 516.

MAXWELL, David, printer, vi. 167 note.

MAXWELL, Lieutenant Giles, ii. 313.

MAXWELL, John, Bishop of Ross and Scottish Privy Councillor in 1633, i. 697, 700, 706, 707, 717, 721; ii. 7, 40, 42; his trial by Scottish Parliament, ii. 301, 304; anti-Presbyterian pamphlet by, iii. 184; a "Delinquent," iii. 421.

MAXWELL, Robert, in the Irish Episcopate in 1660, vi. 127-8.

MAY, Baptist, vi. 271.

MAY, Dr., a physician, ii. 44.

MAY, Sir Humphrey, i. 381.

MAY, Sir Thomas, father of the dramatist, i. 447.

MAY, Thomas, historian, poet, and dramatist, i. 447, 511, 532, 569, 646, 647; his account of Strafford's Trial, ii. 179, 180, 190; iii. 335, 446; order of Council in Nov. 1650 for his ·interment in Westminster Abbey, iv. 230; disinterred, vi. 227.

MAYERNE, Sir Theodore, Physician to James I., i. 101.

MAYNARD, Lord, Parliamentarian Peer, i. 119; ii. 431; iii. 692; v. 50, 695; in debates of the Lords on the Indemnity Bill, vi. 45.

MAYNARD, Sir John, Sergeant at Law: in Long Parliament, ii. 173, 321;

lay member of Westminster Assembly, ii. 524; and the Self-denying Ordinance, iii. 180; among the eleven Presbyterian Leaders denounced by the Army, iii. 548-9; his impeachment, iii. 554; in Lilburne's Trial, iv. 508; in Cony's lawsuit, v. 35-6; an "engager" in Davenant's Italian Opera in 1656, v. 81; in Cromwell's Second Parliament, v. 107, 110, 329; in Council of State, (Feb. 1659-60), v. 544; in the Convention Parliament, vi. 24, 30, 111.

MAYNARD, Rev. John, member of Westminster Assembly in 1643, in succession to Henry Nye, ii. 520.

MAYNARD, Robert, gentleman of Middlesex, ii. 133.

MAYNARD, Thomas, English Consul in Portugal, v. 289.

MAYNE, Coluberry: see Bulstrode.

MAYNE, Jasper, chaplain to Earl of Devonshire, v. 76, 81; vi. 294-5.

MAYNE, Simon, of Dinton, father of Coluberry Mayne, i. 558.

MAYNE, Simon (Regicide), ii. 402; signs the death-warrant of Charles I., iii. 720, vi. 28; in Cromwell's Second Parliament, v. 110, 329; in the Restored Rump, v. 454; after the Restoration, vi. 43; in the Indemnity Bill, vi. 49, 54; his trial, vi. 80, 93; his death, vi. 98 note; in the Bill of Attainder, vi. 115.

MAYOR, Dorothy, daughter of Richard Mayor, married to Richard Cromwell, v. 305.

MAYOR, Richard, of Hursley, Hants: in the Long Parliament, v. 305; in the Barebones Parliament, iv. 506, 512; in Cromwell's Councils of State, iv. 525, 545, 545 note; v. 32, 305; not in the Council of the Second Protectorate, v. 308; supports Richard's Government, v. 417.

MAZARIN, Louis XIV.'s Minister of State, iii. 375, 415, 491, 503, 591, 595, 715; iv. 30, 163, 164, 381-2, 555, 556, 638-9; v. 37, 42, 43-4, 46, 61, 140, 189, 191, 244, 251, 272, 310, 315, 340, 390-1, 392-5, 416, 426, 428, 460, 463, 467, 468, 502-4, 556, 570, 576, 702; vi. 119.

MEADE, Joseph, Fellow and Tutor of Christ's College, Cambridge, i. 123-8, 146 note, 150-5, 158, 167, 180-4, 186-7, 191-2, 206, 215 note, 220-1, 224-5, 231-3, 237-8, 243, 250, 267; his *Apocalyptic Commentaries*, i. 519; ii. 401 note; reputed a Millenary, iii. 153; in correspondence with Hartlib, iii. 216 note ; his death, ii. 76, 78.

MEADE, Richard, fellow-student of Milton at Cambridge, i. 171.

MEADE (Mead), Robert, master of Stationers' Company, iii. 273, 291.

MEADOWS, Mr. Philip, in the Councils of Cromwell, first as Milton's Assistant, then as Latin Secretary in Ordinary, iv. 524-5, 546, 575, 576, 577, 578, 579; v. 178, 256; sent to Portugal as special Agent of the Council, v. 256, 271, 273, 274, 294-5, 296, 625 note; in Denmark and Sweden as Envoy to the Scandinavian Powers, v. 294-5, 296, 312, 314, 342, 370-1, 386, 395, 571; supports Richard's Government, v. 419; recommissioned as Envoy-in-Ordinary to the Kings of Denmark and Sweden by the Restored Rump, v. 467, 595-6; returns to London, v. 501-2; after the Restoration, as " Sir Philip Meadows," vi. 200.

" MEANS TO REMOVE HIRELINGS " : see *Milton*, Writings of.

MEARNE, warden of the Stationers' Company, vi. 710.

MEDBOURNE, actor, vi. 350.

MEDICI, Cosimo de, i. 764.

MEDICI, Mary de, i. 744, 748.

MEDINA CELI, Anthony John Lewis de la Cerda, Duke of (Governor of Andalusia), Letter of State to, iv. 235.

MEDINA, John, his " Sculptures " for *Paradise Lost*, vi. 785.

MEI, Marie, wife of Carolo Diodati, i. 99.

MELANCHTHON, Philip, the Reformer, i. 264.

MELDRUM, John, Parliamentarian officer, ii. 445.

MELDRUM, Robert, admitted to the Westminster Assembly, and Confidential Agent of the Scots in London, iii. 17.

MELDRUM of Tullibody, in Cromwell's Ordinance of Pardon and Grace, iv. 561.

MELLO, Don Francisco de, Portuguese Ambassador in London, v. 312.

MELTON (or Milton), John, quartermaster in the London Trained Bands, ii. 483-4.

MELVILLE, George, 4th Lord, and 1st Earl of Melville: in the Scottish Parliament of 1661, vi. 145.

MELVILLE, Andrew, Presbyterian divine, i. 69, 264.

MÉNAGE, French Savant, v. 285.

MENNES, Sir John, a Royalist sea-captain, and one of the authors of verses in *Wit and Drollery*, v. 261, 262 note.

MEN OF LETTERS : of the Protectorate, v. 75-86; of the Restoration, vi. 273-321 : see *Literature*.

MENSTRIE, Baron : see *Stirling*, Earl of.

MENTEITH, Earl of, iii. 351.

MENZIES of Pitfoddels, ii. 56; Montrose's standard-bearer, iv. 184.

MENZIES, John, Scottish divine, v. 90, 346 note.

MENZIESES, the, in the episode of Montrose in Scotland, iii. 354.

MERCER of Aldie : fined by Cromwell, iv. 561.

MERCERS' COMPANY of London, appointed Trustees of St. Paul's School, i. 75.

MERCHANT-TAILORS' COMPANY, the School of the, founded in London in 1561, i. 73; iv. 38.

MERCIER (French tutor to the Prince of Wales and the Duke of York in Paris), "Memories of Charles I., etc.," by, iv. 155 note.

MERCIER, Anne : see *Salmasius*, Madame.

" MERCURIUS AULICUS," official Royalist newspaper at Oxford, iii. 546; iv. 38; vi. 325.

" MERCURIUS BRITANNICUS," Needham's newspaper in 1643, iv. 38.

" MERCURIUS ELENCTICUS," anti-Cromwellian newspaper in 1650, iv. 154-5, 155 note. ;

" MERCURIUS POLITICUS," Needham's newspaper, iv. 226-7 ; Milton's con-

nexion with, iv. 325-35, 432-4, 434, 452, 462-3 ; v. 19-20, 52, 65, 92, 670-1 and note, 672 ; vi. 165, 200-2, 452.

" MERCURIUS PRAGMATICUS," Needham's newspaper, iv. 37-9, 89, 93, 93 note ; vi. 452.

" MERCURIUS PUBLICUS," London newspaper in 1660, vi. 167 note, 202, 324, 325, 425.

" MERCURIUS VERIDICUS," London newspaper in 1660, stopped by order of the Commons, vi. 167 note.

MERES, Francis, his " Witts' Commonwealth," iii. 447.

" MERLINUS ANGLICUS," a series of prophetic Almanacks, by Lilly, the Astrologer, v. 21.

MERMAID TAVERN : see Taverns.

MERMILLIOD, Genevese pastor, v. 208

MERRICK, Sir John, Parliamentarian officer, ii. 443, 444.

MERRICK (Mericke), Sir William, Doctor of Laws, vi. 450.

MERRYMAN, Captain, in charge of the King at the Isle of Wight, iii. 626, 627.

MERTON COLLEGE, Oxford, i. 535.

MESTREZAT, French Protestant minister at Charenton in 1657, v. 368.

METCALFE, Robert, of St. John's College, Cambridge, Regius Professor of Hebrew, i. 119, 121, 267.

" METROPOLITAN NUNCIO," Commonwealth newspaper, iv. 39.

MEW, William, B.D., of Eastingdon, Gloucestershire, member of Westminster Assembly, ii. 520.

MEWER (Muir), Robert, Parliamentarian officer, ii. 446.

MICHAEL, King of Poland, vi. 725.

MICHAEL ROMANOFF, Emperor of Russia, v. 292.

MICKLETHWAITE, Paul, Fellow of Sidney Sussex, Cambridge, i. 121.

MICKLETHWAIT, Thomas, Rector of Cherry Burton, Yorkshire, member of Westminster Assembly, ii. 520.

MICO, Samuel, English merchant and shipowner, in 1655, v. 244.

" MICROCOSMOGRAPHY," ii. 513 note : see Earle, Bishop.

MIDDLEBURG, in Holland, Brownists in, ii. 539.

MIDDLESEX, Earl of, Parliamentarian

Peer in 1642, ii. 430 ; death of, in 1645, ii. 430 ; iii. 377.

MIDDLESEX, Earl of (son of the preceding) : among the " Champion Peers " in 1646, iii. 377 ; in the House of Lords, iii. 406 ; impeached and committed by the Commons, iii. 554 ; one of the Commissioners of the Lords at the Treaty of Newport, iii. 605 ; in the House of Lords, iii. 692 ; in a deputation of the House of Lords, in May 1660, to Charles II. at Breda, v. 700.

MIDDLETON, Lieutenant-General John : account of his early career to the year 1650, iv. 205-6 ; his part in Charles II.'s adventure of " The Start," iv. 207, 208 ; excommunicated by the Kirk, iv. 213 ; Master of Horse of Charles II.'s Scottish army, iv. 283, 293 ; taken prisoner at the Battle of Worcester, iv. 294 ; in Royalist insurrection in Scotland, iv. 509, 552, 560 ; made an Earl by Charles II., vi. 131 ; member of Charles II.'s Scottish Privy Council, vi. 131, 138, 142 note ; High-Commissioner for the King in the Scottish Parliament of 1661, vi. 131, 138 ; Lauderdale and, in the Privy Council, vi. 138-40 ; in the Scottish Parliament of 1661, vi. 142-9.

MIDDLETON, the Earl of, a subscriber to the fourth edition of Paradise Lost, vi. 785.

MIDDLETON, Mrs., in the Court of Charles II., vi. 355, 461.

MIDDLETON, Thomas, dramatist, i. 432, 444 ; iii. 449 ; in 1660-1, vi. 353.

MIDDLETON, Sir Thomas, M.P. for Denbighshire in the Long Parliament : in military service on the Welsh border, and exempted from the Self-Denying Ordinance, iii. 334 note, 379 ; heads a Royalist rising in Shropshire and Flintshire in 1659, v. 472, 475, 477 ; a member of the Commons' House in the Convention Parliament, vi. 23.

MILAN : the Milanese Territory (Spanish Province) in 1638, i. 745.

MILDMAY, Anthony, Parliamentarian officer, ii. 445.

MILDMAY, Sir Henry, Regicide, member for Malden in the Long Parliament, ii. 173 ; iii. 404 ; captain of a troop of horse in the Parliamentarian army, ii. 445 ; in the removal of the King to Hurst Castle, iii. 629 ; at the King's Trial, iii. 699 ; in the First Council of State of the Commonwealth, iv. 12, 14, 15, 79, 82, 83, 87, 145, 150; in the Second Council, iv. 223, 224, 225, 226, 227 ; in the Third Council, iv. 273, 308, 313, 314, 321 ; in the Fifth Council, iv. 355, 449; in the Restored Rump, v. 454, 455, 490, 666; after the Restoration, vi. 36, 37 ; in the Indemnity Bill, vi. 55 ; his sentence, vi. 224, 228.

MILES, Priscilla, an anti-Scripturist, iii. 158.

MILITIA, proposal of a Bill for the assumption by Parliament of power of the, ii. 318, 328 ; the, of the City of London, ii. 345 ; the *Militia Ordinance*, ii. 421, 440 ; proposed surrender by Charles I. of the, iii. 492, 497, 498, 501, 502, 577 ; Cromwell claims the control of the, v. 11 ; Republican re-officering of the, by the Restored Rump, v. 471 ; reorganisation of the, by the Council of General Monk, v. 555; surrendered back to the Crown, vi. 223.

MILLENARIANS or Chiliasts, sect of, i. 126 ; iii. 152-3; the Fifth Monarchy Men, v. 16-7 and note.

MILLENARY PETITION, of the English Puritan Clergy to James I. in 1603, i. 344.

MILLER, warden of Stationers' Company, iii. 335.

MILLER, John, of Litton, Middlesex, ii. 209.

MILLINGTON, auctioneer in Little Britain, vi. 650-1.

MILLINGTON, Gilbert (Regicide), member for Nottingham in the Long Parliament, iii. 385 ; signs the death-warrant of Charles I., iii. 720 ; vi. 28 ; through the Commonwealth, iv. 390, 438; in the Restored Rump, v. 454 ; in the Restored Long Parliament, v. 545; after the Restoration, vi. 44 ; in the Indem-

nity Bill, vi. 49, 54 ; Trial of, vi. 80, 93 ; death of, vi. 98 note ; in the Bill of Attainder, vi. 115.

MILLIS, a baker, v. 19.

MILTON, origin and distribution of the name, i. 7-8, 10-3 ; the Miltons of Oxfordshire, i. 22 and note.

MILTON, Agnes, great-grandmother of the poet, i. 14, 15 ; ii. 492.

MILTON, Alice, relative of the poet's grandfather, i. 14, 16.

MILTON, Anne, sister of the poet, i. 39 ; married first to Edward Phillips, i. 103-5, 561-2, 564 ; ii. 98-9 ; and afterwards to Thomas Agar, i. 637-8 ; iii. 483, 667 and note ; iv. 105 ; her death, vi. 771.

MILTON, Anne, daughter of the poet, iii. 483-4, 632 ; iv. 105 ; v. 226 ; vi. 447-9, 451, 649-50, 735-44, 750.

MILTON, Catherine, daughter of Christopher Milton, ii. 489 ; vi. 763.

MILTON, Christopher, brother of the poet, i. 40 ; at St. Paul's School, i. 98, 103, 160 ; at Christ's College, Cambridge, i. 243, 327 ; admitted of the Inner Temple, i. 562, 564, 631 ; marries Thomasine Webber, and lives at Horton, i. 735 ; his children, i. 735 note ; ii. 72 ; at Reading, ii. 488-90 ; iii. 485-6 ; his Composition Suit, iii. 632-3 and note, 674 note ; and the Powell family, vi. 449 ; his visit to Bunhill, vi. 727-8 ; and Milton's nuncupative will, vi. 735-40, 742-3 ; subsequent fortunes of, vi. 761-3 ; his family, vi. 761-3.

MILTON (Mitton), Colonel : iii. 334 note, 379.

MILTON, Deborah, youngest daughter of the poet, and wife of Abraham Clarke, i. 6 note, 309 note ; iv. 439 ; v. 226; iv. 447-9, 451, 649-50 ; her account of her father, vi. 681 ; in her father's will, vi. 735-40 ; her marriage, vi. 741-3 ; subsequent fortunes of, vi. 750-4 and note.

MILTON, Elizabeth, sister of the poet's grandfather, i. 15.

MILTON, Elizabeth, of Windsor, i. 23 note.

MILTON, Elizabeth, third wife of the poet : see *Minshull*.

MILTON, Gryffyth, of Chipping Norton,
Oxfordshire, i. 13.

MILTON, Henry, of Stanton St. Johns,
great - grandfather of the poet, i.
14-6 ; ii. 492.

MILTON, Isabell, sister of the poet's
grandfather, i. 14, 15.

MILTON, James, student at Oxford in
1591-2, i. 23 note.

MILTON, James, scrivener, i. 338 note.

MILTON, John (father of the poet), i.
3-5, 5-7, 8, 10, 23-30, 37-40 ; his
home and business in Bread Street,
i. 41-3, 50, 338-9 note ; musical
compositions of, i. 50-2 ; elected
Assistant of the Scriveners' Company, i. 62 ; his sonnet addressed to
the versifier, John Lane, i. 57 ; his
son-in-law, Edward Phillips, i. 104 ;
sends his eldest son (the poet) to
Cambridge University, i. 112, 113 ;
his intentions for his son's career
frustrated, and Milton's Latin poem
to him on the subject, i. 333-7 ; retires from business, quits London, and goes to live at Horton, i.
337-9, 561, 561 note ; his partner in
the business, Thomas Bower, i. 338-
9 note ; his connexions with the Scriveners' Company, i. 338-9 note ; story
of the lawsuit of Cotton v. Milton
and Bower, i. 627-38, 659-61 ; living
at Horton during Milton's contin-
ental journey, i. 735-6 ; ii. 72, 130 ;
leaves Horton to reside at Reading
in 1640 or 1641, ii. 489-90 ; goes
to live with his son in Aldersgate
Street in 1643, ii. 490-1, 508 ; his
connexions with Oxfordshire and the
Powells of Forest Hill, ii. 492 ;
dealings with the Powells on behalf
of his son, ii. 495-6 ; leaves Aldersgate Street and accompanies his son
to the new house in Barbican in
1645, iii. 443 ; death of, in March
1646-7, iii. 641-3.

MILTON, John :
*In his Father's house, Bread Street,
Cheapside* (1608-25) :—Ancestry and
kindred of, i. 1-40 ; birth, i. 3, 3
note ; seal and armorial bearings, i.
5-7, 9 ; the paternal pedigree, i. 8-
30 ; the maternal pedigree, i. 30-9 ;
baptismal entries of, and of his

brothers and sisters, i. 39 - 40 ;
at Spread Eagle in Bread Street,
London, i. 41-72 ; essentially a
Londoner, i. 43 ; Bread Street described, i. 44 ; rambles of the boy
near his home, i. 44-9 ; the home
life of, i. 50-8 ; public events during
the childhood of, i. 58-61 ; Early
Education Period, from 1618 to 1625,
i. 65-108 ; a writer of verses in his
childhood, i. 65 ; portrait of, *ætat.*
10, by Jansen, i. 65-7, 67 note ; his
first tutor, Mr. Thomas Young, i.
68, 72, 83 ; at St. Paul's School, i.
72-4, 78, 103 note ; his school-
masters, i. 78-83 ; juvenile studies
and readings, i. 84-94 ; the earliest
extant verses of, i. 94-8 ; Robert
Pory, and other school-fellows of, at
St. Paul's School, i. 98-103 ; his
school friend in chief, Charles
Diodati, i. 98-103 and notes ; marriage of his sister Anne in 1624, i.
103-5 ; public events during the
school-days of, i. 105-8.

At Cambridge (1625-32) :—i. 108 ;
is admitted a Lesser Pensioner of
Christ's College, Cambridge, i. 111,
218 note ; his fellow-students, i.
111-2 ; the Colleges of Cambridge
in 1625, 113-5 ; the town of Cambridge, i. 115 ; the office-bearers of
University, i. 115-8 ; other notabilities of Cambridge, i. 118-22 ; particular account of Christ's College,
i. 122-31 ; Meade, Chappell, and
Tovey, Fellows of Christ's College, i.
124-31 ; Milton's tutors, i. 131, 160 ;
his fellow-undergraduates, i. 131-2 ;
his rooms in College, and " chamber
fellows," i. 132-3 ; his College terms
and vacations, i. 133-4 ; his fancy to
Hobson, the Cambridge carrier, i.
135 ; daily life and discipline of the
University, i. 136-40 ; the order of
the curriculum of study, i. 140-5.—In
his First Academic Year (1624-5), i.
147-53 ;—Goes to London in March,
1625, i. 147 ; letter to Thomas
Young, i. 147-8 ; returns to Cambridge on 9th April 1625, i. 149 ;
matriculation of, and of his College
fellows, i. 149, 151, 218 note.—In
his Second Academic Year (1625-6),

i. 154-70 ;—Tradition of the quarrel of, with the authorities of his College, i. 159-61; Diodati's Geeek letters to him, and his reply to Diodati, with reference to his quarrel with the College authorities, i. 161-7 ; transference of, from Chappell's tutorship to that of Tovey, i. 167, 170.—In his Third Academic Year (1626-7), i. 171-86;—Edward King entered at Christ's College, i. 171 ; writes Latin Elegies on the deaths of Bishops Andrewes of Winchester and Felton of Ely, i. 168-9, 328 ; death of his infant niece, and his English poem on the occasion, i. 169-70, 170 note; Latin verses of, *On the Death of the Vice-Chancellor* (Dr. Gostlin), and *On the Death of the Cambridge University-Bedel* (Richard Ridding), i. 172-3, 173 notes, 329 ; his Latin Epigrams on successive anniversaries of the Gunpowder Plot, i. 173-4 ; his Poem *In Quintum Novembris*, i. 173-80 ; his Metrical Epistle to Thomas Young at Hamburg, i. 184-5.—In his Fourth Academic Year (1627-8), i. 186-213 ;— John Cleveland, a college-fellow of, i. 186 ; much in London during this year, i. 188; his Seventh Latin Elegy and a Latin Prose Epistle from London to the younger Gill, i. 188 ; the alleged incident of his first love at Cambridge, i. 188-90; possible meeting between, and Meade in London during the summer of this year, i. 191 ; Latin Letter to Alexander Gill from Cambridge, i. 193-4, 203 ; Latin Hexameters, *Naturam non pati Senium*, written by, for the Philosophical Act in the "Commencement" at Cambridge in July 1628, i. 200-3 ; spends the Long Vacation of this year at Cambridge, i. 203-4, 213 ; Letter to Thomas Young, dated Cambridge, July 21, 1628, i. 203-4, 204 note ; his friend Alexander Gill in trouble, i. 210, 212-3.—In his Fifth Academic Year (1628-9), i. 213-26;—Has news of Gill's sentence in Star-Chamber, i. 214-5 ; takes the degree of B.A., and subscribes to the Articles of

Religion, i. 216-8, 218 notes ; his Latin Poem (translated) *In Adventum Veris* (the fifth of his Elegies), i. 218-9 ; present at the "Commencement" in 1629, i. 219 ; his friend Diodati incorporated at Cambridge in July 1629, i. 219 ; opinion of, on University plays and theatricals, i. 224-5.—In his Sixth Academic Year (1629-30), i. 226-36 ; — Spends the Christmas vacation of 1629-39 in London, i. 226 ; addresses a Latin Elegy to his friend Diodati, i. 226-8 ; his English *Ode on the Morning of Christ's Nativity*, i. 228-30, 604 note ; his Fragment entitled *The Passion*, i. 230-1, 604 note ; absent from the University during the Plague, 235-6 ; his Lines *On Shakespeare*, i. 236.—In his Seventh Academic Year (1630-1), i. 237-46;—Returns to Cambridge, i. 238; his friend and junior Edward King promoted to the vacant fellowship, and his own probable disappointment, i. 238-9; his two epitaphs on Thomas Hobson, the Cambridge carrier, i. 239-43 ; his brother Christopher admitted a lesser pensioner at Christ's College, i. 243 ; his epitaph on the Marchioness of Winchester, i. 244-6, 246 note.—In his last year at Cambridge, 1631-2, i. 247-58;— His Sonnet *On his having arrived at the age of twenty-three*, i. 247, 325, 329; does not contribute to a volume of complimentary verses to the Queen, issued in 1631, i. 247-8 ; graduates as Master of Arts in July 1632, and again subscribes to the Articles, i. 257-8, 510; his fellow-graduates, i. 258.—Review of the Academic Studies of, and of their results, i. 259-72;—System of Cambridge in time of, compared with the present, i. 259-61 ; the studies of Sir Simonds D'Ewes of St. John's, taken as the standard of studies in other Colleges, i. 261-6; the course of Milton's studies compared with that of D'Ewes, i. 266-8 ; his learning in the departments of Classics, Logic, and Philosophy, and written testimonies to the same, i.

268-70; Dr. Johnson's statement concerning his unpopularity discussed, i. 270-1, 277, 307; his own estimate of the system and methods of the University, i. 271-2; place of, while at Cambridge, among the younger spirits there, and his relations to his Alma Mater and the intellectual tendencies of the time, i. 272.—The *Prolusiones Oratoriæ*, or Rhetorical Essays of, i. 272-307;—Account of the *Prolusiones* in their order, i. 274-307, 299 note; nicknamed "the Lady of Christ's College," i. 291, 307, 308, 311, 320; his Common-Place Book, i. 303, also vi. 790 note.—Sketch of the character of, in his twenty-fourth year, i. 307-20, 308-10 note; account of the portraits of, before 1640, i. 308-10 note.— Hesitations about a Profession (1692), i. 323-39 :—"Letter to a Friend," accompanying his Sonnet on his 23rd birthday, i. 323-7 and note, 599 note, 604 note, ii. 103, 103-4 note; "Church-outed by the Prelates," i. 326-7, 413, 419; thinks of the Law as a career, i. 327, 327 note; determines in favour of a literary life, i. 327-39; writings of, before 1632 summed up, i. 328-32; his Latin poem, *Ad Patrem*, addressed to his father, i. 334-7.

At Horton, Buckinghamshire (1632-8) :—Removes thither with his family from London, i. 338-9, 339 note; at Horton, i. 552-663; the neighbourhood of Horton, i. 552-61; the Horton household, i. 561, 561-2 and note; amid Horton scenery and society, i. 562-4; journeys of, to London from Horton, i. 552, 564-5, 566; acquaintance with the Gills, i. 565-6, and with Henry Lawes, i. 567, and possibly with the Egerton family, i. 598 note; collects books, i. 566; literary and musical society at Horton, i. 566-7; studies in mathematics and music, i. 566-7; readings in the classics and in Italian writers, i. 567-8, 568 note, and in English literature, i. 568-9;—English poems of, written at Horton, i. 569; *L'Allegro*, and *Il*

Pen.:roso, i. 569-77; *May Morning*, and *To the Nightingale*, i. 577-8; *Arcades*, i. 578, 597-602, 599 note, 603 note, 604 note; *At a Solemn Music*, i. 603, 604 note; *On Time*, i. 603, 604 note; *Upon the Circumcision*, i. 603-4, 604 note; handwriting of, on a preserved draft of the poem *On Time*, i. 603-4; habits of fastidiousness in altering, correcting, and enlarging his manuscripts, i. 604; account of, and references to, the Milton MSS. in Trinity College, Cambridge, i. 569-70 note, 578 note, 599 note, 604 note.— *Comus*, i. 604-23;—the occasion of, i. 604-10; performance of, at Ludlow Castle, Sept. 1634, i. 610; argument of, i. 611-21; three extant versions of, i. 611 note; account of, i. 621-3; coincidences between it and other masques, i. 622; songs of, set to music by Henry Lawes, i. 610; publication by the printer Humphrey Robinson, in 1637, of Lawes's manuscript of the Masque, with motto added by Milton, i. 640-1, 737, 738, 738, note, 739 note; iii. 445; acted in 1750 for the benefit of Milton's grand-daughter, vi. 760. — Letter to Alexander Gill, dated Dec. 4, 1634, i. 623-4; translation of 114th Psalm into Greek hexameters, i. 624, 624 note; incorporated in the degree of Master of Arts at Oxford, i. 624-6; acquaintances at Oxford, i. 625-6; his father's lawsuit, i. 627-31, 632-8, 659-61; death of his mother in April 1637, i. 16-32, 638, 646, 661; visits to London from Horton, and first projects of settling in London and of a foreign tour, i. 640, 646.—Receives news of the death of Edward King, i. 642; two letters to Charles Diodati, i. 642-6; *Lycidas*, i. 646-63, 658 note; arrangements for the foreign tour concluded, i. 662-3.

Foreign Journey (April 1638-July 1639) :— Probable expense of the tour, i. 736; passport, and letter from Henry Lawes, i. 736-7, 737 note; correspondence with, and letters

of introduction from, Sir Henry Wotton, i. 737-9; in Paris, i. 751-4; Lord Scudamore and Grotius, i. 752-4, 752 note; through France, i. 754-9; in Italy, i. 768-831; on the way to Florence, i. 768-9; at Florence, i. 769-92; particulars concerning his principal Florentine friends, i. 773-81; in the Florentine Academies, i. 781-2; reads a Latin poem at a meeting of the Svogliati, i. 782, 792; written encomiums to, from his Florentine friends, i. 783-5, 822 note; a volume of manuscript Sonnets of Malatesti dedicated to, i. 786, 786-7 note; visits Galileo, i. 788-9; his Latin letter to the grammarian Bonmattei of Florence, i. 789-92; in Rome, i. 792-807; entertained, with his servant, at the English College in Rome, i. 800-1; Cherubini, Holstenius, and Cardinal Barberini, i. 801-3, 805, 821 note; the singer, Leonora Baroni, i. 803-5, 821 note; Roman literary acquaintances, i. 805-7; poem in Latin scazons to Salsilli, i. 806-7, 821 note; on the journey from Rome to Naples, i. 807-8; at Naples, i. 813-20; reception of, by Manso, the friend of Tasso, i. 813-6; hears probability of a Civil War in England, i. 816; ii. 472; farewell poem in Latin to Manso, i. 816-9, ii. 94; receives a present and a Latin epigram from Manso, i. 819-20; again at Rome, i. 821 and note; again in Florence and visits Lucca, i. 821-3; through Bologna and Ferrara, i. 824; his Italian Sonnets and Canzone, i. 824-9; at Venice, i. 831; receives news of Diodati's death, i. 829-30, 833; through Verona and Milan, i. 831; at Geneva, i. 831-3; his autograph in the Cerdogni album, i. 833; homewards through France, i. 834; facsimiles of his handwriting, from 1628 to 1637, end of Vol. i.

Back in England (1639-40):— Date of return, ii. 3; old friends, ii. 72-81; the *Epitaphium Damonis*, ii. 80-93 and notes; literary projects, ii. 93-7; commences a life of literary work in London, ii. 97-8; his sister and his two nephews, ii. 98-102; undertakes the teaching of the two boys, ii. 102; in lodgings in St. Bride's Churchyard, ii. 102-4; more literary projects, ii. 104-21; account of the Milton manuscripts preserved in the Library of Trinity College, Cambridge, ii. 103, 103-4 note, iv. 429; the Jottings there of Subjects for possible English Poems, ii. 106-15; first suggestions of *Paradise Lost* and other works of his later life found in these Jottings, ii. 116-7; passage in his "Reason of Church Government" (in 1641) referring to his literary projects, ii. 117-21; the interruption to these schemings, ii. 120.

In Aldersgate Street (1640-5):— Removes from St. Bride's Churchyard to Aldersgate Street in 1640, ii. 203-4; description of the neighbourhood in Milton's time in. 204-8; continued tuition of the nephews, ii. 208-9; throws himself into the Church Reform Movement of 1640-1, ii. 203, 209-12, 237-8, 382; his hand in the Smectymnuus pamphlet, ii. 238, 244, 260; three anti-Episcopal pamphlets by, ii. 237-68, 590; the first of the three, "Of Reformation, etc.," ii. 238-48; the second of the three, "Of Prelatical Episcopacy, etc.," ii. 248-53; the third of the three, the "Apology for Smectymnuus," ii. 253-62; his handwriting in copies of the pamphlets in the British Museum, ii. 248 and note, 251; his political and ecclesiastical views as found in the three pamphlets collectively, ii. 260-1, 356, iii. 109; was regarded as the representative, out of Parliament, of the "Root-and-Branch Party" in Church politics, ii. 277, 356; public talk of the three pamphlets, ii. 358-60; recognition of the pamphlets by Fuller in 1642, ii. 359-60; traces of, as a London citizen and taxpayer in 1641-2, ii. 356-8; Fourth pamphlet, on "The Reason of Church Government, etc.," ii. 361-89, 361 note; aim and scope of the pamphlet, ii. 363; keeps the *Oxford Tracts* in view throughout,

ii. 363 - 9 ; his feeling towards Andrewes and Usher, ii. 369-70 ; his own analysis of the Fourth Pamphlet, ii. 370-1 ; the power, eloquence, and beauty of the pamphlet exemplified in quoted passages, ii. 371-5 ; its Presbyterianism, ii. 375-82 ; autobiographical chapter inserted in the fourth pamphlet, ii. 382-9 ; attack on, by Bishop Hall and his son, ii. 389-98 ; his Fifth pamphlet in reply to the pamphlet of the Halls, ii. 398-409 ; autobiographic passages in self-defence contained in this pamphlet, ii. 400-4, 408 ; hostility to Hall, ii. 404-5 ; opinions on the Church question, ii. 405-8 ; still in Aldersgate Street, ii. 472-90 ; not in the Parliamentarian Army nor in the Trained Bands, ii. 472-3, 481-6 ; his military knowledge discussed, ii. 473-81 ; the Turnham - Green Sonnet, ii. 487-8 ; during the Siege of Reading in April 1643, ii. 488-91 ; his journey to Oxford and marriage to Mary Powell in the summer of 1643, ii. 491-506 ; money transactions between the families of Milton and Powell, ii. 495 ; his marriage troubles begin, ii. 506-7 ; his wife returns to her parents, ii. 507 ; his father comes to reside with him in Aldersgate Street, ii. 507-8 ; signs the Solemn League and Covenant, iii. 12, 56, 56 note ; repents his marriage, iii. 42-7, 78-9 ; first Divorce Treatise, iii. 43-56, 62-4, 186 ; Italian sonnet by, translated into English, iii. 54 ; acquaintance with the Lady Margaret Ley, iii. 57-60 ; two sonnets, iii. 60, 61, 61 notes ; second edition of the Divorce Tract, iii. 64-70, 64 note, 186; his actual Divorce Doctrine discussed, iii. 70-8; ranked among the Sectaries, iii. 155, 165, 186-9 ; results of the Divorce Tract in the story of Mrs. Attaway, iii. 189-92 ; acquaintance with Hartlib, iii. 193, 231-3 ; the Tract on Education, iii. 233-51 ; Dr. Johnson's criticism of Milton's method of education discussed, iii. 251-2 ; his

method with his pupils, iii. 253-4 ; his second Divorce Tract, a compilation from Bucer, iii. 255-61 ; Herbert Palmer's attack on, from the pulpit, iii. 164, 262-6 ; in the Petition of the Stationers' Company and the Ordinance for Printing of the Long Parliament, iii. 164-5, 265-6 ; his neglect of the Printing Ordinance, iii. 271-3 ; prosecuted by the Stationers' Company, iii. 273-5 ; the Areopagitica, iii. 275-91, 431, iv. 118 ; reference to his own enumeration in the Defensio Secunda of his successive writings in favour of the various kinds of Liberty, iii. 276 ; publication of the Areopagitica, iii. 277-8 ; scheme of the treatise explained, iii. 278-83 ; its retrospect of the Italian tour and reminiscences of Galileo, iii. 283 ; was not alone in his detestation of the censorship, iii. 283-4 ; indications in the Areopagitica of the favourite authors of, iii. 284-5 ; his complete severance from the Presbyterians confirmed, iii. 285 ; his own special and extreme " Independency " illustrated, and sympathy with the Army-Independents, iii. 286-7; his exclusion of Roman Catholics from the benefits of the doctrine of " Liberty of Conscience" or "Toleration," iii. 287-90; the effects of the Areopagitica at date of publication and through 1645, iii. 431-4, 435 ; second prosecution of, by Stationers' Company, and the case dismissed by the Lords, iii. 291-7, 297 note ; the Divorce Controversy continued, iii. 298 ; Palmer's sermon against, published, iii. 298 ; in one of Prynne's pamphlets, iii. 298-9 ; other attacks on, iii. 299-301 ; the Tetrachordon, iii. 301-13, 460 ; opinions of, on social questions, iii. 306 ; dedication of the Tetrachordon and previous treatises to the Parliament of England, iii. 308 ; biographical information found in the Tetrachordon, iii. 308-12 ; the Colasterion, iii. 313-21, 460 ; simultaneous publication of the Tetrachordon and Colasterion on March 4, 1644-5, iii. 301, 301 note, 313 ;

A Nameless Answer against the Doctrine and Discipline of Divorce (March 1644-5), account of, iii. 313-21 ; 435, 460, 466-71, iv. 322 ; intention of another marriage, iii. 435-6 ; reconciliation with his wife, iii. 436-42, 460.

In Barbican, London (1645-7) :— Removes from Aldersgate Street, iii. 442-4, 674 ; boards, with his wife, at Widow Webber's in St. Clement's Churchyard, Strand, while the house in Barbican is getting ready, iii. 486 ; description of " Milton's house" in Barbican, and account of its recent destruction, iii. 444, 444 note ; early reputation of, as a poet and as a pamphleteer, iii. 445-6 ; first edition of the collected poems of, in 1645, iii. 445-6, 450-60, 650 ; arrangement of the contents, iii. 451 ; his publisher for the Collected Poems, Humphrey Moseley, iii. 449-51, 455-6, v. 258 ; his previous publishers, iii. 450 ; title-page of the collection, and general description of the book, iii. 451-3 ; his portrait by Marshall prefixed to the poems, iii. 456-9, 459 note ; the " Onslow portrait" of, at the age of twenty-one, iii. 458 ; his full name and new heading added to the *Lycidas* in this volume in 1645, i. 662-3 ; probable addition to the poem to his father in this collection of 1645 ; iii. 643 note ; richness of the volume in Italian reminiscences, iii. 451-3, 650 ; two Divorce sonnets and sonnet to Henry Lawes written in 1645, but not included in the volume of 1645, iii. 460-5 ; continued Presbyterian attacks on, iii. 466-8 ; his anti-Presbyterian sonnet in reply, iii. 468-71 ; his and his wife's personal interest in the siege of Oxford, iii. 471-2 ; condition of his father-in-law's family at the surrender of Oxford in June 1646, iii. 473, 674 note ; Mr. Powell's debts and obligations to, in 1646, iii. 474, 634 ; the Powell family take refuge in the house of, in London, iii. 480-3, 486-7, 633, 635 ; birth of Anne Milton, the poet's first child, iii. 483-4, 483 note ; the troubled affairs of his brother Christopher, iii. 485-6, 632, 674 note ; overcrowded condition of the Barbican household during the Civil War, iii. 486-7, 632 ; death and will of his father-in-law, Mr. Powell, iii. 635-40, 637 note ; witnesses of Mr. Powell's Will, iii. 637 ; sonnet to Mrs. Catherine Thomson, iii. 644-5 ; Latin Ode to Rous, iii. 645-50 and notes ; death of his father, in Mar. 1647, iii. 641 ; reference to the poem of, to his father, written fifteen years before, iii. 643, 643 note ; letters from Carlo Dati of Florence, and reply of, to the last of them, in April 1647, iii. 650-5, 654-5 note ; pedagogy in the Barbican, iii. 655-6, 661 ; list of the known pupils of, iii. 657-60.

In High Holborn (1647-9) :— Breaks up his school establishment in Barbican, iii. 666-8, 674 ; iv. 104 ; his meditations and occupations in the house in High Holborn, iii. 668-72, 672 note, 673 ; collects materials for a Latin Dictionary, iii. 670-2, iv. 429, v. 225 ; ultimate fate of these in 1693, vi. 813 ; still under the ban of the Presbyterians, iii. 673-6 ; a fresh attack upon, in the Sion College *Testimony*, iii. 673, 678-80 ; an Italian letter from Carlo Dati, iii. 680-3 ; his Translation of nine Psalms (lxxx.-lxxxviii.) into English metre, iii. 683 ; through the Second Civil War, iii. 686-9 ; his sonnet to Fairfax, iii. 688 ; birth of Mary Milton, the poet's second child, iii. 689 ; another Italian letter from Carlo Dati, iii. 689-91, 691 note ; is writing the " Tenure of Kings and Magistrates," iii. 718-9 and note ; unqualified adhesion of, to the Republic, iv. 64 ; account of *Tenure of Kings and Magistrates*, iv. 64-77, 94, 94 note ; appointed Secretary for Foreign Tongues to the Council of State, iv. 17, 18, 77-84 ; position and duties of, in the Secretaryship, iv. 84-6 ; mentions of, in the Council Order Books, and his first official work, iv. 87-91 ; employed in press supervisions and pro-

156

secutions by the Council, iv. 92-4; three literary commissions assigned to, by the Council, iv. 94-5, 96-7, 102; his Pamphlet on Ormond's Peace with the Irish Rebels, iv. 98-102; his attack, in the pamphlet, on the Presbytery of Belfast, iv. 103-4. *At Charing Cross and Whitehall* (1649-52) :—Removal to Spring Gardens, Charing Cross, iv. 104-7; first edition of the *Eikonoklastes*, written for the Council, in reply to the *Eikon Basilike*, iv. 129, 132-45; mentions of, in the Council Order Books, iv. 145-52; biographical details contained in these *Minutes*, iv. 152; removal from Charing Cross to official rooms in Whitehall, iv. 152-4; his miscellaneous work in the Secretaryship, iv. 155-6; special literary work for the Council, iv. 156-8; Latin letters for the Council, iv. 152, 158-61; deputed to answer the *Defensio Regia* of Salmasius, iv. 161, 174-5, 175 note; reappointed to the Secretaryship by the Second Council of State, iv. 177; in particular attendance on foreign Embassies, iv. 219, 221; further mentions of, in the Council Order Books, iv. 223-31; the Declaration by the Parliament of the Causes of the War with the Scots translated into Latin by, iv. 228; abstract of twelve of his State Letters of the year 1650-1, iv. 232-6; Mrs. Powell's affairs and, iv. 236-42; his Wheatley estate, iv. 243-6, 246 note; second edition of the *Eikonoklastes* in 1650, iv. 246-50, 246-7 notes, 249-50 note; exposure in this treatise of the theft of the Pamela Prayer in the *Eikon Basilike*, iv. 248-9, 249-50 note; *Pro Populo Anglicano Defensio*, written during the year 1650, iv. 250-67 and notes, 271; his increasing blindness during the pursuance of this task, iv. 251.; reappointed to the Secretaryship by the Third Council of State, iv. 274; in negotiations with foreign embassies, iv. 275; publication of the *Pro Populo Anglicano Defensio* in Mar. 1651, iv. 312, 312 note; more mentions of, in the

Council Order Books, iv. 312-6; admiring reception of the *Defensio* abroad, and by foreigners in London, iv. 316-21; thanked by the Council for his *Defensio*, iv. 321-2; probable illness of, and failing eyesight, iv. 323; more of him in the Council Order Books, iv. 323-4; acting as official Licenser or Censor of the Press through 1651, iv. 324-5; his connexion with Needham and the *Mercurius Politicus*, iv. 325-32, 334-5, 335 note; birth of his only son, iv. 335-6, 335 note; his wife's Bible, iv. 335 note, 440; Mrs. Powell and, iv. 336-41; continued fame of his *Defensio*, iv. 341-6; anonymous *Apologia* against, from Antwerp, iv. 347-8; anonymous English reply to the *Eikonoklastes*, iv. 349-50; Christopher Arnold and his interview with, in London on Aug. 7, 1651, iv. 350-2; contribution of, to Arnold's album, iv. 352-3; tradition of his being allowed "a weekly table" for the entertainment of foreigners of distinction, iv. 353, 353 note; Roger Williams in confidential communication with, iv. 396; his Letter to Hermann Mylius, iv. 418, 422, 705-6. *In Petty France, Westminster* (1652-60) :— Removes from Scotland Yard to the house in Petty France, Westminster, iv. 418; description of the house as it was standing in 1877, iv. 418-20; Lord Scudamore his next-door neighbour, iv. 420-1; more of him in the Council Order Books, iv. 421-7; ill-health in 1652, and absence from Council, iv. 427; appointment of an Assistant to, iv. 427, 451; his blindness complete in 1652, iv. 427-32, 446, 451; ceases his Censorship of the Press in 1652, iv. 432-3; continues connexion with Needham and concern with the *Mercurius Politicus*, iv. 433, 433 note; two more Tracts against, iv. 434-7; in the affair of the Racovian Catechism, iv. 438-9; birth of Deborah, his third daughter, on May 2, 1652, iv. 439-40; account of his four children at that date, iv. 439;

Sonnets to Cromwell and Vane, iv. 440-3 ; in correspondence with Leonard Philaras, iv. 443-5 ; in temporary residence in the City, iv. 445-6 ; in the Council Order Books, iv. 447-51 ; modification of his Secretaryship, iv. 450-2 ; ferocious attack upon, in the *Regii Sanguinis Clamor*, iv. 454-8 ; and the printer Ulac, iv. 466-7 ; deaths of his wife and his only son, iv. 468-9, 469 note ; Latin letters to Richard Heath, iv. 469-70; Phillips's *Apologia* for, iv. 470-4 ; talk concerning, in extracts from letters of Heinsius and Vossius, iv. 474-6 ; his friend Andrew Marvell, iv. 476-80 ; inventory of the Latin State Papers from Jan. 20, 1652 to Feb. 1653, iv. 480-7 ; Durie's French translation of the *Eikonoklastes* in Jan. 1652-3, vi. 188; translates into Latin for the Council the Declaration of the Causes of War with the Dutch, iv. 482-3 ; Letters to, from Andrew Sandelands, iv. 487-94, 706-7 ; his approval of Cromwell's *Coup d'Etat*, iv. 519-20; probable author of a *Letter to a Gentleman in the Country, touching the Dissolution of the late Parliament and of the Reasons thereof*, signed N.LL., and dated London, May 3, 1653, iv. 520-2; retained in his post for Cromwell's Interim Council of Thirteen, with new conditions to suit his blindness, iv. 525-6 ; his new Assistant, Meadows, iv. 526; more concerning him in the Council Order Books, iv. 523-6; four State Letters of, for the Interim Council, iv. 526-8; in a letter to Sir Gilbert Pickering on the subject of a new Translation of thé Bible, iv. 524; acquaintance with Roger Williams renewed, iv. 528-33 ; Mrs. Sadleir and, iv. 530-1 ; translates Psalms i.-viii. and an Ode of Horace, in 1653, iv. 533-4 ; three more Pamphlets against, iv. 534-6 ; at the death of Salmasius, iv. 537-40 ; continues his services in the Council with his old title, but with new arrangements, in 1654, iv. 546, 576-80; a lull of six months in his Secretaryship, iv.

580, 634-5 ; the *Defensio Secunda* published in May 1654, iv. 580, 605 and notes ; account of the book, iv. 581-4 ; invective against Morus, Salmasius, and Ulac, iv. 584-90 ; defence of Cromwell against old charges, iv. 590-1 ; autobiographical passages contained in the *Defensio Secunda*, and a passage on his blindness, iv. 593-7 ; a passage of self-defence, iv. 596-7 ; panegyric on Queen Christina of Sweden, iv. 597-9, 597 note ; panegyrics on Bradshaw, iv. 600-1, Fairfax, iv. 601-2, and a cluster of the Commonwealth's men, iv. 602 ; grand panegyric on Cromwell, iv. 602-5 ; examination of the relation of, to the Protector and his Government, iv. 606-13 ; his cautions to Cromwell summed up, iv. 613-4 ; his dislike of Cromwell's Established Church, iv. 614-6 ; presentation copies of the *Defensio Secunda* to Marvell and others, iv. 616 ; Andrew Marvell again, iv. 616-25 ; Marvell's letters to, about the *Defensio Secunda*, iv. 620-1 ; letters of, to Henry Oldenburg, iv. 626-7 ; in uncertainty concerning Morus's authorship of the *Sanguinis Clamor*, iv. 627-34 ; four more State Letters (the first written for Oliver as Lord Protector), iv. 635-6 ; Leonard Philaras, the Greek physician, calls upon, in London, iv. 639-40 ; letters of, to Philaras with account of his blindness, iv. 640-2 ; the Piedmontese Massacre, v. 40 ; in list of Men of Letters under the Protectorate, v. 75, 77 ; Ulac's Hague edition of the *Defensio Secunda*, with the *Fides Publica* of Morus annexed, v. 150-62 ; his friend Overton in trouble, 162-5 ; three more State Letters, v. 165-7 ; in correspondence with Aitzema and Spanheim, v. 169-75 ; two State Letters of, v. 175-6 ; reduction of his salary, v. 177-83 ; the Piedmontese State Letters of, v. 183-91 ; sonnet on the late Piedmontese Massacre, v. 191-2, 192 note ; in Morus's *Supplementum*, v. 192-8; the *Pro Se Defensio* in reply to the attacks

of Morus, v. 198-212; account of Dr. Peter du Moulin and the question of the real authorship of the *Clamor*, v. 213-25; calm after the Morus Controversy, v. 225; literary work in 1655-6 in the house in Petty France, v. 225-6; account of his nephews, and of the *Satyr against Hypocrites* by John Phillips, v. 226-9, 258, 260, 261-3; Andrew Sande-lands and other acquaintances of, in Scotland, v. 227, 227-8 note; the circle of friends and acquaintances round, during his residence in Petty France, v. 229-36; Lady Ranelagh and, v. 230-4, 235 note, 279; possible meeting between Du Moulin and, v. 235, 235 note; visits from Marvell, Needham, and Cyriack Skinner to, v. 236-7; four domestic sonnets written in 1655, v. 237-40; writes in Latin the *Scriptum Contra Hispanos*, or Declaration of War between England and Spain, in Oct. 1655, v. 240-3, 243 note; thirteen State Letters of, v. 243-54; Count Bundt and, v. 254-6; re-employment of, in the routine work of Council, v. 256-7; personal friends of Milton in the Council, v. 260; account of his elder nephew's edition of Drummond's Poems, v. 264-6; correspondence with Mr. Richard Jones and Henry Olden-burg, v. 266-9; State Letters of, v. 269-75; and Dr. Moulin's petition to the Council in 1656, v. 276; an-other letter to Mr. Richard Jones, v. 277-8; letter to Peter Heimbach, v. 279-81; his second marriage, to Katherine Woodcock in Nov. 1656, v. 281-3, 281-2 notes; letter to Emeric Bigot, v. 283-5, 285 note, 289; the library of, v. 285-7; Mr. Ryley, Mr. Stoupe, and, v. 287-9; State Letters of, v. 289-94, 295; "standing and waiting," v. 296-8; remains in office through the Second Protectorate, v. 363-409; Latin epistle to Mr. Henry de Brass, v. 363-5, 402; letters to Mr. Richard Jones and Oldenburg, v. 365-7, 402, 631; Morus again, v. 368-70; ten State Letters of, v. 370-4; Marvell made assistant to, in the Secretary-ship, v. 374-6, 376 note; respective ages of Dryden, Marvell, and, in Sept. 1657, v. 376; birth of his fifth child, Katherine, in Oct. 1657, v. 376; deaths of his second wife and her infant daughter, v. 381-2, 384; more State Letters of, v. 376-9; Latin letters to Mr. Henry de Brass and Peter Heimbach, v. 379-80, 402; his relations to the various members of Council in 1657, v. 380-1; has little comfort in his nephews, v. 382-4; State Letters of, v. 384-6; these the last letters for Cromwell, v. 396-9, 396-9 notes, 402; glimpse of Marvell as Milton's substitute, v. 402; *Dissertation on certain Passages of*, by Christopher Guntzer of Stras-burg, and the Latin verses annexed by Keck, v. 402-4; his edition of Raleigh's *Cabinet Council* published in May 1658, v. 404-5, 405 note; *Paradise Lost*, begun eighteen years before, is resumed in 1658, v. 405-8; the last of his *Sonnets*, v. 408-9, 409 note; continues in office through Richard's Protectorate, v. 570-96; more State Letters of, v. 570-2; new edition of the *Defensio Prima*, v. 572-4; progress in *Paradise Lost*, v. 574, 580; more State Letters of, v. 575-6; his position politically under Richard's Government, v. 577-80; his *Treatise of Civil Power* addressed to Richard's Parliament in 1659, v. 580-9, 581 note; occurrence of the word *its* in the above Treatise, v. 583 note; State Letters of (the last for Richard), v. 589-90; letter to Jean Labadie, v. 590-5, 595 note; two State Letters of, for the Restored Rump, v. 595-6; remains at his post at Richard's abdication, v. 596; feelings and position of, in the new state of things, v. 598-9; his satisfaction on the whole, and the reasons for it, v. 600-1; Letter of Moses Wall to, v. 601-3, 605; in the renewed agitation against Tithes and Church Establish-ment, v. 604-5; *Means to remove Hirelings out of the Church*, v. 605-16; on Lambert's *Coup d'Etat*, v.

616-9; his scheme for a continued Republic, v. 620-2; the reception of his scheme by the Government of the Restored Rump, v. 622-3; continues nominally in the Secretaryship to Dec. 26, 1659, v. 623-5, 625 note; during the negotiations between the Committee of Safety and Monk, v. 625-7; and the debate on the Constitution, v. 627 - 30; legacy to, in Bradshaw's will, v. 630 - 1 ; nine letters to Oldenburg and Richard Jones, v. 631-5 ; his meditations about the Second Restored Rump and Monk, v. 636-40 ; his pamphlet on the crisis (*Ready and Easy Way*) stopped, v. 640-1 ; his despondency at the position of affairs, v. 641-2 ; publication, in Feb. 1660, of the *Ready and Easy Way*, v. 645-55, 645 note, 670 ; the daring peroration of the pamphlet, v. 654-5 ; its circulation and reception, v. 657-8 ; short private letter of, sent to Monk with a copy of the *Ready and Easy Way*, v. 655-7, 656 note ; hanging predicted for, v. 659 ; *Censure of the Rota on*, v. 659-63 ; 660 note ; suspected of being responsible for the Republican tract called *Plain English* addressed to Monk, v. 663-6, 670 ; the various Republican associates of, suppressed by the Council of State, v. 670-4 ; discharged from his Secretaryship in March 1660, v. 672-4, 674 note ; *Notes on Dr. Griffith's Sermon* by, v. 675-7, 675 note ; second and enlarged edition of the *Ready and Easy Way*, v. 677-88, 689 note ; he and Lambert are the last opponents of the Restoration, v. 688-9 ; reply to his *Notes on Dr. Griffith's Sermon*, v. 689-90 ; reply to the *Ready and Easy Way*, by G. S., v. 691-4 ; further references to the *Ready and Easy Way*, vi. 166, 190, 214, 399, 480.

In hiding and in custody (1660) : —Goes into hiding, v. 702-3 ; the *Eikonoklastes* and *Pro Populo Defensio* burnt by Royal Proclamation, vi. 39, 173-4, 181, 190, 191 ; in abscondence, vi. 162-5; the house in Bartholomew Close, vi. 162-3; review of his antecedents and his chances with the new powers, vi. 163-6 ; in extreme danger at the Restoration, vi. 166 - 7 ; and during the progress of the Indemnity Bill through the Convention Parliament, vi. 166-81; Royal Proclamation against him and John Goodwin on Aug. 13, 1660, vi. 181-2 ; escape of, and speculation as to how it was effected, vi. 183-92 ; in custody of the sergeant-at-arms, vi. 193-5.

Holborn again, and *Jewin Street* (1660 - 64) : — At liberty in Dec. 1660, and goes to a house in Holborn, near Red Lion Fields, vi. 195-6 ; fates of his old friends and associates, vi. 196 - 200 ; Marchamont Needham again, vi. 200 - 2 ; Salmasius's Posthumous Reply to, vi. 203 - 12 and notes ; reception of this book by the old antagonists of, vi. 212-4 and notes ; in Holborn, vi. 214 - 7 ; in apprehension of being mobbed or assassinated, vi. 214-5 ; in a Survey of Literature at the Restoration, vi. 294 ; removal from Holborn to Jewin Street, vi. 406 - 8 ; 423, 440 ; his estimate of the Restoration, vi. 409-412 ; Clarendon and, vi. 413-4 ; at the St. Bartholomew Ejection, vi. 415-6 ; his acquaintances among the ejected, vi. 417 - 9 ; mention of, by Clarendon in his letter to Gauden, vi. 433, 439-40 ; *Paradise Lost* continued in Jewin Street to Books VII. and VIII., vi. 440-4 ; the post-Restoration tone in *Book VII.*, vi. 444 ; his pecuniary circumstances in 1662, vi. 444-5, 445 note ; his three daughters, vi. 446-9, 451 ; the Powell family in 1662, vi. 449-451, 451 note ; visitors in Jewin Street, vi. 452-3 ; Mr. Samuel Parker, vi. 453-4 ; Dr. Paget, vi. 454-5, 473 ; Lady Ranelagh again, vi. 457-8 and note ; Richard Jones, vi. 458, 460-2 ; Henry Oldenburg, vi. 458-60 ; his nephews, vi. 462-5 ; his literary habits, vi. 464-6, 465 note ; the Quaker Ellwood, vi. 467-73 ; his

third marriage, to Elizabeth Minshull, vi. 473-7 and notes; his
interest in the trial of John Twyn,
vi. 477-81.
    In *Artillery Walk, Bunhill Fields*
(1664-74) :— Removal to Artillery
Walk near to Bunhill Fields, vi.
481-6; *Paradise Lost* resumed at
Book IX. and finished in 1665,
vi. 486-90, 500, 500 note; at
Chalfont St. Giles during the Plague
in 1665 - 6, vi. 491 - 8; back in
Artillery Walk, 1666-7, vi. 498 -
500; in correspondence with Peter
Heimbach, vi. 500; letters of
Heimbach to, vi. 501; reply of,
to the same, vi. 501 - 2, 502
note; and the Great Fire of
London, vi. 503 - 5; publication
of the First Edition of *Paradise
Lost*, vi. 505-18; Agreement of,
with Simmons, vi. 509-11, 511 note;
references to, in a critical and
descriptive analysis of the Poem, vi.
518-58; compared with Dante, vi.
518-22; his personality asserts itself
in the choice of the subject, vi. 522-
3; his Pre-Copernicanism, vi. 523-
57; the *learning* shown in *Paradise
Lost*, vi. 556-7, 557 note; his place
in the quarternion of greatest English poets, vi. 558; curious trade
history of the first edition of *Paradise
Lost*, vi. 621-8; first reception of
the poem, and Richardson's story of
Dryden's praise, vi. 628-33; his
contribution to the Blank Verse
Controversy between Dryden and
Howard in 1668, vi. 634; paragraph
on " *The Verse* " prefixed by, together with " The Argument " to
the fifth issue of copies of *Paradise
Lost* in 1668, vi. 634-5; first praises
of his *Paradise Lost* by Edward
Phillips, vi. 635-6 and note; conflux
of visitors to Bunhill, vi. 637-8;
story of the offer to reinstate, in the
post of Latin Secretary, vi. 638-9;
Anthony Wood's story that he was
consulted by a member of the Lords'
House in the matter of the Lord
Roos Divorce Bill, vi. 639-40; the
Latin Grammar of, published in
1669, vi. 640-2, 642 note; his non-

use of the word *its*, vi. 641; his
History of Britain, published in 1670,
vi. 642-7, 647 note; passages of
Miltonism abound in the *History*,
vi. 645-6; non-registration of the
History, vi. 646-7, 647 note; Faithorne's portrait of, prefixed to the
History of Britain, vi. 647-9, 648
note; parts with his three daughters
in 1670, vi. 649-50; in temporary
residence in Little Britain, vi. 650-
1, 678; *Paradise Regained* published
in July 1671, vi. 651-61; the subject
suggested to, by the Quaker Ellwood
at Chalfont St. Giles in 1665, vi.
652, 654-5; his own opinion of the
Poem, .vi. 655; *Samson Agonistes*
published in 1671, vi. 661-78;
peculiarly Miltonic characteristics of
the Poem, vi. 658; examples of its
autobiographic significance, vi. 670-
8; his increasing ill-health, vi. 678;
Richardson's description of, in his
last years, vi. 678-84; Treatise on
Logic, published in 1672, vi. 684-6;
second edition of the Minor Poems,
with additions, in 1673, vi. 687-90,
687 note; Tract on True Religion
and Toleration in 1673, vi. 690-9;
and the Parker-Marvell Controversy
in 1673, vi. 704-9, 708 note; Marvell, in the *Rehearsal Transprosed*,
on his connexion with, vi. 706-8;
Dryden's visit to, in the winter of
1673-4, vi. 709-10; Dryden's Opera
from *Paradise Lost*, vi. 711-2, 717
note; second edition of *Paradise
Lost* in 1674, vi. 712-5; encomiums
on him by Barrow and Marvell, vi.
715-16; his pecuniary circumstances
in 1674, vi. 717-9 and note, 720 and
note; the booksellers or printers
employed by, since 1667, vi. 719;
Brabazon Aylmer and, vi. 719-22;
publication of the *Epistolæ Familiares*
and *Prolusiones Oratoriæ*, vi. 722-4;
Translation of the Sobieski Declaration, vi. 725-7; his last days, vi. 72-
30; his death and burial, vi. 731-2.
    Posthumous details :— his Nun-
cupative Will, vi. 735 - 44; his
widow, i. 309 note; vi. 745 - 9;
her death and will .in 1727, vi.
747 - 9, 749 note; Mrs. Powell,

and her will in 1678, vi. 750-1, 751 note ; his eldest daughter, Anne, vi. 750 ; his daughter, Deborah Clarke, vi. 751-4, 754-8 footnote ; portraits of, vi. 754 note ; his grandson, Caleb Clarke, and his descendants, vi. 752, 755-9, 759 note ; last descendants of, vi. 759-61 ; other surviving relations of, and their descendants, vi. 761-75 and notes; increase of poetical celebrity of, and multiplication of editions of his poems, vi. 775-90 ; tributes of Dryden and Phillips to, in 1675, vi. 776-8 ; the third edition of *Paradise Lost* in 1678, vi. 779-80 ; other editions of his works, vi. 781-2 ; mentions of him from 1678-88, vi. 783-4 ; the fourth edition of *Paradise Lost* in 1678, vi. 784-6 ; third edition of *Paradise Regained*, and *Samson Agonistes*, in 1688, vi. 786 ; the Tonson Copyright, and other copyrights of his poems, vi. 786-90 ; fifth edition of *Paradise Lost* in 1692, vi. 786 ; first collective edition of the Poetical Works of, in 1695, vi. 786-90 ; posthumous prose publications of, and fate of his Manuscripts, vi. 790-816 ; Daniel Skinner and the *Milton MSS.*, vi. 790-806 ; the " *Character of the Long Parliament*," published in 1681, vi. 806-12 ; the *History of Muscovia, etc.*, printed in 1682, vi. 812-3 ; the fate of the *Latin Dictionary* of, vi. 813 ; first collective edition of the Prose Works of, in 1698, by Toland, and subsequent editions of the same, vi. 814 ; *Letters and Papers of State* addressed to Cromwell *from 1649 to 1658*, and found among the Political Collections of Milton, edited by Nickoll in 1743, vi. 814-6, 740 note ; the *Treatise on Christian Doctrine*, vi. 817-40 ; biographical particulars derived from this Treatise, vi. 817 ; the fundamental idea of the Treatise, vi. 817-8 ; his methods of dealing with the Scriptures, vi. 818-22 ; the first, or theoretical, portion of the Treatise, vi. 822-35 ; the second, or practical, part of the Treatise, vi. 835-8 ; concluding historical observations on the whole Treatise, vi. 838-40.

MILTON (*continued*), WRITINGS OF :— I. COLLEGE EXERCISES :—(*Prolusiones Quædam Oratoriæ*) abstracts of, in English, with historical and criticals accounts of each exercise, i. 272-306 ; 328 ; publication of, by Aylmer in 1674, vi. 722, 727, 781. II. PROSE WORKS (in the order of their publication) :—Three Anti-Episcopal Pamphlets entitled (1) *Of Reformation touching Church Discipline in England and the Causes that have hitherto hindered it* (May 1641), account of, ii. 237-48 ; 262-8, 356, 358-61, iii. 450, 679 ; (2) *Of Prelatical Episcopacy* (June 1641), account of, ii. 248-53 ; 262-8, 356, 358-61, iii. 450, 679 ; (3) *Animadversions upon the Remonstrant's Defence against Smectymnuus* (July 1641), account of, ii. 253-62 ; 262-8, 356, 358-61, iii. 450, 679, vi. 705 ; references to the three Pamphlets collectively, ii. 248, 251, 260-1, 356, 358-60, iii. 109, 450, v. 223, vi. 163.—The " Fourth Pamphlet," entitled *The Reason of Church Government urged against Prelaty* (about February 1641-2), ii. 94-5 ; account of, ii. 361-98.—The " Fifth Pamphlet," entitled *Apology against a Pamphlet called A modest Confutation of the Animadversions upon the Remonstrant against Smectymnuus* (March 1641-2), i. 314-6, 224-5, 269 ; account of, ii. 398-409. —*Tract on Education* (June 1644), i. 52, ii. 479-81 ; account of, iii. 231-54 ; 272, 647, 656.—*Areopagitica, or Speech for the Liberty of Unlicensed Printing* (Nov. 1644), account of, iii. 275-91 and notes ; 293, 294, 298, 299, 308, 431-5 ; iv. 118 ; see also under *Areopagitica*. —Four Divorce Pamphlets entitled (1) *The Doctrine and Discipline of Divorce Restored to the good of both Sexes* (Aug. 1643), account of the first edition of, iii. 42-56 ; 61-4, 186, 271-2, 297, 299, 415, 442 ; account of the second edition of, in Feb. 1643-4, iii. 64-70 ; 186-9, 190, **272,**

435, 673, 678-9; (2) *The Judgment of Martin Bucer concerning Divorce* (July 1644), account of; iii. 164-5; further account of, iii. 255 - 62; 262-4, 265, 272, 435; iv. 64; (3) *Tetrachordon, or Expositions upon the four chief places in Scripture which treat of Marriage* (March 1644-5), iii. 56 note; account of, iii. 301-13; 435, 460, 468; (4) *Colasterion: a Reply to a Nameless Answer against the Doctrine and Discipline of Divorce* (March 1644-5), account of, iii. 313-21; 435, 460, 466-8, 468 - 71; iv. 322.— References to the three first of the above Pamphlets collectively, vi. 163, 674.— *Tenure of Kings and Magistrates, proving that it is lawful, and hath been held so through all ages, for any who have the power, to call to account a tyrant, or Wicked King, and after due conviction, to depose and put him to death, if the ordinary magistrate have neglected to do it* (Feb. 1648-9), account of, iv. 64-80, and notes; 94, 94-5 note, 97, 106, 428, 429, v. 223, vi. 163-4, 170, 172, 174, 177, 179, 184, 189, 191-2, 398, 479, 480, 639.—Three publications by order of the Council of State, entitled (1) *Observations on Ormond's Articles of Peace with the Irish Rebels and on a Representation of the Scotch Presbytery of Belfast* (May 1649), iv. 98-102, vi. 164; (2) *Eikonoklastes*, in answer to *Eikon Basilike* (Oct. 1649), iv. 95 note; account of, iv. 132-45; second edition of (1650), iv. 246-50 and notes, 428, 430, v. 223; vi. 39, 164, 173-4, 181-2, 188, 190, 191, 398, 399, 414, 440, 639, 717; (3) *Defensio pro Populo Anglicano* (April 1651), in reply to the *Defensio Regia* of Salmasius: account of, iv. 250-67 and notes; 312, 316-22, 341-6, 347-50, 428, 430, 531, 535, 581, 597 and note, 637; v. 223, 572; new and enlarged edition of, in October 1658, v. 572-4; vi. 39, 164, 173-4, 181-2, vi. 164, 165, 179 note; 188, 190, 191, vi. 203-12, 212 note; 399,

414, 705.— *Pro Populo Anglicano Defensio Secunda* (1654), in reply to *Regii Sanguinis Clamor:* i. 84-5, 552, 816, 834; ii. 3, 211-12; iv. 65 note, 430, 531; account of, iv. 580-616; 624, 625-35, 636, 639, v. 150-62, 192-8, 208, 214, 220, 222, vi. 165, 170, 174, 179 note, 181, 203, 207, 211, 212 note, 399, 417.— *Pro se Defensio contra Alexandrum Morum*, together with *Authoris ad Alexandri Mori Supplementum Responsio* (1655), account of, v. 198-212; 213, 214, 222, 225, 228, vi. 165.— *The Cabinet Council* (edition of Sir Walter Raleigh), published by, in May 1658, v. 404-5.— *A Treatise of Civil Power in Ecclesiastical Causes, showing that it is not lawful for any power on earth to compel in matters of Religion* (Feb. 1658-9), account of, v. 581-7; 600, 601, 674 note; vi. 399.— *Considerations touching the likeliest means to remove Hirelings out of the Church, with a prefatory Address to the Parliament* (August 1659), account of, v. 605-15; 670, 674 note; vi. 399, 414, 480.— *Letter to a Friend concerning the Ruptures of the Commonwealth* (Oct. 1659), account of, v. 617-22, 628.— *The Ready and Easy Way to establish a Free Commonwealth, and the Excellence thereof compared with the inconveniences and dangers of re-admitting kingship in this Nation* (March 1660), account of, v. 645-58, 659-63, 670, 673; second edition of (April 1660), account of, v. 677-88; 678 note, 689 note.— *The Present Means and Brief Delineation of a Free Commonwealth easy to be put in practice and without delay, in a Letter to General Monk* (March 1660), v. 655-7.— *Brief Notes on a late Sermon* (by Dr. Griffiths) in April 1660, v. 675-7, and note, 691; v. 166.— *Accedence Commenc't Grammar* (Latin Grammar) in 1669, vi. 640-2 and note, 651, 706.— *History of Britain to the Conquest* (1670), iii. 670-2; iv. 429; v. 225; vi. 642-9, 651, 684. — *Artis Logicæ*

Plenior Institutio ad Petri Rami Methodum Concinnata (1672), i. 268 ; vi. 684-6, 686-7 note.—*Of True Religion, Heresy, Schism, Toleration, and what best means may be used against the growth of Popery* (1673), vi. 687, account of, vi. 690-9.—*Epistolæ Familiares* (Familiar Letters), (July 1674), i. 272-3, 273 note ; vi. 722-4, 727, 781, 791. Translations into English of the above *Epistolæ* in their order of date :—to Thomas Young from London, Mar. 26, 1625, i. 72 note, 147-8 ; to Alexander Gill from London, May 20, 1628, i. 190-1 ; to Alexander Gill from Cambridge, July 2, 1628, i. 193-4 ; to Thomas Young from Cambridge, July 21, 1628, i. 203-4 ; to Alexander Gill "from our suburban residence, Dec. 4, 1634," i. 623-4 ; to Charles Diodati from London, Sept. 2, 1637, i. 642-3 ; to Charles Diodati from London, Sept. 23, 1637, i. 643-6 ; to Bonmattei in Florence, Sept. 10, 1638, i. 789-92 ; to Lucas Holstenius from Florence, Mar. 30, 1639, i. 802-3, 822-3 ; to Carlo Dati from London, Apr. 21, 1647, iii. 652-4 ; to Hermann Mylius from Westminster (two), Feb. 13, 1652, v. 705, and Feb. 17, 1652, iv. 417, 424 ; to Leonard Philaras from London, June 1652, iv. 444-5 ; to Richard Heath from Westminster, Dec. 13, 1652, iv. 469-70 ; to Henry Oldenburg from Westminster, July 6, 1654, iv. 626-7 ; to Leonard Philaras from Westminster, Sept. 28, 1654, iv. 640-2 ; to Leo Aitzema from Westminster, Feb. 5, 1655, v. 170-1 ; to Ezekiel Spanheim from Westminster, Mar. 24, 1655, v. 172-3 ; to Richard Jones from Westminster, May 1656, v. 267-8 ; to Henry Oldenburg from Westminster, June 25, 1656, v. 268-9 ; to Richard Jones from Westminster, Sept. 21, 1656, v. 277-8 ; to Peter Heimbach from Westminster, Nov. 8, 1656, v. 280 ; to Emeric Bigot from Westminster, Mar. 24, 1657, v. 283-4 ; to Henry de Brass from Westminster, July 15, 1657, v. 363-5 ; to Richard Jones from Westminster, Aug. 1, 1657, v. 366 ; to Henry Oldenburg from Westminster, Aug. 1, 1657, v. 366-7 ; to Henry de Brass from Westminster, Dec. 16, 1657, v. 379 ; to Peter Heimbach from Westminster, Dec. 18, 1657, v. 380 ; to Jean Labadie from Westminster, Apr. 21, 1659, v. 592-4 ; to Henry Oldenburg from Westminster, Dec. 20, 1659, v. 634-5 ; to Richard Jones from Westminster, Dec. 20, 1659, v. 635 ; to Peter Heimbach from London, Aug. 15, 1666, vi. 501-2. —*Letters Patent for the Election of John III. (Sobieski) King of Poland* (July 1674), vi. 725-7, 781.—*Character of the Long Parliament and Assembly of Divines in 1641* (1681), vi. 803-12.—*A Brief History of Moscovia and of other less known countries lying eastward of Russia as far as Cathay* (1682), vi. 812-3.—*The Public or State Letters and Documents of :*—i. 273 ; iv. 89-91, 91 note, 158, 158-9 note ; (i.-v.) iv. 159-61, 161 note ; (vi.-xvii.) iv. 232-6 and notes ; (xviii.-xix.) iv. 324, 424 notes ; (xx.-xl.) iv. 480-6 and notes ; (xli.-xliv.) iv. 527-8 ; (xlv.-xlviii.) iv. 635-6, 636 note ; (xlix.-li.) v. 165-6, 165 note 2 ; (lii.-liii.) v. 175-6, 176 note ; (liv.-lxiv.) v. 184-91 and notes ; (lxv.-lxxvii.) v. 243-54 and notes ; (lxxviii.-xc.) v. 269-75 ; (xci.-c.) v. 289-94 ; (ci.-cxi.) v. 370-4 ; (cxii.-cxvii.) v. 376-9 ; (cxviii.-cxxxii.) v. 385-96 and notes ; (cxxxiii.-cxxxvii.) v. 570-2 ; (cxxxviii.-cxliii.) v. 575-6 ; (cxliv.-cxlvii.) v. 589-90 ; (cxlviii.-cxlix.) v. 595-6. — Accounts of the original State Letters, iv. 91 note, 158-9 note ; futile attempt of Brabazon Aylmer in 1674 to publish them, vi. 720-2, 722 note ; further account of the story of Daniel Skinner and the Milton MSS. in 1676-7, vi. 791-806 ; English translation of them, by Edward Phillips, in 1694, vi. 767 ; accidental discovery of, in the State Paper Office, Whitehall, in 1825, vi. 816. —*De Doctrinâ Christianâ*

(Treatise of Christian Doctrine), iii.
670-2, iv. 429, v. 225, vi. 720, and
note ; Daniel Skinner and the Manuscript of, vi. 791-2, 797, 798, 800,
802 - 3, 805 and note ; account of
the discovery of this Treatise, together with the State Letters, in the
State Paper Offices, Whitehall, and
the publication of, with an English
translation, in 1825, vi. 816 ; abstract of the Treatise, vi. 817-40.
  III.—MINOR POEMS :—(1) The
English Poems.   *Paraphrases of
Psalms cxiv. and cxxxvi.* (1624), i.
95-6, 103, 329 ; *On the Death of
a Fair Infant dying of a Cough*
(1625-6), i. 169-70, 329 ; *At a
Vacation Exercise in the College*
(1628), i. 293-6, 329 ; *On the
Morning of Christ's Nativity* (1629),
i. 228-30, 329 ; *The Passion* (Easter
1630), i. 230, 329, 604 note ; *Song
on May Morning* (1630 or 1633), i.
577-8 ; *On Shakespeare* (1630), i.
236, 329, 331-2, iii. 445 ; *On the
University Carrier* (two pieces)
(1630-1), i. 241-3, 329 ; *An Epitaph
on the Marchioness of Winchester*
(1631), i. 244-6, 329 ; *L'Allegro*
and *Il Penseroso* (1632), i. 569-77,
569 note ; *Arcades* (1633), account
of, i. 578-602, 599 note, 604 note,
ii. 103, iii. 462-4, vi. 491, 662 ;
At a Solemn Music (1633), i.
603-4, ii. 103 ; *On Time* (1633-4),
i. 603-4, ii. 103 ; *Upon the Circumcision* (Jan. 1, 1634), i. 603-4,
604 note, ii. 103 ; *Comus* (1634),
i. 604, 610-23, 640-41, ii. 103,
iii. 54, 445, 462-5, 645, iv. 531,
vi. 662 ; *Lycidas* (1637), i. 646-63,
ii. 103, 210-11, iii. 445, vi. 195,
667.—Sonnets I. and II., *To the
Nightingale*, i. 577 - 8, and note ;
and *On his having arrived at the
Age of Twenty-three* (9th Dec. 1631),
i. 247, 329, 527, ii. 103 ; Five
Italian Sonnets with an accompanying Canzone (1638-9) translated,
i. 824-9, iii. 54 ; Sonnet VIII.,
*When the Assault was intended
to the City* (1642), ii. 487 - 8 ;
Sonnet IX., *To a Lady* (called also
To a Virtuous Young Lady) (1644),

iii. 61 ; Sonnet X., *To the Lady
Margaret Ley* (1644 or 1645), iii.
60-1, 61 note, 189 ; Two Divorce
Sonnets, XI. and XII., *On the
Detraction which followed upon my
writing certain Treatises* (1645-6),
iii. 460-1, 644 ; quoted, iii. 680 ;
Anti-Presbyterian Sonnet, entitled,
*On the New Forcers of Conscience
under the Long Parliament* (1646),
iii. 468-71, 471 note, 644 ; quoted,
iii. 680 ; Sonnet XIII., *To Mr.
H. Lawes, on his Airs* (Feb. 9,
1645 - 6), iii. 462 - 5, v. 226 ;
Sonnet XIV., *On the Religious
Memory of Mrs. Catherine Thomson, my Christian Friend, deceased
December 16, 1646*, iii. 644 - 5 ;
Sonnet XV., *On the Lord General
Fairfax at the Siege of Colchester*
(1648), iii. 688-9, 688 note, **vi.**
775 ; Sonnet XVI., *To the Lord
General Cromwell, May 1652, on
the Proposals of Certain Ministers
at the Committee for Propagation of
the Gospel*, iv. 440 - 3, vi. 775 ;
Sonnet XVII., *To Sir Henry Vane
the Younger* (1652), iv. 440-3, 606,
vi. 688, 775 ; Sonnet XVIII.,
On the late Massacre in Piedmont
(1655), v. 191-2 ; Sonnet XIX.,
On his Blindness (1652-5), iv.
430, v. 273-40, quoted, v. 296 ;
Sonnet XX., *To Mr. Lawrence*
(1655), v. 237-40 ; Sonnet XXI.,
To Cyriack Skinner (1655), v.
237-40 ; Sonnet XXII., *Second
Sonnet to Cyriack Skinner* (1655),
v. 237-40, vi. 775 ; Sonnet XXIII.,
To the Memory of his Second Wife
(1658), v. 408-9.—*The Fifth Ode
of Horace, Lib. 1, Englished* (after
1645), iv. 533-4 ; *Nine of the
Psalms done into Metre, wherein all
but what is in a different character
are the very words of the Text
translated from the original* (April
1648), iii. 683-6 ; *Psalms i.-viii.
Done into Verse* (August 1653),
iv. 533-4 ; Scraps of translated
verse from the Prose Writings, vi.
775.—(2) The Latin Poems (*Elegiæ*):
*Elegia Prima, Ad Carolum Dio-
datum* (1626), translated, i. **161-7**

and 161 note, 328 ; Elegia Secunda, *In Obitum Præconis Academici Cantabrigiensis* (on the death of the Cambridge University Bedel) (1626), i. 172-3, 328 ; Elegia Tertia, *In obitum Præsulis Wintoniensis* (1626), abstract of, i. 168-9, 328 ; Elegia Quarta, *Ad Thomam Junium, præceptorem suum, apud mercatores Anglicos Hamburgæ agentes Pastoris munere fungentem* (1627), i. 68 note, 184-5, 328 ; Elegia Quinta, *In Adventum Veris* (1629), i. 218, 219, 328, vi. 465 ; Elegia Sexta, *Ad Carolum Diodatum ruri commorantem* (1629), i. 226-8, 328 ; Elegia Septima, *Nòndum blanda*, etc. (May 1627 or May 1628), a version of, in English prose, i. 189-90, 328.— (Epigrammata): *In Proditionem Bombardicam* (three pieces), and *In Inventorem Bombardæ* (On the Gunpowder Plot), i. 173, 329 ; *Ad Leonoram Romæ Canentem* (three pieces) (1638), translated, i. 804-5 ; *Apologus de Rustico et Hero* (after 1645), vi. 689 ; *De Moro* (lampoon on Alexander More in *Defensio Secunda* and in *Pro Se Defensio*, iv. 587 and note ; *Ad Christinam, Suecorum Reginam, nomine Cromwelli* (1654), iv. 624-5. —(*Sylvæ*) : *In obitum Procancellarii medici* (1626), abstract of, i. 172-3 ; *In Quintum Novembris* (Nov. 5, 1626), translated into English Hexameters, i. 174-9 ; *In obitum Præsulis Eliensis* (1626), abstract of, i. 168 ; *Naturam non pati Senium* (1628), i. 201-3, 329 ; *De Idea Platonica* (?) translated, i. 305-6 ; *Ad Patrem* (1633), i. 85, translated, i. 334-7 ; iii. 643 ; *Psalm cxiv.* (1634), i. 624, iii. 453 ; *Philosophus ad Regem Quendam*, etc. (1642-45), iii. 453 ; *In Effigiei Ejus Sculptorem* (1645-6), translated, iii. 459, vi. 689; *Ad Salsillum, Poetam Romanum, Ægrotantem* (1638 or 1639), translated, i. 806-7 ; *Mansus* (Jan. 1638-9), translated, i. 816-19 ; ii. 94-5 ; *Epitaphium Damonis* (1639), account of, and translation into English Hexameters, ii. 80-97 ; *Ad Joannem Rousium Oxoniensis Aca-*

demiæ Bibliothecarium (Jan. 23, 1646-7), iii. 644-50 ; *In Salmasii Hundredam* (in 8th chapter of the *Defensio Prima*), translated, iv. 266 ; *In Salmasium* (in the *Defensio Secunda*), translated, iv. 590.— First edition of the Minor Poems (Moseley) in 1645, iii. 445, 451-9 ; Dring's edition in 1673, vi. 687-9 : Warton's edition in 1791, i. 740 note.

IV. LATER POEMS : — *Paradise Lost* (1667), i. 5, 89 note, 789 ; ii. 106-8, 116-19, 473-9; v. 219, 406-8, 407 note, 574 ; vi. 388, 440-4, 448, 464-5, 465 note, 486-9, 496, 500 ; publication of, vi. 505-18 and notes. Essay on the Poem, vi. 518-58 and notes. First edition of, vi. 621-40 and notes, 651, 652, 653, 654, 655, 658, 663, 666, 667, 689, 705, 709, 718, 719, 776, 777 ; Dryden's Opera from, vi. 710-12 ; second edition, vi. 712-17, 775-8 ; third edition, vi. 779-81, 782-4 ; German translation of, vi. 783 ; Latin translation of the first book of, vi. 784; fourth edition of (1688), vi. 784-6 ; subsequent editions of, vi. 786-90 ; other translations of, into German and Latin, vi. 789-90. —*Paradise Regained* (1671), i. 67 ; vi. 496, 616 ; account of the Poem and of its publication, vi. 651-61 ; 666, 668, 677, 684, 689, 718, 775-6, 777 ; second edition (1680), vi. 781-2, 782, 783 ; third and subsequent editions, vi. 786-90.— *Samson Agonistes* (1671), ii. 110, 116 ; vi. 616, 651-2, account of, vi. 661-78 ; 684 ; 689, 718, 775-6, 777 ; second edition (1680), vi. 781-2, 783 ; third and subsequent editions, vi. 786-90.

MILTON, John, of Egham in Surrey, returned in the census for 1433 of the whole gentry of England, i. 12.

MILTON, John de, of Burnham in Buckinghamshire, in 1428 (possibly the same as John Milton of Egham), i. 12.

MILTON (Mylton), John, of Somersetshire, student at Oxford in 1574, i. 23-4 note.

MILTON, John, churchwarden of the

parish of Beckley in Oxfordshire in 1577 and in 1581, i. 20.

MILTON, John, "fisherman," of Culham in Oxfordshire, died in 1602, i. 22 note.

MILTON (Melton), Major John, Quartermaster to Colonel Pennington in 1642, ii. 483-4, 484 note.

MILTON, a "John Milton, junior," arrested and indicted for high treason in 1647, iii. 555.

MILTON, John, only son of Milton the poet, iv. 335-6, 335 note.

MILTON, Katherine, second wife of the poet : see *Woodcock*.

MILTON, Katherine, child of the poet by his second wife, v. 382.

MILTON, Mary, first wife of the poet : see *Powell*, Mary.

MILTON, Mary, second daughter of the poet, iii. 689 ; iv. 105 ; v. 226 ; vi. 447-9, 451, 476, 649-50, 735-44, 750-1.

MILTON, Mary, daughter of Christopher Milton, vi. 763.

MILTON, Mrs., daughter of Thomas, and grand-daughter of Christopher, Milton, vi. 763.

MILTON, Nicholas, of Appleton in Berkshire, i. 20.

MILTON, Nicholas, of Windsor, i. 23 note.

MILTON, Richard, in Berkshire in 1559, i. 13.

MILTON, Richard (eldest son of Henry Milton of Stanton St. John's), grandfather of the poet, i. 16-23, 40 ; ii. 492, 497-8.

MILTON, Richard, scrivener and apprentice of Milton's father, i. 338 note.

MILTON, a Richard, witness, vi. 740.

MILTON, Robert, of Elsfield in Oxfordshire, i. 19-20.

MILTON, Robert, tailor, of Weston in Oxfordshire, died in 1610, i. 22 note.

MILTON, Robert, near Windsor, i. 23 note.

MILTON, Roger, collector, of Oxfordshire, i. 12.

MILTON, Rowland, relative of the poet's grandfather, i. 14, 16, 19, 20.

MILTON, Sarah, mother of the poet, i. 30-3, 35, 36, 38, 38 note ; her real parentage, i. 35, 38 ; Milton's mention of, i. 39 ; her weak eyesight, i. 39 ; her death at Horton, i. 631-2, 639 ; her grave in Horton Church, i. 632.

MILTON, Sarah, infant sister of the poet, i. 40.

MILTON, Sarah, daughter of Christopher Milton, i. 735 note ; ii. 488.

MILTON, Tabitha, infant sister of the poet, i. 40.

MILTON, Thomas, of La Rolfe, Windsor, i. 20.

MILTON, Thomas (another), i. 338 note.

MILTON, Thomas, eldest son of Christopher Milton, vi. 763.

MILTON, Thomasine, wife of Christopher Milton : see *Webber*.

MILTON, William de, i. 7.

MILTON, William, in Berks, i. 13.

MILTON, William, a collector of customs in London, i. 13.

MILTON, William, in Oxford, i. 13.

MILTON, William, of Windsor, i. 23 note.

MILTONISTS : see *Divorcers*.

MINSHULLS of Stoke, in Cheshire, the, vi. 474.

MINSHULL, Elizabeth, Milton's third wife, vi. 473-7 and notes, 638 ; during Milton's last days, vi. 727-31 ; in Milton's Nuncupative Will, vi. 735-41 ; as Milton's widow, vi. 744-9, 749 note, 755-7 note.

MINSHULL, Ellen, wife of Richard Minshull sen., vi. 474.

MINSHULL, Mabel, daughter of the above, vi. 474.

MINSHULL, Mary, wife of Richard Minshull jun., vi. 745.

MINSHULL, Randall (at Wistaston), son and heir of Richard Minshull sen., and father of Elizabeth Minshull, vi. 474 ; his wife : see *Boote*.

MINSHULL, Mr. Richard, master of Sidney-Sussex College, Cambridge, in 1644, iii. 94, 95.

MINSHULL, Richard, sen., yeoman of Wistaston in Cheshire, grandfather of Elizabeth Minshull, vi. 474.

MINSHULL, Richard, jun., brother of Elizabeth Minshull, a "framework-

knitter" at Wistaston in 1680, vi. 745.

MINSHULL, Thomas, son of Richard Minshull sen., apothecary in Manchester, vi. 474.

MIREVELT, in Holland, the school of Rembrandt at, in 1638, i. 746.

"MIST'S WEEKLY JOURNAL," an appeal on behalf of Deborah Clark, published in (April 29, 1727), vi. 754.

MOCHINGER, John, of Dantzic, follower of Comenius, iii. 202.

MODENA : see *Francesco I.*, also *Maria of Modena.*

MODIFORD, James, merchant, v. 589.

"THE MODERATE," a Royalist journal, iv. 39, 88.

MOHUN, Michael, actor in the King's Company, vi. 349, 350, 353, 368, 607, 609.

MOHUN, Lord (Royalist), ii. 429.

MOLIÈRE, vi. 356-7, 360-1.

MOLINEUX, Sir Richard, client of Milton senior, i. 627.

MOLINO, nobleman of Venice, i. 812.

"MONASTICON ANGLICANUM," by Dugdale, vi. 296.

MONINGS, William, Parliamentarian officer, ii. 444.

MONK, General George (Duke of Albemarle in 1660) : in Ireland, iv. 24, 42, 56, 111, 113; in Scotland, iv. 192, 200; Lieutenant-General of Cromwell's Army in Scotland, iv. 290-1, 295, 296, 302, 303, 360-1, 362, 364, 375-6, 401, 552; Commander-in-Chief of the English Fleet during Cromwell's Interim Dictatorship, iv. 499; called to Cromwell's Supreme Assembly, iv. 501; in sea-victories over the Dutch, iv. 502, 507; rewards to, iv. 565 note; anti-Oliverian movement in his Army in Scotland, v. 32-3; in Cromwell's Scottish Privy Council, and also Commander-in-Chief, residing at Dalkeith House, and at the head of Cromwell's Administration of Scotland in 1654, v. 86-7, 96, 115, 139, 162, 163; one of Cromwell's Lords, v. 323; virtual Vice-Protector in Scotland, v. 349-50; his paper of advices to Richard Cromwell, v. 419-20; supports

Richard, v. 421, 438, 459; his Letter of Adhesion for himself and the Scottish Army to the Government of the Restored Rump, v. 461, 463, 464; at the Reofficering of the Army by the Restored Rump, v. 470; in the projected Royalist Insurrection in 1659, v. 473; in intrigues at Dalkeith, v. 475-7; references to, v. 488, 489, 490; passage in a letter of, to Speaker Lenthall from Edinburgh, Oct. 20, 1659, v. 496; declares himself the champion of the Rump Government against the Wallingford House Party, v. 496-7; resolutions of the Committee of Safety concerning, v. 497; negotiations of the Committee with, in prospect of an invasion of England by, v. 497-501; treaty of the Wallingford House Council of Officers with Monk's Commissioners in London, v. 509; is absent from the Army and Navy Representative Council summoned in accordance with that Treaty, v. 510; advances with his Army to Coldstream on the Tweed, v. 512-14; gratitude of the Second Restored Rump Government to, v. 520; relations between the Parliament of the Rump and Monk, v. 524; advances from Coldstream towards London, v. 524-5; is at St. Albans, v. 526-8; in London, v. 528-32; his part in the clash between the Rump and the City of London, v. 533; reduces the City, v. 533-4; makes his peace with the City and breaks with the Parliament, v. 534-6; on the occasion of the "Roasting of the Rump," v. 536; the House endeavours to negotiate with, v. 536-8; takes the direction of affairs into his own hands, v. 539; Milton's Private Letter to, v. 637-42, 644-57; the reseating of the Secluded Members and reconstitution of the Long Parliament by, v. 539-41, 541 note, 546; appointment of, to be Captain-General and Commander-in-Chief under the Parliament of all the land forces of England, Scotland, and Ireland, v. 540, 548, 644; his announcements to the Army and to

the Secluded Members, v. 540-1, 541 note; at the head of the new Council of State, v. 543, 544, 546-7; is conjoined with Montague in the Commandership of the Fleet, v. 548; his part in the reconstitution by the Parliament of the House of Lords, v. 552-3; his Council of State sits on, with full executive powers, after the Dissolution of the Long Parliament on April 6, 1660, v. 554; his co-workers in the Council, v. 544-6; is appointed Major-General and Commander-in-Chief of the Militia of London, v. 555; declines the offer of sovereignty made to him by the Rumpers, v. 556; is in communication with Charles II., v. 558-61; his manipulation of the Army, v. 561-4; defeats the last efforts of the Republicans, v. 564-7; enthusiastic "Declaration" of the London Royalists in favour of Monk, v. 567-8; a sermon of Dr. Griffith dedicated to, and Milton's *Notes* on the same, v. 667-9, 675-7; in various items of Council business immediately previous to the Restoration, v. 669-73; vi. 5; delivery of the Breda Letters of Charles II. to, v. 694-8; in the first week of the Restoration, v. 698-700; honours to, at the arrival of Charles II. in England, vi. 8; in the Royal Progress to London, vi. 8-10; in the Privy Council of Charles II., vi. 17; created Duke of Albemarle, vi. 17, 25; in the *Junto* or Cabinet, vi. 19; in the Convention Parliament, vi. 23, 25; his advice to Charles on the construction of the *Declaration of Indemnity*, vi, 25; action of, in the progress through the Commons of the Indemnity Bill, vi. 38; in the business of disbanding the Puritan Army of the English Revolution and his retention of three regiments of the same, vi. 76, 76 note; on the Commission for the Trials of the Regicides, vi. 77, 78; in a special Conference, in the King's presence, over the Royal *Ecclesiastical Declaration*, vi. 99; is godfather to the infant son of the Duke of York, vi.

119; suppresses the Venner Riot, vi. 120; his request that the body of Pride (of "Pride's Purge") be left undisturbed at the disinterring of the Regicides, vi. 123; his part in the civil government of Ireland, vi. 126-7; in the Scottish Privy Council sitting in London, vi. 131, 139; at the Coronation of Charles II., vi. 152; remains in London during the Plague of 1665, vi. 258; mentions of, during the war with the Dutch from May 1664 to July 1667, vi. 254, 260, 263, 266, 268; mentioned in Dryden's *Annus Mirabilis* (published in 1667), vi. 376-7; on a Commission of Five, appointed to the Office of the Treasury at the death of the Earl of Southampton in 1667, vi. 264; in the Cabal Administration after the Fall of Clarendon, vi. 562; death of, in 1670, vi. 563.

MONK, Rev. Mr. Nicholas, brother of the General, and minister of Kilhampton in Cornwall, v. 476, 490; Bishop of Hereford in 1660, vi. 118.

MONMOUTH, Henry Carey, 2nd Earl of, in the Royalist Army (1642), ii. 428.

MONMOUTH, James Fitzroy, Duke of, son of Lucy Waters or Barlow and Charles II. (" Mr. James Crofts"), vi. 71; marriage of, in 1663, to Anne Scott, Countess of Buccleuch, vi. 248-9, 604.

MONOPOLIES, various, abolished by the Long Parliament in 1640, ii. 188.

MONRO, Major-General Sir George, Scottish officer in the "First Bishops' War," ii. 55, 64, 137; in Ireland with a Scottish force, ii. 417; in the "Episode of Montrose," iii. 360, 366, 517, 518, 597, 604, 620-1.

"MONS MEG": see "*Mounce Meg*."

MONSON, William, Lord (Regicide), in the Restored Rump, v. 454; mentioned in *Treason Arraigned* (1660) (spelt *Mounson*), v. 666; one of the Judges of the King in 1649, vi. 36; in the Indemnity Bill (1660), vi. 37, 44, 55, 224; carted from the Tower to Tyburn, vi. 228.

MONTAGUE of Boughton, Lord (Royalist), brother of the Earl of Manchester, deceased in 1644, ii. 429.

MONTAGUE, Francis Brown, 3rd Viscount, ii. 430; in the House of Lords, iii. 297 note, 377, 510, 541, 555 note, 579, 692; at the abolition of the House of Lords in February, 1648-1649, iv. 4.

MONTAGUE, Sir Edward, Chief-Justice in the reign of Henry VIII., i. 377.

MONTAGUE, Edward (Admiral of the Fleet in 1656, and Earl of Sandwich in 1660): as Colonel in the New Model Army, iii. 326, 336, 402, 542; called to Cromwell's Supreme Assembly, iv. 501; in Barebones Parliament and Council, iv. 506, 525; in Council of the First Protectorate, iv. 545, 545 note, 575; v. 31, 47, 64, 117, 183-4; as Admiral of the Fleet, v. 47-8, 113-14, 141; in Cromwell's Second Parliament, v. 107, 108, 128, 129, 141; at Cromwell's Second Installation, v. 149; in the Council of the Second Protectorate, v. 308, 311; Chief Admiral after the death of Blake, v. 310, 311, 340; one of Cromwell's Lords, v. 323; in the Council of Cromwell after the Dissolution of Parliament, v. 333, 381; supports Richard's Government, v. 417-18, 421; sails with his fleet to the Baltic, v. 435, 459-60, 463, 464, 467, 473; returns from the Baltic to London, and is under suspicion of joining in a Royalist revolt, v. 478; in the Council of State of the Restored Long Parliament of 1660, v. 544, 548; with his Fleet in the Thames, v. 558 and note, 561, 563, 564, 697, 699-700; at the Restoration, vi. 5-9, 17; created Earl of Sandwich, vi. 18; in the Convention Parliament, vi. 23, 25, 77; at the King's Coronation, vi. 151, 157; at the marriage of Charles II. and Catherine of Braganza, vi. 229; in the War with the Dutch, vi. 252-5, 260; killed in 1672, vi. 583.

MONTAGUE, Edward: see Manchester, 2nd Earl of.

MONTAGUE, Henry: see Manchester, 1st Earl of.

MONTAGUE, Dr. Richard, as Bishop of Chichester, i. 214, 369, 373, 389; as Bishop of Norwich in 1638, i. 674, 677, 684, 685; ii. 150-1; death of, in 1641, ii. 324.

MONTAGUE, Sir Sidney, father of Admiral Montague, iii. 326.

MONTAGUE, Stephen, servant of the Council, v. 625.

MONTAGUE, Walter (younger son of the Earl of Manchester), M.A. of Cambridge in 1626-7, i. 182; a Roman Catholic convert, i. 685; ii. 50, 156.

MONTAIGNE, i. 527.

MONTALVAN, Juan Perez de, Spanish author, v. 263.

MONTEAGLE, Anne, Lady: see Spencer, Anne.

MONTEAGLE, William Stanley, Lord, i. 493-4, 591.

MONTGOMERY, Philip Herbert, 1st Earl of: see Pembroke and Montgomery.

MONTGOMERY, Roger de, founder of Ludlow Castle, i. 606.

MONTREUIL, French Ambassador to the Court of Charles I. in 1646; in negotiations for the king with the Scots, iii. 372-3, 375, 414; sent to negotiate for the reception of Charles among the Scots, iii. 493.

MONTROSE, James Graham, Earl, and afterwards Marquis, of: joins in the Scottish struggle against Episcopacy, i. 710, 724; signs the Scottish National Covenant in 1638, i. 732; as an acting chief of the Covenanters, ii. 14, 16, 22; in the "First Bishops' War," ii. 56, 60, 65, 71; his part in the treasonable letter to Louis XIV. discovered, ii. 130; in the Committee of Estates in June 1640, ii. 292; in the "Second Bishops' War," ii. 138; his change of policy in 1641, ii. 293-5; discovered in the plot, called the Merchiston House Compact, against Argyle, ii. 295-300; his MS. Essay on Government, ii. 296-8; committed to the Castle of Edinburgh, ii. 300-1, 303, 304, 305; liberated on

security, ii. 307; iii. 340; among the "malcontents" in 1642; ii. 417; account of the "Episode of Montrose" in Scotland in 1644-5, iii. 340-69; retrospect in 1645 of the career of, since 1641, iii. 340-4; his plan for rousing Scotland on behalf of King Charles I., iii. 341-5; his victorious generalship in Scotland through 1644, iii. 345-55; defeats Argyle at the Battle of Inverlochy, Feb. 2nd, 1644-5, iii. 355-7; his rebellion discussed in the Scottish Parliament, iii. 357-8; his "fiery progress" continued towards the north, iii. 358-9; three more victories—of Auldearn, Alford, and Kilsyth,—iii. 359-61; sets up his head-quarters at Bothwell, near Glasgow, iii. 361-2; review of his political intentions, founded upon his Manifesto for the Parliament, iii. 363-5; feelings in England over the news of his triumph, iii. 366; is defeated by David Leslie at Philiphaugh, iii. 367-9, 370, 371; in hiding in the Highlands, iii. 414; Charles I.'s continued hope in, during the Newcastle negotiations, iii. 414, 414 note, 417, 421, 498; disbands his army at the close of the Civil War and goes to Norway, iii. 498; joins Charles II. at the Hague in 1649, iv. 25-6; his part in breaking off the treaty of the King with the Presbyterians, iv. 28-9, 31, 49, 181; is appointed by Charles II. Lieutenant-Governor and Captain-General of Scotland, and his Ambassador-Extraordinary to the northern Foreign Powers, iv. 181; his disastrous Expedition to Scotland in 1649, resulting in his capture, trial, and execution at Edinburgh, iv. 181-8; mention of his head in a letter to Milton, iv. 492-3; fate of his remains in 1661, vi. 145.

MOORE, David, husband of Ann Agar, vi. 772-5.

MOORE, Edmund, son of Sir Thomas Moore, vi. 775.

MOORE, John (Regicide), signs the death-warrant, iii. 720; is dead in 1660, vi. 28; in the Indemnity Bill, vi. 54.

MOORE (spelt Moor), Thomas, a weaver of Wisbeach and Lynn, and a preacher in Cromwell's Army, iii. 385.

MOORE, Sir Thomas, son of David Moore, vi. 773-5.

MORAY HOUSE (in Edinburgh), iii. 622; iv. 201.

MORAY, James Stewart, 2nd Earl of, i. 707.

MORAY, James Stewart, 3rd Earl of, i. 707; ii. 15; iv. 561.

•MORAY, Sir Robert, one of the founders of the Royal Society, and its first President, iii. 429 note; vi. 394, 396, 458-9.

MORDAUNT, Mr. John (brother of the 2nd Earl of Peterborough), in Royalist plots, v. 337, 472, 474, 477, 541 note.

MORDAUNT, Lord, afterwards 3rd Earl of Peterborough, subscriber to the fourth edition of Paradise Lost, vi.785.

MORDINGTON, James Douglas, 1st Lord, in Cromwell's Ordinance of Pardon and Grace, iv. 560.

MORE, Mr., a member of the Westminster Assembly, ii. 520.

MORE, Alexander : see Morus.

MORE, Alexander (father of the Platonist), i. 248.

MORE, Dr. Henry (the Platonist), i. 248, 250, 648, 649, 651; ii. 76, 401 note; his early life, sketched by himself, i. 249-50; under the Protectorate, v. 74, 75; after the Restoration, vi. 299, 302-6, 322, 388, 418, 617.

MORE, Roger (Rory O'More), in the Irish Insurrection, ii. 309, 312.

MORE, Stephen, Independent pastor, ii. 588.

MORE, Sir Thomas, references to, i. 73, 514.

MORE, William, fellow-student of Milton at Cambridge, i. 171, 653.

MORETO, Spanish dramatist, vi. 357.

MORGAN, Thomas, Major-General, iv. 552; Governor of Mardike, v. 340; at the capture of Ypres, v. 416; knighted by Richard, v. 416 note; at the Republican remodelling of the Army, v. 470; with Monk, v. 499, 525, 564; vi. 132.

MORISON of Prestongrange, Sir George, in Cromwell's Ordinance of Pardon and Grace, iv. 561.

MORLAND, Samuel, Commissioner from Cromwell to Louis XIV. and the Duke of Savoy respecting the Piedmontese Massacre, v. 42-4, 186, 188 note, 190-1 ; agent in Switzerland, v. 244, 294 ; dishonourable conduct of, v. 557 and note ; v. 624, 625 note ; vi. 74, 199, 730.

MORLEY, Dr. George (Royalist and Latitudinarian), i. 533, 534-5 ; his appointment to the Westminster Assembly cancelled, ii. 520, 525 ; at the Treaty of Newport, iii. 609 ; iv. 225 note ; under the Protectorate, v. 76 ; after the Restoration, vi. 61, 99, 100 ; made Bishop of Worcester in 1660, vi. 105 ; at the Coronation of Charles II., vi. 154 ; marries a daughter of Izaak Walton, vi. 293 ; further references to, vi. 318, 425, 428-30, 430, 432 ; made Bishop of Winchester, vi. 437-8 ; his part in the Church policy of the Cabal, vi. 566.

MORLEY, Colonel Herbert, in successive Councils of State of the Commonwealth, iv. 177, 224, 225, 229, 230, 309-10, 354, 355, 449 ; in the Restored Rump and in the new Council of State, v. 454, 456, 465, 470, 490-1 ; in the Second Restored Rump and Council, v. 495, 504-5, 514, 519, 520, 522, 523, 529, 537 ; in the Restored Long Parliament and Council, v. 543, 545.

MORLEY, Thomas, musical composer, i. 51.

MORLEY AND MOUNTEAGLE, Lord (Royalist), ii. 429.

MORPHIE, Laird of, i. 732.

MORRICE, William (afterwards Sir William), in the Restored Long Parliament, v. 545-6, 559; Governor of Plymouth, v. 563 ; in the Privy Council of, and Secretary of State to Charles II., vi. 9, 18, 19 ; knighted, vi. 74 ; in the Convention Parliament, vi. 23, 24, 40, 77, 89, 110; his possible connexion with Milton's escape in 1660, vi. 185,

187, 189 ; at the fall of Clarendon, vi. 271, 562-3 ; and the Newspaper Press, vi. 331 ; is a booklicenser, vi. 398 note, 514.

MORRIS (Royalist), Commander of the Castle of Pontefract, iii. 623.

MORTALISTS or MATERIALISTS, sect of, iii. 156-7 ; v. 15.

MORTIMER, Hugh de, Lord of Wigmore, i. 607.

MORTIMER'S CROSS, Battle of, i. 607.

MORTLOCK, Henry, bookseller and publisher, vi. 403, 625-6.

MORTON, Dr. Thomas, Bishop of Durham, i. 389, 390, 400, 684 ; ii. 124, 151, 225 ; his part in the Protest of Lord Keeper Williams, ii. 334-6 and note ; iii. 196-7, 217.

MORTON, William Douglas, 9th Earl of : High Treasurer of Scotland till 1635, i. 706 ; father-in-law of the 7th Earl of Argyle, ii. 11, 15, 303, 418 ; iv. 182-3.

MORTON, Countess of, in the service of the family of Charles I., iii. 375.

MORTON, William, a member of Westminster Assembly, ii. 520.

MORUS, Aaron, iv. 459.

MORUS, Alexander, Professor of Greek at Geneva, i. 832 ; believed by Milton to be the author of Regii Sanguinis Clamor, iv. 453 ; abstract of the Clamor, with illustrative passages, iv. 453-8 ; account of Morus at Geneva and at Middleburg, and of his connexions with the family of Salmasius, iv. 459-64 ; foreign gossip about, iv. 464-5 ; Milton's reception of the Clamor, iv. 466-9 ; and his projected reply, iv. 474; more gossip about, from abroad, iv. 474-6; Milton's attack, in the Defensio Secunda, on Morus as the reputed author of the Clamor, iv. 584-90, 593-7 ; the question of the authorship under discussion with Milton and his friends, iv. 626-8 ; more gossip concerning Morus, now Professor of Sacred History in Amsterdam, iv. 628-30 ; his alarm at the publication of the Defensio Secunda, iv. 630-4 ; Ulac's edition at the Hague of Milton's Defensio Secunda, with the Fides Publica of Morus annexed,

v. 150 - 6; account of the *Fides Publica*, with quoted passages, v. 156-62, 166-7, 171-2, 192; Morus publishes a *Supplementum* to the *Fides Publica*, v. 192-3; account of the *Supplementum*, v. 193-8; Milton replies to this in his *Pro Se Defensio*, v. 198-212; references to literary authorities concerning the life and career of Morus, v. 212-3 note; the question of the true authorship of the *Clamor* again discussed, v. 213-25; conclusion of the Morus Controversy, v. 225; mentioned by Milton in a letter to Oldenburg (Aug. 1657), v. 367; leaves Amsterdam and becomes one of the ministers of the Protestant Church of Charenton, near Paris, v. 368-70; is in disgrace with the Walloon Synod, v. 633; references to, in letters of Milton, v. 634-5; confirmed in his ministry at Charenton by the decision of the Synod of Loudun in 1659, vi. 419; account of his great reputation for pulpit oratory at Paris, vi. 419-20; visits London in 1661, vi. 421-2; returns to Paris in June 1662, and dies in Sept. 1670, vi. 422-3.

MOSELEY, actor, vi. 350.

MOSELEY, Anne, wife of Humphrey Mòseley, vi. 403, 404, 515.

MOSELEY, Anne, daughter of the above, vi. 403.

MOSELEY, Edward, iv. 364; v. 86.

MOSELEY, Humphrey, bookseller of London, account of, iii. 448-51 and notes; publishes the first edition of Milton's Poems in Jan. 1645-6, iii. 450-1, 455-8, vi. 647; publishes Cowley's Poems, v. 83; further account of, in the London book trade of 1656, v. 257-8; after the Restoration, vi. 352.

MOSSE, Francis, scrivener, i. 339 note.

MOSSE, Colonel Richard, v. 470, 490-1; at the Second Restoration of the Rump, v. 517, 522; at the Restoration of the Long Parliament, v. 540.

MOSTON, Baptist minister, ii. 581.

MOUCHERON, one of the savants of Queen Christina's Court, iv. 344.

MOULE, J., bookseller, iv. 246.

MOULTON, Anne, daughter of Robert Moulton, and wife of Richard Powell, ii. 493 : see *Powell*, Mrs.

MOULTON, Robert, of Honyborne in Worcestershire, ii. 493.

"MOUNCE (MONS) MEG," firing of the old gun of that name, on Edinburgh Castle on the occasion of the Restoration in 1660, vi. 11-2 note.

MOUNSON : see *Monson*.

MOUNTAIN, Dr., Bishop of London in 1625-6, i. 157-8, 371.

MOUNTNORRIS, Sir Francis Annesley, Earl of (Viscount Valentia), account of, in 1635, i. 695; his son, Arthur Annesley, v. 545.

MOUNTRATH, Earl of : see *Coote*, Sir Charles.

MOWBRAY AND MALTRAVERS, Lord, son of the Earl of Arundel, ii. 429.

MOYER, Samuel, in the Interim Council of Thirteen, iv. 498 note, 499; called to Cromwell's Supreme Assembly, iv. 501; in the Barebones Parliament, iv. 506, 514.

MOYSLEY, Dr., Vicar of Newark, his visit to Scotland, ii. 60-1.

"MUCKLE - JOHN," Court fool to Charles I., ii. 6 note.

MUDDIMAN, Henry, journalist, v. 672; vi. 202, 325, 331.

MUGGLETON, Frederick, chief of the sect of Muggletonians, v. 19-20.

MULCASTER, Richard, master at St. Paul's School, i. 78; iii. 242 note.

MULGRAVE, Edward Sheffield, 1st Earl of, ii. 142; in the Long Parliament, ii. 158; death of, ii. 430; his son, James Sheffield, ii. 445.

MULGRAVE, Edmund Sheffield, 2nd Earl of, iii. 555 note; in the last days of Charles I., iii. 692; at the abolition of the House of Lords, iv. 4; in the First Council of State of the Commonwealth, iv. 12; in the Second Council of State, iv. 177; in the Council of the First Protectorate, iv. 545; v. 5, 31, 64, 183-4, 259; in the Council of the Second Protectorate, v. 303, 305, 308, 322; one of Cromwell's Lords, v. 323, 326, 333, 346-7; death of, v. 417 note.

MULGRAVE, Sheffield, Earl of : *his*

Essay on Poetry, in 1682, vi. 782-3.

MUNDAY, Anthony, dramatist, i. 445.

MUNDEN, Thomas, Baptist preacher, iii. 148.

MURE of Rowallan, Sir William, author of a MS. version of the Psalms in 1643-4, iii. 27 and note.

MURILLO, mentioned, i. 745.

MURRAY of Polmaise, iv. 561.

MURRAY of Stanhope, iv. 561.

MURRAY, Lieutenant-Colonel (Royalist), ii. 442.

MURRAY, Thomas, Provost of Eton, i. 536.

MURRAY, Dr. William, Bishop of Llandaff, i. 389.

MURRAY, William, brother of the Earl of Tullibardine, iii. 368.

MURRAY, William or Will, attendant on Charles I., ii. 306; iii. 501-2, 504.

MURTON, John, Early Baptist, ii. 544, 581; iii. 103, 114, 147.

MUSCKLE, Richard, a weaver living, with his wife, in Aldersgate Street, ii. 207.

MUSCOVY, the Czar of, see *Russia*.

MUSGRAVE, Sir Philip (Royalist), iii. 591, 593.

MUSIC, for references to, see under *Davenant, Dowland, Lawes, Milton* (John, senior), *Morley* (Thomas).

MUSKERRY, Lord, in the Royalist movement in Ireland, iv. 23, 303; killed, vi. 254.

MYLIUS, Hermann, Envoy from the Count of Oldenburg to the English Republic, and a correspondent of Milton, iv. 351, 379, 416-8, 481; v. 705; vi. 723.

MYLTON and MYTTON : see *Milton*.

"MYSTERIES OF LOVE AND ELOQUENCE," by Edward Phillips in 1658, v. 383.

N

NAISMYTH, Mr. James, Scottish minister, vi. 134.

NAPIER, Archibald, 1st Lord, Scottish Privy Councillor, i. 707, 709; ii. 15; one of the Scottish Committee of Estates, ii. 292; his part in the Montrose plots against Argyle, ii. 295, 301, 307; at the outbreak of the English Civil War, ii. 417; through the "Episode of Montrose" in Scotland, iii. 341, 362, 363, 365, 366, 367; death of, iii. 368.

NAPIER, Archibald, 2nd Lord, as master of Napier, iii. 367; in correspondence with Charles II., iv. 182; excepted from Cromwell's Ordinance of Pardon and Grace, iv. 560.

NAPIER, Captain, a Scotsman in London, ii. 44, 45.

NAPIER, John, of Merchiston, the Inventor of Logarithms, i. 707.

NAPLES, i. 745.

NASEBY, the Battle of, iii. 335-7.

NASH, Thomas, dramatist, i. 592.

NASSAU, Count of, iv. 572-3.

"NATURA BREVIUM," by Fitz-Herbert, account of a copy of, which belonged to Milton, i. 327 note.

"NATURAM NON PATI SENIUM," account of Milton's Latin verses so entitled, with translation, i. 200-3; subsequent references to, i. 305, 782.

NAUDET, French scholar, iv. 269.

NAUNTON, Sir Robert, i. 381.

NAVIGATION ACT, the, against the Dutch, iv. 305, 371-2.

NAVY, the English, iv. 499, 502, 507, 562; v. 35, 471, 510, 548, 564; vi. 57-8, 254; see under *Blake, Monk, Montague*.

NAYLER, James, Early Quaker, v. 26-7; his fanatical outbreak, v. 68; his trial, and tortures inflicted upon, for blasphemy, v. 116-8; Cromwell's visit to, and care of, during his imprisonment, v. 317, 350; his release from prison, v. 479.

NEAL, John, Parliamentarian officer, ii. 445.

NEEDHAM, Marchamont (London journalist), account of his life and of his connexions with journals as far as to the year 1649, iv. 37-9; in trouble with the Commonwealth Government for his *Mercurius Pragmaticus*, iv. 89, 93; has escaped from custody, and order for his rearrest, iv. 146; discharged from custody, and reconciled

to the Commonwealth, iv. 149-50, 155 - 6 ; commences the Government paper called *Mercurius Politicus*, iv. 226-7 ; another literary commission to, iv. 229 ; Milton associated with him in the *Mercurius Politicus*, as Censor and superintending Editor in 1651, iv. 325 - 35 ; further history of the *Mercurius Politicus*, iv. 432-3 and notes ; edits the *Public Intelligencer*, v. 52 ; mention of, among Men of Letters under the Protectorate, v. 75, 77 ; his pension, v. 177 - 9, 181 - 2 ; among Milton's visitors in Petty France, v. 230 ; pamphlet of, in behalf of Cromwell's Established Church, v. 316-7 ; in connexion with the proposed restrictions of the Press, v. 352 ; legacy to, by President Bradshaw, v. 630 ; on the eve of the Restoration, v. 659, 665, 666, 670-2, 674 ; in exile, v. 702-3 ; vi. 200-2 and note ; mentions of, among Men of Letters of the Restoration, vi. 165, 299, 308 ; is living in London as a medical practitioner, vi. 452.

NEEDHAM, Ralph, publisher, vi. 515.

NEILE, Sir Paul, member of the Royal Society of London in 1662, vi. 392, 394, 396.

NEILE, Dr. Richard, Bishop, successively, of Rochester, i. 359, of Lincoln, i. 359, of Durham, i. 158-9, 361, 369, and of Worcester, i. 215, 377 ; in the Privy Council of Charles I., i. 371, 372, 374, 377, 390, 392 ; in Star Chamber votes, i. 385 ; Archbishop of York, i. 390, 399 ; in prosecutions by the Star Chamber, i. 405, 677 ; raises money for the King in the " First Bishops' War," ii. 49 ; death of, ii. 150, 324.

NELSON, Lieut.-Colonel, his evidence on the trial of the Regicide Axtell, vi. 88-9.

NELTHORPE, James, in the Restored Rump, v. 454.

NETHERLANDS, Spanish, account of, in 1638, i. 746.

" NEUTRALS," the, one of the Scottish parties of 1646, iii. 417, 498.

NEVILL, Mr., fellow-commoner of St. John's, Cambridge, i. 262.

NEVILLE, Henry, in the Fourth Council of the Commonwealth, iv. 354, 423-4 ; in Richard Cromwell's Parliament, v. 430, 432, 436 ; in the Restored Rump, v. 454 ; and its Council, v. 456, 465, 466, 479, 480, 488 ; member of the Rota Club, v. 483, 485 ; during the Wallingford House Interregnum, v. 495, 497, 505, 512, 514 ; at the Second Restoration of the Rump, v. 519, 520, 523, 537 ; not in the Restored Long Parliament of the Secluded Members, v. 544 and note ; mentioned in a letter of Milton, v. 705 ; mention of, among Men of Letters of the Restoration, vi, 299, 308.

" NEW ATLAS," the : several volumes of the book entitled, purchased by Thurloe for use of the Council in their foreign business in 1655, v. 46-7.

" NEW CHAINS DISCOVERED," pamphlet so entitled, iv. 43-4, 87.

NEW ENGLAND, in America : history of the early Puritan Church of, from 1620 to 1640, i. 428 - 31 ; ii. 545-77 ; from 1640 to 1643, ii. 599-602 ; during the Protectorate, v. 101-2.

NEW MODEL ARMY, see under *Army (English Parliamentarian)*.

" NEW WORLD OF WORDS," dictionary so called, by Edward Phillips, v. 383.

NEWARK, King Charles at, ii. 354 ; siege of, by Auxiliary Scottish Army, iii. 371 ; King's arrival at, and surrender to the Scottish Army, iii. 373-4.

NEWBERY, Battle of, iii. 35 ; Second Battle of, iii. 177.

NEWBURGH, Edward Barret (or Barrett), Lord, i. 380 ; ii. 152, 278, 281, 283, 337 ; iii. 702.

NEWBURGH, Sir James Livingston, Viscount, iv. 212, 560 ; vi. 142 note.

NEWBURN, the Fight of, ii. 140-1.

NEWCASTLE, town of : in the " First Bishops' War," ii. 43 ; the King at, ii. 58-62 ; in the " Second Bishops' War," ii. 135, 140 ; taken by the Scottish Covenanting Army, ii. 141 ; Charles I. captive with the

Scottish Army at, iii. 411-8; negotiations with him at, iii. 496-510; Charles left at, in charge of the English Commissioners, iii. 510.

NEWCASTLE, Sir William Cavendish, Earl, Marquis, and 1st Duke of, i. 436, 438, 621; in the "First Bishops' War," ii. 47, 62; in the Long Parliament, ii. 152, 279, 281, 283; with the King after his break with the Parliament, ii. 350, 413; in the Civil War, ii. 428; his daughter married to Viscount Brackley, ii. 430; iii. 462; his regiment in the King's Army, ii. 442; in possession of Newcastle, as Royalist Governor of that town, ii. 443, 467, 468; defeats Lord Fairfax at Atherston Moor, iii. 6; defends York against siege by the Parliamentarian forces, iii. 86; assists Montrose with supplies of men and arms, iii. 345; shares in the defeat at Marston Moor, and escapes to the Continent, iii. 96; named among the Delinquents to Parliament, iii. 421; in the Convention Parliament, vi. 22; at the Coronation of Charles II., vi. 152; raised to the Dukedom, vi. 313; mentioned among Men of Letters of the Restoration, vi. 313, 356.

NEWCASTLE, Margaret, Marchioness, and afterwards Duchess, of (second wife of the preceding), account of, among writers of the Restoration, vi. 313.

NEWCOME, Thomas, printer, iv. 146, 147, 325, 433, 581; v. 52, 405, 572, 581 and note; vi. 167 note, 202 and note, 325, 331, 332, 399.

NEWCOMEN, Matthew, minister of Oldham in Essex, ii. 202; one of the authors of the Smectymnuus book, ii. 219; a member of the Westminster Assembly, ii. 520, 605; iii. 20, 160, 170; after the Restoration, vi. 63; among the ejected Nonconformists of 1662, vi. 232 note, 416.

NEWDEGATE, John, i. 603 note.

NEWDEGATE, Sir Richard, of Arbury, i. 603 note.

NEWDEGATE, Richard, Parliamentarian officer, ii. 445.

NEWMANN, John, fellow-graduate of Milton at Cambridge, i. 258.

NEWPORT, Isle of Wight, Treaty of: see Treaty.

NEWPORT, Earl of (Royalist), ii. 62, 128, 428; arrested under the Protectorate, v. 50; in the Cabal Administration for Charles II., vi. 563.

NEWRY, Irish Insurgent camp stationed at, ii. 311.

NEWSCORE, William, member of Westminster Assembly, ii. 520.

NEWSPAPERS: of the Civil War, iii. 271 note; London weekly papers in 1648-9, iv. 37-9 and note; in Bradshaw's Press Act, iv. 117; censorship of the Press in 1649, iv. 324-35; regulation of the Press by Cromwell in 1655, v. 51-2; newspaper press of the Restoration, vi. 324-32: see also under Needham and Press.

"NEW STYLE" of dating, see "Old Style."

NEWTON, Bishop, references to his Life of Milton and Milton researches, i. 11; vi. 760-1 and note.

NEWTON, Sir Isaac, story of, in his boyhood, v. 358; as Fellow of the Royal Society, vi. 619.

NICHOLAS, Edward, Clerk of the Council to Charles I., ii. 47; in the Long Parliament, ii. 159, 279, 283, 320; becomes Secretary of State and is knighted, ii. 336, 337; with Charles after his break with the Parliament, ii. 345, 350, 413; named as a "Delinquent" by Parliament, iii. 421; in exile, iii. 494, 591; in correspondence with Ormond in Ireland, iv. 131; in the negotiations between Monk and Charles II., v. 560; in the Privy Council and Cabinet of Charles II. after the Restoration, vi. 18, 19; on the commission for the trials of the Regicides, vi. 77; one of the Scottish Council in London, vi. 131-142 note; incidents of his Secretaryship of State for Charles II., vi. 113, 227; retires from the Secretaryship, vi. 237; mentions of, in connexion with the

Eikon Basilike and Milton's *Eikono-klastes*, iv. 131; vi. 188, 204, 432.

NICHOLAS, Judge, seized at Salisbury in a Royalist rising in March 1654-5, v. 34.

NICHOLAS, Robert, one of the Restored Rump, v. 454, 544 note.

NICHOLLS, John, jun., v. 814.

NICHOLS, Anthony, iii. 548-9.

NICOLAI, N., City Clerk of Amsterdam, v. 196.

NICOLSON, William, nominated to the Westminster Assembly, ii. 520, 525; Bishop of Gloucester, vi. 118.

NIEUPORT, Lord, Dutch Ambassador, iv. 502; his reception by Cromwell, iv. 572-3; in the Morus Controversy, iv. 632; v. 158, 202; is in London, v. 312; State letter of commendation of, v. 377-8; in London again, v. 399-402, 502.

NIEUPORT, Lady, iv. 572-3.

NIEUPORT jun., son of the Ambassador, v. 399-400.

"NINETEEN PROPOSITIONS," the, embodying the terms required by the Parliament of Charles I. in July 1646, iii. 420-2, 422 note, 493, 497, 498, 499, 504-6, 507, 509, 529, 539, 559-60, 564, 580-1.

NISBET, Sir Henry, iv. 561.

NISBET, Sir Philip, iii. 367, 368.

NITHSDALE, Robert Maxwell, 2nd Earl of, iii. 421.

NIVEN, John, merchant of Londonderry, v. 372.

"NO BLIND GUIDES," an attack on Milton in 1660, v. 689-90; vi. 480.

NOKES, James, actor, vi. 350, 351, 369.

NOKES, Robert, actor, vi. 350.

NONCONFORMISTS: ejection from their livings of a great body of the Nonconforming clergymen of the Church of England on St. Bartholomew's Day 1662, vi. 231-6, 234 note; as affected by the terms of the King's Toleration Edict, vi. 241-5; relaxation of severities against the, in 1667-70, vi. 563-64, 566-7; royal Declaration of Religious Indulgence for, vi. 586-90.

NORFOLKE, James, sergeant-at-arms, vi. 113, 192-5.

NORGATE, Mr. Edward, clerk to Secretary Coke during the First Bishops' War, ii. 61, 69, 70.

NORRIS, an actor, vi. 350.

NORRIS, an actress, vi. 350.

NORRIS, Sir William, i. 627.

NORTH, Lord (of Kirtling), i. 122; ii. 142, 172, 431; Lord-Lieutenant of Cambridgeshire in 1642, ii. 439; in the House of Peers, iii. 297 note, 406, 555 note, 692.

NORTH, Sir Dudley (son of Lord North of Kirtling), i. 122; in the Long Parliament, ii. 172.

NORTH, Arthur, vi. 433 note.

NORTH, Sir Roger, iii. 510 note.

NORTHAMPTON, William Compton, 2nd Earl of, i. 605; ii. 48, 428, 463.

NORTHAMPTON, James Compton, 3rd Earl of, iii. 331; v. 50, 473, 505.

NORTHESK, Sir John Carnegie of Ethie (Lord Lour), 1st Earl of, v. 706.

NORTHUMBERLAND, Algernon Percy, Earl of, i. 751; ii. 24, 48, 128, 136, 152, 159, 180, 279, 281, 430, 439, 464, 523; iii. 41, 279 note, 375, 380, 405-6, 555 note, 556, 605, 692; iv. 4; v. 695; vi. 18, 151.

NORTHUMBERLAND, George Fitzroy, Earl and afterwards Duke of, son of Charles II. and the Duchess of Cleveland, vi. 604.

NORTON, a publisher, vi. 403.

NORTON, Sir Gregory (Regicide), iii. 720; vi. 28; after the Restoration, vi. 54, 179 note.

NORTON, John, of King's College, Cambridge, i. 154.

NORTON, John, New England minister, ii. 557-8.

NORTON, Colonel Richard, iii. 327, 402; iv. 355, 506; v. 108, 478, 544; vi. 23.

NORTON, T., verses by, on the death of Edward King, i. 654-5.

NORWAY, in 1638, i. 747: see also under *Sweden and Norway*.

NORWICH, Earl of: see *Goring*, Lord.

NORWICH, psalm tune of that name by Milton's father, i. 52.

NORWOOD, Mr., attacked for heresy by the London booksellers, v. 59 note.

NOTTINGHAM, Charles Howard, 1st Earl of, i. 51.

NOTTINGHAM, Charles Howard, 2nd Earl of, ii. 48, 430.

NOTTINGHAM, Charles Howard, 3rd Earl of (half-brother of the preceding), ii. 430 and note ; iii. 297 note, 376, 406, 555 note, 549, 692; at the abolition of the House of Peers, iv. 4.

NOVA SCOTIA (Acadie), v. 102.

NOY, Attorney-General, i. 580, 581, 670, 682.

NUNAPPLETON HOUSE, home of Fairfax in Yorkshire, iv. 194-6.

NUNNELLY, Richard, vi. 86.

NUTT, John, in the Restored Rump, v. 454.

NUTT, Richard, bargeman to the Council, v. 179 ; his salary, v. 625 and note.

NYE, Henry, elected to the Westminster Assembly, brother of Philip Nye, ii. 520.

NYE, Philip, ii. 368 note ; pastor at Arnheim (1638-40) ; ii. 578, 580 ; minister of Kimbolton parish, in Huntingdonshire (1640-1), ii. 585, 591 ; member of the Westminster Assembly (1642), ii. 520, 605 ; iii. 8 ; as an Independent, iii. 9, 22, 23, 87, 111, 127-9, 131, 149, 157, 161, 286, 298, 391, 392 ; accompanies the Commissioners of the Parliament to Newport in 1648, iii. 606 ; employed by the Council of State, iv. 228 ; in the business of the *Propagation of the Gospel* in 1651-2, iv. 392, 438, 566, 571 ; v. 12, 71, 424, 508 ; after the Restoration, vi. 40, 41, 47, 55, 122 ; a Nonconformist, vi. 232 note, 416.

O

OATES, Samuel, Baptist preacher, iii. 148.

OATES, Titus, vi. 768-9.

OATLANDS, iii. 556.

O'BRYEN, Henry, son of the Earl of Thomond, v. 266.

ODEMIRA, Count of, Prime Minister of Portugal, Letters of State to, v. 274.

OGILBY, John, author, vi. 292-4.

OGILVIE, Mrs. (of Barra), removal of the Scottish Regalia by, iv. 366.

OGILVY, Lord, in the Episode of Montrose in Scotland, iii. 344, 345, 347, 367, 368 ; taken prisoner and sent to England, iv. 296, 298 ; at Cromwell's Court, v. 249.

OGILVY, Sir David, a son of the 1st Earl of Airlie, iii. 352-3.

OGILVY, Sir Thomas, a son of the 1st Earl of Airlie, in the Episode of Montrose, iii. 352-3, 356.

OGILVY of Innerquharity, iii. 368.

OGILVY, James : see *Deskford*, Lord.

OKEY, Colonel John (Regicide), ii. 445 ; in the New Model Army, iii. 327, 328 note, 534, 537 ; at the King's Trial, iii. 707, 712 note; signs the death-warrant, iii. 720, vi. 28 ; in the Commons, iv. 73; at the Fairfaxian Creation, iv. 52; Scottish lands awarded to, iv. 296 ; 302, 392, 402, 403, 551-2 ; in Oliver's First Parliament, v. 5, 33 ; in Oliver's Second Parliament, v. 107 ; in Richard's Parliament, v. 430 ; through the period of Anarchy to the Restoration, v. 470, 490, 391, 495, 517, 522, 566 ; in the Indemnity Bill, vi. 44, 54 ; in the Bill of Attainder, vi. 115 ; subsequent fate of, vi. 115 note, 228-9.

OLDENBURG, Count Anthony of (son of Count Frederick of Oldenburg), sent by his father to London in 1654, iv. 635.

OLDENBURG, Frederick, Count of ; his relations with the Commonwealth of England, iv. 379, 417-8 ; business of Council in connexion with, and State Letters to, iv. 423-4, 480-1, 525, 527, 635-6 ; v. 370-1, 705-6.

OLDENBURG, Henry, in correspondence with Milton, and agent for the City of Bremen in Lower Saxony with the Commonwealth, iv. 625-7, 628; v. 166 ; visits Milton, v. 230 ; marries the daughter of John Durie, v. 236 ; removes from London to Oxford, as a student and tutor, v. 266-7 ; letters of Milton to, v. 268-9 ; accompanies his pupil, the young Ranelagh, on a foreign tour, v. 365-7 ; letter of Milton to, at Saumur in France, v. 366-7, 631 ; incidents of his travels taken from his letters to

Milton and others, v. 631-4; Milton's letter in reply to, at Paris, v. 634-5; vi. 203; returns, with his pupil, to England, and becomes a member of the newly-founded Royal Society of London, vi. 394, 396, 397, 458; is elected a Fellow of that Society, vi. 459; in Milton's *Epistolæ Familiares*, published in 1674, vi. 723-4; an occasional licenser of books in 1676, vi. 770 note.

OLDENBURG, Rupert, son of Henry Oldenburg, vi. 459.

" OLD STYLE " and " New Style," explanation of the two systems of dating, iv. 180 note.

OLDWORTH, Michael, in the Restored Rump, v. 454.

OLIVAREZ, minister of Philip IV. of Spain, i. 744.

OLIVER, Mr. William, a Scot residing in Paris, i. 758.

OLIVERIANS, the party of, in the nation in 1654, v. 6; in Oliver's First Parliament, v. 122; Quakers included among that section of the party known as *Contrariants*, v. 318, 417.

OLIVIER, Isaac, verses by, on the death of Edward King, i. 653.

O'MORE, Rory (of Ballynagh), concerned in the Irish Insurrection : see *More*, Roger.

O'NEALE, Daniel, Royalist officer, ii. 442.

O'NEILE, Hugh, son of Owen Roe O'Neile, iv. 191.

O'NEILE, Owen Roe, in the Irish Insurrection, ii. 310; iii. 517, 520; iv. 24; in a Treaty with Monk, iv. 111, 113.

O'NEILE, Sir Phelim, in the Irish Insurrection, ii. 309, 311, 312, 313.

ONSLOW, the Right Hon. Arthur (Speaker of the House of Commons, died in 1768), mention of, in connexion with a portrait of Milton, i. 309-10 note.

ONSLOW, the Earl of, son of the preceding, i. 310 note.

ONSLOW, Arthur, in the Convention Parliament, vi. 23.

ONSLOW, Sir Richard, one of Cromwell's Lords, v. 324, 544; in the Convention Parliament, vi. 23.

OPDAM, Dutch Admiral, v. 428; vi. 254.

ORANGE, William I. of, his wife, Charlotte of Bourbon, ii. 158.

ORANGE, the Princess of : see *Mary*, Princess.

ORANGE, William, of Nassau, Prince of (afterwards William III. of England) : see *William III*.

ORDINANCES, first eighty-two, of Cromwell and his Council, iv. 558-65.

ORIEL COLLEGE, Oxford, i. 543, 626.

ORLEANS, Philip, Duke of, husband of the Princess Henrietta, vi. 571, 575.

ORMOND, James Butler, Marquis and 1st Duke of, letter of Charles I. to, in April 1646, iii. 414 note ; account of, as Marquis of, and Lord-Lieutenant of Ireland for Charles I., to July 1646, iii. 517-21 ; surrenders Dublin to the English Parliament, iii. 561 ; 573 ; with the Queen and Prince in Paris, iii. 591-2 ; back in Ireland in Sept. 1648, iv. 22; in correspondence with Charles I. at this date, iii. 608; his Negotiations with the Council of the Roman Catholic Confederates at Kilkenny, resulting in• his *Articles of Peace* for the King and the Roman Catholics in Ireland, iv. 23-4 ; proclaims Charles II. at Carrick in Feb. 1649, iv. 24 ; his effort to conciliate Colonel Jones, Governor of Dublin, in a Letter dated Carrick, March 9, 1648-9, iv. 24-5 ; in action against Monk and threatening Jones in Dublin, iv. 56 ; in Milton's Pamphlet on Ireland, iv. 98-102 ; 106 ; 131 ; beaten by Jones before Dublin in the Campaign of 1649, iv. 111-3 ; in the continued Campaign of Cromwell (1649-50), iv. 191 ; goes abroad, iv. 303 ; excepted from pardon in the Act of the English Parliament (1652) for the " Settling of Ireland," iv. 368 ; abroad with Charles II., and planning a landing in England, v. 34 ; visits London in disguise, v. 335-8 ; in Royalist plottings after the death of Cromwell, v. 416, 473, 503 ; before the Restoration, v. 560 ; as Duke of Ormond and Earl of Brecknock, in Charles's

Privy Council, vi. 17, 19, 20, 77, 99, 106; in the Scottish Council sitting in London, vi. 131; at the Coronation of Charles II., vi. 151; reinstalled in the Lord-Lieutenancy of Ireland, vi. 126-7, 237, 264, 562; 563; in the Cabal, vi. 597, 600, 602; 785.

ORMOND, the Marchioness of, iv. 131; vi. 107-8, 119.

ORRERY, Roger Boyle, Lord Broghill, afterwards Earl of, iii. 572 note, 659; v. 230; in the Irish Campaigns, iv. 112-3, 303, 366; in Cromwell's First Parliament, v. 5, 12; President of Cromwell's Council in Scotland, v. 86, 89, 95-6, 108, 115, 230; member for Cork in Cromwell's Second Parliament, v. 108, 122, 125, 128, 130; his place and work in literature, v. 76, 230, 258; vi. 312, 354, 362-3, 373, 515, 610-1; at Cromwell's Court, v. 303; one of Cromwell's Lords, v. 323, 335, 345; his sister, Lady Ranelagh, writes to him on the occasion of Cromwell's death, vi. 455-6; through the Protectorate of Richard Cromwell, v. 419, 421, 422, 438, 439, 440, 441, 442; with Henry Cromwell in Ireland, v. 459; political veerings, v. 464, 564; after the Restoration, vi. 23; President of Munster, vi. 124; created Earl of Orrery in the Irish Peerage in 1660, vi. 127; his possible share in rescuing Milton from punishment, vi. 447-8 and note; Dryden dedicates a play to, vi. 367-8, 373; in Cabal politics, vi. 574.

OSBALDISTON, Lambert, headmaster of Westminster School, i. 489, 683.

OSBALDSTON, Edward, messenger to the Council, iv. 578; v. 625.

OSBORNE, Sir Edward, ii. 442.

OSBORNE, Sir Thomas; see Danby, Earl of.

OSSORY, James, Earl of (2nd Duke of Ormond), v. 249; a subscriber to the fourth edition of Paradise Lost, vi. 785.

OTWAY, Thomas, vi. 611.

OUGHTRED, mathematician, i. 120.

OVERBUBY, Sir Nicholas, i. 609.

OVERBURY, Sir Thomas, i. 527; murdered in the Tower of London, i. 60; ii. 153.

OVERTON, Richard, printer, iii. 528, 678, 687; iv. 44-6, 87, 97; trial of, iv. 119-20.

OVERTON, Colonel (also Major-General) Robert, iii. 768 note; with Cromwell's Army in Scotland, iv. 192, 288, 302, 362, 365, 402; v. 32; his disagreement with Cromwell in 1653-4, iv. 551-2; is removed from Scotland to the Commandership of Hull in England, iv. 552; is sent back to Scotland as second in command to Monk, v. 32, 162; is arrested at Aberdeen and committed to the Tower in 1654-5, v. 33, 107, 162-5, 165 note; Milton's friendship for, and high opinion of, iv. 602, 606-8, 612; vi. 197; mention of, by Marvell, in a letter to Milton, iv. 621; is released from the Tower in 1659, v. 436; as Colonel of a Foot Regiment under Fleetwood, v. 470, 472 note, 490; is removed from the Governorship of Hull by Monk, v. 563; proposed disposal of his regiment by Monk, v. 498; mentions of, in Mercurius Publicus in 1660, vi. 197.

OVERTON, Mrs. Anne, wife of Colonel Overton, v. 165.

OWEN, Lieutenant-Colonel under New Model, iii. 326.

OWEN, Andrew, iv. 364.

OWEN, Rev. J., of Rochdale, v. 603 note.

OWEN, Sir John, one of the five chief Delinquents, next to the King, tried by the Rump Parliament in 1649, iv. 40.

OWEN, John, Epigrammatist, iv. 474.

OWEN, John, Bishop of St. Asaph, ii. 150, 270, 334-6.

OWEN, John, Independent minister in London: a Thanksgiving Sermon by, iv. 53; associated with Goodwin as Chaplain to Cromwell and to the Council, iv. 61, 106, 145, 177, 229, 296, 322, 370, 390, 392-3, 438, 514, 566-7, 571; member for Oxford University in Oliver's First Parliament, v. 5, 12-3, 53, 59, 71; Dean of Christ Church, Oxford, v.

73; vi. 318, 319; mention of, among Men of Letters under the Protectorate, v. 75; Cromwell's friendship for, v. 76-7; sermons by, v. 107, 122; in a Conference with Scottish Divines, v. 115, 131; grant of Irish lands to, v. 139; his views and proposals in connexion with Cromwell's scheme for an Established Church, v. 344, 424, 585; supports Richard's Protectorate, v. 418, 439, 441, 445; preaches the Reinauguration sermon at the Restoration of the Rump, v. 447, 508; is displaced from his Deanery of Christ Church, v. 550; among the silenced Nonconformists in 1662, vi. 232 note, 417; his place in literature after the Restoration, vi. 299, 302, 322, 388, 616, 700-1; his grave in Bunhill Fields, vi. 499.

OWEN, Morgan, Bishop of Llandaff, ii. 150, 270, 334-6.

OWEN, Dr. Thankful, iv. 571; v. 73.

OXENBRIDGE, John, Independent divine, account of, iv. 618-9 and note, 621; after the Restoration, vi. 122; among the ejected Nonconformists, vi. 232 note, 417.

OXENBRIDGE, Mrs., iv. 618-9 and note.

OXENBRIDGE, a second Mrs., iv. 619 note.

OXENSTIERN, the Swedish Chancellor, i. 742, 743, 747, 753; ii. 367; iii. 195, 203, 225; his death, v. 246.

OXENSTIERN (the younger), v. 246.

OXFORD (the City of), the King makes his headquarters at, through the Civil War, ii. 458, 460, 463, 464, 465, 467, 470, 471; iii. 370, 371, 372, 545; the King's escape from, iii. 373, 374, 375; siege of, by Fairfax, and subsequent surrender of, to him, iii. 471-3.

OXFORD (the University of), reference to, in its connection with the London Book-trade in 1632, i. 544-5; Laud's connexions with, i. 407-8; Laud succeeds the Earl of Pembroke in the Chancellorship of, in 1630, and commences reforms in, i. 408-9; Milton incorporated M.A. in 1635, i. 624-6; John Selden elected member for, in the Long Parliament, ii. 163; proceedings for the Visitation and Purgation of, in 1647, iii. 545-6; Cromwell succeeds the Earl of Pembroke in the Chancellorship of, in 1650-1, iv. 278; the Fairfaxian Creation at, iv. 51-2; v. 73; Owen elected member for, in Cromwell's First Parliament, v. 5, 73; Cromwell's influence in, v. 73-5; *The Philosophical Society of Oxford* in 1649: see *Invisible College.*

OXFORD, Earl of (Royalist), ii. 430; v. 473, 477, 700; at the Coronation of Charles II., vi. 152; 351.

"OXFORD GAZETTE," the, vi. 331.

"OXFORD TRACTS," ii. 363-9.

P

"PACIFICATION OF BIRKS" (Treaty with the Scots so called), at the close of the First "Bishops' War," ii. 70, 72, 122.

PACK, Sir Christopher, Alderman of London, in Cromwell's Second Parliament, v. 107; his motion in the House on Feb. 23, 1656-7, v. 121-3, 126, 129; one of Cromwell's Lords, v. 324; in the Indemnity Bill, vi. 39, 47, 55.

PACKER, Mr., pupil of Milton, iii. 657.

PACKER, William, a colonel in Cromwell's regiment of horse, v. 335, 470, 490, 521.

PACKINGTON, Sir John, v. 78.

PAGET, Ephraim, anti-toleration writings by, iii. 138-40, 146, 155.

PAGET, John (of Amsterdam), Independent preacher, ii. 556, 593.

PAGET, Margery, wife of Rev. Thomas Paget, vi. 474.

PAGET, Dr. Nathan, physician to the Tower, iv. 151; account of, vi. 454-5; introduces Ellwood to Milton, vi. 469; arranges Milton's third marriage, vi. 473-5; and Milton's widow, vi. 744.

PAGET, Rev. Thomas, rector of Stockport in Cheshire, vi. 474.

PAGET, Rev. Thomas (another), brother of Dr. Nathan Paget, vi. 474, 744.

PAGET, William, 5th Lord, in the Long Parliament, ii. 143, 158, 429.

PAINE, Jarvis, sergeant-major in the Parliamentarian Army, ii. 444.

PAINTER, Rev. Henry, member of Westminster Assembly, ii. 520.

PAKEMAN, Mr., vi. 339.

PAKINGTON, Sir John (Royalist), ii. 415.

PALATINE, Prince Elector (nephew of Charles I., and elder brother of the Princes Rupert and Maurice), ii. 272 ; iii. 375 ; at the Coronation of Charles II., vi. 152.

PALATINE, the Princess, iv. 639.

PALISSY, Bernard ("the Potter"), died in 1590, iii. 217 and note.

PALLAVICINI, Sforza (Cardinal), i. 796.

PALLAVICINI, Mrs., widow, a relation of Cromwell, ii. 207, 357.

PALMER, Mrs. : see *Cleveland*, Duchess of.

PALMER, Dudley, in the First Council of the Royal Society, vi. 396.

PALMER, Geoffrey (afterwards Sir Geoffrey), a lawyer, and member for Stamford in the Long Parliament, ii. 173 ; in the debates on the Grand Remonstrance, ii. 320, 321, 322 ; in the Treaty of Newport, iii. 606 ; Attorney-General after the Restoration, vi. 39, 41, 74, 77, 173, 174, 178.

PALMER, Herbert, B.D., censured by the Court of High Commission, i. 407 ; account of, in the list of Westminster Assembly divines in 1643, ii. 520 ; in the Assembly, ii. 523, 605 ; iii. 19, 22, 84 ; made President of Queen's College, Cambridge, iii. 93, 95 note, 153, 160 ; anti-toleration sermon by, iii. 162-4, 183-4 ; his attack on Milton, iii. 262-4, 298 ; answered in Milton's *Tetrachordon*, iii. 309, 311 and note.

PALMER, Dr. John, in the Restored Rump, v. 454 ; in the debates on the Indemnity Bill, vi. 51.

PALMER, Roger, husband of the Duchess of Cleveland, vi. 71.

PALMER, W., publisher, v. 691 ; vi. 162.

PALUZZI, Lorenzo, Venetian Senator, iv. 486.

PANDOLFINI, Filippo, Florentine, i. 787.

PANMURE, Earl of, iv. 560, 561.

PANZANI, Papal agent at the Court of Charles I., i. 684, 799.

PAPILLON, Sieur, a Parisian advocate and elder in the church of Charenton, v. 369.

PAPISTS, outward conformity of, with the Church of England until 1570, i. 17 ; account of, to the year 1632, i. 340-1, 342 ; their relative position among the various English religious societies in 1644, iii. 136-7 ; Cromwell's relations to, in 1656, v. 60-1.

"PARADISE LOST" AND "PARADISE REGAINED" : see *Milton*, Writings of.

PARK, John, ii. 56.

PARKER, Alexander, early Quaker, v. 27.

PARKER, Henry, Secretary of Stationers' Company, iii. 335 note.

PARKER, John, Bishop of Elphin (Irish), vi. 129.

PARKER, John, warden of Stationers' Company, iii. 255 note, 273, 291, 293.

PARKER, John, father of Samuel Parker, vi. 453, 707.

PARKER, Peter, printer and bookseller, vi. 516, 622-3, 626.

PARKER, Samuel, vi. 453-4, 616 ; his controversy with Andrew Marvell, vi. 699-708 and note ; 768.

PARKINSON, John, Parliamentarian officer, ii. 444.

PARLIAMENTS : King James's Parliament of 1621-2, i. 505, 522.—The First Parliament of Charles I., in 1625, i. 156, 368-9, 506, 522.— The Second, of Charles I., in Feb. 1625-6, i. 157, 159, 369-70.—The Third, of Charles I., in March 1627-8, i. 187-8, 191-3, 213, 215-6, 370-3, 375-6, 506, 522.— The "Short Parliament," in 1640, ii. 126-31, 131-3.—The "Long Parliament" (from Nov. 1640 to Apr. 1660), ii. 142-5, 209-12 ; composition and chiefs of, ii. 149-73 ; history of the first nine months of (to Aug. 1641), ii. 173-93 ; account of the English Church Reform Movement in the, during that period, ii. 193-202, 213-8, 220, 222-36 ; "Bishops Exclusion Bill,"

rejected in the Lords, ii. 222-7, 231; "Root and Branch Bill," ii. 231-5; Archbishop Williams's "Draft Bill," ii. 235-6; Impeachment of Thirteen Bishops by, ii. 269-70; Bill for Prosecution of members of the late Convocation of the Provinces of Canterbury and York, ii. 270; Treaty of Peace between England and Scotland concluded (Aug. 7, 1641), ii. 271; preparations in, for a Recess, ii. 271-4; Commissioners appointed to attend the King in Scotland, ii. 273; Committees of Vigilance to meet during the Recess (Oct. 1641 to March 1641-2), ii. 274-88; after the Recess, ii. 315-55; another Bishops Exclusion Bill passed in the Commons, ii. 316; Grand Petition and Remonstrance of the Commons to the King, ii. 316-30; Archbishop Williams in the House of Peers, ii. 331-6; attempted arrest of five members of the House of Commons by the King, ii. 336-45; triumph of the Commons, ii. 345-7; the Militia Question, ii. 328, 345, 347-8, 352, 354-5; Bishops Exclusion Bill passed in the Lords, ii. 349-53; relations of the King and the two Houses of, in the period immediately preceding the Civil War, ii. 410-6, 417, 420, 421, 422; Declaration of, to the Scottish General Assembly of 1642, ii. 420; army-volunteering for the, ii. 421 and note; answer of the, to the King's Proclamation, ii. 422; classification of the two Houses of, in 1642, into Royalists and Parliamentarians, ii. 427-34; appointment of the Westminster Assembly by the two Houses, ii. 510-4; action of, in the matter of the Solemn League and Covenant, iii. 6-13; proceedings of, in connexion with the Westminster Assembly, iii. 26-33; iv. 58-60; Visitation of the University of Cambridge in 1644, iii. 32-3, 92-6, iv. 52; review of the condition of, in 1643-4; iii. 33-5; the "Committee of the Two Kingdoms," iii. 40-1; Accommodation Order of, on behalf of the Independents, iii. 168-71; Presbyterian Settlement voted by, iii. 173-5; Self-Denying Ordinance and New Model, iii. 176-83; Vengeances and Executions, iii. 183-5; Milton and the Parliament in his Second Divorce Tract, iii. 258; Book-Censorship and the Printing Ordinance of June 1643, iii. 265-75; Milton addresses the *Areopagitica* to the, ii. 277-9, 290; conduct of the House of Lords in the second prosecution of Milton by the Stationers' Company, iii. 291-7; anti-toleration pamphlet of Featley dedicated to, iii. 300; Milton's *Tetrachordon* dedicated to, iii. 301, 308; the King's Papers published by order of, after the Battle of Naseby, iii. 335; Proclamation of, against the King, iii. 373; review of the Acts and Decrees of, at the close of the Civil War, iii. 376; review of the continued Church Controversies in, from April 1645 to August 1646, iii. 382-3, 384; case of Paul Best in, iii. 384-5; Toleration Controversy continued in, iii. 390-1, 394-6; Presbyterian Enactments by, iii. 396-400; Recruiting of the Commons, iii. 400-3; "The Power of the Keys," iii. 403; quarrel of the, with the City of London and the Westminster Assembly, iii. 407, 408-11; Cromwell receives the thanks of, at the close of the First Civil War, iii. 411; the visit of Argyle to, in June 1646, iii. 418-20; the "Nineteen Propositions" of, to the King, iii. 420-2, 504-5, 509-10; reconciliation of, with the Westminster Assembly, iii. 422-6; dispute of, with the Scots on the disposal of the King's person and other matters, iii. 506-8; surrender of the King's person by the Scots to, iii. 510; Church business in, iii. 511-3; continued negotiations between the King and, iii. 516; quarrel of the, with its own Army, iii. 516, 530-8; in a Retrospect of Irish affairs, iii. 518-9; Presbyterian majority in, iii. 529-30; Church and University matters in, iii. 544-6; continued quarrel with the Army, iii. 547-75;

negotiations with the King in the Isle of Wight, and the " Four Bills," iii. 577-9; *Concordat* between the Army and, iii. 582-4; " Committee of the Two Kingdoms " dissolved, iii. 585-6; conduct of, during the Second Civil War, iii. 598-603; Ordinance for the Suppression of Blasphemies and Heresies, iii. 600-1, 686-7; in the Treaty of Newport, iii. 605-10; the *Grand Army Remonstrance* addressed to (Nov. 1648), iii. 616-20, 629-30; the two Houses in the grasp of the Army, iii. 692-4; last efforts by the, for the King, iii. 692-5; " Pride's Purge," iii. 697; iv. 6, 57; Resolution and Ordinance for the King's Trial, iii. 699, 702-4; abolition of the House of Peers, and the Lower House declares itself to be the supreme power in the Government (Feb. 1648-9), iv. 3-5 : see *Rump;* the *Agreement of the People of England* delivered to the Commons by the Army, iv. 7-11; the First Council of State of the Commonwealth, iv. 11-2; History of, through the period of the First Council of State (to Feb. 1649-50), iv. 11-9, 39-58, 92-4, 114-28 and notes; "the Engagement" prescribed by, for the members of Council, iv. 14-5; arrangements by, for housing of the Council at Whitehall, iv. 16-7, 54; relations of the, and the Council, iv. 18; attitude of, to the proposal to dissolve, iv. 19, 39-40; first acts of the, in co-operation with its Council of State, iv. 40-2; manifesto entitled *Declaration for the Satisfaction of the Kingdom, touching the late Proceedings of the Parliament,* iv. 41; act of, against ministers preaching sedition, iv. 47; Visitation of Oxford University, in 1648, iv. 51-2; Acts of (May 1849), iv. 53; average attendance of members from the King's death to the date of Cromwell's departure for Ireland (July 1649), iv. 57-8; peers in the Rump Parliament, iv. 58; attendance of members in the House during Cromwell's absence, iv. 114; Bradshaw's Press Act, iv.

117-8; attitude of, towards the Presbyterians, iv. 122-4; the "Engagement" of the, extended as a universal form of Oath of Allegiance to the Commonwealth, iv. 124; foreign relations of, iv. 125-6; history of, through the period of the Second Council of State (to Feb. 1650-1), iv. 127-8, 177-80, 190-3, 214-22 and notes; further Acts of, to please the Presbyterians, iv. 178-80; at Cromwell's return from Ireland, iv. 191-3; has charge of the King's children, iv. 214; relations of, to Foreign Powers, iv. 214-21; prospects of a new Parliament, iv. 221-2; history of, to Dec. 1, 1651, iv. 272-8, 284-7, 296-8, 302-10 and notes; in negotiations with Portugal, iv. 275, and with the Netherlands, iv. 278; scheme of, for Incorporation of Scotland with the Commonwealth, iv. 302-3; Navigation Act against the Dutch, iv. 305 : see *United Provinces;* review of the achievements of the 3rd year of the, iv. 306; question of a new, iv. 306-9; history of, to April 20, 1653, iv. 354-414 and notes; the "Rump" in its relations to Cromwell, iv. 359-60, 399-401; the *Tender,* or offer of the English Parliament to incorporate England and Scotland into one Commonwealth, iv. 360-1, 363-6; proceedings of, for the settlement of Ireland, iv. 366-71; reception by the, of the Dutch Ambassadors, iv. 371; in measures of reform in the internal affairs of England, iv. 383-7, 398; Committee of, for the *Propagation of the Gospel,* iv. 387-95, 397-8; Cromwell and the Rump, iv. 398-401; the Officers' Petition to the Rump, iv. 403; Bill for a New Parliament, iv. 405-10; forcible dissolution of the Rump by Cromwell, iv. 410-4.—The " Little " or " Barebones " Parliament (Nov. 3 to Dec. 12, 1653), iv. 505-18, 565.—The First Parliament of Oliver Cromwell (Sept. 1654 to Jan. 1654-5), iv. 543-4, 547, 572, v. 3-14, 28-9, 31.—The Second of Oliver Cromwell (Sept. 1656 to Feb. 1657-8), v. 323-33,

353-4, 443.—The Parliament of Richard Cromwell (1658-9), v. 415-6, 428-42.—The "Restored Rump" (May to Oct. 1659), v. 445-51, 453-92, 627-30.—The Second "Restored Rump" (Dec. 1659 to Feb. 1659-60), v. 510-7, 518-39; the "Roasting of the Rump," v. 641.—The "Restored Long Parliament," or "Parliament of the Secluded Members" (Feb. 1659-60), v. 539-41, 543-54; resolutions of the House for a "Full and Free" Parliament, v. 551-4; 568; last acts of the Rump, v. 657-8; first meetings of a "full and free" House of Commons and the reconstituted House of Lords, on April 25, 1660, v. 694-5; proceedings in, previous to the Restoration, v. 696-700.—The "Convention Parliament" at the Restoration of Charles II., vi. 10-1, 21-69, 70, 109-16, 117-8.—The "Cavalier Parliament," vi. 158-61; through the first six sessions to the fall of Clarendon, in August 1667, vi. 221-72; through the six sessions of the Cabal Administration from 1667 to 1674, vi. 561-603.—Irish Parliaments: (1634-5) i. 690-1; (1661) vi. 158. — Scottish Parliaments: (1633) i. 699, 701-3; (1639) ii. 122, 127, 136; (1641) ii. 271, 281, 291, 317; (1645) iii. 347, 355, 360; (1661) vi. 142-8.—The "Anti-parliament" summoned by Charles I. at Oxford during the Civil War, iii. 83-4.

"PARLIAMENTARY INTELLIGENCER," principal London newspaper in 1660, vi. 167, note, 202, 324.

PARMA and PIACENZA, Dukes of, i. 745; iv. 638-9.

PARNEL, James, Early Quaker, v. 26.

PARR, Dr. Richard, Bishop of Man in 1635, i. 674.

PARRET, Edward, Quaker, vi. 495.

PARRY, Owen, Parliamentarian officer, ii. 444.

PARSONS, Elizabeth, vi. 94 note.

PARSONS, Sir William, ii. 309.

"PARTHENISSA," a novel, by Lord Broghill, v. 230, 258; vi. 312, 362.

PARTRIDGE, Ralph, New England minister, ii. 558.

PASHLEY, Christopher, member of Westminster Assembly, ii. 521.

PASKE, Dr. Thomas, Master of Clare Hall, Cambridge, i. 116, 120, 157, 182; ejection of, iii. 94.

PASTON, Sir William: see Yarmouth, Earl of.

PASTORALISTS and ENGLISH PASTORAL POETRY: see Spenser.

PATIENCE, Thomas, Baptist preacher, iii. 148.

PATRICK, Simon, Cambridge Platonist, vi. 307.

PAUL III. Pope of Rome, i. 99.

PAULET, Lord, ii. 143, 429, 465.

PAUL'S CROSS, at Old St. Paul's Church, i. 49.

PAUW, Adrian, Dutch Ambassador in London, iv. 373-4, 482, 638.

PAYNE, Phineas, supposed executioner of Charles I., vi. 94 note.

PEACE OF WESTPHALIA in 1648, iv. 30.

PEAK, Mr., iii. 193.

PEALE, Edward, of Compton, member of Westminster Assembly, ii. 521.

PEARD, George, member of Long Parliament, ii. 321, 358 note.

PEARSON, Alexander, v. 86.

PEARSON, John, Bishop of Chester, i. 248, 648, 651; v. 76; vi. 299, 301.

PEARSON, Richard, vi. 750.

PECK, Francis, Antiquary, i. 9, 20, 30 note.

PEELE, Elizabethan dramatist, i. 622.

PEERS, in the Long Parliament of 1640, ii. 428-31; after the Civil War, iii. 376; iv. 3-5; v. 694, see Parliaments.

PEG, Mrs. Catherine, and her children, vi. 604.

PEGGE, Jonas, of Derby, i. 111.

PEGGE, Richard, sizar, and fellow-student of Milton at Christ's College, Cambridge, i. 111, 258.

PEIRSON, Anthony, vi. 32.

PELHAM, Henry, iii. 551.

PELHAM, Peregrine (Regicide), signs the death-warrant, iii. 720; vi. 28; in the Indemnity Bill, vi. 54.

PELLEGRINI, i. 762.

PELL, John, account of, iv. 449; agent of the Commonwealth in Switzerland, v. 41-2, 44, 192, 244-6, 294.

PELLETTA, Claudia, v. 205.

PEMBROKE COLLEGE, Cambridge, i. 114, 115, 116, 120, 122, 237, 248, 499.

PEMBROKE, Henry Herbert, 2nd Earl of, succeeds Sir Henry Sidney in the Presidency of Wales, i. 605.

PEMBROKE, William Herbert, 3rd Earl of, i. 330; account of, i. 378, 384, 385, 438, 439; Chancellor of Oxford University, i. 408; ii. 163.

PEMBROKE, Philip Herbert, 1st Earl of Montgomery, and (in 1630) 4th Earl of, i. 330; account of, i. 378; 383, 384; 414, 527, 666; commander of a horse regiment in the First "Bishops' War," ii. 61, 62, 65, 69, 71; in the Upper House of the Long Parliament, and Lord Chamberlain to the King, ii. 152, 168, 278, 279; out of office, ii. 281; Parliamentarian Peer, ii. 430; Lord-Lieutenant for Wiltshire, ii. 439; lay-member of Westminster Assembly, ii. 523; in the House of Peers, iii. 297 note; at the close of the Civil War, iii. 380; his second son, James Herbert, iii. 401; in the House of Peers, iii. 406; in the Commission of the Lords to the King at Newcastle, iii. 421, 510; and Sir Thomas Herbert, iii. 514 note; in the Lords, iii. 555; in the Hampton Court negotiations, iii. 564; in Commission of the Lords at the Treaty of Newport, iii. 605; in the Lords, iii. 692; previous to the King's Trial, iii. 703; at the abolition of the House of Peers, iv. 4; in the First Council of the Commonwealth, iv. 12, 13 note, 14; Chancellor of Oxford University, iv. 52; member for Berkshire in the Rump Parliament, iv. 58; mention of, in the Council Order Books, iv. 150, 151; his death in Jan. 1649-50, iv. 127-8, 177, 354.

PEMBROKE, Philip (5th Earl of), in the Fourth Council of the Commonwealth, iv. 354; President of Council, iv. 446; in the Restored Rump, v. 454.

PEMBROKE, William (6th Earl of), vi. 764.

PEMBROKE, Philip (7th Earl of), vi. 764; a subscriber to the fourth edition of *Paradise Lost* in 1688, vi. 785.

PEMBROKE, Dowager Countess of (widow of the 2nd Earl), i. 523.

PEMBROKE, Henrietta de Querouaille, Countess of (wife of the 7th Earl), vi. 764.

PENDENNIS CASTLE, in Cornwall, iii. 372, 374; v. 107.

PENDLEBURY, Rev. Mr., married a daughter of Christopher Milton, vi. 763.

PENN, Sir William, in the war with the Dutch (1652-3), iv. 35-6, 507; in command of a fleet in Cromwell's West India Expedition (1654), v. 37, 44-6; in the Convention Parliament, vi. 23; Vice-Admiral of the English Fleet in the war with the Dutch (1665), vi. 254-6, 256 note.

PENNINGTON, Admiral Sir John, ii. 23, 51.

PENNINGTON, Isaac (Regicide), Alderman, and afterwards Lord Mayor, of London, ii. 173, 174, 213, 328, 412, 446; Colonel in the City Trained Bands, ii. 446, 483; in the march to Turnham Green, ii. 457; in 1640 as an Independent, ii. 583; ejected by the City of London Council in 1647 from the City Militia, iii. 533; during a week of mob-dictation in London, iii. 550-1; takes part in a Resolution of the House for the King's Trial, iii. 699, 707; has relentings, and is absent at the sentence of the judges, iii. 712 note, 718; in the First Council of State of the Commonwealth, iv. 13, 14, 15, 79, 88, 105, 145, 147; in the Second, iv. 224, 225; in the Third, iv. 273; in the Fourth, iv. 354; in the Restored Rump Parliament, v. 454, 490; at the Restoration, vi. 28; surrenders himself, vi. 43, 49; in the Indemnity Bill, vi. 54; his trial, vi. 80, 93; death of, in the Tower in 1661, vi. 98 note, 115, 468.

PENNINGTON, Isaac (eldest son of the preceding), account of his conversion to Quakerism, and of his acquaintance with Ellwood, vi. 467-9, 472-3, 495; committed to jail in Aylesbury, vi. 495, 497.

PENNINGTON, Mary (Lady Springett), wife of Isaac Pennington (younger), vi. 467, 472, 497.

PENROSE, Mr., denounced by the Westminster Assembly for heresy, iii. 161, 165.

PENRUDDOCK, Colonel John, beheaded at Exeter in March 1654-5 for his part in a Royalist rising, v. 34-5.

PENRY, John, Separatist, ii. 537, 539.

PENSHURST, in Kent, ii. 519; the children of Charles I. at, iv. 214.

PEPES, Edward, Esq., dedication to, of *Wit and Drollery* in 1656, v. 260.

PEPYS, Chief Justice, in the Irish Council, v. 419.

PEPYS, Samuel, under the Protectorate, v. 76, 558, 564; at the Restoration, v. 699; vi. 6, 7-8; for references to the *Diary* of, see *Notes* throughout the period covered by the *Diary*; at the executions of the Regicides, vi. 96, 123; at the Coronation of Charles II., vi. 156-7; Hartlib and, vi. 200; Clarendon and, vi. 263; mentions of, among Men of Letters of the Restoration, vi. 319, 388; Butler and, vi. 339-40; glimpses of the theatres of London from the *Diary*, vi. 352-6; is elected a·fellow of the Royal Society in 1662, vi. 396; later references to, vi. 499, 617, 648; as Secretary to the Admiralty in 1675, vi. 792; story of Daniel Skinner and, in connexion with the publication in 1675 of the Milton MSS., vi. 792, 797-9, 801-2.

PEPYS, Mrs., wife of Samuel Pepys, vi. 123, 156, 351.

PERCY, Henry, Lord (brother of Earl of Northumberland), in the Long Parliament, in 1640-1, ii. 173, 284, 286; in the Royalist Army, ii. 441; with the Queen at the French Court, iii. 494; in the Second Civil War, iii. 591.

"PERFECT OCCURRENCES," a Commonwealth journal, iv. 154.

PERFOY, William (Regicide), iii. 720: see *Purefoy*, William.

PERNE, Andrew, member of Westminster Assembly, ii. 521.

PERNHAM, Richard, vicar of Stowmarket in Suffolk, i. 185.

PERRE, Paulus Vande, Pensionary of Middleburg, and Dutch ambassador in London (1651-2), iv. 371, 422, 502.

PERROT, Charles, vi. 331-2.

PERRY, Henry, lawyer, i. 632-3.

PERTH, town of, submits to Cromwell in 1651, iv. 289-91.

PERTH, John Drummond, 2nd Earl of: Scottish Privy Councillor (1634-8), i. 707; ii. 15, 303, iii. 351; excluded from Cromwell's Ordinance of Pardon and Grace, iv. 560.

PERTH, James Drummond, 4th Earl of: subscriber, in 1688, to the fourth edition of *Paradise Lost*, vi. 785.

PERU, Ex-Viceroy of, v. 113.

PERWICK, Mr., vi. 804.

PETERBOROUGH, John Mordaunt, 1st Earl of (Parliamentarian), account of, ii. 428, 443, 444, 445.

PETERBOROUGH, Henry Mordaunt, 2nd Earl of (Royalist), son of the preceding Earl, ii. 428; in the Second Civil War, iii. 591, 596; v. 50; his brother, John Mordaunt, v. 337.

PETERHOUSE, Cambridge, i. 114, 115, 119, 213, 220, 500.

PETERS, Garbrand, shipmaster, v. 575.

PETERS, Hugh, ii. 516, 518; account of, as a New England minister, ii. 558, 562-3, 575, 579; returns to England, ii. 586, 593, 597; iii. 386; army chaplain, iii. 524, 697, 712; iv. 61, 126; chaplain to the Council of State of the Commonwealth, iv. 229, 231, 352, 370, 385-6, 396, 421; Roger Williams's account of, iv. 532-3; 565 note, 571, 597 note; v. 71; Cromwell's friendship for, v. 77; 378 note, 526; after the Restoration, vi. 32; in the Indemnity Bill, vi. 41-2, 54; his trial, vi. 80-1, 85-7; his execution, vi. 96-7; in the Bill of Attainder, vi. 115.

PETO, Sir Edward, Parliamentarian officer, ii. 444.

PETRE, Lord, non-effective Royalist Peer, ii. 430; iii. 138; v. 50.

PETT, Peter, shipbuilder and shipmaster, father of Sir Peter Pett, v. 576.

PETT, Sir Peter, Fellow of the Royal Society in 1662, v. 231, 266, 576.

PETTIE, Maximilian, of Tetsworth in Oxfordshire, member of the Rota Club, v. 485.

PETTY FRANCE, Milton's house in, iv. 418-20.

PETTY, John, of Stoke Talmage, co. Oxon., Esq., iii. 58.

PETTY, Mary, first wife of the Earl of Marlborough, iii. 58-9.

PETTY, Sir William, his connexion with Hartlib and "The Invisible College," iii. 664-6; Christopher Arnold and, iv. 351; his autograph, iv. 352; mentioned among Men of Letters under the Protectorate, v. 76; in the Rota Club, v. 485-6, 660 note; after the Restoration, vi. 312-3; in the Royal Society, vi. 392, 394, 396, 458-9.

PEYTON, Sir Thomas, v. 472.

PHAYRE, Lieutenant-Colonel, the warrant for the execution of the King addressed to, iii. 720; iv. 401; vi. 87-8.

PHELPS, John, one of the Clerks of the Court at the King's Trial, vi. 27, 33, 37, 55, 224; his death, vi. 98 note.

PHESANT, a junior Fellow of Trinity College, Dublin, ii. 76.

PHILARAS, Leonard (Villeré), in correspondence with Milton, iv. 443-5, 637-9, 640-2; vi. 723.

PHILIP IV. of Spain, iv. 30; Letters of State to, 160-1, 233-4, 234, 234-5, 324; his relations with the Commonwealth, iv. 220-1, 379; vi. 568.

PHILIPHAUGH, the Battle of, iii. 367-8 and note.

PHILIPS, of Cardigan, James, vi. 317.

PHILIPS, Mrs., Katherine (née Fowler), poetess, account of, vi. 317, 388.

PHILLIPS, Anne, Milton's sister: see Milton.

PHILLIPS, Edward, Milton's brother-in-law, i. 104 and note, 169, 637; ii. 98-9.

PHILLIPS, Edward, jun., elder of the two nephews of Milton, and his pupil, ii. 99, 101, 102; in Aldersgate Street, ii. 204, 208-9, 503; account of his studies with his Uncle, iii. 253-4; in Barbican, iii. 443, 632, 657; at Oxford, iv. 104; back in London, iv. 431; v. 76; in 1655, v. 226-7, 258; novelettes by, and his Edition of the Poems of Drummond of Hawthornden in 1656, v. 263-5; reference to his memoir of his Uncle, v. 382-4; further mention of, vi. 316, 388; story of Milton in 1662 from the memoir, 463-4; 481, 635-6, 763-7; in Thomas Agar's Will, vi. 772, 774; later references to, vi. 776-8; his translation of Milton's State Letters, vi. 806.

PHILLIPS, George, executed at Newgate in 1662, vi. 471.

PHILLIPS, John, Bishop of Man, i. 390, 674.

PHILLIPS, John, Rector of Wrentham, Suffolk, and member of the Westminster Assembly, ii. 251; iii. 392 note.

PHILLIPS, John, younger of the two nephews of Milton, and his pupil, ii. 99, 101, 102, 203, 208-9, 502, 503, 506, 507, 508; account of his studies with his Uncle, iii. 253-4, 443, 632, 657; with his Uncle at Charing Cross, iv. 104-5; possible author of A Short and True Way to the Latin Tongue, iv. 149 note; is Milton's private secretary, iv. 431; writes the Responsio ad Apologiam for his Uncle in 1652, iv. 470-4; vi. 214; in 1655, v. 76, 226-7; in Scotland, v. 226-7; his Satyr against Hypocrites, v. 228-9 and note; is summoned before the Council of State in 1656, for his part in the editorship of Sportive Wit, v. 259-62, 262 note; Milton's uncomfortable relations with, in 1657-8, v. 382-4; after the Restoration, vi. 316, 462-3; account of his later life, vi. 763, 767-70.

PHILOLAUS, J., iv. 96.

PHILOSOPHICAL SOCIETY, see Invisible College.

PHILOSOPHICAL TRANSACTIONS of the Royal Society, vi. 397.

PIANEZZA, Marquis di, commander of troops in the Piedmontese Massacre of 1655, v. 39.

PIATTI, Giovanni, iv. 486.

PICKERING, Mr., the London publisher: references to his Edition of Milton's

Works (1851), iv. 158 note; purchaser in 1831 of an autograph of Milton, vi. 511 note.

PICKERING, Benjamin, member of Westminster Assembly, ii. 521.

PICKERING, Colonel John, in the New Model Army, iii. 326, 336.

PICKERING, Sir Gilbert, in the First Council of State of the Commonwealth, iv. 12, 14, 79, 145, 151; in the Second, iv. 223, 224, 227; in the Third, iv. 273, 314, 315, 321; in the Fourth, iv. 354, 446; in the Fifth, iv. 355, 449, 450; in debates of the Rump, iv. 394; President of Cromwell's Interim Council of Thirteen, iv. 499, 523, 524, 706-7; called to the Supreme Assembly of Notables, iv. 501; in the Barebones Parliament, iv. 506, 512; in the Council of the First Protectorate, iv. 545, 545-6 not , 575; his friendship with Milton, iv. 105, 602, 606, 612; in Cromwell's Council, v. 32 note, 64, 177, 183-4, 248, 259-60, 273, 374; in the Second Parliament of Cromwell, v. 107, 118; in the Council of the Second Protectorate, v. 308; one of Cromwell's Lords, v. 324, 333, 352; in the Committee for a New Parliament in 1658, v. 354; Dryden and, v. 375; Milton and, v. 381; supports the Government of Richard Cromwell, v. 417; in the Restored Rump, v. 454, 455, 480-1; in the Indemnity Bill, vi. 36-7, 47-8, 55; among the old friends and associates of Milton after the Restoration, vi. 197.

PICKERING, Henry, knighted by Cromwell, v. 354 note.

PICKERING, William, of Trinity College, Oxford, i. 207-2.

PICOT, Mr., in Guernsey, Anabaptist, iii. 161, 165.

PIDCOCK, Thomas, messenger to the Council of State, iv. 578; v. 625.

PIEDMONT : Cromwell and the Piedmontese Massacre, v. 38-44; Milton's Piedmontese Letters, v. 183-91; Milton's Piedmontese Sonnet, v. 191-2; allusions to the Massacre in the *Scriptum Contra Hispanos*, and in Milton's Latin State Letters, v. 240-6; the Piedmontese Fund, v. 342.

PIERCE, a sculptor, vi. 754 note.

PIERCE, Dr. William, Bishop of Bath and Wells, i. 388, 390, 399, 674, 677; ii. 150; impeachment of, ii. 270, 334-6; vi. 61, 104.

PIERPONT, Anne : see *Roos*, Lady.

PIERREPONT, Lord : see *Kingston*, Earl of.

PIERREPOINT, the Hon. William (second son of the Earl of Kingston), in the Long Parliament, ii. 173; at the Siege of Reading, ii. 464; in the Westminster Assembly, ii. 524; in the Committee of the Two Kingdoms, iii. 41, 605; v. 130; one of Cromwell's Lords, v. 324; supports Richard's Protectorate, v. 418; in the Council of the Restored Long Parliament, v. 543; in the Convention Parliament, vi. 23, 24; after the Restoration, vi. 51.

PIERSON, Colonel John, v. 470.

PIGGOT, Samuel, merchant, v. 575.

PIGNEROL, Treaty of, v. 43-4.

PIGOTT, Gervase, in the Restored Rump, v. 454, 544 note.

PILGRIM FATHERS, the, ii. 545-6.

"PILGRIM'S PROGRESS," the, vi. 616-7.

PILSWORTH, William, Irish Bishop, i. 420.

PITFODDELS, the Laird of : see *Menzies of Pitfoddels.*

PITILLOH, Robert, Advocate, pamphlet by, in 1659, v. 346 note.

PITKUM, Simon de, Danish agent in London, v. 290.

PITT, George, of Strathfieldsaye, i. 603 note.

PITTET, pastor at Geneva, v. 208.

PITTI, Alessandro, Florentine, i. 822.

PITTS, a London bookseller, iv. 158 note; vi. 794-5.

PLACE, Samuel de la, member of Westminster Assembly, ii. 517.

PLAGUE : the epidemic of 1625, i. 152-4; in Cambridge in 1630, i. 232-5, 237-8, and in 1636-7, i. 626-7, 629, 638-40; in London, ii. 272, 274, 315 and note; the Great, of 1665, vi. 256-8, 259-61, 489-90, 497-9.

" PLAIN ENGLISH AND TREASON ARRAIGNED," a Pamphlet addressed to

Monk in 1660, v. 664-6, 670; vi. 316.

PLANTATIONS, the outlying, of New England, ii. 550.

PLATTES, Gabriel, a writer of Scientific Treatises in 1639, iii. 217 and note.

PLAYER, Thomas, hosier of London, and Captain in the Trained Bands, ii. 483.

PLUNKET, Colonel Richard, Anglo-Irish Conspirator, ii. 309.

PLYMOUTH, New, v. 101.

PLYMOUTH, raising of the Siege of, by the New Model Army, in 1645-6, iii. 371.

POCOCK, Rector of Childrey, Orientalist, v. 53, 73, 76, 78; vi. 294-5.

POLAND in 1638, i. 746-7; account of, in 1648-74, vi. 725-7.

POLL-TAX, imposed by the Parliament for the payment of the Scottish arrears and indemnity in 1641, ii. 193.

POLLARD, Captain, member for Beer-alston in the Long Parliament, ii. 173, 284.

POLLARD, Sir Hugh, Major in the Army of Charles I. in 1642, and killed in 1646, ii. 442.

POLLARD, Sir Hugh, M.P. for Devonshire, and in the Privy Council of Charles II. in 1661, vi. 237; death of, in 1667, vi. 264.

PONDER, Nathaniel, publisher in 1673, vi. 704.

PONTEFRACT, surrender of the Castle of, to Cromwell, iii. 623; member for, in Richard's Parliament, v. 430.

POOLE, Matthew, Nonconformist, vi. 232 note, 417.

POPE, Alexander, i. 470; vi. 186.

POPES OF ROME: see Urban VIII.; the (Innocent X.), complies with Blake's demands in 1654, v. 37; the (Clement IX.), and the Triple Alliance (1667-70), vi. 569.

POPE, Major, Royalist officer, ii. 442.

"POPISH ARMY," the, called also the "Queen's Army," in 1642-3, ii. 468.

POPHAM, Colonel Alexander, in Councils of State of the Commonwealth, iv. 13, 14, 87, 150, 223, 354; one of Cromwell's Lords, v. 324; in the Royalist rising of 1659, v. 473, 478; in the Second Restored Rump, v. 519; in the Council of the Restored Long Parliament, v. 543; in the Convention Parliament, vi. 23.

POPHAM, Edward (Admiral), General of the Fleet of the Republic, iv. 41, 42, 125; in a mission to Portugal, iv. 218; and to the King of Spain, iv. 233-4.

PORDAGE, Dr., of the sect of Boehmenists, v. 21.

PORTA, Baptista, ii. 256 and note.

PORTER, Dr., of Queen's College, Cambridge, i. 158.

PORTER, Mr. Endymion, in the Long Parliament, and Royalist Officer, ii. 415, 442, 449; iii. 346.

PORTLAND, Richard Weston, 1st Earl of: see Weston, Sir Richard.

PORTLAND, Jerome Weston, 2nd Earl of, ii. 429; killed in the war with the Dutch, 1664, vi. 254.

PORTMAN, John, Secretary to Blake, v. 335.

PORTSMOUTH, Louise de Querouaille, Duchess of, vi. 578, 604.

PORTUGAL, iv. 274-5, 380.

PORY, John, secretary to the Colony of Virginia, i. 244.

PORY, Robert, i. 112, 113.

PORY, Robert (son of the preceding), schoolfellow of Milton, i. 98, 112, 113, 133, 149, 218, 258, 565, 648; at the Restoration, vi. 417-8.

POSTAL-SERVICE between London and Edinburgh in 1635, i. 708.

POTS, J., verses by, on Edward King's death, i. 651.

POTTER, Dr. Barnabas, Bishop of Carlisle, i. 390, 399 note, 400; ii. 151, 335.

POTTER, Daniel, messenger to the Council, iv. 578.

POTTER, Vincent (Regicide), iii. 720; vi. 28, 44, 49, 54, 80, 93, 98 note, 115.

POTTS, Sir John, member of Parliament in 1648, iii. 605; in the Council of the Restored Long Parliament, v. 544.

POULTENEY, Will, in the Rota Club, v. 485, 660 note.

POUSSIN, the two French painters of that name in the reign of Louis XIII., i. 744.

POVEY, Justinian, auditor, in Aldersgate Street, ii. 207, 357, 358 ; vi. 267.

POWELL of Forest Hill, account of the family of, ii. 494-502 ; iii. 437, 438-9, 471-80 ; in London, iii. 480-3 ; in the year 1662, vi. 449-51 and notes.

POWELL, of Hart Hall, Oxford, i. 208.

POWELL, Ann (Mrs. Powell), daughter of Robert Moulton and wife of Richard Powell of Forest Hill, ii. 493 ; iii. 47 and note, 632 ; in her husband's will, iii. 336-7, 339, 640 ; assisted by Milton, iv. 81 ; her petition to the Parliament, iv. 145-6 ; Milton's interest in her affairs, iv. 236-42, 243-5 ; her suit again, iv. 336-41 ; her will, vi. 750.

POWELL, Ann, fifth child of Richard and Ann Powell, ii. 499 ; married to Thomas Kinaston, vi. 750.

POWELL, Anne, wife of Richard Powell jun., vi. 750.

POWELL, Archdale, eighth child of Richard and Ann Powell, ii. 499.

POWELL, Colonel (Royalist), ii. 442 ; iii. 592.

POWELL, Sir Edward, Bart., ii. 497 ; iii. 640 ; iv. 241-2, 340.

POWELL, Elizabeth, daughter of Richard and Ann Powell, ii. 499 ; married to Christmas Holloway, vi. 750, 751 note.

POWELL, Elizabeth, daughter of Richard and Ann Powell, ii. 449 ; married to Thomas Howell, vi. 750, 751 note.

POWELL, George, tenth child of Richard and Ann Powell, ii. 499.

POWELL, James, second child of Richard and Ann Powell, ii. 499, 500 and note.

POWELL, John, sixth child of Richard and Ann Powell, ii. 499.

POWELL, Mary, sister of Richard Powell of Forest Hill, ii. 493 note.

POWELL, Mary, third child of Richard and Ann Powell, and first wife of Milton, ii. 491, 499 ; her marriage, ii. 502-8, 507 note ; leaves Milton, iii. 42-56, 76, 78-9 ; returns to him, iii. 437-42, 443 ; her first child born, iii. 483-4 and note, 632 ;

reference to, in her father's will, iii. 636-8 ; her second child born, iii. 689 ; at Charing Cross with her husband and children, iv. 105 ; birth of her son, iv. 335-6 and note ; birth of her fourth child, iv. 439-40 ; her death, iv. 468-9 and note.

POWELL, Richard, of Forest Hill (father-in-law of Milton), account of, ii. 491-502 ; his composition suit, iii. 632-4, 674 note ; his death and his will, iii. 635-40.

POWELL, Richard, jun., eldest son of Richard Powell of Forest Hill, ii. 499, 500 and note ; iii. 636-7, 639, 640 and note ; vi. 740, 742-3, 750, 751.

POWELL, Richard, son of Richard Powell jun., vi. 750.

POWELL, Sarah, or Zara, fourth child of Richard and Ann Powell, ii. 499 ; married to Richard Pearson, vi. 750.

POWELL, Thomas, and his family, ii. 494 and note.

POWELL, Thomas (another), v. 625.

POWELL, Vavasour, Baptist preacher, iii. 148 ; iv. 547-8 ; vi. 232 note.

POWELL, William, seventh child of Richard and Ann Powell, ii. 499.

POWER, William, Fellow of Christ's College, Cambridge, i. 123, 183, 237 ; ejected as a suspected Jesuit in 1643, i. 184 and note ; ii. 76.

" POWER OF THE KEYS," iii. 404-6.

POWIS, William Herbert, 1st Lord, i. 494 ; in a Royalist rising, ii. 429.

POWLETT, Robert, publisher, vi. 403.

POYER, Colonel (Royalist), iii. 592.

POYNER, George, English merchant, v. 244.

POYNTZ, General, in Fairfax's Army, iii. 379, 552, 554.

PRATT, David, ii. 57.

" PREACHER, the, or the Art and Method of Preaching," by William Chappell, i. 129.

PRELATISTS in 1644, iii. 136-7.

PRESBYTERIANISM: opposition in Scotland to the Church policy of Charles I. and Laud, culminating in the *Scottish Covenant* of March 1638, i. 697-702 ; re-establishment of the Kirk of Scotland on the Presbyterian model by the Glasgow Assembly of

1638, ii. 41-2 ; effects upon England of this Presbyterian revolt in Scotland, ii. 3-71, 122-45 ; the Presbyterian or Root and Branch Party in England, ii. 199-202, 218, 234-6, 288-90 ; confirmation of, in Scotland at the King's visit in 1641, ii. 287, 308, 416 ; the theory of, as expounded by Milton, ii. 376-82 ; extension of the Presbyterian Revolution to England, ii. 418-20 ; the, Church of Scotland to be represented in the Westminster Assembly with a view to establishing uniformity. between the two Churches of Scotland and England, ii. 509-10 ; account of English, to 1643, ii. 531-4 ; condition of, in July 1643, and its prospects in the Westminster Assembly, ii. 602-8 ; the extension of the Scottish system of Presbyterianism in Church government to England is made a condition by the Scots of their assisting the English Parliament in the Civil War, iii. 8-15, 15 note, 38-40 ; list of Scottish Presbyterians in the Westminster Assembly, iii. 16-7 ; their position and work in the Assembly, iii. 18-26 ; co-operation of Parliament with the Presbyterian action of the Assembly, iii. 26-8 ; the *Solemn League and Covenant* made stringent throughout England, iii. 38-40; struggle between Independency and Presbyterianism in the Westminster Assembly, iii. 84-90; state of, in 1644, ii. 129-30 ; the new national Church of England to be on the, model, iii. 129 ; antagonism of the Presbyterians to the multiplication of sects and heresies consequent upon Toleration, iii. 136-7, 160-6; the Presbyterian Settlement voted by Parliament, iii. 171-5, 382 ; continued work of the Presbyterians in the Westminster Assembly over (1) the details of the Settlement, and (2) concerning the question of Toleration of Dissent in England, iii. 382 - 3, 384-96; completion of the Frame of Church-government and Enactments of the Assembly and Parliament for the same, iii. 396-400, 404 ; at its fullest tide in England, Jan. 1645-6, iii. 400 ; check given to the Presbyterians, and the Westminster Assembly rebuked, by Parliament, iii. 403-11 ; attitude of the King to the Presbyterian Question, iii. 414-5 ; Presbyterian Remonstrance of the City of London to Parliament, iii. 415-6 ; establishment of, included in the Nineteen Propositions of Parliament to the King, iii. 421 ; Presbyterianising of London and Lancashire, iii. 422-5, 511-3 ; First Presbyterian Provincial Synod of London, iii. 544-5 ; Presbyterian frenzy in London at the action of the Army and Independents, iii. 547-52, 555 ; establishment of, included in the *Heads of Proposals* of the Army to the King, iii. 559 ; interference of Scotland in favour of, in the Hampton Court Negotiations, iii. 562-3, 566-7 ; the Second Provincial, Synod of London, iii. 568 ; wrath of the Scottish Envoys at neglect of question of Presbyterian Conformity in the Four Bills, iii. 581 ; Secret Treaty between Charles and the Scottish Commissioners in the Isle of Wight to confirm Presbyterian Church-government in England, iii. 586-90 ; Presbyterian action in Parliament previous to the Second Civil War, iii. 599-603 ; question of Presbyterian Establishment in the negotiations for the Treaty of Newport, iii. 607 ; system of Presbyterian Church - government perfected in London, iii. 673-6 ; Presbyterian Inquisitorship, iii. 676-9 ; attacks by the Presbyterians on Milton, and his reply, iii. 466-71 ; state of the Presbyterian Church establishment in England at cessation of Westminster Assembly, iv. 58-61 ; and in Scotland at same date, iv. 61-3 ; horror of the Presbyterians, in and out of Parliament, at the King's Trial, and their last efforts for the King, iii. 693-5, 715-7, 718 ; iv. 59-60 ; action of the Belfast Presbytery against the execution of the King, iv. 98-104 ; exclusion from Parliament of 143 Presbyterian members in 1648, iii. 696-8; v. 448 ; attitude

of Presbyterian Scotland towards the infant English Republic, iv. 19-22; opposition of the Rump Government to the Presbyterians, iv. 122-3; subsequent attempts of the Rump to conciliate the Presbyterians, iv. 123-4; Presbyterian Synods in London and Lancashire in 1649, iv. 60, 122; acts of the Rump to please the Presbyterians, iv. 178-80; Charles II.'s first experiences of, and his acceptance of the Scottish Covenant, iv. 190; the Super-ultra-Presbyterian Party in Scotland after the Battle of Dunbar, iv. 203-4; effect of Cromwell's occupation of the South of Scotland in 1650-1 upon the Presbyterian Kirk System and feeling in Scotland, iv. 279-81; simultaneous breaking down of Presbyterianism, but for different reasons, in the Scotland of Charles II. north of the Firths, iv. 281-4; attitude of the Presbyterians of Lancashire and of London before the Battle of Worcester, iv. 292, 293, 299; the Marquis of Argyle and Scottish Presbyterianism, iv. 299-301; splitting of parties in Scottish Presbyteries and Synods at prospect of the Incorporating Union of Scotland with the English Commonwealth, iv. 361-4; English Voluntaryism in 1651, with desire to sweep away the Presbyterian Establishment from London and Lancashire and England generally, iv. 388-90; dispersion of the Scottish General Assembly of 1653 by an English Colonel, iv. 509-10; the party of Presbyterians in the First Parliament of the Protectorate (1654-5), v. 6-7; recognition of Presbyterians, with other sects, in Cromwell's proposed Established Church, v. 15, 344; condition of the Presbyterian organisations in London and in Lancashire under the Protectorate, v. 54-5; the party of Protesters, or Super-ultra-Presbyterians, in Scotland under the Protectorate, v. 91, 92, 95-8, 115, 345-50; Presbyterian members of the Restored Rump in 1659, v. 448, 466; in the Restored Long Parliament of Feb. 1659-60, v. 538, 548; restoration of Presbyterianism and revival of the Solemn League and Covenant by the Restored Long Parliament, v. 548-9; Monk's speech to the "secluded members," promising, conditionally, Presbyterian Church government, v. 541; re-establishment of Presbyterianism by the House and the Council, v. 548-50; the blunder of the Presbyterians when restoring Charles II., vi. 58-60; Charles's attitude after the Restoration towards Presbyterians, vi. 60-3, 65-7, 101-4, 111-2, 122; Presbyterian members in the Convention Parliament, vi. 63-4; state of Presbyterian feeling in Scotland on the restoration of Episcopacy in England by Charles II., and the King's Letter to the Presbytery of Edinburgh, vi. 135-40; Acts of the Scottish Parliament of 1661 to annul *The Solemn League and Covenant* with England, vi. 146; the *Act Rescissory* for the purpose of extirpating Presbytery in Scotland, vi. 146-8; anti-presbyterian character of the new English Parliament of 1661, and order of the two Houses for the burning, by the common hangman, of the Solemn League and Covenant, vi. 158-60; Presbyterians among the Nonconformist clergy of 1662, vi. 235; Clarendon's attitude towards Presbyterianism, vi. 235-6; miserable condition of the vast body of English Presbyterians under the Act of Uniformity, vi. 241-2, 587; Clarendon's anti-Toleration policy against the Presbyterians and other Nonconformist bodies, vi. 244-5.

PRESS, the: *Ordinance for Printing* by the Long Parliament in 1643, iii. 269-70, iv. 118; press offences and press prosecutions in 1648-9, iv. 92-4; Bradshaw's Press Act, of Sept. 1649, iv. 92, 116-8; the same Act renewed in Jan. 1651-2, iv. 386-7; order of Council, in Sept. 1655, to regulate the newspaper press, v. 51-2; statistics of the English press, from 1640 to 1667, vi. 323-4; New Press Act of the Cavalier Parliament in 1662,

vi. 227, 323; history of the Newspaper Press from the beginning of
the Civil Wars to the Restoration, iv.
37-9, 116-8, 324-35; v. 51-2, 670-
2; vi. 324-5 and notes; the Newspaper Press of the Restoration, vi.
325-32, 505-6; "Liberty of the
Press": see *Milton's writings (Areopagitica)*: see also *Book Trade.*

PRESTON, the Battle of, iii. 604.

PRESTON of Craigmillar, iv. 561.

PRESTON, Dr. John, of Emanuel
College, Cambridge, Puritan leader,
i. 117, 120, 343, 516, 543.

PRESTON, General, iii. 517, 520.

PRETTY, Captain William, in the Parliamentarian Army, ii. 445.

PRETTY, Captain William (secundus or
junior), in the Parliamentarian Army,
ii. 446.

PRETTY, Colonel, in the Irish Army,
vi. 90.

PRICE, an actor, vi. 350.

PRICE, Elizabeth, deposition of, after
the Irish Insurrection. ii. 314.

PRICE, Dr. John, chaplain to Monk,
v. 476-7, 526, 528.

PRICE, Robert, Irish bishop, vi. 128.

PRICE, Thomas, Irish bishop, vi. 128.

PRICE, Samuel, Parliamentarian officer,
ii. 444.

PRICE, William, member of Westminster Assembly, iii. 521.

PRICHETT, John, Bishop of Gloucester,
vi. 419.

PRIDE, Thomas, Lieutenant-Colonel
under the *New Model*, iii. 327, 328,
note; at the Battle of Naseby, iii. 336;
in the Quarrel of the Parliament and
Army, iii. 534, 537; his part in
"Pride's Purge," iii. 696-9; iv. 70;
in the King's Trial, iii. 707, 712
note; in the death-warrant of Charles
I., iii. 720, vi. 28; with Cromwell's
army in Scotland, iv. 192; quartered
in England, iv. 402; in Cromwell's
Second Parliament, v. 108, 131;
knighted by Cromwell, v. 324; one
of Cromwell's Lords, v. 323-4;
supports Richard's Government, v.
418; at the Republican remodelling
of the Army, v. 469; deceased at
date of the Restoration, vi. 30, 54;
order for his disinterment, vi. 113-4;

the order cancelled by request of
General Monk, vi. 123.

"PRIDE'S PURGE," iii. 696-9.

PRIDEAUX, Sir Edmund, Attorney-
General, and lay-member of West-
minster Assembly, ii. 524; in
Councils of State of the Common-
wealth, iv. 273, 313, 355; in
Cromwell's Second Parliament, v.
107; created baronet in 1658, v.
354 note, 356; supports Richard's
Government, v. 418; in Richard's
Parliament, v. 430; in the Restored
Rump, v. 454, 455.

PRIDEAUX, Dr. John, i. 625; ii. 225;
Bishop of Worcester, ii. 325, 335,
349, 513 note; iii. 609.

PRIDEAUX, William, English agent in
Russia, v. 292.

PRIESTLEY, John, messenger to the
Council, iv. 578.

PRIMATE, Josiah, leather-seller, his
petition to Parliament in 1651, iv.
357-8.

PRIMROSE, Sir Archibald, Clerk of the
Scottish Privy Council of Charles I.,
afterwards Lord Clerk-Register or
Keeper of the Rolls, and in 1660 a
member of the Scottish Privy Council
sitting in London, vi. 131; receives
charge of the Scottish Records de-
posited in the Tower of London,
vi. 141; in the Scottish Government
of 1661, vi. 143-4, 146-8.

PRINCE, Thomas, Governor of New
Plymouth in 1634, ii. 548.

PRINCE, Thomas, English Leveller and
ultra-democrat, iv. 45, 46, 87, 97,
119-20.

PRIOR, Poet, i. 309 note.

PRITZ, printer at Leipsic of an edition,
in 1690, of Milton's State Letters,
iv. 158 note.

PRIVY COUNCIL: see *Councils.*

PROCTOR, Daniel, fellow-graduate of
Milton at Cambridge, i. 218, 258.

"PRODROMUS PANSOPHIÆ": see
Comenius.

PROGERS, Harry and Valentine
(brothers), assassins of Anthony
Ascham, iv. 193, 234.

PROPHET, Nicolas, member of Westminster Assembly, ii. 521.

PROTESTANT, Cromwell's idea of a,

O

European Council, v. 341-2; account of the "Protestant Separatists," as constituting, in 1632, an exceptional class of the English population, i. 341-2; the Protestant Union in the Thirty Years' War, i. 61; Protestants in Ireland under the Protectorate, v. 99-100.

PROTESTATION, an anti - Episcopal, offered to the Scottish Parliament at Perth, in 1606, i. 69.

PROTESTERS, or ANTI - ENGAGERS (called also REMONSTRANTS), one of the Church parties in Scotland in 1650, iii. 589; iv. 209, 210-4, 281-4, 288-9, 361; v. 89-91, 95-7, 115; vi. 133-5.

PROVIDENCE, the Plantation of, in New England, v. 101.

PROWETT, Septimus, bookseller, vi. 511 note.

PRYNNE, William, account of, as lawyer and Puritan pamphleteer, i. 543-4, 546 note; author of *Histrio-Mastix* in 1632, i. 450-1, 579-80; his prosecution and sentence for the above book by the Star-Chamber in 1634, i. 673; is again before the Star-Chamber, and again cruelly punished, i. 688-92; another anti-Episcopal pamphlet by, in 1635, ii. 260; released in 1640 by the Long Parliament, and receives compensation, ii. 175, 588; attitude of the Root and Branch party to, after his release, ii. 200-1; becomes a strenuous advocate of strict Presbyterianism, and a voluminous writer of pamphlets in that cause and against Toleration, ii. 237, 237 note, 260, 589; iii. 130, 140-1; on the Ordinance for Licensing of 1643, iii. 433-4; takes an active part in the trial of Laud, iii. 184; contributes a pamphlet to the discussion on Church government, iii. 298-9, 298 note; Milton's answer to the same, iii. 313, 315-7; in the war of pamphlets on the side of Presbyterianism and anti-Toleration against Independency and Toleration, iii. 386-90; his views on the question of a Frame of Church Government in 1645, iii. 397, 398, 401; against Lilburne in 1646, iii. 528; is one of the non-Parliamentary Commissioners appointed by Parliament for the visitation of Oxford University in 1647, iii. 546; member of Parliament for Newport in Cornwall, iii. 402 note; in debates of the House on the *Grand Army Remonstrance*, iii. 620; his speech to the Commons on behalf of Charles I., iii. 694-5, 695 note; is excluded from the House by "Pride's Purge," iii. 696; issues a pamphlet and other protests in behalf of the sentenced King, iii. 706-7, 716, 719; sneered at by Milton in "Tenure of Kings and Magistrates," iv. 70; more pamphlets by, in 1649, and answers to the same, iv. 147; is apprehended by the Second Council of State of the Commonwealth, and imprisoned in Dunster Castle in Somersetshire (June 1650), iv. 227-8; order of Council to discharge him from prison, iv. 450; pamphlet of, against Quakers, v. 60; another pamphlet of, against the re-admission of Jews into England, v. 72 note; continues his pamphleteering through the Protectorate, v. 76, 79; in the trial of Dr. Hewitt, v. 337; pamphlets by, against the Rumpers for his seclusion from Parliament, v. 448-9 note, 531-2; again refused admission to the House at the Second Restoration of the Rump, v. 519; is reinstated in the Restored Long Parliament (1660), v. 544-5, 549, 554; reference to, in Milton's "Means to Remove Hirelings" (1659), v. 612; in the Convention Parliament, vi. 23, 24-5; in the Committee of fifty-two members of that Parliament to frame the Indemnity Bill, vi. 30, 31, 35, 40, 43, 51-2, 173; in debates on the Church Question, vi. 63; at the reassembling of the Convention Parliament after a recess, vi. 109, 110, 112, 114; his continued enmity to Milton in 1661, vi. 214; account of his various employments and literary work after the Restoration, vi. 268-9, 292, 293.

"PUBLIC INTELLIGENCER," authorised weekly newspaper of the Common-

wealth period, v. 52, 69, 670-2 and note, vi. 325.

"PUBLIC LIBRARY," new name of the King's Library in St. James's Palace, iv. 41.

PUCKERING, Jane, her case before the Council of State, iv. 232-3.

PUCKERING, Sir Thomas, knight and baronet, of Priory, Warwickshire (father of the preceding), i. 244, 244 note, 565 ; iv. 233.

PUGSLEY'S FIELD (near Bristol), a romantic story of, iii. 338 note.

PULLEN, J., verses on Edward King's death by, i. 651.

PULLEYN, warden of the Stationers' Company, v. 581 note.

PULLEYN, Samuel, Archbishop of Tuam, vi. 129.

PURBECK, Viscount, elder brother of the 1st Duke of Buckingham, ii. 430.

PUREFOY (or PERFOY), Colonel William (Regicide), iii. 525 ; at the King's Trial, iii. 707, 712 note ; in the Death Warrant, iii. 720 ; at the abolition of House of Peers, iv. 5 ; in the First Council of State of the Commonwealth, iv. 13, 147, 150, 151 ; in the Second, iv. 177, 223, 224, 226, 227, 230 ; in the Third, iv. 273, 313 ; in the Fourth and Fifth, iv. 354-5, 446, 447, 449 ; signs a Latin Letter of State, iv. 484 ; in Oliver's First Parliament, v. 5 ; supports Richard's Government, v. 419 ; in the Restored Rump, v. 454 ; is dead in May 1660, vi. 28, 54.

PURITANISM : Fuller's explanation of the use of the term " Puritans " from the year 1564, ii. 531-2 ; condition and aims of the Puritan party in the Church of England at the time of James's accession, as inferred from the " Millenary Petition " presented by them to the King on his coming to England, i. 334-5 ; in the Hampton Court Conferences of 1603-4, i. 58-9, 345 ; result of these Conferences against the cause of, i. 345-8 ; at Cambridge University in 1614, i. 117-8 ; attitude of Lord - Keeper Williams to, i. 352-4 ; the development of Calvin-

istic doctrine among the Puritans, and the distinction of the *Doctrinal Puritans* used as a term of reproach for Puritans holding Calvinistic views, i. 354-8 ; supervision of the Puritan clergy by Laud in 1629, i. 402 - 3, and of the bishops who favoured Puritanism, i. 403-4 ; condition of the Puritan clergy under Laud's government, i. 418-9 ; in the Irish Church during the reign of James I., i. 421-2 ; influx of Puritan refugees from England and Scotland to the towns of Northern Germany and the Netherlands, and chaplaincies established there, i. 426-8 ; Puritan emigrants to the colonies of New England, i. 430-1, 548-50 ; decline of the Drama due to the growth of the Puritan sentiment in London, i. 449-51 ; Sabbatarianism one form or sign of, i. 675 ; Laudian persecution of Puritan ministers between 1635 and 1638, i. 679-80 ; interest of the English Puritan party in the Scottish struggle of 1638, ii. 46, 49 ; attitude of the Roman Catholics towards, ii. 50 ; two varieties of opinion among Puritans in 1643 on the question of right Church government, ii. 531 ; Laud's always increasing antagonism to, i. 544 ; the *Puritanism of Milton*, vi. 840.

PURVES, Dr., Scottish physician, v. 349 note.

PURY, Peter, fellow-graduate of Milton at Cambridge, i. 218, 258.

PURY, Thomas (sen.), in the Restored Rump, v. 454.

PURY, Thomas (jun.), in the Restored Rump, v. 454.

PUTEANUS, Erycius : see *Putten*.

PUTNEY (on the Thames), headquarters of the Republican army at, in 1647, iii. 561-2, 573-4.

PUTNEY, Baron : see *Wimbledon*, Viscount.

PUTTEN, Hendrik van der, Dutch author ; his *Comus*, in 1608, i. 622.

PYE, Sir Robert, member for Woodstock in the Long Parliament, ii. 173 ; in the Parliamentarian Army, ii. 446 ; a friend of the Powell family, ii. 496-7 ; iii. 474-9, 633,

637-40; iv. 239-42; vi. 449 note; in Presbyterian debates in the Commons, iii. 552, 599 note; excluded from the House of Commons by "Pride's Purge," iii. 696; in the Convention Parliament, vi. 23.

PYE, Colonel Sir Robert (son of the preceding), iii. 327, 335, 537.

PYE, John (Esq.), second son of Sir Robert Pye, iv. 239, 340.

PYM, Alexander (a son of John Pym, M.P.), officer in the Parliamentarian Army, ii. 445.

PYM, John: in Charles I.'s First and Third Parliaments, i. 375, 522; a leader in the Short Parliament, ii. 131; account of, in the Long Parliament, ii. 160-1, 174; his proposal for Strafford's impeachment, ii. 176-7; in Strafford's trial, ii. 179, 181, 281; in various measures for reform, ii. 185, 187, 188; his first great speech in the Parliament, ii. 194; in the Church Reform Movement, ii. 201; through the Recess in 1641, ii. 274, 315; at the head of the Party of Movement, ii. 277; after the Recess, ii. 315; his demand for the sequestration of the Bishops, ii. 316, 318-9; in debates on the Grand Remonstrance, ii. 320, 321, 328; one of the Five Members who escaped arrest in Charles I.'s *Coup d'État*, ii. 336, 338-45; his warning to the Lords on *Obstruction*, ii. 347-8; engaged in licensing books (1641-2), iii. 267-8; on a Parliamentary Commission for the management of the Colonies in 1643, iii. 119; a lay-member of Westminster Assembly, ii. 524; his death in 1643, ii. 524; iii. 41; a vote of Parliament in 1646 of £10,000 to pay his debts, iii. 381; his body disinterred in Westminster Abbey in 1661, vi. 227.

PYNE, John, rector of Beer-Ferris, Devon, and member of Westminster Assembly, ii. 521.

PYNE, Colonel John, in the Restored Rump, v. 454, 544 note; in the Indemnity Bill, vi. 40, 47, 55.

Q

QUAKERISM: account of the Sect of Quakers or Friends in 1654-5, v. 22-7; in Cromwell's scheme of Toleration, v. 66-70; imported into Scotland, v. 91-2; in New England, v. 101; relaxations for the Quakers by the Council of Cromwell, v. 114; the case of James Nayler, v. 116-8; under the Protectorate, v. 317; an Act of 1662 against Quakers, vi. 225; relative position of, among the sects in 1662, vi. 235; account of, in 1670-2, vi. 587-8; effect upon, of Charles II.'s Declaration of Religious Indulgence of 1672, vi. 589-90.

QUARLES, Francis, account of, i. 490-1, 492, 569; ii. 154; iii. 448.

QUARLES, James, Parliamentarian officer, ii. 444.

QUEENS: see under Christian names of.

"QUEEN'S ARMY," the, in England, ii. 468.

QUEEN'S OWN REGIMENT, iii. 331.

QUEEN'S COLLEGE, Cambridge, i. 114, 116, 117, 120, 122, 226, 244, 251, 252.

QUEENSBERRY, Earl of, iv. 560.

QUEROUAILLE, Henrietta de: see *Pembroke*, Countess of.

QUEROUAILLE, Louise de: see *Portsmouth*, Duchess of.

QUESTIONISTS or SCEPTICS, the sect so called, iii. 159.

QUIN, an actress in the King's Company, vi. 350.

R

RABELAIS, i. 526.

RABY (in Durham), the estate of Sir Harry Vane, v. 520-1.

RACAN, French poet, i. 744.

RACOVIAN CATECHISM, the, iv. 423, 438-9 and note.

RAGLAN CASTLE, surrender of, iii. 374.

RAGOTSKI, George, Prince of Transylvania, v. 40, 190, 313.

RAINBOW, Dr. Edward, Bishop of Carlisle, i. 122; iii. 93.

RAINOLDS, Doctor, Elizabethan divine, ii. 229, 248-53, 365.

RAINSBOROUGH, Colonel Thomas,

under the *New Model*, iii. 326, 328 note, 336, 537 ; iii. 553, 549, 565, 566, 569, 583, 584, 594, 623.

RAINSFORD, Prosper, ii. 207.

RALEIGH, Sir Walter, his club at the Mermaid, Old Bread Street, i. 46 ; his execution in 1618, i. 60 ; mentions of, i. 514, 529 ; account of his " Cabinet Council," first published by Milton in 1658 ; v. 405-6 and note.

RALEIGH, Carew, son of Sir Walter Raleigh, and member for Haslemere in Surrey in the Rump Parliament, account of, iv. 114 ; in the Restored Rump, v. 454, 465, 604 ; at the second Restoration of the Rump, v. 519, 537 ; in the Restored Long Parliament, v. 545.

RAM, Thomas, Irish bishop, i. 420.

RAMSAY of Balmain, ii. 38.

RAMSAY, Andrew, minister of Edinburgh in 1632, and Latin versifier, i. 511, 711, 722 ; ii. 16, 38.

RAMUS, French logician, his influence on the universities of Europe, i. 264-5 ; Milton's Compendium of his Logic, i. 268.

RANDALL, Antinomian preacher, iii. 151, 152, 161, 165, 678.

RANDOLPH, two persons thus named, both " gentlemen," and both of London, i. 63.

RANDOLPH, Mr., Clerk of the Papers of State at Whitehall, iv. 145.

RANDOLPH, Thomas (dramatist and versifier), at Westminster School, and afterwards at Trinity College, Cambridge, i. 122, 138, 152, 247, 251-2 and note, 253-4, 297, 448, 449, 508, 648, 738 note; iii. 446-7, 448.

RANELAGH, Arthur Jones, 2nd Viscount, in the Irish peerage, iii. 659 ; vi. 456, 638.

RANELAGH, Catherine, wife of the 2nd Viscount (known as Lady Ranelagh, and as Milton's Friend), iii. 658-60 ; v. 229-34, 278-9 ; vi. 445-8, 638, 724 and note.

RANELAGH, 3rd Viscount and 1st Earl of (known as Mr. Richard Jones), account of, among the pupils of Milton, iii. 660 ; v. 232, 234 ; in

correspondence with Milton, v. 267-8, 277-8, 365-7, 631-3 ; vi. 723-4 ; 394, 458-62, 638.

RANELAGH GARDENS, iii. 660.

RANTERS, the sect of, v. 17-9.

RATCLIFFE, Francis, Lord : see *Derwentwater*, Earl of, vi. 605.

RATHBONE, William, member of Westminster Assembly, ii. 520.

RATICH, Wolfgang, German scholar, iii. 226-7.

RAVENSCROFT, Edward, dramatist, vi. 611, 612.

RAVENSCROFT, Thomas, author of a compendium of church music in 1621, i. 51-2.

RAWORTH, Ruth, printer, iii. 451.

RAY, John, Nonconformist minister in 1662, known afterwards as a Naturalist, vi. 232 note.

RAYMOND, John, Clerk in Cromwell's Council-office, iv. 578.

READ, John, of Hertfordshire, created a baronet by Cromwell in 1657, v. 354 note.

READ, Colonel Thomas, under the *New Model*, iii. 326, 534 ; iv. 402 ; in Oliver's First Parliament, v. 5 ; at the Republican remodelling of the Army, v. 470 ; his regiment, v. 498 ; with General Monk, v. 540, 562.

READE, Robert, private secretary to Sir Francis Windebanke, i. 386 ; ii. 44, 61, 70, 177-8 and note; iii. 216.

" RECOGNITION, THE," a document of Oliver Cromwell, described in his 3rd Speech, v. 9-10.

REDMAYNE, John, publisher, vi. 403.

REED, Roger, messenger to the Council of State of the Commonwealth, iv. 578 ; v. 625.

READING : the Siege of, ii. 464 ; some of the Milton family at, during the Civil War, ii. 489-90 ; v. 430.

REETZ, Peter, Danish ambassador in London, iv. 378.

REEVE, optician, vi. 289.

REEVE, John, a leader of a sect of Fanatics in 1652, v. 19-20.

REEVES, an actress, vi. 350.

REEVES, Mr. Justice, in the prosecution of Milton by the Stationers' Company, iii. 295.

REGICIDES : list of the, in the death-

warrant of Charles I., iii. 720 and note; quest of the, in 1660, vi. 25-8; list of the living and dead in 1660, vi. 28; in the Indemnity Bill, vi. 29-56; trials and executions of the, vi. 76-98 and note; Bill of Attainder on the dead, vi. 109-10, 112; the Disinterring Order, vi. 112-5.

" RELIGIO MEDICI," by Sir Thomas Browne of Norwich, vi. 296.

" REGII SANGUINIS CLAMOR," iv. 453-8, 466-7, 580-616; v. 213-5.

" REHEARSAL, THE," by the Duke of Buckingham, vi. 612-5, 702.

" REHEARSAL TRANSPROSED, THE," by Marvell, vi. 702-8.

REID, Mary : see Bulstrode.

REID, Thomas, of Burton, Berks, i. 557.

REMBRANDT, i. 746.

" REMONSTRANCE, THE GRAND," of the Parliament to Charles I. in Dec. 1641, ii. 316-30, 509.

" REMONSTRANCE, THE GRAND ARMY," addressed to the House of Commons in Nov. 1648, iii. 616-20; iv. 6.

" REMONSTRANCE," addressed by the Western Whigs to the Committee of Estates in Stirling in October 1650, iv. 209-10.

" REMONSTRANCE," of excluded members against the exclusion of anti-Oliverians from Cromwell's Second Parliament in Sept. 1656, v. 112.

" REMONSTRANTS " (called also Protesters or Anti-Resolutioners), a section of the Scottish Presbyterian clergy in 1650, iv. 213-4, 282, 288, 361; v. 89, 95-7, 115.

RENA, a Florentine, i. 822.

RENIERI, of Genoa, i. 767.

RENTON, of Lamberton, iv. 561.

REPUBLIC, the English : see Commonwealth.

" RESOLUTIONERS," a section of the Scottish Presbyterian Clergy in 1650, iv. 213-4, 282, 288, 361; v. 89, 95-7, 115.

RESTORATION : for account of the, see Charles II.

REYNOLDS, Dr. Edward, member of Westminster Assembly, ii. 521, 605; in the Visitation of Oxford, iv. 52;

Dean of Christ Church, v. 550; in 1660, vi. 4, 62, 99-100, 105; Bishop of Norwich, vi. 118, 430, 434.

REYNOLDS, Dr. John, Elizabethan divine : see Rainolds.

REYNOLDS, Sir John, Commissary General in the government of Ireland in 1652, iv. 366; in the question of the Kingship offered to Cromwell, v. 125; member for Tipperary and Waterford in 1657, appointed by Cromwell as General of the Auxiliary Army in Flanders, v. 140-1, 295, 310-1; his death by drowning, v. 339.

REYNOLDS, Robert, lay member of Westminster Assembly, ii. 524; in the Restored Rump and its Council, v. 454, 456; in the Council of the Second Restored Rump Parliament, v. 519; as Attorney General in the Restored Long Parliament, v. 545.

REYNOLDSON, Abraham, Lord Mayor of London, ejected from his office in 1649, iv. 47.

REYNOR, William, member of Westminster Assembly, ii. 521.

RHODES, bookseller, and owner of a theatre in London, before the Restoration, vi. 348, 350.

RHODES, Sir John, Royalist officer, ii. 442.

RICCARDI, Niccolo, i. 797.

RICH, Henry, 1st Earl of Holland : see Holland.

RICH, Lord (eldest son of the Earl of Warwick), raised to the peerage in January 1641-2, ii. 429; commands a troop of horse for the King in 1642, ii. 442; iii. 380.

RICH, Major, in the Earl of Newcastle's Foot Regiment in Oct. 1642, ii. 442.

RICH, Colonel Charles, in the New Model Army, iii. 327, 336; among the Recruiters in the Commons, iii. 402, 534, 537, 549; iv. 402, 403; v. 107, 134.

RICH, Colonel Nathaniel, in Fleetwood's Army, v. 470.

RICH, Mr. Robert, only son of Lord Rich, and grandson of the Earl of

Warwick, married, in 1657, to Cromwell's youngest daughter, v. 306 ; 338-9 ; vi. 422.

RICHARDS, an actor, vi. 350.

RICHARDSON, Jonathan (painter), his Life of Milton in 1734, vi. 185-7.

RICHARDSON, Chief-Justice, i. 675.

RICHARDSON, Dr. John, Master of Trinity College, Cambridge, i. 117.

RICHARDSON, Samuel, Baptist preacher, iii. 148, 157, 395-6.

RICHARDSON, Anabaptist, iv. 45.

RICHBELL, Major, under the New Model, iii. 326.

RICHELIEU, Cardinal, i. 204, 742-3, 744, 747, 749, 755, 756, 757, 758 ; and Salmasius, iv. 163, 164.

RICHMOND, Countess of, patroness of the poet Davenant, i. 448.

RICHMOND, James Stuart, 1st Duke of, with Charles I. in Scotland in 1641, ii. 272, 279, 283-4, 298, 300, 306, 336, 346, 350; with the King before the Civil War, ii. 413; in the Royalist Army, ii. 428 ; his brother, Lord Bernard Stewart, ii. 441 ; at the close of the War, iii. 376, 556, 561, 606 ; with the King at Hurst Castle, iii. 627-9 ; in the King's last days, iii. 712 ; at the burial of the King, iii. 727.

RICHMOND, the Duchess Dowager of (widow of the above), v. 576.

RICHMOND, Esmé Stuart, 2nd Duke of, v. 576.

RICHMOND, Charles Stuart, 3rd Duke of (cousin of the preceding), at the Coronation of Charles II., vi. 151 ; marries Miss Stewart, vi. 272.

RICHMOND, Charles Lennox, Duke of, son of Charles II. and the Duchess of Portsmouth, vi. 605.

RICHTER, Dr. George, iv. 350-2.

RICHTER, Jean Paul, i. 526.

RIDDING, Richard, of St. John's College, Cambridge, i. 172 ; commemorated in Latin verse by Milton, i. 173.

RIGHTWIS, John, master at St. Paul's school, i. 78.

RINUCCINI, archbishop, iii. 518-20 ; iv. 24.

RIPA, Baptista de, interpreter to Anthony Ascham, iv. 234.

RIPON, the truce of, ii. 143, 144, 189, 190, 513 note.

" RIVAL FRIENDS," Cambridge Comedy, by Peter Hausted, i. 251-3.

RIVERIUS, Moderator of the Walloon Synod, v. 207.

RIVERS, Thomas Darcy, 1st Earl of (Royalist), i. 244 ; ii. 47-8, 429 ; arrested, v. 50.

ROBERTS, Lord, Parliamentarian Peer, ii. 431 ; Lord-Lieutenant for Cornwall, ii. 439 ; his regiment, ii. 444 ; in the "Committee of the Two Kingdoms," iii. 41 ; at the close of the Civil War, iii. 380 ; in Church Questions, iii. 405 ; in the Privy Council of the Restoration, vi. 19, 45, 46, 77, 126-7, 237, 244-5 ; in the attack on Clarendon, vi. 249 ; in the Cabal Administration, vi. 562-4.

ROBERTS, William, of Corpus Christi College, Cambridge, and University Proctor, i. 226 ; Bishop of Bangor, i. 128, 674 ; ii. 150 ; impeachment of, ii. 270, 335 ; after the Restoration, vi. 61, 104.

ROBERTS, Sir William, in the Second Council of the Barebones Parliament, iv. 525 ; one of Cromwell's Lords, v. 324 ; in the Indemnity Bill, vi. 39.

ROBINS, John, a leader of a sect of Fanatics in 1650, v. 19-20.

ROBINS, Robert, Regicide pamphlet by, iv. 94 note.

ROBINSON, at Christ's College, Cambridge, i. 111.

ROBINSON, Alderman, v. 541 note ; in the Convention Parliament, vi. 23, 24 ; knighted in 1660, vi. 74.

ROBINSON, Henry, pamphleteer and book-licenser, iii. 146, 387, 433-4.

ROBINSON, Humphrey, printer and publisher, v. 155 note ; vi. 402, 403 ; Master of the Stationers' Company, vi. 515.

ROBINSON, John (minister at Leyden), his importance in the history of Independency, i. 429 ; his Address to the New Plymouth Colonists on their sailing from Delfthaven in 1620, i. 429 and note ; further mentions of, ii. 539, 540-2, 543, 544, 545, 546, 556, 569, 570 ; iii. 101.

ROBINSON, Sir John, Keeper of the Tower, vi. 142 note, 173.

ROBINSON, Luke, in the Long Parliament and in the successive Councils of the Commonwealth, iv. 11, 13, 82, 147, 150, 151, 230; in the Second Parliament of the Protectorate, v. 121; in the Restored Rump, v. 454; in the Second Restored Rump and its Council, v. 519, 525, 528, 529, 536, 666; in the Restored Long Parliament, v. 544.

ROBINSON, Dr. Tancred, vi. 628-30.

ROBINSON, William, servant of the Council of State, v. 624, 625 note.

ROBOROUGH, Henry, scribe of the Westminster Assembly, ii. 515; iii. 677; iv. 71.

ROCHE, Giles de la, commander of French privateer vessels, v. 272.

ROCHEFORT, Lord (Miles de Malta), a Cambridge graduate in 1626-7, i. 181.

ROCHEFOUCAULT, Cardinal, i. 757.

ROCHELLE, siege of, by the French in 1626, i. 204, 380.

ROCHESTER, Henry Wilmot, 1st Earl of, concerned in a Royalist insurrection in 1655, v. 34.

ROCHESTER, John Wilmot, 2nd Earl of, Dryden dedicates a play to, in 1672, vi. 610, 612.

ROCHFORT, Henry Carey, Viscount (Lord Hunsdon), son of the Earl of Dover, ii. 431, 444; impeachment of, iii. 554, 693, v. 695.

RODER (a German), married to a daughter of Hartlib, vi. 200.

ROE, Sir Thomas, iii. 194-7, 217.

ROESKILDE, the Peace of, v. 385, 427.

ROGER, Major, iii. 534.

ROGERS, Rev. Mr. Daniel, of Weathersfield, i. 402.

ROGERS, Rev. Mr. John, of Deadham, in 1632, i. 402.

ROGERS, John, an army preacher, v. 335.

ROHAN, Duchess de, vi. 422.

ROHAN, Henri de : see La Cloche, James.

ROLLE, Henry (Lord Chief-Justice), in the Trial of Charles I., iii. 703; in the First Council of State of the Commonwealth, iv. 12; and the Second, iv. 230; and the Third, iv. 273; and the Fourth and Fifth, iv.

354-5; captured in a Royalist rising at the assizes at Salisbury in 1655, v. 34; removed from his office for reasons of policy by Cromwell, v. 36; in the Council of the Second Restored Rump, v. 520.

ROLLES, William, rector of Chalfont St. Giles, vi. 494.

ROLLO, Sir Andrew, 1st Lord, iv. 561.

ROLLO, Major, a friend of Montrose, iii. 374, 351.

ROLLO, Sir William, in the Episode of Montrose in Scotland, iii. 360, 367, 368.

ROLLOCK, Mr. Alexander, minister at Perth, iv. 213.

ROLLOCK (Roque), Mr. Henry, minister at Edinburgh in 1638, i. 711, 727; ii. 16, 38, 43.

ROLPH, Major, under the New Model, iii. 326-8.

ROMAN CATHOLICS : see Papists.

ROMANOFF, Michael, Czar of Russia (1613-45), i. 747.

ROME, Milton in, in 1638, i. 792-807.

ROMSWINCKEL, Peter George, Doctor of Laws, v. 269.

ROOKE, Mr., lecturer of Geometry at Gresham College, vi. 393-4.

ROOKE, Thomas, registers a book on Arithmetic by James Hodder, vi. 515-6.

ROOS, John Manners, Lord (eldest son of the Earl of Rutland), in a divorce suit in 1669-70, vi. 572-4, 639-40.

ROOS, Lady (Anne Pierpoint, daughter of the Marquis of Dorchester), wife of Lord Roos, vi. 639.

"ROOT AND BRANCH," name given to the party of extreme Church Reformers in and out of Parliament in 1640-1, ii. 199-202, 203, 213; a "Root and Branch" Bill, ii. 231-5, 269; v. 63.

ROOTEN, John, a witness in the trials of the Regicides, vi. 91.

ROPER, Abel, publisher, vi. 399; Warden of the Stationers' Company, vi. 651.

ROQUE : see Rollock.

ROSCOMMON, Wentworth Dillon, 4th Earl of, mentioned among Men of Letters of the Restoration, vi. 319; his tribute to Milton, vi. 783.

ROSENCRANTZ, Eric, Danish ambassador in London, iv. 378.

ROSS, William, Lord, iv. 561.

ROSS, Dr. Alexander, i. 28; account of, iii. 447, 447 note.

ROSSI, Gianvittorio, Roman author, i. 801.

ROSSITER, Colonel Edward, in the *New Model* Army, iii. 327, 335; in the recruiting of the Commons, iii. 402; in a Royalist insurrection, v. 473; in the Council of State of 1659-60, v. 543; with General Monk, v. 563.

ROTA CLUB, the, debating club of the Harringtonians in 1659, v. 484-6, 508-9, 659; publication of the *Censure of the Rota* upon Milton's *Ready and Easy Way*, v. 659-63; cessation of the Club in January 1659-60, v. 555, 660 note.

ROTHES, John Leslie, 6th Earl of, opponent of Charles I. in the Scottish Parliament, and leader of the Covenanting Movement, i. 703, 710, 722; ii. 16, 22, 38, 40, 52, 53, 65; in the First "Bishops' War," ii. 66, 68, 69, 71, 126, 130; one of the Scottish Commissioners for a proposed Treaty with the Scots at the close of the Second "Bishops' War," ii. 143; in continued negotiations for the Treaty in London, ii. 190, 192, 292; his warning to Montrose, ii. 293-4; his illness and death in 1641, ii. 302-3.

ROTHES, John Leslie, 7th Earl of (son of the preceding), taken prisoner at the Battle of Worcester, and confined in the Tower, iv. 294, 298; excepted from Cromwell's Ordinance of Pardon and Grace, iv. 561; with Monk at Coldstream, v. 512; in the Scottish Privy Council, sitting in London, of Charles II., vi. 130, 138, 161.

ROTHIEMAGORDON, Laird of, iv. 561.

ROTHWELL, Henry, servant of Milton's father, ii. 99, 362.

ROTHWELL, John, one of Milton's publishers, ii. 361-2, 398; iii. 198, 450; v. 59 note; vi. 399.

"ROUNDHEADS," first use of the term, ii. 332.

ROUNDWAY DOWN, battle at, in 1643, iii. 6.

ROUS, Colonel Anthony, in the Barebones Parliament, iv. 512.

ROUS, Francis, of Truro, member of Charles I.'s Third Parliament, i. 375; in the Long Parliament, ii. 164; lay member of Westminster Assembly, ii. 524; his metrical version of the Psalms, iii. 26-7, 425, 512; in debates of the House on Assembly business, iii. 175, 274; in a Committee for *The Propagation of the Gospel*, iv. 390; called to Cromwell's Supreme Assembly, iv. 501; in the Barebones Parliament, iv. 505, 507, 516, 525; signs Latin State Letters, iv. 527; in Cromwell's Council, iv. 545, 568, 571; v. 31, 64, 98, 183-4, 259, 273; in Cromwell's Second Parliament, v. 107, 129; in the Privy Council of Second Protectorate, v. 308; one of Cromwell's Lords, v. 324; in Cromwell's Privy Council after the dissolution of his Second Parliament, v. 333; his death in January 1658-9, v. 417 note; in connexion with, in Milton's Treatise of Civil Power, v. 586.

ROUS, John, Librarian of the Bodleian at Oxford, and friend of Milton, i. 626, 738 note; Milton's Latin Ode to, iii. 644-50; iv. 350; vi. 689.

ROVAI, Francesco, Florentine poet, iii. 681.

Row of Carnock, Presbyterian divine, ii. 38.

Row, John, Principal of Old Aberdeen College, v. 346 note.

Row, Robert, vi. 134.

ROWE, Owen (Regicide), in the death-warrant of Charles I., iii. 720; vi. 28, 43, 49, 54; his trial, vi. 80, 93; his death, vi. 98 note, 115.

ROWLAND, John, iv. 536 and note.

ROWLEY, William, dramatist, i. 446; iii. 449; vi. 352.

ROXBURGH, Robert Ker, 1st Earl of, in the Scottish Privy Council in 1637, i. 706, 720; ii. 15, 31, 303, 305, 307, 342, 417; in Scottish affairs, iii. 344, 362.

ROXBURGH, William Drummond, 2nd Earl of: iv. 208, 560; with Monk at Coldstream, v. 512.

ROYAL SOCIETY OF LONDON, the, origin of, iii. 662 ; Charter to, in 1662, vi. 391-8 ; Transactions of, vi. 397 ; Sprat's *History of the Institution, Design, and Progress* of, vi. 398.

ROYALISTS (or STUARTISTS), in Oliver's First Parliament, v. 6 ; abortive risings of the, in 1654-5, v. 34-5, 119, 142 ; new conspiracy of, in 1657-8, v. 335-8 ; revived hopes of the, in 1659, v. 463-4, 504-5 ; in 1660, v. 557-61.

ROYCROFT, Thomas, publisher, vi. 399.

ROYDEN, Captain, an officer in the London Trained Bands, ii. 446.

ROYSTON (royal hunting lodge), Charles I. at, ii. 354 ; iii. 556.

ROYSTON, Richard, printer and publisher, iv. 88, 147, 148-9, 434 ; vi. 398-9, 403, 424, 514 ; Warden of the Stationers' Company, vi. 515.

RUBENS, Peter Paul, residing in England in 1629, and admitted to the honorary degree of M.A. at Cambridge in that year, i. 220, 223, 746.

RUDYARD, Sir Benjamin, account of, at meeting of the Long Parliament in 1640, ii. 163, 174, 197, 216, 321 ; lay member of Westminster Assembly, ii. 524 ; in the King's last days, iii. 694 ; excluded from the House by " Pride's Purge," iii. 696-7 ; a witty saying of, v. 22.

RUGELEY, Dr. Luke, son of Dr. Thomas Luke, ii. 101 ; vi. 772-3.

RUGELEY, Mary, daughter of Dr. Thomas Rugeley, and first wife of Thomas Agar, i. 638 ; ii. 100.

RUGELEY, Simon, Parliamentarian officer, ii. 446.

RUGELEY, Dr. Thomas, physician in London, ii. 100-1 and notes ; his sons, Thomas, Luke (see *Rugeley*, Dr. Luke), and George, ii. 101.

RUGGLE, George, of Clare Hall, Cambridge, i. 221.

RULE, Dr. Gilbert, Nonconformist, vi. 232 note.

RUMP, THE, name given to the surviving remnant of the Long Parliament under the Commonwealth, iv. 359, 399, 403 ; 409 ; dissolution of the, by Cromwell in 1653, iv. 411-

4 ; First Restoration of the, v. 447-92 ; list of the Restored Rumpers in May 1659, v. 453-4 ; 477-9, Second Restoration of the, in Dec. 1659, v. 517-39 ; Roasting of the, v. 536-7. See *Parliaments*.

" RUMP, THE," a Collection of Cavalier Songs, in June 1660, vi. 333.

RUPERT, Prince, nephew of Charles I., and Master of Horse in the King's Army in the Civil War, ii. 422, 423, 428, 440 ; in the Fight of Powick Bridge, ii. 454 ; 456, 460, 461, 463 ; in the skirmish of Chalgrove field, ii. 471 ; in the Siege of Bristol, iii. 6 ; in the Battle of Marston Moor, iii. 96-7, 332, 333 ; in the Battle of Naseby, iii. 335, 336 ; at the Surrender of Bristol, iii. 338 ; at the close of Civil War, iii. 375 ; in the Surrender of Oxford, iii. 472 ; in the Second Civil War, iii. 591, 595 ; his friendship for Montrose, iv. 28 ; takes a fleet to Ireland to co-operate there with Ormond, iv. 22, 56 ; escapes thence with his fleet to the Portuguese coast, iv. 125 ; in engagements with Blake, iv. 217-8 ; in State Letters of the Council, iv. 232, 233, 235 ; at the Restoration, vi. 71, 151, 237 ; in the War with the Dutch, vi. 252, 254-5, 260, 596 ; mentioned in Dryden's *Annus Mirabilis*, vi. 376-7 ; his " Drops " (1662), vi. 395 ; is godfather to the child of Oldenburg (Secretary of the Royal Society), vi. 459 ; his portrait by Faithorne, vi. 648.

RUSHWORTH, John (lawyer of Lincoln's Inn, and Assistant Clerk of the Commons in the Long Parliament), references to his *Collections*, ii. 134, 140, 174, 273, 332, 342, 343 note ; Secretary to Fairfax, iii. 326, 432, 548, 557, 619, 630 ; iv. 7, 154 ; his Press Act, iv. 325-6, 385-6 ; among Men of Letters under the Protectorate, v. 75 ; in the Convention Parliament, vi. 23, 32, 46 ; among Men of Letters of the Restoration, vi. 294-6.

RUSSEL, tailor, and landlord of Milton in St. Bride's Churchyard, ii. 101.

RUSSELL, a Major in the King's Army, ii. 442.

RUSSELL, Lady Catherine, daughter of Earl of Bedford, ii. 156.

RUSSELL, Lord, son of the 4th Earl of Bedford, ii. 154.

RUSSELL, Colonel John, brother of the Earl of Bedford, v. 336.

RUSSELL, Sir Francis, of Chippenham, Cambridgeshire, v. 305; one of Cromwell's Lords, v. 324; supports Richard's Government, v. 419, 544 note.

RUSSIA or MUSCOVY in 1638, i. 747: see also under *Michael Romanoff* and *Alexis* (Czars of).

RUST, George, Cambridge Platonist, vi. 307.

RUTHERFORD, Mr. Samuel, minister of Anwoth in Kirkcudbright, and conspicuous Covenanter, i. 712, 714; ii. 16; a Scottish Assessor in the Westminster Assembly, and resident in London (1643-7), iii. 10, 17, 25, 84, 130, 160, 176, 298, 412, 513; author, in 1644, of a Treatise entitled *Lex Rex*, vi. 134; is named in Milton's anti-Presbyterian Sonnet (1646), iii. 468, 470; returns to Scotland in Nov. 1647, iii. 568; is a leader of the party of *Remonstrants*, iv. 209, 213; in the General Assembly of 1651, iv. 288-9; Principal of St. Andrews University, v. 90; his *Lex Rex* burned by the hangman, vi. 134; deprived of his Principalship, vi. 135; his illness and death at St. Andrews, vi. 135, 214.

RUTHEN (or Ruthven), Governor of Plymouth in 1642, Colonel, ii. 466.

RUTHVEN, General, Commander of Edinburgh Castle for the King, in the Second Bishops' War, ii. 137.

RUTHVEN, Sir Francis, excepted from Cromwell's Ordinance of Pardon and Grace, iv. 561.

RUTLAND, John Manners, Earl of, i. 130; ii. 142; Parliamentarian Peer, ii. 158, 430; iii. 40, 297 note, 692; his son, Lord Roos, vi. 572.

RUTLEY, Richard, of Suffolk, i. 112.

RUTLEY, Roger, at Christ's College, Cambridge, i. 112, 218, 258.

RUTTER, Mrs., an actress, vi. 350.

RUTTS, David, iv. 486.

RUVIGNY, French Ambassador in London, vi. 569.

RUYTER, DE, Dutch Admiral, iv. 375; vi. 254, 260, 266, 583, 596.

RYCAUT, Sir Paul, and the fourth edition of *Paradise Lost*, vi. 785.

RYLEY, William, Norroy King at Arms, v. 284, 287; and the Scottish Records, vi. 142 note.

RYMER, Thomas, author of the *Fœdera*: account of, in 1678, vi. 778-9.

S

SA, Don Pantaleon, brother of Don Roderigo Sa, iv. 380, 556-7, 636.

SA, Don Roderigo, Portuguese Ambassador in London in 1652, iv. 380, 448, 556-7, 636; v. 273.

SACKVILLE, Edward: see *Dorset*, 4th Earl of.

SACKVILLE, Sir John, i. 155 note.

SACKVILLE, Thomas: see *Dorset*, 1st Earl of, i. 378.

SADLEIR, Mrs. (daughter of Sir Edward Coke), story of Roger Williams, Milton, and, iv. 529-31.

SADLER, John, in the Council of the Barebones Parliament, iv. 525.

SADLER, Colonel Thomas, in Fleetwood's Army in Ireland, iv. 401; in Oliver's First Parliament, v. 5; again in Ireland, v. 471.

ST. ALBANS, Monk at, v. 526-7.

ST. ALBANS, Earl of: see *Clanricarde*, Marquis of.

ST. ALBANS, Henry Jermyn, Earl of, reputed second husband of Queen Henrietta Maria, vi. 72: see also under *Jermyn*.

ST. ALBANS, Charles Beauclerk, Duke of, son of Nell Gwynn and Charles II., vi. 605.

ST. BARTHOLOMEW, the Massacre of, i. 99; "St. Bartholomew Sunday" in 1662, vi. 231-5 and notes, 414-6.

ST. DOMINGO, Penn's assault on, in 1655, v. 44-5.

ST. JAMES'S PALACE, King Charles I. at, previous to his execution, iii. 707, 712, 717, 721, 723; Librarians of: see *Young*, Patrick, and *Durie*,

John; contents of the Library, iii. 229, 351; the King's Library in, iv. 41.

ST. JOHN (of Bletso), Oliver, Lord (son and heir of the Earl of Boling-broke), i. 589; killed at Edgehill, ii. 444, 445; his wife, Lady Arabella Egerton: see *Egerton*.

ST. JOHN, Lord, arrested by Cromwell's Major-Generals in 1655-6, v. 50; at the Count Bundt's supper party, v. 249.

ST. JOHN, Oliver (lawyer), member for Totness in the Long Parliament, account of, ii. 163, 164, 174, 187, 279, 280, 451; in Westminster Assembly, ii. 525, 606; iii. 41, 169-70, 274-5, 397; in the King's Trial, iii. 699, 703, 718; in the First Council of State of the Commonwealth, iv. 12, 13 note, 147; Lord Chief-Justice and Ambassador Extraordinary to the United Provinces in 1650-1, iv. 216, 275-8; in the Third Council of State, iv. 230, 273-4; in a Parliamentary deputation to Cromwell after Worcester, iv. 297; in the Commission for Incorporation of Scotland into the English Commonwealth, iv. 303, 360, 308-9; in the Fourth and Fifth Councils of State, iv. 354-5, 449; in a Conference of Lawyers with Cromwell's Council in 1655, v. 71; one of Cromwell's Lords, v. 324; supports Richard's Protectorate, v. 418; in the Restored Rump and its Council, v. 454, 455, 456, 479, 480, 509; in the Second Restored Rump and the new Council of State, v. 519, 523, 543; in the Restored Long Parliament, v. 545, 556; and the Indemnity Bill after the Restoration, vi. 38, 47, 55; reference to, among Milton's old friends and associates, vi. 197.

ST. JOHN'S COLLEGE, Cambridge, i. 113, 116, 121, 172, 182, 238, 247, 261, 262, 349, 359, 389, 400, 446, 508.

SAINTLOE, Mr., English Presbyterian, • ii. 532.

ST. MICHAEL'S MOUNT (Cornwall), surrender of, in 1646, to the Parliamentarian Army, iii. 371.

ST. NICHOLAS, Mr. Thomas, in the Council of the Barebones Parliament, iv. 506; Clerk of the Parliament in 1659-60, v. 546.

SAINT PAUL'S CATHEDRAL, "Old St. Paul's" in 1608, i. 48; enactments of Laud for the embellishment of, in 1631, i. 394-5, 407; ii. 225; the *History of*, by the historian Dugdale, vi. 296.

ST. PAUL'S SCHOOL, London, i. 49, 73, 74-7, 83, 102, 103, 106, 112, 113 note, 209, 214, 215, 243, 272, 305, 481, 626.

SALISBURY, Bishop of (1640), iii. 217.

SALISBURY, David, servant of the Council of State, v. 625.

SALISBURY, Professor Edward, reference to his account of the Diodati family, i. 102-3 note.

SALISBURY, William Cecil, 2nd Earl of, account of, i. 380, 384, 438; ii. 68, 71, 143; in the King's Privy Council in 1640-1, ii. 152, 278, 279, 413; joins the Parliamentarians, ii. 430; in the Westminster Assembly, ii. 523; in the House of Lords, iii. 297; at the close of the First Civil War, iii. 380; in the Lords, iii. 406, 555 note, 605, 692; iv. 4; in Councils of State of the Commonwealth, iv. 12, 13 note, 14, 79, 83, 224, 225, 230, 355; in the Rump Parliament, iv. 58, 114; in Cromwell's First Parliament, v. 5; in Cromwell's Second Parliament, v. 107, 110; in the Restored Rump, v. 454; his second son, Mr. Robert Cecil, v. 519; forsakes the Rump, v. 544 note; in the Convention Parliament, vi. 22; at the Coronation of Charles II., vi. 151.

SALMASIUS, Claudius (Claude de Saumaise), order of Council to Milton concerning the book of, iv. 150-1; account of, and of his book *Defensio Regia pro Carolo I.*, iv. 162-75 and notes; Milton's reply to, in *Pro Populo Anglicano Defensio*, iv. 250-68, 311-2, 312 note, 316-20, 341, 466; unpopularity abroad of the *Defensio Regia*, iv. 267; removes his residence from Leyden to the Court of Queen Christina at Stock-

holm, iv. 268-71, 329-30; is crest-
fallen at the reception of Milton's
Defensio Popula, iv. 341-6; account
of books written in defence of, and
of replies to the same, iv. 346-8,
474; quits Stockholm and returns to
Leyden, iv. 433-4, 452-3; connexion
with, and mentions of, in *Regii
Sanguinis ad Cœlum*, iv. 453-8, 466;
relations of Alexander Morus and, iv.
460-5; begins his reply to Milton, but
dies in Sept. 1653 before it is completed, iv. 474-5, 537-8, 539-40,
581; referred to in Milton's *Defensio
Secunda* (1654), iv. 585-90; also in
the *Supplementum* of Morus (1655),
v. 193-8; posthumous publication in
1659 of his reply to Milton, v. 633;
vi. 203-12 and notes; his sons,
Claude and Josias : see *Saumaise*,
Claude de, and Josias de.

SALMASIUS, Madame (Anne Mercier),
wife of Salmasius, iv. 162, 263, 265,
271, 461-3, 628, 634; v. 195, 206.

SALMON, Lieutenant-Colonel Edward,
iii. 534; v. 125, 470.

SALMON, Joseph, of the sect of Seekers,
iii. 678.

SALSILLI, Giovanni (Roman), friend of
Milton, i. 805-7, 821 note, 828; iii.
455, 650.

SALSTONSTALL, Mr. Richard, fellow-
student of Milton at Cambridge, i.
262.

SALT HEATH, near Stafford, Earl of
Northampton slain at, in 1642-3, ii.
463.

SALTMARSH, John, Antinomian
preacher and Army chaplain, iii.
151, 153, 396 note, 524, 525, 678.

SALTONSTAL, Richard, Commissioner
at Leith, and trustee for forfeited
lands in Scotland in 1653-4, iv.
562.

SALVATOR ROSA, i. 763, 815.

SALVETTI, Amerigo, agent in London
for the Grand Duke of Tuscany, iv.
379, 422, 485.

SALWAY, Arthur, M.A. (Oxon.), in
the Westminster Assembly, ii. 521.

SALWAY, Humphrey, lay-member of
Westminster Assembly, ii. 524.

SALWAY, Major Richard, in the
Long Parliament, and the Third

Council of State of the Commonwealth, iv. 273, 314, 315, 321; in
the Fourth Council, iv. 354, 446;
in the Commission of Eight Members
of Parliament for the Incorporation
of Scotland with England (1651),
iv. 303, 360; in the Council of the
Barebones Parliament, iv. 505-6;
in the Restored Rump and Council
of the same, v. 454, 456, 465, 479,
480; in the Committee of Safety of
the Wallingford House Government,
v. 494, 505, 511; in disgrace at
the Second Restoration of the Rump,
v. 521; Prynne's enmity to, in the
debates on the Indemnity Bill, vi.
40.

SAMBIX, John à, publisher at Leyden,
iv. 535.

" SAMSON AGONISTES " : see *Milton*,
Writings of.

SANDELANDS, Andrew, a Fellow of
Christ's College, Cambridge, i. 112,
123, 200, 238-9; his letters to
Milton, iv. 487-94; v. 227, 227-8
note, 706-7; vi. 418.

SANDERS, Sir John, Parliamentarian
officer, ii. 446.

SANDERS, Colonel Thomas, v. 522,
540.

SANDERSON, John, a Turkey merchant,
i. 4.

SANDERSON, Dr. Robert, ii. 225, 521,
525; iii. 606; among Men of Letters
under the Protectorate, v. 76, 78-9;
after the Restoration, vi. 61; Bishop
of Lincoln in 1660, vi. 105, 291,
322; his portrait by Faithorne, vi.
648.

SANDFORD, an actor in the Duke's
Company, vi. 350.

SANDILANDS, John : see *Torphichen*,
Lord.

SANDWICH, Earl of : see *Montague*,
Admiral.

SANDYS, Edwin, captain of horse in
the Parliamentarian Army in 1642,
ii. 445, 454.

SANDYS, Sir William, i. 627.

SANSOME, Rear-Admiral, killed, vi.
254.

SANTA CRUZ, Blake's victory at, v.
141.

SARPI, Paolo, i. 529.

SARTORIS, Monsieur, friend of Salmasius, v. 194.
SATIRISTS, or SOCIAL POETS, and SATIRE as a form of literature, i. 469-84.
"SATYR AGAINST HYPOCRITES," by John Phillips, v. 228-9, 229 note, 383.
SAUMAISE : see *Salmasius*.
SAUMAISE, Claude and Josias de, sons of Salmasius, iv. 271, 346 ; vi. 204.
SAUNDERS, Rev. Mr., i. 402.
SAUNDERS, Colonel Thomas, iii. 326 ; iv. 402 ; v. 470.
SAUNDERSON, Miss, an actress, married to Betterton, the actor, vi. 350-1.
SAUNDERSON, Dr. Robert : see *Sanderson*, Dr. Robert.
SAVAGE, Lieutenant-Colonel, Royalist officer, ii. 442.
SAVAGE, Viscount, of Rock - Savage, Cheshire, i. 244.
SAVAGE, Sir Edward, iii. 193.
SAVILE, Sir Harry, Provost of Eton in 1618, i. 536.
SAVILE, Henry, vi. 630.
SAVILE, Thomas, 1st Lord Pomfret, ii. 159.
SAVILE, Sir William, ii. 62.
SAVILE, Lord : see *Sussex*, Earl of.
SAVOY and PIEDMONT, the dukedom of, v. 183-4 : see also *Milton* (*Piedmontese Letters of*), and *Piedmont*.
SAVOY CONFERENCES, the, of Bishops and Nonconformist clergymen in 1661, vi. 159, 433-4.
SAWBRIDGE, publisher, vi. 403.
SAWREY, Colonel Roger, in the Republican Army, v. 470, 498.
SAXBY, Edward, Army agitator, iii. 534-5.
SAY, Lord (1450), i. 48.
SAY, William (Regicide), iii. 720 ; vi. 28 ; in successive Councils of State, iv. 273, 313, 314, 321, 355, 449, 519 ; in Parliament, iv. 394 ; in the Restored Rump, v. 454, 465 ; after the Restoration, vi. 31, 54 ; subsequent escape to Holland, vi. 115 and note.
SAYE AND SELE, William Fiennes, 1st Viscount, i. 680; in the First Bishops' War, ii. 49, 58, 67, 142 ; in the Long Parliament, ii. 155, 156, 161,
163-4 ; in English Church Reform movement, ii. 201 ; his part in Bishops Exclusion Bill, ii. 227, 236, 279, 280, 281, 337, 431 ; in the Parliamentarian Army, ii. 444, 445 ; lay member of Westminster Assembly, ii. 523, 596, 605 ; in the management of the Colonies, iii. 119 ; in the prosecution of Milton by Stationers' Company, iii. 297 note ; in the " Committee of the Two Kingdoms," iii. 331 note, 380 ; his son, the Hon. John Fiennes, iii. 401 ; in House of Lords business, iii. 411, 555 note ; at the Treaty of Newport, iii. 605; in the House of Lords in 1648, iii. 692 ; one of Cromwell's Lords, v. 323, 326 ; in the restored House of Lords in 1660, v. 695 ; in the Privy Council of the Restoration, vi. 17 ; in the Trials of the Regicides, vi. 77 ; his death, vi. 237.
SCARSDALE, Lord Deincourt, 1st Earl of, ii. 429.
SCEPTICS, account of the sect of, in 1644-5, iii. 159 ; v. 15.
SCHAEP, Gerard, Dutch ambassador in London, iv. 215, 371, 422.
SCHALLER, James (or Jacobus), Professor of Philosophy at Strasburg, iv. 534-5 ; v. 402-3.
SCHLEZER, John Frederick, agent for the Marquis of Brandenburg, in London, v. 273-4, 402.
SCHNEIDER, Zacharias, of Leipsic, iii. 202.
SCHOLOER, Mr., Rector of Ould in Northamptonshire, iv. 4.
SCHOMBERG, Count, in command of the auxiliary land force of Charles II. in 1673, vi. 596.
SCHURMANN, Mademoiselle, v. 594-5 and note.
SCIPIONI, Alberto, friend of Sir Henry Wotton, i. 738-9.
SCOBELL, Mr. Henry, Clerk of the Parliament, iv. 154, 325, 326, 424, 505 ; Assistant Secretary to the Council of State, iv. 546, 576, 779 ; reference to his *Acts and Ordinances*, iv. 565 note ; Clerk of Oliver's First Parliament, v. 6 ; and of the Second, v. 327, 329, 363 ; his salary, v. 182, 624, 625 note ; in disgrace with the

Restored Rump, v. 599-600; after the Restoration, vi. 199.

SCOT, Sir John, of Scotstarvet, i. 511; in the episode of Montrose in Scotland, iii. 351; excepted from Cromwell's Ordinance of Pardon and Grace, iv. 561; in London, v. 94; the Drummond MSS. and, v. 263-4.

SCOTLAND: the Church, or Kirk of, in 1632, i. 423-5; the policy of "Thorough" pursued by Charles and Laud in, i. 667, 697; ecclesiastical system of, in 1632, i. 697-9; Charles I.'s Coronation visit to, and the Scottish Parliament of 1633, i. 699-704; Laud's policy for, i. 704-6, 716-19; the Privy Council of, from 1634 to 1638, i. 706-8; the Court of High Commission of, i. 708-9; opposition elements in, i. 709-13; theological fervour in, i. 713-6; the signing of the Covenant throughout, i. 719-32; in 1638-9, and the "First Bishops' War," ii. 3-71, 122; feeling of the English people for and against the people of, in 1640, ii. 122-3; through the "Second Bishops' War" (1639-40), ii. 126-42; the King's second visit to, in 1641, ii. 287-308; iii. 427; attitude of, towards the King and towards the English Parliament before the Civil War, ii. 416-20; the Church of, represented in the Westminster Assembly, ii. 509-10; iii. 15-18; the Auxiliary Army of, in the Civil War (1643-5), iii. 35-7, 339-40; see *Charles I.*; Alliance of, with England, and "Committee of the Two Kingdoms," iii. 40-1; episode of Montrose in, iii. 340-69; interference of, with English affairs in 1647, iii. 562-4, 578-82; end of the Alliance and dissolution of the Committee of the Two Kingdoms, iii. 585; Secret Treaty of Charles I. with, in 1647-8, iii. 586, 588-90; Cromwell's first visit to, iii. 620-3; danger from, to the Infant Commonwealth, iv. 19-22; Presbyterianism in, in 1648-9; iv. 61-3; Charles II. and the Argyle Government of, in 1649, iv. 180-1; Montrose's expedition to, in 1649-50, iv. 181-6; arrival of Charles II. in (June 1650-1), iv. 187-90; Cromwell's campaign in, iv. 196-201; parties in, after Dunbar, iv. 201-6; position of Charles II. in, after Dunbar, iv. 207-10; Cromwell's continued campaign in, after Dunbar, iv. 210-1; Coronation of Charles II. in, iv. 213-4; during Cromwell's occupation of, south of the Firths, iv. 281-4, 286, 287-92; account of, north of the Firths, iv. 281-4; political incorporation of, with the English Commonwealth, iv. 302-3, 360-6; the Glencairn-Middleton Insurrection in, iv. 508-10, v. 86; feeling in, about the Protectorate, iv. 551-2; Monk's success in the government of, iv. 552; Cromwell's system of government of, in 1654, v. 86-9; theological parties in (1654-6), v. 89-98, 115-6; Cromwell's schemes for church government of, in 1657, v. 345-50; re-officering of the Army for, by the Restored Rump, v. 470; Monk quits, in December 1659, v. 512; dissolution of the political connexion of, with England, at the Restoration, vi. 129; the Scottish Council in London, vi. 130-3; arrests of Argyle and Swinton in London, vi. 132-3; government in, by the revived Committee of Estates, vi. 132-40; loss at sea of the national Records of, vi. 141; acts of the Scottish Parliament of 1661, vi. 142-51.

SCOTT of Montross, iv. 561.

SCOTT of Thirlstane, iv. 561.

SCOTT, Arthur, Fellow of Christ's College, Cambridge, i. 111, 112, 123.

SCOTT, Major Thomas (Regicide), a Recruiter in 1646, iii. 402, 583, 584, 613; at the King's Trial, iii. 712 note, 720; vi. 28; in the First Council of State of the Commonwealth, iv. 11, 13, 79, 83, 87, 123, 146, 147, 150, 151; in the Second, iv. 223, 224, 225, 231; in the Third, iv. 273, 314; in Parliament, iv. 308; in the Fourth and Fifth Councils of State, iv. 354-5, 449, 456; on the Committee for the Propagation of the Gospel, iv. 397; at the dissolution of the Rump, iv. 407, 413; in Oliver's First Parliament, v. 5, 7;

in Cromwell's Second Parliament, v. 107, 110, 112, 329, 331; in Richard's Parliament, v. 430, 432, 441; in the Restored Rump, v. 454, 455, 465, 479, 480, 488, 495, 497, 505, 514; in the Second Restored Rump and the new Council of State, v. 519-20, 525, 528, 529, 536; in the Restored Long Parliament, v. 544, 545, 552, 561, 666; his last speech at the Dissolution of the Long Parliament, v. 554, 658; after the Restoration, vi. 31, 54, 80; trial and execution of, vi. 81, 85, 96-7; in the Bill of Attainder, vi. 115.

SCOTT, Sir Walter, reference to his description, in the *Legend of Montrose*, of the Marquis of Argyle, ii. 13-4.

SCOTT of Harden, Sir William, iv. 561.

SCRIMGEOUR, David, ii. 441.

"SCRIPTUM CONTRA HISPANOS," a Declaration of War by Cromwell against the Spaniards (1655), v. 108, 240-2.

SCRIVENERS, description of the calling of, i. 28-9; Company and Arms of the London, i. 7; Charter of, i. 62.

SCROOPE, Colonel Adrian (Regicide), Parliamentarian officer, ii. 445; Major in the *New Model* Army, iii. 327; signs the death-warrant of Charles I., iii. 720; vi. 28; in the campaign to Ireland, iv. 56; in the Goverment of Scotland and in Monk's Army, v. 86, 87, 115, 418; in Richard's Parliament, v. 430; after the Restoration, vi. 36, 38, 43, 49, 52, 54; his trial and execution, vi. 80, 81, 85, 96-7; in the Bill of Attainder, vi. 115.

SCUDAMORE, Sir James, in the reign of Elizabeth, i. 749

SCUDAMORE, John, Lord (Viscount Sligo), Ambassador at Paris in 1638, i. 749-51, 752, 753, 755, 756, 757, 758, 759; ii. 368 note; recalled to England, in 1639, i. 834, 834 note; v. 306 note; his house next door to Milton's in Petty France, iv. 418, 420-1; mention of in Milton's *Defensio Secunda*, iv. 637.

SCUDAMORE, Lady (in 1602), probably mother of the Ambassador, i. 752 note.

SCUDAMORE, Lady, wife of the Ambassador, i. 755-6.

SCUDAMORE (the "young Lord S."), possibly son of the Ambassador, i. 738 note.

SCUDAMORE, Mary, daughter of the Ambassador, married to (1) Thomas Russel, (2) William Dutton, v. 306 note.

SCUDAMORE, Mrs. (known, in 1612, as "old Mrs. Skydmore of Chilton," in Bucks), i. 752 note.

SCUDAMORE, Richard, of London, in 1606-7, i. 4.

SCUDDER, Henry, member of Westminster Assembly, ii. 521.

SCUDERI, Georges de, French romance writer, vi. 359.

SCUDERI, Madeleine de, French romance writer, vi. 359.

SCULTETUS, Abrahamus, German Divine, ii. 253-4 and note.

SCUTT, Richard, Usher of the Council Chamber, v. 178, 179.

SEAFORTH, the Earl of, ii. 7; iii. 355-6, 358, 359; iv. 205, 206; in the Scottish Parliament of 1650, iv. 212, 560.

"SEALED KNOT," the, secret association of Royalists in 1657-8, v. 336.

SEAMAN, Dr. Lazarus, member of Westminster Assembly, account of, ii. 521; iii. 20, 22, 94, 95 note; Moderator of Second Provincial Presbyterian Synod of London, iii. 568, 606, 674, 677; iv. 71; v. 74; ejected as a Nonconformist, vi. 232, 416.

SEARLE, George, v. 691 and note, 694.

SEATON, Mr., minister of Old Aberdeen, v. 346 note.

SECKER, Dr., vi. 763.

"SECOND BEACON FIRED," a pamphlet published in London in 1654, v. 59 and note.

SECTS and SECTARIES, synopsis of English, in 1644, iii. 136-59; Denunciation of, by the Westminster Assembly, iii. 160-6; Milton among the Sectaries, iii. 186-9; a new synopsis of Sects for 1654, v. 15-27.

SEDASCUE, Major, in the New Model Army, iii. 327.

SEDGWICK, Major, v. 102, 103.

SEDGWICK, Obadiah, member of Westminster Assembly, ii. 521, 605; iii. 270.

SEDGWICK, William, Chaplain in the Parliamentarian Army, ii. 444; iii. 588 note.

SEDGWICK, William, of Ely (called Doomsday Sedgwick), iii. 588 and note.

SEDLEY, Sir Charles, i. 603 note; among Men of Letters of the Restoration, vi. 321, 389-90; in Dryden's *Essay of Dramatic Poesy*, vi. 378; Plays by, vi. 610, 611; account of, vi. 632 note.

SEDLEY, Sir William, i. 603 note.

SEEKERS, the sect of, iii. 153-5, 396 note; v. 15, 18.

SEGAR, Sir William, Garter King-at-Arms, i. 6, 7.

"SEICENTISTI," the, term applied by the Italians to writers of the 17th century, i. 762-3.

SEIGNIOR, George, vi. 803.

SEILE, Henry, publisher, v. 691; vi. 398, 403.

SELDEN, John, indicted in Star Chamber and committed to the Tower, i. 216; in Charles I.'s Third Parliament, i. 375-6; friend of Herrick, i. 508; quotation from his writings, i. 517; account of, i. 521-5; specimens of his table-talk, i. 524-5; among the Latitudinarians, i. 531, 532, 533; his high esteem for the theosophist Fludd, i. 540; acquaintance with Hobbes, i. 541; his Inn of Court, i. 562; at the Great Masque of the Inns of Court, i. 580, 581; in the Long Parliament, ii. 163, 174; in Strafford's Trial, ii. 179, 185; in miscellaneous reforms by the Long Parliament, ii. 187; in English Church reform movement, ii. 197; for Limited Episcopacy, ii. 217, 236; before the Civil War, ii. 416; lay member of the Westminster Assembly, ii. 511, 524, 606-8; iii. 20, 22; referred to, with praise, by Milton, iii. 67-8, 284; his *Uxor Ebraica*, iii. 297 note; chairman of a Parliamentary Committee, iii. 579; and the Erastians, iii. 397, 408, 410-1, 552; adviser of the Council of State of the Commonwealth, iv. 48, 447, 556; and Christopher Arnold, iv. 350; his autograph, iv. 352; his *Mare Clausum*, iv. 450; Queen Christina's interest in, iv. 597 note; *not* in Oliver's First Parliament, v. 5; his death, v. 75.

SELKIRK, William, Earl of (a younger son of the Marquis of Douglas), excepted from Cromwell's Ordinance of Pardon and Grace, iv. 561; as Duke of Hamilton and a member of the Scottish Council in London, vi. 130, 148: see *Hamilton*, Dukes of.

SELVAGGI, Roman friend of Milton, i. 805, 806 note, 821 note; iii. 455, 650.

SEMPILL, Lord, iv. 561.

"SENILE ODIUM," a Cambridge Comedy, by Peter Hausted, i. 244.

SEPARATISTS, i. 678-9; ii. 46, 538-44.

SEPPENS, Robert, fellow-graduate of Milton at Cambridge, i. 218, 258.

SERLE, Daniel, v. 103.

SERVIEN, French minister at Turin, v. 43.

SETON, George: see *Winton*, Earl of.

SETON'S LOGIC, i. 262 and note, 265 note.

SETTLE, Elkanah, in controversy with Dryden, vi. 611-12.

SEWSTER, Mrs. Anna, v. 307.

SEWSTER, Robina, niece of Cromwell, and wife of William Lockhart, v. 47, 307.

SEXBY, Colonel Edward, v. 33; in the Sexby-Sindercombe Plot, v. 119-20; real author of *Killing no Murder*, v. 141-2 and note; his death, v. 320.

SEYMOUR, Lord, brother of the Marquis of Hertford, ii. 429, 465.

SEYMOUR, Mr. Edward, Speaker of the House of Commons in 1673, vi. 598.

SEYMOUR, Francis (Lord Seymour of Trowbridge), in Charles II.'s Privy Council, vi. 18.

SHADWELL, an actress in the Duke's Company, vi. 350.

SHADWELL, Thomas, dramatist, vi.
321, 611-2, 730.
SHAFTESBURY, Earl of: see *Cooper*,
Sir Anthony Ashley.
SHAKESPEARE, T., of the sect of
Ranters, v. 18.
SHAKESPEARE, William: references to,
i. 23, 24, 27, 46, 60, 88, 89, 134,
169, 236, 330, 378, 433, 434, 438,
443, 485, 503; iii. 445, 447, 449,
515, 515 note; iv. 137, 137 note;
vi. 353, 358.
SHANDON (or SHANNON), Francis
Boyle, Viscount (son of the 1st
Earl of Cork), iii. 659; v. 230;
v. 604.
SHANDON, Elizabeth, Viscountess, vi.
604.
SHAPCOTT, Colonel Robert, M.P. for
Tiverton, vi. 195.
SHARP, James, minister of Crail in
Fifeshire, taken prisoner at Worcester
and sent to London, iv. 296; back
in Scotland, v. 90; sent by the
"Resolutioners" on a mission to
the Protector in London, v. 95,
96-8, 115-6, 345, 349; with General
Monk in London, v. 541; vi. 5;
acts as agent for the Kirk to Charles
II., vi. 136-7, 141; is made a
professor in the New College, St.
Andrews, vi. 149; in London again,
vi. 161.
SHARP, John, Archbishop of York, iv.
419.
SHATTEREL, Robert (called also
William), actor, vi. 349, 355.
SHEFFIELD, James (son of Earl of
Mulgrave), Parliamentarian officer,
ii. 445.
SHEFFIELD, Lady Mary, daughter of
Lord Sheffield, and wife of Lord
Fairfax, ii. 171.
SHEFFIELD, Lord, President of the
North, ii. 171.
SHEFFIELD, Thomas (son of Earl of
Mulgrave), Colonel, under Sir
Thomas Fairfax, in the *New Model
Army*, iii. 327; at the Battle of
Naseby, iii. 335; waverings towards
Parliament in 1647, iii. 537; in
1660, v. 563.
SHELDON, Dr. Gilbert, account of, in
1632, i. 533, 534-5; chaplain to

Charles I., iii. 556, 587; among
Men of Letters under the Protectorate, v. 76; possible author of the
denunciation of Milton by G. S., v.
691 and note; after the Restoration,
vi. 61, 99; Bishop of London, vi.
105, 425, 428; at Coronation of
Charles II., vi. 154-8; among
Milton's old antagonists, vi. 214;
performs the marriage ceremony of
Charles II., vi. 229; in the Privy
Council, vi. 236-7; in London
during the Great Plague, vi. 258; a
promoter of the "Five Miles Act,"
vi. 258; Archbishop of Canterbury,
vi. 270, 432, 506, 507, 566, 606,
700.
SHELTON, a Puritan emigrant to
America, i. 430.
SHEPARD, Thomas, account of, as a
New England minister, ii. 558.
SHEPHARD, Sir Fleetwood (Fleet
Shephard), vi. 629-31, 778.
SHEPPARD, Thomas, army agitator,
iii. 534-5.
SHEPPEY, an actor, vi. 350.
SHERBORNE, Castle of, storming of,
iii. 338.
SHERFIELD, Mr., a client of the elder
Milton, i. 627.
SHERLY, an actor, vi. 349.
SHERWYN, Richard, iv. 242.
SHIP MONEY, exaction of, i. 670, 735;
ii. 188.
SHIRLEY, James (dramatist), i. 446,
451, 569, 580, 586, 621; iii. 446,
449; v. 76; vi. 292-3, 322, 358.
SHORT, Peter, printer, i. 90.
SHOTTON, William, fellow-graduate of
Milton at Cambridge, i. 258.
SHREWSBURY, Earl of, Royalist, i.
523; ii. 429; iv. 294.
SHUTE, Christopher, fellow-student of
Milton at Cambridge, i. 171, 240
note.
SHUTE, Josias, B.D., ii. 516.
SHUTE, Mr., a citizen of London, ii.
455.
SIBBALD, Dr. James, of Aberdeen, ii.
28.
SIBBALD, Colonel, iii. 347, 352.
SIBBES, Dr. Richard, Master of Cather-
ine Hall, Cambridge, i. 121, 180-
343, 516, 569, 609.

SIBTHORP, Dr., i. 371 ; agent of Laud, i. 403.

SICILY, in 1638 (Spanish Province), i. 745.

SIDDALL, William, Fellow and tutor of Christ's College, Cambridge, i. 123, 186, 225, 237 ; ii. 76.

SIDES, Mr. Henry J., of the Bodleian Library, Oxford (1880), i. 338 note.

SIDNEY, Algernon, third son of the Earl of Leicester, i. 751 ; vi. 18, 262 ; Colonel under the *New Model*, iii. 327, 402 ; absent from the King's Trial, iii. 708 note ; in the Fifth Council of State of the Common- wealth, iv. 355, 449 ; not in Oliver's First Parliament, v. 5 ; mention of, among Men of Letters under the Pro- tectorate, v. 75 ; in the Restored Rump and its Council of State, v. 454, 456, 467, 544 note ; his mission to the Baltic, v. 478, 502 ; among Men of Letters of the Restoration, vi. 197-8, 299, 308 ; mentioned by Milton, iv. 602, 612.

SIDNEY, Lady Dorothy, ii. 169.

SIDNEY, Sir Henry (father of Sir Philip Sidney), i. 605, 608.

SIDNEY, Henry, brother of Algernon Sidney, vi. 262.

SIDNEY, Humphrey, English trader, v. 589.

SIDNEY, Sir Philip, i. 115, 514, 605 ; his *Arcadia*, iv. 139, 248-9, 250 note.

SIDNEY, Robert : see *Leicester*, Earl of.

SIDNEY-SUSSEX COLLEGE, Cambridge, i. 114, 118, 121, 399, 447, 525 ; ii. 78, 225.

SILER, Edward, iv. 562.

"SILURIST," the : see *Vaughan*, Henry.

SILVERCRON, Peter Spiering, Swedish ambassador in London, iv. 377-8.

SIMON, J. (engraver), died in 1753, vi. 756 note.

SIMMONS, Martha, Quaker fanatic, v. 68.

SIMMONS, Matthew, printer for the Council of State, and one of Milton's publishers, i. 5 ; iii. 255 (spelt Symmons), 450 ; iv. 64, 97, 98 note, 99, 146, 148-9, 154-5, 249 note, 325, 327 ; vi. 171, 398, 509.

SIMMONS, Samuel (probably son of the preceding), publisher, vi. 403 ; agreement between Milton and, in the matter of *Paradise Lost*, vi. 509- 11, 511 note ; 516, 622-8 ; 640-1, 712-3, 779, 781.

SIMPSON, Fellow of Christ's College, Cambridge, i. 123, 181.

SIMPSON, David, i. 34, 35.

SIMPSON, James, v. 345 ; vi. 134.

SIMPSON, John, i. 35.

SIMPSON, John, Anabaptist preacher, iv. 548.

SIMPSON, Sidrach, member of West- minster Assembly, ii. 521, 580, 585, 591, 605 ; iii. 22, 23, 87, 111, 127-8, 131, 298, 392 ; iv. 370, 392, 438 ; v. 12.

SIMS, John, Baptist preacher, iii. 148.

SIMSON, Mr., of the sect of Antinomians, iii. 161, 165, 678.

SIMSON, Mr. James, minister of Airth, v. 115.

SINCLAIR, John, 6th Lord, i. 710, 722 ; ii. 16, 38, 65, 418 ; iv. 560 ; v. 360, 547.

SINDERCOMBE, Miles (in Monk's army in Scotland), his plot against Crom- well in 1656-7, v. 119-20.

SION COLLEGE (in London), iii. 394-5, 405, 407, 416 ; the First Provincial Presbyterian Synod of London held at, in May 1647, iii. 545 ; the Second of the same, in Nov. 1647, iii. 568, 676-8 ; and Milton, iii. 679-80 ; efforts of the Presbyterians of, in the last days of Charles I., iii. 716 ; iv. 71-2 ; vi. 66.

SION HOUSE, seat of the Earl of Northumberland, iii. 561.

SKELTON, John (poet), reference to, i. 470.

SKELTON, Puritan preacher, ii. 531-4.

SKENE, of Skene, ii. 38.

SKINNER, Mr., clergyman in London, i. 211.

SKINNER, Madam, of Thornton Col- lege, iv. 623.

SKINNER, Captain Augustine, v. 454.

SKINNER, Cyriac, Milton's pupil and friend, iii. 657, iv. 621, 622-3, v. 230 ; Milton's Sonnets to, v. 236-40, vi. 688 ; friendship with Milton and Oldenburg, v. 269 ; a

member of the Rota Club, v. 485;
and Milton, v. 703, vi. 453; scurrilities against, in 1661-2, vi. 462.

SKINNER, Daniel, merchant, iii. 658,
vi. 791, 801, 803, 805.

SKINNER, Daniel, jun., son of the preceding, iii. 658, iv. 158 note; is
Milton's amanuensis, vi. 720 and
note, 721; story of, and the Milton
MSS., vi. 790-805 and note, 806.

SKINNER, Robert, Bishop of Bristol,
i. 674, ii. 149, 150; impeachment
of, ii. 270; Bishop of Oxford, ii.
325, 334-6; after the Restoration,
vi. 61, 105.

SKINNER, Thomas, iii. 658.

SKINNER, Sir Vincent, iii. 657.

SKIPPON, Philip, Captain of the Artillery Garden, and Major-General of
the City Militia, ii. 344-5, 354, 402,
443, 446, 456; in the March to
Turnham Green, ii. 457; at the
Siege of Reading, ii. 465; through
the Civil War, iii. 168, 182-3, 326,
328 note, 332, 335, 336, 378,
381; in the House of Commons,
iii. 402 note; at Newcastle, in
1646-7, iii. 508, 510, 522, 532; in
the question of the Irish Field-
Marshalship, iii. 533; in London,
iii. 534; in the quarrel of Parliament and Army, iii. 535-7; in a
Commission of the Parliament to
treat with the Army, iii. 549; in
charge of London during the Second
Civil War, iii. 593; his part at the
King's Trial, iii. 689, 708 note, 718;
in the First Council of State of the
Commonwealth, iv. 12, 14; doggerel
lines about, iv. 115; commands in
London during Cromwell's war in
Scotland, iv. 192; in the Second
Council of State, iv. 224; in the
Third, iv. 273, 314, 315, 321; and
in the Fifth, iv. 355, 370; in the
Council of the First Protectorate, iv.
545, v. 31, 64, 177, 183-259, 273;
one of Cromwell's Major-Generals,
v. 49; in Cromwell's Second Parliament, v. 107; in the Council of
Second Protectorate, v. 308, 333;
one of Cromwell's Lords, v. 324;
supports Richard's government, v.
417-8; in the restored Rump, v. 454,

455, 472; scurrilous allusion to, in
Treason Arraigned, v. 666.

SKYDMORE: see Scudamore.

SKYTE, Dr. Johannes, iii. 225.

SLANNING, Sir Nicholas, ii. 466.

SLATER, Samuel, vi. 782.

SLEIGH, George, fellow-graduate of
Milton at Cambridge, i. 218.

SLIGO, Viscount: see Scudamore.

SLINGSBY, Sir Henry, Royalist rising
headed by, v. 34, 336; his trial and
execution, v. 337-8.

SLINGSBY, Henry, in the First Council
of the Royal Society, 1662, vi. 396.

SMALL, Mr., his papers seized by the
Council of State, in 1649, iv. 89, 92.

SMECTYMNUUS, the feigned name of
the Authors of an Anti-Episcopal
book in 1640, ii. 219-22, 219
note, 253-61, 255-7, 391; letter of
the Smectymnuans and their adherents to the Westminster Assembly in
1642, ii. 420; the Five Smectymnuans in the Assembly, ii. 605, iii.
84; Milton and the Smectymnuans,
iii. 187, 266, v. 63; in 1660, vi.
62-3, see Calamy, Marshall, Newcomen, Spurstow and Young.

SMETHWICK, Francis, publisher, iii.
447.

SMITH, bailie of Edinburgh in 1640,
ii. 143, 190.

SMITH, Mr., Presbyterian minister of
Mitcham in 1572, ii. 532.

SMITH, Mr., Presbyterian preacher in
London, in 1640, ii. 191.

SMITH, an actor in the Duke's Company, vi. 350.

SMITH, Abraham, waterman, vi. 91.

SMITH, Bernard, fellow-graduate of
Milton at Cambridge, i. 258.

SMITH, Charles, publisher, vi. 764.

SMITH, George, one of the English
lawyers sent to Scotland as resident
Judges for the Commonwealth in
1651-2, iv. 364, 561, v. 86-7;
at Dumfries, v. 92; in Oliver's
second Parliament, v. 108.

SMITH, Dr. Henry, Master of Magdalen College, Cambridge, and Vice-
Chancellor of the University, i. 171,
172.

SMITH, Major Henry (Regicide), in
the New Model Army, iii. 326; in

the Quarrel between Parliament and Army, iii. 534; in the death-warrant of Charles I., iii. 720, vi. 28; in the Restored Rump, v. 454, 470; after the Restoration, vi. 43, 49, 54; his trial, vi. 80, 93; his death, vi. 98 note; in the Bill of Attainder, vi. 115.

SMITH, James, one of the authors of *Wit and Drollery*, in 1656, v. 261-2 and note.

SMITH, Adjutant Jeremiah, v. 477.

SMITH, John, Cambridge Platonist, vi. 306.

SMITH, John, of Edinburgh, Burgh Commissioner in 1638-9, ii. 16.

SMITH, Peter, member of Westminster Assembly, ii. 521.

SMITH, Philip, sizar and fellow-student of Milton at Christ's College, Cambridge, i. 112, 218, 258, 558; in the Restored Rump (?), v. 454.

SMITH, Ralph, publisher, iii. 131, vi. 403.

SMITH, Sir Richard, Knight and Privy Councillor, iii. 193.

SMITH, Thomas (of Northampton), father of Philip Smith, i. 112.

SMITHSON, Colonel, v. 522.

SMYTH, John, early Independent and Separatist, and leader among the Anglo-Dutch Baptists at Leyden, ii. 539-40, 543, iii. 101-2, 147.

SMYTHE, John, Clerk of the Commons in Cromwell's Second Parliament, v. 327, 329.

SOAME, Thomas, in Long Parliament, ii. 173, 513 note.

" SOBIESKI DECLARATION," The, translated by Milton in 1674, vi. 725-7.

SOBIESKI, John (King John III. of Poland) : see *Poland*.

SOCINIANS, the sect of, i. 537, 540, iii. 157, v. 14-15; Cromwell's Toleration of the, v. 65.

SOLEMN LEAGUE AND COVENANT, the : see *Covenant*.

SOMERS, Mr., afterwards Lord, and the fourth edition of *Paradise Lost*, sometimes called " the Somers edition," vi. 785.

SOMERSET, Carr (Ker), Earl of, trial of, with his wife, in 1615, for the murder of Sir Thomas Overbury, i. 60, ii. 153-4, 430.

SOMERSET, Edward, eldest son of the 1st Earl of Worcester, see *Herbert of Raglan*, Lord.

SOMERSET, William Seymour, Duke of : (known as 11th Earl, and afterwards Marquis, of Hertford), ii. 48, 142, 143; account of, ii. 157, 168, 279; appointed Governor of the Prince of Wales and created Marquis, ii. 281, 283; in Charles I.'s Council, ii. 336, 350, 413, 428, 429; appointed Lieutenant of the County of Somersetshire, ii. 439; his contribution of horse and foot to the King's Army, ii. 442-3; General-in-chief in the west of England, ii. 465, 467; after the Civil War, iii. 376, 561, 606; in the last days of the King, iii. 712; at the King's funeral, iii. 727; arrested by Cromwell's Major-Generals, v. 50; in 1657-8, v. 303; the dukedom of Somerset revived in his honour in 1660, vi. 18; Chancellor of Oxford University in succession to Richard Cromwell, vi. 65; one of the thirty-four Commissioners for the Trials of the Regicides, vi. 77; his death, vi. 18, 108.

SOMERSET, Duke of (in 1688), a subscriber to the fourth edition of *Paradise Lost*, vi. 785.

SOUL-SLEEPERS, or Mortalists, sect of, iii. 156.

SOUTH, Robert, mention of, among Men of Letters under the Protectorate, v. 76; at the Restoration, vi. 319, 388, 617, 636 note.

SOUTHAMPTON, Earl of (Shakespeare's friend), i. 122, 438.

SOUTHAMPTON, Thomas Wriothesley, Earl of (son of the preceding), i. 122; account of, ii. 157-8; in Charles I.'s Council, iii. 337, 350, 429, 453; after the Civil War, iii. 376, 561, 606, 627; in the last days of Charles I., iii. 712-3; at the King's funeral, iii. 727; at the Restoration of Charles II., vi. 9, 17, 19; and the Trials of the Regicides, vi. 77; in court affairs, vi. 106; member of the Scottish Council in London, vi. 131; at the Coronation of Charles

II., vi. 151; Clarendon and, vi. 239, 245, 253, 264; opposes the Five Miles Act, vi. 259; his death, vi. 264.

SOUTHAMPTON, Charles Fitzroy, Duke of, eldest son of Charles II. and the Duchess of Cleveland, and her heir-designate, vi. 604.

SOUTHCOTT, Mrs. Grace, ii. 44.

SOUTHCOT, Thomas, Parliamentarian officer, iii. 444.

SOUTHERNE, Thomas, dramatist, subscriber to the fourth edition of *Paradise Lost*, vi. 785.

SOUTHESK, David Carnegy, 1st Earl of, i. 707; ii. 15, 21, 293, 418; iv. 561.

SOUTHWOLD BAY, Battle of, between the Dutch and English, vi. 583.

SPAGNOLETTO, Italian painter, i. 763.

SPAIN: the Spanish Infanta, i. 61, 105, 106; the Spanish Match proposed for Prince Charles, i. 61, 105, 356; war declared with, by James I., i. 106; account of, in 1638, i. 744-5; relations of, with the English Commonwealth, iv. 379-80; Cromwell's rupture with, v. 46-7; war with, v. 140-1; Louis XIV. and the "Spanish Succession," vi. 568.

SPALDING, local historian of Aberdeen, ii. 56.

SPANG, William, minister at Campvere in Holland, and in correspondence with Baillie, ii. 65; iii. 91, 121, 121 note, 428, 429 note; iv. 569; v. 97.

SPANHEIM, Ezekiel, son of Frederick Spanheim, v. 171-3, 204-5; vi. 723.

SPANHEIM, Frederick, Professor of Philosophy at Geneva, i. 832; iv. 460; v. 152, 171, 208.

SPARKE, Michael, publisher, iii. 220, 298 note.

SPARRA, lady attendant to Queen Christina of Sweden, iv. 271.

SPARROW, Richard, goldsmith of London, i. 4.

SPAVIN, Robert, Secretary to Cromwell, vi. 32.

SPEED, the historian, i. 525; vi. 765.

SPEEDE, Samuel, publisher, vi. 514.

SPELMAN, Sir Henry, antiquary and Saxon scholar, i. 525.

SPENCER, Captain, Baptist preacher in 1639, iii. 147.

SPENCER, Lord; see *Sunderland*, Earl of.

SPENCER, Alice: see *Derby*, Countess-Dowager of.

SPENCER, Anne (sister of the preceding), i. 590-1, 592, 596, 597 note, 603 note.

SPENCER, Elizabeth: (sister of the preceding), i. 591, 592, 596.

SPENCER, Sir John, of Althorpe, father of the Dowager Countess of Derby, i. 588.

SPENCER, Lord: Charles I. a visitor at his house at Althorpe, in 1647, iii. 515.

SPENSER, Edmund (Poet), his pastoral forms, and the "Spenserians," i. 452-68; Milton and, i. 89, 575, 451, 503, 519, 592-3, 593-4; Charles I. and the *Faerie Queen*, iii. 515.

SPILSBURY, John, Anabaptist, iii. 147, 148; iv. 45.

SPOOR, Frederic, printer, v. 403.

"SPORTIVE WIT, or the Muses' Merriment," by John Phillips, v. 259-62 and note, 383.

SPOTSWOOD, James, Irish bishop, i. 420.

SPOTSWOOD, John, Archbishop of St. Andrews, i. 697, 700; High Chancellor of Scotland, i. 706, 707, 708, 719; ii. 7, 15, 42.

SPOTSWOOD, Sir Robert, his trial by Scottish Parliament, ii. 301, 307; in the episode of Montrose; iii. 362, 367, 368; iv. 488.

SPRAT, Thomas, mentioned among Men of Letters of the Restoration, vi. 320; and the Royal Society, vi. 396; his *History of the Institution, Design, and Progress, of the Royal Society*, vi. 398, 514; Chaplain to the Duke of Buckingham, vi. 613.

SPRINGETT, Lady, wife of Alderman Pennington, vi. 467.

SPRINGETT, Gulielma, daughter of Lady Springett, vi. 467, 472-3, 497.

SPURSTOW, Dr. William, Puritan divine, i. 121; minister of Hampden in Bucks, ii. 202; one of the authors of the *Smectymnuus* pamphlet, ii. 219, 605; chaplain to Parliamentarian regiment, ii. 444; account of, as member of Westminster Assembly,

ii. 521 ; iii. 94, 160, 170 ; iv. 172 ; after the Restoration, vi. 62-3, 99 ; ejected as a Nonconformist, vi. 23 note, 416.

SPYNIE, Lord, iv. 560.

SQUIB, Mr. Arthur, in the Barebones Parliament, and afterwards arrested in Venner's Riot in 1657, v. 134-6.

STACEY, John, witness, i. 15.

STACEY, Thomas, of Stanton St. John's, i. 18.

STAFFORD, John, publisher, vi. 399.

STAFFORD, a gentleman of Northamptonshire, and member of the Rota Club, v. 485.

STAFFORD, Viscount, a younger son of the Earl of Arundel, ii. 430.

STAGE COACHES, between London and Edinburgh, in 1658, v. 94 note.

STAGG, Mrs. Ann (wife of a London brewer), heads a deputation of women with a petition to the Commons in 1641-2, ii. 348 ; among the London sectaries in 1645, iii. 467.

STAMFORD, Henry Grey, 1st Earl of, ii. 69 ; account of, ii. 155, 430, 444, 445 ; his son, see *Grey of Groby ;* defeated at Stratton in 1643, ii. 466 ; in the House of Peers, iii. 297 note, 406, 692 ; in Oliver's First Parliament, v. 5 ; in attempted Royalist insurrection, v. 473, 478.

STAMMERS, a witness in the Trials of the Regicides, vi. 89.

STANBRIDGE, Mr., living in Three Leg Alley, Fetter Lane, vi. 197.

STANDEN, Mr., English Presbyterian, ii. 532.

STANHOPE, Lord Charles, ii. 48, 430.

STANHOPE, Major (Royalist), ii. 442.

STANLEY, Lieutenant-Colonel (Royalist), ii. 442.

STANLEY, Major (Royalist), iii. 442.

STANLEY, Lady Anne : see *Chandos and Castlehaven.*

STANLEY, Lady Elizabeth : see *Huntingdon,* Countess of.

STANLEY, Thomas, mentioned among Men of Letters under the Protectorate, v. 76 ; and at the Restoration, vi. 314, 387.

STANLEY, Venetia, wife of Sir Kenelm Digby, vi. 296.

STANLEY, William : see *Monteagle.*

STANTON, Dr., see *Staunton.*

STAPLETON, Sir Philip, ii. 162-3, 273, 315, 349, 444 ; in the " Committee of the Two Kingdoms," iii. 41, 180, 182 note, 266, 381, 404, 408, 416, 510 note, 530, 531 ; among the Presbyterian leaders denounced by the Army, iii. 548-9 ; his death, iii. 554.

STAPLEY, Colonel Anthony (Regicide), iii. 720 ; in the First Council of State of the Commonwealth, iv. 13, 87, 147, 150, and in the Second, iv. 224, 226, 227, 229, 230, 231 ; and in the Fourth and Fifth, iv. 354, 446, 523 ; in the Interim Council of Thirteen, iv. 499 ; called to Cromwell's Supreme Assembly, iv. 501 ; in the Barebones Parliament, iv. 506 ; in Oliver's First Parliament, v. 5 ; his son, v. 337 ; dead before 1660, vi. 28, 54.

STAPLEY, Mr. John, of Sussex (son of the Regicide), his connection with the " Sealed Knot " conspiracy, v. 337-8.

STAPYLTON, Sir Robert, mention of, among Men of Letters of the Restoration, vi. 311.

STAR CHAMBER, Court of the, its history and constitution, i. 403-4, 403 note ; prosecutions by, i. 212, 214, 216, 385, 404-6 and notes, 673, 681, 682-3 ; abolished in 1641, ii. 188.

STARKEY, Mr., and his daughters, victims of the Irish Insurrection of 1641, ii. 313.

STARKEY, John, publisher, vi. 616, 640, 651, 661, 781.

" START, The, and its consequences " : see *Charles II.*

STATIONERS' COMPANY, the incorporation of, i. 544 ; its privileges, i. 546 ; list of publications registered from July to Dec. 1632, i. 549-50 ; petition of, against sectarian pamphlets, iii. 164-5 ; and Book Censorship, iii. 265-9 ; Milton prosecuted by, iii. 270-5 ; attacked by Milton, iii. 290-1 ; second prosecution of Milton by, iii. 291-7.

STAUNTON, Dr. Edmund, member of

Westminster Assembly, ii. 521, 605; iii. 5; iv. 71; vi. 232 note.

STAYNER, Captain, in command of six English frigates, makes a capture of Spanish Treasure, v. 113-4.

STEBBIN, Robert, servant to the Council of State (1654), iv. 578; v. 179.

STEELE, his account in the *Spectator* of Thomas Hobson, the Cambridge Carrier, i. 135.

STEELE, William, appointed a Judge by Cromwell, v. 36, 71; one of Cromwell's Lords, v. 324; supports Richard's Government, v. 418; in the Civil Government of Ireland, v. 471; Chancellor of Ireland, and member of the Committee of Safety in 1659, v. 494.

STEERE, William, Irish Bishop, i. 420.

STEPHENS, Mr., in the Long Parliament, and on the Committee for Printing in 1643, iii. 266.

STEPHENS, John, member of the Rump in 1659, v. 478.

STEPHENS, Philemon, publisher, iii. 164 note.

STEPHENS, Richard, servant of the Council, v. 625.

STERNE, Richard, Master of Jesus College, Cambridge, and Archbishop of York, i. 120; ejected from Cambridge University, iii. 94, 95 note.

STERNHOLD AND HOPKINS, the old version of the Psalms of David by, i. 52; iii. 26-7.

STERRY, Mr. Peter, member of Westminster Assembly, ii. 522, 525 note; iii. 392, 392 note; one of Cromwell's favourite preachers, iv. 61, 106, 145, 177, 229, 421, v. 22, 31, 71, 77, 374; has lodgings in Whitehall, iv. 153, 231; on the *Commission of Triers*, iv. 571.

STEUART, Dr. Adam, author of a Presbyterian pamphlet addressed to the Parliament and the Westminster Assembly in 1644, iii. 25, 120, 130; mentioned by Prynne (as Dr. Steward), iii. 298; by Milton in his anti-Presbyterian Sonnet as " A. S. " iii. 468-9, 470.

STEWART, Dr., Royalist and Episcopalian, iii. 27; with Charles II. at the Hague, iv. 27.

STEWART, Miss, vi. 262, 272, 353 : see *Richmond*, 3rd Duke of.

STEWART, Sir Archibald (a Lord of Session in Edinburgh), tried by the Scottish Parliament of 1641 as an " Incendiary," ii. 296, 298, 299, 300, 301, 307.

STEWART, Lord Bernard (Royalist), ii. 441; iii. 335.

STEWART, Sir James, Provost of Edinburgh in 1660, vi. 132, 133.

STEWART, John : see *Traquair*, Earl of.

STEWART of Ladywell, Mr. John, Commissary of Dunkeld, beheaded for his part in a plot of Montrose against Argyle in 1641, ii. 298-301.

STEWART, Colonel Walter, concerned in the above-mentioned plot, ii. 299-301.

STEWART, William, victim of the Irish insurrection of 1641, ii. 313.

STILLINGFLEET, Edward, mentioned among Men of Letters under the Protectorate, v. 76, and again at the Restoration, vi. 319-20, 388, 616; a subscriber to the fourth edition of *Paradise Lost*, in 1688, vi. 785.

STIRLING CASTLE, held by the Scottish Army in the First Bishops' War, ii. 56; surrender of, to Monk in 1651, iv. 295.

STIRLING, William Alexander, 1st Earl of : account of (in 1632), as Sir William Alexander of Menstrie, Principal Secretary of State for Scotland, i. 462-4, 512; his son, i. 707; resident in London, i. 706, 708; the original of his " Aurora," ii. 11; reference to the grant of Nova Scotia, to, by King James in 1621, v. 102; death of, in 1639-40, ii. 128.

STIRLING of Carden, Sir Archibald, iv. 561.

STIRLING of Keir, Sir George, ii. 38, 296, 298, 299, 300; his trial by the Scottish Parliament of 1641, ii. 301, 307; in the Episode of Montrose, iii. 362.

STOCKARTUS (or STOCKARUS), Johannes Jacobus, Envoy in London from the Cantons of Switzerland, iv. 383, 525, 528.

STOCKE, Rev. Richard, minister of Allhallows Church, Bread Street, i. 54, 55, 71, 104, 157, 343; ii. 518; iv. 447.

STONE, Anne, sempster, i. 4.

STONE, Captain, in the Second Council of the Barebones Parliament, iv. 525.

STONE, Samuel, New England minister, ii. 559.

STOUPE, Mr., travelling agent of Cromwell and Thurloe, v. 190, 284, 287-9 and notes.

STOURTON, Lord (Royalist), ii. 429.

STOW (the historian), his description of old Bread Street, i. 44.

STRACHAN, ·Colonel Archibald, iv. 184, 204, 207, 211, 213, 283.

STRADA, Italian historian, i. 762, 796.

STRADLING, Dr. George, vi. 327.

STRAFFORD, Thomas, 1st Viscount Wentworth, afterwards Earl of: at St. John's College, Cambridge, i. 116; in his twentieth year, and on his travels, i. 833; account of, to 1630, i. 382; as President of the North, i. 386, 405, 407, 605; as Lord Deputy of Ireland from 1632-8, i. 666-7; in correspondence with Laud, and their use of the term *Thorough*, i. 668-9, 671, 673; account of his government of Ireland from 1632 to 1638, i. 687-96; ii. 6; his handwriting described, ii. 9 note; his views on the Scottish Presbyterian movement of 1638 expressed in correspondences with the Earl of Northumberland and Lord Lorne, ii. 24-5, 26-7; his part in matters relating to the First "Bishops' War" with the Scots, ii. 47, 51, 54; his sayings concerning the Scottish Commander Leslie, ii. 55; gives, in a letter to Laud, his high opinion of Chappell as Provost of Trinity College, Dublin, ii. 76-7, 126; in correspondence with the King previous to the Second "Bishops' War," ii. 127-8; leaves Ireland, is in the King's Cabinet, is appointed Lieutenant-General in the Royal Army and Lord-Lieutenant of Ireland, heads the loan to Charles for expenses of the War, and is raised to the Earldom of Strafford, ii. 128-

9; through the Second "Bishops' War," ii. 135, 136, 140, 141; in the House of Peers and the King's Cabinet, ii. 152; impeachment of, by the Commons of England in November 1640, ii. 176-7; the trial and execution of, ii. 178-85; further mentions of, ii. 278, 280, 281, 284.

STRAFFORD, William Wentworth, 2nd Earl of, ii. 430; at the Coronation of Charles II., vi. 152.

STRALSUND, defence of, by Alexander Leslie in 1628, ii. 53.

STRANGE, Baron, 7th Earl of Derby, iv. 294, 297: see *Derby*.

STRANGE, Alice, Lady: see *Derby*, Countess Dowager of.

STRANGE, Lord Ferdinando: see *Derby*, Earl of.

STRANGE, Francis, scrivener, i. 338 note.

STRANGEWAYS, Sir John, in the Long Parliament, ii. 172, 416.

STRATHBOGIE, the Marquis of Huntley's domain of, ii. 56-7, 137; Treaty of, iv. 208-9.

STRATTON, Royalist victory at, ii. 466.

STREATER, Colonel John, in the remodelled Army of 1659, v. 522, 540, 566.

STRICKLAND, John, member of Westminster Assembly, ii. 522.

STRICKLAND, Mr. Walter, English Resident at the Hague in 1648, iv. 48-9, 83, 91, 125; recalled to England, and receives the thanks of the Parliament for his services, iv. 215-6; in the Parliament and its Third Council of State, iv. 273; sent as Ambassador-Extraordinary to the United Provinces, iv. 274, 276-8, 329; in the Fifth Council of State of the Commonwealth, iv. 355, 449; in Cromwell's Interim Council of Thirteen, iv. 499, 523; called to Cromwell's Supreme Assembly, iv. 501; in the Barebones Parliament, iv. 506; in the Second Council of the Barebones Parliament, iv. 525; mentions of, by Milton in the *Defensio Secunda*, iv. 602, 606, 612; in the Council of the First Protectorate, iv. 545, 572, 575; v. 7, 31, 64, 107, 124-5, 183-4, 247, 248,

259-60, 270, 273 ; one of Cromwell's Lords, v. 304 ; in the Second Parliament of Cromwell, v. 121, 129 ; in the Council of the Second Protectorate, v. 308, 322, 333, 346, 352, 374, 381, 401 ; in Richard's Council, v. 417 ; in the Restored Rump, v. 454, 455, 480 ; on the Committee of Safety of the Wallingford House Government, v. 494, 544 note ; among Milton's old friends and associates after the Restoration, vi. 197.

STRICKLAND, Sir William, made a baronet by Cromwell, v. 324 ; in the Restored Rump, v. 454, 455, 544 note.

STRODE, William, indicted in the Star Chamber, and committed to the Tower, in March 1628-9, i. 216.

STRODE, William, account of, in the Long Parliament, ii. 163 ; 174, 186, 232, 320, 328 ; attempted arrest of, by Charles I. in the House of Commons, ii. 339-45 ; in the Westminster Assembly, ii. 524.

STRONG, William, account of, as member of the Westminster Assembly, ii. 521 ; iv. 370.

STROZZI, nobleman of Rome, i. 812.

STRUTHERS, Rev. John, of Prestonpans, iii. 95 note.

STRYPE (the historian), i. 41, 78 note.

STUART, House of, ii. 137.

STUART, Rev. Dr., iv. 538.

STUART, Lady Arabella, ii. 157.

STUART, Sir Lewis, iv. 561.

STUARTISM and STUARTISTS : see Royalists.

STUBBE, Henry, mention of, among Men of Letters under the Protectorate, v. 76 ; at the Restoration, vi. 317-8 and note, 322, 616.

STUBBE, Philip, of Trinity College, Cambridge, author of Fraus Honesta, i. 221-5.

STUBBINS, Dr., of Oxford, i. 501.

STUBBS, John, Early Quaker, v. 27.

STURBRIDGE FAIR, near Cambridge, i. 137, 153.

STURGES, Richard, ii. 588.

STUTEVILLE, Sir Martin, of Dalham in Suffolk, in correspondence with Joseph Meade, i. 127, 146 note,

150-5, 167, 180-4, 187, 191-2, 215 note, 220, 231-3, 235, 237, 243, 243 note.

STUTEVILLE, John (son of Sir Martin), student of Christ's College, Cambridge, i. 150-1, 180.

STYLES, Matthias, member of Westminster Assembly, ii. 522.

SUCKLING, Sir John, i. 444, 448 ; account of, i. 503-5, 506 ; in the Royal Army, ii. 62, 183 ; verses by, v. 261 ; plays by, vi. 352 ; registration of his works in 1667, vi. 515.

SUFFOLK, Thomas Howard, 1st Earl of : Chancellor of Cambridge University, i. 115, 157.

SUFFOLK, Theophilus Howard, 2nd Earl of, i. 380, 385, 438, 737 ; in the First "Bishops' War," ii. 47 ; in the Peers, ii. 152 ; 153, 155, 430 ; iii. 297 note, 405, 421 ; impeachment of, by the Commons in 1647, iii. 554 ; 692 ; v. 176.

SUFFOLK, James Howard, 3rd Earl of, v. 176, 695.

SUMNER, Rev. Charles Richard (afterwards Bishop of Winchester), editor in 1825 of Milton's Treatise of Christian Doctrine, vi. 816.

SUNDERLAND, the Earl of (Lord Spencer), in the King's Army, (1642-3), ii. 429, 439 ; iii. 35.

"SUPPLEMENTUM," the, of Morus, in 1655, v. 192-8.

"SUPPLICANTS," the Scottish Presbyterian, in 1637, i. 722-4.

SUPPLY and REVENUE, measures of, and of retrenchment, in 1651-3, iv. 383 ; in 1654-6, v. 35 ; the business of, in the Convention Parliament of 1660, vi. 56-8.

SURAT (Hindostan), a factory of the London East India Company at, in 1612, v. 101.

SUSSEX, Earl of (Lord Savile), ii. 48, 142-3, 279, 336, 337, 413, 429.

SUTCLIFFE, Dean of Exeter, founder of Chelsea College in 1610, iii. 222.

SUTHERLAND, Earl of, i. 722 ; ii. 16 ; iii. 359 ; iv. 184.

SWADLING, Rev. Mr., vicar of Aldgate's, ii. 44.

SWEDEN, in 1638, i. 747 ; cadets of Scottish families serving in, ii. 52-3 ;

importation into Scotland of guns from, ii. 54 ; Salmasius in : see *Salmasius ;* ambassadors from, to London in 1651, iv. 377-8 ; Letter of the Council of State to the Queen of, in March 1651-2, iv. 481 ; friendly relations of, with the Commonwealth in 1651-3, iv. 377-8 ; embassy from Cromwell to, in Nov. 1653, iv. 512-3 ; Treaty of Upsal between Cromwell and the Queen of, in April 1654, iv. 553-4 ; letters of the Council of State to, from July 1654 to Oct. 1656, iv. 636, v. 189, 246-50, 252-3, 269-71, 274, 289 ; friendly relations of Cromwell and the King of, in the matter of a proposed Protestant Union, v. 313-5 ; Jephson sent by Cromwell on an Embassy to, in 1657, v. 342, 370 ; letters of the Council of State to, from Aug. 1657 to June 1658, v. 370, 385-6, 395-6 ; continuance of Oliver's relations with, during the Protectorate of Richard, v. 427-8 ; letters of Richard's Council of State to the King of, v. 571-2, 590 ; the policy of the Restored Rump towards, in 1659, v. 467.

SWEETING, John, publisher, v. 260.

SWIFT, Jonathan, i. 526.

SWINFEN, John, in the Council of State of 1659-60, v. 544.

SWINTON of Swinton, John, iv. 203 ; called to Cromwell's Supreme Assembly in 1653, iv. 502 ; a Commissioner for the forfeited estates in Scotland in 1654, iv. 561 ; in Oliver's First Parliament, v. 5 ; in the Scottish Council sitting in Edinburgh, v. 86, 349 ; in Cromwell's Second Parliament, v. 108, 114-5 ; supports Richard's Government, v. 418 ; in Richard's Parliament, v. 430 ; adopts Quakerism, vi. 132 ; his arrest and prosecuted in 1661, vi. 132-3 ; 135, 137 note, 140, 142, 150.

SWITZERLAND : in 1638, i. 745 ; non-episcopal church government in, ii. 46 ; Evangelical Cantons of, iv. 383, 527-8, v. 188, 244-6, 389-90 ; Cromwell's agents in, and embassy to, v. 41-3.

SYDENHAM, Thomas, brother of Colonel Sydenham, vi. 313-4.

SYDENHAM, Colonel William, in the Long Parliament, iii. 402 ; at the abolition of the House of Peers, iv. 5 ; in Cromwell's Interim Council of Thirteen, iv. 499, 523 ; called to the Supreme Assembly, iv. 501 ; in the Barebones Parliament and its Council, iv. 506, 515, 516, 525 ; in the Council of the First Protectorate, iv. 545, 568, 575, v. 31, 64, 177, 183, 184, 259, 260 ; Milton's mention of him in the *Defensio Secunda,* iv. 602 ; 606, 612 ; v. 381 ; in Cromwell's Second Parliament, v. 107, 118, 121, 129 ; in Cromwell's Council of the Second Protectorate, v. 308, 333, 346, 374 ; one of Cromwell's Lords, v. 324 ; supports Richard's Government, v. 417-8 ; in the Restored Rump and its Council, v. 454, 456, 470, 479, 480 ; on the Committee of Safety, v. 494, 521 ; after the Restoration, vi. 38, 47, 55, 197.

SYDNEY, Algernon, son of the Earl of Leicester : see *Sidney.*

SYDSERF, Thomas, Bishop of Galloway and Privy Councillor, i. 705, 706, 719 ; ii. 42 ; vi. 151.

SYLVESTER, Joshua, English translator of Du Bartas, i. 90, 451, 457 ; vi. 530.

SYMBALL, Henry, servant of the Council of State, iv. 578 ; v. 625.

SYMMEREN (?), Duchess of, mentioned, v. 269.

SYMMONS, Rev. Edward, and the *Eikon Basilike,* iv. 148-9.

SYMON, William, servant of the Council of State, iv. 576 ; v. 624.

SYMONDS, Baptist minister, ii. 581.

SYMONS, Nevill, publisher, vi. 399, 403.

SYNGE, Edward, Bishop of Limerick in 1660-1, vi. 129.

SYNODS : of the English and Scottish clergy in the United Provinces, i. 427 ; the French Walloon, of the United Provinces, v. 633 ; of the Presbyterian Church in England, see *Presbyterianism.*

T

"TABLES," the, name given to the Committees of Nobles, Lairds, Burgesses, and Ministers sitting in Edinburgh and maintaining the struggle for religious independence against Charles I. and his Scottish Privy Council in 1638, i. 724-6, ii. 54, 70-1.

TABOR, of Corpus Christi College, and Registrar of Cambridge University, i. 118, 149.

TAFFE (or Taafe), Theobald, Viscount, afterwards Earl of Carlingford, ii. 442.

TALBOT, Father, a French priest, i. 759.

TALBOT, Sir Gilbert, in the First Council of the Royal Society, vi. 396.

TALBOT, Colonel Thomas, in Cromwell's Second Parliament, v. 128; in Monk's Scottish Army, v. 470, 497, 498, 499.

TALLIS, musical composer, i. 52.

TANFIELD, Lord Chief Baron, i. 533.

TANGIER COMMITTEE, the, in London (1666-7), vi. 263.

TANY, Thomas, of the sect of "Muggletonians," v. 20.

TARENTE, the Prince of, letter of the Council of State to, v. 175-6; at the Coronation of Charles II., vi. 152.

TASBOROUGH, Sir John (of Suffolk), i. 154-5, 155 note.

TASSO, i. 762, 808-10.

TASSONI, Italian poet (1565), i. 762.

TATE, Mr. Zouch, M.P. for Northampton, iii. 181.

TAULER, Platonic writer, vi. 303.

TAVERNS: the Apollo Club, i. 440, 479; the Bull, in Bishopsgate Street, i. 134; the Devil, at Temple Bar, i. 440; the Grecian Coffee-House, v. 629; the Mermaid, in Old Bread Street, Cheapside, i. 45-6 and note, 439, 485, v. 338; the Rose, at Cambridge, i. 138.

TAYLOR, agent and correspondent of Wentworth in 1635, i. 695.

TAYLOR, Francis, account of, as member of Westminster Assembly, ii. 522.

TAYLOR, Jeremy, as student at Cambridge, i. 171, vi. 418; incorporated M.A. at Oxford and made a Fellow of All Souls, i. 625; his views on Toleration, iii. 126; his place in English literature, i. 517; mentioned among Men of Letters under the Protectorate, v. 76, 78-9, 80, 80 note; previous to the Restoration, v. 568; as Bishop of Down and Connor in 1660, vi. 128; among Men of Letters of the Restoration, vi. 299, 322, 388; registration of a book by, in 1667, vi. 514; his death in August 1667, vi. 405.

TAYLOR, John (the "Water-Poet"), account of, i. 482-4.

TAYLOR, Nathaniel, father of Jeremy Taylor, i. 171.

TAYLOR, Randal, a publisher, vi. 403, 786.

TAYLOR, Thomas, early Quaker, v. 26.

"TEARES AND LAMENTATIONS OF A SOROWFULL SOULE," a Collection of Songs by Sir William Leighton in 1614, i. 51.

TEDDIMAN, Sir Thomas, second in command of the English fleet in the Dutch war of 1665, vi. 255.

TEMPLE, James (Regicide), Captain of a troop in the Parliamentarian army in 1642, ii. 445; signs the death-warrant of Charles I., iii. 720, vi. 28; in the Restored Rump, v. 454; after the Restoration, vi. 43, 49, 54; his trial and condemnation, vi. 80, 93, 115; his death in prison, vi. 98 note.

TEMPLE, Sir John, in Oliver's First Parliament, v. 6; in the Council of State of 1659-60, v. 544.

TEMPLE, Peter (Regicide), a "Recruiter," iii. 402; signs the death-warrant of Charles I., iii. 720, vi. 28; in the Restored Rump, v. 454; after the Restoration, vi. 43, 49, 54; his trial and condemnation, vi. 80, 93, 115; his death in prison, vi. 98 note.

TEMPLE, Sir Richard, in the debates on the Indemnity Bill, vi. 173.

TEMPLE, Thomas, Parliamentarian officer, ii. 446.

TEMPLE, Dr. Thomas, member of

Westminster Assembly, ii. 522, iii. 270, 391, iv. 71.

TEMPLE, Sir William, mention of, among Men of Letters under the Protectorate, v. 76; after the Restoration, vi. 315, 569, 601.

TENCH, a joiner of London, vi. 86, 94 note.

"TENDER OF UNION," the, name given to the Offer of the English Rump Parliament to incorporate England and Scotland into one Commonwealth, iv. 360-1, 364, 365.

TENNYSON, Alfred, reference to his Horatian Ode to Milton, vi. 555.

TERRILL, Thomas, ii. 445.

TESTI, Italian poet, i. 762, 797, 804 note, 806.

TETUAN, Governor of, iv. 152, 158.

TEYNHAM, Lord (Royalist), ii. 430.

THANET, Earl of (Royalist), in the First "Bishops' War," ii. 47-8; town house of, ii. 208; in the Civil War, ii. 429.

THEATRES: ordinance for closing (Sept. 1642), v. 81; Davenant's Italian Opera (1656), v. 81, vi. 73; the, reopened (1660), vi. 72-3: see Drama of the Restoration.

"THEATRUM POETARUM", by Edward Phillips, vi. 764-5, 777.

THEOBALDS (in Hertfordshire), Charles I. at, ii. 323, 354, 355.

"THEOPHILUS VERAX," and "THEODORUS VERAX": see Lilburne.

THEVENOT, physician at Paris, iv. 640.

THIRTY YEARS' WAR, the, i. 61, 382, 667; account of, i. 739-44; ii. 52.

THOMAS, Edmund, in Cromwell's House of Lords, v. 324.

THOMAS, Edward, publisher, vi. 399.

THOMAS, William, a Welsh Baptist, ii. 581.

THOMASON, George, London bookseller and Collector of Pamphlets, account of, iii. 44-5 and note, 65, 220, v. 155 note, vi. 399-400, 403.

THOMOND, Henry, 7th Earl of: his son, Henry O'Bryen, v. 266.

THOMPSON, Cornet (brother of Captain William Thompson), shot for taking part in an insurrection of Levellers in 1648-9, iv. 50.

THOMPSON, "Dutch," of Clare Hall, Cambridge, i. 129.

THOMPSON, Francis, Parliamentarian officer, ii. 445.

THOMPSON, George, Colonel in the Parliamentarian Army, ii. 445; in the Third Council of State of the Commonwealth, iv. 273, 313, 314, 315, 321; in the Fifth, 355, 449, 450; in the Restored Rump, v. 454; in Cromwell's Council, v. 456; in Monk's Council of 1659-60, v. 519, 544; in the Restored Long Parliament, v. 545.

THOMPSON, John, appointed joint-secretary of State with Thurloe in the Restored Long Parliament, v. 546.

THOMPSON, Robert, on the Committee of Safety, v. 494.

THOMPSON, Captain William, writer of a Levelling Pamphlet in 1648-9, and killed in an insurrection of Levellers, iv. 50-1.

THOMS, Mr. William J., reference to his inquiry concerning the death-warrant of Charles I. in Notes and Queries (1872), iii. 720 note.

THOMSON, a printer, iv. 42.

THOMSON, Milton's landlord at Charing Cross, iv. 104-5.

THOMSON, Mrs. Catherine, Milton's Sonnet to, iii. 644-5, vi. 688.

THOMSON, John, one of the Commissioners for the forfeited estates in Scotland in 1654, iv. 561.

THOMSON, Samuel, publisher, vi. 403, 625-6.

THOMSON, Sir Thomas, excepted from Cromwell's Ordinance of Pardon and Grace in 1654, iv. 560.

THORNBOROUGH, Dr. John, i. 390, 677; Bishop of Worcester, ii. 150, 324.

THORNDIKE, deputy-orator of Cambridge, i. 150.

THORNE, Giles, expelled from Oxford for Puritanism, i. 408.

THORNTON, Thomas, of St. John's College, Cambridge, and Lecturer on Logic, i. 119.

"THOROUGH," the System of, i. 664-732; origin and meaning of the expression as applied to the govern-

ment of Charles and Laud from 1628 to 1640, i. 668-9 ; ii. 177.

THOROUGHGOOD, Thomas, member of Westminster Assembly, ii. 522, iv. 71.

THORPE, Sergeant Francis, in Oliver's First Parliament, v. 5 ; member of the Restored Rump Parliament, v. 454, 455 ; in the Indemnity Bill (1660), vi. 41.

THOUARS, Claude de la Tremouille, Duke of (Peer of France), and his wife, the Duchess of, ii. 158.

THRALE, Richard, warden of the Stationers' Company, vi. 402.

THROGMORTON, Job, merchant of London, iv. 486.

THURLOE, John (Cromwell's Secretary), as lawyer of Lincoln's Inn, iv. 276 ; appointed Secretary to an Embassy to the Netherlands, iv. 276 ; as General Secretary to the Councils of State of the Commonwealth, iv. 425-7, 433, 447, 448, 486, v. 706 ; retained as Secretary to Cromwell's Interim Council of Thirteen, iv. 499, 523, and to the Councils of the Barebones Parliament, iv. 524, 525, 526 ; in the Chief Secretaryship of the First Protectorate, with a place at the Council Board, iv. 545-6, 547, 550, 573, 575, 576, 577, 578 ; his system of work in the Secretaryship, iv. 578-80 ; further references to, as Cromwell's Secretary and right-hand man, iv. 635, v. 34, 52, 178, 179, 183, 227, 246, 273, 288-9 ; a member of Cromwell's First Parliament (Sept. 3, 1654), v. 5 ; references to, in connexion with the Milton and Morus Controversy, iv. 632, v. 192, 202 ; a member of Cromwell's Second Parliament (Sept. 17, 1656, to June 26, 1657), v. 107, 119, 120, 128, 130, 134, 141 ; in the Privy Council of the Second Protectorate (June 1657), v. 308, 333-4, 345, 354, 363, 374-5, 381, 394, 399-401, 402 ; in the last days of Cromwell, v. 358 ; at Richard's accession to the Protectorate, v. 415 ; continues in his post of Secretary and member of the Council, v. 417 ; of the Court Party in the Council, v. 421 ; writes

Richard's Speech to the Officers, v. 422 ; in the foreign business of the Council, v. 426, 428 ; represents the Government against the Opposition in Richard's Parliament, v. 429-30, 431, 432-5 ; in the Struggle between the Court Party and the Army, or Wallingford House Party, v. 437-40 ; draws up the Commission to the Speaker of the House (Lord Fiennes) to dissolve the Parliament, v. 442 ; no longer in the Council, v. 625 note ; assists the Rump Government with secret intelligence during a projected Royalist Insurrection, v. 474 ; appointed by the Restored Long Parliament to be Secretary of State, v. 546 ; arrested by the Commons of the Convention Parliament on a special charge of high treason, vi. 42 ; his escape from penalty, and subsequent life, vi. 42, 48, 198, 198 note.

THYNNE, Sir James, ii. 326.

TICHBORNE, Alderman, Robert (Regicide), in the death-warrant of the King, iii. 720, vi. 28 ; iv. 303, 360, 506, 514, 571 ; v. 71 ; one of Cromwell's Lords, v. 324, 494, 505, 511, 666 ; after the Restoration, vi. 43, 49, 54, 80, 93 ; death of, vi. 98 note, 115.

TILDESLEY, Sir Thomas, iv. 292, 293.

TILLOTSON, John, Archbishop : among Men of Letters under the Protectorate, v. 76 ; marries Cromwell's niece, v. 307 ; at the Restoration, vi. 315, 388 ; in 1667-74, vi. 616, 617.

TIMMIS, Randall, a yeoman, vi. 746.

TIPPERMUIR, battle of, iii. 351.

TIPPING, George, Baptist preacher, iii. 148.

TISDALE, Christopher, member of Westminster Assembly, ii. 522.

TITUS, Captain Silas or Silius, reputed author of Killing no Murder in 1657, his part in "Disinterring Order" of 1660, vi. 112-3.

TODD (Editor of Milton), his investigation of Milton's early readings, i. 89 note, 96.

TOLERATION, pleadings for in 1644-5 by the Independents in the Westminster Assembly and in the Army,

iii. 89-90 ; history of the principle of, from 1611 onwards, and state of the Controversy concerning, in 1644, iii. 98-129, 160; the Opposition to, in 1644, iii. 129-36 ; attitude of the Tolerationists to the Sects and Sectaries, iii. 136-7 ; Roger Williams, the Tolerationist, iii. 154; the Westminster Assembly's war against, iii. 160-6 ; Cromwell interferes for, iii. 166-71 ; Milton's notion of, as found in the *Areopagitica*, iii. 287-90 ; the Controversy continued in Parliament and the Assembly in 1645-6, iii. 383, 384-96 ; Cromwell pleads for, iii. 384-5 ; in the New Model, iii. 386 ; the Question again discussed (through 1649-53) in the scheme for the " Propagation of the Gospel," iv. 389-98 ; the principle of, negatived by the Parliament in 1652-3, iv. 398 ; debates in the House involving the principle of, iv. 403-11 ; Cromwell's principle that toleration of Dissent was compatible with the existence of a State Church, iv. 570 ; Milton's difference with Cromwell on this point, iv. 613 ; the Question again at issue in 1654-5, v. 121-6 ; Cromwell's, of Dissent applied to the principal sects in 1654-6, v. 58-72 ; Cromwell's latest views on, v. 343-5, vi. 60; reassertion of the principle of, by the Restored Rump in 1659, v. 466 ; its chances after the Restoration, vi. 60, 100, 103-4 ; Acts of Parliament to suppress Nonconformity, vi. 225-6, 249-50, 258 ; Edict of Charles II. in 1662 in favour of, vi. 241-4 ; policy of religious, in the Cabal in 1667-70, vi. 564-8 ; Charles II.'s Declaration of Religious Indulgence, or a general Toleration to Nonconformists and Catholics, vi. 586-90, 591-4.

TOMBES, John, Baptist leader, iii. 148, 678 ; one of Cromwell's Triers, iv. 571 ; v. 56 ; a Nonconformist, vi. 232 note, 417.

TOMKINS, Mr., member of the Convention Parliament, vi. 51.

TOMKYNS, Rev. Thomas, licenser of *Paradise Lost*, vi. 506-8, 514, 515, 616, 651.

TOMLINS, Richard, v. 264.

TOMLINSON, Colonel Matthew (Regicide), under the *New Model*, iii. 327, 328 note, 713, 720 note, 723 ; iv. 402 ; in Cromwell's Interim Council of Thirteen, iv. 498 ; in the Barebones Parliament, iv. 505-6 ; v. 98 ; one of Cromwell's Lords, v. 324 ; knighted by Cromwell, v. 354 note ; supports Richard's Government, v. 419 ; through the period of Anarchy, v. 471, 521 ; after the Restoration, vi. 28, 34 note, 36, 38, 45, 46, 48, 50, 55, 89, 97 ; subsequent fate of, vi. 98.

TONGUE, Thomas, distiller, executed for conspiracy in 1662, vi. 471.

"TONNAGE AND POUNDAGE," in disputes between Charles I. and Parliament, i. 213, 215, 669 ; ii. 188.

TONSON, Jacob (of the family of Tonsons, publishers in London), vi. 511 note, 755 note ; account of, in connexion with the fourth edition of *Paradise Lost*, vi. 781-2, 784 ; subsequent ownership of Milton's works by the Tonsons, vi. 786-90.

TOOGOOD, Captain, vi. 89.

TOPSALL, licenser of books, i. 550 note.

TORRICELLI, i. 767-8, 797.

TORPHICHEN, John Sandilands, Lord, i. 710.

TORRINGTON, storming of, by the New Model Army, iii. 371.

TOURNEUR, Cyril, dramatist, iii. 449.

TOVEY, Nathaniel, account of, as Fellow of Christ's College, Cambridge, i. 130 ; further references to, i. 123, 160, 167, 170, 237, 243, 266, 268 ; ii. 76, 401 note, 414.

TOWER OF LONDON, the : see *London*, City of.

TOWERS, Dr. John, Bishop of Peterborough, i. 120, 674 ; ii. 150 ; impeachment of, ii. 270 ; 334-6.

TOWES, Alderman, Colonel of City Trained Bands, ii. 447.

TOWNLEY, Zouch, a disciple of Ben Jonson, i. 566.

TOWNSEND, Mr., a friend of Pepys, vi. 340.

TOWNSEND, Sir Horatio, in the Council of the Restored Rump, v. 456, 457,

478 ; in the Restored Long Parliament, v. 700 ; in the Convention Parliament, vi. 23, 152.

TOZER, Henry, member of Westminster Assembly, ii. 522.

TRACEY of Moulton, son of an attorney, and pupil of Meade in 1624-5, i. 151, 180.

TRACEY, Richard, in the story of *Vox Piscis*, i. 155.

" TRACTS, the Oxford," of 1641, ii. 363-9.

TRANCOUS : see *De Trancous*.

TRAQUAIR, John Stewart, Earl of, High Treasurer of Scotland, in 1635, i. 706, 707-8, 709, 721, 724, 725, 726 ; ii. 15, 31, 71, 122, 136, 300, 301, 304 ; iii. 344, 362, 421.

TRASKE, John, founder of the sect of Traskites, or Anti-Sabbatarians, in 1644, iii. 155-6.

TRAVERS, Mr., English Presbyterian, ii. 532.

TRAVIS, Philip, London merchant, v. 250.

" TREASON ARRAIGNED," see L'Estrange.

TREATY : of Uxbridge in 1644, between Charles I. and the Army of the Parliament, iii. 183 ; Ormond's Articles of Peace with the Irish Rebels, in 1646, iii. 520; the Secret, between Charles I. and the Scottish Commissioners in 1647, iii. 586 ; of Newport, between the Parliament and Charles II. in 1648, iii. 603-9, 694, v. 527, 550 ; Articles of Peace between the Marquis of Ormond for Charles I. and the Roman Catholics of Ireland, in 1648-9, iv. 23 ; of Breda, between Charles II. and the Scottish Parliament in 1650, iv. 180 ; of the Commonwealth with the United Provinces in 1654, iv. 552 ; with Sweden in 1654, iv. 553 ; with Portugal in 1654, iv. 554 ; with Denmark in 1654, iv. 554 ; of Pignerol, granted by the Duke of Savoy to the Vaudois Protestants in 1655, v. 43-4, 342 ; of Peace and Commerce, between Cromwell and Louis XIV. of France, in 1655, v. 46 ; of the Pyrenees, between France and Spain, in 1659, v. 502-3 ; the

Secret, of Dover, between Charles II. and Louis XIV., in 1670, vi. 575-81 ; the " Mock Treaty," or *Traité Simulé*, also between Charles II. and Louis XIV., in 1670, vi. 580.

TREMOUILLE, Charlotte de la, wife of the 7th Earl of Derby, ii. 158.

TRENCHARD, John, in the Restored Rump, v. 454.

TREVANION, John, ii. 466.

TREVOR, Sir John, in the Councils of the Commonwealth, iv. 313, 314, 315, 321, 355, 449, 450 ; in the Restored Rump, v. 454 ; in the Council of the Restored Long Parliament, v. 544 ; after the Restoration, vi. 563, 574-5 ; his death, vi. 590.

TRIERS, Cromwell's Commission of, iv. 571 ; v. 53, 138, 315, 343-4.

TRINITY COLLEGE (Cambridge), i. 113, 115, 117, 121, 122, 138, 140, 182, 187, 220, 221, 223, 237, 238, 247, 251, 252, 261.

TRINITY COLLEGE (Dublin), i. 125, 129, 420, 519, 533, 691, 692 ; ii. 76.

TRINITY COLLEGE (Oxford), i. 102, 207-12, 537, 626.

TRINITY HALL (Cambridge), i. 114, 116, 120, 226.

TRIPLE ALLIANCE, the, vi. 568-9, 579.

TRISTRAM, a gardener of Brentford, i. 100.

" TRIUMPHS OF ORIANA," a collection of madrigals in 1601, i. 50.

TRONCHIN, Theodore, professor of Theology at Geneva, i. 832 ; v. 208.

TROUGHTON, army-chaplain, iii. 588.

TRUELOVE, William, of Hatfield-Peverill in Essex, i. 37, 39, 63.

TRUMBULL, Dr., afterwards Sir William, Ambassador and Secretary of State to William III., vi. 737.

TUCKNEY, Dr., Anthony, member of Westminster Assembly, ii. 522, 605 ; Master of Emanuel College, Cambridge, iii. 93 ; v. 74 ; in the Presbyterian *Testimony* of Sion College against Heretics, iii. 677 ; in the Commission of Triers, iv. 571 ; among the Nonconformist clergy in 1662, vi. 232 note.

TUDOR, Mary, daughter of Charles II.

and Mary Davis, vi. 605 : see *Derwentwater*, Earl of.

TUKE, Sir Samuel, mention of, among Men of Letters of the Restoration, vi. 311.

TULLIBARDINE, Earl of, ii. 15 ; in the Episode of Montrose in Scotland (1644-5), iii. 351, 361 ; 509 ; iv. 491, 561 ; v. 512, 707.

TUNIS, the Dey of, in an engagement with Blake's fleet, v. 37.

TURCHI, Italian painter, i. 763.

TURENNE, French Commander, i. 743 ; v. 310-1, 340, 341, 416 ; vi. 585.

TURKEY, in 1638, i. 747.

TURNER, an actor, vi. 350.

TURNER, of the sect of Separatists, i. 678.

TURNER, Alexander, servant of the Council of State, v. 625.

TURNER, Sir Edward, vi. 77, 173, 249.

TURNER, William, printer to Oxford University, iii. 198.

TURNHAM GREEN, The March to, ii. 457-8, 487-8.

TURRETIN, Benedict, Professor of Theology at Geneva, i. 832 ; v. 174.

TURRETIN, Francis, son of Benedict, and also Professor of Theology at Geneva, v. 174-5, 212 note.

TURRETIN (brother of Francis), living in London and a friend of Milton in 1655-6, v. 175.

"TURRIFF, the Trot of," a skirmish in the "First Bishops' War," ii. 57, 60.

TUSCANY, one of the Native Sovereignties of Italy (1638), i. 745 ; the Grand Duke of, from 1621 to 1670 : see *Ferdinando II*.

TWEEDDALE, John Hay, 1st Earl of, iv. 208 ; in Cromwell's Second Parliament, v. 108, 129 ; in Richard's Parliament, v. 430 ; in the Scottish Council in London, vi. 130.

TWISSE, Dr. William, in the Bishops Exclusion Bill Controversy, ii. 225 ; Prolocutor of Westminster Assembly, ii. 514, 515, 604-5 ; iii. 3, 153, 216 note ; death of, iii. 426 ; his body disinterred, vi. 227.

TWISTLETON, John, v. 354 note.

TWISTLETON, Colonel Philip, under the *New Model*, iii. 327 ; iv. 402 ;

knighted by Cromwell, v. 354 note ; through the period of Anarchy, v. 470, 498.

TWYN, John, printer, his trial for high treason, and execution in 1663-4, vi. 477-80.

TYDDOLL, an actor, vi. 349.

TYERS, Thomas, in the tradition of Milton's escape at the Restoration, vi. 190.

TYLER, Evan, warden of the Stationers' Company, vi. 515.

TYLER, Wat, referred to, i. 48.

TYNE, Nicholas, ii. 587.

TYRONE, Earl of, in the Irish Insurrection, ii. 309, 310.

TYRRELL, Thomas, in the Restored Rump, v. 465 ; in employment of the Council of the same, v. 520 ; in the Committee for the Indemnity Bill, vi. 30.

TYRWHIT, Thomas, of St. John's College, Cambridge, i. 247.

TYTAN, Edward, servant of the Council of State, v. 625.

U

ULAC, Adrian, printer and publisher at the Hague of the *Regii Sanguinis Clamor* in 1652, iv. 453, 584, 627 ; Milton's invective against, iv. 588-9, 627, 633-4 ; his Hague edition of Milton's *Defensio Secunda*, v. 150-1 ; his defence of himself, v. 152-6 ; retrospective account of, v. 155 note ; 161-2 ; 192-3, 203-4.

ULITIUS, James (at the Hague), letter of, to Heinsius, iv. 463, 464.

UNDERHILL, Cave, an actor, vi. 350, 351.

UNDERHILL, Edmund, minister of Cuddesdon, ii. 498 note.

UNDERHILL, Thomas, one of Milton's publishers, ii. 237, 239-40, 251, 382 note ; iii. 164 note, 233, 233 note ; 450, 679 ; v. 59 note ; vi. 399.

UNDERWOOD, Mr. Sheriff, his house in Bucklersbury, iv. 504.

UNITED DUTCH PROVINCES, The Seven : in 1638, i. 745-6 ; scheme of a Union of, with the English Commonwealth, iv. 30, 49, 125, 215-6,

275-8 ; iv. 216, 275-8 ; Navigation Act against, in 1651, iv. 305-6, 350, 371-2 ; war with, in 1652-4, iv. 372-7, 383, 482-3, 502, 507, 552-3 ; v. 40, 156, 189-90, 250-1, 254, 272-3, 312, 314, 377-8, 378, 467 ; war with, from 1664 to 1673, vi. 252-6, 265-7, 569, 583-6, 601 : see also *Holland*.

UNIVERSITIES : see *Cambridge, Dublin, Edinburgh, Glasgow, Oxford* and *St. Andrews*.

UPHILL, an actress, vi. 350.

UPTON, Edmund, witness, vi. 628.

URBAN VIII., Pope of Rome (1623-44), i. 744, 745, 756-7, 763, 794-5, 797, 798; ii. 50.

"URN - BURIAL, Discourse of," by Thomas Browne of Norwich, vi. 296.

URQUHART, Sir Thomas, his " Epigrams, Divine and Moral," iii. 446.

URRY (or HURRY), John, Parliamentarian officer, ii. 445 ; his desertion to the King, ii. 470-1 ; in the episode of Montrose in Scotland, iii. 358-9, 360 ; in Montrose's expedition to Scotland, iv. 183, 184, 185.

USE OF HOLY SCRIPTURE, the, a treatise by William Chappell, i. 129.

USHER, James, Archbishop of Armagh, i. 125, 420, 490 ; appointed to the Primacy of all Ireland in 1624, i. 421, 423 ; among prose-writers in 1632, i. 519-20, 546-7, 547 note; his action with Wentworth in the government of Ireland, i. 693 ; Chappell of Cambridge and, ii. 76-8 ; in 1639, ii. 124 ; his advice to the King previous to the execution of Strafford, ii. 184 ; his part in the English Church Reform movement in 1640-1, ii. 197-8, 225, 229-30, 248 - 53 ; his contribution to the " Oxford Tracts " and Milton's reply to the same in his Fourth Pamphlet, ii. 363, 365, 369 ; appointed Bishop of Chester, ii. 411 ; remains with the King at Oxford, and his proposed appointment to the Westminster Assembly is cancelled, ii. 522, 525 ; iii. 15, 138 ; his probable views on the question of Toleration in 1644, iii. 126 ; 218 ; with the King at Newport, iii. 609 ; Christopher Arnold's

eulogy of, in 1651, iv. 350, **352** ; 447 ; his friendship with Morus, **v.** 159 ; his later life, and death in 1655-6, v. 63-4, 75 ; recurrence by the English Presbyterians in 1660 to the plan of a limited Episcopacy as sketched by, in his " Model " of 1641, vi. 60-1, 63, 66, 100.

UXBRIDGE, Treaty of : see *Treaty*.

V

VACHE, the, seat of the Fleetwoods at Chalfont St. Giles, vi. 493.

VALENTIA, Sir Francis Annesley, Viscount (Baron Mountnorris), father of Arthur Annesley, v. 545.

VALENTINE, Benjamin, i. 216; ii. 163.

VALENTINE, Thomas, member of Westminster Assembly, ii. 522 ; vi. 494.

VALORI, member of the *Svogliati* at Florence, i. 822.

VANDYCK, i. 746 ; ii. 167.

VANE, Charles, English agent in Portugal, iv. 125, 161, 217-9, 231, 232, 275, 393.

VANE, Sir Henry, Knight (senior), account of, in the Privy Council of Charles I., i. 381 ; ii. 24, 62, 68, 128, 149, 159, 174, 180, 181, 278, 279, 281, 336; lay member of Westminster Assembly, ii. 524 ; iii. 41, 268, 381, 694 ; iv. 127 note ; in Oliver's First Parliament, v. 5.

VANE, Sir Henry (younger), governor of Massachusetts for one year, in 1636-7, ii. 549, 558, 575, 586, iii. 151; account of, in the Long Parliament, ii. 165 ; in debates of the Commons, ii. 174 ; in Strafford's Trial, ii. 181 ; in English Church Reform movement, ii. 201 ; for *Root and Branch*, ii. 217, 231-3, 236, 239 ; Cromwell and, ii. 277 ; lay member of Westminster Assembly, ii. 522, 524 ; and the Independents in the Assembly, in 1642, ii. 605 ; chief friend of Roger Williams in London in 1643-4, ii. 602 ; in a Commission of the English Parliament to the Scots in 1643-4, iii. 7-10 ; in the " Committee of the Two Kingdoms," iii. 41, 331 note ; in a Commission

of both Houses for the Management of the Colonies, iii. 119 ; and the English sects and sectaries, iii. 162 ; with Cromwell in the Toleration Question, iii. 169-70 ; in debate on the *Self-denying Ordinance*, iii. 181, 182 note; in Committee of the Commons to rebuke the Westminster Assembly, iii. 408, 410 ; 416 ; Argyle and, in 1646, iii. 420 ; in the Commons, iii. 423, 549, 560 ; in Parliamentary Commission to treat with the King at Newport in 1648, iii. 605, 694 ; his conduct on the occasion of "Pride's Purge," iii. 698 ; in the last days of Charles I., iii. 718 ; in the First Council of State of the Commonwealth, iv. 12, 15, 18, 79, 82, 87, 105, 150 ; in the Second, iv. 26-7, 223, 224, 225, 226, 231 ; in the Third, iv. 273, 586-7, 303, 308-9, 313, 314, 315 ; in the Fourth and Fifth, iv. 354-5, 360, 363, 450 ; in debates on Irish business, iv. 370, 384 ; in debates on the question of a New Parliament, iv. 406, 407, 408, 409 ; at the Dissolution of the Rump, iv. 412 ; Milton's Sonnet to, iv. 440-3 ; in the Barebones Parliament, iv. 512 ; his friendship with Roger Williams, iv. 395, 396, 532 ; through Cromwell's First Protectorate, iv. 549, 606 ; *not* in Oliver's First Parliament, v. 5 ; his peculiar metaphysics, and his followers, called by Baxter "Vanists," v. 21-2 ; committed to imprisonment for a Republican pamphlet in 1656, v. 106-7, 114 ; in 1658, v. 354 ; in Richard's Parliament, v. 430, 431, 432, 434, 441, 445, 448, 449 ; in the Restored Rump, and its Council of State, v. 454, 456, 457, 465-6, 478, 479 ; in the Wallingford House Government and its Committee of Safety, v. 494, 495, 505, 507-10, 511, 516-7 ; in disgrace with the Parliament of the Second Restored Rump, v. 520-1, 538 ; mention of, in Milton's *Treatise of Civil Power*, v. 586 ; and in *Treason Arraigned*, v. 666 ; after the Restoration, vi. 38, 46-8, 50-1, 55 ; in prison, vi. 98, 197 ; capital prosecution of, vi. 224 ; his trial and execution in June 1662, vi. 230-1 ; further mentions of, vi. 317-8 note, 688.

VANE, Lady, wife of the younger Vane, vi. 530.

VANISTS, the Sect of : see *Vane*, Sir Henry (younger).

VAN TROMP, Vice-Admiral, iv. 372-7, 502, 507, vi. 254.

VASSAL, Samuel, in the Long Parliament, ii. 173.

VAUGHAN, Bishop, kinsman of Archbishop Williams, i. 350.

VAUGHAN, Lieutenant-Colonel (Royalist), ii. 442.

VAUGHAN, Henry ("the Silurist"), mentioned among Men of Letters of the Restoration, vi. 312, 388.

VAUGHAN, John, friend of Hyde, i. 532.

VAUGHAN, Colonel Joseph, fellow-conspirator with Gibbons, iv. 304.

VAUGHAN, Richard : see *Carbery*, Earl of.

VAUDOIS, the : see *Waldenses*.

VAUX, Edward, 4th Lord, ii. 430 ; his house at Harrowden, iii. 515.

VAUX, George, Housekeeper at Whitehall, iv. 314, 315, 322 ; v. 177, 182, 625, 625 note.

VAVASOUR, Lieutenant-Colonel (Royalist), ii. 442.

VAVASOUR, Sir William, v. 289.

VELASQUEZ, i. 745.

VENABLES, Colonel Robert, in the Irish Campaign, iv. 112 ; in Oliver's First Parliament, v. 5 ; General in the West India Expedition of 1655, v. 44-6.

VENICE : i. 745 ; Letters of State to the Doge and Senate of, iv. 379, 486 ; v. 243-4, 377.

VENN, John (Regicide), member for London in the Long Parliament, ii. 173, 447 ; in the death-warrant of Charles I., iii. 720 ; dead in 1660, vi. 28, 54, 179 note.

VENNER, Major, member of the Rota Club, v. 485.

VENNER, Thomas, and his Fifth Monarchy Riots, v. 133-4 ; vi. 119-22.

VERDUSSEN, Jerome, printer, iv. 347.

VERE, Lord (Sir Horatio), his regiment in the Netherlands in 1621, ii. 53.

VERJUICE, an actress, vi. 350.

VERMUYDEN, Sir Cornelius, iii. 327.

VERMUYDEN, Colonel, son of the preceding, iii. 327, 334.

VERNEY, Sir Edmund, Standard-Bearer for Charles I., ii. 68, account of his conversation with Hyde previous to the setting up of the King's Standard at Nottingham in August 1642, ii. 423-4; in the King's "Troop of Guards," ii. 441; killed at the Battle of Edgehill, ii. 455.

VERNEY, Sir Ralph (son of the Standard-Bearer), in the Long Parliament, ii. 172; his Notes of the Long Parliament, ii. 172.

VERNON, Mr., living in Aldersgate Street in 1640-1, ii. 207.

VERTUE, George, the Engraver, i. 309-10 note; vi. 752-3, 754 note.

VESSEY, Captain Robert, of the Nightingale war-ship, v. 244.

VICARS, John, pamphleteer, iii. 386.

VICCARS, Samuel, fellow-graduate of Milton at Cambridge, i. 218, 258.

VILLERÉ: see Philaras, Leonard.

VILLERS, Lord Francis (Royalist), in the Second Civil War, iii. 591, 596.

VILLIERS, Barbara: see Cleveland, Duchess of, vi. 71.

VINES, Richard, i. 186; member of Westminster Assembly, ii. 522; 605; iii. 19, 22, 84, 94, 95 note, 160, 391, 606, 721; v. 12.

VIRGIN ISLANDS (West Indies), v. 103.

VIRGINIA, v. 102.

VIVERS, Richard, iii. 476, 478, 479.

VIVERS, Robert, Parliamentarian officer, ii. 446.

VIVIANI, pupil of Galileo, i. 768.

VOLTAIRE, story of Milton's daughter and, vi. 752.

VOLUNTARYISM, the doctrine of absolute, iii. 117-8, 396 note.

VORSTIUS, Conrad, theologian of Leyden, i. 59.

VOSSIUS, Gerhard John, iv. 351.

VOSSIUS, Isaac, of Holland, iii. 681, 681 note; iv. 269, 317-20, 341-4, 434, 463-5, 474-5, 633.

VOWEL, Peter, executed for his part in a Stuartist plot in 1654, iv. 550.

"VOX PISCIS," three treatises said to have been found in a codfish, and reprinted, with the above title, in London in 1627, i. 155.

"VULGAR ERRORS," by Browne of Norwich, vi. 296.

VYNER, Thomas, Lord Mayor of London, knighted by Cromwell in Feb. 1653-4, iv. 573.

W

WADLOE, Simon, landlord of the Devil Tavern, Temple Bar, i. 440.

WAGSTAFF, Lieutenant, in the Parliamentarian Army, ii. 444.

WAGSTAFF, Sir Joseph, ii. 442; royalist rising headed by, v. 34.

WAKE, Thomas, of Caius College, Cambridge, i. 171.

WAKEFIELD, Parliamentarian victory at, in 1643, ii. 469.

WAKEFIELD, William, merchant, v. 253, 290.

WALDENSES (or VAUDOIS), account of the, and of the Massacre of, in 1654-5, v. 38-40: see Milton (Piedmontese State Letters).

WALKER, Mr. ("of the Temple"), a relation of Milton, vi. 215 note.

WALKER, Sergeant, supposed executioner of Charles I., vi. 88-9.

WALKER, an artist, vi. 648.

WALKER, Dr. Anthony, curate to Dr. Gauden, vi. 439 note.

WALKER, Clement, Esq., recruiting member of Parliament for Wells in 1645, iii. 401, 694; secluded from the House by Pride's Purge, iii. 696; his mythical account of the "paper book," iii. 713-4, 714 note; among the remonstrants against the execution of the King, iii. 716; his History of Independency, in 1648-9, iv. 132; committed to the Tower on a charge of High Treason, iv. 121, 147, 155-6.

WALKER, George, account of, as member of Westminster Assembly, ii. 522; iii. 20, 29; Moderator of the sixth Provincial Synod of London, iv. 122.

WALKER, Matthias, bookseller, vi. 516, 622-3, 625-6.

WALLENSTEIN, ii. 53.

WALL, Moses, his Letter to Milton, v. 601-3, 608.

WALLER, Major in Royalist Army, ii. 442.

WALLER, Lady Anne, iii. 218.

WALLER, Edmund (Poet), i. 122; account of, i. 505-6; his "Latitudinarianism," i. 532, 534; and Henry Lawes, i. 567, ii. 80; and Ben Jonson, i. 647; ii. 79; cousin to Cromwell, ii. 164, v. 307; member for St. Ives in the Long Parliament, ii. 169; his place in the House of Commons, ii. 174; in a debate on the Root-and-Branch Bill, ii. 233; opposes the "Grand Remonstrance," ii. 321; his poems published by Moseley, iii. 449-50, 449 note, 456; arrest and punishment of, for his part in an anti-Parliamentarian plot, ii. 470; pardoned by the Parliament, iv. 359; under the Protectorate, v. 75; his Panegyric to Cromwell in May 1655, v. 85-6; in a Committee of Commons in favour of the Question of Cromwell's Kingship, v. 129; his poem, in May 1660, To the King on his Majesty's Happy Return, vi. 12-13; referred to among Men of Letters of the Restoration, vi. 276, 294, 298-9, 322, 378, 380, 383, 384; Lady Ranelagh's criticism of, vi. 456-7; reference to, in 1667-74, vi. 617; a subscriber to the fourth edition of Paradise Lost, vi. 785; his death, vi. 785.

WALLER, Sir Hardress (Regicide), Colonel under the New Model, iii. 327, 336, 537, 543, 549; one of the ejectors at "Pride's Purge," iii. 696; at the King's Trial, iii. 707, 712 note; signs the death-warrant of Charles I., iii. 720, vi. 28; at the Fairfaxian Creation, iv. 52; in the management of Irish affairs, iv. 366, 401; in Cromwell's First Parliament, v. 5; in Cromwell's Second Parliament, v. 108, 139; supports Richard's Government, v. 419, 431; through the period of Anarchy, v. 471, 514, 520; after the Restoration, vi. 43, 49, 53, 54; his Trial,

vi. 79, 94, 114; his death, vi. 98 note; in the Bill of Attainder, vi. 115.

WALLER, Sir William, account of, in the Long Parliament, ii. 170; his career in the Parliamentarian Army, ii. 445, 461-2, 465, 471, iii. 6, 35, 41, 84, 85, 86, 168, 177, 178, 330-1, 333, 378, 381; a member of the Committee of the Two Kingdoms (1644), iii. 41; after the Civil War, iii. 522, 532; denounced by the Army, iii. 548-9, 552; escapes abroad, iii. 554; mentioned, iii. 562; ejected from the House by "Pride's Purge," iii. 696; his concern in Royalist conspiracies, v. 337, 473, 477; in the Restored Long Parliament and the Council of State, v. 544, 545, 546; in the Convention Parliament, vi. 23.

WALLINGFORD CASTLE, surrender of, by Charles I., in 1646, iii. 374.

WALLINGFORD HOUSE PARTY: account of the weekly meetings of the Army leaders at Wallingford House, London, in 1659, v. 418; and of the formation of the, or "Army Party," led by Fleetwood, Desborough, and Lambert, in opposition to the "Court Party" in Richard's Parliament, v. 421, 425, 437; general Convention of Officers at Wallingford House, and their Petition to Richard, v. 438-41; the meetings of the Council of Officers at Wallingford House dissolved by Richard, v. 441; counteraction of the Officers, and Richard's Parliament forcibly dissolved by them, v. 441-2; condition and prospects of the Wallingford House leaders after the dissolution, v. 443-6; they finally join with the Republicans in restoring the Rump, v. 446-8; difficulties arising between the Officers and the resuscitated Rump, v. 449; their Petition and Address to the Rump, v. 449-51; renewed quarrel of the Army Officers with the Parliament, v. 486, 488-90; Parliament dissolved by the Council of Officers, v. 490-2; the "Wallingford House Interregnum"

(Oct. 13 to Dec. 26, 1659), v. 493-517 ; government continued in concert by the Council of the Rump and the Council of Officers, v. 494 ; until the formation, by the Wallingford House leaders, of the new Supreme Executive called *The Committee of Safety*, v. 494-5 ; military arrangements of this new Committee, v. 495-7 ; in negotiations with Monk, v. 497-501 ; in foreign business, v. 501-5 ; in debates on the matter of a new Republican Constitution, v. 505-10 ; the Army and Navy Council called by, v. 510-2 ; disintegration of the Wallingford House Party by the policy and action of Monk, v. 513-5 ; perilous prospects of the Wallingford House Chiefs at the approach of Monk and his army towards London, v. 515-6 ; dispersion of the Party and its Army at the second Restoration of the Rump, v. 517, 519, 520, 526.

WALLIS, Mr. John, at Cambridge, i. 243 ; appointed clerk to the Westminster Assembly in 1643, ii. 515 ; account of his subsequent career, ii. 515 ; a member of the " Invisible College " in 1645, ii. 662, 677 ; signs a Presbyterian demonstration for Charles I., iv. 71 ; among Men of Letters and of Science of the Protectorate, v. 73, 75, 81, 231, 266, vi. 318, 322, 391-3 ; appointed one of the King's Chaplains in 1660, vi. 62 ; mentions of, among Men of Letters of the Restoration, vi. 290, 299 ; Professor of Geometry in Oxford since 1649, vi. 301-2 ; a member of the Royal Society in 1662, vi. 394, 396.

WALLIS, Colonel Peter, in the Republican Army, v. 471.

WALLOP, Robert (Regicide), in the " Committee of the Two Kingdoms," iii. 41 ; in Councils of State of the Commonwealth, iv. 13, 14, 145, 147, 151, 223, 354 ; in Oliver's First Parliament, v. 5 ; in the Restored Rump and its Council, v. 454, 456, 519, 544 note ; in the Convention Parliament, vi. 23 ; trial and punishment of, by that Parliament, as having been one of the Judges in the King's Trial, vi. 35-6, 37, 54-5, 223-4, 228.

WALSALL, Dr. Samuel, Master of Corpus Christi College, Cambridge (died 1626), i. 116, 120, 226.

WALSALL, Dr., mentioned in the Council Order Books of May 1650, iv. 225.

WALSH, case of abduction against, iv. 232.

WALSINGHAM, Sir Thomas, member of the Restored Rump, v. 454, 544 note.

WALTER, Mr., a Welsh Baptist minister, ii. 581.

WALTON, Rev. Brian, Bishop of Chester, and editor of Polyglot Bible, i. 105, 119 ; iv. 446-7 ; v. 76, 79, 98 ; vi. 61, 292, 322, 417.

WALTON, Izaak, i. 486, 493, 500, 530 ; mentions of, through the Protectorate, v. 76, 79, vi. 322 ; in 1660, vi. 292, 293 ; in 1667, vi. 616.

WALTON, Colonel Valentine (Regicide), in the Parliamentarian Army, ii. 446 ; married to Cromwell's sister, iii. 97, v. 307, signs the death-warrant of Charles I., iii. 720, vi. 28 ; in successive Councils of State of the Commonwealth, iv. 13, 82, 87, 150, 224, 225, 226, 227, 273, 313, 314, 354-5, 449 ; conspicuous among Cromwell's Officers in 1652, iv. 402 ; in the Restored Rump, and its Council of State, v. 454, 456, 465, 479, 490 ; at the second Restoration of the Rump, v. 495, 514, 519, 520, 522, 529, 534, 537 ; Monk gives his regiment to Viscount Howard, v. 563 ; in the Indemnity Bill, vi. 44, 54, 115 ; subsequent fate of, vi. 115 note.

WALWYN, William, of the sect of " Seekers," and a pamphleteer, iii. 153 ; iv. 45-6, 45 note, 87, 97, 115, 119-20.

WANDLOE, James, Parliamentarian officer, ii. 446.

WANDSWORTH (near London), Fuller's account of the first Presbytery in England, set up at, in 1572, ii. 532.

WARD, Rev., suspended by Laud, i. 402.

WARD, Edward, of Norfolk, knighted
by Cromwell, in 1657, v. 354 note.

WARD, John, member of Westminster
Assembly, ii. 520.

WARD, Nathaniel, account of, as a
New England minister, ii. 559.

WARD, Robert, of Queen's College,
Cambridge, i. 154.

WARD, Dr. Samuel, account of, as
Master of Sidney Sussex College,
Cambridge, i. 118; 267; ii. 225;
further account of, as nominated
for the Westminster Assembly, ii.
522, 525; ejected from Cambridge
University, iii. 94.

WARD, Dr. Seth (mathematician),
member of the *Philosophical Society
of Oxford* in 1649, vi. 392; author
of a pamphlet in 1653, iv. 568
note; Professor in Oxford University, v. 73, 231; Bishop of Salisbury, vi. 258; an anti-Hobbist, vi.
290; member of the Royal Society,
vi. 394.

WARD, Professor of Gresham College,
visits Milton's daughter, vi. 753-4.

WARING, Edmund, denounced by the
Convention Parliament, vi. 47.

WARING, Thomas, iv. 151, 156.

WARNER (English poet), died in 1609,
i. 451.

WARNER, Alderman, and Colonel of
City Trained Bands, ii. 447.

WARNER, Dr. John (Oxford divine),
appointed Bishop of Rochester in
1637, i. 674; ii. 150, 151; impeachment of, in 1641, ii. 270, 335,
349; iii. 609; a Royalist sermon
of, in 1648-9, iv. 37; after the Restoration, vi. 61, 105, 154-5.

WARREN, Mr., preaches before the
House of Commons, v. 120.

WARREN, Walter (Mathematician), i.
130.

WARRISTON, Lord : see *Johnstone of
Warriston.*

WARTON (literary historian), reference
to, vi. 190; his Edition of Milton's
Minor Poems (1791), vi. 740 note.

WARWICK, Sir Philip, member of Parliament for Radnor in 1640-1, ii.
164, 168; account by, of his first
sight of Cromwell in the House of
Commons, ii. 175; 322; joins

Charles I. before the Civil War, ii.
415.

WARWICK, Robert Rich, 1st Earl of,
i. 379.

WARWICK, Robert Rich, 2nd Earl of,
at Cambridge, i. 220; previous to
First "Bishops' War," ii. 48; at
the calling of the Long Parliament
in 1639-40, ii. 142, 143; account
of, in the Parliament, ii. 154, 156;
in the King's Privy Council (1640-1),
ii. 279; through the Civil War, ii.
429, 431, 439, 455, iii. 380; in the
"Committee of the Two Kingdoms,"
iii. 41; in the House of Lords, iii.
119, 405, 585; in the office of Lord
High Admiral, iii. 297 note, 595,
iv. 41; at Cromwell's second Installation, v. 148-9; at Cromwell's
Court, v. 303; marriage and death
of his grandson, v. 306; one of
Cromwell's Lords, v. 323, 326; in
a Letter to Cromwell, v. 338-9; at
the Restoration, v. 700; his chaplain, Dr. Gauden, vi. 423.

WASHBOURNE, Rev. Thomas, author
of *Divine Poems*, published in 1654,
v. 226-7, 179.

WASHINGTON, Lieutenant-Colonel in
Royalist Army, ii. 442.

WASHINGTON, Mr., "of the Temple,"
translator, in 1692, of Milton's *Pro
Populo Anglicano* into English, iv.
258 note.

WATERFORD, siege of, by Cromwell,
iv. 112.

WATERHOUSE, Joseph, Parliamentarian
officer, ii. 446.

WATERS, Lucy, vi. 71, 73 note, 604.

WATIES, Edward, in the Council of
Wales, i. 609.

WATKINS, Mr., mention of, in a
Minute of Council (April 20, 1649),
iv. 87.

WATSON, Miss Caroline, her engraving
of a portrait called Milton's, vi. 754
note.

WATSON, Leonard, in the Parliamentarian Army, iii. 326; a witness at
the trials of the Regicides in 1660,
vi. 32.

WATSON, Dr. Richard, reference to a
sermon of, preached before Charles
II. at the Hague, iv. 131.

WAUCHOPE of Niddry, Sir John, excepted from Cromwell's Ordinance of Pardon and Grace, iv. 561.

WAYTE, Colonel Thomas (Regicide), iii. 712 note, 720, vi. 28 ; in the Restored Rump, v. 454 ; after the Restoration, vi. 43, 49, 54, 80, 93, 98 note, 115.

WEAVER, an actress, vi. 350.

WEAVER, Edmund (or John), "anti-Oliverian" in Cromwell's Second Parliament, v. 329 ; recruiter in the Restored Rump, v. 454, 465 ; in the Council of the Second Restored Rump, v. 519, 523 ; in the Council of the Restored Long Parliament, v. 544.

WEBB, John, of the sect of "anti-Trinitarians," ii. 587, iii. 157 ; denounced by Sion College, iii. 678.

WEBB, John, Parliamentary Sequestrator in 1646, iii. 476, 478, 479.

WEBB, Nathaniel, bookseller, v. 59 note.

WEBBER, Widow, mother of Thomasine Milton, iii. 437, 442.

WEBBER, Thomasine, wife of Christopher Milton, i. 735 and note ; ii. 72, 488-90 ; iii. 437 ; vi. 762.

WEBSTER, John, dramatist, i. 433, 445, 446 ; iii. 449.

WEBSTER, John, Anabaptist preacher, i. 265-6 ; iv. 568 ; v. 59 note.

WECKHERLIN (or WECHERLYN), Mr. George Rodolph, licenser of books in 1632, i. 550-1 note ; account of his career to 1648-9, iv. 82 and note ; mentions of, in the Council Order Books, iv. 152, 156 ; appointed Milton's Assistant in the Foreign Secretaryship, iv. 425, 426, 450, 451-2.

WEDDERBURN, burgess of Dundee, ii. 143, 190.

WEDDERBURN, Sir Alexander, in Cromwell's First Parliament, v. 5.

WEDDERBURN, David, Scottish Latinist, i. 511.

WEDDERBURN, James, Bishop of Dunblane, i. 706, 717, 721 ; ii. 42.

"WEEKLY INTELLIGENCER," the, a Commonwealth newspaper, iv. 39, 498.

WEELKS, Thomas, musical composer, i. 51.

WELBEY, John, at Cambridge, i. 218, 258, 627.

WELBY, James, member of Westminster Assembly, ii. 522.

WELDE, Thomas, New England minister, ii. 559, 586, 593, 598.

WELDEN, Ralph, Colonel under New Model, iii. 326, 332, 337.

WELLS, Henry, minister in Suffolk, iv. 228.

WELSFORD, John, ii. 207.

WEMYSS, John Wemyss, 1st Earl of, i. 710, 722 ; ii. 16, 38, 287, 418.

WEMYSS, David, 2nd Earl of, v. 512.

WEMYSS, John, vi. 141-2 note.

WENHAM, Sir Francis, i. 532, 534.

WENMAN, Viscount (Irish peerage), in the Treaty of Newport, iii. 605.

WENMAN, Sir Thomas, in the Convention Parliament, vi. 23.

WENTWORTH, Lord, son of the Earl of Cleveland, ii. 429, 441 ; iv. 188, 189, 206, 212 ; in the Privy Council of the Restoration, vi. 19.

WENTWORTH, Sir Peter, iii. 565 ; in Councils of State of the Commonwealth, iv. 177, 226, 227, 229, 230, 273, 354-5 ; at the Dissolution of the Rump, iv. 407, 412 ; in the Restored Rump, v. 454, 491 ; his bequest to Milton, vi. 719 note.

WENTWORTH, Thomas, Viscount : see Strafford, Earl of.

WESLEY, John (grandfather of the brothers John and Charles Wesley), ejected in 1662 as a Nonconformist, vi. 232 note.

WESLEY, John (Founder of the Wesleyan Church), and his brother Charles, vi. 408.

WESLEY, Mrs. Susanna, mother of the Wesleys, and daughter of Dr. Annesley, vi. 408 note.

WEST, Edmund, Parliamentarian officer, ii. 446 ; in the Restored Rump, v. 454.

WEST INDIES, Penn's Expedition to the, in 1655, v. 44-6 ; Cromwell and the, in 1654-6, v. 102-4.

WESTFIELD, Dr. Thomas, i. 121 ; Bishop of Bristol, ii. 411 ; member of Westminster Assembly, ii. 522, 525.

WESTMINSTER ASSEMBLY OF DIVINES: see *Assembly*.

WESTMORLAND, Mildmay, 2nd Earl of, his subscription towards First Bishops' War, ii. 48, 429.

WESTON, Benjamin, in the Restored Rump, v. 454.

WESTON, Sir Richard, 1st Lord : Lord High Treasurer in the Privy Council of Charles I., i. 377, 383, 384, 385, 410, 436 ; raised to the Earldom of Portland in 1633, i. 377 ; 665 ; his death in 1634-5, i. 670-1.

WEXFORD, storming of, by Cromwell, in 1649, iv. 112.

WHALLEY, Colonel, Edward (Regicide), account of, iii. 327 ; in the Battle of Naseby, iii. 335 ; 386, 534, 537 ; in the abduction of the King by the Army, iii. 541, 542, 543, 561 ; at Pride's Purge, iii. 696 ; a Commissioner in the King's Trial, iii. 707, 712 note ; signs the death-warrant, iii. 720, vi. 28 ; with Cromwell's Army in Scotland, iv. 192, 296 ; 392, 402, 403 ; Milton's praise of, in the *Defensio Secunda*, iv. 602, 612 ; in Oliver's First Parliament, v. 5 ; one of Cromwell's Major-Generals, v. 49 ; in Cromwell's Second Parliament, v. 107, 127, 128, 129 ; his relationship to the Protector, v. 307 ; one of Cromwell's Lords, v. 323, 354 ; through Richard's Protectorate, v. 418, 422, 423, 439, 440, 442 ; through the period of Anarchy, v. 469, 497 ; at the Restoration, vi. 44, 54, 115 ; subsequent fate of, vi. 115 note, 197.

WHALLEY, Mr. Henry, in the affair of the printing of the Racovian Catechism, iv. 438.

WHARTON, Nehemiah, account of, ii. 421-2 note.

WHARTON, Philip, 4th Lord, ii. 142-3 ; account of, in the composition of the Long Parliament, ii. 156, 431, 444, 445 ; lay member of Westminster Assembly, ii. 523 ; in the " Committee of the Two Kingdoms," iii. 41, 297 note, 331 note, 380, 406, 549, 555 note ; one of Cromwell's Lords, v. 323, 326 ; in the reassembled House of Peers in April

1660, v. 695 ; opposes the " Five Miles Act " in 1665, vi. 258.

WHEATLEY, the village and the estate of, in Oxfordshire, ii. 491 ; iii. 474, 478 ; iv. 237-8, 240-1, 243-6 ; 336-41 ; vi. 444, 450-1.

WHEELER, Jonas, Irish Bishop, i. 420.

WHEELER, Sir William, husband of Charles I.'s laundress in 1649, iii. 713.

WHEELER, William, member of Westminster Assembly in 1643, ii. 524 ; knighted by Cromwell in 1657, v. 354 note ; in the Parliament of the Secluded Members, v. 545.

WHEELWRIGHT, John, New England minister, account of, ii. 559, 575, 576 ; iii. 151.

WHELOCK, Abraham, Saxon scholar and Orientalist, i. 119, 120, 152, 247, 267, 648.

WHETHAM, Colonel Nathaniel, in Cromwell's Government of Scotland, v. 86, 87 ; in Cromwell's Second Parliament, v. 108, 349 ; through Richard's Protectorate, v. 418, 430 ; through the period of Anarchy, v. 470, 513-4, 520, 522.

WHETSTONE, Roger, Parliamentarian officer, and married to Cromwell's sister, v. 307.

WHICHCOT, Christopher, a merchant of London, and captain of Trained Bands in 1643, ii. 483.

WHICHCOT, Colonel, Governor of Windsor Castle in 1649, iii. 702, 727, 728.

WHICHCOTE, Dr. Benjamin, at Emanuel College, Cambridge, i. 171 ; iii. 94, 95 ; v. 73 ; among Men of Letters during the Protectorate, v. 75 ; at the Restoration, vi. 294-5 ; a Cambridge Platonist, vi. 306.

WHIDDON, Francis, member of Westminster Assembly, ii. 522.

WHIGS and Whiggism, iii. 621, origin of the term, 623 note ; vi. 619-20.

WHITAKER, Jeremiah, account of, ii. 522 ; member of the Westminster Assembly, ii. 605 ; iii. 20, 22 ; in a Presbyterian demonstration for Charles I., iv. 71.

WHITBY, Major, in Lambert's army, v. 565.

WHITE, Rev. Mr., of Knightsbridge, suspended by Laud, i. 402.

WHITE, Mr. (known as "Century White"), member for Southwark in the Long Parliament, and chairman of a Committee of the Commons for investigating the lives and opinions of the clergy, iii. 28-30; publishes his "First Century of Scandalous Malignant Priests" in November 1643, iii. 30; licenses books, iii. 268; his death in 1644-5, iii. 297-8.

WHITE, Mr., minute of Council in favour of, for an anonymous Treatise written by him in 1650-1, iv. 323.

WHITE "of Barking," reference to a case against, in a State Letter (14th May 1656), to Louis XIV. of France, v. 253.

WHITE, Dr. Francis, Bishop of Norwich in 1628-9 to 1631, i. 389; promoted to Ely, i. 399, 419; his death in 1638, i. 674; reference to, i. 677.

WHITE, Mr. Jeremiah, one of Cromwell's chaplains, iv. 353 note.

WHITE, Mr. John (Puritan minister of Dorchester, and known as "Patriarch White"), at Williams's Conferences in the Jerusalem Chamber at Westminster, ii. 225; account of, as member of Westminster Assembly, ii. 522-3, 549, 558, 605; iii. 162; iv. 352.

WHITE, John, lay member of Westminster Assembly, ii. 524.

WHITE, Robert, printer and publisher in 1650, iv. 94 note, 327.

WHITE, Colonel John (Royalist), lodged in the Tower for his concern in the "Sealed Knot" plot, v. 336.

WHITE, Colonel William, in the Restored Rump, v. 454, 519, 604.

WHITE, Robert, engraver and artist (born in 1645), vi. 756 footnote, 785.

WHITEFORD, Walter, Bishop of Brechin, i. 706, 719, 721; ii. 42.

WHITEHALL, the Palace of: Masques acted at the Court of Charles I. in, i. 580-7, 595; squibs and petitions against the "First Bishops' War" flung over the walls of, ii. 51; return of Charles I. to, after the First Bishops' War, ii. 71; guarded by the *Cavaliers* during tumults in London in 1641 and in 1641-2, ii. 331, 341; Charles I. and the royal family leave, on January 10, 1641-2, ii. 345, 410; the King taken to, on the day of his sentence, iii. 712; the procession from St. James's Palace to, iii. 723-4; the execution of the King at, iii. 724-6; iv. 3; the meeting-place of the First Council of State of the Commonwealth transferred from Derby House to, iv. 16-8, 54, 105, 107; account of "Old Whitehall," iv. 152-3; Milton has residence in Scotland Yard, iv. 153-4, 323, 335, 353, 377; Cromwell occupies the Palace of, by vote of the Parliament, iv. 191; foreign ministers and agents at, in 1653, iv. 377; Milton removes from his residence in, to Petty France, iv. 418-9; Conferences of Cromwell and his officers at, iv. 410-3; Cromwell's Interim Council of Thirteen is quartered in, iv. 498, 499, v. 707; the Supreme Assembly of Notables summoned by Cromwell to attend at the Council Chamber in, iv. 501, 504-5; Sindercombe's plot against Cromwell at, v. 119-20; presentation to Cromwell at, by his Second Parliament, of the *Petition and Advice*, v. 127-8, 131; the Court of the Protector at, v. 303; death of Cromwell's mother in, v. 304; members of the Lord Protector's family resident in, v. 305-7; the Commons summoned to, for the dissolving of Parliament, v. 329-30; Cromwell's death at, v. 354-61; Richard and his Council at, v. 414, 416; Richard retires from, v. 451; the Rumpers meet at, v. 517; Monk in quarters at, v. 528-9, 535, 537, 539, 540, 548; Charles II.'s return to, in 1660, vi. 10, 11; the Royal Family and Court at, vi. 71-3; ceremony of touching for the King's Evil at, vi. 74-5; the Scottish Council has its meetings at, vi. 131-2; the Marquis of Argyle comes to, and is sent to the Tower, vi. 131-2; the Court absent from, during the Great Plague, vi. 256-7; last interview of Charles II. and Clarendon at, vi. 270-1.

WHITEHEAD, George, early Quaker, v. 26.

WHITELAW, David, servant, v. 365.

WHITEMAN (or Wightman), burned for Arianism, i. 60, iii. 157.

WHITFIELD, Sergeant, iii. 296.

WHITFIELD, Sir Ralph, ii. 134.

WHITGIFT, Archbishop of Canterbury, i. 73, 347, 532, 537.

WHITLOCKE, Bulstrode, son of Sir James Whitlocke, and lawyer of the Middle Temple, i. 557, 558, 567; his part in the Great Masque of the Inns of Court in 1633, i. 580-3, 586; account of, in composition of Long Parliament, ii. 166-7; at Strafford's Trial, ii. 179; his part in the "Grand Remonstrance," ii. 320; in a deputation of both Houses of Parliament sent to Oxford to treat with the King, ii. 464; a lay member of Westminster Assembly, ii. 524, 606, iii. 397; reference to his "Memorials," iii. 180; in the Commons in 1645, iii. 397; in the Committee for the King's Trial, iii. 699, 703; in the First Council of State of the Commonwealth, iv. 12, 14, 79, 82, 83, 150, 151; appointed Lord Commissioner of the Great Seal of the Commonwealth, iv. 40; a National Republican Manifesto prepared by, iv. 41; at a Great City Banquet to Cromwell, iv. 54; Milton and, iv. 79, 82, 83, 105; in Parliament in 1650, iv. 219; in the Second Council of State, iv. 224, 225, 314; in the Third Council of State, iv. 273; in a deputation to Cromwell after Worcester, iv. 297; in the debates on the Question of a New Parliament, iv. 308-9; in the Fourth and Fifth Councils of State, iv. 354-5, 385-6, 400, 403, 418, 449; in Cromwell's Conferences with his Officers previous to the Dissolution of the Rump in 1653, iv. 410, 411; sent by Cromwell as Ambassador Extraordinary to Sweden, iv. 512-3, 553-4, 597 note; in Cromwell's First Parliament, v. 5; deprived, for reasons of State, of his Commissionership of the Great Seal, v. 36; "Whitlocke's Treaty" of the Protector's Government with Christina of Sweden, ratified by her successor, Charles X., v. 246; his account of the reception by the Protector, in July 1655, of Count Bundt and the Swedish Embassy, v. 247-50, 252-3, 254-7, 256 notes, 270; in Cromwell's Second Parliament, v. 107, 113, 122, 125-6, 128, 130, 148-9; at Cromwell's Court, v. 304; one of Cromwell's Lords, v. 324; proposed peerage for, by Cromwell, v. 354 note; in Cromwell's Council, v. 334; his last interview with Cromwell, v. 358; supports Richard's Protectorate, v. 417, 421, 422, 442, in the Restored Rump and its Council of State, v. 454, 455, 456, 465, 474, 479, 480; President of the Committee of Safety through the period of the Wallingford House Government, v. 494-517, 924; at the Second Restoration of the Rump, v. 517, 521, 544 note; mentions of, by Milton, iv. 602, 612; v. 705; in the Indemnity Bill, vi. 37, 41; among Milton's old friends and associates, vi. 197; among Men of Letters of the Restoration, vi. 294-5.

WHITLOCKE, Elizabeth (see *Bulstrode*), wife of Sir James Whitlocke, i. 557.

WHITLOCKE, Sir James, Judge of the King's Bench, i. 557.

WHITTAKER, Laurence, Clerk of the Privy Council, i. 210.

WHITTAKER, Richard, bookseller, iii. 271; Warden of Stationers' Company, iii. 273, 291, 293, 483 note; v. 155 note.

WICKSTEAD, Thomas, Chaplain to the Council of Wales, i. 608.

WIDDERS, Robert, Early Quaker, v. 26.

WIDDRINGTON, Sir William (made a Baron in 1643), ii. 442; iv. 284, 292; killed at Worcester, iv. 293.

WIDDRINGTON, Ralph, physician, i. 248, 651.

WIDDRINGTON, Sir Thomas, on the Committee for Printing in 1644, iii. 266; in Third Council of State of the Commonwealth, iv. 273; at the Dissolution of the Rump, iv. 410;

through Cromwell's First and Second Protectorates, v. 5, 36, 108, 111, 113, 120, 128, 148 ; through the Period of Anarchy, v. 454, 519 ; on the Council of State of the Restored Long Parliament, v. 543 ; in the Convention Parliament, vi. 23 ; on the Committee for the Indemnity Bill, vi. 30, 43.

WIGAN, defeat of Royalist Army at, iv. 293.

WIGHTMAN, burnt for Arianism, see *Whiteman*.

WIGTON, John Fleming, Earl of (Scottish Privy Councillor), i. 707 ; ii. 15, 292.

WILBRAHAM, Sir Thomas, vi. 745.

WILBYE, John, musical composer, i. 51.

WILCOX, Mr., early Presbyterian leader in London, ii. 532.

WILDMAN, Major John, in Republican plottings, v. 33, 485.

WILDMAN, William, fellow-graduate of Milton at Cambridge, i. 218, 258.

WILKES, Colonel Timothy, in the Republican Army, v. 470, 498, 501.

WILKINS, Dr. John, member of the "Invisible College" in 1645, iii. 662 ; iv. 568 note ; vi. 391, 392 ; through Cromwell's Protectorate, v. 73, 75, 231, 266 ; married to Cromwell's youngest sister, v. 62, 307 ; Burnett's talk with him about Cromwell, v. 62 ; supports Richard's Protectorate, v. 418 ; mentioned among Men of Letters of the Restoration, vi. 299, 301 ; 314, 315, 322 ; at the foundation of the Royal Society, London, in 1662, vi. 391-7 ; 459 ; appointed Bishop of Chester in 1668, vi. 567.

WILKINSON, John, master of Magdalen Hall, iv. 104.

WILKINSON, Henry, member of Westminster Assembly, ii. 523.

WILKINSON, Henry, (son of the preceding), account of, as member of Westminster Assembly, ii. 523 ; Professor in Oxford University, v. 73 ; a Nonconformist, vi. 232 note.

WILKINSON, Henry, Puritan and Parliamentarian, known as "Dean Harry," ii. 523.

WILKS, Lieutenant - Colonel, trustee for forfeited lands in Scotland, iv. 562.

WILKS, John, shipmaster, v. 576.

WILLIAM, Landgrave of Hesse, State letter to, v. 291-2.

WILLIAM I. of Orange, ii. 158.

WILLIAM II. of Orange, husband of the Princess Mary, eldest daughter of Charles I., ii. 350 ; iii. 529 ; assists the Prince of Wales, iii. 595, 597 ; entertains Charles II. at the Hague, iv. 25, 27, 30, and later at Breda, iv. 125 ; his acquaintance with Salmasius, iv. 166 ; his death at the Hague, iv. 216.

WILLIAM of NASSAU, Prince of Orange (son of the preceding, and afterwards William III. of England), his birth iv. 553 ; at the departure of Charles II. from the Hague in 1660, vi. 6, 72 ; in the Dutch War (1672), vi. 583-6 ; his marriage with the Princess Mary already proposed in 1674, vi. 605 ; the marriage advised by the Earl of Danby, vi. 729.

WILLIAMS, Major, under the *New Model*, iii. 327.

WILLIAMS, Sir Abraham, v. 177-8, 247.

WILLIAMS, Daniel, a Nonconformist, vi. 232 note.

WILLIAMS, Griffith (of Carnarvonshire), knighted by Cromwell in 1658, v. 354 note.

WILLIAMS, Griffith, Bishop of Ossory, vi. 127, 128.

WILLIAMS, Mr. John, in the Council of the Barebones Parliament, iv. 506.

WILLIAMS, John (Captain of Foot), one of the assassins of Ascham in 1650, iv. 234.

WILLIAMS, John, Bishop of Lincoln (1621-41), and Lord Keeper of the Great Seal to King James, i. 349, 389, 414, 677 ; account of, as "Lord Keeper Williams" to the year 1625, i. 349-54 ; state of the Church under, in 1625-32, i. 354-9 ; his broad policy, as seen in his exertions to promote Laud, i. 364-5 ; in cooperation with King James against the coalition of Prince Charles, Laud, and Buckingham, i. 366 ; passages

from Laud's Diary referring to, i. 367-8; deprived of the Great Seal by Charles I. in 1625, i. 370, 377; his attitude to Laud, i. 400; mentioned in connexion with New England ministers, ii. 555, 557; activity of the Privy Council of Charles I. against, i. 403; Laud's dream concerning, i. 404; Laud and, critically compared, i. 410, 412; and again, i. 513; State prosecution of, in the Star-Chamber (1632), on a charge of having revealed the King's secrets, i. 682-4; references to, while a prisoner in the Tower, ii. 44, 150, 151; takes his seat in the Long Parliament in November 1640, ii. 151 and note; his advice to Charles in the trial of Strafford, ii. 184; his attitude to the Church Reform Movement, ii. 198-9; assumes the leadership of the Movement in the Lords, ii. 224; his Committee of Clergy and Peers and their Conferences with him (as Dean of Westminster) in the Jerusalem Chamber, ii. 224-6; his opposition to the Bishops Exclusion Bill, ii. 226-7; his Draft Bill of a new Church-Organisation, ii. 235-6; anxiety of King Charles to be on good terms with, in 1641, ii. 285-6; in the Archbishopric of York, ii. 325, 331 and note; his "blunder" during anti-Episcopal riots in London, ii. 330-5; again lodged, with eleven other Bishops, in the Tower, ii. 335-6; released on bail, ii. 412; later mention of, iii. 218; his nephew, Dr. John Dolben, vi. 419; Hacket's Life of: see *Hacket*.

WILLIAMS, Nicholas, merchant, v. 254.

WILLIAMS, Roger, account of, as a New England minister, to 1640, ii. 560-3; his special form of heresy described as *Individualism*, ii. 573-4; at the plantation of Providence on Rhode Island, ii. 576-7, 600-1; visits England (1643-4), ii. 600-2; account of his *Bloody Tenent*, and of his part in the Toleration Controversy going on in England, iii. 112-29; his connexion with the sect of "Seekers," iii. 153-5; his *Bloody Tenent*, iii. 162, 165, 170, 189; denounced by the Westminster Assembly to Parliament, and his book burnt by the hangman, iii. 262, 264, 299; Milton and, iii. 189, 288; his theory of *Absolute Voluntaryism*, iii. 396 note; denounced by Sion College, iii. 678; his second visit to England, in 1652, iv. 395-6, 396-7 note; Milton and, iv. 528-33; his return to America in 1654, iv. 533; his account of the Republican discontents at the Protectorate, iv. 548-9; his theory of *Toleration* and Cromwell's compared, v. 58.

WILLIAMS, William and Daniel, English merchants and shipowners, v. 243.

WILLIAMSON, Sir Joseph, Under-Secretary of State in 1666, vi. 331; his connexion with the newspaper press and book-licensing, vi. 331-2, 616; full Secretary of State in 1674, vi. 603, 729-30; his connexion with the story of Milton's State Letters and other surviving manuscripts, iv. 158 note; vi. 721, 794-806, 805 note.

WILLINGE, William, ii. 505 note.

WILLINGHAM, Mr., in the service of the Council of State, iv. 152, 156.

WILLINGHAM, George, merchant, ii. 421 note.

WILLIS, Dr., in the Invisible College, v. 231; Fellow of the Royal Society in 1662, vi. 392, 394.

WILLIS, Sir Richard, in the Royalist conspiracy called "The Sealed Knot," v. 336, 474.

WILLOUGBY, Ensign, English spy in Scotland, ii. 54.

WILLOUGHBY, Major (Royalist), ii. 442.

WILLOUGHBY - D'ERESBY, Peregrine Bertie, 1st Lord (in Elizabeth's reign), i. 380.

WILLOUGHBY-D'ERESBY, Robert Bertie, 2nd Lord, i. 380: see *Lindsey*, 1st Earl of.

WILLOUGHBY of Parham, Henry, 4th Lord (Royalist), in the House of Peers, ii. 142, 431, 445; iii. 297 note, 380, 405, 551, 554; v. 50, 107, 473, 477.

WILLYS, Thomas, chief clerk of the Crown Office, ii. 100, 150, 173.

WILMOT, Colonel (Royalist), ii. 284, 441.

WILMOT, Henry, member for Tamworth in the Long Parliament, ii. 173.

WILMOT, Sir Charles, Lord (Royalist), in the First "Bishops' War," ii. 62.

WILMOT, Henry, afterwards 2nd Lord, in the Civil War, ii. 440, 441, iii. 331 ; with Henrietta Maria at the French Court, iii. 494; in the Second Civil War, iii. 591 ; with Charles II.'s Court at the Hague, iv. 27 ; with Charles II. in Scotland, iv. 188, 189 ; dismissed from the Scottish Court, iv. 206, 212; in Charles II.'s Scottish army, iv. 284; escapes with Charles II. to France, iv. 299.

WILSON, Dr., Chaplain to Mountain, Bishop of London, i. 157.

WILSON, Rev. Aaron, vi. 314.

WILSON, Arthur, iv. 526 note.

WILSON, John, dramatist (son of Rev. Aaron Wilson), mentioned among Men of Letters of the Restoration, vi. 314, 365-6, 366 note.

WILSON, Alderman Rowland, in the City Trained Bands in 1642, ii. 447; in the first Council of State of the Commonwealth, iv. 13, 14, 79.

WILSON, Thomas, member of Westminster Assembly, ii. 523.

WILSON, Thomas, Baptist preacher, iii. 147.

WIMBLEDON, Edward Cecil, Viscount (Baron Putney), account of, i. 380.

WINCHESTER, William Paulet, 4th Marquis of, i. 245 note.

WINCHESTER, Lucy, Marchioness of (wife of the 4th Marquis), i. 245 note.

WINCHESTER, John Paulet, 5th Marquis of, i. 244; ii. 48, 150, 428 ; iii. 369, 457.

WINCHESTER, Jane, Marchioness of (wife of the 5th Marquis), Elegies upon the occasion of her death, in 1631, by Milton and others, i. 244-6 and notes.

WINCHESTER, school of, Sir Henry Wotton at, ii. 74.

•WINCHILSEA, Earl of, ii. 430.

WINCOP, John, member of Westminster Assembly, ii. 523.

WINDEBANKE, Christopher (son of the Secretary), i. 822 note.

WINDEBANKE, Sir Francis, Secretary of State to Charles I., i. 381, 386-7, 668, 683, 684, 756, 799, 822 note; ii. 24, 43-5 and note, 48, 52, 58, 61, 127, 128, 129-30, 144 ; in the Long Parliament, ii. 259 ; proceedings against, and escape of, ii. 176-8 and note ; 278, 279, 280, 281 ; iii. 216.

WINDEBANKE, Thomas (son of the Secretary), i. 799 ; ii. 70 ; iii. 331-2 and note.

WINDSOR CASTLE, Charles I. at, in 1641-2, ii. 345, and again in 1647, iii. 556, and again in 1648, iii. 701-2, 702, 705 ; removal of the King from, to St. James's, iii. 707 ; burial of Charles I. in the Royal Chapel of, iii. 727-9 ; opening of the vault in 1813, iii. 729 note ; used as a prison in 1656, v. 107.

WINGATE, Edward, Parliamentarian officer, ii. 445.

WINGFIELD, Roger, Parliamentarian officer, ii. 444.

WINNIFFE, Dr. Thomas, Bishop of Lincoln in 1641-2, ii. 411.

WINRAM, Mr. George (of Liberton, Senator of the College of Justice), iv. 180.

WINSLOW, Edward, one of the early Governors of New Plymouth, ii. 548, 599.

WINSTANLEY, George, fellow-student of Milton at Cambridge, i. 171.

WINSTANLEY, William, mention of Milton in his Lives of English Poets in 1687, vi. 783.

WINTERSHALL, William, actor, vi. 349.

WINTERTON, Ralph, Regius Professor of Medicine at Cambridge, i. 120.

WINTHROP, John, governor of Massachusetts, ii. 165, 549, 562, 575, 599, 600; iv. 533 note; v. 378 note.

WINTON, George Seton, Earl of, Scottish Privy Councillor, i. 707 ; iv. 561.

WIRTZ, Paul de, minister of the Count of Oldenburg, iv. 527.

WISHART, George, chaplain to Montrose, and his biographer, iv. 28, 185.

WISHART, Mr. William, minister of Kinneill, vi. 134.

"WIT and DROLLERY," edited by John Phillips in 1656, v. 260-2, 262 note.

WITCHCRAFT : an Act for restraining, in the Scottish General Assembly of 1642, ii. 420; "extraordinary multiplying of witches", especially in Fifeshire, in 1643-4, iii. 8 ; Scottish witch-trials and witch-burnings in 1654-6, v. 92.

WITHER, George (poet), account of, i. 472-82 ; 490, 509, 547, 569 ; ii. 154 ; among Men of Letters under the Protectorate, v. 75, 84 ; after the Restoration, vi. 291, 322.

WITHERINGS, Thomas, Postmaster, i. 708.

WITHERINGTON, Roger, ii. 64.

WITHERINGTON, William, i. 629.

WITT, Cornelius de, and John de : see De Witt.

WOBURN, seat of the Earl of Bedford at, iii. 556.

WOGAN, Thomas (Regicide), signs the death-warrant of Charles I., iii. 720, vi. 28, 49 ; in the Restored Rump, v. 454 ; after the Restoration, vi. 44, 49, 54, 94 note, 115 note.

WOLFE, landlord of the *Rose* at Cambridge, i. 138.

WOLISOG, Frederick Matthias, envoy of the Count of Oldenburg to Cromwell in 1654, iv. 635.

WOLLASTON, Alderman, Colonel of City Trained Bands, ii. 447.

WOLSELEY, Lieutenant - Colonel, his part at the Dissolution of the Rump by Cromwell in 1653, iv. 412; called to Cromwell's Supreme Assembly, iv. 501 ; in the Barebones Parliament, and of its Council, iv. 506, 525 ; in Cromwell's Council, iv. 545, 575, v. 7, 31, 64 ; in Cromwell's Second Parliament, v. 107, 121, 125, 128, 130, 177, 183, 273 ; in the Privy Council of the Second Protectorate, v. 308, 322, 333, 346-7, 352, 374 ; one of Cromwell's Lords, v. 324 ; supports Richard's government, v. 417, 442 ; in the Convention Parliament, vi. 23.

WOLSELEY, Charles (of Staffordshire), member of the Rota Club in 1659, v. 485.

WOLZOGUE, M. de, minister of the Walloon Church at Utrecht, v. 594.

WOMAT, the Laird of, iv. 560.

WOOD, Anthony, quoted, v. 484 ; mentioned among Men of Letters under the Protectorate, v. 76, and after the Restoration, vi. 316, 388.

WOOD, James, Presbyterian minister, iv. 209, 213 ; v. 90.

WOOD, Robert, of Lincoln College, a member of the Rota Club, v. 485.

WOOD, Thomas, goldsmith of Cheapside, i. 47.

WOODBRIDGE, Mr., Presbyterian, and one of the chaplains of Charles II., vi. 62.

WOODCOCK, Captain (of Hackney), father of Milton's second wife, v. 282, 382.

WOODCOCK, Francis, member of Westminster Assembly, ii. 520 ; iii. 184; v. 282 note.

WOODCOCK, Katherine, Milton's second wife, v. 281-2, 376, 382, 409.

WOODCOCK, Michael, v. 282 note.

WOODCOCK, Ralph, officer of City Trained Bands, ii. 447.

WOODCOCK, Thomas, Puritan divine, v. 282 note, 337.

WOODFORD, Jack, friend of Alexander Gill jun., i. 211.

WOODFORD, Dr. Samuel, his *Paraphrase upon Canticles*, in 1670, vi. 782.

WOODSTOCK, ii. 149; surrender of, to the *New Model* Army in 1646, iii. 372 ; members for, in the Long Parliament, ii. 173, 446, 496-7 ; iii. 327.

WOODWARD, Hezekiah, iii. 231, 293-6 ; his daughter marries John Oxenbridge, iv. 619 note.

WORCESTER, surrender of, iii. 374 ; Charles II. at, iv. 293 ; the Battle of, iv. 294-9.

WORCESTER, Earl of (in 1626-7), i. 182.

WORCESTER, Henry Somerset, 5th Earl of (in 1638-9), ii. 47 ; created Marquis of, in 1642, ii. 429, 462 ; defender of Raglan Castle in 1646, iii.

374, 376 ; death of, in 1646, ii. 429; his son (see *Herbert of Raglan*, Lord).

WORCESTER HOUSE (in London), used by the Scottish Commissioners to the Long Parliament, iii. 18.

WORDSWORTH, Dr. Christopher, author of *Who Wrote Eikon Basilike?* (1824), vi. 439 note.

WORDSWORTH, William, his reminiscence of Milton's rooms at Christ's College, Cambridge, i. 132; 272, 311.

" WORLD IN A MAZE, THE, or OLIVER'S GHOST," title of a rigmarole poem of 1659, v. 451.

" WORLD OF WORDS, THE," a dictionary, by John Phillips, in 1678, vi. 766-77.

WORSLEY, Charles, one of Cromwell's Major-Generals, v. 49.

WORTH, Edward, Irish Bishop in 1660, vi. 129.

WORTH, Zachary, servant of the Council, v. 625.

" WORTHIES OF ENGLAND," by Thomas Fuller, vi. 295.

WORTHINGTON, John, at Cambridge, i. 248 ; iii. 194 note ; iv. 514 ; v. 74 ; vi. 299, 306, 453 note.

WORTLEY, Sir Francis, ii. 442.

WOTTON, Sir Henry, account of, i. 528-31 ; as provost of Eton, i. 536, 564; his acquaintance with Milton, and his letter to Milton in April 1638, i. 737-9, 752 ; his last days and death, ii. 73-5 ; references to his letter to Milton in 1638, iii. 454, iv. 637.

WRANGEL, Swedish Admiral, v. 428.

WRAY, Sir Christopher, in the Long Parliament, ii. 326.

WRAY, Sir John, in the Long Parliament, ii. 173.

WRAY, William, Parliamentarian officer, ii. 446.

WREN, Sir Christopher, as " Mr. Wren," and deputy to Sir John Denham, vi. 309; in the Philosophical Society of Oxford, vi. 392 ; as lecturer on Astronomy in Gresham College, vi. 393; in the Council of the Royal Society, vi. 394, 396, 458.

WREN, Dr. Matthew, Master of Peterhouse, Cambridge, i. 120, 157, 187;

Vice-Chancellor of the University, i. 213 ; as Bishop of Norwich, i. 419, 677, 678, 716 ; ii. 52 and note ; as Bishop of Ely, i. 674 ; ii. 150; impeachment of, by the Long Parliament, ii. 178, 270 ; imprisoned in the Tower with Williams and others of the Bishops, ii. 334, 335 note ; mentions of, ii. 517 ; iii. 421 ; released by the Restored Long Parliament in 1660, after nineteen years' imprisonment in the Tower, v. 547 ; in the Episcopate after the Restoration, vi. 61, 105, 136.

WRIGHT, Dr., Cromwell's physician, iv. 278 ; v. 317, 354 note.

WRIGHT, Dr. (" an aged clergyman in Dorsetshire "), account, by the painter Richardson, of a visit of, to Milton in Artillery Walk, vi. 679.

WRIGHT, Mr., of Emanuel College, Cambridge (in 1629), i. 220.

WRIGHT, Sir Henry (son of the physician), made a baronet by Cromwell in 1658, v. 354 note.

WRIGHT, Dr. Robert, Bishop of Bristol, i. 389 ; Bishop of Lichfield and Coventry, i. 677; ii. 150; impeachment of, by the Long Parliament, ii. 270, 334-6.

WRIGHT, Thomas, servant of the Council of State, v. 625.

WRIGHTER, Clement, of the Sect of " Anti-Scripturists," iii. 158, 159, 165, 262, 687.

WRIOTHESLEY, Lord : see *Southampton*, Earl of.

WROTH, Mr., Independent minister, ii. 581.

WROTH, Sir Thomas, in the Restored Rump, v. 454.

WULLENIUS, mentioned in a letter of Heinsius to Gronovius, iv. 318.

WYBERD, William, denounced in the Convention Parliament in 1660, vi. 47.

WYCHERLEY, William, account of, among the younger writers of the Restoration period, vi. 321 ; as a dramatist, vi. 611, 730.

WYCLIFFE (the Reformer), i. 130, 514.

WYETH, Joseph (citizen and merchant of London), reference to his edition

of the *Life of Thomas Ellwood* in 1714, vi. 815.

WYKE, Andrew, Baptist preacher, iii. 148.

WYKES, Dr., book censor, iii. 268.

WYLDE, George, Irish Bishop (1660), vi. 128.

WYLDE, John (lawyer), member for Worcestershire in the Long Parliament, ii. 173; lay-member of the Westminster Assembly, ii. 524; as Lord Chief Baron of the Court of Exchequer and on the Commission for the King's Trial, iii. 703; in the First Council of State of the Commonwealth, iv. 12, 151; and in the Second, iv. 223, 224, 225, 230; in the Restored Rump, v. 454; in the trial of John Twyn, printer, for high treason in 1663-4, vi. 478.

WYLDE, Sir William, member of the Convention Parliament, and takes part in the debates on the Indemnity Bill, vi. 41, 173.

WYNDHAM, Hugh, Judge of Assize for Lancashire, iv. 558.

WYNDHAM, Sir William (of Somersetshire), knighted by Cromwell in 1658, v. 354 note.

WYNN, Sir Richard, ii. 326.

Y

YAPP, William and Ann, witnesses to the signature of Milton's widow, in 1680, vi. 779.

YARDLEY, Richard, printer, i. 90.

YARMOUTH, Earl of (Sir William Paston), vi. 604.

YATES, Jane, servant of Milton, ii. 208, 357.

YELVERTON, Sir Henry, v. 478.

YEOMANS, Charles, scrivener, i. 339 note.

YESTER, John Hay, Lord, in the opposition party of the Scottish Parliament of 1633, i. 710; among the Presbyterian "Supplicants" in 1637, i. 722; in the Glasgow General Assembly of 1638, ii. 38; in the First "Bishops' War," ii. 65; present at the General Assembly of 1642, ii. 418.

YORK: rendezvous of the English Army at, in 1638-9, ii. 47; Charles I. and Strafford at, ii. 140, 144; member for, in the Long Parliament, ii. 171; Charles I. at, ii. 354; siege of, iii. 86; member for, in the Cavalier Parliament, vi. 597.

YORK, Richard Plantagenet, Duke of, i. 607.

YORK, James, Duke of: see *James II.*

YORK, Duchess of: see *Hyde*, Anne.

"YORK," a psalm tune so named, the composition of Milton's father, i. 52.

"YORKSHIRE REDCAPS," Sir Thomas Fairfax's horse troop, in 1639, so named, ii. 171.

YOUGHAL: see *Cork*, 1st Earl of.

YOUNG, an actor, vi. 350.

YOUNG, Jack, an Oxfordshire squire, story of, and the epitaph on Ben Jonson, i. 647.

YOUNG, Patrick: see *Junius.*

YOUNG, Robert, printer in Edinburgh, i. 718.

YOUNG, Rev. Thomas, account of his parentage and early career, and as Milton's first preceptor, i. 68-72, 71 note, 559-60; mentions of, i. 103, 272; Latin letters of Milton to (1625-8), i. 147-8, 184-5, 203-4; as English chaplain at Hamburg, i. 185, 426; as Vicar of Stowmarket, i. 185-6, 236, 418-9, ii. 75; his share in the authorship of the Smectymnuan Pamphlet, ii. 201-2, 219, 225, 238, 288, 605; further account of, in 1643, as member of Westminster Assembly, ii. 523; in Assembly debates, iii. 20; appointed to the Mastership of Jesus College, Cambridge, in 1643-4; iii. 94-5, 95 note; mentioned, iii. 188; publication, in 1674, of Milton's letters to, vi. 723.

YOUNG, Walter, lay member of the Westminster Assembly, ii. 524.

YOUNG, Rev. William (father of Thomas Young), i. 69.

YOUNG, William (Doctor of Physic), in the Trials of the Regicides, vi. 41.

YOUNGSTON, Mr., Scottish divine, v. 346 note.

YPRES, capture of, by the English and French, v. 416.

THE END.

John Milton. Inde:

		DATE DUE	